Presented to

Becky Mayfield

BY

DATE

HURLBUT'S
Story of the Bible

HURLBUT'S

Story of the Bible

FOR YOUNG AND OLD

A continuous narrative of the Scriptures
told in one hundred sixty-eight stories

BY

JESSE LYMAN HURLBUT, D.D.

Text drawings in two colors by
STEELE SAVAGE

ZONDERVAN
PUBLISHING HOUSE 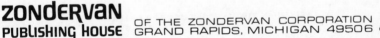 OF THE ZONDERVAN CORPORATION
GRAND RAPIDS, MICHIGAN 49506

LIBRARY OF CONGRESS CATALOG CARD NUMBER: 63–7320

First Zondervan printing   1967
Second printing   1968
Third printing   1969
Fourth printing   January   1972
Fifth printing   June   1972
Sixth printing   1973
Seventh printing   1974

Illustration copyright, 1949, for "The Four Gems of the Bible" section
by Zondervan Publishing House.

PRINTED IN THE UNITED STATES OF AMERICA

To the Young People of the World

THIS BOOK IS DEDICATED IN THE HOPE

THAT IT MAY INTEREST THEM

IN THE READING OF

The Best of All
Books

PRONUNCIATION KEY

Vowels in unaccented syllables are not marked if their pronunciation presents no special difficulty. Consonants which are not marked are to be pronounced as in ordinary English words.

VOWELS

ā as in āte . . . . Ā'bĕl	ī as in elixīr . . . Ō'phĭr
å as in senåte . . . Nå-ō'mī	ĭ as in pĭn . . . Ē-lĭṣ'a-bĕth
â as in râre . . . . Shâr'on	ō as in gō . . . . Jō'ṣeph
ă as in căt . . . Băb'y̆-lon	ȯ as in ȯbey . . Mȯ-rī'ah
à as in sofà . . . . Jȯsh'u-à	ô as in ôrder . . Môr'de-cāi
ä as in ärm . . . . Tär'sus	ŏ as in tŏp . . . . Jŏp'pà
a̧ as in fa̧ll . . . . . Sa̧ul	ū as in ūse . . . . Jū'dah
ē as in ēven . . . . Ēve	û as in bûrn . . . . Ûr
ė as in ėvent . . Rė-bĕk'ah	ŭ as in cŭt . . . . Ē'hŭd
ĕ as in dĕn . . . Bĕn'ja-mĭn	u̧ as in ru̧le . . . Ru̧th
ẽ as in writẽr . . . Ăb'nẽr	y̅ like ī . . . . . Çy̅'rus
ī as in nīne . . . . Lē'vī	y̆ like ĭ . . . . . Mā'ry̆

CONSONANTS

ç as in çity . . . . Çy̅'prus	
ḡ as in ḡo . . . . Ḡil'e-ad	
ġ as in ġentle . . . Ē'ġy̆pt	
ṣ as in roṣe . . . . Iṣ'ra-el	

vi

A Son's Memory of the Author

by Charles C. Hurlbut

ONE of the earliest recollections of my childhood is sitting with a group of other children, with my father in the center and a huge Bible on the table in front of us. The Bible was unusual, for it had a full-page woodcut on alternate pages. From the Creation to the Last Judgment, it was all there—the greatest picture book that any child could ask for.

My father, Jesse Lyman Hurlbut, was a wonderful story-teller; so nothing thrilled us more than to sit on his knees to hear him tell the stories as he turned the pages. Not only his own children, but all their friends flocked to these little gatherings, so that "hearing Bible stories" became a standard diversion in the neighborhood.

The old Bible was completely worn out before the story-telling period was ended, for it extended over two complete generations of children. In the process, by long practice, my father learned the language that holds a child's attention and the way to make a story real to him. When he finally wrote the stories for children beyond the reach of his voice, he merely set down on paper the very words that he had been repeating for half a century to children grouped around his knees.

In writing Hurlbut's STORY OF THE BIBLE, my father did not merely make a selection of the most striking and interesting stories in the Bible. He told all the principal stories in a connected order and in such relation with each other as to form a continuous history. It was his hope that the reader would find in it not only stories from the Bible, but also THE STORY OF THE BIBLE in one narration.

Inasmuch as this book was designed to lead the reader to the Bible itself, the language of the Bible, or a language similar to that of the Bible was used. In the same manner, my father refrained from adding any imaginary scenes, incidents, or conversations.

He wanted his readers to enjoy the stories in virtually their original form, without being rewritten or changed.

My father was very earnest in his belief that many books of Bible stories are greatly marred by an attempt to make them teach doctrines which are not stated or even hinted at in the Scripture stories themselves. He therefore tried to explain that which needed explanation, but to avoid all doctrinal bias. In a few instances, where the New Testament warranted a spiritual interpretation of an Old Testament story, he provided it in the simplest and fewest words possible, so that all denominations of Christians might feel at home in the pages of his book.

For the most part, the author used the King James' Version of the Bible, but where he believed the American Standard Revision to be a manifest improvement, he followed it to bring the reader a step nearer to the thought of the Biblical writers.

That my father succeeded in producing a book of Bible stories that has stood the test of time is evidenced by the continuing popularity of HURLBUT'S STORY OF THE BIBLE.

Since its publication it has found its way into millions of homes and has been translated into many foreign languages, including Afrikaans.

In its lifetime it has undergone several revisions, the third edition, published two decades ago, having been issued as a memorial to my father.

Publisher's Foreword

More than four million copies of *Hurlbut's Story of the Bible* have been printed since the book was first published. This volume has truly become a classic in its position as a leader in the Bible story book field, a standard of excellence and quality other publications have striven to reach. *Hurlbut's* has been selected by many as the retelling of the Bible story most faithful to the original Scriptures and the most understandable for children of all ages.

The full-color illustrations in this latest edition are new to *Hurlbut's*. They are used with the authorization and full approval of the copyright owners and illustrate in dramatic fashion these fascinating Bible stories.

It is with a very real sense of mission that we assume the publication responsibility for this rich and worthwhile volume, with its tremendous message for young and old alike.

THE PUBLISHERS

Table of Contents

Part Second
Stories of Joshua and the Judges

Part Third
Stories of the Three Great Kings of Israel

Part Fourth
Stories of the Kingdom of Israel

Part Fifth
Stories of the People and Kingdom of Judah

Part Sixth
The Life and Teachings of Jesus

Part Seventh
Stories of the Early Church

Part First

STORIES FROM THE
FIRST FIVE BOOKS
IN THE BIBLE

The Story of a Beautiful Garden

THIS great round world on which we live is very old; in the beginning God created the earth, and the sun, moon and stars. But long before there was any earth or sun or stars, God was living, for God never began to be. He always was. And long, long ago, God spoke, and the earth and the heavens came. But the earth was not beautiful as it is now, with mountains and valleys, rivers and seas, with trees and flowers. It was a great round ball, with land and water mingled in one mass. And all the earth was blacker than midnight, for there was no light upon it. No man could have breathed its air, no animals could walk upon it, and no fish could swim in its black oceans. There was no life upon the earth.

While all was dark upon earth, God said, "Let there be light," and then the light began to come upon the world. Part of the time it was light and part of the time it was dark, just as it is now. And God called the dark time Night and the light time Day. And that was the first day upon this earth after a long night.

Then at God's word, the dark clouds all around the earth began to break, the sky came in sight, and the water that was in the clouds began to be separate from the water that was on the earth. And the arch of the sky which was over the earth God called Heaven. Thus the night and the morning made a second day.

Then God said, "Let the water on the earth come together in one place, and let the dry land rise up." And so it was. The water that had been all over the world came together and formed a great ocean, and the dry land rose up from it. And the great water God called Sea, and the dry land he named Earth: and God saw that the Earth and the Sea were both good. Then God said, "Let grass and trees and flowers and fruits grow on the earth." And at once the earth began to be green and bright with grass and flowers and trees bearing fruit. This made the third day upon the earth.

3

Then God said, "Let the sun and moon and stars come into sight from the earth." So the dark clouds over the earth rolled away, the sun began to shine by day, and the moon and the stars began to shine in the night. And this was done on the fourth day.

And God said, "Let there be fishes in the sea and let there be birds to fly in the air." So the fishes, great ones and small, began to swim in the sea; and the birds began to fly in the air over the earth, just as they do now. And this was the fifth day.

Then God said, "Let the animals come upon the earth, great animals and small ones; those that walk and those that creep and crawl on the earth." And the woods and the fields began to be alive with animals of all kinds. And now the earth began to be more beautiful, with its green fields and bright flowers, and singing birds in the trees, and animals of every kind walking in the forests.

But there were no people in the world—no cities nor houses, and no children playing under the trees. The world was all ready for men and women to enjoy it: and so God said, "I will make man, to be different from all other animals. He shall stand up and shall have a soul, and shall be like God; and he shall be the master of the earth and all that is upon it."

So God took some of the dust that was on the ground, and out of it he made man; and God breathed into him the breath of life, and man became alive and stood up on the earth.

And so that the man whom God had made might have a home, God planted a beautiful garden on the earth at a place where four rivers met. Perhaps we might rather call it a park, for it was much larger than any garden that you have ever seen; it was miles and miles in every direction. In this garden, or park, God planted trees and caused grass to grow and made flowers to bloom. This was called "The Garden of Ē'děn," and as in one of the languages of the Bible the word that means "garden," or "park," is a word quite like the word "Paradise," this Garden of Ē'děn has often been called "Paradise." This garden God gave to the man that he had made; and told him to care for it and to gather the fruits upon the trees and the plants and to live upon them. And God gave to the first man the name Ăd'ăm: and God brought to Ăd'ăm

all the animals that he had made and let Ăd'ăm give to each one
its name.

But Ăd'ăm was all alone in this beautiful garden. And God
said, "It is not good for man to be alone. I will make someone
to be with Ăd'ăm and to help him." So when Ăd'ăm was asleep,
God took a rib from Ăd'ăm's side, and from it God made a
woman; and he brought her to Ăd'ăm, and Ăd'ăm called her Ēve.
And Ăd'ăm and Ēve loved one another; and they were happy in
the beautiful garden which God had given them for a home.

Thus in six days the Lord God made the heavens and the earth
and the sea, and all that is in them. And on the seventh day God
rested from his work.

For a time, we do not know how long, Ăd'ăm and Ēve were
at peace in their beautiful garden. They did just as God told
them to do, and talked with God as a man would talk with his
friend; and they did not know of anything evil or wicked. It was
needful for Ăd'ăm and Ēve to understand that they must always
obey God's commands. So God said to Ăd'ăm and Ēve:
"You may eat the fruit of all the trees in the garden except one.
In the middle of the garden grows a tree, with fruit upon it that
you must not eat and you must not touch. If you eat of the fruit
upon that tree, you shall die."

Now among the animals in the garden there was a snake: and
this snake said to Ēve, "Has God told you that there is any kind
of fruit in the garden, of which you are forbidden to eat?"

And Ēve answered the snake, "We can eat the fruit of all the
trees except the one that stands in the middle of the garden. If
we eat the fruit of that tree, God says that we must die."

Then the snake said, "No, you will not surely die. God knows
that if you eat of the fruit of that tree, you will become as wise as
God himself, for you will know what is good and what is evil."

Ēve listened to the snake, and then she looked at the tree and
its fruit. As she saw it, she thought that it would taste good; and
if it would really make one wise, she would like to eat it, even
though God had told her not to do so. She took the fruit and ate
it; and then she gave some to Ăd'ăm, and he, too, ate it.

Ăd'ăm and Ēve knew that they had done wrong in not obey-

Eve disobeys God

ing God's words: and now for the first time they were afraid to meet God. They tried to hide themselves from God's sight among the trees of the garden. But the Lord God called and said, "Ăd'ăm, where are you?" And Ăd'ăm said, "Lord, I heard thy voice in the garden, and I was afraid and I hid myself."

And God said, "Why were you afraid to meet me? Have you eaten the fruit of the tree of which I told you that you must not touch it?" And Ăd'ăm said, "The woman whom thou gavest to be with me, she gave me some of the fruit, and I ate it."

Then God said to the woman, "What is this that you have done?" And Ēve said, "The snake told me that it would do me no harm if I should eat the fruit, and so I took some of it and ate it."

Then the Lord God said to the snake, "Because you have led Ăd'ăm and Ēve to do wrong, you shall no more walk as do other animals; you shall crawl in the dust and the dirt forever. I will put enmity between you and the woman, between you and all men. But one of them will have the victory over you."

And the Lord God said to the woman, "Because you led your husband to disobey me, there shall be pain and sorrow in your life, and your husband shall rule over you."

And God said to Ăd'ăm, "Because you listened to your wife when she told you to do what was wrong, you, too, must suffer. You must work for everything that you get from the ground. You will find thorns and thistles and weeds growing on the earth.

If you want food, you must dig and plant and reap and work as long as you live. You came out from the ground, for you were made of dust, and back again into the dust shall your body go when you die."

And because Ăd'ăm and Ēve had disobeyed the word of the Lord, they were driven out of the beautiful Garden of Ē'dĕn, which God had made to be their home. They were sent out into the world; and to keep them from going back into the garden, God placed his angels before its gate, with swords which flashed like fire.

So Ăd'ăm and his wife lost their garden, and no man has ever been able to go into it from that day.

Story Two   GENESIS 4 : 1-18

The First Baby in the World, and His Brother

SO ĂD'ĂM and his wife went out into the world to live and to work. For a time they were all alone, but after a while God gave them a little child of their own, the first baby that ever came into the world. Ēve named him Cāin; and after a time another baby came, whom she named Ā'bĕl.

When the two boys grew up, they worked, as their father worked before them. Cāin chose to work in the fields and to raise grain and fruits. Ā'bĕl had a flock of sheep and became a shepherd.

While Ăd'ăm and Ēve were living in the Garden of Ē'dĕn, they could talk with God and hear God's voice speaking to them. But now that they were out in the world, they could no longer talk with God freely, as before. So when they came to God, they built an altar of stones heaped up, and upon it they laid something as a gift to God, and burned it, to show that it was not their own, but was given to God, whom they could not see. Then before the altar they made their prayer to God and asked God to forgive their sins, all that they had done that was wrong; and prayed God to bless them and do good to them.

Each of these brothers, Cāin and Ā'bĕl, offered upon the altar to God his own gift. Cāin brought the fruits and the grain which he had grown; and Ā'bĕl brought a sheep from his flock, and killed it and burned it upon the altar. For some reason God was pleased with Ā'bĕl and his offering, but was not pleased with Cāin and his offering. Perhaps God wished Cāin to offer something that had life, as Ā'bĕl offered; perhaps Cāin's heart was not right when he came before God.

And God showed that he was not pleased with Cāin, and Cāin, instead of being sorry for his sin and asking God to forgive him, was very angry with God and angry also toward his brother Ā'bĕl. When they were out in the field together, Cāin struck his brother Ā'bĕl and killed him. So the first baby in the world grew up to be the murderer of his own brother.

And the Lord said to Cāin, "Where is Ā'bĕl your brother?"

And Cāin answered, "I do not know; why should I take care of my brother?"

Then the Lord said to Cāin, "What is this that you have done? Your brother's blood is like a voice crying to me from the ground. Do you see how the ground has opened, like a mouth, to drink your brother's blood? As long as you live, you shall be under God's curse for the murder of your brother. You shall wander over the earth, and shall never find a home, because you have done this wicked deed."

And Cāin said to the Lord, "My punishment is greater than I can bear. Thou hast driven me out from among men; and thou hast hid thy face from me. If any man finds me, he will kill me, because I shall be alone, and no one will be my friend."

And God said to Cāin, "If anyone harms Cāin, he shall be punished for it." And the Lord God placed a mark on Cāin, so that whoever met him should know him, and should know also that God had forbidden any man to harm him. Then Cāin and his wife went away from Ăd'ăm's home, to live in a place by themselves, and there they had children. And Cāin's family built a city in that land; and Cāin named the city after his first child, whom he had called Ē'nŏch.

Story Three
GENESIS 5 : 1 to 9 : 17

The Great Ship That Saved Eight People

AFTER Ā'bĕl was slain, and his brother Cāin had gone into another land, again God gave a child to Ăd'ăm and Ēve. This child they named Sĕth; and other sons and daughters were given to them, for Ăd'ăm and Ēve lived many years. But at last they died, as God had said that they must die, because they had eaten of the tree that God had forbidden them to eat.

By the time that Ăd'ăm died, there were many people on the earth; for the children of Ăd'ăm and Ēve had many other children; and when these grew up, they also had children; and these too had children. And in those early times people lived much longer than they do now. Very few people now live to be a hundred years old; but in those days, when the earth was new, men often lived to be eight hundred or even nine hundred years old. So after a time that part of the earth where Ăd'ăm's sons lived began to be full of people.

It is sad to tell that as time went on more and more of these people became wicked, and fewer and fewer of them grew up to become good men and women. All the people lived near together, and few went away to other lands; so it came to pass that even the children of good men and women learned to be bad, like the people around them.

And as God looked down on the world that he had made, he
how wicked the men in it had become, and that every thought
and every act of man was evil and only evil continually.

But while most of the people in the world were very wicked,
there were some good people also, though they were very few.
The best of all the men who lived at that time was a man whose
name was Ē'nŏch. He was not the son of Cāin, but another
Ē'nŏch, who came from the family of Sĕth, the son of Ăd'ăm who
was born after the death of Ā'bĕl. While so many around Ē'nŏch
were doing evil, this man did only what was right. He walked
with God, and God walked with him and talked with him. And
at last, when Ē'nŏch was three hundred and sixty-five years old,
God took him away from the earth to heaven. He did not die,
as all the people have died since Ăd'ăm disobeyed God, but "He
was not, for God took him." This means that Ē'nŏch was taken
up from earth without dying.

Ē'nŏch left a son whose name was Mĕ-thu'se-lah. We do not
know anything about Mĕ-thu'se-lah, except that he lived to be
nine hundred and sixty-nine years old, which was longer than the
life of any other man who ever lived. But at last, Mĕ-thu'se-lah
died like all his people, except his father Ē'nŏch. By the time that
Mĕ-thu'se-lah died, the world was very wicked. And God looked
down on the earth, and said:

"I will take away all men from the earth that I have made; because the men of the world are evil, and evil continually."

But even in those bad times, God saw one good man. His name
was Nō'ah. Nō'ah tried to do right in the sight of God. As
Ē'nŏch had walked with God, so Nō'ah walked with God and
talked with him. And Nō'ah had three sons: their names were
Shĕm and Hăm and Jā'pheth.

God said to Nō'ah, "The time has come when all the men and
women on the earth are to be destroyed. Everyone must die,
because they are all wicked. But you and your family shall be
saved, because you alone are trying to do right."

Then God told Nō'ah how he might save his life and the lives
of his sons. He was to build a very large boat, as large as the
largest ships that are made in our time; very long and very wide

and very deep; with a roof over it; and made like a long, wide house in three stories, but so built that it would float on the water. Such a ship as this was called "an ark." God told Nō'ah to build this ark and to have it ready for the time when he would need it.

"For," said God to Nō'ah, "I am going to bring a great flood of water on the earth, to cover all the land and to drown all the wicked people on the earth. And as the animals on the earth will be drowned with the people, you must make the ark large enough to hold a pair of each kind of animals, and several pairs of some animals that are needed by men, like sheep and goats and oxen; so that there will be animals as well as men to live upon the earth after the flood has passed away. And you must take in the ark food for yourself and your family and for all the animals with you, enough food to last for a year, while the flood shall stay on the earth."

And Nō'ah did what God told him to do, although it must have seemed very strange to all the people around, to build this great ark where there was no water for it to sail upon. And it was a long time, even a hundred and twenty years, that Nō'ah and his sons were at work building the ark, while the wicked people around wondered, and no doubt laughed at Nō'ah for building a great ship where there was no sea. At last the ark was finished, and stood like a great house on the land. There was a door on one side, and a window on the roof, to let in the light. Then God said to Nō'ah, "Come into the ark, you and your wife, and your three sons, and their wives with them; for the flood of waters will come very soon. And take with you animals of all kinds and birds and things that creep; seven pairs of those that will be needed by men, and one pair of all the rest; so that all kinds of animals may be kept alive upon the earth."

So Nō'ah and his wife, and his three sons, Shĕm, Hăm, and Jā'pheth, with their wives, went into the ark. And God brought to the door of the ark the animals and the birds and the creeping things of all kinds; and they went into the ark, and Nō'ah and his sons put them in their places and brought in food for them all. And then the door of the ark was shut, so that no more people and no more animals could come in.

In a few days the rain began to fall, as it had never rained before. It seemed as though the heavens were opened to pour great floods upon the earth. The streams filled and the rivers rose, higher and higher, and the ark began to float on the water. The people left their houses and ran up to the hills, but soon the hills were covered and all the people on them were drowned.

Some had climbed up to the tops of higher mountains, but the water rose higher and higher, until even the mountains were covered and all the people, wicked as they had been, were drowned in the great sea that now rolled over all the earth where men had lived. And all the animals, the tame animals—cattle and sheep and oxen—were drowned; and the wild animals—lions and tigers and all the rest—were drowned also. Even the birds were drowned, for their nests in the trees were swept away, and there was no place where they could fly from the terrible storm. For forty days and nights the rain kept on, until there was no breath of life remaining outside of the ark.

After forty days the rain stopped, but the water stayed upon the earth for more than six months; and the ark, with all that were in it, floated over the great sea that covered the land. Then God sent a wind to blow over the waters and to dry them up: so by degrees the waters grew less and less. First the mountains rose above the waters, then the hills rose up; and finally the ark ceased to float, and lay aground on a mountain which is called Mount Âr'a-răt. But Nō'ah could not see what had happened on the earth, because the door was shut, and the window may have been in the roof. But he felt that the ark was no longer moving, and he knew that the water must have gone down. So, after waiting for a time, Nō'ah opened a window and let loose a bird called a raven. Now the raven has strong wings; and this raven flew round and round until the waters had gone down and it could find a place to rest, and it did not come back to the ark.

After Nō'ah had waited for it a while, he sent out a dove; but the dove could not find any place to rest, so it flew back to the ark, and Nō'ah took it into the ark again. Then Nō'ah waited a week longer, and afterward he sent out the dove again. And at the evening, the dove came back to the ark, which was its home;

and in its bill was a fresh leaf which it had picked from an olive tree.

So Nō'ah knew that the water had gone down enough to let the trees grow once more. He waited another week and sent out the dove again; but this time the dove flew away and never came back. And Nō'ah knew that the earth was becoming dry again. So he took off a part of the roof and looked out and saw that there was dry land all around the ark. Nō'ah had now lived in the ark a little more than a year, and he was glad to see the green land and the trees once more. And God said to Nō'ah:

"Come out of the ark with your wife and your sons and their wives and all the living things that are with you in the ark."

So Nō'ah opened the door of the ark, and with his family came out and stood once more on the ground. All the animals and birds and creeping things in the ark came out also and began again to bring life to the earth.

When Nō'ah came out of the ark, his first act was to give thanks to God for saving all his family when the rest of the people on the earth were destroyed. He built an altar and laid upon it an offering to the Lord, and he gave himself and his family to God and promised to do God's will.

And God was pleased with Nō'ah's offering, and God said:

"I will not again destroy the earth on account of men, no matter how bad they may be. From this time no flood shall again cover the earth; but the season of spring and summer and fall and winter shall remain without change. I give to you the earth; you shall be the rulers of the ground and of every living thing upon it."

Then God caused a rainbow to appear in the sky, and he told Nō'ah and his sons that whenever they or the people after them should see the rainbow, they should remember that God had placed it in the sky and over the clouds as a sign of his promise that he would always remember the earth and the people upon it, and would never again send a flood to destroy men from the earth.

So, as often as we see the beautiful rainbow, we are to remember that it is the sign of God's promise to the world.

The Tower That Was Never Finished

AFTER the great flood, the family of Nō'ah and those who came after him grew in number until, as the years went on, the earth began to be full of people once more. But there was one great difference between the people who had lived before the flood and those who lived after it. Before the flood, all the people stayed close together, so that very many lived in one land and no one lived in other lands. So far as we know, all the people on the earth before the great flood, lived in the lands where the two great rivers flowed, called the Tī'gris and Eū-phrā'tēṣ. This part of the world was very full of people; but few or none crossed the mountains on the east or the desert on the west; and the great world beyond was without people living in it. After the flood, families began to move from one place to another, seeking for themselves new homes. Some went one way and some another.

This moving about was a part of God's plan to have the whole earth used for the home of men, and not merely a small part of it. Then, too, a family who wished to serve God and do right could go away to another land if the people around them became evil; and in a place by themselves they could bring up their children in the right way.

From Mount Âr'a-răt, where the ark rested, many of the people moved southward into a country between two great rivers, the rivers Tī'gris and Eū-phrā'tēṣ: and there they built houses for themselves. They undertook to build a great city, which should rule all the peoples around them. They found that the soil in that country could be made into bricks, and that the bricks could be heated and made hard; so that it was easy to build houses to live in and walls around their city.

And the people said to each other, "Let us build a great tower

15

The Tower of Babel

that shall stand on the earth and shall reach up to the sky; so that we may be kept together and not scattered abroad on the earth."

So they began to build their great tower out of bricks, which they piled up, one story above another. But God did not wish all the people on the earth to live close together, just as they had lived before the great flood. God knew that if they all kept together, those that were wicked would lead away from God those that were good, and all the world would become evil again, as it had been before the flood.

This was the way that God kept people from staying in one place. While they were building this great city and tower which they intended to rule the world, God caused their speech to change. At that time, all men were speaking one language, so that everybody could understand what every other person said.

God caused men to change their language, so that different groups could not understand one another. After a time, the people who belonged to one family found that they could not understand what the people of another family were saying, just as now Germans do not understand English, and French people, Italian, until they have learned their different languages.

As people began to grow apart in their speech, they moved away into other places, where the families speaking one language could understand each other. So the men who were building the city and the great tower could no longer understand each other's speech; they left the building without finishing it, and many of them went away into other lands. So the building stayed forever unfinished.

And the city was named Bā'bel, a word which means "confusion." It was afterward known as Băb'ў-lon, and for a long time
was one of the greatest cities of that part of the world, even after
many of its people had left it to live elsewhere.

Part of the people who left Băb'ў-lon went up to the north and
built a city called Nĭn'e-veh, which became the ruling city of a
great land called Ăs-sўr'ĭ-à, whose people were called Ăs-sўr'ĭ-àns.

Another company went away to the west and settled by the
great river Nile and founded the land of Ē'ğўpt, with its strange
temples and pyramids, its Sphinx, and its monuments.

Another company wandered northwest until they came to the
shore of the great sea which we call the Mĕd-ĭ-ter-rā'ne-an Sea.
There they founded the cities of Sī'dŏn and Tȳre, where the
people were sailors, sailing to countries far away, and bringing
home many things from other lands to sell to the people of Băb'ў-
lon and Ăs-sўr'ĭ-à and Ē'ğўpt and other countries.

So after the flood, the earth again became covered with people
living in many lands and speaking many languages.

Story Five   GENESIS 11 : 27 to 13 : 18

The Story of a Long Journey

NOT FAR from the city of Băb'ў-lon, where they
began to build the tower of Bā'bel, was another
city, called Ûr of the Chăl'dees. The Chăl'dees
were the people who lived in the country which
was called Chăl-dē'à, where the two rivers Eū-
phrā'tēs and Tī'gris come together. Among these people at Ûr,
was living a man named Ā'brăm. Ā'brăm was a good man, for he
prayed to the Lord God and tried always to do God's will.

But the people who lived in Ûr, Ā'brăm's home, did not pray to
God. They prayed to idols, images made of wood and stone.

They thought that these images were gods, and that they could hear their prayers and could help them. And as these people who worshiped idols did not call on God, they did not know his will and they did many wicked things.

The Lord saw that Ā′brăm was good and faithful, though wicked people were living all around him. And God did not wish to have Ā′brăm's family grow up in such a place, for then they too might become wicked. So the Lord spoke to Ā′brăm and said:

"Ā′brăm, gather together all your family and go out from this place to a land far away, that I will show you. And in that land I will make your family to become a great people, and I will bless you and make your name great, so that all the world shall give honor to your name. If you will do as I command you, you shall be blessed, and all the families of the earth shall obtain a blessing through you."

Ā′brăm did not know just what this blessing meant that God promised to him. But we know that Ā′brăm's family grew after many years into the Ĭṣ′ra-el-īte people, out of whom came Jē′ṣus, the Saviour of the world, for Jē′ṣus was a descendant of Ā′brăm: that is, Jē′ṣus came a long time afterward from the family of which Ā′brăm was the father; and thus Ā′brăm's family became a blessing to all the world by giving to the world a Saviour.

Although Ā′brăm did not know just what the blessing was to be that God promised to give him, and although he did not know where the land was to which God was sending him, he obeyed God's word. He took all his family and with them his father Tē′rah, who was very old, and his wife, whose name was Sā′rāi; and his brother Nā′hôr and his wife, and another brother's son whose name was Lŏt; for Lŏt's father, Hā′ran, who was the younger brother of Ā′brăm, had died before this time. And Ā′brăm took all that he had, his tents and his flocks of sheep and herds of cattle, and went forth on a long journey to a land of which he did not even know the name.

He journeyed far up the great river Eū-phrā′tēṣ to the mountain region, until he came to a place called Hā′ran, in a country called Mĕs-o-pŏ-ta′mĭ-à. The word Mĕs-o-pŏ-ta′mĭ-à means "Between the rivers"; and this country was between the two great rivers

Tī'gris and Eū-phrā'tēṣ. At Hā'ran they all stayed for a time. Perhaps they stopped there because Tē'rah, Ā'brăm's father, was too old to travel farther, for they stayed at Hā'ran until Tē'rah died.

After the death of Tē'rah, his father, Ā'brăm again went on his journey; and Lŏt, his brother's son, went with him; but Nā'hôr, Ā'brăm's brother, stayed in Hā'ran, and his family and children and children's children, whom they call "his descendants," lived at Hā'ran for many years.

Abraham Obeys God — Takes His family
to Canaan

From Hā'ran, Ā'brăm and Lŏt turned toward the southwest and journeyed for a long time, having the mountains on their right hand and the great desert on their left. They crossed over rivers and climbed the hills, and at last they came into the land of Cā'năan, which was the land of which God had spoken to Ā'brăm.

This land was called Cā'năan because the people who were living in it were the descendants, or children's children, of a man who had lived long before, whose name was Cā'năan. A long time after this it was called "the Land of Iṣ'ra-el," from the people who lived in it; and because in that same land the Lord Jē'ṣus lived many years afterward, we now call it "The Holy Land."

When Ā'brăm came into the land of Cā'năan, he found in it a few cities and villages of the Cā'năan-ītes. But Ā'brăm and his people did not go into the towns to live. They lived in tents, out in the open fields, where they could find grass for their sheep and cattle. Not far from a city called Shē'chem, Ā'brăm set up his tent under an oak tree on the plain. There the Lord came to Ā'brăm, and said:

"I will give this land to your children and to their children, and this shall be their land forever."

And Ā'brăm built there an altar and made an offering and worshiped the Lord. Wherever Ā'brăm set up his tent, there he built his altar and prayed to God; for Ā'brăm loved God and served God and believed God's promises.

Ā'brăm and Lŏt moved their tents and their flocks to many places where they could find grass for their flocks and water to drink. At one time they went down to the land of Ē'gўpt, where they saw the great river Nile. Perhaps they saw also the Pyramids and the Sphinx and the wonderful temples in that land, for many of them were built before Ā'brăm lived.

Ā'brăm did not stay long in the land of Ē'gўpt. God did not wish him to live in a land where the people worshiped idols; so God sent Ā'brăm back again to the land of Cā'năan, where he could live apart from cities and bring up his servants and his people to worship the Lord. He came to a place where afterward a city called Bĕth'el stood; and there as before he built an altar and prayed to the Lord.

Now Lŏt, the son of Ā'brăm's younger brother who had died, was with Ā'brăm; and Lŏt, like Ā'brăm, had flocks of sheep and herds of cattle and many tents for his people. Ā'brăm's shepherds and Lŏt's shepherds quarreled, because there was not grass enough in one place for both of them to feed their flocks; and besides these people, the Cā'năan-ītes were also in the land, so that there was not room for them all.

When Ā'brăm heard of the quarrel between his men and the men under Lŏt, he said to Lŏt:

"Let there be no quarrel between you and me nor between your men and my men; for you and I are like brothers to each other. The whole land is before us; let us go apart. You shall have the first choice, too. If you will take the land on the right hand, then I will take the land on the left; or if you choose the left hand, then I will take the right."

This was noble and generous in Ā'brăm, for he was the older and might claim the first choice. Then, too, God had promised all the land to Ā'brăm, so that he might have said to Lŏt, "Go away, for this land is all mine." But Ā′brăm showed a kind, good heart in giving to Lŏt his choice of the land.

And Lŏt looked over the land from the mountain where they were standing and saw down in the valley the river Jôr′dan flowing between green fields, where the soil was rich. He saw the cities of Sŏd′om and Gŏ-mŏr′rah upon the plain, near the head of the Dead Sea, into which the Jôr′dan flows. And Lŏt said, "I will go down yonder to the plain."

And he went down the mountain to the plain, with his tents and his men and his flocks of sheep and his cattle, leaving the land on the mountains, which was not so good, to his uncle Ā′brăm. Perhaps Lŏt did not know that the people in Sŏd′om were the most wicked of all the people in the land; but he went to live near them and gradually moved his tent closer to Sŏd′om, until after a time he was living in that wicked city.

After Lŏt had separated from Ā′brăm, God said to Ā′brăm: "Lift up your eyes from this place and look east and west and north and south. All the land that you can see, mountains and valleys and plains, I will give it to you and to your children and their children and those who come after them. Your descendants shall have all this land, and they shall be as many as the dust of the earth; so that if one could count the dust of the earth, they could as easily count those who shall come from you. Rise up and walk through the land wherever you please, for it is all yours."

Then Ā′brăm moved his tent from Bĕth′el, and went to live near the city of Hē′bron, in the south, under an oak tree; and there again he built an altar to the Lord.

How Lot's Choice Brought Trouble and Abram's Choice Brought Blessing

S O LŎT lived in Sŏd'om, and Ā'brăm lived in his tent on the mountains of Cā'năan. At that time in the plain of Jôr'dan, near the head of the Dead Sea, were five cities, of which Sŏd'om and Gŏ-mŏr'rah were two; and each of the five cities was ruled by its own king. But over all these little kings and their little kingdoms was a greater king, who lived far away near the land of Chăl-dē'a, from which Ā'brăm had come, and who ruled all the lands far and near.

After a time these little kings in the plain would not obey the greater king; so he and all his army made war upon them. A battle was fought on the plain not far from Sŏd'om, and the kings of Sŏd'om and Gŏ-mŏr'rah were beaten in the battle, and their soldiers were killed. Then the king who had won the victory over his enemies came to Sŏd'om and took everything that he could find in the city, and carried away all the people in the city, intending to keep them as slaves. After a battle in those times, the army that won the victory took away all the goods and made slaves of all the people on the side that had been beaten.

So Lŏt, with all that he owned, was carried away by enemies, who went up the valley from Sŏd'om and did not stop to rest until they came to the headwaters of the river Jôr'dan, at a place afterward called Dăn. So, all that Lŏt's selfish choice gained for him was to lose all that he had and to be made a prisoner and a slave.

Someone ran away from the battle and came to Ā'brăm, who was living in his tent under the oak tree near Hē'bron. As soon as Ā'brăm heard what had happened, he called together all the men who were with him, his servants, his shepherds, and his people and his friends; and he led them after the enemy that had taken away Lŏt. He followed as fast as his men could march and

22

found the enemy, with all the goods they had taken and all their prisoners, at Dăn, one of the places where the Jôr'dan River begins.

Ā'brăm rushed upon the enemies at night, while they were asleep, and fought them and drove them away so suddenly that they left behind them everything and ran far among the mountains. And in their camp Ā'brăm found his nephew Lŏt safe, with his wife and daughters and all his goods, and, besides, all the goods and all the other people that had been carried away from Sŏd'om.

Then the king of Sŏd'om came to meet Ā'brăm at a place near the city of Jĕ-ru'sȧ-lĕm, which was afterward called "The King's Valley." And with him came the king of Jĕ-ru'sȧ-lĕm, which at that time was called Sā'lem. The name of this king was Mĕl-chĭz'-e-dĕk, and unlike most other kings in the land at that time, he was a worshiper of the Lord God, as Ā'brăm was. And the king Mĕl-chĭz'e-dĕk blessed Ā'brăm, and said, "May the Lord God Most High, who made heaven and earth, bless Ā'brăm; and blessed be the Lord God Most High, who has given your enemies into your hand."

And Ā'bram made a present to the King Mĕl-chĭz'e-dĕk, because he worshiped the Lord. And Ā'brăm gave to the king of Sŏd'om all the people and all the goods that had been taken away; and he would not take any pay for having saved them.

You would have thought that after this, Lŏt would have seen that it was wrong for him to live in Sŏd'om; but he went back to that city and made his home there once more, even though his heart was made sad by the wickedness that he saw all around him.

After Ā'brăm had gone back to his tent under the oak trees at Hē'bron, one day the Lord God spoke to him and said:

"Fear not, Ā'brăm; I will be a shield to keep you safe from enemies; and I will give you a very great reward for serving me."

And Ā'brăm said, "O Lord God, what good can anything do to me, since I have no child to whom I can give it; and after I die, the man who will own everything that I have is not my son, but a servant." For although Ā'brăm had a large family of people around him and many servants, he had no son, and he was now an old man and his wife Sā'rāi was also old.

And God said to Ā'brăm, "The one to receive what you own shall not be a stranger, but shall be your own son."

And that night God brought Ā'brăm out of his tent, under the heavens, and said to him:

"Look now up to the sky and count the stars, if you can. The people who shall spring from you, your descendants, in the years to come, shall be many more than all the stars that you can see."

Ā'brăm did not see how this promise of God could be kept; but he believed God's word and did not doubt it. And God loved Ā'brăm because he believed the promise. Although Ā'brăm could not at that time see how God's promise could be kept, yet we know that it was kept, for the Ĭṣ'ra-el-īte people in the Bible story and the Jews everywhere in the world now all came from Ā'brăm.

After that, one day, just as the sun was going down, God came to Ā'brăm again and told him many things that should come to pass. God said to Ā'brăm:

"After your life is ended, those who are to come from you, your descendants, shall go into a strange land. The people of that land shall make slaves of them and shall be cruel to them. And they shall stay in that strange land four hundred years; and afterward they shall come out of that land, not any more as slaves, but very rich. And after the four hundred years, they shall come back to this

land, and this shall be their home. All this shall come to pass after your life, for you shall die in peace and be buried in a good old age. And all this land where you are living shall belong to your people."

So that Ā'brăm might remember this promise of God, God told Ā'brăm to make ready an offering of a lamb and a goat and a pair of pigeons, and to divide them in pieces and place them opposite to each other. And that night Ā'brăm looked and saw a smoke and fire, like a flaming torch, that passed between the pieces of the offering.

Thus a promise was made between God and Ā'brăm. God promised to give Ā'brăm a son and a people and a land, and Ā'brăm promised to serve God faithfully.

Such a promise as this, made by two people to each other, was called a covenant; and this was God's covenant with Ā'brăm.

Story Seven   GENESIS 16 : 1 to 17 : 27

The Angel by the Well

YOU REMEMBER that Ā'brăm's wife, who had journeyed with him from Ûr of the Chăl'dees, and who lived in his tent all those years, was named Sā'rāi. Now Sā'rāi had a maid, a servant that waited on her, whose name was Hā'gar. She came from the land of Ē'ġўpt, where were the pyramids and the temples. But Sā'rāi and her maid Hā'gar had some trouble; they could not agree, and Sā'rāi was so sharp and severe with Hā'gar that at last Hā'gar ran away from Sā'rāi's tent.

She went out into the desert and took the road that led down to Ē'ġўpt, her own country, the land from which she had come. On the way she stopped beside a spring of water. There the angel from the Lord met her and said to her:

"Hā'gar, are you not the servant of Sā'rāi, Ā'brăm's wife? What are you doing here? Where are you going?"

And Hā'gar said to the angel:

"I am going away from my mistress, Sā'rāi, because I do not wish to stay with her and serve her any longer."

Then the angel said to Hā'gar:

"Go back to your mistress, Sā'rāi, and submit to her, for it is better for you than to go away. God knows all your troubles, for

he sees and hears you, and he will help you. By and by you shall have a son, and you shall call his name Ĭsh'ma-el, because God has heard you."

The word Ĭsh'ma-el means "God hears." So whenever Hā'gar should speak her boy's name, she would think "God has heard me."

Then the angel told Hā'gar that her son Ĭsh'ma-el should be strong and fierce, and that no one should be able to overcome him or his children or his descendants.

So Hā'gar was comforted and went back again to serve Sā'rāi. And afterward the well where she saw the angel was called by a name which means "The well of the Living One who sees me." And after this, Hā'gar had a son; and as the angel told her, she called his name Ĭsh'ma-el; that is, "God hears." We shall read more about Hā'gar and Ĭsh'ma-el a little later. After this, while Ā'brăm was living near Hē'bron, the Lord came to him again and spoke to him, while Ā′brăm bowed with his face to the ground. God said: "I am the Almighty God; walk before me and be perfect, and I will make you a father of many nations. And your name shall be changed. You shall no more be called Ā′brăm, but Ā′bră-hăm, a word that means 'Father of a multitude,' because you shall be the father of many nations of people. And your wife's name shall also be changed. She shall no more be called Sā′rāi, but Sā′rah; that is, 'Princess.' And you and Sā′rah shall have a son, and you shall call his name Ī′şaac; and he shall have sons when he becomes a man, and his descendants, those who spring from him, shall be very many people." So from this time he was no longer Ā′brăm, but Ā′bră-hăm, and his wife was called Sā′rah.

Story Eight   GENESIS 18 : 1 to 19 : 30

The Rain of Fire That Fell on a City

ONE DAY Ā′bră-hăm—for we shall call him now by his new name—was sitting in the door of his tent, when he saw three men coming toward him. He knew from their looks that they were not common men. They were angels, and one of them seems to have been the Lord himself, coming in the form of a man.

When Ā′bră-hăm saw these men coming, he went out to meet them and bowed to them; and he said to the one who was the leader:

"My Lord, do not pass by, but come and rest a little under the tree. Let me send for water to wash your feet; and take some food; and stay with us a little while."

So this strange person, who was God in the form of a man, sat with his two followers in Ā'brā-hăm's tent under the oak trees at Hē'bron. They took some food which Sā'rah, Ā'brā-hăm's wife, made ready for them, and then the Lord talked with Ā'brā-hăm. He told Ā'brā-hăm again that in a very little time God would send to him and Sā'rah a little boy, whose name should be I'saac. In the language that Ā'brā-hăm spoke, the name I'saac means "Laughing"; because Ā'brā-hăm and Sā'rah both laughed aloud when they heard it. They were so happy they could scarcely believe the news.

Then the three persons rose up to go, and two of them went on the road which led toward Sŏd'om, down on the plain of Jôr'dan, below the mountains. But the one whom Ā'brā-hăm called "My Lord," stopped after the others had gone away and said:

"Shall I hide from Ā'brā-hăm what I am going to do? For Ā'brā-hăm is to be the father of a great people, and all the world shall receive a blessing through him. And I know that Ā'brā-hăm will teach his children and all those that live with him to obey the will of the Lord and to do right. I will tell Ā'brā-hăm what I am going to do. I am going down to the city of Sŏd'om and the other cities that are near it, and I am going to see if the city is as bad as it seems to be; for the wickedness of the city is like a cry coming up before the Lord."

And Ā'brā-hăm knew that Sŏd'om was very wicked, and he feared that God was about to destroy it. And Ā'brā-hăm said:

"Wilt thou destroy the righteous with the wicked, the good with the bad, in Sŏd'om? Perhaps there may be fifty good people in the city. Wilt thou not spare the city for the sake of fifty good men who may be in it? Shall not the Judge and Ruler of all the earth do right?"

And the Lord said: "If I find in Sŏd'om fifty good people, then I will not destroy the city, but will spare it for their sake."

Then Ā'brā-hăm said:

"Perhaps I ought not to ask anything more, for I am only a common man, talking with the Lord God. But suppose that there should be forty-five good people in Sŏd'om, wilt thou destroy the city because it needs only five good men to make up the fifty?"

And the Lord said, "I will not destroy it, if there are forty-five good men in it." And Ā′bră-hăm said, "Suppose there are forty good people in it—what then?" And the Lord answered, "I will spare the city, if I find in it forty good men." And Ā′bră-hăm said, "O Lord, do not be angry, if I ask that if there are thirty good men in the city, it may be spared." And the Lord said, "I will not harm the city, if I find thirty good men there." And Ā′bră-hăm said, "Let me venture to ask that thou wilt spare it if twenty are there." The Lord said, "I will not destroy it for the sake of twenty good men, if they are there." Then Ā′bră-hăm said, "Oh, let not the Lord be angry, and I will speak only this once more. Perhaps there may be ten good men found in the city." And the Lord said, "If I find ten good men in Sŏd′om, I will spare the city."

And Ā′bră-hăm had no more to say. The Lord in the form of a man went on his way toward Sŏd′om; and Ā′bră-hăm turned back and went to his tent.

You remember that Lŏt, the nephew of Ā′bră-hăm, chose the land of Sŏd′om for his home and lived there, though the people were so wicked. You remember, too, how Lŏt was carried away a prisoner when Sŏd′om was taken by its enemies and how he was rescued by Ā′brăm. But after all that had happened, Lŏt went to live in Sŏd′om again; and he was there when the angels came to Ā′bră-hăm's tent, as we read in the last story.

Two of the angels who had visited Ā′bră-hăm went down to Sŏd′om and walked through the city, trying to find some good men; for if they could find only ten, the city would be saved. But the only good man whom they could find was Lŏt. He took the angels, who looked like men, into his house, and treated them kindly and made a supper for them.

The men of Sŏd′om, when they found that strangers were in Lŏt's house, came before the house in the street and tried to take the two men out, that they might do them harm, so wicked and cruel were they. But the men of Sŏd′om could do nothing against them, for when they tried to break open the door, and Lŏt was greatly frightened, the two angels struck all those wicked men blind in a moment, so that they could not see, and felt around in the dark for the door.

Then the angels said to Lŏt:

"Have you here any others besides yourself, any sons or sons-in-law or daughters? Whomever you have, get them out of this city quickly, for we are here to destroy this place, because it is so very wicked."

Then Lŏt went to the houses where the young men lived who had been betrothed to his daughters, and said to them:

"Hurry, and get out of this place, for the Lord will destroy it."

But his sons-in-law, the husbands of his daughters, would not believe his words; they only laughed at him. What a mistake it was for Lŏt to live in a wicked city, where his daughters were married to young men living there!

And when the morning was coming, the two angels tried to make poor Lŏt hasten away. They said:

"Rise up quickly, and take your wife, and your two daughters that are here. If you do not haste, you will be destroyed with the city."

But Lŏt was slow to leave his house and his married daughters and all that he had; and the two angels took hold of him and of his wife and his two daughters; and the angels dragged them out of the city. God was good to Lŏt, to take him out of the city before it was destroyed.

And when they had brought Lŏt and his wife and his daughters out of the city, one of the angels said to him:

"Escape for your life; do not look behind you; do not stop anywhere in the plain; climb up the mountain or you may be destroyed!"

And Lŏt begged the angels not to send him so far away. He said, "O my Lord, I cannot climb the mountain. Have mercy upon me and let me go to that little city that lies yonder. It is only a little city, and you can spare it. Please let me be safe there."

And the angel said, "We will spare that city for your sake; and we will wait until you are safe before we destroy these other cities."

So Lŏt ran to the little city, and there he found safety. In the language of that time, the word "Zō'ar" means little; so that city

God sends Judgement
upon Sodom and
Gomorroh.

was afterward called Zō'ar. It was the time of sunrise when Lŏt came to Zō'ar.

Then, as soon as Lŏt and his family were safely out of Sŏd'om, the Lord caused a rain of fire to fall upon Sŏd'om and the other cities on the plain. With the fire came great clouds of sulphur smoke, covering all the plain. So the cities were destroyed and all the people in them; not one man or woman or child was left.

While Lŏt and his daughters were flying from the city, Lŏt's wife stopped and looked back; and she became a pillar of salt, standing there upon the plain. Lŏt and his two daughters escaped, but they were afraid to stay in the little city of Zō'ar. They climbed up the mountain, away from the plain, and found a cave, and there they lived. So Lŏt lost his wife and all that he had, because he had made his home among the wicked people of Sŏd'om.

And when Ā'brä-hăm, from his tent door on the mountain, looked down toward the plain, the smoke was rising from it, like the smoke of a great furnace.

And that was the end of the cities of the plain, Sŏd'om and Gŏ-mŏr'rah, and the other cities with them. Zō'ar alone was saved, because Lŏt, a good man, prayed for it.

Story Nine   GENESIS 21 : 1-21

The Boy Who Became an Archer

AFTER Sŏd'om and Gŏ-mŏr'rah were destroyed, Ā'brä-hăm moved his tent and his camp away from that part of the land and went to live near a place called Gē'rär, in the southwest, not far from the Great Sea. And there at last, the child whom God had promised to Ā'brä-hăm and Sā'rah was born, when Ā'brä-hăm his father was a hundred years old.

They named this child Ī′saac, as the angel had told them he
should be named. And Ā′bră-hăm and Sā′rah were so happy to
have a little boy that after a time they gave a great feast to all the
people in honor of the little Ī′saac.

You remember the story about Sā′rah's maid Hā′gar, the Ē′gў̆p-
tian woman, and how she ran away from her mistress and saw an
angel by a well, and afterward came back to Sā′rah, and had a
child whose name was Ĭsh′ma-el. So now there were two boys in
Ā′bră-hăm's tent, the older boy, Ĭsh′ma-el, the son of Hā′gar, and
the younger boy, Ī′saac, the son of Ā′bră-hăm and Sā′rah.

Ĭsh′ma-el was a rough, wild boy. He did not like the little
Ī′saac, who was quiet and gentle, and he did not treat him kindly.
This made Sā′rah very angry, and she said to her husband:

"I do not wish to have this boy Ĭsh′ma-el growing up with my
son Ī′saac. Send away Hā′gar and her boy, for they are a trouble
to me."

And Ā′bră-hăm felt very sorry to have trouble come between
Sā′rah and Hā′gar and between Ī′saac and Ĭsh′ma-el; for Ā′bră-
hăm was a kind and good man, and he was friendly to them all.

But the Lord said to Ā′bră-hăm, "Do not be troubled about
Ĭsh′ma-el and his mother. Do as Sā′rah has asked you to do, and
send them away. It is best that Ī′saac should be left alone in your
tent, for he is to receive everything that is yours. I the Lord will
take care of Ĭsh′ma-el and will make a great people of his descendants, those who shall come from him."

So the next morning, Ā′bră-hăm sent Hā′gar and her boy away,
expecting them to go back to the land of Ē′gў̆pt, from which
Hā′gar had come. He gave them some food for the journey and
a bottle of water to drink by the way. The bottles in that country were not like ours, made of glass. They were made from the
skin of a goat, sewed tightly together. One of these skin bottles
Ā′bră-hăm filled with water and gave to Hā′gar.

And Hā′gar went away from Ā′bră-hăm's tent, leading her
little boy. But in some way she lost the road and wandered over
the desert, not knowing where she was, until all the water in the
bottle was used up; and her poor boy, in the hot sun and the burning sand, had nothing to drink. She thought that he would die of

his terrible thirst, and she laid him down under a little bush; and then she went away, for she said to herself:

"I cannot bear to look at my poor boy suffering and dying for want of water."

And just at that moment, while Hā′gar was crying and her boy was moaning with thirst, she heard a voice saying to her:

"Hā′gar, what is your trouble? Do not be afraid. God has heard your cry and the cry of your child. God will take care of you both, and will make of your boy a great nation of people."

It was the voice of an angel from heaven; and then Hā′gar looked, and there close at hand was a spring of water in the desert. How glad Hā′gar was, as she filled the bottle with water and took it to her suffering boy under the bush!

After this, Hā′gar did not go down to Ē′gȳpt. She found a place near this spring, where she lived and brought up her son in the wilderness, far from other people. And God was with Ĭsh′ma-el and cared for him. And Ĭsh′ma-el grew up in the desert and learned to shoot with the bow and arrow. He became a wild man, and his children after him grew up to be wild men also. They were the Ă-rā′bĭ-ans of the desert, who even to this day have never been ruled by any other people, but wander through the desert and live as they please. So Ĭsh′ma-el came to be the father of many people, and his descendants, the wild Ă-rā′bĭ-ans of the desert, are living unto this day in that land, just as the Jews, who are the descendants of Ī′saac, are living all over the world.

How an Angel's Voice Saved a Boy's Life

YOU REMEMBER that in those times of which we are telling, when men worshiped God, they built an altar of earth or of stone and laid an offering upon it, as a gift to God. The offering was generally a sheep or a goat or a young ox, some animal that was used for food. Such an offering was called "a sacrifice."

But the people who worshiped idols often did what seems to us very strange and very terrible. They thought that it would please their gods if they would offer as a sacrifice the most precious living things that were their own; and they would take their own little children and kill them upon their altars as offerings to the gods of wood and stone, that were no real gods, but only images.

God wished to show to Ā'brǎ-hǎm and all his descendants, those who should come after him, that he was not pleased with such offerings as those of living people, killed on the altars. And God took a way to teach Ā'brǎ-hǎm, so that he and his children after him would never forget it. Then at the same time he wished to see how faithful and obedient Ā'brǎ-hǎm would be to his commands; how fully Ā'brǎ-hǎm would trust in God, or as we should say, how great was Ā'brǎ-hǎm's faith in God.

So God gave to Ā'brǎ-hǎm a command which he did not mean to have obeyed, though this he did not tell to Ā'brǎ-hǎm. He said:

"Take now your son, your only son Ī'ṣaac, whom you love so greatly, and go to the land of Mō-rī'ah; and there, on a mountain that I will show you, offer him for a burnt offering to me."

God called Ī'ṣaac Ā'brǎ-hǎm's only son, because he was the son of his wife Sā'rah; and also Ĭsh'ma-el, the son of Hā'gar, had gone away, and Ī'ṣaac was the only son at his home.

Though this command filled Ā'brǎ-hǎm's heart with pain, yet

35

he would not be as surprised to receive it as a father would in our day; for such offerings were very common among all those people in the land where Ā'bră-hăm lived. Ā'bră-hăm never for one moment doubted or disobeyed God's word. He knew that Ī'şaac was the child whom God had promised, and that God had promised, too, that Ī'şaac should have children, and that those coming from Ī'şaac should be a great nation. He did not see how God could keep his promise with regard to Ī'şaac, if Ī'şaac should be killed as an offering: unless, indeed, God should raise him up from the dead afterward. But Ā'bră-hăm undertook at once to obey God's command. He took two young men with him and an ass laden with wood for the fire; and he went toward the mountain in the north, Ī'şaac his son walking by his side. For two days they walked, sleeping under the trees at night in the open country. And on the third day, Ā'bră-hăm saw the mountain far away. And as they drew near to the mountain, Ā'bră-hăm said to the young men:

"Stay here with the ass, while I go up yonder mountain with Ī'şaac to worship; and when we have worshiped, we will come back to you."

For Ā'bră-hăm believed that in some way God would bring back Ī'şaac to life. He took the wood from the ass and placed it on Ī'şaac, and the two walked up the mountain together. As they were walking, Ī'şaac said, "Father, here is the wood, but where is the lamb for the offering?" And Ā'bră-hăm said, "My son, God will provide himself the lamb."

Abraham offers his
Son to God

And they came to the place on the top of the mountain. There
Ā′bră-hăm built an altar of stones and earth heaped up, and on it
he placed the wood. Then he tied the hands and the feet of Ī′ṣaac,
and laid him on the wood on the altar. And Ā′bră-hăm lifted up
his hand, holding a knife to kill his son. A moment longer, and
Ī′ṣaac would be slain by his own father's hand. But just at that
moment the angel of the Lord out of heaven called to Ā′bră-hăm,
and said, "Ā′bră-hăm! Ā′bră-hăm!" And Ā′bră-hăm answered,
"Here I am, Lord." Then the angel of the Lord said:
"Do not lay your hand upon your son. Do no harm to him.
Now I know that you love God more than you love your only
son, and that you are obedient to God, since you are ready to give
up your son, your only son, to God." What a relief and a joy
these words from heaven brought to the heart of Ā′bră-hăm!
How glad he was to know that it was not God's will for him to
kill his son! Then Ā′bră-hăm looked around, and there in the
thicket was a ram caught by his horns. And Ā′bră-hăm took the
ram and offered him up for a burnt offering in place of his son.
So Ā′bră-hăm's words came true when he said that God would
provide for himself a lamb. The place where this altar was built
Ā′bră-hăm named Jĕ-hō′vah=jī′reh, words meaning, in the language that Ā′bră-hăm spoke, "The Lord will provide."

This offering, which seems so strange, did much good. It
showed to Ā′bră-hăm and to Ī′ṣaac also, that Ī′ṣaac belonged to
God, for to God he had been offered; and in Ī′ṣaac, all those who
should come from him, his descendants, had been given to God.
Then it showed to Ā′bră-hăm, and to all the people after him, that
God did not wish children or men killed as offerings for worship;
and while all the people around offered such sacrifices, the Ĭs′ra-
el-ītes, who came from Ā′bră-hăm and from Ī′ṣaac, never offered
them, but offered oxen and sheep and goats instead. And it looked
onward to a time when, just as Ā′bră-hăm gave his son as an offering, God should give his Son Jē′ṣus Chrīst to die for the sins of
the world. All this was taught in this act of worship on Mount
Mō-rī′ah.

Some think that on the very place where this offering was given,
the altar in the temple many years afterward stood on Mount

Mō-rī'ah. If that be true, the rock is still there, and over it is a building called "The Dome of the Rock." Many people now visit this rock under the dome, and think of what took place there so long ago. At this time Ā'brā-hăm was living at a place called Bē'er=shē'bà, on the border of the desert, south of the land of Cā'năan. From Bē'er=shē'bà he took this journey to Mount Mō-rī'ah, and to Bē'er=shē'bà he came again after the offering on the mountain. Bē'er=shē'bà was the home of Ā'brā-hăm during most of his late years. After a time, Sā'rah, the wife of Ā'brā-hăm, and the mother of Ī'şaac, died, being one hundred and twenty years old. And Ā'brā-hăm bought of the people of Hē'bron a cave, called the cave of Măch-pē'lah; and there he buried Sā'rah his wife. This place is still known as the city of Hē'bron, but the people who live there will not allow any strangers to visit the cave or the building over it.

Story Eleven

GENESIS 24 : 1 to 25 : 18

Story of a Journey After a Wife

AFTER the death of Sā'rah, Ī'şaac, her son, was lonely; and as he was now old enough to marry, Ā'brā-hăm sought a wife for him; for in those countries the parents have always chosen the wives for their sons, and husbands for their daughters. Ā'brā-hăm did not wish Ī'şaac to marry any woman of the people in the land where he was living, for they were all worshipers of idols, and would not teach their children the ways of the Lord. For the same reason Ā'brā-hăm did not settle in one place, and build for himself and his people a city. By moving from place to place, Ā'brā-hăm kept his people apart.

You remember (Story Five) that when Ā'brā-hăm made his long journey to the land of Cā'năan, he stayed for a time at a place

called Hā'ran, in Mĕs-o-pŏ-tā'mĭ-à, between the two rivers Tī'gris
and Eū-phrā'teṣ, far to the northeast of Cā'năan. When Ā'bră-
hăm left Hā'ran to go to Cā'năan, his brother Nā'hôr and his
family stayed in Hā'ran. They worshiped the Lord, as Ā'bră-hăm
and his family did; and Ā'bră-hăm thought that it would be well
to find among them a wife for his son Ī'ṣaac.

As Ā'bră-hăm could not leave his own land of Cā'năan and go
to Hā'ran in Mĕs-o-pŏ-tā'mĭ-à to find a wife for his son Ī'ṣaac, he
called his chief servant, E-li-ē'zĕr, the man whom he trusted, who
cared for all his flocks and cattle, and who ruled over his other
servants and sent him to Hā'ran to find a wife for his son Ī'ṣaac.

And the servant took ten camels and many presents and went
on a long journey, and at last came to the city of Hā'ran, where
the family of Nā'hôr, the brother of Ā'bră-hăm, was living. And
at the well, just outside of the city, at the time of evening, he made
his camels kneel down. Then the servant prayed to the Lord that
he would send to him just the right young woman to be the wife
of his master's son Ī'ṣaac.

And just as the servant was praying, a beautiful young woman
came to the well, with her water jar upon her shoulder. As she
drew the water and filled her jar, the servant came up and bowed

to her, and said, "Will you kindly give me a drink of water from your jar?"

And she said, "Drink, my lord," and she held her jar for him to drink. And then she said, "I will draw some water for your camels also to drink."

And she emptied her jar into the trough by the well and drew more water, until she had given drink to all the camels.

And the servant of Ā'bră-hăm looked at her and wondered whether she might be the right woman for Ī'saac to marry. And he said to her, "Will you tell me your name, young lady, and whose daughter you are? And do you suppose that I could find a place to stay at your father's house?" And then he gave her a gold ring and gold bracelets for her wrists. And the beautiful young woman said, "My name is Rĕ-bĕk'ah; and my father is Bĕth-u'el, who is the son of Nā'hôr. You can come right to our house. We have room for you, and a place and food for your camels."

Then the man bowed his head and thanked God, for he saw that his prayer was answered, since this kind and lovely young woman was a cousin to Ī'saac, his master's son. And he told Rĕ-bĕk'ah that he was the servant of Ā'bră-hăm, who was so near a relative of her own family.

Then Rĕ-bĕk'ah ran home and told her parents of the stranger, and showed them the presents that he had given to her. And her brother Lā'ban went out to the man and brought him into the house, and found a place for his camels. And they washed his feet, for that was the custom of the land, where people did not wear shoes, but sandals: and they set the table for a supper and asked him to sit down and eat with them. But the man said, "I will not eat until I have told my errand."

After this he told them all about Ā'bră-hăm's riches; and how Ā'bră-hăm had sent him to Hā'ran to find a wife for Ī'saac, his son; and how he had met Rĕ-bĕk'ah, and felt sure that Rĕ-bĕk'ah was the one whom the Lord would choose for Ī'saac's wife; and then he asked that they would give him Rĕ-bĕk'ah to be taken home to be married to Ī'saac.

When he had told his errand, Lā'ban, Rĕ-bĕk'ah's brother, and

Bĕth-u'el, her father, said, "This comes from the Lord; it is his
will; and it is not for us to oppose it. Here is Rĕ-bĕk'ah; take her,
and let her be the wife of your master's son, for the Lord has
shown it to be his will."

Then Ā'bră-hăm's servant gave rich presents to Rĕ-bĕk'ah and
to her mother and her brother Lā'ban. And that night they had a
feast, with great joy. And the next morning Ā'bră-hăm's servant
said, "Now I must go home to my master." But they said, "Oh,
not so soon! Let Rĕ-bĕk'ah stay with us for a few days, ten days
at least, before she goes away from her home."

And he said to them, "Do not hinder me; since God has given
me what I came for, I must go back to my master."

And they called Rĕ-bĕk'ah and asked her, "Will you go with
this man?" And she said, "I will go."

So the servant of Ā'bră-hăm went away and took with him
Rĕ-bĕk'ah, with good wishes and blessings and prayers from all
in her father's house. And after a long journey, they came to the
place where Ā'bră-hăm and Ī'saac were living. And when Ī'saac
saw Rĕ-bĕk'ah, he loved her; and she became his wife, and they
were faithful to each other as long as they both lived.

Afterward Ā'bră-hăm, great and good man that he was, died,
almost a hundred and eighty years old. And Ī'saac and Ish'ma-el
buried Ā'bră-hăm in the cave where Ā'bră-hăm had buried Sā'rah
at Hē'bron. Then Ī'saac became the owner of all the riches of
Ā'bră-hăm, his tents and flocks of sheep and herds of cattle and
camels and servants. Ī'saac was a peaceful, quiet man. He did not
move his tents often, as his father had done, but stayed in one place
nearly all his life.

How Jacob Stole His Brother's Blessing

AFTER Ā'bră-hăm died, his son Ī'ṣaac lived in the land of Cā'năan. Like his father's, Ī'ṣaac's home was a tent; and around him were the tents of his people, and many flocks of sheep and herds of cattle feeding wherever they could find grass to eat and water to drink, because these were so necessary in sheep raising.

Ī'ṣaac and his wife Rĕ-bĕk'ah had two children. The older was named Ē'ṣau and the younger Jā'cob. Ē'ṣau was a man of the woods and fond of hunting; and he was rough and covered with hair. Even as a boy he was fond of hunting with his bow and arrow. Jā'cob was quiet and thoughtful, staying at home and caring for the flocks of his father. Ī'ṣaac loved Ē'ṣau more than Jā'cob, because Ē'ṣau brought to his father that which he had killed in his hunting; but Rĕ-bĕk'ah liked Jā'cob, because she saw that he was wise and careful in his work.

Among the people in those lands, when a man dies, his older son receives twice as much as the younger of what the father has owned. This was called his "birthright," for it was his right as the oldest born. So Ē'ṣau, as the older, had a "birthright," to more of Ī'ṣaac's possessions than Jā'cob. And besides this, there was the privilege of the promise of God that the family of Ī'ṣaac should receive great blessings.

Now Ē'ṣau, when he grew up, did not care for his birthright or the blessing which God had promised. But Jā'cob, who was a wise man, wished greatly to have the birthright which would come to Ē'ṣau when his father died. Once, when Ē'ṣau came home hungry and tired from hunting in the fields, he saw that Jā'cob had a bowl of something that he had just cooked for dinner. And Ē'ṣau said, "Give me some of that red stuff in the dish. Will you not give me some? I am hungry."

42

And Jā'cob answered, "I will give it to you, if you will first of all sell to me your birthright."

And Ē'sau said, "What is the use of the birthright to me now when I am almost starving to death? You can have my birthright if you will give me something to eat."

Then Ē'sau made Jā'cob a solemn promise to give to Jā'cob his birthright, all for a bowl of food. It was not right for Jā'cob to deal so selfishly with his brother; but it was very wrong in Ē'sau to care so little for his birthright, and with it God's blessing.

Some time after this, when Ē'sau was forty years old, he married two wives. Though this would be very wicked in our times, it was not supposed to be wrong then; for even good men then had more than one wife. But Ē'sau's two wives were women from the people of Cā'năan, who worshiped idols and not the true God. And they taught their children also to pray to idols, so that those who came from Ē'sau, the people who were his descendants, lost all knowledge of God and became very wicked. But this was long after that time.

Ī'saac and Rĕ-bĕk'ah were very sorry to have their son Ē'sau marry women who prayed to idols and not to God; but still Ī'saac loved his active son Ē'sau more than his quiet son Jā'cob.

Ī'ṣaac became at last very old and feeble and so blind that he could see scarcely anything. One day he said to Ē'ṣau:

"My son, I am very old and do not know how soon I must die. But before I die, I wish to give to you, as my older son, God's blessing upon you and your children and your descendants. Go out into the fields, and with your bow and arrows shoot some animal that is good for food and make me a dish of cooked meat, such as you know I love; and after I have eaten it, I will give you the blessing."

Ē'ṣau ought to have told his father that the blessing did not belong to him, for he had sold it to his brother Jā'cob. But he did not tell his father. He went out into the fields hunting, to find the kind of meat which his father liked the most.

Now Rĕ-bĕk'ah was listening, and heard all that Ī'ṣaac had said to Ē'ṣau. She knew that it would be better for Jā'cob to have the blessing than for Ē'ṣau; and she loved Jā'cob more than Ē'ṣau. So she called to Jā'cob and told him what Ī'ṣaac had said to Ē'ṣau and she said:

"Now, my son, do what I tell you and you will get the blessing instead of your brother. Go to the flocks and bring to me two little kids from the goats: and I will cook them just like the meat which Ē'ṣau cooks for your father. And you will bring it to your father; and he will think that you are Ē'ṣau and will give you the blessing; and it really belongs to you."

But Jā'cob said, "You know that Ē'ṣau and I are not alike. His neck and arms are covered with hair, while mine are smooth. My father will feel of me, and he will find that I am not Ē'ṣau; and then, instead of giving me a blessing, I am afraid he will curse me."

But Rĕ-bĕk'ah answered her son, "Never mind, you do as I have told you, and I will take care of you. If any harm comes, it will come to me; so do not be afraid, but go and bring the meat."

Then Jā'cob went and brought a pair of little kids from the flock, and from them his mother made a dish of food, so that it would be to the taste just as Ī'ṣaac liked it. Then Rĕ-bĕk'ah found some of Ē'ṣau's clothes, and dressed Jā'cob in them; and she placed on his neck and his hands some of the skins of the kids, so that his neck and hands would feel rough and hairy to the touch.

Then Jā'cob came into his father's tent, bringing the dinner and speaking as much like Ē'saŭ as he could, he said:

"Here I am, my father."

And Ī'saac said, "Who are you, my son?"

And Jā'cob answered, "I am Ē'saŭ, your oldest son. I have done as you bade me; now sit up and eat the dinner that I have made; and then give me your blessing, as you promised me."

And Ī'saac said, "How is it that you found it so quickly?"

Jā'cob answered, "Because the Lord your God showed me where to go and gave me good success."

Ī'saac did not feel certain that it was his son Ē'saŭ, and he said, "Come nearer and let me feel you, so that I may know that you are really my son Ē'saŭ."

And Jā'cob went up close to Ī'saac's bed, and Ī'saac felt of his face and his neck and his hands and he said:

"The voice sounds like Jā'cob, but the hands are the hands of Ē'saŭ. Are you really my son Ē'saŭ?"

And Jā'cob again told a lie to his father, and said, "I am."

Then the old man ate the food that Jā'cob had brought to him, and he kissed Jā'cob, believing him to be Ē'saŭ, and he gave him the blessing, saying to him:

"May God give you the dew of heaven and the richness of the earth and plenty of grain and wine. May nations bow down to you and people become your servants. May you be the master over your brother; and may your family and descendants that shall come from you rule over his family and his descendants. Blessed be those that bless you, and cursed be those that curse you."

Just as soon as Jā'cob had received the blessing, he rose up and hastened away. He had scarcely gone out, when Ē'saŭ came in from his hunting, with the dish of food that he had cooked, and he said:

"Let my father sit up and eat the food that I have brought and give me the blessing."

And Ī'saac said, "Why, who are you?"

Ē'saŭ answered, "I am your son, your oldest son Ē'saŭ."

And Ī'saac trembled and said, "Who then is the one that came in and brought to me food? And I have eaten his food and have blessed him; yes, and he shall be blessed."

When Ē'sạu heard this, he knew that he had been cheated; and he cried aloud, with a bitter cry, "O my father, my brother has taken away my blessing, just as he took away my birthright! But cannot you give me another blessing, too? Have you given everything to my brother?" And Ī'ṣaac told him all that he had said to Jā'cob.

He said, "I have told him that he shall be the ruler, and that all his brothers and their children will be under him. I have promised him the richest ground for his crops and rains from heaven to make them grow. All these things have been spoken, and they must come to pass. What is left for me to promise you, my son?"

But Ē'sạu begged for another blessing, and Ī'ṣaac said:

"My son, your dwelling shall be of the riches of the earth and of the dew of heaven. You shall live by your sword, and your descendants shall serve his descendants. But in time to come, they shall break loose and shall shake off the yoke of your brother's rule and shall be free."

All this came to pass many years afterward. The people who came from Ē'sạu lived in a land called Ē'dom, on the south of the land of Ĭs'ra-el, where Jā'cob's descendants lived. And after a time the Ĭs'ra-el-ītes became rulers over the Ē'dom-ītes; and, later still the Ē'dom-ītes made themselves free from the Ĭs'ra-el-ītes. But all this took place hundreds of years after both Ē'sạu and Jā'cob had passed away. The blessing of God's covenant or promise came to Ĭs'ra-el, and not to the people from Ē'sạu.

It was better that Jā'cob's descendants, those who came after him, should have the blessing, than that Ē'sạu's people should have it; for Jā'cob's people worshiped God, and Ē'sạu's people walked in the way of the idols and became wicked. But it was very wrong in Jā'cob to obtain the blessing in the way that he obtained it.

Jacob's Wonderful Dream

AFTER Ē'saụ found that he had lost his birthright and his blessing, he was very angry against his brother Jā'cob; and he said to himself and told others, "My father Ī'ṣaac is very old and cannot live long. As soon as he is dead, then I shall kill Jā'cob for having robbed me of my right."

When Rĕ-bĕk'ah heard this, she said to Jā'cob, "Before it is too late, go away from home and get out of Ē'saụ's sight. Perhaps when Ē'saụ sees you no longer, he will forget his anger; and then you can come home again. Go and visit my brother Lā'ban, your uncle, in Hā'ran, and stay with him for a little while, until Ē'saụ's anger is past."

You remember that Rĕ-bĕk'ah came from the family of Nā'hôr, Ā'brȧ-hăm's younger brother, who lived in Hā'ran, a long distance to the northeast of Cā'nǎan; and that Lā'ban was Rĕ-bĕk'ah's brother, as was told in Story Eleven.

So Jā'cob went out of Bē'er=shē'bȧ, on the border of the desert, and walked alone toward a land far to the north, carrying his staff in his hand. One evening, just about sunset, he came to a place among the mountains, more than sixty miles distant from his home. And as he had no bed to lie down upon, he took a stone and rested his head upon it for a pillow and lay down to sleep. We would think that a hard pillow, but Jā'cob was very tired and soon fell asleep.

And on that night Jā'cob had a wonderful dream. In his dream he saw stairs leading up to heaven from the earth where he lay; and angels were coming down and going up upon the stairs. And above the stairs, he saw the Lord God standing. And God said to Jā'cob:

"I am the Lord, the God of Ā'brȧ-hăm and the God of Ī'ṣaac your father; and I will be your God, too. The land where you are lying all alone shall belong to you and to your children after

God speaks to Jacob through a dream.

you; and your children shall spread abroad over the lands, east and west and north and south, like the dust of the earth: and in your family all the world shall receive a blessing. And I am with you in your journey, and I will keep you where you are going and will bring you back to this land. I will never leave you and I will surely keep my promise to you."

And in the morning Jā′cob awaked from his sleep and he said, "Surely the Lord is in this place and I did not know it! I thought that I was all alone, but God has been with me. This place is the house of God; it is the gate of heaven!"

And Jā′cob took the stone on which his head had rested and he set it up as a pillar and poured oil on it as an offering to God. And Jā′cob named that place Bĕth′el, which in the language that Jā′cob spoke means "The House of God."

And Jā′cob made a promise to God at that time and said:

"If God really will go with me, and will keep me in the way that I go, and will give me bread to eat, and will bring me to my father's house in peace, then the Lord shall be my God; and this stone shall be the house of God; and of all that God gives me, I will give back to God one-tenth as an offering."

Then Jā′cob went onward in his long journey. He waded across the river Jôr′dan in a shallow place, feeling the way with his staff; he climbed mountains and journeyed beside the great desert on the east, and at last he came to the city of Hā′ran. Beside the city was the well, where Ā'bră-hăm's servant had met Jā'cob's mother, Rĕ-bĕk'ah (see Story Eleven); and there, after Jā'cob had waited for a time, he saw a young woman coming with her sheep to give them water.

Then Jā'cob took off the flat stone that was over the mouth of the well and drew water and gave it to the sheep. And when he found that this young woman was his own cousin Rā'chel, the daughter of Lā'ban, he was so glad that he wept for joy. And at that moment he began to love Rā'chel and longed to have her for his wife.

Rā'chel's father, Lā'ban, who was Jā'cob's uncle, the brother of Rĕ-bĕk'ah, Jā'cob's mother, gave a welcome to Jā'cob and took him into his home.

And Jā'cob asked Lā'ban if he would give his daughter Rā'chel to him as his wife; and Jā'cob said, "If you will give me Rā'chel, I will work for you seven years."

And Lā'ban said, "It is better that you should have her than that a stranger should marry her."

So Jā'cob lived seven years in Lā'ban's house, caring for his sheep and oxen and camels; and such was his love for Rā'chel that the seven years seemed like a few days.

At last the day came for the marriage; and they brought in the bride, who after the manner of that land was covered with a thick veil, so that her face could not be seen. And she was married to Jā'cob; and when Jā'cob lifted up her veil, he found that he had married, not Rā'chel whom he loved, but her older sister Lē'ah, who was not beautiful, and whom Jā'cob did not love at all.

Jā'cob was very angry that he had been deceived, though that was just the way in which Jā'cob himself had deceived his father and cheated his brother Ē'sau (see Story Twelve). But his uncle Lā'ban said:

"In our land we never allow the younger daughter to be married before the older daughter. Keep Lē'ah for your wife, and work for me seven years longer, and you shall have Rā'chel also."

For in those times, as we have seen, men often had two wives, or even more than two. No one thought that it was wrong then to have more than one wife, although now it is considered very wicked. So Jā'cob stayed seven years more, fourteen years in all, before he received Rā'chel as his wife.

While Jā'cob was living at Hā'ran, eleven sons were born to him. But only one of these was the child of Rā'chel, whom Jā'cob loved. This son was Jō'ṣeph, who was dearer to Jā'cob than any other of his children, partly because he was the youngest, and also because he was the child of his beloved Rā'chel.

Story Fourteen

GENESIS 30 : 25 to 33 : 20

A Midnight Wrestling Match

JĀ'COB stayed a long time in the land of Hā'ran, much longer than he had expected to stay. And in that land Jā'cob became rich. As wages for his work with Lā'ban, Jā'cob took a share of the sheep and oxen and camels. And since Jā'cob was very wise and careful in his work, his share grew larger, until Jā'cob owned a great flock and much cattle. At last, after twenty years, Jā'cob decided to go back to the land of Cā'nặan and to his father Ī'ṣaac, who was still living, though now very old and feeble.

Jā'cob did not tell his uncle Lā'ban that he was going away; but while Lā'ban was absent from home, Jā'cob gathered together his wives and children and all his sheep and cattle and camels, and he stole away quietly. When Lā'ban found that Jā'cob had left him, he was not at all pleased; for he wished Jā'cob still to care for the things that he owned, for Jā'cob managed them better than Lā'ban himself, and God blessed everything that Jā'cob undertook. Then, too, Lā'ban did not like to have his two daughters, the wives of Jā'cob, taken so far away from him.

So Lā'ban and the men who were with him followed after Jā'cob; but that night God spoke to Lā'ban in a dream and said: "Do no harm to Jā'cob when you meet him."

Therefore, when Lā'ban came to where Jā'cob was in his camp on Mount Ḡĭl'e-ăd, on the east of the river Jôr'dan, Lā'ban spoke kindly to Jā'cob. And Jā'cob and Lā'ban made a covenant, that is, a promise between them. They piled up a heap of stones and on it they set up a large rock like a pillar; and beside the heap of stones they ate a meal together; and Jā'cob said to Lā'ban:

"I promise not to go past this heap of stones and this pillar, to do you any harm. The God of your grandfather, Nā'hôr, and the God of my grandfather, Ā'bră-hăm, be the judge between us."

And Lā'ban made the same promise to Jā'cob; and then he kissed his daughters, Jā'cob's two wives, and all of Jā'cob's children, and bade them good-by; and Lā'ban went back to Hā'ran and Jā'cob went on to Cā'năan.

And Jā'cob gave two names to the heap of stones where they had made the covenant. One name was "Găl'e-ĕd," a word which means, "The heap of Witness." The other was "Mĭz'peh," which means "Watch-tower." For Jā'cob said, "The Lord watch between you and me, when we are absent from each other."

While Jā'cob was going back to Cā'năan, he heard news that filled him with fear. He heard that Ē'sau, his brother, was coming to meet him, leading an army of four hundred men. He knew how angry Ē'sau had been long before, and how he had threatened to kill him. And Jā'cob feared that Ē'sau would now come upon him and kill not only Jā'cob himself but his wives and his children. If Jā'cob had acted rightly toward his brother, he need not have feared Ē'sau's coming; but he knew how he had wronged Ē'sau, and he was terribly afraid to meet him.

That night Jā'cob divided his company into two parts; so that if one part were taken the other part might escape. And he sent onward before him, as a present to his brother, a great drove of oxen and cows, and sheep and goats, and camels and asses; hoping that by the present his brother might be made more kind toward him. And then Jā'cob prayed earnestly to the Lord God to help him. After that he sent all his family across a brook that was in his path, called the brook Jăb'bŏk, while he stayed alone on the other side of the brook to pray again.

And while Jā'cob was alone, he felt that a man had taken hold of him, and Jā'cob wrestled with this strange man all the night. And the man was the angel from God. They wrestled so hard that Jā'cob's thigh was strained in the struggle. And the angel said: "Let me go, for the day is breaking."

And Jā'cob said: "I will not let thee go until thou dost bless me." And the angel said:

"What is your name?"

And Jā'cob answered, "Jā'cob is my name."

Then the angel said:

"Your name shall no more be called Jā'cob, but Iṣ'ra-el, that is, 'He who wrestles with God.' For you have wrestled with God and have won the victory."

Jacob wrestles with angel of god

And the angel blessed him there. And the sun rose as the angel left him; and Jā'cob gave a name to that place. He called it Pĕ-nī'el, or Pĕ-nū'el, words which in the language that Jā'cob spoke mean "The Face of God." "For," said Jā'cob, "I have met God face to face." And after this Jā'cob was lame, for in the wrestle he had strained his thigh.

And as Jā'cob went across the brook Jăb'bŏk, early in the morning, he looked up, and there was Ē'sau right before him. He bowed with his face to the ground, over and over again, as people do in those lands when they meet someone of higher rank than their own. But Ē'sau ran to meet him and placed his arms around his neck and kissed him; and the two brothers wept together. Ē'sau was kind and generous to forgive his brother all the wrong that he had done; and at first he would not receive Jā'cob's present, for he said: "I have enough, my brother." But Jā′cob urged him, until at last he took the present. And so the quarrel was ended and the two brothers were at peace.

Jā′cob came to Shē′chem, in the middle of the land of Cā′năan, and there he set up his tents; and at the foot of the mountain, although there were streams of water all around, he dug his own well, great and deep; the well where Jē′ṣus sat and talked with a woman many ages after that time, and the well that may be still seen.

After that Jā′cob had a new name, Iṣ′ra-el, which means, as we have seen, "The one who wrestles with God." Sometimes he was called Jā′cob and sometimes Iṣ′ra-el. . And all those who come from Iṣ′ra-el, his descendants, were called Iṣ′ra-el-ītes.

Not long afterward the aged Ī′saac died, and was buried by his sons, Jā′cob and Ē′ṣau, in the cave at Hē′bron where Ā′bră-hăm and Sā′rah were buried already. Ē′ṣau with his children and his cattle went away to a land on the southeast of Cā′năan, which was called Ē′dom. And Jā′cob, or Iṣ′ra-el, and his family lived in the land of Cā′năan, dwelling in tents and moving from place to place where they could find good pasture, or grass, for their flocks.

Story Fifteen GENESIS 37 : 1-36

The Rich Man's Son Who Was Sold as a Slave

AFTER Jā′cob came back to the land of Cā′năan with his eleven sons, another son was born to him, the second child of his wife Rā′chel, whom Jā′cob loved so well. You remember we told in Story Thirteen how long Jā′cob worked for Lā′ban caring for his sheep and oxen in order that he might have Rā′chel for his wife. But now a great sorrow was to come to Jā′cob, for soon after the

baby came, his mother Rā'chel died, and Jā'cob was filled with
sorrow. Even to this day you can see the place where Rā'chel
was buried on the road between Jĕ-ru'sa-lĕm and Bĕth'lĕ-hĕm.
Jā'cob named the child whom Rā'chel left, Bĕn'ja-mĭn; and
now Jā'cob had twelve sons. Most of them were grown-up men,
but Jō'şeph was a boy, seventeen years old, and his brother Bĕn'ja-
mĭn was very young.

Of all his children, Jā'cob loved Jō'şeph the best, because he
was Rā'chel's child, because he was so much younger than most
of his brothers, and because he was good and faithful and thoughtful. Jā'cob gave to Jō'şeph a robe or coat of many colors made
somewhat like a long cloak with wide sleeves. This was a special
mark of Jā'cob's favor to Jō'şeph, and it made his older brothers
very envious of him.

Then, too, Jō'şeph did what was right, while his older brothers
often did very wrong acts, of which Jō'şeph sometimes told their
father, and this made them very angry at Jō'şeph. But they hated
him still more because of two strange dreams that he had and of
which he told them. He said one day:

"Listen to this dream that I have dreamed. I dreamed that we
were out in the field binding sheaves, when suddenly my sheaf
stood up and all your sheaves came around it and bowed down to

my sheaf." And they said scornfully, "Do you suppose that the dream means that you will some time rule over us, and that we shall bow down to you?" Then a few days after Jō'ṣeph said, "I have dreamed again. This time I saw in my dream the sun and the moon and eleven stars all come and bow down to me."

And his father said to him, "I do not like you to dream such dreams. Shall I and your mother and your brothers come and bow down before you, as if you were a king?"

His brothers hated Jō'ṣeph and would not speak kindly to him; but his father thought much of what Jō'ṣeph had said.

At one time, Jō'ṣeph's ten older brothers were taking care of the flock in the fields near Shē'chem, which was nearly fifty miles from Hē'bron, where Jā'cob's tents were spread. And Jā'cob wished to send a message to his sons, so he called Jō'ṣeph and said to him, "Your brothers are near Shē'chem with the flock. I wish that you would go to them and take a message, and find if they are well, and if the flocks are doing well; and bring me word."

That was quite an errand for a boy to go alone over the country, and find his way, for fifty miles, and then walk home again. But Jō'ṣeph was a boy that could take care of himself and could be trusted; so he went forth on his journey, walking northward over the mountains, past Bĕth'lĕ-hĕm and Jĕ-ru'sà-lĕm and Bĕth'el—though we are not sure that any of those cities were then built, except Jĕ-ru'sà-lĕm, which we know was already a strong city.

When Jō'ṣeph reached Shē'chem, he could not find his brothers, for they had taken their flocks to another place. A man met Jō'ṣeph wandering in the field and asked him, "Whom are you seeking?" Jō'ṣeph said, "I am looking for my brothers, the sons of Jā'cob. Can you tell me where I will find them?" And the man said, "They are at Dō'than; for I heard them say that they were going there." Then Jō'ṣeph walked over the hills to Dō'than, which was fifteen miles farther. And his brothers saw him afar off coming toward them. They knew him by his bright garment; and one said to another:

"Look, that dreamer is coming! Come, let us kill him and throw his body into a pit and tell his father that some wild beast has eaten him; and then we will see what becomes of his dreams."

One of his brothers, whose name was Reu′ben, felt more kindly toward Jō′seph than the others; but he did not dare to oppose the others openly. Reu′ben said:

"Let us not kill him; but let us throw him into this pit, here in the wilderness, and leave him there to die."

But Reu′ben intended, after they had gone away, to lift Jō′seph out of the pit and take him home to his father. The brothers did as Reu′ben told them; they threw Jō′seph into the pit, which was empty. He cried and begged them to save him, but they would not. They calmly sat down to eat their dinner on the grass, while their brother was calling to them from the pit.

After the dinner, Reu′ben chanced to go to another part of the field, so that he was not at hand when a company of men passed by with their camels, going from Gĭl′e-ăd, on the east of the river Jôr′dan, to Ē′ġўpt, to sell to the Ē-ġўp′tians spices and fragrant gum from trees. Then Jū′dah, another of Jō′seph's brothers, said, "What good will it do us to kill our brother? Would it not be better for us to sell him to these men and let them carry him away? After all, he is our brother, and we would better not kill him?"

His brothers agreed with him; so they stopped the men who were passing, and drew up Jō′seph from the pit; and for twenty pieces of silver, they sold Jō′seph to these men; and they took him away with them down to Ē-ġўpt.

After a while, Reu′ben came to the pit, where he had left Jō′seph and looked into it; but Jō′seph was not there. Then Reu′ben was in great trouble and he came back to his brothers saying, "The boy is not there! What shall I do?"

Then his brothers told Reu′ben what they had done, and they all agreed together to deceive their father. They killed one of the goats and dipped Jō′seph's coat in its blood, and they brought it to their father and they said to him, "We found this coat out in the wilderness. Look at it, and see if you think it was your son's." And Jā′cob knew it at once. He said, "It is my son's coat. Some wild beast has eaten him. There is no doubt that Jō′seph has been torn in pieces!"

And Jā′cob's heart was broken over the loss of Jō′seph, all the more because he had sent Jō′seph alone on the journey through the wilderness. They tried to comfort him, but he would not be comforted. He said:

"I will go down to the grave mourning for my poor lost son."

So the old man sorrowed for his son Jō'şeph; and all the time his wicked brothers knew that Jō'şeph was not dead; but they would not tell their father the dreadful deed that they had done to their brother, in selling him as a slave.

Story Sixteen   GENESIS 40 : 1 to 41 : 44

From the Prison to the Palace

THE men who bought Jō'şeph from his brothers were called Ĭsh'ma-el-ītes, because they belonged to the family of Ĭsh'ma-el, who, you remember, was the son of Hā'gar, the servant of Sā'rah. These men carried Jō'şeph southward over the plain which lies beside the great sea on the west of Cā'năan; and after many days they brought Jō'şeph to Ē'ġўpt. How strange it must have seemed to the boy who had lived in tents, to see the great river Nile and the cities, thronged with people, and the temples and the mighty pyramids!

The Ĭsh'ma-el-ītes sold Jō'şeph as a slave to a man named Pŏt'ĭ-phar, who was an officer in the army of Phā'raōh, the king of Ē'ġўpt. Jō'şeph was a beautiful boy, cheerful and willing in spirit, and able in all that he undertook; so that his master, Pŏt'ĭ-phar, became very friendly with him, and after a time he placed Jō'şeph in charge of his house and everything in it. For some years Jō'şeph continued in the house of Pŏt'ĭ-phar, a slave in name, but in reality the master of all his affairs and ruler over his fellow servants.

But Pŏt'ĭ-phar's wife, who at first was very friendly to Jō'şeph, afterward became his enemy, because Jō'şeph would not do wrong to please her. She told her husband falsely that Jō'şeph had done a wicked deed. Her husband believed her, and was very angry at

Jō'şeph, and put him in the prison with those who had been sent to that place for breaking the laws of the land. How hard it was for Jō'şeph to be charged with a crime, when he had done no wrong, and to be thrust into a dark prison among wicked people!

But Jō'şeph had faith in God, that at some time all would come out right; and in the prison he was cheerful and kind and helpful, as he had always been. The keeper of the prison saw that Jō'şeph was not like the other men around him, and he was kind to Jō'şeph. In a very little while Jō'şeph was placed in charge of all his fellow prisoners and took care of them; just as he had taken care of everything in Pŏt'ĭ-phar's house. The keeper of the prison scarcely looked into the prison at all, for he had confidence in Jō'seph that he would be faithful and wise in doing the work given to him. Jō'şeph did right and served God; and God blessed Jō'şeph in everything.

While Jō'şeph was in the prison, two men were sent there by the king of Ē'ġўpt, because he was displeased with them. One was the king's chief butler, who served the king with wine; the other was the chief baker, who served him with bread. These two men were under Jō'şeph's care, and Jō'şeph waited on them, for they were men of rank.

One morning, when Jō'şeph came into the room in the prison where the butler and the baker were kept, he found them looking quite sad. Jō'şeph said to them:

"Why do you look so sad today?" Jō'şeph was cheerful and happy in his spirit and he wished others to be happy, even in prison.

And one of the men said, "Each one of us dreamed last night a very strange dream; and there is no one to tell us what our dreams mean."

For in those times, before God gave the Bible to men, he often spoke to men in dreams; and there were wise men who could sometimes tell what the dreams meant.

"Tell me," said Jō'şeph, "what your dreams were. Perhaps my God will help me to understand them."

Then the chief butler told his dream. He said, "In my dream I saw a grapevine with three branches; and as I looked, the

branches shot out buds, and the buds became blossoms, and the blossoms turned into clusters of ripe grapes. And I picked the grapes and squeezed their juice into King Phā′raōh's cup, and it became wine; and I gave it to King Phā′raōh to drink, just as I used to do when I was beside his table."

Then Jō′ṣeph said, "This is what your dream means. The three branches mean three days. In three days King Phā′raōh will call you out of prison, and will put you back in your place; and you shall stand at his table, and shall give him his wine, as you have given it before. But when you go out of prison, please to remember me, and try to find some way to get me, too, out of prison. For I was stolen out of the land of Cā′nặan and sold as a slave; and I have done nothing wrong, to deserve being put in this prison. Do speak to the king for me, that I may be set free."

Of course the chief butler felt very happy to hear that his dream had so pleasant a meaning; and then the chief baker spoke, hoping to have an answer as good.

"In my dream," said the baker, "there were three baskets of

white bread on my head, one above the other, and on the topmost basket were all kinds of roasted meat and food for Phā'raōh; and the birds came and ate the food from the baskets on my head."

And Jō'seph said to the baker:

"This is the meaning of your dream, and I am sorry to tell it to you. The three baskets are three days. In three days, by order of the king, you shall be lifted up and hanged upon a tree; and the birds shall eat your flesh from your bones as you are hanging in the air."

And it came to pass, just as Jō'seph had said. Three days after that, King Phā'raōh sent his officers to the prison. They came and took out both the chief butler and the chief baker. The baker they hung up by his neck to die and left his body for the birds to pick in pieces. The chief butler they brought back to his old place, where he waited at the king's table and handed him his wine to drink.

You would have supposed that the butler would remember Jō'seph, who had given him the promise of freedom, and had shown such wisdom. But in his gladness, he forgot all about Jō'seph. And two full years passed by, while Jō'seph was still in prison, until he was a man thirty years old.

But one night, King Phā'raōh himself dreamed a dream, in fact two dreams in one. And in the morning he sent for all the wise men of Ē'gy̆pt and told them his dreams; but there was not a man who could give the meaning of them. And the king was troubled, for he felt that the dreams had some meaning, which it was important for him to know.

Then suddenly the chief butler, who was by the king's table, remembered his own dream in the prison two years before, and remembered, too, the young man who had told its meaning so exactly. And he said:

"I do remember my faults this day. Two years ago King Phā'raōh was angry with his servants, with me and the chief baker, and he sent us to the prison. While we were in the prison, one night each of us dreamed a dream, and the next day a young man in the prison, a Hē'brew from the land of Cā'năan, told us what our dreams meant; and in three days they came true, just as the

Hē′brew had said. I think that if this young man is still in the prison, he could tell the king the meaning of his dreams."

You notice that the butler spoke of Jō′seph as "a Hē′brew." The people of Ĭṣ′ra-el, to whom Jō′seph belonged, were called Hē′brews as well as Ĭṣ′ra-el-ītes. The word Hē′brew means "one who crosses over," and was given to the Ĭṣ′ra-el-ītes because Ā′brā-hăm their father had come from a land on the other side of the river Eū-phrā′tēṣ, and had crossed over the river on his way to Cā′năan.

King Phā′raōh sent in haste to the prison for Jō′seph; and Jō′seph was taken out, and he was dressed in new garments and was led in to Phā′raōh in the palace. And Phā′raōh said to Jō′seph, "I have dreamed a dream, and there is no one who can tell what it means. And I have been told that you have power to understand dreams and what they mean."

And Jō′seph answered Phā′raōh, "The power is not in me; but God will give Phā′raōh a good answer. What is the dream that the king has dreamed?"

"In my first dream," said Phā′raōh, "I was standing by the river; and I saw seven fat and handsome cows come up from the river to feed in the grass. And while they were feeding, seven other cows followed them up from the river, very thin and poor and lean, such miserable creatures as I had never seen. And the seven lean cows ate up the seven fat cows; and after they had eaten them, they were as lean and miserable as before. Then I awoke.

"And I fell asleep again and dreamed again. In my second dream, I saw seven heads of grain growing upon one stalk, large and strong and good. And then seven heads came up after them, that were thin and poor and withered. And the seven thin heads swallowed up the seven good heads, and afterward were as poor and withered as before.

"And I told these two dreams to all the wise men, and there is no one who can tell me their meaning. Can you tell me what these dreams mean?"

And Jō′seph said to the king:

"The two dreams have the same meaning. God has been show-ing to King Phā′raōh what he will do in this land. The seven good cows mean seven years, and the seven good heads of grain mean the same seven years. The seven lean cows and the seven thin heads of grain also mean seven years. The good cows and the good grain mean seven years of plenty; and the seven thin cows and thin heads of grain mean seven poor years. There are coming upon the land of Ē′gy̆pt seven years of such plenty as have never been seen; when the fields shall bring greater crops than ever before; and after those years shall come seven years when the fields shall bring no crops at all. And then for seven years there shall be such need, that the years of plenty will be forgotten, for the people will have nothing to eat.

"Now, let King Phā′raōh find some man who is able and wise, and let him set this man to rule over the land. And during the seven years of plenty, let a part of the crops be put away for the years of need. If this shall be done, then when the years of need come there will be plenty of food for all the people and no one will suffer, for all will have enough."

And King Phā′raōh said to Jō′seph:

"Since God has shown you all this, there is no other man as wise as you. I will appoint you to do this work and to rule over the land of Ē′gy̆pt. All the people shall be under you; only on the throne of Ē′gy̆pt, I will be above you."

And Phā′raōh took from his own hand the ring which held his seal, and put it on Jō′seph's hand, so that he could sign for the king and seal in the king's place. And he dressed Jō′seph in robes of fine linen, and put around his neck a gold chain. And he made Jō′seph ride in a chariot which was next in rank to his own. And they cried out before Jō′seph, "Bow the knee." And thus Jō′seph was ruler over all the land of Ē′gy̆pt.

So the slave boy, who was sent to prison without deserving it, came out of prison to be a prince and a master over all the land. You see that God had not forgotten Jō′seph, even when he seemed to have left him to suffer.

How Joseph's Dream Came True

WHEN Jō'şeph was made ruler over the land of Ē'ġȳpt, he did just as he had always done. It was not Jō'şeph's way to sit down and rest and enjoy himself, and to make others wait on him. He found his work at once and began to do it faithfully and thoroughly. He went out over all the land of Ē'ġȳpt and saw how rich and abundant were the fields of grain, giving much more than the people could use for their own needs. He told the people not to waste it, but to save it for the coming time of need.

And he called upon the people to give him for the king one bushel of grain out of every five, to be stored up. The people brought their grain, after taking for themselves as much as they needed; and Jō'şeph stored it up in great storehouses in the cities, so much at last that no one could keep account of it.

The king of Ē'ġȳpt gave a wife to Jō'şeph from the noble young women of his kingdom. Her name was Ăs'e-năth; and to Jō'şeph and his wife God gave two sons. The oldest son he named Mȧ-năs'seh, a word which means "making to forget."

"For," said Jō'şeph, "God has made me forget all my troubles and my toil as a slave."

The second son he named Ē'phră-ĭm, a word that means "Fruitful."

"Because," said Jō'şeph, "God has not only made the land fruitful, but he has made me fruitful in the land of my troubles."

The seven years of plenty soon passed by and then came the years of need. In all the lands around people were hungry, and there was no food for them to eat; but in the land of Ē'ġȳpt everybody had enough. Most of the people soon used up the grain that they had saved: many had saved none at all, and they all cried to the king to help them.

63

"Go to Jō'şeph," said King Phā'raōh, "and do whatever he tells you to do."

Then the people came to Jō'şeph, and Jō'şeph opened the store-houses and sold to the people all the grain that they wished to buy. And not only the people of Ē'ġўpt came to buy grain, but people of all the lands around as well, for there was great need and famine everywhere.

And the need was as great in the land of Cā'năan, where Jā'cob lived, as in other lands. Jā'cob was rich in flocks and cattle and gold and silver; but his fields gave no grain, and there was danger that his family and his people would starve. And Jā'cob—who was now called Ĭş'ra-el also—heard that there was food in Ē'ġўpt, and he said to his sons:

"Why do you look at each other, asking what to do to find food? I have been told that there is grain in Ē'ġўpt. Go down to that land and take money with you, and buy grain, so that we may have bread and may live."

Then the ten older brothers of Jō'şeph went down to the land of Ē'ġўpt. They rode upon asses, for horses were not much used in those times, and they brought money with them. But Jā'cob would not let Bĕn'ja-mĭn, Jō'şeph's younger brother, go with them, for he was all the more dear to his father, now that Jō'şeph was no longer with him; and Jā'cob feared that harm might come to him.

Then Jō'şeph's brothers came to Jō'şeph to buy food. They did not know him, grown up to be a man, dressed as a prince and seated on a throne. Jō'şeph was now nearly forty years old, and it had been almost twenty-three years since they had sold him. But Jō'şeph knew them all, as soon as he saw them. He resolved to be sharp and stern with them, not because he hated them, but because he wished to see what their spirit was, and whether they were as selfish and cruel and wicked as they had been in other days.

They came before him and bowed with their faces to the ground. Then, no doubt, Jō'şeph thought of the dream that had come to him while he was a boy, of his brothers' sheaves bending

down around his sheaf. He spoke to them as a stranger, as if he did not understand their language, and he had their words explained to him in the language of Ē'ḡўpt.

"Who are you? And from what place do you come?" said Jō'ṣeph, in a harsh, stern manner.

They answered him, very meekly, "We have come from the land of Cā'năan to buy food."

"No," said Jō'ṣeph, "I know what you have come for. You have come as spies, to see how helpless the land is, so that you can bring an army against us and make war on us."

"No, no," said Jō'ṣeph's ten brothers, "we are no spies, we are the sons of one man, who lives in the land of Cā'năan; and we have come for food, because we have none at home."

"You say you are the sons of one man, who is your father? Is he living? Have you any more brothers? Tell me all about yourselves."

And they said, "Our father is an old man in Cā'năan. We did have a younger brother, but he was lost; and we have one brother still, who is the youngest of all, but his father could not spare him to come with us."

"No," said Jō'ṣeph, "you are not good, honest men. You are

spies. I shall put you all in prison, except one of you; and he shall go and bring that youngest brother of yours; and when I see him, then I will believe that you tell the truth."

So Jō'ṣeph put all the ten men in prison and kept them under guard for three days; then he sent for them again. They did not know that he could understand their language and they said to each other, while Jō'ṣeph heard, but pretended not to hear:

"This has come upon us because of the wrong that we did to our brother Jō'ṣeph, more than twenty years ago. We heard him cry and plead with us when we threw him into the pit, and we would not have mercy on him. God is giving us only what we have deserved."

And Reu'ben, who had tried to save Jō'ṣeph, said, "Did I not tell you not to harm the boy? And you would not listen to me. God is bringing our brother's blood upon us all."

When Jō'ṣeph heard this, his heart was touched, for he saw that his brothers were really sorry for the wrong that they had done him. He turned away from them, so that they could not see his face, and he wept. Then he turned again to them and spoke roughly as before, and said:

"This I will do, for I serve God, I will let you all go home, except one man. One of you I will shut up in prison; but the rest of you can go home and take food for your people. And you must come back and bring your youngest brother with you, and I shall know then that you have spoken the truth."

Then Jō'ṣeph gave orders, and his servants seized one of his brothers, whose name was Sĭm'e-on, and bound him in their sight and took him away to prison. And he ordered his servants to fill the men's sacks with grain and to put every man's money back into the sack before it was tied up, so that they would find the money as soon as they opened the sack. Then the men loaded their asses with the sacks of grain and started to go home, leaving their brother Sĭm'e-on a prisoner.

When they stopped on the way to feed their asses, one of the brothers opened his sack and there he found his money lying on the top of the grain. He called out to his brothers, "See, here is my money given again to me!" And they were frightened; but they did not dare to go back to Ē′ġўpt and meet the stern ruler of the land. They went home and told their old father all that had happened to them; and how their brother Sĭm′e-on was in prison and must stay there until they should return, bringing Bĕn′ja-mĭn with them.

When they opened their sacks of grain, there, in the mouth of each sack, was the money that they had given; and they were filled with fear. Then they spoke of going again to Ē′ġўpt and taking Bĕn′ja-mĭn, but Jā′cob said to them:

"You are taking my sons away from me. Jō′ṣeph is gone and Sĭm′e-on is gone, and now you would take Bĕn′ja-mĭn away. All these things are against me!"

Reṳ′ben said, "Here are my own two boys. You may kill them, if you wish, in case I do not bring Bĕn′ja-mĭn back to you."

But Jā′cob said, "My youngest son shall not go with you. His brother is dead, and he alone is left to me. If harm should come to him, it would bring down my gray hairs with sorrow to the grave."

Story Eighteen

GENESIS 43 : 1 to 45 : 24

A Lost Brother Found

THE FOOD which Jā′cob's sons had brought from Ē′ġўpt did not last long, for Jā′cob's family was large. Most of his sons were married and had children of their own; so that the children and grandchildren were sixty-six, besides the servants who waited on them and the men who cared for Jā′cob's flocks. So around the tent of Jā′cob was quite a camp of other tents and an army of people.

When the food that had come from Ē′ġўpt was nearly eaten up, Jā′cob said to his sons:

"Go down to Ē′ġўpt again and buy some more food for us."

And Jū′dah, Jā′cob's son, the man who years before had urged his brothers to sell Jō′şeph to the Ïsh′ma-el-ïtes, said to his father:

"It is of no use for us to go to Ē′ğÿpt, unless we take Bĕn′ja-mĭn with us. The man who rules in that land said to us, 'You shall not see my face unless your youngest brother be with you.'"

Ïş′ra-el said, "Why did you tell the man that you had a brother? You did me great harm when you told him."

"Why," said Jā′cob's sons, "we could not help telling him. The man asked us all about our family. Is your father yet living? Have you any more brothers? And we had to tell him, his questions were so close. How should we know that he would say, 'Bring your brother here for me to see him.'"

And Jū′dah said, "Send Bĕn′ja-mĭn with me, and I will take care of him. I promise you that I will bring him safely home. If he does not come back, let me bear the blame forever. He must go or we shall die for want of food; and we might have gone down to Ē′ğÿpt and come home again, if we had not been kept back."

And Jā′cob said, "If he must go, then he must. But take a present to the man, some of the choicest fruits of the land, some spices and perfumes and nuts and almonds. And take twice as much money, besides the money that was in your sacks. Perhaps that was a mistake, when the money was given back to you. And take your brother Bĕn′ja-mĭn; and may the Lord God make the man kind to you, so that he will set Sĭm′e-on free and let you bring Bĕn′ja-mĭn back. But if it is God's will that I lose my children, I cannot help it."

So ten brothers of Jō′şeph went down a second time to Ē′ğÿpt, Bĕn′ja-mĭn going in place of Sĭm′e-on. They came to Jō′şeph's office, the place where he sold grain to the people; and they stood before their brother and bowed as before. Jō′şeph saw that Bĕn′ja-mĭn was with them, and he said to his steward, "Make ready a dinner, for all these men shall dine with me today."

When Jō′şeph's brothers found that they were taken into Jō′şeph's house, they were filled with fear; they said to each other:

"We have been taken here on account of the money in our sacks. They will say that we have stolen; and then they will sell us all for slaves."

But Jō'şeph's steward, the man who was over his house, treated the men kindly, and when they spoke of the money in their sacks, he would not take it again, saying, "Never fear; your God must have sent you this as a gift. I had your money." The steward received the men into Jō'şeph's house and washed their feet, according to the custom of the land. And at noon, Jō'şeph came in to meet them. They brought him the present from their father, and again they bowed before him, with their faces on the ground.

And Jō'şeph asked them if they were well, and said, "Is your father still living, the old man of whom you spoke? Is he well?"

And they said, "Our father is living, and he is well." And again they bowed to Jō'şeph. And Jō'şeph looked at his younger brother, Bĕn'ja-mĭn, the child of his own mother, Rā'chel; and he said, "Is this your youngest brother, of whom you spoke to me? God be gracious unto you, my son."

And Jō'şeph's heart was so full that he could not keep back his tears. He went in haste to his own room, and wept there. Then he washed his face and came out again, and ordered the table to be set for dinner. They set Jō'şeph's table for himself, as the ruler, and another table for his Ē-ġў̆p'tian officers, and another for the eleven men from Cā'năan; for Jō'şeph had brought Sĭm'e-on out of the prison and had given him a place with his brothers.

Jō'şeph himself arranged the order of the seats for his brothers, the oldest at the head; and all in order of age down to the youngest. The men wondered at this, and could not see how the ruler of Ē'ġў̆pt should know the order of their ages. And Jō'şeph sent dishes from his table to his brothers; and he gave to Bĕn'ja-mĭn five times as much as to the others. Perhaps he wished to see whether they were as jealous of Bĕn'ja-mĭn as in other days they had been toward him.

After dinner, Jō'şeph said to his steward, "Fill the men's sacks with grain, as much as they can carry; and put each man's money in his sack. And put my silver cup in the sack of the youngest, with his money."

The steward did as Jō'şeph had said; and early in the morning the brothers started to go home. A little while afterward, Jō'şeph said to his steward:

"Hasten, follow after the men from Cā'nǎan and say, 'Why have you wronged me, after I had treated you kindly? You have stolen my master's silver cup, out of which he drinks.'" The steward followed the men and overtook them and charged them with stealing. And they said to him:

"Why should you talk to us in this manner? We have stolen nothing. Why, we brought back to you the money that we found in our sacks; and is it likely that we would steal from your lord his silver or gold? You may search us; and if you find your master's cup on any of us, let him die, and the rest of us may be sold as slaves."

Then they took down the sacks from the asses and opened them; and in each man's sack was his money, for the second time. And when they came to Bĕn'ja-mĭn's sack, there was the ruler's silver cup! Then, in the greatest sorrow, they tied up their bags again and laid them on the asses and came back to Jō'şeph's palace.

And Jō'şeph said to them:

"What wicked thing is this that you have done? Did you not know that I would surely find out your deeds?"

Then Jū'dah said, "O my lord, what can we say? God has punished us for our sins; and now we must all be slaves, both us that are older and the youngest in whose sack the cup was found."

"No," said Jō'şeph, "only one of you is guilty, the one who has taken away my cup; I will hold him as a slave, and the rest of you can go home to your father."

Jō'şeph wished to see whether his brothers were still selfish and were willing to let Bĕn'ja-mĭn suffer, if they could escape.

Then Jū'dah, the very man who had urged his brothers to sell Jō'şeph as a slave, came forward and fell at Jō'şeph's feet and pleaded with him to let Bĕn'ja-mĭn go. He told again the whole story, how Bĕn'ja-mĭn was the one whom his father loved the most of all his children, now that his brother was lost. He said:

"I promised to bear the blame, if this boy was not brought home in safety. If he does not go back, it will kill our poor old father, who has seen much trouble. Now let my youngest brother go home to his father, and I will stay here as a slave in his place!"

Jō'şeph knew now what he had longed to know, that his

brothers were no longer cruel nor selfish, but one of them was willing to suffer, so that his brother might be spared. And Jō'ṣeph could not any longer keep his secret, for his heart longed after his brothers, and he was ready to weep again, with tears of love and joy. He sent all his E-ġy̆p'tian servants out of the room, so that he might be alone with his brothers, and then said:

"Come near to me, I wish to speak with you"; and they came near, wondering. Then Jō'ṣeph said:

"I am Jō'ṣeph; is my father really alive?" How frightened his brothers were, as they heard these words, spoken in their own language by the ruler of E'ġy̆pt, and for the first time knew that this stern man, who had their lives in his hand, was their own brother whom they had wronged! Then Jō'ṣeph said again:

"I am Jō'ṣeph your brother, whom you sold into E'ġy̆pt. But do not feel troubled because of what you did. For God sent me before you to save your lives. There have been already two years of need and famine, and there are to be five years more, when there shall neither be plowing of the fields nor harvest. It was not you who sent me here, but God, and he sent me to save your lives. God has made me like a father to Phā'raōh and ruler over all the land of E'ġy̆pt. Now, go home, and bring down to me my father and all his family, for that is the only way to save their lives."

Then Jō'şeph placed his arms around Bĕn'ja-mĭn's neck and kissed him and wept upon him. And Bĕn'ja-mĭn wept on his neck. And Jō'şeph kissed all his brothers, to show them that he had fully forgiven them; and after that his brothers began to lose their fear of Jō'şeph, and talked with him more freely.

Afterward Jō'şeph sent his brothers home with good news and rich gifts and abundant food. He sent also wagons in which Jā'cob and his wives and the little ones of his family might ride from Cā'năan down to Ē'ġy̆pt. And Jō'şeph's brothers went home happier than they had been for many years.

Story Nineteen   GENESIS 45 : 25 to 50 : 26

From the Land of Famine to the Land of Plenty

SO JŌ'ŞEPH'S eleven brothers went home to their old father with the glad news that Jō'şeph was alive and was ruler over the land. It was such a joyful surprise to Jā'cob that he fainted. But after a time he revived; and when they showed him the wagons that Jō'şeph had sent to bring him and his family to Ē'ġy̆pt, old Jā'cob said, "Jō'şeph my son is yet alive; I will go and see him before I die."

Then they went on their journey, with their wives and children and servants and sheep and cattle, a great company. They stopped to rest at Bē'er=shē'ba, which had been the home of Ī'şaac and of Ā'bră-hăm, and made offerings to the Lord and worshiped. And that night the Lord appeared to Jā'cob and said to him:

"Jā'cob, I am the Lord, the God of your father, fear not to go down to Ē'ġy̆pt; for I will go down with you; and there you shall see your son Jō'şeph; and in Ē'ġy̆pt I will make of your descendants, those that come from you, a great people; and I will surely bring them back again to this land."

They came down to Ē'ġўpt, sixty-six of Jā'cob's children and grandchildren.   Jō'seph rode in his chariot to meet his father, and fell on his neck and wept upon him.   And Jā'cob said, "Now I am ready to die, since I know that you are still alive; and I have seen your face."   And Jō'seph brought his father in to see King Phā'raōh; and Jā'cob, as an old man, gave his blessing to the king.

The part of the land of Ē'ġўpt where Jō'seph found for his brothers a home was called Gō'shen.   It was on the east, between Ē'ġўpt and the desert, and it was a very rich land, where the soil gave large harvests.   But at that time, and for five years after, there

were no crops, because of the famine that was in the land.   During those years, the people of Ĭs'ra-el in the land of Gō'shen were fed as were all the people of Ē'ġўpt, with grain from the storehouses of Jō'seph.

Jā'cob lived to be almost a hundred and fifty years old.   Before he died, he blessed Jō'seph and all his sons and said to them:

"When I die, do not bury me in the land of Ē'ġўpt, but take my body to the land of Cā'năan, and bury me in the cave at Hē'bron, with Ā'bră-hăm and Ī'saac, my father."

And Jō'seph brought his two sons, Mă-năs'seh and Ē'phră-ĭm, to his father's bed.   Jā'cob's eyes were dim with age, as his father Ī'saac had been, and he could not see the two young men.   And he said, "Who are these?"

And Jō'seph said, "They are my two sons, whom God has given me in this land."

"Bring them to me," said Jā'cob, "that I may bless them before I die."

Jā'cob kissed them and put his arms around them, and said:

"I had not thought that I should ever see your face, my son; and God has let me see both you and your children also."

And Jā'cob placed his right hand on Ē'phră-ĭm's head, the younger, and his left hand on Mȧ-năs'seh the older. Jō'seph tried to change his father's hands, so that his right hand should be on the older son's head. But Jā'cob would not allow him, and he said:

"I know what I am doing, God will bless the older son; but the greater blessing shall be with the younger, for his descendants shall be greater and stronger than the descendants of his brother."

And so it came to pass many years after this; for the tribe of Ē'phră-ĭm, the younger son, became greater and more powerful than the tribe of Mȧ-năs'seh, the older son.

When Jā'cob died, a great funeral was held. They carried his body up out of Ē'ġўpt to the land of Cā'năan, and buried it—as he had said to them—in the cave of Măch-pē'lah, where Ā'bră-hăm and Ī'şaac were buried already.

When the sons of Jā'cob came to Ē'ġўpt after the burial of their father, they said one to another:

"It may be that Jō'seph will punish us, now that his father is dead, for the wrong that we did to him many years ago."

And they sent a message, asking Jō'seph to forgive them, for his father's sake. And again they came and bowed down before him, with their faces to the ground; they said, "We are your servants; be merciful to us."

Jō'seph wept when his brothers spoke to him, and he said:

"Fear not. Am I in God's place to punish and to reward? It is true that you meant evil to me, but God turned it to good, so that all your families might be kept alive. Do not be afraid; I will care for you and for your children."

After this Jō'seph lived to a good old age, until he was a hundred and ten years old. Before he died, he said to his children and to all the children of Iş'ra-el, who had now increased to very many people:

"I am going to die; but God will come to you and will bring you up out of this land, into your own land, which he promised to your fathers, to Ā'bră-hăm and Ī'ṣaac and Jā'cob. When I die, do not bury me in Ē'ġypt, but keep my body until you go out of this land, and take it with you."

So when Jō'ṣeph died, they embalmed his body as the Ē-ġўp'-tiang embalmed the bodies of their kings and great men, filling it with drugs and spices, so that it would not decay; and they placed his body in a stone coffin and kept it in the land of Gō'shen among the people of Iṣ'ra-el. Thus Jō'ṣeph not only showed his faith in God's promise, that he would bring his people back to the land of Cā'nằan; but he also encouraged the faith of those who came after him. For as often as the Iṣ'ra-el-ītes looked on the stone coffin that held the body of Jō'ṣeph, they said to one another:

"There is the token, the sign, that this land is not our home. This coffin will not be buried until we bury it in our own land, the land of Cā'nằan, where God will lead us in his own time."

Story Twenty EXODUS 1 : 1 to 2 : 22

The Beautiful Baby Who Was Found in a River

THE CHILDREN of Iṣ'ra-el stayed in the land of Ē'ġўpt much longer than they had expected to stay. They were in that land about four hundred years. And the going down to Ē'ġўpt proved a great blessing to them. It saved their lives during the years of famine and need. After the years of need were over, they found the soil in the land of Gō'shen, that part of Ē'ġўpt where they were living, very rich, so that they could gather three or four crops every year.

Then, too, some of the sons of Iṣ'ra-el, before they came to

Ē'gӯpt, had begun to marry the women in the land of Cā'nӑan, who worshiped idols, and not the Lord. If they had stayed there, their children would have grown up like the people around them, and soon would have lost all knowledge of God.

But in Gō'shen, they lived alone and apart from the people of Ē'gӯpt. They worshiped the Lord God, and were kept away from the idols of Ē'gӯpt. And in that land, as the years went on, from being seventy people, they grew in number, until they became a great multitude. Each of the twelve sons of Jā'cob was the father of a tribe, and Jō'seph was the father of two tribes, which were named after his two sons, Ē'phră-ĭm and Mȧ-năs'seh.

As long as Jō'seph lived, and for some time after, the people of Ĭs'ra-el were treated kindly by the Ē-ġӯp'tians, out of their love for Jō'seph, who had saved Ēġӯpt from suffering by famine. But after a long time, another king began to rule over Ē'gӯpt, who cared nothing for Jō'seph or Jō'seph's people. He saw that the Ĭs'ra-el-ītes (as the children of Ĭs'ra-el were called) were very many; and he feared lest they would soon become greater in number and in power than the Ē-ġӯp'tians.

He said to his people, "Let us rule these Ĭs'ra-el-ītes more strictly. They are growing too strong."

Then they set harsh rulers over the Ĭs'ra-el-ītes, who laid heavy burdens on them. They made the Ĭs'ra-el-ītes work hard for the Ē-ġӯp'tians and build cities for them, and give to the Ē-ġӯp'tians a large part of the crops from their fields. They set them at work in making brick and in building storehouses. They were so afraid that the Ĭs'ra-el-ītes would grow in number that they gave orders to kill all the little boys that were born to the Ĭs'ra-el-ītes; though their little girls might be allowed to live.

But in the face of all this hate and wrong and cruelty, the people of Ĭs'ra-el were growing in numbers and becoming greater and greater.

At this time, when the wrongs of the Ĭs'ra-el-ītes were the greatest, and when their little children were being killed, one little boy was born. He was such a lovely child that his mother kept him hid, so that the enemies did not find him. When she could no longer hide him, she found a plan to save his life, believing that

God would help her and save her beautiful little boy. She made a little box like a boat, and covered it with something that would not let the water into it. Such a boat as this, covered over, was called "an ark." She knew that at certain times the daughter of King Phā′raōh—all the kings of Ē′gўpt were called Phā′raōh— would come down to the river for a bath. She placed her baby boy in the ark, and let it float down the river where the princess, Phā′raōh's daughter, would see it. And she sent her own daughter, a little girl named Mĭr′ĭ-am, twelve years old, to watch close at hand. How anxious the mother and the sister were as they saw the little ark floating away from them on the river.

Phā′raōh's daughter, with her maids, came down to the river; and they saw the ark floating on the water, among the reeds. She sent one of her maids to bring it to her, so that she might see what was in the curious box. They opened it, and there was a beautiful baby, who began to cry to be taken up.

The princess felt kind toward the little one, and loved it at once. She said, "This is one of the Hē′brews' children." You have

heard how the children of Ĭş'ra-el came to be called Hē'brewş. Phā'raōh's daughter thought that it would be cruel to let such a lovely baby as this die out on the water. And just then a little girl came running up to her, as if by accident, and shę looked at the baby also, and said:

"Shall I go and find some woman of the Hē'brewş to be a nurse to the child for you, and take care of it?"

"Yes," said the princess, "go and find a nurse for me."

The little girl—who was Mĭr'ĭ-am, the baby's sister—ran as quickly as she could and brought the baby's own mother to the princess. Mĭr'ĭ-am showed in this act that she was a wise and thoughtful little girl. The princess said to the little baby's mother:

"Take this child to your home and nurse it for me, and I will pay you wages for it."

How glad the Hē'brew mother was to take her child home! No one could harm her boy now, for he was protected by the princess of Ē'ġȳpt, the daughter of the king.

When the child was large enough to leave his mother, Phā'raōh's daughter took him into her own home in the palace. She named him "Mō'şeş," a word that means "Drawn out," because he was drawn out of the water.

So Mō'şeş, the Hē'brew boy, lived in the palace among the nobles of the land, as the son of the princess. There he learned much more than he could have learned among his own people; for there were very wise teachers among the Ē-ġȳp'tianş. Mō'şeş gained all the knowledge that the Ē-ġȳp'tianş had to give. There in the court of the cruel king who had made slaves of the Ĭş'ra-el-ītes, God's people, was growing up an Ĭş'ra-el-īte boy who should at some time set his people free.

Although Mō'şeş grew up among the Ē-ġȳp'tianş and gained their learning, he loved his own people. They were poor and were hated and were slaves, but he loved them, because they were the people who served the Lord God, while the Ē-ġȳp'tianş worshiped idols and animals. Strange it was that so wise a people as these should bow down and pray to an ox or to a cat or to a snake, as did the Ē-ġȳp'tianş!

When Mō'şeş became a man, he went among his own people,

leaving the riches and ease that he might have enjoyed among the Ē-ġўp'tianṣ. He felt a call from God to lift up the Iṣ'ra-el-ītes and set them free. But at that time he found that he could do nothing to help them. They would not let him lead them, and as the king of Ē'ġўpt had now become his enemy, Mō'ṣeṣ went away from Ē'ġўpt into a country in Ā-rā'bĭ-á called Mĭd'ĭ-an.

He was sitting by a well, in that land, tired from his long journey, when he saw some young women come to draw water for their flocks of sheep. But some rough men came and drove the women away and took the water for their own flocks. Mō'ṣeṣ saw it, and he helped the women and drew the water for them.

These young women were sisters, the daughters of a man named Jĕth'rŏ, who was a priest in the land of Mĭd'ĭ-an. He asked Mō'ṣeṣ to live with him and to help him in the care of his flocks. Mō'ṣeṣ stayed with Jĕth'rŏ and married one of his daughters. So from being a prince in the king's palace in Ē'ġўpt, Mō'ṣeṣ became a shepherd in the wilderness of Mĭd'ĭ-an.

Story Twenty-one

EXODUS 3 : 1 to 4 : 31

The Voice from the Burning Bush

IT MUST have been a great change in the life of Mō'ṣeṣ, after he had spent forty years in the palace as a prince, to go out into the wilderness of Mĭd'ĭ-an and live there as a shepherd. He saw no more the crowded cities, the pyramids, the temples of Ē'ġўpt, and the great river Nile. For forty years Mō'ṣeṣ wandered about the land of Mĭd'ĭ-an with his flocks, living alone, often sleeping at night on the ground and looking up by day to the great mountains.

He wore the rough skin mantle of a shepherd; and in his hand was the long shepherd's staff. On his feet were sandals which he wore instead of shoes. But when he stood before an altar to worship God, he took off his sandals. For when we take off our hats, as in church or a place where God is worshiped, the people of those lands take off their shoes, as a sign of reverence.

Mō'ṣeṣ was a great man, one of the greatest men that ever lived. But he did not think himself great or wise. He was contented with the work that he was doing; and sought no higher place. But God had a work for Mō'ṣeṣ to do, and all through those years in the wilderness God was preparing him for that work.

All through those years, while Mō'ṣeṣ was feeding his flock in Mĭd'ĭ-an, the people of Iṣ'ra-el were still bearing heavy burdens and working as slaves in Ē'ġypt, making brick and building cities. The king who had begun the hard treatment of the Iṣ'ra-el-ītes died, but another king took his place, and was just as cruel. He was called by the same name, Phā'raōh, for this was the name given to all the kings of Ē'ġypt.

One day, Mō'ṣeṣ was feeding his flock on a mountain, called Mount Hō'reb. This mountain was also called Mount Sī'nāi, and is spoken of by both names in the Bible. On the mountain Mō'ṣeṣ saw a bush which seemed to be on fire. He watched to see it burn up, but it was not destroyed, though it kept burning on and on. And Mō'ṣeṣ said to himself:

"I will go and look at this strange thing, a bush on fire, yet not burning up."

As Mō'ṣeṣ was going toward the bush, he heard a voice coming out of the bush, calling him by name, "Mō'ṣeṣ, Mō'ṣeṣ!" He listened and said, "Here I am."

The voice said, "Mō'ṣeṣ, do not come near; but take off your shoes from your feet, for you are standing on holy ground."

So Mō'ṣeṣ took off his shoes and stood before the burning bush. And the voice came from the bush, saying:

"I am the God of your father, the God of Ā'bră-hăm, and of I'ṣaac, and of Jā'cob. I have seen the wrongs and the cruelty that my people have suffered in Ē'ġỹpt, and I have heard their cry on account of their taskmasters. And I am coming to set them free from the land of the Ē-ġỹp'tianṣ, and to bring them up to their own land, the land of Cā'năan, a good land, and large. Come, now, and I will send you to Phā'raōh, the king of Ē'ġỹpt, and you shall lead out my people from Ē'ġỹpt."

Mō'ṣeṣ knew what a great work this would be, to lead the Iṣ'ra-el-ītes out of Ē'ġypt, from the power of its king. He dreaded to take up such a task; and he said to the Lord:

"O Lord, who am I, a shepherd here in the wilderness, to do this great work, to go to Phā'raōh and to bring the people out of Ē'ġypt? It is too great a work for me."

And God said to Mō'ṣeṣ:

"Surely I will be with you and will help you to do this great work. I will give you a sign of my presence with you. When you have led my people out of Ē'ġypt, you shall bring them to this mountain, and they shall worship me here. And then you shall know that I have been with you."

And Mō'ṣeṣ said to God:

"When I go to the children of Iṣ'ra-el in Ē'ġypt, and tell them that the God of their fathers has sent me, they will say to me, 'Who is this God? What is his name?' For they have suffered so much, and have sunk so low, that I fear they have forgotten their God."

You remember that Mō'ṣeṣ had been out of Ē'ġypt and afar from his people for forty years, a long time, and in that time he did not know whether they had continued the worship of God.

And God said to Mō'ṣeṣ:

"My name is 'I AM,' the One who is always living. Do you go to your people and say to them, 'I AM hath sent me to you.' Do not be afraid; go to your people, and say to them what I have said to you, and they will listen to you and believe. And you shall take the elders of your tribes, the leading men among them, and shall go to King Phā'raōh, and shall say to him, 'Let my people go, that they may worship me in the wilderness.' At first he will not let you go; but afterward, I will show my power in Ē'ġypt, and then he will let you go out of the land."

But Mō'ṣeṣ wished some sign, which he could give to his people and to the Ē-ġyp'tianṣ, to show them that God had sent him. He asked God to give him some sign. And God said to him:

"What is that which you have in your hand?"

Mō'ṣeṣ said: "It is a rod, my shepherd's staff, which I use to guide the sheep."

And God said, "Throw it on the ground." Then Mō'ṣeṣ threw it down, and instantly it was turned into a snake. Mō'ṣeṣ was afraid of it, and began to run from it.

And God said, "Do not fear it, but take hold of it by the tail." Mō'ṣeṣ did so, and at once it became again a rod in his hand.

And God said again to Mō'ṣeṣ, "Put your hand into your bosom, under your garment, and take it out again."

Then Mō'ṣeṣ put his hand under his garment, and when he took it out, it had changed and was now as white as snow and covered with a scaly crust, like the hand of a leper. He looked at it with fear and horror. But God said to him again:

"Put your hand into your bosom once more." Mō'ṣeṣ did so, and when he took it out, his hand was like the other, with a pure skin, no longer like a leper's hand.

And God said to Mō'ṣeṣ, "When you go to speak my words, if they will not believe you, show them the first sign, and let your rod become a snake and then a rod again. And if they still refuse to believe your words, show them the second sign; turn your hand into a leper's hand, and then bring it back as it was before. And if they still will not believe, then take some water from the river, and it shall turn to blood. Fear not, go and speak my words to your own people and to the Ē-ġy̆p'tianṣ."

But Mō'ṣeṣ was still unwilling to go, not because he was afraid, but because he did not feel himself to be fit for such a great task. And he said to the Lord:

"O Lord, thou knowest that I am not a good speaker; I am slow of speech, and cannot talk before men."

And God said, "Am not I the Lord, who made man's mouth? Go, and I will be with your lips, and will teach you what to say."

But Mō'ṣeṣ still hesitated, and he said, "O Lord, choose some other man for this great work; I am not able to do it."

And God said, "You have a brother, whose name is Aâr'on. He can speak well. Even now he is coming to see you in the wilderness. Let him help you and speak for you. Let him do the speaking, and do you show the signs which I have given you."

At last Mō'ṣeṣ yielded to God's call. He went from Mount Sī'nāi with his flocks, and took them home to Jĕth'rȯ his father-in-law; and then he went toward Ē'ġўpt, and on the way he met his brother coming to see him. Then the two brothers, Mō'ṣeṣ and Aâr'on, came to the elders of Ĭṣ'ra-el in the land of Gō'shen. They told the people what God had said, and they showed them the signs which God had given.

And the people said, "God has seen all our troubles, and at last he is coming to set us free." And they were glad, and gave thanks to God who had not forgotten them.

Story Twenty-two

EXODUS 6 : 28 to 10 : 29

The River That Ran Blood

AFTER Mō'ṣeṣ and Aâr'on had spoken to the people of Ĭṣ'ra-el the words which God had given them, they went to meet Phā'raōh, the king of Ē'ġўpt. You remember that all the kings of Ē'ġўpt bore the name of Phā'raōh. Mō'ṣeṣ and Aâr'on did not at first ask Phā'raōh to let the people go out of Ē'ġўpt, never to return, but they said:

"Our God, the Lord God of Ĭṣ'ra-el, has bidden us to go out with all our people, a journey of three days into the wilderness, and there to worship him. And God speaks to you through us, saying, 'Let my people go, that they may serve me.'"

But Phā'raōh was very angry. He said, "What are you doing, you Mō'ṣeṣ and Aâr'on, to call your people away from their work? Go back to your tasks and let your people alone. I know why the Ĭṣ'ra-el-ītes are talking about going out into the wilderness. It is because they have not work enough to keep them busy. I will give them more work to do."

The work of the Ĭṣ'ra-el-ītes, at that time, was mostly in making brick and putting up the walls of buildings for the rulers of Ē'ġўpt. In mixing the clay for the brick they used straw, chopped up fine, to hold the clay together. Phā'raōh said:

"Let them make as many bricks as before; but give them no straw. Let the Iṣ'ra-el-ītes find their own straw for the brick-making."

Of course this made their task all the harder, for it took much time to find the straw; and the Iṣ'ra-el-ītes were scattered all through the land finding straw and stubble, for use in making the brick; and yet they were called upon to bring as many bricks each day as before. And when they could not do all their task, they were cruelly beaten by the Ė-ġy̆p'tians. Many of the Iṣ'ra-el-ītes now became angry with Mō'ṣeṣ and Aâr'on, who, they thought, had brought more burden and trouble upon them. They said:

"May the Lord God judge you and punish you! You promised to lead us out and set us free; but you have only made our suffering the greater!"

Then Mō'ṣeṣ cried to the Lord, and the Lord said to him:

"Take Aâr'on your brother, and go again to Phā'raōh; and show him the signs that I gave you."

So they went in to Phā'raōh and again asked him in the Lord's name, to let the people go. And Phā'raōh said:

"Who is the Lord? Why should I obey his commands? What sign can you show that God has sent you?"

Then Aâr'on threw down his rod, and it was turned into a snake. But there were wise men in Ē'ġy̆pt who had heard of this; and they made ready a trick. They threw down their rods, and their rods became snakes, or seemed to. They may have been tame snakes, which they had hidden under their long garments, and then brought out, as if they had been rods.

But Aâr'on's rod, in the form of a snake, ran after them and swallowed them all; and then it became a rod again in Aâr'on's hand. But King Phā'raōh refused to obey God's voice.

Then Mō'ṣeṣ spoke to Aâr'on, by God's command, "Take your rod and wave it over the waters of Ē'ġy̆pt, over the river Nile and the canals and the lakes."

Then Aâr'on did so. He lifted up the rod and struck the water, in the sight of Phā'raōh. And in a moment all the water turned to blood, and the fish in the river all died; and a terrible stench, a foul smell, arose over the land. And the people were in danger of

dying. But in the land of Gō'shen, where the Ĭṣ'ra-el-ītes were, the water remained as it had been, and was not turned to blood. So God made a difference between Ĭṣ'ra-el and Ē'ġy̆pt.

The people of Ē'ġy̆pt dug wells to find water; and the wise men of Ē'ġy̆pt brought some water to Phā'raōh, and made it look as though they had turned it to blood. And Phā'raōh would not listen nor let the people go.

After seven days Mō'ṣeṣ took away the plague of blood, but he warned Phā'raōh that another plague was coming, if he refused to obey. And as Phā'raōh still would not obey, Aâr'on stretched forth his rod again, and then all the land was covered with frogs. Like a great army they ran over all the fields and they even filled the houses. Phā'raōh said:

"Pray to your God for me; ask him to take the frogs away, and I will let the people go."

Then Mō'ṣeṣ prayed; and God took away the frogs. They died everywhere; and the Ē-ġy̆p'tianṣ heaped them up and buried them. But Phā'raōh broke his promise and would not let the people go.

Then, at God's command by Mō'ṣeṣ, Aâr'on lifted his rod again and struck the dust; and everywhere the dust became alive with lice and fleas. But still Phā'raōh would not hear, and God sent great swarms and clouds of flies all over the land, so that their houses were filled with them, and the sky was covered. But where the Ĭṣ'ra-el-ītes lived there were no lice nor fleas nor flies.

Then Phā'raōh began to yield a little. He said:

"Why must you go out of the land to worship God? Worship him here in this land."

But Mō′ṣeṣ said, "When we worship the Lord, we must make an offering: and our offerings are of animals which the people of Ē′ġȳpt worship, oxen and sheep. It would make the Ē-ġȳp′tianṣ angry to see us offering a sacrifice of animals which they call gods."

"Well," said Phā′raōh, "you may go; but do not go far away and come back." But when Mō′ṣeṣ and Aâr′on had taken away the plague, Phā′raōh broke his promise again, and still held the people as slaves.

Then another plague came. A terrible disease struck all the animals in Ē′ġȳpt, the horses and asses, the camels, the sheep, and the oxen; and they died by the thousand in a day, all over the land. But no plague came upon the flocks and herds of the Iṣ′ra-el-ītes.

But Phā′raōh was still stubborn. He would not obey God's voice. Then Mō′ṣeṣ and Aâr′on gathered up in their hands ashes from the furnace and threw it up like a cloud into the air. And instantly boils began to break out on men and on beasts all through the land.

Still Phā′raōh refused to obey; and then Mō′ṣeṣ stretched out his rod toward the sky. At once a terrible storm burst forth upon the land; all the more terrible because in that land rain scarcely ever falls. Sometimes there will not be even a shower of rain for years at a time. But now the black clouds rolled, the thunder sounded, the lightning flashed, and the rain poured down, and with the rain came hail, something that the Ē-ġȳp′tianṣ had never seen before. It struck all the crops growing in the fields and the fruits on the trees and destroyed them.

Then again Phā′raōh was frightened and promised to let the people go; and again when God took away the hail at Mō′ṣeṣ prayer, he broke his word and would not let the Iṣ′ra-el-ītes leave the land.

Then after the hail came great clouds of locusts, which ate up every green thing that the hail had spared. And after the locusts came the plague of darkness. For three days there was thick darkness, no sun shining nor moon nor stars. But still Phā′raōh would not let the people go. Phā′raōh said to Mō′ṣeṣ:

"Get out of my sight. Let me never see your face again. If you come into my presence, you shall be killed."

And Mō'ses said, "It shall be as you say, I will see your face no more."

And God said to Mō'ses, "There shall be one plague more, and then Phā'raōh will be glad to let the people go. He will drive you out of the land. Make your people ready to go out of Ē'gўpt; your time here will soon be ended."

Story Twenty-three

The Night When a Nation Was Born

WHILE all these terrible plagues, of which we read in the last story, were falling upon the people of Ē'gўpt, the Is'ra-el-ītes in the land of Gō'shen were living in safety under God's care. The waters there were not made blood; nor did the flies or the locusts trouble them. While all was dark in the rest of Ē'gўpt, in the land of Gō'shen the sun was shining.

This made the Ē-gўp'tians feel that the Lord God of the Is'ra-el-ītes was watching over his own people. They brought gifts to the Is'ra-el-ītes of gold and silver and jewels and precious things of every kind, to win their favor, and to win the favor of their God. So the Is'ra-el-ītes, from being very poor, began suddenly to be very rich.

Now Mō'ses said to the people:

"In a few days you are to go out of Ē'gўpt, so gather together, get yourselves in order by your families and your twelve tribes: and be ready to march out of Ē'gўpt."

And the people of Is'ra-el did as Mō'ses bade them. Then said Mō'ses:

"God will bring one plague more upon the Ê-g̣y̆p′tiaṇṣ, and then they will let you go. And you must take care and obey God's command exactly, or the terrible plague will come upon your houses with the Ê-g̣y̆p′tian houses. At midnight, the angel of the Lord will go through the land and the oldest child in every house shall die. Phā′raōh's son shall die and every rich man's son and every poor man's son, even the son of the beggar that has no home. But your families shall be safe if you do exactly as I command you."

Then Mō′ṣeṣ told them what to do. Every family was bidden to find a lamb and to kill it. They were to take some of the blood of the lamb and sprinkle it at the entrance of the house, on the door frame overhead and on each side. Then they were to roast the lamb, and with it to cook some vegetables, and to eat it standing around the table, with all their garments on, ready to march away as soon as the meal should be ended. And no one was to go out of his house that night, for God's angel would be abroad, and he might be killed if the angel should meet him.

The children of Iṣ′ra-el did as Mō′ṣeṣ commanded them. They killed the lamb and sprinkled the blood and ate the supper in the night, as God had told them to do. And this supper was called "the Passover Supper," because when the angel saw the doors sprinkled with blood, he *passed over* those houses and did not enter them. And in memory of this great night, when God kept his people from death, the Iṣ′ra-el-ītes were commanded to eat just such a supper on that same night every year. This became a great feast of the Iṣ′ra-el-ītes and was called "The Passover."

Does not that slain lamb and his blood sprinkled to save the people from death, make you think of Jē'ṣus Chrīst, who was the Lamb of God, slain to save us all?

And that night a great cry went up from all the land of Ē'ġȳpt. In every house there was one, and that one the oldest son, who died. And Phā'raōh the king of Ē'ġȳpt saw his own son lie dead, and knew that it was the hand of God. And all the people of Ē'ġȳpt were filled with terror, as they saw their children lying dead in their houses.

The king now sent a messenger to Mō'ṣeṣ and Aâr'on, saying:

"Make haste; get out of the land; take everything that you have; leave nothing. And pray to your God to have mercy upon us and to do us no more harm."

So suddenly at the last, early in the morning, the Ĭṣ'ra-el-ītes, after four hundred years in Ē'ġȳpt, went out of the land. They went out in order, like a great army, family by family and tribe by tribe. They went out in such haste that they had no time to bake bread to eat on the journey. They left the dough in the pans, all ready mixed for baking, but not yet risen as bread is before it is baked: and they set the bread pans on their heads, as people do in that land when they carry loads. And as a memory of that day, when they took the bread without waiting for it to rise, the rule was made that for one week in every year, and that same time in the year when they went out of Ē'ġȳpt, all the people of Ĭṣ'ra-el should eat bread that is "unleavened," that is, bread made without yeast, and unrisen. And this rule is kept to this day by the Jewṣ, who belong to the Ĭṣ'ra-el-īte family.

And the Lord God went before the host of Ĭṣ'ra-el, as they marched out of Ē'ġȳpt. In the daytime there was a great cloud, like a pillar, in front; and at night it became a pillar of fire. So both by day and night, as they saw the cloudy and fiery pillar going before, they could say, "Our Lord, the God of heaven and earth, goes before us."

When the pillar of cloud stopped, they knew that was a sign that they were to pause in their journey and rest. So they set up their tents and waited until the cloud should rise up and go forward. When they looked and saw that the pillar of cloud was higher up in the air, and as though moving forward, they took down their tents and formed in order for the march. Thus the pillar was like a guide by day and a guard by night.

You remember that when Jō'ṣeph died (see the end of Story Nineteen), he commanded the Ĭṣ'ra-el-ītes not to bury his body in Ē'ġȳpt, but to keep it in a stone coffin, unburied, as long as they should stay in the land. When they were going out of Ē'ġȳpt, the two tribes of Ē'phră-ĭm and Mȧ-năs'seh, who had sprung from Jō'ṣeph, his descendants—as they are called—took with them on their journey this stone coffin which held the body of Jōṣeph their father. And thus the Ĭṣ'ra-el-ītes went out of Ē'ġȳpt, four hundred years after they had gone down to Ē'ġȳpt to live.

Story Twenty-four

EXODUS 14 : 1 to 16 : 36

How the Sea Became Dry Land and the Sky Rained Bread

WHEN the children of Ĭṣ'ra-el came out of Ē'ġȳpt, it was their aim to go at once to the land of Cā'năan, from which their fathers had come. The shortest road was that following the shore of the Great Sea and entering Cā'năan on the southwest. But in this region lived the Phĭ-lĭs'tĭnes, a strong and warlike people; and the Ĭṣ'ra-el-ītes, after ages of slavery, were not fit to carry on war. The other way was by the southeast, through the desert of Mount Sī'nāi, where Mō'ṣeṣ knew the land, for it was there he had been a shepherd for many years.

So the Ĭṣ'ra-el-ītes, led by the pillar of cloud and fire, turned to the southeast, directly toward the Red Sea, which rolled between them and the desert. In a very few days they came to the shore of the sea, with the water before them and high mountains on each side.

As soon as the Ĭṣ'ra-el-ītes had left their homes, and were on the march, King Phā'raōh was sorry that he had let them go; for now they would no more be his servants and do his work. Word came to Phā'raōh that the Ĭṣ'ra-el-ītes were lost among the mountains and held fast by the sea in front of them. Phā'raōh called out his army, his chariots, and his horsemen, and followed the Ĭṣ'ra-el-ītes, intending either to kill them or to bring them back. Very soon the army of Ē'ġȳpt was close behind the host of Ĭṣ'ra-el, and the hearts of the people were filled with fear. They cried to Mō'ṣeṣ, saying:

"Why did you bring us out into this terrible place, shut in by the mountains and the sea, and with our enemies close behind us? It would be better to serve the Ē-ġȳp'tianṣ than to die here in the wilderness!"

"Fear not," answered Mō'ṣeṣ. "Stand still and see how God will save you. As for the Ē-ġȳp'tianṣ, whom you now see following you, you will see them no more forever. The Lord will fight for you, and you shall stand still and see your enemies slain." That night the pillar of fire, which was before the host of Ĭṣ'ra-el, went behind them and stood between the camp of the Ē-ġȳp'tianṣ and the camp of the Ĭṣ'ra-el-ītes. To Ĭṣ'ra-el it was bright and dazzling with the glory of the Lord, but to the Ē-ġȳp'tianṣ it was dark and terrible; and they dared not enter it.

And all that night there blew over the sea a mighty east wind so that the water was blown away; and when the morning came, there was a ridge of dry land between water on one side and water on the other, making a road across the sea to the land beyond, and on each side of the road the water stood like walls, as if to keep their enemies away from them.

Then Mō'ṣeṣ told the people to go forward, and the pillar of cloud again went before them; and the people followed, a great army. They walked across the Red Sea as on dry land and passed safely over into the wilderness on the other side. So God brought his people out of Ē'ġȳp᷍ into a land that they had never seen.

When the Ē-ġȳp'tianṣ saw them marching into the sea, they followed with their chariots and their horses. But the sand was no longer hard; it had become soft, and their chariot wheels were

fastened in it, and many of them broke off from the chariots. And
the horses became mired and fell down, so that the army was in
confusion; and all were frightened. The soldiers cried out:

"Let us fly from the face of the Ĭs′ra-el-ītes! The Lord is
fighting for them and against us!"

By this time, all the Ĭs′ra-el-ītes had passed through the Red Sea
and were standing on the high ground beyond it, looking at their
enemies slowly struggling through the sand, all in one heaped-up
mass of men and horses and chariots. Then Mō′ses lifted up his
hand, and at once a great side of water swept up from the sea on
the south; the road over which the Ĭs′ra-el-ītes had walked in
safety was covered with water; and the host of Phā′raōh, with all
his chariots and his horses and their riders, were drowned in the
sea, before the eyes of the people of Ĭs′ra-el. They saw the dead
bodies of the Ē-ġўp′tians tossed up by the waves on the shore.

Mō′ses wrote a great song, and all the people sang it together over their great victory, which God had wrought for them. It began thus:

"I will sing unto the Lord, for he hath triumphed gloriously
The horse and his rider hath he thrown into the sea,
The Lord is my strength and song,
And he is become my salvation."*

And now the people of Is'ra-el were no longer in a level land with fields of grain and abundance of food and streams of water. They were in the great desert, with a rocky path under them, and mountains of rock rising all around, with only a few springs of water, and these far apart. Such a host of men and women and children, with their flocks, would need much water, and they found very little.

They saw in the distance some springs of water and ran to drink of it, for they were very thirsty. But when they tasted, they found it bitter, so that they could not drink it. Then the people cried to Mō'ṣeṣ and Mō'ṣeṣ cried to the Lord; and the Lord showed Mō'ṣeṣ a tree, and told him to cut it down and throw it into the water. Mō'ṣeṣ did so, and then the water became fresh and pure and good, so that the people could drink it. This place they named Mā'rah, a word which means "Bitterness," because of the water which they found there.

After passing Mā'rah, they came to another and more pleasant place, where they saw twelve springs of fresh water and a grove of seventy palm trees around them. And there they rested under the cool shade.

But soon they were in a hot desert of sand which lies between the waters of Ē'lim and Mount Sī'nāi; and again they were in great trouble, for there was no food for such an army of people.

Then Mō'ṣeṣ called upon God, and the Lord said, "I will rain bread from heaven upon you; and you shall go out and gather it every day."

The next morning when the people looked out of their tents, they saw all around the camp, on the sand, little white flakes, like snow or frost. They had never seen anything like it before and

---

* See Exodus, chapter 15, for the words of this song.

they said, just as anybody would say, "What is it?" In the language of the Iṣ'ra-el-ītes, the Hē'brew language, "What is it?" is the word "Manhu." So the people said to one another "Manhu? Manhu?" And this gave a name afterward to what they saw, the name *Manna*.

And Mō'ṣeṣ said to them, "This is the bread which the Lord has given you to eat. Go out and gather it, as much as you need. But take only as much as you need for today, for it will not keep; and God will give you more tomorrow."

So the people went out and gathered the manna. They cooked it in various ways, baking it and boiling it; and the taste of it was like wafers flavored with honey. Some took more than they needed, not trusting God's word that there would be more on the next day. But that which was left over after it was gathered, spoiled and smelled badly, so that it was useless. This was to teach the people that each day they should trust God for their daily bread.

But the manna which was left on the ground did not spoil. When the sun came up, it melted away, just as frost or snowflakes. Before the sixth day of the week came, Mō'ṣeṣ said to all the people:

"Tomorrow, on the sixth day of the week, take twice as much manna as usual; for the next day is the Lord's Sabbath, the day of rest, and the manna will not come on that day."

So the next morning, all the people went out as before to gather the manna. On that day, they found that the manna which was not used did not spoil, but kept fresh until the next morning.

On the Sabbath day, some of the people who had failed to hear Mō'ṣeṣ, and had not gathered the manna in advance for the Sabbath, went out, and they could find none. So that day, these people had nothing to eat; and all Iṣ'ra-el learned the lesson, which we also should remember, that one day in each week belongs to God and is to be kept holy to the Lord.

All the time that the Iṣ'ra-el-ītes lived in the wilderness, which was forty years, they ate the manna which God gave them day by day. Not until they entered the land of Cā'năan did the manna cease to fall.

The Mountain That Smoked and the Words That Were Spoken from It

WHILE the Ĭṣ′ra-el-ītes were journeying through the desert, they had great trouble from want of water. Between the wells of Ē′lim and Mount Sī′nāi, they found no streams nor springs. Their sheep and men suffered from thirst, and the little children were crying for water. The people came to Mō′ṣeṣ and said in great anger:

"Give us water or we shall die. Why have you brought us up from Ē′ġўpt to kill us here in the desert?"

And Mō′ṣeṣ called on God and said:

"Lord, what shall I do to this people? They are almost ready to stone me in their anger. How can I give them water?"

Then God told Mō′ṣeṣ what to do; and this was what Mō′ṣeṣ did:

He brought the people together before a great rock, and with his rod he struck the rock. Then out of the rock came forth a stream of water, which ran like a little river through the camp and gave them plenty of water for themselves and for their flocks.

While they were in camp around this rock at Rĕph′i-dĭm, the wild people who had their homes in the desert and were called the Ăm′a-lĕk-ītes, made sudden war on the Ĭṣ′ra-el-ītes. They came down upon them from the mountains, while they were weary with marching, and killed some of the Ĭṣ′ra-el-ītes. Then Mō′ṣeṣ called out those of the people who were fit for war and made a young man named Jŏsh′u-à their leader; and they fought a battle with the Ăm′a-lĕk-ītes.

While they were fighting, Mō′ṣeṣ stood on a rock, where all could see him, and prayed the Lord God to help his people. His hands were stretched out toward heaven; and while Mō′ṣeṣ' hands

96

were reaching upward, the Ĭs'ra-el-ītes were strong and drove back the enemy. But when Mō'ṣeṣ' arms fell down, then the enemy drove back the men of Ĭs'ra-el.

So Aâr'on, Mō'ṣeṣ' brother, and Hûr (who is thought to have been Mō'ṣeṣ' brother-in-law, the husband of his sister Mĭr'ĭ-am), stood beside Mō'ṣeṣ and held up his hands until the Ĭs'ra-el-ītes won the victory and overcome the men of Ăm'a-lĕk.

In the third month after the Ĭs'ra-el-ītes had left the land of Ē'ġўpt, they came to a great mountain which rises straight up from the plain. This was Mount Sī'nāi; where Mō'ṣeṣ saw the burning bush and heard God's voice.

The Ĭs'ra-el-ītes made their camp in front of Mount Sī'nāi, and stayed there for many days. And God said to Mō'ṣeṣ:

"Let none of the people go up on the mount or come near to touch it. If even one of your cattle or sheep shall touch the mountain, it must be killed. This is a holy place, where God will show his glory."

And a few days after this, the people heard the voice as of many trumpets sounding on the top of the mountain. They looked, and saw that the mountain was covered with clouds and smoke, and lightnings were flashing from it, while the thunder rolled and crashed. And the mountain shook and trembled.

The people came out of their tents and stood far off, trembling with fear. Then God spoke in the hearing of all the people, as with a voice of thunder, and said:

"I am the Lord thy God, who brought thee out of the land of Ē′gy̆pt, out of the house of bondage."

And then God spoke to all the people the words of the Ten Commandments, to which you have listened many times. In a shorter form, with explanations where necessary, the Ten Commandments are these:

I. Thou shalt have no other gods before me; that is, God is our supreme ruler.
II. Thou shalt not make unto thee any graven image; that is, thou shalt not worship idols.
III. Thou shalt not take the name of the Lord thy God in vain; that is, thou shalt not use the name of God profanely.
IV. Remember the Sabbath day to keep it holy.
V. Honor thy father and thy mother.
VI. Thou shalt not kill; that is, thou shalt not take the life of any person.
VII. Thou shalt not commit adultery; that is, thou shalt not be unfaithful to husband or wife.
VIII. Thou shalt not steal.
IX. Thou shalt not bear false witness against thy neighbor; that is, thou shall not tell a lie about anyone.
X. Thou shalt not covet; that is, thou shalt not desire other people's possessions.

And all the people heard these words spoken by the Lord God; and they saw the mountain smoking and the lightning flashing and they were frightened. They said to Mō′şeş:

"Let not God speak to us any more; for the sound of his voice will take away our lives. Let God speak to you, Mō′şeş, and do you speak to us God's words."

"Fear not," said Mō′şeş, "for God has come to you, to speak with you, that you may fear him and do his will."

Then God called Mō'sĕs up to the top of the mount; and
Mō'sĕs went up, and with him was his helper, the young man
Jŏsh'u-à.   Jŏsh'u-à stayed on the side of the mountain, but Mō'sĕs
went up alone to the top, among the clouds.

And there Mō'sĕs stayed upon the mountain, alone with God,
for forty days, talking with God and listening to the words which
God spoke to him, the laws for the people of Ĭs'ra-el to obey.
And God gave to Mō'sĕs two flat tablets of stone, upon which
God had written with his own hand the Ten Commandments.

Story Twenty-six

EXODUS 32 : 1 to 34 : 35

How Aaron Made a Golden Calf,
and What Became of It

WHILE Mō'sĕs was in the mountain alone with
God, a strange and wicked thing was done in
the camp on the plain.   At first the people were
alarmed when they saw the mountain smoking
and heard the thunder.   But soon they grew
accustomed to it, and when day after day passed, and Mō'sĕs did
not come down, at last they said to Aâr'on:

"Come now, make us a god that we may worship and that we
may have to lead us.   As for Mō'sĕs, the man who brought us out
of the land of Ē'ġy̆pt, we do not know what has become of him."

Aâr'on was not a man of strong will, as Mō'sĕs was.   When his
brother Mō'sĕs was not by his side, Aâr'on was weak and ready
to yield to the wishes of the people.   Aâr'on said:

"If you must have a god that you can look at, then break off
the gold earrings that are in your ears and in the ears of your wives
and children, and bring them to me."

Then the people brought their gold to Aâr'on; and Aâr'on
melted the gold rings into one mass and shaped it with a graving

tool into the form of a calf; and this he brought out and stood up before the people. Then they all cried out:

"This is your god, O Ĭṣ'ra-el, that brought you out of the land of Ē'ġўpt."

And Aâr'on built an altar before the image, and he said to all the people, "Tomorrow shall be a feast to the Lord."

Perhaps Aâr'on thought that if the people could have before them an image that they could see, they might still be kept to the worship of the Lord God. But in this he was greatly mistaken. The people came to the feast and offered sacrifices; and then they began to dance around the altar and to do wicked deeds together, as they had seen the people of Ē'ġўpt doing before their idols. And all this time the mountain was smoking and flashing with fire, almost over their heads!

And the Lord, up in the mountain, spoke to Mō'ṣeṣ and said:

"Hasten, and get down to the camp; for your people have done very wickedly. They have made for themselves an idol, and they are worshiping it now. I am angry with them and am ready to destroy them all, and to make of your children a great nation."

And Mō'ṣeṣ pleaded with the Lord for Ĭṣ'ra-el, and God did not destroy the people; but he sent Mō'ṣeṣ down to them, holding in his hands the two stone tables on which God had written the Ten Commandments. As he went down the mountain, Jŏsh'u-à joined him and said to him:

"I can hear noise of war in the camp. It is not the sound of men who are shouting for victory, nor is it the cry of those who are beaten in battle; it is the voice of singing that I hear."

And in a moment more, as they stood where they could look down upon the camp, there was standing the golden calf, and around it were the people making offerings and feasting and dancing and singing.

And Mō'ses was so angry when he saw all the wickedness and shame of his people that he threw down the two tables out of his hands and broke them in pieces upon the rocks. What was the use of keeping the tables of stone, he may have thought, while the people were breaking the laws written upon them?

Mō'ṣeṣ came straight into the midst of the throng, and at once all the dancing and merry-making stopped. He tore down the golden calf, broke it in pieces, and burned it in the fire, and then ground it to powder and threw it into the water; and he made the people drink the water filled with its dust. He meant to teach the people that they would suffer punishment like bitter water, for their wicked deed.

Then Mō′ṣeṣ turned to Aâr′on:

"What led you to such an act as this?" said Mō′ṣeṣ. "Why did you let the people persuade you to make them an image for worship?"

And Aâr′on said, "Do not be angry with me; you know how the hearts of this people are set to do evil. They came to me and said, 'Make us a god,' and I said to them, 'Give me whatever gold you have.' So they gave it to me, and I threw the gold into the fire, and this calf came out!"

Then Mō′ṣeṣ stood at the entrance to the camp and called out:

"Whoever is on the Lord's side, let him come and stand by me!" Then one whole tribe out of the twelve tribes of Iṣ′ra-el, the tribe of Lē′vī, all sprung from Lē′vī, one of Jā′cob's sons, came and stood beside Mō′ṣeṣ. And Mō′ṣeṣ said to them:

"Draw your swords and go through the camp and kill every-one whom you find bowing down to the idol. Spare no one. Slay your friends and your neighbors, if they are worshiping the image."

And on that day three thousand of the worshipers of the idol were slain by the sons of Lē'vī.

Then Mō'ṣeṣ said to the people, "You have sinned a great sin; but I will go to the Lord and I will make an offering to him, and will ask him to forgive your sin."

Mō'ṣeṣ went before the Lord and prayed for the people:

"O Lord, this people have sinned a great sin. Yet now forgive their sin, if thou art willing. And if thou wilt not forgive their sin, then let me suffer with them, for they are my people."

And the Lord forgave the sin of the people, and took them once again for his own, and promised to go with them and to lead them into the land which he had promised to their fathers.

And God said to Mō'ṣeṣ, "Cut out two tables of stone, like those which I gave to you and which you broke; and bring them up to me in the mountain, and I will write on them again the words of the law."

So Mō'ṣeṣ went up a second time into the holy mount; and there God talked with him again. Mō'ṣeṣ stayed forty days on this second meeting with God, as he had stayed in the mountain forty days before. And all this time, while God was talking with Mō'ṣeṣ, the people waited in the camp; and they did not again set up any idol for worship.

Once more Mō'ṣeṣ came down the mountain, bringing the two stone tables upon which God had written the words of his law, the Ten Commandments. And Mō'ṣeṣ had been so close to God's glory and had been so long in the blaze of God's light, that when he came into the camp of Iṣ'ra-el, his face was shining, though he did not know it. The people could not look on Mō'ṣeṣ face, it was so dazzling. And Mō'ṣeṣ found that when he talked with the people it was needful for him to wear a veil over his face. When Mō'ṣeṣ went to talk with God, he took off the veil; but while he spoke with the people, he kept his face covered, for it shone as the sun.

The Tent Where God Lived Among His People

I T MAY seem strange that the Ĭṣ'ra-el-ītes, after all that God had done for them, and while Mount Sī'nāi was still showing God's glory, should fall away from the service of God to the worship of idols, as we read in the last story. But you must keep in mind that all the people whom the Ĭṣ'ra-el-ītes had ever met, both in Cā'năan and in Ē'ḡўpt, were worshipers of images; and from their neighbors the Ĭṣ'ra-el-ītes also had learned to bow down to idols. In those times everywhere people felt that they must have a god that they could see.

God was very good to the Ĭṣ'ra-el-ītes after they had forsaken him, to take them again as his own people; and God gave to the Ĭṣ'ra-el-ītes a plan for worship, which would allow them to have something that they could see to remind them of their God; and yet at the same time, would not lead them to the worship of an image, but would teach them a higher truth, that the true God cannot be seen by the eyes of men.

The plan was this: to have in the middle of the camp of Ĭṣ'ra-el a house to be called, "The House of God," which the people could see and to which they could come for worship. Every time that an Ĭṣ'ra-el-īte looked at this house he might say to himself and might teach his children, "That is the house where God lives among his people," even though no image stood in the house.

And as the Ĭṣ'ra-el-ītes were living in tents and were often moving from place to place, this House of God would need to be something like a tent, so that it could be taken down and moved, as often as the camp was changed. Such a tent as this was called a Tabernacle. The Tabernacle, then, was the tent where God was supposed to live among his people, and where the people could meet God.

103

We know that God is a Spirit and that he is everywhere. Yet it was right to say that God lived in the Tabernacle of the Is'ra-el-ites, because there God showed his presence in a special way, by having the pillar of cloud over it all day and the pillar of fire all night. And it was believed by the Is'ra-el-ites that in one room of this Tabernacle the glory and brightness of God's presence might be seen.

This Tabernacle stood exactly in the middle of the camp of the Is'ra-el-ites in the wilderness. In front of it, and a little distance from it, on the east, stood the tent where Mō'ses lived, and from which he gave the laws and commands of God to the people.

Around the Tabernacle there was what we might call an open square, though it was not exactly square, for it was about a hundred and fifty feet long by seventy-five feet wide; that is, its length was twice its width. Around it was a curtain of fine linen, in bright colors, hanging upon posts of brass. The posts were held in place by cords fastened to the ground with tent pins or spikes. Some think that these posts were not of brass but of copper; for we are not sure that men knew how to make brass in those times. This open square was called the Court of the Tabernacle. The curtain around it was between seven and eight feet high, a little higher than a man's head. In the middle, on the end toward the east, it could be opened for the priests to enter into the court; but no others except the priests and their helpers were ever allowed to enter it.

Inside this court, near the entrance, stood the great Altar. You remember that an altar was made generally of stone, or by heaping up the earth; and that it was the place on which a fire was kindled to burn the offering or sacrifice. The offering or sacrifice, you remember, was the gift offered to God whenever a man worshiped; and it was given to God by being burned upon his altar.

But as a stone altar or an earth altar could not be carried from place to place, God told the Is'ra-el-ites to make an altar of wood and brass or copper. It was like a box, without bottom or top, made of thin boards so that it would not be too heavy, and then covered on the inside and the outside with plates of brass or copper, so that it would not take fire and burn. Inside, a few inches below the top, was a metal grating on which the fire was built; and the ashes would fall through the grating to the ground inside.

This altar had four rings on the corners, through which long poles were placed, so that the priests could carry it on their shoulders when the camp was moved. The altar was a little less than five feet high and a little more than seven feet wide on each side. This was the great altar, sometimes called "The Altar of Burnt Offering," because a sacrifice was burned upon it every morning and every evening. Near the altar in the court of the Tabernacle stood the Laver. This was a large tank, or basin, holding water which was used in washing the offerings. For the worship of the Tabernacle much water was needed; and for this purpose the Laver was kept full of water.

The Tabernacle itself stood in the court. It was a large tent, not unlike the tents in which the people lived while they were journeying through the wilderness, though larger. Its walls however, were not made of skins or woven cloth, as were most tents, but of boards standing upright on silver bases and fastened together. The boards were covered with gold. The roof of the Tabernacle was made of four curtains, one laid above another, the inner curtain being beautifully decorated, and the outer curtain of rams' skins to keep out the rain. The board walls of the Tabernacle were on the two sides and the rear end; the front was open, except when a curtain was hung over it. The Tabernacle, half tent and half house, was about forty-five feet long, fifteen feet wide, and fifteen feet high. Its only floor was the sand of the desert.

This Tabernacle was divided into two rooms by a veil which hung down from the roof. The larger room, the one on the eastern end, into which the priest came first from the court, was twice as large as the other room. It was thirty feet long, fifteen feet wide, and fifteen feet high, and was called the Holy Place. In the Holy Place were three things: on the right side, as one entered, a table covered with gold, on which lay twelve loaves of bread, as if each tribe gave its offering of food to the Lord; on the left side, the Golden Lampstand, with seven branches, each having its light.

This is sometimes called the Golden Candlestick, but as it held lamps and not candles, it should be called "the Lampstand."

At the farther end of the Holy Place, close to the veil, was the Golden Altar of Incense: a small altar on which fragrant gum was burned and from which a silvery cloud floated up. The fire on this altar was always to be lighted from the great altar of brass or copper that was standing outside the Tabernacle in the court. Everything in this room was made of gold or covered with gold, even to the walls on each side.

The inner room of the Tabernacle was called the Holy of Holies; and it was so sacred that no one except the high priest ever entered it, and he on only one day in each year. It was fifteen feet wide, fifteen feet long, and fifteen feet high. All that it held was a box or chest, made of wood and covered with plates of gold on both the outside and the inside; and with a cover of solid gold, on which stood two strange figures called cherubim, also made of gold. This chest was called the Ark of the Covenant, and in it were placed for safe-keeping the two stone tables on which God wrote the Ten Commandments. It was in this room, the Holy of Holies, that God was supposed to dwell and to show his glory. But in it there was no image to tempt the Is'ra-el-ītes to the worship of idols.

Whenever the camp in the desert was to be changed, the priests first carefully covered with curtains all the furniture in the Tabernacle—the Table, the Lampstand, the Altar of Incense, and the Ark of the Covenant; and they passed rods through the rings which were on the corners of all these articles. They took down the Tabernacle and tied its gold-covered boards and its great curtains, its posts and its pillars, in packages to be carried. And then the men of the tribe of Lē'vī, who were the helpers of the priests, took up their burdens and carried them out in front of the camp. The twelve tribes were arranged in marching order behind them; the Ark of the Covenant unseen under its wrappings, upon the shoulders of the priests, led the way, with the pillar of cloud over it. And thus the children of Ĭṣ'ra-el removed their camp from place to place for forty years in the wilderness.

When they fixed their camping place after each journey, the Tabernacle was first set up, with the court around it and the altar in front of it. Then the tribes placed their tents in order around it, three tribes on each of its four sides.

And whenever an Ĭṣ'ra-el-īte saw the altar with the smoke rising from it and the Tabernacle with the silver-white cloud above it, he said to himself, "Our God, the Lord of all, lives in that tent. I need no image, made by men's hands, to remind me of God."

Story Twenty-eight

LEVITICUS I : I-13; 8 : I-13;
EXODUS 27 : 20, 21

How They Worshiped God in the Tabernacle

NOW WE will tell about some of the services that were held at the Tabernacle, the tent where God lived among his people.

Every morning at sunrise the priests came to the great altar that was before the Tabernacle and raked the fire and placed fresh wood upon it, so that it would burn brightly. This fire was never allowed to go out. God had kindled it himself; and the priests watched it closely and kept wood at hand, so that it was always burning.

Even while the altar was being carried from one place to another, the embers and live coals of the fire were kept in a covered pan and were taken to the new place for the altar without being allowed to die out; and from the embers of the old fire, a new fire was made on the altar.

From this altar outside the Tabernacle the priest took every morning and every afternoon a fire shovel full of burning coals and placed them in a bowl hanging on chains, so that, with the fire in it, the bowl could be carried by hand. This bowl with the chains was called "a censer." Upon these burning coals the priest placed some fragrant gum called incense, which, when laid on the live coals, made a bright, silvery cloud and sent forth a strong, pleasant odor. The incense in the censer the priest carried into the Holy Place, and there laid it on the Golden Altar of Incense, which stood next to the veil. This was to teach the Is̱'ra-el-ītes that, like the cloud of incense, their prayers should go up to God.

About nine o'clock in the morning the priest brought a lamb, or sometimes a young ox, and killed it and caught its blood in a basin. Then he laid the offering on the wood which was burning on the altar in front of the Tabernacle, and on the fire he poured the blood from the basin; and then he stood by while the blood and the animal were burned to ashes.

This was the offering, or sacrifice, for all the people of Is'ra-el together, and it was offered every morning and every afternoon. It meant that as the lamb, or the ox, gave up his life, so all the people were to give themselves to God, to be his, and only his. And it meant also, that as they gave themselves to God, God would forgive and take away their sins.

There was another meaning in all this service. It was to point to the time when, just as the lamb died as an offering for the people, Je'sus, the Son of God, should give his life on the cross, the Lamb of God, dying to take away the sins of the world. But this meaning, of course, the Is'ra-el-ites of that time could not understand, because they lived before Christ came.

Sometimes a man came to the priest with a lamb or an ox as an offering for himself. It must always be a perfect animal and the best, without any defects, for God will take from man only his best. The man who wished to worship God led his lamb to the entrance of the court, by the altar; and laid his hands upon its head, as if to say, "This animal stands in my place; and when I give it to God, I give myself." Then the priest killed it and laid it on the burning wood on the altar and poured the animal's blood upon it. And the man stood at the entrance of the court of the Tabernacle and watched it burn away, and he offered with it his thanks to God and his prayer for the forgiveness of his sins. And God heard and answered the prayer of the man who worshiped him with the offering at his altar.

Every day the priest went into the Holy Place and filled the seven lamps on the Lampstand with fresh oil. These lamps were never allowed to go out; that is, some of them must always be kept burning. While the lamps on one side were put out in order to be refilled, those on the other side were kept burning until these had been filled and lighted once more. So the lamps in the house of God never went out. Does not this make you think of One who long after this said, "I am the light of the world"?*

On the gold-covered table in the Holy Place were always standing twelve loaves of unleavened bread; that is, bread made without any yeast. One loaf stood for each tribe of Iṣ'ra-el. On every Sabbath morning the priests came in with twelve fresh loaves, which they sprinkled with incense and laid on the table in place of the stale loaves. Then, standing around the table, they ate the twelve old loaves. Thus the bread on the table before the Lord was kept fresh at all times.

God chose Aâr'on and his sons to be the priests for all Iṣ'ra-el, and their children and the descendants who should come after them were to be priests as long as the worship of the Tabernacle, and of the Temple that followed it, should be continued. Aâr'on, as the high priest, wore a splendid robe; and a breastplate of precious stones was over his bosom; and a peculiar hat, called "a miter," was on his head. It may seem strange to us, that when Aâr'on and his sons were in the Tabernacle they wore no shoes or stockings, but stood barefooted. This was because it was a holy place, and as we have seen, in those lands people take off their shoes, as we take off our hats, when they enter places sacred to God and his worship.

Aâr'on and his sons, as Mō'ṣeṣ also, belonged to the tribe of Lē'vī, the one among the tribes which stood faithful to God when the other tribes bowed down to the golden calf. This tribe was chosen to help the priests in the services of the Tabernacle; though only Aâr'on and his sons could enter the Holy Place; and only the high priest could go into the Holy of Holies, where the Ark of the Covenant was; and he could enter on but one day in each year.

* See John 8:12.

What Disobedience Brought to Aaron's Sons

SOON after the Tabernacle was set up in the middle of the camp of Ĭṣ'ra-el and the priests began the daily service of worship, a sad event took place, which gave great sorrow to Aâr'on the priest, to his family, and to all the people. The two older sons of Aâr'on, whose names were Nā'dăb and Ȧ-bī'hū, were one day in the Holy Place. It was a part of their work to take in a censer (which was a metal bowl for carrying fire) some burning coals from the great altar of burnt offering in front of the Tabernacle, and with these coals to light the fire in the small golden altar of incense, which stood inside the Holy Place.

Now the fire on the Great Altar was considered sacred and burned perpetually, and, therefore, it had been commanded that the small altar of incense must be lit from this fire and no other. These young men knew this, but did not take their office seriously, and, perhaps, just to save a little trouble or for some other reason that we do not know, they took some common fire, and with this they went into the Holy Place to burn the incense upon the golden altar. God was angry with these young men for disobeying his commands and treating the sacred offering of incense to him with disrespect.

While they were standing by the golden altar, fire came out from it, and they both fell down dead in the Holy Place. And when Mō'şeṣ heard of it, he said, "This is the sign that God's house is holy and that God's worship is holy; and God will make people to fear him, because he is holy." And Mō'şeṣ would not allow Aâr'on, the father of these two men, to touch their dead bodies. He said, "You have on the robes of the high priest, and you are leading in the service of worship. God's work must go on and must not stop for your trouble, great as it is."

111

Then Aâr'on stood by the altar and offered the sacrifice, though his heart was very sad. And the cousins of Aâr'on, by the command of Mō'ṣeṣ, went into the Holy Place and carried out the dead bodies of the two young men, dressed as they were in their priests' robes. And they buried these men outside the camp, in the desert.

Perhaps the young men had been drinking, for Mō'ṣeṣ said:

"After this, let no priest drink wine or strong drink before he enters the Tabernacle. Be sober, when you are leading the worship of the people, so that you will know the difference between the things that are holy and those that are common; and so that you may teach the people all the laws which the Lord has given them."

The rule that Mō'ṣeṣ gave to the priests to be kept when they were leading the worship of the people, not to drink wine or strong drink, is a good rule for everyone to keep, not only when worshiping God, but at all times.

Besides these two sons of Aâr'on who had died, there were two other sons named Ē-le-ā'zar and Ĭth'a-mär. These young men took their older brothers' places in the services of the Tabernacle; they were very careful to do as the Lord had bidden them.

Story Thirty

The Scapegoat in the Wilderness

YOU HAVE read that only the high priest could enter the inner room of the Tabernacle, called the Holy of Holies, where was the Ark of the Covenant, and where God was supposed to live. And even the high priest could go into this room on but one day in the year. This day was called "the Great Day of Atonement."

The service on that day was to show the people that all are sinners and that they must seek from God to have their sins taken away. God teaches us these things by word in his book, the Bible; but in those times there was no Bible, and very few could have read a written book; so God taught the people then by acts which they could see.

As a beginning of the service on the Day of Atonement, everybody was required to fast from sunset on the day before until three o'clock on that afternoon, the hour when the offering was placed on the altar. No person could eat anything in all that time. Even children, except nursing babies, were not allowed to have any food. They were to show a sorrow for sin, and were to appear before God as seeking for mercy.

Early in the morning of that day the high priest offered on the altar before the Tabernacle what was called "a sin offering," for himself and his family. It was a young ox, burned upon the altar. He took some of the blood of this ox and carried it through the Holy Place, lifted the veil, entered into the Holy of Holies, and sprinkled the blood on the golden lid to the Ark of the Covenant before the Lord. This was to show the priest himself as a sinner, seeking mercy and forgiveness from God. The priest must himself have his own sins forgiven, before asking forgiveness for others.

Then the priest came again to the great altar before the Tabernacle. Here two goats were brought to him. Lots were cast upon them and on the forehead of one goat was written, "For the Lord," and on the other words that meant, "To be sent away." These two goats were looked upon as bearing the sins of the people. One was killed and burned on the altar; and the priest, with some of the blood of the slain goat, again entered the Holy of Holies, and sprinkled the blood on the Ark of the Covenant, as before, thus asking God to receive the blood and the offering and to forgive the sins of the people.

Then the high priest came out of the Tabernacle again and laid his hands on the head of the living goat, the one whose forehead was marked "To be sent away," as if to place upon him the sin of all the people. Then this goat, which was called the "Scapegoat," was led away into the wilderness, to some desolate place from

which he would never find his way back to the camp; and there he was left, to wander as he chose. This was to show the sins of the people as taken away, never to come back to them.

When this service was over, the people were looked upon as having their sins forgiven and forgotten by the Lord. Then the regular afternoon offering was given on the altar; and after that the people could go home happy and end their long fast with all the food that they wished to eat.

In all this God tried to make the people feel that sin is terrible. It separates from God; it brings death; it must be taken away by blood. Thus so long before Christ came to take away our sins by his death, God showed to men the way of forgiveness and peace.

The Cluster of Grapes from the Land of Canaan

THE IŞ'RA-EL-ĪTES stayed in their camp before Mount Sĭ'nāi almost a year, while they were building the Tabernacle and learning God's laws given through Mō'şeş. At last the cloud over the Tabernacle rose up; and the people knew that this was the sign for them to move. They took down the Tabernacle and their own tents and journeyed northward toward the land of Cā'năan for many days, led by the pillar of cloud by day and the pillar of fire by night.

At last they came to a place just on the border between the desert and Cā'năan, called Kā'desh, or Kā'desh=bär'ne-à. Here they stopped to rest, for there were many springs of water and some grass for their cattle. While they were waiting at Kā'desh=bär'ne-à and were expecting soon to march into the land which was to be their home, God told Mō'şeş to send onward some men who should walk through the land and look at it, and then come back and tell what they had found; what kind of land it was, what fruits and crops grew in it, and what people were living in it. The Iş'ra-el-ītes could more easily win the land, if these men, after walking through it, could act as their guides and point out the best places in it and the best plans of making war upon it. There was need of wise and bold men for such a work as this, for it was full of danger.

So Mō'şeş chose out some men of high rank among the people, one ruler from each tribe, twelve men in all. One of these was Jŏsh'u-à, who was the helper of Mō'şeş in caring for the people, and another was Cā'leb, who belonged to the tribe of Jū'dah. These twelve men went out and walked over the mountains of Cā'năan, and they looked at the cities and saw the fields. In one place, just before they came back to the camp, they cut down a

115

cluster of ripe grapes which was so large that two men carried it between them, hanging from a staff. They named the place where they found this bunch of grapes Ĕsh'cŏl, a word which means "A cluster." These twelve men were called "spies," because they went "to spy out the land."

After forty days they came back to the camp; and this was what they said:

"We walked all over the land and found it a rich land. There is grass for all our flocks, and fields where we can raise grain, and trees bearing fruits, and streams running down the sides of the hills. But we found that the people who live there are very strong, and are men of war. They have cities with walls that reach almost up to the sky; and some of the men are giants, so tall that we felt that we were like grasshoppers beside them."

One of the spies, who was Cā'leb, said, "All that is true, yet we need not be afraid to go up and take the land. It is a good land, well worth fighting for. God is on our side, and he will help us to overcome those people."

But all the other spies, except Jŏsh'u-à, said, "No; there is no use in trying to make war upon such strong people. We can never take those walled cities, and we dare not fight those tall giants."

And the people, who had journeyed all the way through the wilderness to find this very land, were so frightened by the words of the ten spies, that now on the very border of Cā'năan they dared not enter it. They forgot that God had led them out of

Ḗġȳpt, that he had kept them in the dangers of the desert, that he had given them water out of the rock and bread from the sky, and his law from the mountain.

All that night, after the spies brought back their report, the people were so filled with fear that they could not sleep. They cried out against Mō'șeș, and blamed him for bringing them out of the land of Ē'ġȳpt. They forgot all their troubles in Ē'ġȳpt, their toil and their slavery; and they resolved to go back to that land. They said, "Let us choose a ruler in place of Mō'șeș, who has brought us into all these evils, and let us turn back to the land of Ē'ġȳpt!"

But Cā'leb and Jŏsh'u-à, two of the spies, said, "Why should we fear? The land of Cā'nǎan is a good land; it is rich with milk and honey. If God is our friend and is with us, we can easily conquer the people who live there. Above all things, let us not rebel against the Lord or disobey him and make him our enemy."

But the people were so angry with Cā'leb and Jŏsh'u-à that they were ready to stone them and kill them. Then suddenly the people saw a strange sight. The glory of the Lord, which stayed in the Holy of Holies, the inner room of the Tabernacle, now flashed out and shone from the door of the Tabernacle in the faces of the people.

And the Lord out of this glory spoke to Mō'șeș, and said:

"How long will this people disobey and despise me? They shall not go into the good land that I have promised them. Not one of them shall enter in except Cā'leb and Jŏsh'u-à, who have been faithful to me. All of the people who are twenty years old and over it, shall die in the desert; but their little children shall grow up in the wilderness, and when they become men, they shall enter in and own the land that I promised to their fathers. You people are not worthy of the land that I have been keeping for you. Now turn back into the desert, and stay there until you die. After you are dead, Jŏsh'u-à shall lead your children into the land of Cā'nǎan. And because Cā'leb showed another spirit, and was true to me, and followed my will fully, Cā'leb shall live to go into the land, and shall have his choice of a home there. Tomorrow, turn back into the desert by the way of the Red Sea."

And God told Mō'ṣeṣ that for every day that the spies had spent in Cā'năan, looking at the land, the people should spend a year in the wilderness; so that they should live in the desert forty years, instead of going at once into the Promised Land.

When Mō'ṣeṣ told all God's words to the people, they felt worse than before. They changed their minds as suddenly as they had made up their minds. "No," they all said, "we will not go back to the wilderness. We will go straight into the land and see if we are able to take it, as Jŏsh'u-à and Cā'leb have said."

"You must not go into the land," said Mō'ṣeṣ, "for you are not fit to go; and God will not go with you. You must turn back into the desert, as the Lord has commanded."

But the people would not obey. They rushed up the mountain and tried to march at once into the land. But they were without leaders and without order, a mob of men untrained and in confusion. And the people in that part of the land, the Cā'năan-ītes and the Ăm'ôr-ītes, came down upon them and killed many of them, and drove them away. Then, discouraged and beaten, they obeyed the Lord and Mō'ṣeṣ, and went once more into the desert.

And in the desert of Pā'ran, on the south of the land of Cā'năan, the children of Iṣ'ra-el stayed nearly forty years; and all because they would not trust in the Lord.

It was not strange that the Iṣ'ra-el-ītes should act like children, eager to go back one day and then eager to go forward the next day. Through four hundred years they had been weakened by living in the hot land of Ē'ġȳpt; and their hard lot as slaves had made them unfit to care for themselves. They were still in heart slavish and weak. Mō'ṣeṣ saw that they needed the free life of the wilderness; and that their children, growing up as free men and trained for war, would be far better fitted to win the land of promise than they had shown themselves to be. So they went back into the wilderness to wait and to be trained for the work of winning their land in war.

How the Long Journey of the Israelites Came to an End

SO THE Ĭṣ'ra-el-ītes, after coming to the border of the Promised Land, went back into the wilderness to wait there until all the men who had sinned against the Lord in not trusting his word should die. Mō'ṣeṣ knew that the men who had been slaves in Ē'ġўpt were in their spirits slaves still, and could not fight as brave men to win their land. There was need of men who had been trained up to a free life in the wilderness; men who would teach their children after them to be free and bold.

They stayed for nearly all the forty years of waiting in the wilderness of Pā'ran, south of Cā'năan. Very few things happened during those years. The young men as they grew up were trained to be soldiers, and one by one the old men died, until very few of them were left.

When the forty years were almost ended, the people came again to Kā'desh=bär'ne-à. For some reason they found no water there. Perhaps the wells from which they had drawn water before were now dried up. The people complained against Mō'ṣeṣ, as they always complained when trouble came to them, and blamed him for bringing them into such a desert land, where there was neither fruit to eat nor water to drink. There was nothing but great rocks all around.

Then the Lord said to Mō'ṣeṣ:

"Take the rod, and bring the people together, and stand before the rock and speak to the rock before them; and then the water will come out of the rock and the people and their flocks shall drink."

Then Mō'ṣeṣ and Aâr'on brought all the people together before a great rock that stood beside the camp. And Mō'ṣeṣ stood in front of the rock, with the rod in his hand; but he did not do

119

exactly what God had told him to do, to speak to the rock. He spoke to the people instead, in an angry manner.

"Hear now, ye rebels," said Mō'ṣeṣ. "Shall we bring you water out of this rock?"

And Mō'ṣeṣ lifted up the rod and struck the rock. Then he struck it again, and at the second blow, the water came pouring out of the rock, just as it had come many years before from the rock at Rĕph'i-dĭm, near Mount Sī'nāi; and again there was plenty of water for the people and their flocks.

But God was not pleased with Mō'ṣeṣ, because Mō'ṣeṣ had shown anger and had not obeyed God's command just as God had given it. And God said to Mō'ṣeṣ and to Aâr'on:

"Because you did not show honor to me, by doing as I commanded you, neither of you shall enter the land that I have promised to the children of Ĭs'ra-el."

One act of disobedience cost Mō'ṣeṣ and Aâr'on the privilege of leading the people into their own land of promise! About this time, Mĭr'ĭ-am, the sister of Mō'ṣeṣ and Aâr'on, died at Kā'desh=bär'ne-à. You remember that when she was a little girl, she helped to save the baby Mō'ṣeṣ, her brother, from the river. She also led the women in singing the song of Mō'ṣeṣ after the crossing of the Red Sea. And soon after her death, Mō'ṣeṣ and Aâr'on, and Ē-le-ā'zar, Aâr'on's son, walked together up a mountain called Hôr; and on the top of the mountain Mō'ṣeṣ took off the priest's robes from Aâr'on, and placed them on his son Ē-le-ā'zar; and there on the top of Mount Hôr, Aâr'on died, and Mō'ṣeṣ and Ē-le-ā'zar buried him. Then they came down to the camp and Ē-le-ā'zar took his father's place as the priest.

While they were at Kā'desh=bär'ne-à, on the south of Cā'năan, they tried again to enter the land. But they found that the Cā'năan-ītes and Ăm'ôr-ītes who lived there were too strong for them; so again they turned back to the wilderness, and sought another road to Cā'năan. On the south of the Dead Sea and southeast of Cā'năan, were living the Ē'dom-ītes, who had sprung from Ē'ṣau, Jā'cob's brother, as the Ĭs'ra-el-ītes had sprung from Jā'cob. Thus you see the Ē'dom-ītes were closely related to the Ĭs'ra-el-ītes.

And Mō'şeş sent to the king of Ē'dom, to say to him:

"We men of Iş'ra-el are your brothers. We have come out of the land of Ē'ġӯpt, where the people of Ē'ġӯpt dealt harshly with us, and now we are going to our own land, which our God has promised to us, the land of Cā'năan. We pray you let us pass through your land, on our way. We will do no harm to your land nor your people. We will walk on the road to Cā'năan, not turning to the right hand nor the left. And we will not rob your vineyards nor even drink from your wells, unless we pay for the water that we use."

But the king of Ē'dom was afraid to have such a great host of people, with all their flocks and cattle, go through his land. He drew out his army, and came against the Iş'ra-el-ītes. Mō'şeş was not willing to make war on a people who were so close in their race to the Iş'ra-el-ītes, so instead of leading the Iş'ra-el-ītes through Ē'dom, he went around it, making a long journey to the south and then to the east and then to the north again.

It was a long, hard journey, through a deep valley which was very hot; and for most of the journey they were going away from Cā'năan, and not toward it; but it was the only way, since Mō'şeş would not let the Iş'ra-el-ītes fight the men of Ē'dom.

While they were on this long journey, the people again found fault with Mō'şeş. They said, "Why have you brought us into this hot and sandy country? There is no water; and there is no bread except this vile manna, of which we are very tired! We wish that we were all back in Ē'ġӯpt again!"

Then God was angry with the people; and he let the fierce snakes that grew in the desert crawl among them and bite them. These snakes were called "fiery serpents," perhaps because of their bright color or perhaps because of their eyes and tongues, which seemed to flash out fire. Their bite was poisonous, so that many of the people died.

Then the people saw that they had acted wickedly in speaking against Mō'şeş; for when they spoke against Mō'şeş, they were speaking against God, who was leading them. They said:

"We have sinned against the Lord and we are sorry. Now pray to the Lord for us, that he may take away the serpents."

So Mō'şeş prayed for the people, as he had prayed so many times before. And God heard Mō'şeş' prayer and God said to him:

"Make a serpent of brass, like the fiery serpents; and set it up on a pole, where the people can see it. Then everyone who is bitten may look on the serpent on the pole, and he shall live."

And Mō'şeş did as God commanded him. He made a serpent of brass, which looked like the fiery snakes; and he lifted it up on

a pole where all could see it. And then, whoever had been bitten by a snake looked up at the brazen snake, and the bite did him no harm.

This brazen snake was a teaching about Chrīst, though it was given so long before Chrīst came. You remember the text which says, "As Mō'şeş lifted up the serpent in the wilderness, even so must the Son of man be lifted up: that whosoever believeth in him should not perish, but have eternal life." *

Northeast of the Dead Sea, above a brook called the brook Är'nŏn, lived a people who were called the Ăm'ôr-ītes. Mō'şeş sent to their king, whose name was Sī'hŏn, the same message that he had sent to the king of Ē'dom, asking for leave to go through his land. But he would not allow the Ĭş'ra-el-ītes to pass through.

* See John 3:14, 15.

He led his army against Ĭṣ'ra-el, and crossed the brook Är'nŏn and fought against Ĭṣ'ra-el at a place called Jā'hăz. The Ĭṣ'ra-el-ītes here won their first great victory. In the battle they killed many of the Ăm'ôr-ītes, and with them their king, Sī'hŏn, and they took for their own all their land, as far north as the brook Jăb'bŏk. Do you remember how Jā'cob one night prayed by the brook Jăb'bŏk?

And after this they marched on toward the land of Cā'năan, coming from the east. And at last they encamped on the east bank of the river Jôr'dan, at the foot of the mountains of Mō'ab. Their long journey of forty years was now ended, the desert was left behind them, before them rolled the Jôr'dan River, and beyond the Jôr'dan they could see the hills of the land which God had promised to them for their own.

Story Thirty-three   NUMBERS 22 : 2 to 25 : 18; 31 : 1-9

What a Wise Man Learned from an Ass

WHEN the Ĭṣ'ra-el-ītes had traveled around the land of Ē'dom and encamped beside the river Jôr'dan, a little north of the Dead Sea, they did not sit down to rest, for Mō'ṣeṣ knew that a great work was before them, to take the land of Cā'năan. He had already won a great victory over the Ăm'ôr-ītes at Jā'hăz, and slain their king, and won their land. Again Mō'ṣeṣ sent out an army into the north, a region called Bā'shăn. There they fought with King Og, who was one of the giants, and killed him and took his country. This made the Ĭṣ'ra-el-ītes masters of all the land on the east of the river Jôr'dan and north of the brook Är'nŏn.

South of the brook Är'nŏn and east of the Dead Sea were living the Mō'ab-ītes. This people had sprung from Lŏt, the nephew of Ā'bră-hăm, of whom we read in earlier stories. In the five hundred years since Lŏt's time, his family or descendants had become a people who were called the Mō'ab-ītes, just as Jā'cob's descendants were the Ĭs'ra-el-ītes. The Mō'ab-ītes were filled with alarm and fear as they saw this mighty host of Ĭs'ra-el marching around their land, conquering the country and encamping on their border. The Mō'ab-ītes were ruled by a king whose name was Bā'lăk, and he tried to form some plan for driving away the people of Ĭs'ra-el from that region.

There was at that time a man living far in the east, near the great river Eū-phrā'teṣ, whose name was Bā'laam. This man was known far and wide as a prophet, that is a man who talked with God, and heard God's voice, and spoke from God, as did Mō'ṣeṣ. People believed that whatever Bā'laam said was sure to come to pass; but they did not know that Bā'laam could only speak what God gave him to speak.

Bā'lăk, the king of the Mō'ab-ītes, sent men to Bā'laam at his home by the river, with great presents. He said to Bā'laam:

"There is a people here who have come up out of Ē'ġўpt, and they cover the whole land. I am afraid of them, for they have made war and beaten all the nations around. Come and curse them for me in the name of your God; for I know that those whom you bless are blessed and prosper, and those whom you curse are cursed and fail."

The men from Mō'ab brought this message and promised to Bā'laam a great reward if he would go with them. And Bā'laam answered them, "Stay here tonight, and I will ask my God what to do."

That night God came to Bā'laam and said to him: "Who are these men at your house, and what do they want from you?"

The Lord knew who they were and what they wanted, for God knows all things. But he wished Bā'laam to tell him. And Bā'laam said:

"They have come from Bā'lăk, the king of Mō'ab, and they ask me to go with them and to curse for them a people that have come out of Ē'ġўpt."

And God said to Bā'laam, "You must not go with these men; you shall not curse this people, for this people are to be blessed."

So the next morning Bā'laam said to the men of Mō'ab, "Go back to your land; for the Lord will not let me go with you."

When these men brought back to their king, Bā'lăk, the message of Bā'laam, the king still thought that Bā'laam would come, if he should offer him more money. So he sent other messengers of high rank, the princes of Mō'ab, with larger gifts. And they came to Bā'laam and said:

"Our King Bā'lăk says that you must come: he will give you great honors and all the money that you ask. Come now, and curse this people for King Bā'lăk."

And Bā'laam said:

"If Bā'lăk should give me his house full of silver and gold, I cannot speak anything except what God gives me to speak. Stay here tonight, and I will ask my God what I may say to you."

Now Bā'laam knew very well what God wished him to say; but Bā'laam, though he was a prophet of the Lord, wished to be rich. He wanted to go with the men and get Bā'lăk's money, but he did not dare to go against God's command. And that night God said to Bā'laam:

"If these men ask you to go with them, you may go; but when you go to Bā'lăk's country, you shall speak only the words that I give you to speak."

At this Bā'laam was very glad, and the next day he went with the princes of Mō'ab, to go to their land, which was far to the southwest. God was not pleased with Bā'laam's going, for Bā'laam knew very well that God had forbidden him to curse Iṣ'ra-el; but he hoped in some way to get King Bā'lăk's money.

And God sent his angel to meet Bā'laam in the way. In order to teach Bā'laam a lesson, the angel appeared first to the ass on which Bā'laam was riding. The ass could see the angel with his fiery sword standing in front of the way, but Bā'laam could not see him. The ass turned to one side, out of the road, into an open field; and Bā'laam struck the ass and drove it back into the road, for he could not see the angel, whom the ass saw.

Then the angel appeared again, in a place where the road was

narrow, with a stone wall on each side. And when the ass saw
the angel, it turned to one side and crushed Bā'laam's foot against
the wall. And Bā'laam struck the ass again.

Again the angel of the Lord appeared to the ass in a place where
there was no place to turn aside; and the ass was frightened and
fell down, while Bā'laam struck it again and again with his staff.

Then the Lord allowed the ass to speak; and the ass said to
Bā'laam, "What have I done that you have struck me these three
times?"

And Bā'laam was so angry that he never thought how strange
it was for an animal to talk; and he said, "I struck you because you
will not walk as you should. I wish that I had a sword in my
hand; then I would kill you."

And the ass spoke again to Bā'laam, "Am I not your ass, the
one that has always carried you? Did I ever disobey you before?
Why do you treat me so cruelly?"

And then God opened Bā'laam's eyes and let him see the angel
standing with a drawn sword in front of him. Then Bā'laam

leaped off from the ass to the ground, and fell down upon his face before the angel. And the angel said to Bā'laam, "Bā'laam, you know that you are going in the wrong way. But for the ass, which saw me, I would have killed you. The road that you are taking will lead you to death."

And Bā'laam said, "I have sinned against the Lord; now let the Lord forgive me, and I will go home again."

But the angel knew that in his heart Bā'laam wanted to go on to meet King Bā'lăk; and the angel said:

"You may go with these men to Mō'ab; but be sure to say only what God gives you to speak."

So Bā'laam went on and came to the land of Mō'ab; and King Bā'lăk said to him:

"So you have come at last! Why did you wait until I sent the second time? Do you know that I will pay you all that you want, if you will only do what I wish?"

And Bā'laam said, "I have come to you as you asked; but I have no power to speak anything except what God gives me."

King Bā'lăk thought that all Bā'laam said about speaking God's word was spoken only to get more money. He did not understand that a true prophet could never say anything except what was the will of God. He took Bā'laam up to the top of a mountain, from which they could look down upon the camp of the Iṣ'ra-el-ītes, as it lay with tents spread on the plain and the Tabernacle in the middle, overshadowed by the white cloud.

Then Bā'laam said, "Build for me seven altars, and bring me for an offering seven young oxen and seven rams."

They did so, and while the offering was on the altar, God gave a word to Bā'laam; and then Bā'laam spoke out God's word:

"The king of Mō'ab has brought me from the east, saying, 'Come, curse Jā'cob for me; come, speak against Iṣ'ra-el.' How shall I curse those whom God has not cursed? How shall I speak against those who are God's own people? From the mountain top I see this people dwelling alone and not like other nations. Who can count the men of Iṣ'ra-el, like the dust of the earth? Let me die the death of the righteous; and let my last end be like his!"

And King Bā'lăk was surprised at Bā'laam's words. He said:

"What have you done? I brought you to curse my enemies, and instead, you have blessed them!"

And Bā'laam answered, "Did I not tell you beforehand that I could only say the words that God should put into my mouth?"

But King Bā'lăk thought that he would try again to obtain from Bā'laam a curse against Ĭṣ'ra-el. He brought him to another place, where they could look down on the Ĭṣ'ra-el-ītes, and again offered sacrifices. And again God gave a message to Bā'laam; and Bā'laam said:

"Rise up, King Bā'lăk, and hear. God is not a man, that he should lie, or that he should change his mind. What God has said, that he will do. He has commanded me to bless this people; yea, and blessed shall they be. The Lord God is their king, and he shall lead them and give them victory."

Then King Bā'lăk said to Bā'laam:

"If you cannot curse this people, do not bless them, but let them alone!"

And Bā'laam said again, "Did I not tell you, that what God gives me to speak, that I must speak?"

But King Bā'lăk was not yet satisfied. He brought Bā'laam to still another place and offered sacrifices as before. And again the Spirit of God came on Bā'laam. Looking down on the camp of Ĭṣ'ra-el, he said:

"How goodly are your tents, O Ĭṣ'ra-el! and your tabernacles, O Jā'cob! God has brought him out of Ē'ġўpt; and God shall give him the land of promise. He shall destroy his enemies; Ĭṣ'ra-el shall be like a lion when he rises up. Blessed be everyone who blesses him; and cursed be everyone that curses him!"

And Bā'lăk, the king of Mō'ab, was very angry with Bā'laam the prophet.

"I called you," said Bā'lăk, "to curse my enemies; and you have blessed them over and over again. Go back to your own home. I meant to give you great honor and riches; but your God has kept you back from your reward!"

And Bā'laam said to Bā'lăk:

"Did I not say to your messengers, 'If Bā'lăk should give me his house full of silver and gold, I cannot go beyond God's command, to say good or evil? What God speaks, that I must speak.' Now let me tell you what this people shall do to your people in the years to come. A Star shall come out of Jā'cob, and a Scepter shall be stretched forth from Ĭs'ra-el that shall rule over Mō'ab. All these lands, Ē'dom and Mount Sē'ĭr and Mō'ab and Ăm'mŏn shall sometime be under the rule of Ĭs'ra-el."

And all this came to pass, though it was four hundred years afterward, when Dā'vid, the king of Ĭs'ra-el, made all those countries subject to his rule.

But Bā'laam soon showed that although for a time God spoke through his lips, in his heart he was no true servant of God. Although he could not speak a curse against the Ĭs'ra-el-ītes, he still longed for the money that King Bā'lăk was ready to give him if he would only help Bā'lăk to weaken the power of Ĭs'ra-el. And he tried another plan to do harm to Ĭs'ra-el.

Bā'laam told King Bā'lăk that the best plan for him and his people would be to make the Ĭs'ra-el-ītes their friends, to marry among them, and not to make war upon them. And this the Mō'ab-ītes did; until many of the Ĭs'ra-el-ītes married the daughters of Mō'ab, and then they began to worship the idols of Mō'ab.

This was worse for the Ĭs'ra-el-ītes than making war upon them. For if the people of Ĭs'ra-el should be friendly with the idol-worshiping people around them, the Mō'ab-ītes east of the Dead Sea, the Ăm'mŏn-ītes near the wilderness, and the Ē'dom-ītes on the south, they would soon forget the Lord, and begin to worship idols.

There was danger that all the people would be led into sin. And God sent a plague of death upon the people, and many died. Then Mō'ṣeṣ took the men who were leading Ĭs'ra-el into sin, and put them to death. And after this the Ĭs'ra-el-ītes made war upon the Mō'ab-ītes and their neighbors, the Mĭd'ĭ-an-ītes, who were joined with them. They beat them in a great battle, and killed many of them. And among the men of Mō'ab they found Bā'-laam the prophet; and they killed him also, because he had given advice to the Mō'ab-ītes which brought harm to Ĭs'ra-el.

It would have been better for Bā'laam to have stayed at home, and not to have come when King Bā'lăk called him; or it would have been well for him to have gone back to his home when the angel met him. He might then have lived in honor; but he knew God's will, and tried to go against it, and died in disgrace among the enemies of God's people.

Story Thirty-four   NUMBERS 26 : 1-4, 63-65; 32 : 1-42;
DEUTERONOMY 31 : 1 to 34 : 12

How Moses Looked Upon the Promised Land

WHILE the Ĭs'ra-el-ītes were in their camp on the plain beside the river Jôr'dan, at the foot of the mountains of Mō'ab, God told Mō'ṣeṣ to count the number of the men who were old enough and strong enough to go forth to war. And Mō'ṣeṣ caused the men to be counted who were above twenty years of age, and found them to be a little more than six hundred thousand in number. Besides these were the women and children.

And among them all were only three men who were above sixty years of age, men who had been more than twenty years old forty years before, when the Ĭs'ra-el-ītes came out of Ē'ġўpt. The men who had been afraid to enter the land of Cā'năan, when they were at Kā'desh=bär'ne-à the first time, had all died. Some of them had been slain by the enemies in war; some had died in the wilderness during the forty years; some had perished by the plague; some had been bitten by the fiery serpents. Of all those who had come out of Ē'ġўpt as men, the only ones living were Mō'ṣeṣ and Jŏsh'u-à and Cā'leb. Mō'ṣeṣ was now a hundred and twenty years old. He had lived forty years as a prince of Ē'ġўpt, forty years as a shepherd, in Mĭd'ĭ-an, and forty years as the leader of Ĭs'ra-el in the wilderness. But although he was so very old, God had kept his strength. His eyes were bright, his mind was clear, and his arm and heart were strong.

The people of Ĭṣ'ra-el had now full possession of all the land on the east of the river Jôr'dan, from the brook Är'nŏn up to the great Mount Hĕr'mon. Much of this land was well fitted for pasture; for grass was green and rich, and there were many streams of water. There were two of the twelve tribes and half of another tribe, whose people had great flocks of sheep and goats and herds of cattle. These were the tribes which had sprung from Reṳ'ben and Găd, the sons of Jā'cob, and half of the tribe of Mȧ-năs'seh, the son of Jō'ṣeph. For there were two tribes that had sprung from Jō'ṣeph, his descendants, the tribes of Ē'phră-ĭm and Mȧ-năs'seh.

The men of Reṳ'ben, Găd, and half the men of Mȧ-năs'seh came to Mō'ṣeṣ and said:

"The land on this side of the river is good for the feeding of sheep and cattle; and we are shepherds and herdsmen. Cannot we have our possessions on this side of the river, and give all the land beyond the river to our brothers of the other tribes?"

Mō'ṣeṣ was not pleased at this; for he thought that the men of these tribes wished to have their home at once in order to avoid going to war with the rest of the tribes; and this may have been in their minds.

So Mō'ṣeṣ said to them:

"Shall your brothers of the other tribes go to the war? And shall you sit here in your own land and not help them? That would be wicked, and would displease the Lord your God."

Then the men of the two tribes and the half tribe came again to Mō'ṣeṣ, and said to him:

"We will build sheepfolds here for our sheep, and we will choose some cities to place our wives and our children in; and we ourselves will go armed with our brothers of the other tribes, and will help them to take the land on the other side of the Jôr'dan. We will not come back to this side of the river until the war is over, and our brothers have taken their shares of the land, each tribe its own part; and we will take no part on the other side of the river, because our place has been given to us here. And when the land is all won and divided, then we will come back here to our wives and our children."

Then Mō'ṣeṣ was satisfied with the promise that they had given, and he divided the land on the east of the Jôr'dan to these tribes. To the men of Reụ'ben he gave the land on the south; to the men of Găd the land in the middle; and to the half tribe of Mȧ-năs'seh the land on the north, the country called Bā'shăn. And after their wives and children and flocks had been placed safely, the men of war came to the camp, ready to go with the other tribes across the river when God should call them.

And now the work of Mō'șeș was almost done. God said to him:

"Gather the children of Ĭṣ'ra-el together and speak to them your last words, for you are not to lead the people across the Jôr'dan. You are to die in this land, as I said to you at Kā'desh." (See Story Thirty-one.)

Then Mō'șeș called the leaders of the twelve tribes before his tent and said to them many things, which you can read in the book of the Bible called Deuteronomy. There all the long speech of Mō'șeș is given. He told them what wonderful things God had done for their fathers and for them. He gave them again all the words of God's law. He told them that they must not only keep God's law themselves, but must teach it to their children, so that it might never be forgotten. And Mō'șeș sang a song of farewell, and wrote down all his last words.

Then he gave a charge to Jŏsh'u-ȧ, whom God had chosen to take his place as the ruler and leader of the people: though no man could take Mō'șeș' place as a prophet of God and the giver of God's law. He laid his hands on Jŏsh'u-ȧ's head; and God gave to Jŏsh'u-ȧ some of his spirit that had been on Mō'șeș.

Then Mō'șeș, all alone, went out of the camp, while all the people looked at him and wept. Slowly he walked up the mountain side, until they saw him no more. He climbed to the top of Mount Nē'bŏ and stood alone upon the height, and looked at the Land of Promise, which lay spread out before him. Far in the north he could see the white crown of Mount Hẽr'mon, where most of the year there is snow. At his feet, but far below, the river Jôr'dan was winding its way down to the Dead Sea. Across the river, at the foot of the mountains, was standing the city of Jĕr'ĭ-chō, surrounded with a high wall. On the summits of the

mountains beyond he could see Hē'bron, where Ā'brȧ-hăm and
Ĭṣ'aac, and Jā'cob were buried; he could see Jĕ-ru̇'sȧ-lĕm, and
Bĕth'el, and the two mountains where Shē'chem lay hidden in the
center of the land.   And here and there, through the valleys, he
could see afar in the west the gleaming water of the Great Sea.

Then Mō'ṣeṣ, all alone, lay down on the mountain's top, and
died.   Aâr'on and Hûr, who had held up the hands of Mō'ṣeṣ in
battle, had both died; and there was no man on Mount Nē'bö̇ to
bury Mō'ṣeṣ; so God himself buried him, and no man knows where
God laid the body of Mō'ṣeṣ, who had served God so faithfully.

And after Mō'ṣeṣ there was never a man who lived so near to
God, and talked with God so freely, as one would talk face to
face with his friend, until long afterward Jē'ṣus Chrīst, the Son
of God, and greater than Mō'ṣeṣ, came among men.

Story Thirty-five

JOB 1 : 1 to 2 : 13; 42 : 1-17

The Story of Job

A T SOME TIME in those early days—we do not know
just at what time, whether in the days of Mō'ṣeṣ or
later—there was living a good man named Jōb. His
home was in the land of Ŭz, which may have been
on the edge of the desert, east of the land of Ĭṣ'ra-el.
Jōb was a very rich man.   He had many sheep and camels and oxen
and asses.   In all the east no other man was so rich as Jōb.

And Jōb was a good man.   He served the Lord God, and
prayed to God every day, with an offering upon God's altar, as
men worshiped in those times.   He tried to live as God wished
him to live, and was always kind and gentle.   Every day, when
his sons were out in the field, or were having a feast together in
the house of any of them, Jōb went out to his altar and offered a
burnt offering for each one of his sons and his daughters and
prayed to God for them; for he said:

"It may be that my sons have sinned or have turned away from God in their hearts; and I will pray God to forgive them."

At one time, when the angels of God stood before the Lord, Sā'tan the Evil One came also and stood among them, as though he were one of God's angels. The Lord God saw Sā'tan and said to him, "Sā'tan, from what place have you come?" "I have come," answered Sā'tan, "from going up and down in the earth and looking at the people upon it."

Then the Lord said to Sā'tan, "Have you looked at my servant Jōb? And have you seen that there is not another man like him in the earth, a good and a perfect man, one who fears God and does nothing evil?" Then Sā'tan said to the Lord: "Does Jōb fear God for nothing? Hast thou not made a wall around him and around his house, and around everything that he has? Thou hast given a blessing upon his work and hast made him rich. But if thou wilt stretch forth thy hand and take away from him all that he has, then he will turn away from thee and will curse thee to thy face."

Then the Lord said to the Evil One, "Sā'tan, all that Jōb has is in your power; you can do to his sons and his flocks and his cattle whatever you wish; only lay not your hand upon the man himself."

Then Sā'tan went forth from before the Lord; and soon trouble began to come upon Jōb. One day, when all his sons and daughters were eating and drinking together in their oldest brother's house, a man came running to Jōb and said:

"The oxen were plowing and the asses were feeding beside them, when the wild men from the desert came upon them and drove them all away; and the men who were working with the oxen and caring for the asses have all been killed; and I am the only one who has fled away alive!"

While this man was speaking, another man came rushing in; and he said:

"The lightning from the clouds has fallen on all the sheep and on the men who were tending them; and I am the only one who has come away alive!"

Before this man had ended, another came in; and he said:

"The enemies from Chăl-dē'ả have come in three bands, and have taken away all the camels. They have killed the men who were with them; and I am the only one left alive!"

Then at the same time, one more man came in and said to Jōb:

"Your sons and your daughters were eating and drinking together in their oldest brother's house, when a sudden and terrible wind from the desert struck the house and it fell upon them. All your sons and your daughters are dead, and I alone have lived to tell you of it."

Thus in one day, all that Jōb had—his flocks and his cattle and his sons and his daughters—all were taken away; and Jōb, from being rich, was suddenly made poor. Then Jōb fell down upon his face before the Lord and he said:

"With nothing I came into the world and with nothing I shall leave it. The Lord gave and the Lord has taken away; blessed be the name of the Lord."

So even when all was taken from him, Jōb did not turn away from God nor did he find fault with God's doings.

And again the angels of God were before the Lord, and Sā'tan, who had done all this harm to Jōb, was among them. The Lord said to Sā'tan, "Have you looked at my servant Jōb? There is no other man in the world as good as he; a perfect man, one that fears God and does no wrong act. Do you see how he holds fast to his goodness, even after I have let you do him so great harm?" Then Sā'tan answered the Lord, "All that a man has he will give for his life. But if thou wilt put thy hand upon him and touch his bone and his flesh, he will turn from thee and will curse thee to thy face."

And the Lord said to Sā'tan, "I will give Jōb into your hand; do to him whatever you please; only spare his life."

Then Sā'tan struck Jōb, and caused dreadful boils to come upon him, over all his body, from the soles of his feet to the crown of his head. And Jōb sat down in the ashes in great pain; but he would not speak one word against God. His wife said to him:

"What is the use of trying to serve God? You may as well curse God, and die!"

But Jōb said to her, "You speak as one of the foolish women. What? Shall we take good things from the Lord? and shall we not take evil things also?" So Jōb would not speak against God. Then three friends of Jōb came to see him and to try to comfort him in his sorrow and pain. Their names were Ĕl'i-phăz and Bĭl'dăd and Zō'phar. They sat down with Jōb, and wept and spoke to him. But their words were not words of comfort. They believed that all these great troubles had come upon Jōb to punish him, and they tried to persuade Jōb to tell what evil things he had done, to make God so angry with him.

For in those times most people believed that trouble and sickness and the loss of friends and the loss of what they had owned, came to men because God was angry with them on account of their sins. These men thought that Jōb must have been very wicked because they saw such evils coming upon him. They made long speeches to Jōb, urging him to confess his wickedness.

Jōb said that he had done no wrong, that he had tried to do right; and he did not know why these troubles had come; but he would not say that God had dealt unjustly in letting him suffer. Jōb did not understand God's ways, but he believed that God was good; and he left himself in God's hands. And at last God himself spoke to Jōb and to his friends, telling them that it is not for man to judge God, and that God will do right by every man. And the Lord said to the three friends of Jōb:

"You have not spoken of me what is right, as Jōb has. Now bring an offering to me; and Jōb shall pray for you, and for his sake I will forgive you."

So Jōb prayed for his friends, and God forgave them. And

because in all his troubles Jōb had been faithful to God, the Lord blessed Jōb once more, and took away his boils from him and made him well. Then the Lord gave to Jōb more than he had ever owned in the past, twice as many sheep and oxen and camels and asses. And God gave again to Jōb seven sons and three daughters; and in all the land there were no women found so lovely as the daughters of Jōb. After his trouble, Jōb lived a long time, in riches and honor and goodness under God's care.

Part Second

STORIES OF JOSHUA AND THE JUDGES

The Story of a Scarlet Cord

AFTER the death of Mō'ṣeṣ, while the children of Iṣ'ra-el were still encamped upon the east bank of the river Jôr'dan, God spoke to Jŏsh'u-à and said:

"Now that Mō'ṣeṣ my servant is dead, you are to take his place and to rule this people. Do not delay, but lead them across the river Jôr'dan and conquer the land which I have given to them."

Then God told Jŏsh'u-à how large would be the land which the Iṣ'ra-el-ītes were to have, if they should show themselves worthy of it. It was to reach from the great river Eū-phrā'teṣ, far in the north, down to the border of Ē'ġÿpt on the south, and from the desert on the east to the Great Sea on the west. And God said to Jŏsh'u-à:

"Be strong and of a good courage. I will be with you as I was with Mō'ṣeṣ. Read constantly the book of the law which Mō'ṣeṣ gave you, and be careful to obey all that is written in it. Do this and you will have good success."

Then Jŏsh'u-à gave orders to his officers. He said, "Go through the camp and tell the people to prepare food for a journey; for in three days we shall pass over the river Jôr'dan and shall go into the land which the Lord has promised us."

To say this, was very bold; for at that time of the year, in the spring, the Jôr'dan was much larger than at other times. All its banks were overflowed, and it was running as a broad, deep, swift river, down to the Dead Sea, a few miles to the south. No one could possibly walk through it; only a strong man could swim in its powerful current; and the Iṣ'ra-el-ītes had no boats in which they could cross it.

On the other side of the river, a few miles distant, the Iṣ'ra-el-ītes could see the high walls of the city of Jĕr'ĭ-chō, standing at the foot of the mountains. Before the rest of the land could be won, this city must be taken, for it stood beside the road leading up to the mountain country.

Jŏsh'u-à chose two careful, brave, and wise men, and said to them, "Go across the river and get into the city of Jĕr'ĭ-chō; find out all you can about it and come back in two days."

The two men swam across the river and walked over to Jĕr'ĭ-chō and went into the city. But they had been seen, and the king of Jĕr'ĭ-chō sent men to take them prisoners. They came to a house which stood on the wall of the city, where was living a woman named Rā'hăb; and she hid the men.

But these strange men had been seen going into her house, and the king sent his officers after them. The woman hid the men on the roof of the house and heaped over them stalks of flax, which are like long reeds, so that the officers could not find them. After the officers had gone away, thinking that the two spies had left the city, the woman Rā'hăb came to the two men and said to them:

"All of us in this city know that your God is mighty and terrible, and that he has given you this land. We have heard how your God dried up the Red Sea before you, and led you through the desert, and gave you victory over your enemies. And now all the people in this city are in fear of you, for they know that your God will give you this city and all this land."

"Now," said Rā'hăb, "promise me in the name of the Lord, that you will spare my life and the lives of my father and mother and my brothers and sisters, when you take this city."

And the men said, "We will pledge our life for yours, that no harm shall come to you; for you have saved our lives."

This woman's house stood on the wall of the city. From one of its windows Rā'hăb let down outside a rope, upon which the men could slide down to the ground. It happened that this rope was of a bright scarlet color.

The two spies said to Rā'hăb, "When our men come to take this city, you shall have this scarlet rope hanging in the window. Bring your father and mother and family into the house, and keep them there while we are taking the city. We will tell all our men not to harm the people who are in the house where the scarlet cord hangs from the window; and thus all your family will be safe when the city is taken."

Then the two men, at night, slid down the rope and found their way to the river, and swam over it again, and told their story to Jŏsh'u-à. They said, "Truly the Lord has given to us all the land; for all the people in it are in terror before us, and will not dare to oppose us."

One fact was a great help to the Ĭs'ra-el-ītes in their plans for taking the land of Cā'năan. It was not held by one people, or ruled over by one king, who could unite all his people against the Ĭs'ra-el-ītes. There were many small nations living in the land, and each little tribe, and even each city, was ruled by its own king. So it would be easy for the Ĭs'ra-el-ītes to destroy them one by one, so long as they kept apart and did not band themselves into one army.

The Ĭs'ra-el-ītes were now a strong and united people, trained for war and willing to obey one leader, so that all the twelve tribes were ready to fight as one man.

How the River Jordan Became Dry, and the Walls of Jericho Fell Down

AFTER the two spies had come back from Jĕr′ĭ-chō to the camp of Ĭṣ′ra-el, Jŏsh′u-à commanded the people to take down their tents and remove from their camping place to the bank of the river Jôr′dan. Then the priests took apart the Tabernacle and covered the ark and all the furniture in the Holy Place; and ran the poles through the rings for carrying the altar, and made ready for leaving the camp. At the same time the people took down their tents and rolled them up, and brought together their flocks and cattle and stood ready to march.

Then Jŏsh′u-à gave the word, and they marched down toward the river, which was rolling high and strong in front of them. Jŏsh′u-à said:

"Let the priests carry the Ark of the Covenant in front, and let there be a space between it and the rest of the people of three thousand feet. Do not come nearer than that space to the ark."

And all the people stood still, wondering, while the ark was brought on the shoulders of the priests far out in front of the ranks of men, until it came down to the very edge of the water. They could not see the ark, for it was covered, but they knew that it was under its coverings on the shoulders of the priests.

Then said Jŏsh′u-à to the priests, "Now walk into the water of the river."

Then a most wonderful thing took place. As soon as the feet of the priests touched the water by the shore, the river above stopped flowing, and far away, up the river, they could see the water rising and piling up like a great heap. And below the place where they were standing the water ran on, until it left a great place dry, and the stones on the river's bed were uncovered.

144

Then, at Jŏsh'u-à's command, the priests carried the ark down to the middle of the dry bed of the river and stood there with it on their shoulders.

And Jŏsh'u-à gave order to the people to march across the river. In front came the soldiers from Reu'ben, Găd, and the half tribe of Mă-năs'seh, who had already received their homes on the east of the river, but were with the other tribes to help in the war. After them came all the other tribes, each by itself, until they had all passed over the river; and all this time the priests stood on the river's dry bed holding the ark.

Then Jŏsh'u-à called for twelve men, one man from each tribe, and he said to them:

"Go down into the river and bring up from it twelve stones, as large stones as you can carry, from the place where the priests are standing."

They did so; and with these stones Jŏsh'u-à made a stone heap on the bank; and he said:

"Let this heap of stones stand here to keep in memory what has taken place today. When your children shall ask you, 'Why are these stones here?' you shall say to them, 'Because here the Lord God made the river dry before the Ark of the Covenant, so that the people could cross over into the land that God had promised to their fathers.' "

And Jŏsh'u-à told these twelve men to take also twelve other stones and heap them up in the bed of the river where the priests stood with the ark, so that these stones also might stand to remind all people forever of God's wonderful help to them.

When all this had been done, and the two heaps of stone had been piled up, one on the bank, the other in the bed of the river, Jŏsh'u-à said to the priests, "Come now up from the river, and bring the ark to the shore."

They did so; and then the waters began to flow down from above, until soon the river Jôr'dan was rolling by as it had rolled before. So now at last the children of Ĭs'ra-el were safely in the land which God had promised to their fathers more than five hundred years before.

They set up a new camp, with the Tabernacle in the middle,

the altar before it, and the tents of the tribes around it in order.
The place of the camp was near the river, on the plain of Jôr'dan,
and was called Gĭl'găl. And there the main camp of the Ĭṣ'ra-el-
ītes was kept all the time that they were carrying on the war to
win the land of Cā'năan.

When they came into the land, it was the time of the early harvest; and in the fields they found grain and barley in abundance.
They gathered it and ground it and made bread of it; and some of
it they roasted in the ear; and on that day the manna which God
had sent them from the sky through forty years ceased to fall,
now that it was needed no more.

There, in full view of the new camp, stood the strong walls of
Jĕr'ĭ-chō. Jŏsh'u-à went out to look at the city; and he saw a man
all armed coming toward him. Jŏsh'u-à walked boldly up to the
man and said to him, "Are you on our side, or are you one of our
enemies?"

And he said, "No; but as captain of the Lord's host, have I
come."

Then Jŏsh'u-à saw that he was the angel of the Lord; and
Jŏsh'u-à, bowing down before him, said, "What word has my Lord
to his servant?"

And the captain of the Lord's host said to Jŏsh'u-à, "Take off
your shoes from your feet, for it is holy ground where you are
standing."

Jŏsh'u-à did so; for the one who was speaking to him was not
merely an angel, but the Lord himself appearing as a man. And
the Lord said to Jŏsh'u-à, "I have given to you Jĕr'ĭ-chō and its
king and its mighty men of war; and I will destroy the city of
Jĕr'ĭ-chō before you."

Then the Lord told Jŏsh'u-à the way in which the city should
be taken; and Jŏsh'u-à went back to the camp of Gĭl'găl and made
ready to march as God commanded. During the next seven days
all that was done was according to the word spoken by the Lord
to Jŏsh'u-à.

They drew out the army as if to fight against the city. In front
came the soldiers from the tribes on the east of the river. Then
came a company of priests with trumpets made of rams' horns,

which they blew long and loud. Then came the Ark of the Covenant, borne on the shoulders of the priests. And, last of all came the host of Ĭṣ′ra-el, marching in order. No one shouted, nor was any noise heard, except the sound of the rams'-horn trumpets. They marched around the walls of Jĕr′ĭ-chō once on that day and then all marched back to the camp.

The next morning they all formed in the same order, and again marched around the walls of the city; and so they did again and again, marching once each day for six days.

On the seventh day, by God's command, they rose very early in the morning and did not stop when they had marched around the walls once; but kept on marching round and round, until they had gone about the walls seven times. As they went by, they saw at one window on the wall a scarlet cord hanging down; and they knew that this was the house of Rā′hăb, who had saved the lives of the two spies.

When the seventh march was ended, they all stood still. Even the trumpets ceased, and there was a great silence for a moment, until the voice of Jŏsh′u-à rang out, "Shout, for the Lord has given you the city!"

Then a great shout went up from the host; and they looked at the wall and saw that it was trembling and shaking and falling! It fell down flat at every place but one. There was one part of

the wall left standing, where the scarlet cord was hanging from the window.

And Jŏsh'u-à said to the two spies, "Go and bring out Rā'hăb and her family, and take them to a safe place."

They went into Rā'hăb's house on the wall and brought her out, and with her her father and mother and all their family. They cared for them and kept them safely in the camp of the Ĭs'ra-el-ītes until all the war against the people of the land was ended.

While some of the soldiers were taking care of Rā'hăb, all the rest of the army was climbing up over the ruined wall. The people in the city were so filled with fear when they saw the walls falling down on every side, that they did not try to defend it, but sank down helpless and were slain or taken prisoners by the Ĭs'ra-el-ītes.

Thus the city was taken, with all that was within it. But the Ĭs'ra-el-ītes were forbidden to use for themselves any of the treasures in the city. Jŏsh'u-à said to them, "Nothing in this city belongs to you. It is the Lord's, and is to be destroyed as an offering to the Lord."

So they brought together all the gold and silver and precious things, and all that was in the houses. They took nothing for themselves, but kept the gold and silver and the things made of brass and iron for the Tabernacle. All the rest of what they found in the city they burned and destroyed, leaving of the city of Jĕr'ĭ-chō nothing but waste and desolation. Jŏsh'u-à said:

"Let the Lord's curse rest on any man who shall ever build again the city of Jĕr'ĭ-chō. With the loss of his oldest born, shall he lay its foundation, and with the loss of his youngest son, shall he set up the gates of it."

After this Rā'hăb, the woman who had saved the spies, was taken among the people of Ĭs'ra-el just as though she had been an Ĭs'ra-el-īte born. And one of the nobles of the tribe of Jū'dah, whose name was Săl'mŏn, took her for his wife. And from her line of descendants, of those who came from her, many years after this, was born Dā'vid the king. She was saved and blessed, because she had faith in the God of Ĭs'ra-el.

The Story of a Wedge of Gold

WHILE the Ĭs̱′ra-el-ītes at God's word were destroying the city of Jĕr′ĭ-chō, there was one man who disobeyed God's command. A man named Ā′chăn, of the tribe of Jū′dah, saw in one house a beautiful garment that had come from Băb′ў̆-lon, and a wedge-shaped piece of gold and some silver. He looked at it, longed to have it for his own, took it secretly to his tent, and hid it. He thought that no one had seen him do this thing. But God saw it all; and Ā′chăn's theft from God, to whom everything in Jĕr′ĭ-chō belonged, brought great trouble to Ĭs̱′ra-el.

From Jĕr′ĭ-chō there was a road up the ravines and valleys leading to the mountain country. On one of the hills above the plain stood a little city called Ā′ī. Jŏsh′u-à did not think it needful for all the army to go to take Ā′ī, because it was a small place. So he sent a small army of three thousand men. But the men of Ā′ī came out against them and killed a number of them and drove them away, so that they failed to take the city.

And when the rest of the people heard of this defeat, they were filled with fear. Jŏsh′u-à was alarmed, not because he was afraid of the Cā′năan-ītes, but because he knew that God was not with the men who went against Ā′ī. And Jŏsh′u-à fell on his face before the Lord and said:

"O Lord God, why hast thou led us across Jôr′dan only to let us fall before our enemies? What shall I say, O Lord, now that the men of Ĭs̱′ra-el have been beaten and driven away?"

And God said to Jŏsh′u-à:

"Ĭs̱′ra-el has sinned. They have disobeyed my words and have broken their promise. They have taken the treasure that belongs to me and have kept it. And that is the reason why I have left them to suffer from their enemies. My curse shall rest on the people until they bring back that which is stolen and punish the

149

man who robbed me." And God told Jŏsh'u-à how to find the
man who had done this evil thing.

The next morning, very early, Jŏsh'u-à called all the tribes of
Ĭs'ra-el to come before him. When the tribe of Jū'dah came near,
God showed to Jŏsh'u-à that this was the tribe. Then as the divisions of Jū'dah came by, God pointed out one division; and in that
division one family, and in that family one household, and in that
household one man. Ā'chăn was singled out as the man who
had robbed God.

And Jŏsh'u-à said to Ā'chăn, "My son, give honor to the Lord
God and confess your sin to him; and tell me now what you have
done. Do not try to hide it from me."

And Ā'chăn said, "I have sinned against the Lord. I saw in
Jĕr'ĭ-chō a garment from Băb'y̆-lon and a wedge of gold and some
pieces of silver, and I hid them in my tent." Then Jŏsh'u-à sent
messengers, who ran to the tent of Ā'chăn, and found the hidden
things and brought them out before all the people.

Then, because Ā'chăn's crime had harmed all the people, and
because his children were with him in the crime, they took them

all, Ā′chăn, and his sons and his daughters, and the treasure that he had stolen, and even his sheep and his oxen, and his tent and all that was in it. And the people threw stones upon them until all were dead; then they burned their bodies and all the things in the tent. And over the ashes they piled up a heap of stones, so that all who saw it would remember what came to Ā′chăn for his sin.

Thus did God show to his people how careful they must be to obey his commands, if they would have God with them. After this Jŏsh′u-à sent another army, larger than before, against Ā′ī. And they took the city and destroyed it, as they had destroyed Jĕr′ĭ-chō. But God allowed the people to take for themselves what they found in the city of Ā′ī.

Then they marched on over the mountains, until they came near to the city of Shē′chem, in the middle of the land of Cā′nǎan. The people of the land were so filled with fear that none of them resisted the march of the Ĭṣ′ra-el-ītes. Near Shē′chem are the two mountains, Ē′bal on the north and Gĕr′ĭ-zĭm on the south. Between these is a great hollow place. There Jŏsh′u-à gathered all the people of Ĭṣ′ra-el, with their wives and their children.

In the midst of this place they built an altar of unhewn stones heaped up, for they had left the Tabernacle and the brazen altar standing in the camp at Gĭl′găl, by Jôr′dan. On this new altar they gave offerings to the Lord and worshiped.

Then before all the people, Jŏsh′u-à read the law which Mō′ṣeṣ had written. And all the people, with their wives, and even the little children, listened to the law of the Lord. Half of the tribes stood on the slope of Mount Ē′bal on the north, and these, as Jŏsh′u-à read the words of warning which God had given to those who should disobey, all answered with one voice, "Amen." The other half stood on the slope of Mount Gĕr′ĭ-zĭm on the south; and as Jŏsh′u-à read God's words of blessing to those who should obey the law, these answered, "Amen."

When they had done all this, and thus given the land to the Lord and pledged themselves to serve God, they marched again down the mountains, past the smoldering ruins of Ā′ī, past the heap of stones that covered Ā′chăn, and past the broken walls of Jĕr′ĭ-chō, back to the camp at Gĭl′găl beside the river.

How Joshua Conquered the Land of Canaan

THE NEWS of all that Jŏsh'u-à and the men of Ĭṣ'ra-el had done at Jĕr'ĭ-chō and at Ā'ī, how they had destroyed those cities and slain their people, went through all the land. Everywhere the tribes of Cā'-năan prepared to fight these strangers who had so suddenly and so boldly entered their country.

Near the middle of the mountain region, between Jĕ-ru'sà-lĕm and Shē'chem, were four cities of a race called either the Hī'vītes, or the Gĭb'e-on-ītes, from their chief city, Gĭb'e-on. These people felt that they could not resist the Ĭṣ'ra-el-ītes; so they undertook to make peace with them. Their cities were less than a day's journey from the camp of Gĭl'găl, and quite near to Ā'ī; but they came to Jŏsh'u-à at the camp, looking as if they had made a long journey.

They were wearing old and ragged garments and shoes worn out; and they brought dry and moldy bread and old bags of food and wine skins torn and mended. They met Jŏsh'u-à and the elders of Ĭṣ'ra-el in the camp and said to them:

"We live in a country far away; but we have heard of the great things that you have done; the journey you have made, and the cities you have taken on the other side of the river Jôr'dan; and now we have come to offer you our friendship and to make peace with you."

And Jŏsh'u-à said to them, "Who are you? And from what land do you come?"

"We have come," they said, "from a country far away. See this bread. We took it hot from the oven, and now it is moldy. These wine skins were new when we filled them, and you see they are old. Look at our garments and our shoes, all worn out and patched."

Jŏsh'u-à and the elders did not ask the Lord what to do, but made an agreement with these men to have peace with them, not to destroy their cities, and to spare the lives of their people. And a very few days after making peace with them, they found that the four cities where they lived were very near.

At first the Ĭṣ'ra-el-īte rulers were very angry and were inclined to break their agreement, but afterward they said:

"We will keep our promise to these people, though they have deceived us. We will let them live, but they shall be made our servants and shall do the hard work for the camp and for the Tabernacle."

Even this was better than to be killed and to have their cities destroyed; and the Gĭb'e-on-īte people were glad to save their lives. So from that time the people of the four Gĭb'e-on-īte cities carried burdens and drew water and cut wood and served the camp of Ĭṣ'ra-el.

The largest city near the camp of Gĭl'găl was Jĕ-ru'sà-lĕm, among the mountains, where its king, Mĕl-chĭz'e-dĕk, in the days of Ā'brà-hăm, five hundred years before, had been a priest of the Lord, and had blessed Ā'brà-hăm. But now, in the days of Jŏsh'u-à, the people of that city worshiped idols and were very wicked.

When the king of Jĕ-ru'sà-lĕm heard that the Gĭb'e-on-ītes, who lived near him, had made peace with Ĭṣ'ra-el, he sent to the kings of Hē'bron and Lā'chish and several other cities, and said to them:

"Come, let us unite our armies into one great army and fight the Gĭb'e-on-ītes and destroy them; for they have made peace with our enemies, the people of Ĭṣ'ra-el."

As soon as the people of Gĭb'e-on heard this, they sent to Jŏsh'u-à, saying:

"Come quickly and help us; for we are your servants; and the king of Jĕ-ru'sà-lĕm is coming with a great army to kill us all, and destroy our cities. The whole country is in arms against us; come at once, before it is too late!"

Jŏsh'u-à was a very prompt man, swift in all his acts. At once he called out his army, and marched all night up the mountains.

He came suddenly upon the five kings and their army at a place called Bĕth=hō'rŏn. There a great battle was fought, Jŏsh'u-à leading his men against the Cā'năan-ītes. He did not give his enemies time to form in line, but fell upon them so suddenly that they were driven into confusion, and fled before the men of Ĭṣ'ra-el.

And the Lord helped his people by a storm which drove great hailstones down on the Cā'năan-ītes; so that more were killed by the hailstones than by the sword.

It is written in an old song that on that day Jŏsh'u-à said before all his men:

> "Sun, stand thou still over Ḡib'e-on,
> And thou, moon, in the valley of Āj'a-lŏn,
> And the sun stood still, and the moon stayed,
> Until the people had taken vengeance upon their enemies."

If ever in all the history of the world there was a battle when the sun might well stand still, and the day be made longer, to make the victory complete, it was that day more than any other. For on that day the land was won by the people of the Lord. If Ĭṣ'ra-el had been defeated and destroyed, instead of Cā'năan, then the Bible would never have been written, the worship of the true God would have been blotted out, and the whole world would have

worshiped idols. The battle that day was for the salvation of the world as well as of Ĭṣ'ra-el. So this was the greatest battle in its results that the world has ever seen. There have been many battles where more men fought and more soldiers were slain, than at the battle of Bĕth=hō'rŏn. But no battle in all the world had such an effect in the years and the ages after, as this battle.

After the victory Jŏsh'u-à followed his enemies as they fled, and killed many of them, until their armies were broken up and destroyed. The five kings who had led against Jŏsh'u-à were found hidden in a cave, were brought out and were slain, so that they might no more trouble the Ĭṣ'ra-el-ītes. By this one victory all the part of the land of Cā'năan on the south was won, though there were a few small fights afterward.

Then Jŏsh'u-à turned to the north, and led his army by a swift march against the kings who had united there to fight the Ĭṣ'ra-el-ītes. As suddenly as before he had fallen on the five kings at Bĕth=hō'rŏn, he fell upon these kings and their army, near the little lake in the far north of Cā'năan, called "the waters of Mē'rom." There another great victory was won; and after this it was easy to conquer the land. Everywhere the tribes of Cā'năan were made to submit to the Ĭṣ'ra-el-ītes, until all the mountain country was under Jŏsh'u-à's rule.

In the conquest of Cā'năan, there were six great marches and six battles; three in the lands on the east of the Jôr'dan, while Mō'ṣeṣ was still living, the victories over the Ăm'ôr-ītes, the Mĭd'ĭ-an-ītes, and the people of Bā'shăn, on the northeast, and three on the west of the Jôr'dan, the victories at Jĕr'ĭ-chō, at Bĕth=hō'rŏn, and Lake Mē'rom, under Jŏsh'u-à.

But even after these marchings and victories, it was a long time before all the land was taken by the Ĭṣ'ra-el-ītes.

The Old Man Who Fought Against the Giants

THE GREAT war for the conquest of Cā'năan was now ended, though in the land some cities were still held by the Cā'năan-īte people. Yet the Ĭṣ'ra-el-ītes were now the rulers over most of the country, and so Jŏsh'u-à made plans to divide the land among the twelve tribes of Ĭṣ'ra-el.

One day the rulers of the tribe of Jū'dah came to Jŏsh'u-à's tent at Gĭl'găl, and with them came an old man, Cā'leb, whom you remember as one of the twelve spies sent by Mō'ṣeṣ from Kā'desh=bär'ne-à to go through the land of Cā'năan. This had been many years before, and Cā'leb, like Jŏsh'u-à, was now an old man, past eighty years of age. He said to Jŏsh'u-à:

"You remember what the Lord said to Mō'ṣeṣ, the man of God, when we were in the desert at Kā'desh=bär'ne-à, and you and I with the other spies brought back our report. I spoke to Mō'ṣeṣ the word that was in my heart, and I followed the Lord wholly, when the other spies spoke out of their own fear and made the people afraid. On that day you remember that Mō'ṣeṣ said to me, 'The land where your feet have trodden and over which you have walked shall be yours, because you trusted in the Lord.'

"That was forty-five years ago," Cā'leb went on to say, "and God has kept me alive all those years. Today, at eighty-five years of age, I am as strong as I was in that day. And now I ask that the promise made by Mō'ṣeṣ be kept, and that I have my choice of the places in the land."

"Well," said Jŏsh'u-à, "you can take your choice in the land. What part of it will you choose?"

And Cā'leb answered:

"The place that I will choose is the very mountain on which we saw the city with the high walls, where the giants were living then,

156

and where other giants, their sons, are living now, the city of Hē'bron. I know that the walls are high and that the giants live there. But the Lord will help me to take the cities, and to drive out the people who live in them. Let me have the city of Hē'bron."

This was very bold in so old a man as Cā'leb, to choose the city which was not yet taken from the enemies, and one of the hardest cities to take, when he might have chosen some rich place already won. But Cā'leb at eighty-five showed the same spirit of courage and willingness to war, and faith in God, that he had shown in his

prime at forty years of age. Then Jŏsh'u-à said to Cā'leb, "You shall have the city of Hē'bron, with all its giants, if you will gather together your men and take it." And the old soldier brought together his men and led them against the strong city of Hē'bron, where was the tomb of Ā'bră-hăm, Ī'saac, and Jā'cob. By the help of the Lord, Cā'leb was able to drive out the giants, tall and mighty as they were. They fled from Cā'leb's men and went down to the shore on the west of the land, and lived among the people of that region, who were called the Phĭ-lĭs'tĭneṣ; while Cā'leb and his children, and his descendants long after him, held the city of Hē'bron in the south of the land.

After this, by command of the Lord, Jŏsh'u-à divided the land among the tribes. Two tribes and half of another tribe had already received their land on the east of Jôr'dan; so there were nine tribes and a half tribe to receive their shares. Jū'dah, one of the largest, had the mountain country west of the Dead Sea, from Hē'bron to Jĕ-ru̯'să-lĕm; Sĭm'e-on was on the south toward the desert; Bĕn'ja-mĭn was north of Jū'dah on the east, toward the Jôr'dan, and Dăn north of Jū'dah on the west, toward the Great Sea.

In the middle of the country, around the city of Shē'chem, and the two mountains, Ē'bal and Gĕr'ĭ-zĭm, where Jŏsh'u-à had read the law to the people, was the land of the tribe of Ē'phră-ĭm. This was one of the best parts of all the country, for the soil was rich and there were many springs and streams of water. And here, near Mount Ē'bal, they buried the body of their tribe father Jō'ṣeph, which they had kept in its coffin of stone, unburied, ever since they left Ē'ḡy̆pt, more than forty years before. As Jŏsh'u-à himself belonged to the tribe of Ē'phră-ĭm, his home was also in this land.

North of Ē'phră-ĭm, and reaching from the river Jôr'dan to the Great Sea, was the land of the other half of the tribe of Mà-năs'seh. Both tribes of Ē'phră-ĭm and Mà-năs'seh had sprung from Jō'ṣeph. So Jō'ṣeph's descendants had two tribes.

The northern part of the land was divided among four tribes. Ĭs'sa-char was in the south, Ăsh'ēr on the west beside the Great Sea, Zĕb'u-lŭn was in the middle among the mountains, and Năph'-ta-lī was in the north and by the lake afterward called the Sea of Găl'ĭ-lee. At that time this lake was called the Sea of Kĭn'no-rĕth, because the word "kinnor" means "a harp"; and as they thought that this lake was shaped somewhat like a harp, they named it "the Harp-shaped Sea."

But although all the land had been divided, it had not all been completely conquered. Nearly all the Cā'năan-īte people were there, still living upon the land, though in the mountain region they were under the rule of the Ĭs'ra-el-ītes. But on the plain beside the Great Sea, on the west of the land were the Phĭ-lĭs'tĭneṣ, a very strong people whom the Ĭs'ra-el-ītes had not yet met in war, though the time was coming when they would meet them and suffer from them.

And even among the mountains were many cities where the Cā'năan-īte people still lived, and in some of these cities they were strong. Years afterward, when Jŏsh'u-à the great warrior was no longer living, many of these people rose up to trouble the Ĭs'ra-el-ītes. The time came when the tribes of Ĭs'ra-el wished often that their fathers had driven out or entirely destroyed the Cā'năan-ītes, before they ceased the war and divided the land.

But when Jŏsh'u-à divided the land and sent the tribes to their new homes, peace seemed to reign over all the country. Up to this time we have spoken of all this land as the land of Cā'năan, but now and henceforth it was to be called "The Land of Ĭs'ra-el," or "The Land of the Twelve Tribes," for it was now their home.

Story Six   JOSHUA 20 : 1 to 21 : 45

The Avenger of Blood and the Cities of Refuge

THERE was among the Ĭs'ra-el-ītes one custom which seems so strange and so different from our ways that it will be interesting to hear about it. It was their rule with regard to any man who by accident killed another man. With us, whenever a man has been killed, the man who killed him, if he can be found, is taken by an officer before the judge, and he is tried. If he killed the man by accident, not wishing to do harm, he is set free. If he meant to kill him, he is punished; he may be sentenced to die for the other man's death; and when he is put to death, it is by the officer of the law.

But in the lands of the east, where the Ĭs'ra-el-ītes lived, it was very different. There, when a man was killed, his nearest relative always took it upon himself to kill the man who had killed him; and he undertook to kill this man without trial, without a judge, and by his own hand, whether the man deserved to die or did not deserve it. Two men might be working in the forest together and one man's ax might fly from his hand and kill the other; or one

man hunting might kill another hunter by mistake. No matter whether the man was guilty or innocent, the nearest relative of the one who had lost his life must find the man who had killed him and kill him in return, wherever he was. If he could not find him, sometimes he would kill any member of his family whom he could find. This man was called "the avenger of blood," because he took vengeance for the blood of his relative, whether the one whom he slew deserved to die or not. When Mō'şeş gave laws to the children of Iş'ra-el, he found this custom of having an "avenger of blood" rooted so deeply in the habits of the people that it could not be broken up. In fact, it still remains even to this day among the village people in the land where the Iş'ra-el-ītes lived.

But Mō'şeş gave a law which was to take the place of the old custom and to teach the people greater justice in their dealings with each other. And when they came into the land of Cā'năan, Jŏsh'u-à carried out the plan which Mō'şeş had commanded.

Jŏsh'u-à chose in the land six cities, three on one side of the river Jôr'dan, and three on the other side. All of these were well-known places and easy to find. Most of them were on mountains and could be seen far away. They were so chosen that from almost any part of the land a man could reach one of these cities in a day, or at the most in two days. These cities were called "Cities of Refuge," because in them a man who had killed another by mistake could find refuge from the avenger of blood.

When a man killed another by accident, wherever he was, he ran as quickly as possible to the nearest of these cities of refuge. The avenger of blood followed him and might perhaps overtake him and kill him before he reached the city. But almost always the man, having some start before his enemy, would get to the city of refuge first.

There the elders of the city looked into the case. They learned all the facts; and if the man was really guilty and deserved to die, they gave him up to be killed by the avenger. But if he was innocent, and did not mean to kill the man who was dead, they forbade the avenger to touch him and kept him in safety.

A line was drawn around the city, at a distance from the wall, within which line the avenger could not come to do the man harm; and within this line were fields, where the man could work and raise crops, so that he could have food.

And there at the city of refuge the innocent man who had killed another without meaning to kill, lived until the high priest died. After the high priest died and another high priest took his place, the man could go back to his own home and live in peace.

These were the cities of refuge in the land of Ĭṣ'ra-el: On the north, Kē'desh in the tribe of Năph'ta-lī; in the center, Shē'chem, at the foot of Mount Ḡĕr'ĭ-zĭm, in the tribe of Ē'phră-ĭm; and on the south, Hē'bron, Cā'leb's city, in the tribe of Jū'dah. These were among the mountains, on the west of the river Jôr'dan. On the east of the river Jôr'dan, the cities were Gō'lan of Bā'shan in Mȧ-năs'seh, Rā'moth of Ḡil'e-ăd in the tribe of Găd, and Bē'zēr in the high lands of the tribe of Reu'ben.

This law taught the Ĭṣ'ra-el-ītes to be patient and to control themselves, to protect the innocent and to seek for justice, and not yield to sudden anger.

Among the tribes there was one which had no land given to it in one place. This was the tribe of Lē'vī, to which Mō'ṣeṣ and Aȧr'on belonged. The men of this tribe were priests, who offered the sacrifices, and Lē'vītes, who cared for the Tabernacle and its worship. Mō'ṣeṣ and Jŏsh'u-ȧ did not think it well to have all the Lē'vītes living in one part of the country, so he gave them cities, and in some places the fields around the cities, in many parts of the land. From these places they went up to the Tabernacle to serve, each for a certain part of the year; and the rest of the year stayed in their homes and cared for their fields.

When the war was over and the land was divided, Jŏsh'u-ȧ

fixed the Tabernacle at a place called Shī'lōh, not far from the center of the land, so that from all the tribes, the people could come up at least once a year for worship. They were told to come from their homes three times in each year and to worship the Lord at Shī'lōh.

These three times were for the feast of the Passover in the spring, when the lamb was killed and roasted and eaten with un-leavened bread; the feast of the Tabernacles in the fall, when for a week they slept out of doors in huts made of twigs and boughs, to keep in mind their life in the wilderness; and the feast of Pente-cost, fifty days after the Passover, when they laid on the altar the first ripe fruits from the fields. These three feasts were kept at the place of the altar and the Tabernacle.

And at Shī'lōh, before the Tabernacle, they placed the altar, on which the offerings were laid twice every day.

God had kept his promise, and had brought the Iṣ'ra-el-ītes into a land which was their own, and had given them rest from all their enemies.

Story Seven   JOSHUA 22 : 1 to 24 : 33

The Story of an Altar Beside the River

WHEN the war for the conquest of Cā'năan was ended, and the tribes were about to leave for their places in the land, Jŏsh'u-à broke up the camp at Gĭl'găl, which had been the meeting place of the Iṣ'ra-el-ītes through all the war. You remember that two of the tribes and half of another tribe had received their land on the east of Jôr'dan, but their soldiers crossed the Jôr'dan with the men of the other tribes. Jŏsh'u-à now called these soldiers and said to them:

"You have done all that Mō'șeș the servant of the Lord commanded you; you have stood faithfully by your brothers of the other tribes; and now the time has come for you to go back to your wives and your children in your own tribe lands on the other side of Jôr'dan. Go to your homes, where your wives and children are waiting for you. Only remember always to keep the commandments of the Lord, and be true to the Lord and serve him with all your heart and all your soul."

Then Jŏsh'u-à gave them the blessing of the Lord and sent them away. They left Shī'lōh, where the Tabernacle was standing, and came to the river Jôr'dan. There on a great rock where it could be seen from far, they built a high altar of stone.

Soon it was told among the tribes that the men of the two tribes and a half tribe had built for themselves an altar. God had commanded the people to have but one altar for all the tribes and one high priest, and one offering for all the tribes upon the altar. This was for the purpose of keeping all the people together, as one family, with one worship.

The people of Ĭș'ra-el were greatly displeased when they found that these tribes had built an altar, while there was already one altar for all the tribes at Shī'lōh. They were almost ready to go to war against the tribes on the east of the Jôr'dan on account of this altar.

But before going to war, they sent one of the priests, Phĭn'e-has, the son of Ē-le-ā'zar, and with him ten of the princes of Ĭș'ra-el, one from each tribe, to ask the men of the tribes on the east for

what purpose they had built this altar. These men came to the men of Reu′ben and Găd and the half tribe of Må-năs′seh, and said to them:

"What is this that you have done in building for yourselves an altar? Do you mean to turn away from the Lord and set up your own gods? Have you forgotten how God was made angry when Iṣ′ra-el worshiped other gods? Do not show yourselves rebels against God by building an altar while God's altar is standing at Shī′lōh."

Then the men of the two tribes and a half answered:

"The Lord, the only God, he knows that we have not built this altar for the offering of sacrifices. Let the Lord himself be our judge, that we have done no wrong. We have built this altar so that our children may see it, standing as it stands on your side of the river and not on our side: and then we can say to them, 'Let that altar remind you that we are all one people, we and the tribes on the other side of Jôr′dan.' This altar stands as a witness between us that we are all one people and worship the one Lord God of Iṣ′ra-el."

Then the princes of the nine and a half tribes were satisfied. They were pleased when they knew that it was an altar for witness and not for offerings. They named the altar Ed, a word which means witness. "For," they said, "it is a witness between us that the Lord is our God, the God of us all."

Jŏsh′u-à was now a very old man, more than a hundred years old. He knew that he must soon die and he wished to give to the people his last words. So he called the elders and rulers and judges of the tribes to meet him at Shē′chem, in the middle of the land and near his own home.

When they were all together before him, Jŏsh′u-à reminded them of all that God had done for their fathers and for themselves. He told them the story of Ā′brà-hăm, how he left his home at God's call; the story of Jā′cob and his family going down to Ē′gy̆pt; and how after many years the Lord had brought them out of that land; how the Lord had led them through the wilderness and had given them the land where they were now living at peace. Jŏsh′u-à then said:

"You are living in cities that you did not build and you are eating of vines and olive trees that you did not plant. It is the Lord who has given you all these things. Now, therefore, fear the Lord and serve him with all your hearts. And if any of you have any other gods, such as Ā'brǎ-hǎm's father worshiped beyond the River, and as your fathers sometimes worshiped in Ē'ġẙpt, put them away and serve the Lord only. And if you are not willing to serve the Lord, then choose this day whatever god you will serve; but as for me and my house, we will serve the Lord."

Then the people answered Jǒsh'u-à:

"We will not turn away from the Lord to serve other gods; for the Lord brought us out of Ē'ġẙpt where we were slaves; and the Lord drove out our enemies before us; and the Lord gave us this land. We will serve the Lord, for he is the God of Iṣ'ra-el."

"But," said Jǒsh'u-à, "you must remember that the Lord is very strict in his commands. He will be angry with you if you turn away from him after promising to serve him; and will punish you if you worship images, as the people do around you."

And the people said, "We pledge ourselves to serve the Lord and the Lord only."

Then Jǒsh'u-à wrote down the people's promise in the book of the law, so that others might read it and remember it. And he set up a great stone under an oak tree in Shē'chem, and he said:

"Let this stone stand as a witness between you and the Lord, that you have pledged yourselves to be faithful to him."

Then Jǒsh'u-à sent the people away to their tribe lands, telling them not to forget the promise that they had made. After this Jǒsh'u-à died, at the age of a hundred and ten years. And as long as the people lived who remembered Jǒsh'u-à, the people of Iṣ'ra-el continued serving the Lord.

The Present That Ehud Brought
to King Eglon

OU WOULD suppose that, after all that God had done for the Ĭṣ'ra-el-ītes, and after their own promises to serve him faithfully, they would never turn to the idols which could not save their own people, the Cā'-nǎan-ītes. Yet, when Jŏsh'u-à was no longer living, and the men who knew Jŏsh'u-à had also died, the people began to forget their own God and to worship images of wood and stone.

Perhaps it was not so strange after all. In all the world, so far as we know, at that time the Ĭṣ'ra-el-ītes were the only people who did not worship idols. All the nations around them, the Ē-ġў͝p'-tiaṇs, from whose land they had come, the Ē'dom-ītes on the south, the Mō'ab-ītes on the east, the Phĭ-lĭs'tĭneṣ on the west beside the Great Sea—all these bowed down to images, and many of them offered their own children upon the idol altars.

Then, too, you remember that the Cā'nǎan-ītes had not been driven out of the land. They were there still, in their own cities and villages everywhere, and their idols were standing under the trees on many high places. So the Ĭṣ'ra-el-ītes saw idols all around them and people bowing down before them; while they themselves had no God that could be seen. The Tabernacle was far away from some parts of the land; and the people were so busy with their fields and their houses that few of them went up to worship.

And so it came to pass that the people began to neglect their own worship of the Lord and then to begin the worship of the idols around them. And from idol worship they sank lower still into wicked deeds. For this the Lord caused them to suffer. Their enemies came upon them from the lands around and became their masters; for when God left them, they were helpless. They were made poor, for these rulers who had conquered them robbed them of all their grain and grapes and olive oil.

After a time of suffering the Is̱'ra-el-ītes would think of what God had done for them in other times. Then they would turn away from the idols and would call upon God. And God would hear them and raise up some great man to lead them to freedom and to break the power of those who were ruling over them. This great man they called "a judge"; and under him they would serve God and be happy and successful once more.

As long as the judge lived and ruled, the people worshiped God. But when the judge died, they forgot God again and worshiped idols and fell under the power of their enemies as before, until God sent another judge to deliver them. And this happened over and over again for two hundred years after Jŏsh'u-à died. Seven nations in turn ruled over the Is̱'ra-el-ītes, and after each "oppression," as this rule was called, a "deliverer" arose to set the people free.

The idols which the Is̱'ra-el-ītes worshiped most of all were those named Bā'al and Ăsh-ĕ'rah. Bā'al was an image looking somewhat like a man; and Ăsh-ĕ'rah was the name given to the one that looked like a woman. These images were set up in groves and on hills by the Cā'năan-īte people, and to these the Is̱'ra-el-ītes bowed down, falling on their faces before them.

The first nation to come from another land against the Is̱'ra-el-ītes was the people of Mĕs-o-pŏ-tā'mĭ-à, between the great rivers Eū-phrā'teş and Tī'gris on the north. Their king led his army into the land and made the Is̱'ra-el-ītes serve him eight years. Then they cried to the Lord, and the Lord sent to them Ŏth'nĭ-el, who was a younger brother of Cā'leb, of whom we read in Story Five in this Part. He set the people free from the Mĕs-o-pŏ-tā'mĭ-àns and ruled them as long as he lived and kept them faithful to the Lord. Ŏth'nĭ-el was the first of the judges of Is̱'ra-el.

But after Ŏth'nĭ-el died, the people again began to worship images, and again fell under the power of their enemies. This time it was the Mō'ab-ītes who came against them from the land east of the Dead Sea. Their king at this time was named Eg'lŏn, and he was very hard in his rule over the Is̱'ra-el-ītes. Again they cried to the Lord, and God called a man named Ē'hŭd, who belonged to the tribe of Bĕn'ja-mĭn, to set the people free.

Ē'hŭd came one day to visit King Eg'lŏn, who was ruling ove:
the land. He said:

"I have a present from my people to the king. Let me go inte
his palace and see him."

They let Ē'hŭd into the palace, and he gave to the king a pres
ent; then he went out, but soon came back and said:

"I have a message to the king that no one else can hear. Let me
see the king alone."

As he had just brought a present, they supposed that he was a
friend to the king. Then, too, he had no sword on the side where

men carried their swords. But Ē'hŭd was left-handed, and he carried on the other side a short, sharp sword which he had made, like
a dagger. This sword was out of sight under his garment.

He went into the room where King Eg'lŏn was sitting alone,
and he said, "I have a message from the Lord to you, and this is the
message."

And then he drew out his sword and drove it up to the handle
into the king's body so suddenly that the king died without giving
a sound. Ē'hŭd left the sword in the dead body of the king and
went out quietly by the rear door. The servants of the king
thought he was asleep in his room, and for a while did not go in
to see why he was so still; but when they found him dead, Ē'hŭd
was far away.

Ē'hŭd blew a trumpet and called his people together, and led
them against the Mō'ab-ītes. They were so helpless without their

king that Ē'hŭd and his men easily drove them out of Ĭṣ'ra-el and
et the people free. Ē'hŭd became the second judge over the land.
And after that it was many years before enemies again held rule
over Ĭṣ'ra-el.

The next enemies of Ĭṣ'ra-el were the Phĭ-lĭs'tĭneṣ, who lived on
the shore of the Great Sea on the west. They came up from the
plain against the Ĭṣ'ra-el-ītes; but Shăm'gär, the third judge, met
them with a company of farmers, who drove the Phĭ-lĭs'tĭneṣ back
with their oxgoads, and so kept them from ruling over the land.

Story Nine   JUDGES 4 : 1 to 5 : 31

How a Woman Won a Great Victory

AGAIN many of the people of Ĭṣ'ra-el were drawn away
from the worship of the Lord, and began to live like
the people around them, praying to idols and doing
wickedly. And again the Lord left them to suffer
for their sins. A Cā'năan-īte king in the north,
whose name was Jā'bin, sent his army down to conquer them
under the command of his general, named Sĭs'e-rà. In Sĭs'e-rà's
army were many chariots of iron, drawn by horses; while soldiers
in the chariots shot arrows and threw spears at the Ĭṣ'ra-el-ītes.
The men of Ĭṣ'ra-el were not used to horses and greatly feared these
war chariots.

All the northern tribes in the land of Ĭṣ'ra-el fell under the power
of King Jā'bin and his general, Sĭs'e-rà; and their rule was very
harsh and severe. This was the fourth of these "oppressions," and
it bore most heavily upon the people in the north. But it led those
who suffered from it to turn from their idols and to call upon the
Lord God of Ĭṣ'ra-el.

At that time a woman was ruling as judge over a large part of the land; the only woman among the fifteen judges who, one afte another, ruled the Ĭṣ'ra-el-ītes. Her name was Dĕb'o-rah. She sa under a palm tree north of Jĕ-ru̱'så-lĕm, between the cities o Rā'mah and Bĕth'el, and gave advice to all the people who sough her. So wise and good was Dĕb'o-rah that men came from all part of the land with their difficulties and the questions that arose be tween them. She ruled over the land, not by the force of any army or by any appointment, but because all men saw that God's Spiri was upon her.

Dĕb'o-rah heard of the troubles of the tribes in the north under the hard rule of the Cā'năan-ītes. She knew that a brave man wa living in the land of Năph'ta-lī, a man named Bā'răk, and to him she sent this message:

"Bā'răk, call out the tribes of Ĭṣ'ra-el who live near you; raise ar army and lead the men who gather about you to Mount Tā'bôr The Lord has told me that he will give Sĭs'e-rà and the host of the Cā'năan-ītes into your hands."

But Bā'răk felt afraid to undertake alone this great work of set- ting his people free. He sent back to Dĕb'o-rah this answer:

"If you will go with me, I will go; but if you will not go with me, I will not go."

"I will go with you," said Dĕb'o-rah; "but because you did not trust God and did not go when God called you, the honor of this war will not be yours, for God will deliver Sĭs'e-rà into the hands of a woman."

Dĕb'o-rah left her seat under the palm tree and went up to Kē'desh, where Bā'răk lived. Together Dĕb'o-rah and Bā'răk sent out a call for the men of the north, and ten thousand men met together with such arms as they could find. This little army, with a woman for its chief, encamped on Mount Tā'bôr, which is one of three mountains standing in a row on the east of a great plain called "the plain of Ĕs-dra-ē'lon," "the plain of Jĕz'rĕ-el," and "the plain of Mĕ-gĭd'dŏ"—for it bears all these three names. On this plain, both in Bible times and also in the times since the Bible, many great battles have been fought. Over this plain winds the brook Kī'shŏn, which at some seasons, after heavy rain, be- comes a foaming, rushing river.

From their camp on the top of Mount Tā'bôr the little army of
Iṣ'ra-el could look down on the great host of Cā'năan-ītes with
their many tents, their horses and chariots, and their general, Sĭs'-
e-rà. But Dĕb'o-rah was not afraid. She said to Bā'răk:
"March down the mountain with all your men and fight the
Cā'năan-ītes. The Lord will go before you, and he will give
Sĭs'e-rà and his host into your hand."
Then Bā'răk blew a trumpet and called out his men. They ran
down the side of Mount Tā'bôr and rushed upon their enemies.
The Cā'năan-ītes were taken so suddenly that they had no time to
draw out their chariots. They were frightened and ran away,
trampling each other under foot, chariots and horses and men in
a wild flight.
And the Lord helped the Iṣ'ra-el-ītes; for at that time the brook
Kī'shŏn was swollen into a river, and the Cā'năan-ītes crowded
after each other into it. While many were killed in the battle,
many were also drowned in the river.
Sĭs'e-rà, the general of the Cā'năan-ītes, saw that the battle had
gone against him and that all was lost. He leaped from his chariot
and fled away on foot. On the edge of the plain he found a tent
standing alone, and he ran to it for shelter and hiding.
It was the tent of a man named Hē'bĕr, and Hē'bĕr's wife, Jā'el,
was in front of it. She knew Sĭs'e-rà and said to him, "Come in,
my lord; come into the tent; do not be afraid."
Sĭs'e-rà entered the tent and Jā'el covered him with a rug, so
that no enemy might find him. Sĭs'e-rà said to her, "I am very
thirsty; can you give me a little water to drink?"
Instead of water she brought out a bottle of milk and gave him
some: and then Sĭs'e-rà lay down to sleep, for he was very tired
from the battle and from running. While he was in a deep sleep,
Jā'el crept into the tent quietly and killed him by driving a tent pin
through his head. After a moment's struggle Sĭs'e-rà was dead,
and she left his body upon the ground.
In a little time Jā'el saw Bā'răk, the chief of the Iṣ'ra-el-īte army,
coming toward the tent. She went out to meet him and said,
"Come with me, and I will show you the man whom you are
seeking."

She lifted the curtain of the tent and led Bā'răk within; and there he saw lying dead upon the ground the mighty Sĭs'e-rȧ, who only the day before had led the army of the Cā'nāan-ītes.

That was a terrible deed which Jā'el did. We should call it treachery and murder; but such was the bitter hate between Ĭṣ'ra-el-īte and Cā'nāan-īte at that time that all the people gave great honor to Jā'el on account of it, for by that act she had set the people free from the king who had been oppressing Ĭṣ'ra-el. After this the land had rest for many years.

Dĕb'o-rah, the judge, wrote a great song about this victory. Here are some verses from it:

"Because the elders took the lead in Ĭṣ'ra-el,
  Because the people offered themselves willingly,
    Bless ye the Lord.

Hear, O ye kings; give ear, O ye princes;
I, even I, will sing unto the Lord;
    I will sing praise to the Lord, the God of Ĭṣ'ra-el.
* * * * * * * * * * *
The kings came and fought.
Then fought the kings of Cā'năan,
In Tā'a-năch by the waters of Mĕ-ġĭd'dŏ.
    They took no gain of money."

They fought from heaven,
The stars in their courses fought against Sĭs'e-rà.
The river Kī'shŏn swept them away,
That ancient river, the river Kī'shŏn.
   O my soul, march on with strength;
   *   *   *   *   *   *   *   *   *   *   *

Blessed among women shall Jā'el be,
The wife of Hē'bēr the Kĕn'īte,
Blessed shall she be among women in the tent.
He asked water, and she gave him milk,
   She brought him butter in a lordly dish.
   *   *   *   *   *   *   *   *   *   *   *

At her feet he bowed, he fell, he lay;
At her feet he bowed, he fell.
   Where he bowed, there he fell down dead.

Through the window a woman looked forth and cried,
The mother of Sĭs'e-rà cried through the lattice,
Why is his chariot so long in coming?
   Why tarry the wheels of his chariot?
   *   *   *   *   *   *   *   *   *   *   *

So let all thine enemies perish, O Lord;
But let them that love him be as the sun,
   When he goeth forth in his might."

Story Ten

JUDGES 6 : 1 to 8 : 28

Gideon and His Brave Three Hundred

AGAIN the people of Ĭs'ra-el did evil in the sight of the Lord in worshiping Bā'al; and the Lord left them again to suffer for their sins. This time it was the Mĭd'ĭ-an-ītes, living near the desert on the east of Ĭs'ra-el, who came against the tribes in the middle of the country. The two tribes that suffered the hardest fate were Ē'phră-ĭm and the part of Mȧ-năs'seh on the west of Jôr'dan. For seven years the Mĭd'ĭ-an-ītes swept over their land every year, just at the time of harvest, and carried away all the crops of grain, until the Is̠'ra-el-ītes had no food for themselves and none for their sheep and cattle. The Mĭd'ĭ-an-ītes brought also their own flocks and camels without number, which ate all the grass of the field. These Mĭd'ĭ-an-ītes were the wild Arabs, living on the border of the desert, and from their land they made sudden and swift attacks upon the people of Is̠'ra-el.

The people of Is̠'ra-el were driven away from their villages and their farms and were compelled to hide in the caves of the mountains. And if any Is̠'ra-el-īte could raise any grain, he buried it in pits covered with earth or in empty wine presses, where the Mĭd'ĭ-an-ītes could not find it.

One day a man named Gīd'e-on was threshing out wheat in a hidden place, when suddenly he saw an angel sitting under an oak tree. The angel said to him, "You are a brave man, Gīd'e-on; and the Lord is with you. Go out boldly, and save your people from the power of the Mĭd'ĭ-an-ītes."

Gīd'e-on answered the angel, "O Lord, how can I save Is̠'ra-el? Mine is a poor family in Mă-năs'seh, and I am the least in my father's house."

And the Lord said to him, "Surely I will be with you and I will help you drive out the Mĭd'ĭ-an-ītes."

Gĭd'e-on felt that it was the Lord who was talking with him in the form of an angel. He brought an offering and laid it on a rock before the angel. Then the angel touched the offering with his staff. At once a fire leaped up and burned the offering; and then the angel vanished from his sight. Gĭd'e-on was afraid when he saw this; but the Lord said to him, "Peace be unto you, Gĭd'e-on; do not fear, for I am with you."

On the spot where the Lord appeared to Gĭd'e-on, under an oak tree near the village of Ŏph'rah, in the tribe land of Mă-năs'seh, Gĭd'e-on built an altar and called it by a name which means "The Lord is peace." This altar was standing long afterward in that place.

Then the Lord told Gĭd'e-on that before setting his people free from the Mĭd'ĭ-an-ītes, he must first set them free from the service of Bā'al and Ăsh-ē'rah, the two idols most worshiped among them. Near the house of Gĭd'e-on's own father stood an altar to Bā'al, and the image of Ăsh-ē'rah.

On that night Gĭd'e-on went out with ten men and threw down the image of Bā'al, and cut in pieces the wooden image of Ăsh-ē'rah, and destroyed the altar before these idols. And in place he built an altar to the God of Ĭṣ'ra-el, and on it laid the broken pieces of the idols for wood, and with them offered a young ox as a burnt offering.

On the next morning, when the people of the village went out to worship their idols, they found them cut in pieces and the altar taken away; in its place stood an altar of the Lord and on it the pieces of the Ăsh-ē'rah were burning as wood under a sacrifice to the Lord. The people looked at the broken and burning idols and they said, "Who has done this?"

Someone said, "Gĭd'e-on, the son of Jō'ash, did this last night." Then they came to Jō'ăsh, Gĭd'e-on's father, and said, "We are going to kill your son because he has destroyed the image of Bā'al, who is our god."

And Jō'ăsh, Gĭd'e-on's father, said, "If Bā'al is a god, he can take care of himself; and he will surely punish the man who has destroyed his image. Why should you help Bā'al? Let Bā'al help himself."

And when they saw that Bā'al could not harm the man who had broken down his altar and his image, the people turned from Bā'al back to their own Lord God.

Gĭd'e-on sent men through all his own tribe of Mȧ-năs'seh and the other tribes in that part of the land, to say, "Come and help us drive out the Mĭd'ĭ-an-ītes." The men came and gathered around Gĭd'e-on. Very few of them had swords and spears, for the Ĭs'ra-el-ītes were not a fighting people and were not trained for war. They met beside a great spring on Mount Gĭl-bō'ȧ, called "the fountain of Hā'rod." Mount Gĭl-bō'ȧ is one of the three mountains on the east of the plain of Ĕs-dra-ē'lon, or the plain of Jĕz're-el, of which we read in the last story. On the plain, stretching up the side of another of these mountains, called "the Hill of Mō'reh," was the camp of a vast Mĭd'ĭ-an-īte army. For as soon as the Mĭd'ĭ-an-ītes heard that Gĭd'e-on had undertaken to set his people free, they came against him with a mighty host. Just as Dĕb'o-rah and her little army had looked down from Mount Tā'bôr on the great army of the Cā'năan-ītes, so now, on Mount Gĭl-bō'ȧ, Gĭd'e-on looked down on the host of the Mĭd'ĭ-an-ītes in their camp on the same plain.

Gĭd'e-on was a man of faith. He wished to be sure that God was leading him; and he prayed to God and said, "O Lord God, give me some sign that thou wilt save Ĭs'ra-el through me. Here is a fleece of wool on this threshing floor. If tomorrow morning the fleece is wet with dew, while the grass around it is dry, then I shall know that thou art with me and that thou wilt give me victory over the Mĭd'ĭ-an-ītes."

Very early the next morning Gĭd'e-on came to look at the fleece. He found it wringing wet with dew, while all around the grass was dry. But Gĭd'e-on was not yet satisfied. He said to the Lord, "O Lord, be not angry with me; but give me just one more sign. Tomorrow morning, let the fleece be dry and let the dew fall around it; and then I will doubt no more."

The next morning Gĭd'e-on found the grass and the bushes and the trees wet with dew, while the fleece of wool was dry. And

Adam and Eve were happy in the beautiful garden God had given them (p. 5)

Abram journeyed for a long time (p. 19)

Joseph had two strange dreams (p. 54)

Moses lived in the palace (p. 78)

The spies came back to the camp (p. 116)

Gideon chose three hundred men (p. 177)

The three brave men brought the water to David (p. 239)

The Queen of Sheba came to visit Solomon (p. 286)

Rehoboam saw that he had lost his kingdom (p. 293)

The ravens brought food to Elijah (p. 300)

Elisha led the blinded soldiers into the city (p. 334)

There was a little girl in Naaman's house (p. 330)

The Lord gave Daniel the secret of the King's dream (p. 387)

Jonah was swallowed by a great fish (p. 30
History of the Books of the Bible)

Hosea was the first of the minor prophets (p. 29
History of the Books of the Bible)

Malachi prophesied that the Messiah is coming (p. 33
History of the Books of the Bible)

Gĭd′e-on was now sure that God had called him and that God would give him victory over the enemies of Ĭṣ′ra-el.

The Lord said to Gĭd′e-on, "Your army is too large. If Ĭṣ′ra-el should win the victory, they would say, 'We won it by our own might.' Send home all those who are afraid to fight." For many of the people were frightened as they looked on the host of their enemies; and the Lord knew that these men in the battle would only hinder the rest.

So Gĭd′e-on sent word through the camp, "Whoever is afraid of the enemy may go home." And twenty-two thousand people went away, leaving only ten thousand in Gĭd′e-on's army. But the army was stronger though it was smaller, for the cowards had gone and only the brave men were left.

But the Lord said to Gĭd′e-on, "The people are yet too many. You need only a few of the bravest and best men to fight in this battle. Bring the men down the mountain, beside the water, and I will show you there how to find the men whom you need."

In the morning Gĭd′e-on by God's command called his ten thousand men out and made them march down the hill, just as though they were going to attack the enemy. And when they were beside the water, he noticed how they drank; and set them apart in two companies, according to their way of drinking. As they came to the water, most of the men threw aside their shields and spears and knelt down and scooped up a draught of the water with both hands together like a cup. These men Gĭd′e-on commanded to stand in one company.

There were a few men who did not stop to take a large draught of water. Holding spear and shield in the right hand, to be ready for the enemy if one should suddenly appear, they merely caught up a handful of the water in passing and marched on, lapping up the water from one hand.

God said to Gĭd′e-on, "Set by themselves these men who lapped up each a handful of water. These are the men whom I have chosen to set Ĭṣ′ra-el free."

Gĭd′e-on counted these men and found that there were only three hundred of them; while all the rest bowed down on their faces to drink. The difference between them was that these three hundred were earnest men, of one purpose; not turning aside from their aim even to drink, as the others did. Then, too, they were watchful men, always ready to meet their enemies. Suppose that the Mĭd'ĭ-an-ītes had rushed out on that army while nearly all of them were on their faces drinking, their arms thrown to one side— how helpless they would have been! But no enemy could have surprised the three hundred, who held their spears and shields ready, even while they were taking a drink.

Some have thought that this test showed also who were worshipers of idols, and who worshiped God; for men fell on their faces when they prayed to the idols, but men stood up while they worshiped the Lord. Perhaps this act showed that most of the army were used to worship kneeling down before idols and that only a few used to stand up before the Lord in their worship; but of this we are not certain. It did show that here were three hundred brave, watchful men, obedient to orders and ready for the battle.

Then Gĭd'e-on, at God's command, sent back to the camp on Mount Gĭl-bō'ȧ all the rest of his army, nearly ten thousand men; keeping with himself only his little band of three hundred. But before the battle, God gave to Gĭd'e-on one more sign, that he might be the more encouraged.

God said to Gĭd'e-on, "Go down with your servant into the camp of the Mĭd'ĭ-an-ītes and hear what they say. It will cheer your heart for the fight."

Then Gĭd'e-on crept down the mountain with his servant and walked around the edge of the Mĭd'ĭ-an-īte camp, just as though he were one of their own men. He saw two men talking and stood near to listen. One man said to the other:

"I had a strange dream in the night. I dreamed that I saw a loaf of barley bread come rolling down the mountain; and it struck the tent and threw it down in a heap on the ground. What do you suppose that dream means?"

"That loaf of bread," said the other, "means Gĭd'e-on, a man of Ĭṣ'ra-el, who will come down and destroy this army; for the Lord God has given us all into his hand."

Gĭd'e-on was glad when he heard this, for it showed that the

Ίid′ĭ-an-ītes, for all their number, were in fear of him and of his rmy, even more than his men had feared the Mĭd′ĭ-an-ītes. He ave thanks to God and hastened back to his camp and made ready o lead his men against the Mĭd′ĭ-an-ītes.

Gĭd′e-on's plan did not need a large army; but it needed a few areful, bold men, who should do exactly as their leader com- nanded them. He gave to each man a lamp, a pitcher, and a rumpet, and told the men just what was to be done with them. Che lamp was lighted, but was placed inside the pitcher, so that it ould not be seen. He divided his men into three companies; and ery quietly led them down the mountain, in the middle of the ight; and arranged them all in order around the camp of the Mĭd′ĭ- .n-ītes.

Then at one moment a great shout rang out in the darkness, "The sword of the Lord and of Gĭd′e-on," and after it came a :rash of breaking pitchers and then a flash of light in every direc- ion. The three hundred men had given the shout and broken their)itchers, so that on every side lights were shining. The men blew heir trumpets with a mighty noise; and the Mĭd′ĭ-an-ītes were oused from sleep to see enemies all round them, lights beaming ınd swords flashing in the darkness, while everywhere the sharp ;ound of the trumpets was heard.

They were filled with sudden terror and thought only of escape, ıot of fighting. But wherever they turned, their enemies seemed :o be standing with swords drawn. They trampled each other down to death, flying from the Iṣ′ra-el-ītes. Their own land was in the east, across the river Jôr′dan, and they fled in that direction, down one of the valleys between the mountains.

Gĭd′e-on had thought that the Mĭd′ĭ-an-ītes would turn toward their own land if they should be beaten in the battle; and he had already planned to cut off their flight. The ten thousand men in the camp he had placed on the sides of the valley leading to the Jôr′dan. There they slew very many of the Mĭd′ĭ-an-ītes as they fled down the steep pass toward the river. And Gĭd′e-on had also sent to the men of the tribe of Ē′phră-ĭm, who had thus far taken no part in the war, to hold the only place at the river where men could wade through the water. Those of the Mĭd′ĭ-an-ītes who

had escaped from Gĭd'e-on's men on either side of the valley wer
now met by the Ē'phră-ĭm-ītes at the river and many more of ther
were slain. Among the slain were two of the princes of the Mĭd'ĭ
an-ītes, named Ō'reb and Zē'eb.

A part of the Mĭd'ĭ-an-īte army was able to get across the rive
and to continue its flight toward the desert; but Gĭd'e-on and hĭ
brave three hundred men followed closely after them; fought an
other battle with them, destroyed them utterly and took their twe
kings, Zē'bah and Zăl-mŭn'nà, whom they killed. After this grea
victory the Ĭs̯'ra-el-ītes were freed forever from the Mĭd'ĭ-an-ītes
They never again ventured to leave their home in the desert tɔ
make war on the tribes of Ĭs̯'ra-el.

The tribe of Ē'phră-ĭm, in the middle of the land, was one oʿ
the most powerful of the twelve tribes. Its leaders were quite dis
pleased with Gĭd'e-on, because their part in the victory had beeɪ
so small. They said to Gĭd'e-on, in an angry manner, "Why diɑ
you not send word to us, when you were calling for men to figh'
the Mĭd'ĭ-an-ītes?"

But Gĭd'e-on knew how to make a kind answer. He said tɔ
them, "What have I done as compared with you? Did you noʇ
kill thousands of the Mĭd'ĭ-an-ītes at the crossing of the Jôr'dan?
Did you not take their two princes, Ō'reb and Zē'eb? What coulɑ
my men have done without the help of your men?" By gentle
words and words of praise Gĭd'e-on made the men of Ē'phră-ĭn
friendly.

And after this, as long as Gĭd'e-on lived, he ruled as judge iɪ
Ĭs̯'ra-el. The people wished him to make himself a king. "Rule
over us as king," they said, "and let your son be king after you, and
his son king after him." But Gĭd'e-on said, "No; you have a king
already; for the Lord God is the King of Ĭs̯'ra-el. No one but Goɑ
shall be king over these tribes."

Of all the fifteen men who ruled as judges in Ĭs̯'ra-el, Gĭd'e-on,
the fifth judge, was the greatest in courage, in wisdom, and in faith
in God.

If all the people of Ĭs̯'ra-el had been like him, there would have
been no worship of idols and no weakness before enemies. Ĭs̯'ra-el

would have been strong and faithful before God. But as soon as Gĭd'e-on died, and even before his death, his people began once more to turn away from the Lord and to seek the idol gods.

Story Eleven

Jephthah's Rash Promise, and What Came from It

ALTHOUGH Gĭd'e-on had refused to become a king, even when all the tribes desired him, after his death one of his sons whose name was Ă-bĭm'e-lĕch, tried to make himself a king. He began by killing all his brothers except one who escaped. But his rule was only over Shē'chem and a few places near it and lasted only a few years; so that he was never named among the kings of Ĭṣ'ra-el. Ă-bĭm'e-lĕch is sometimes called the sixth of the judges, though he did not deserve the title. After him came Tō'la, the seventh judge, and Jā'ĭr, the eighth. Of these two judges, very little is told.

After this the Ĭṣ'ra-el-ītes again began to worship the idols of the Cā'năan-ītes and again fell under the power of their enemies. The Ăm'mon-ītes came against them from the southeast and held rule over the tribes on the east of Jôr'dan. This was the sixth of "the oppressions"; and the man who set Ĭṣ'ra-el free was Jĕph'thah. He called together the men of the tribes on the east of Jôr'dan— Reu'ben, Găd, and the half tribe of Mă-năs'seh—and fought against the Ăm'mon-ītes.

Before Jĕph'thah went to the battle he said to the Lord, "If thou wilt give me victory over the Ăm'mon-ītes, then when I come back from the battle, whatever comes out of the house to meet me shall be the Lord's and I will offer it up as a burnt offering."

This was not a wise promise, nor a right one; for God had told the Ĭṣ'ra-el-ītes long before what offerings were commanded, as

oxen and sheep, and what were forbidden. But Jĕph'thah had
lived on the border near the desert, far from the house of God at
Shī'lŏh, and he knew very little about God's law.

Jĕph'thah fought the Ăm'mon-ītes and won a victory and drove
the enemies out of the land. Then, as he was going back to his
home, his daughter, who was his only child, came out to meet him,
leading the young girls, her companions, dancing and making
music, to welcome his return. When Jĕph'thah saw her, he cried
out in sorrow, "O my daughter, what trouble you bring with you!
I have given a promise to the Lord, and now I must keep it!"

As soon as his daughter had learned what promise her father had
made, she met it bravely, as a true daughter of Ĭs'ra-el. She said:

"My father, you have made a solemn promise to the Lord, and
you shall keep it, for God has given to you victory over the enemies
of your people. But let me live a little while and weep with my
young friends over the death that I must suffer."

For two months she stayed with the young girls upon the mountains, for perhaps she feared that if she was at home with her father
he would fail to keep his promise. Then she gave herself up to
death and her father did with her as he had promised.

In all the history of the Ĭṣ'ra-el-ītes this was the only time when a living man or woman was offered in sacrifice to the Lord. Among all the nations around Ĭṣ'ra-el the people offered human lives, even those of their own children, to the idols which they worshiped. But the people of Ĭṣ'ra-el remembered what God had taught Ā'bră-hăm when he was about to offer up Ī'ṣaac; and they never, except this once, laid a human offering upon God's altar. If Jĕph'thah had lived near the Tabernacle at Shī'lōh and had been taught God's law, he would not have given such a promise, for God did not desire it; and his daughter's life would have been saved. From all these stories it is easy to see how the Ĭṣ'ra-el-ītes lived during the two hundred years while the judges ruled. There was no strong power to which all gave obedience; but each family lived as it chose. Many people worshiped the Lord; but many more turned from the Lord to the idols and then turned back to the Lord after they had fallen under the hand of their enemies. In one part of the land they were free; in another part they were ruled by the foreign peoples.

Story Twelve   JUDGES 12 : 1 to 16 : 31

The Strong Man: How He Lived and How He Died

AFTER Jĕph'thah three judges ruled in turn, named Ĭb'zăn, Ē'lŏn, and Ăb'dŏn. None of these were men of war and in their days the land was quiet.

But the people of Ĭṣ'ra-el again began to worship idols; and as a punishment God allowed them once more to pass under the power of their enemies. The seventh oppression, which now fell upon Ĭṣ'ra-el, was by far the heaviest, the longest, and the most widely spread of any, for it was over all the tribes. It came from the Phĭ-lĭs'tĭneṣ, a strong and warlike people, who lived on the west of Ĭṣ'ra-el upon the plain beside the Great Sea. They worshiped an idol called Dā'gon, which was made in the form of a fish's head on a man's body.

These people, the Phĭ-lĭs'tĭneṣ, sent their armies up from the plain beside the sea to the mountains of Ĭṣ'ra-el and overran all the land.

They took away from the Ĭṣ'ra-el-ītes all their swords and spears, so that they could not fight; and they robbed their land of all the crops, so that the people suffered for want of food. And as before, the Ĭṣ'ra-el-ītes in their trouble cried to the Lord, and the Lord heard their prayer.

In the tribe land of Dăn, which was next to the country of the Phĭ-lĭs'tĭneṣ, there was living a man named Mȧ-nō'ah. One day an angel came to his wife and said, "You shall have a son; and when he grows up, he will begin to save Ĭṣ'ra-el from the hand of the Phĭ-lĭs'tĭneṣ. But your son must never drink any wine or strong drink as long as he lives. And his hair must be allowed to grow long and must never be cut, for he shall be a Năz'a-rīte under a vow of the Lord."

When a child was given especially to God, or when a man gave himself to some work for God, he was forbidden to drink wine, and as a sign, his hair was left to grow long while the vow or promise to God was upon him. Such a person as this was called a Năz'a-rīte, a word which means "one who has a vow," and Mȧ-nō'ah's child was to be a Năz'a-rīte and was to be under a vow as long as he lived.

The child was born and was named Săm'son. He grew up to become the strongest man of whom the Bible tells. Săm'son was no general, like Gĭd'e-on or Jĕph'thah, to call out his people and lead them in war. He did much to try to set his people free; but all that he did was by his own strength, without any help from other men.

When Săm'son became a young man, he went down to Tĭm'-nath, in the land of the Phĭ-lĭs'tĭneṣ. There he saw a young Phĭ-lĭs'tĭne woman whom he loved and wished to have as his wife. His father and mother were not pleased that he should marry among the enemies of his own people. They did not know that

God would make this marriage the means of bringing harm upon the Phĭ-lĭs′tĭneş and of helping the Iş′ra-el-ītes.

As Săm′son was going down to Tĭm′nath to see this young woman, a hungry young lion came out of the mountain, growling and roaring. Săm′son seized the lion and tore him in pieces as easily as another man would have killed a little kid of the goats; and then went on his way. He made his visit and came home, but said nothing to anyone about the lion.

After a time Săm′son went again to Tĭm′nath for his marriage with the Phĭ-lĭs′tĭne woman. On his way he stopped to look at the dead lion; and he found that all its flesh had been eaten by the wild beasts; but among its bones he saw that a swarm of bees had made their home and had left some of their honey. He took some of the honey and ate it as he walked; but told no one of it.

At the wedding feast, which lasted a whole week, there were many Phĭ-lĭs′tĭne young men; and they amused each other with questions and riddles.

"I will give you a riddle," said Săm′son. "If you answer it during the feast, I will give you thirty suits of clothing. And if you cannot answer it, then you must give me thirty suits of clothing."

"Let us hear your riddle," they said. And this was Săm′son's riddle for the young men of the Phĭ-lĭs′tĭneş to answer:

"Out of the eater came forth meat.
And out of the strong came forth sweetness."

They could not find the answer, though they tried to find it all that day and the two days that followed. And at last they came to Săm′son's wife and said to her, "Coax your husband to tell you the answer. If you do not find it out, we will set your house on fire and burn you and all your people."

And Săm′son's wife urged him to tell her the answer. She cried and pleaded with him and said, "If you really love me, you would not keep this a secret from me."

At last Săm′son yielded and told his wife how he had killed the lion and afterward found the honey in its body. She told her people, and just before the end of the feast they came to Săm′son with the answer. They said, "What is sweeter than honey? And what is stronger than a lion?"

And Săm'son said to them, "If you had not plowed with my heifer, you had not found out my riddle."

By his "heifer"—which is a young cow—of course Săm'son meant his wife. Then Săm'son was required to give them thirty suits of clothing. He went out among the Phĭ-lĭs'tĭneʂ, killed the first thirty men whom he found, took off their clothes, and gave them to the guests at the feast. But all this made Săm'son very angry. He left his new wife and went home to his father's house. Then the parents of his new wife gave her to another man.

But after a time Săm'son's anger passed away and he went again to Tĭm'nath to see his wife. But her father said to him, "You went away angry, and I supposed that you cared nothing for her. I gave her to another man and now she is his wife. But here is her younger sister; you can take her for your wife instead."

But Săm'son would not take his wife's sister. He went out very angry, determined to do harm to the Phĭ-lĭs'tĭneʂ, because they had cheated him. He caught all the wild foxes that he could find, until he had three hundred of them. Then he tied them together in pairs, by their tails; and between each pair of foxes he tied to their tails a piece of dry wood which he set on fire. These foxes with firebrands on their tails he turned loose among the fields of the Phĭ-lĭs'tĭneʂ when the grain was ripe. They ran wildly over the fields, set the grain on fire and burned it; and with the grain the olive trees in the fields.

When the Phĭ-lĭs'tĭneʂ saw their harvests destroyed, they said, "Who has done this?"

And the people said, "Săm'son did this, because his wife was given by her father to another man."

The Phĭ-lĭs'tĭneʂ looked on Săm'son's father-in-law as the cause of their loss; and they came and set his house on fire and burned the man and his daughter whom Săm'son had married. Then Săm'son came down again and alone fought a company of Phĭ-lĭs'tĭneʂ and killed them all, as a punishment for burning his wife.

After this Săm'son went to live in a hollow place in a split rock,

called the rock of Ē'tăm. The Phĭ-lĭs'tĭneṣ came up in a great army
and overran the fields in the tribe land of Jū'dah.

"Why do you come against us?" asked the men of Jū'dah.
"What do you want from us?" "We have come," they said, "to
bind Săm'son and to deal with him as he has dealt with our people."

The men of Jū'dah said to Săm'son, "Do you not know that the
Phĭ-lĭs'tĭneṣ are ruling over us? Why do you make them angry
by killing their people? You see that we suffer through your
pranks. Now we must bind you and give you to the Phĭ-lĭs'tĭneṣ;
or they will ruin us all."

And Săm'son said, "I will let you bind me, if you will promise
not to kill me yourselves; but only to give me safely into the hands
of the Phĭ-lĭs'tĭneṣ."

They made the promise; and Săm'son gave himself up to them
and allowed them to tie him up fast with new ropes. The Phĭ-lĭs'-
tĭneṣ shouted for joy as they saw their enemy brought to them, led
in bonds by his own people. Little did they know what was to
happen. For as soon as Săm'son came among them, he burst the
bonds as though they had been light strings; and he picked up from
the ground the jawbone of an ass and struck right and left with it
as with a sword. He killed almost a thousand of the Phĭ-lĭs'tĭneṣ
with this strange weapon. Afterward he sang a song about it, thus:

> "With the jawbone of an ass, heaps upon heaps,
> With the jawbone of an ass, have I slain a thousand men."

After this Săm'son went down to the chief city of the Phĭ-lĭs'-
tĭneṣ, which was named Gā'zȧ. It was a large city; and like all
large cities was surrounded with a high wall. When the men of
Gā'zȧ found Săm'son in their city, they shut the gates, thinking
that they could now hold him as a prisoner. But in the night,
Săm'son rose up, went to the gates, pulled their posts out of the
ground, and put the gates with their posts upon his shoulder. He
carried them twenty miles away and left them on the top of a hill
not far from the city of Hē'bron.

After this Săm'son saw another woman among the Phĭ-lĭs'tĭneṣ
and he loved her. The name of this woman was Dĕ-lī'lah. The
rulers of the Phĭ-lĭs'tĭneṣ came to Dĕ-lī'lah and said to her:

"Find out, if you can, what it is that makes Săm'son so strong; and tell us. If you help us to get control of him so that we can have him in our power, we will give you a great sum of money."

And Dĕ-lī'lah coaxed and pleaded with Săm'son to tell her what it was that made him so strong. Săm'son said to her, "If they will tie me with seven green twigs from a tree, then I shall not be strong any more."

They brought her seven green twigs, like those of a willow tree; and she bound Săm'son with them while he was asleep. Then she called out to him, "Wake up, Săm'son, the Phĭ-lĭs'tĭnes̤ are coming against you!"

And Săm'son rose up and broke the twigs as easily as if they had been charred in the fire, and went away with ease.

And Dĕ-lī'lah tried again to find his secret. She said, "You are making fun of me. Tell me truly how you can be bound."

And Săm'son said, "Let them bind me with new ropes that have never been used before; and then I cannot get away."

While Săm'son was asleep again, Dĕ-lī'lah bound him with new ropes. Then she called out as before, "Get up, Săm'son, for the Phĭ-lĭs'tĭnes̤ are coming!" And when Săm'son rose up, the ropes broke as if they were thread. And Dĕ-lī'lah again urged him to tell her; and he said:

"You notice that my long hair is braided in seven locks. Weave it together in the loom, just as if it were the threads in a piece of cloth."

Then, while he was asleep, she unbound the braids, wove his hair in the loom and fastened it with a large pin to the weaving frame. But when he awoke, he rose up and carried away the pin and the beam of the weaving frame, for he was as strong as before.

And Dĕ-lī'lah said, "Why do you tell me that you love me, as long as you deceive me and keep from me your secret!" And she pleaded with him day after day, until at last he yielded to her and told her the real secret of his strength. He said:

"I am a Năz'a-rīte, under a vow to the Lord not to drink wine and not to allow my hair to be cut. If I should let my hair be cut short, then the Lord would forsake me, and my strength would go from me and I would be like other men."

Then Dĕ-lī'lah knew that she had found the truth at last. She sent for the rulers of the Phĭ-lĭs'tīneṣ, saying, "Come up this once and you shall have your enemy; for I am sure now that he has told me all that is in his heart."

Then, while the Phĭ-lĭs'tĭneṣ were watching outside, Dĕ-lī'lah let Săm'son go to sleep, with his head upon her knees. While he was sound asleep, they took a razor and shaved off all his hair. Then she called out as at other times, "Rise up, Săm'son; the Phĭ-lĭs'tĭneṣ are upon you."

He awoke and rose up, expecting to find himself as strong as before; for he did not at first know that his long hair had been cut off. But he had broken his vow to the Lord and the Lord had left him. He was now as weak as other men and helpless in the hands of his enemies. The Phĭ-lĭs'tĭneṣ easily made him their prisoner; and that he might never do them more harm, they put out his eyes. Then they chained him with fetters and sent him to prison at Gā'zȧ. And in the prison they made Săm'son turn a heavy millstone to grind grain, just as though he were a beast of burden.

But while Săm'son was in prison, his hair grew long again; and with his hair his strength came back to him, for Săm'son renewed his vow to the Lord.

One day a great feast was held by the Phĭ-lĭs'tīneṣ in the temple of their fish god Dā'gon. For they said, "Our god has given Săm'-son our enemy into our hands. Let us be glad together and praise Dā'gon."

And the temple was thronged with people and the roof over it was also crowded with more than three thousand men and women. They sent for Săm'son to rejoice over him; and Săm'son was led into the court of the temple, before all the people, to amuse them. After a time Săm'son said to the boy who was leading him:

"Take me up to the front of the temple, so that I may stand by one of the pillars and lean against it."

And while Săm'son stood between two of the pillars, he prayed to the Lord God of Ĭṣ'ra-el and said, "O Lord God, remember me, I pray thee, and give me strength only this once, O God; and help me, that I may obtain vengeance upon the Phĭ-lĭs'tĭneṣ for my two eyes!"

Then he placed one arm around the pillar on one side and the other arm around the pillar on the other side, and he said, "Let me die with the Phĭ-lĭs'tĭneṣ."

And he bowed forward with all his might and pulled the pillars over with him, bringing down the roof and all upon it upon those that were under it. Săm'son himself was among the dead; but in his death he killed more of the Phĭ-lĭs'tĭneṣ than he had killed during his life.

Then in the terror which came upon the Phĭ-lĭs'tĭneṣ the men of Săm'son's tribe came down and found his dead body and buried it in their own land. After that it was years before the Phĭ-lĭs'tĭneṣ tried again to rule over the Ĭṣ'ra-el-ītes.

Săm'son did much to set his people free, but he might have done much more if he had led his people instead of trusting alone to his own strength; and if he had lived more earnestly, and not done his deeds as though he was playing pranks and making jokes upon his enemies. There were deep faults in Săm'son, but at the end he sought God's help and found it; and God used Săm'son to begin to set his people free.

The tribe to which Săm'son belonged was the tribe of Dăn, a people who lived on the edge of the mountain country between the mountains and the plains by the seacoast, which was the home of the Phĭ-lĭs'tĭneṣ. The tribe land of Dăn was northwest of Jū'dah, southwest of Ē'phră-ĭm, and west of Bĕn'ja-mĭn. Săm'son ruled over his own tribe, but not much over the other tribes. Yet his deeds of courage and strength kept the Phĭ-lĭs'tĭneṣ, during his lifetime, from getting control over the lands of Jū'dah and Bĕn'ja-mĭn; so that Săm'son helped to save Ĭṣ'ra-el from its enemies.

The Idol Temple at Dan, and
Its Priest

WHILE the judges were ruling in Ĭṣ'ra-el, at one time there was living in the mountains of Ē'phră-ĭm, near the road which ran north and south, a man named Mī'cah. His mother, who was dwelling with him, found that someone had stolen from her a large sum of money. Now, the money had been taken by her son Mī'cah, and after a time he said to her:

"Those eleven hundred pieces of silver which you lost and of which you spoke, are with me; for I took them myself."

And his mother answered, "May the blessing of God rest upon you, my son, for bringing again to me my silver. This money shall be the Lord's. I will give it back to you, to be used in the service of the Lord."

But instead of taking the money to the Tabernacle of the Lord at Shī'lōh, Mī'cah used it to make two images of silver, one carved and the other cast in metal. These he set up in his house to be worshiped. He appointed one of his sons as a priest and thus made of his house an idol temple.

One day a man on a journey was passing by Mī'cah's house. Mī'cah saw from his dress that he belonged to the tribe of Lē'vī, from which the priests come. He said to him, "Who are you? From what place do you come?"

The young man said, "I am a Lē'vīte, from Bĕth'lĕ-hĕm in the land of Jū'dah and I am trying to find a place where I can earn my living."

"Stay here with me," said Mī'cah, "and be a priest in my house. I will give you your food and a place to sleep, and for each year a suit of clothes and ten pieces of silver."

The Lē'vīte was well pleased at this and stayed in Mī'cah's house and became his priest. And Mī'cah said to himself:

192

"I am sure that now the Lord will be pleased with me, since I have a house with gods and a Lē'vīte as my priest."

Already many in Iṣ'ra-el had forgotten that God would not bless those who set up idols when they should worship the Lord God.

The tribe of Dăn was living at that time between the country of the Phĭ-lĭs'tīneṣ and the tribe of Bĕn'ja-mĭn, having Jū'dah on the south and Ē'phră-ĭm on the north. The Phĭ-lĭs'tīneṣ pressed closely upon them and they sought some place where they could live with more room and at peace.

They sent out from their tribe land five men as spies, to go through the country and find some better place for the home of their tribe. These five men walked through the land and they came to the house of Mī'cah. Mī'cah took them into his house, for it was the custom thus to care for people who were on a journey.

These men from Dăn, who were called Dăn'ītes, had seen Mī'cah's priest before in his earlier home. They knew him and asked him how he came to be there. The young Lē'vīte told them that Mī'cah had hired him to become his priest. He took them into the temple room and showed them the images and the altar and he offered a sacrifice and a prayer for them.

Then the five men left Mī'cah's house and went on their way. They walked through all the tribes in the north; and far up among the mountains, near one of the great fountains where the river Jôr'dan begins, they found a little city called Lā'ish. The people of Lā'ish were not Iṣ'ra-el-ītes, but came from the country of Zī'dŏn. The Dăn'ītes saw that their little city was far from Zī'dŏn and that its people were living alone, with none of their own race to help them.

The men of Dăn walked back over the mountains to their own people, near the Phĭ-lĭs'tīne country; and they brought back an account of their journey through the land. They said:

"We have found a good place, far up in the north, where there is room for us and a rich soil and plenty of water. Come with us and let us take that place for our home."

So a large part of the tribe of Dăn, with their wives and their children, went up toward this place. Among them were six hundred men with shields and swords and spears for war. As they came near to Mī'cah's house, one of the five men who had been there before said to them:

"Do you know that in one of these houses there is an altar and a carved image and another image, both of silver? Now think what you had better do."

Then the five men came again into Mī'cah's temple while the six hundred soldiers stood outside. They were just about to carry away the silver images when the Lē'vīte said to them, "What are you doing?"

And the men said to him, "Never mind what we are doing

Keep still and come with us. Is it not better for you to be a priest to a whole tribe than to one man?"

Then the young priest said no more. He took away all the priestly robes and the silver ornaments and the images, and went away with the people of Dăn. When Mī'cah came home, he found that his temple had been robbed and his images and his priest were taken away.

He gathered some of his neighbors, and they hastened after the people of Dăn. When they caught up with them, Mī'cah cried aloud to them.

The men of Dăn turned and said to Mī'cah:

"What is the matter with you, that you come after us with a company and make such a noise?"

And Mī'cah answered, "You have taken away my gods which

I made, and my priest; and now what is left me?   And you say to
me, 'What is the matter?' "

Then the men of Dăn said, "Be careful what you say, or you
may make some of our men angry and they will fall on you and
then you will lose your life!"

Mĭ'cah saw that the men of Dăn were too strong for him to fight
them, so he went back to his house without his priest and without
his images. The Dăn'ītes went up to the little city of Lā'ish, in the
north. They took it and killed all the people who were living
there. Then they built the city again and changed its name to
Dăn, the name of the father of their tribe.

There, at Dăn, they built a temple and in it they set up the
images, and this Lē'vīte became their priest. And the strangest
part of all the story is, that this Lē'vīte was a grandson of Mō'ṣeṣ,
the man of God and the great prophet. So soon did the people of
Iṣ'ra-el fall into sin, and so deeply, that the grandson of Mō'ṣeṣ
became the priest in a temple of idols. And at this time the house
of God was at Shī'lōh; yet at Dăn during those years and for many
years afterward was a temple of idols, and within its walls a line
of priests descended from Mō'ṣeṣ were worshiping and offering
sacrifices to images.

And as the temple of idols in Dăn was much nearer to the people
in the northern part of the land than was the house of the Lord,
the Tabernacle at Shī'lōh, very many of those who lived in the
north went to this idol temple to worship. So the people of Iṣ'ra-el
were led away from God to serve idols. This was very displeasing
to God.

How Ruth Gleaned in the Field of Boaz

IN THE time of the judges in Ĭṣ'ra-el, a man named Ê-lĭm'e-lĕch was living in the town of Bĕth'lĕ-hĕm, in the tribe of Jū'dah, about six miles south of Jĕ-ru̇'sȧ-lĕm. His wife's name was Nȧ-ō'mī and his two sons were Mäh'lon and Chĭl'ĭ-on. For some years the crops were poor and food was scarce in Jū'dah; and Ê-lĭm'e-lĕch, with his family, went to live in the land of Mō'ab, which was on the east of the Dead Sea, as Jū'dah was on the west.

There they stayed ten years, and in that time Ê-lĭm'e-lĕch died. His two sons married women of the country of Mō'ab, one woman named Ôr'pah, the other named Ru̇th. But the two young men also died in the land of Mō'ab, so that Nȧ-ō'mī and her two daughters-in-law were all left widows.

Nȧ-ō'mī heard that God had again given good harvests and bread to the land of Jū'dah and she rose up to go from Mō'ab back to her own land and her own town of Bĕth'lĕ-hĕm. Her two daughters-in-law loved her and both would have gone with her, though the land of Jū'dah was a strange land to them, for they were of the Mō'ab-īte people.

Nȧ-ō'mī said to them, "Go back, my daughters, to your own mothers' homes. May the Lord deal kindly with you, as you have been kind to your husbands and to me. May the Lord grant that each of you may yet find another husband and a happy home." Then Nȧ-ō'mī kissed them in farewell, and the three women all wept together. The two young widows said to her, "You have been a good mother to us and we will go with you and live among your people."

"No, no," said Nȧ-ō'mī. "You are young, and I am old. Go back and be happy among your own people."

Then Ôr'pah kissed Nȧ-ō'mī and went back to her people; but

uth would not leave her. She said, "Do not ask me to leave you, r I never will. Where you go, I will go; where you live, I will 'e; your people shall be my people; and your God shall be my od. Where you die, I will die, and be buried. Nothing but :ath itself shall part you and me."

When Nȧ-ō'mī saw that Ruth was firm in her purpose, she ased trying to persuade her; so the two women went on together.

hey walked around the Dead Sea and crossed the river Jôr'dan ıd climbed the mountains of Jū'dah and came to Bĕth'lĕ-hĕm. Nȧ-ō'mī had been absent from Bĕth'lĕ-hĕm for ten years, but :r friends were all glad to see her again. They said, "Is this .ȧ-ō'mī, whom we knew years ago?" Now the name Nȧ-ō'mī eans "Pleasant." And Nȧ-ō'mī said:

"Call me not Nȧ-ō'mī; call me Mā'rȧ, for the Lord has made ıy life bitter. I went out full, with my husband and two sons; ow I come home empty, without them. Do not call me 'Pleas-ıt'; call me 'Bitter.' " The name "Mā'rȧ," by which Nȧ-ō'mī 'ished to be called, means "Bitter." But Nȧ-ō'mī learned later ıat "Pleasant" was the right name for her after all.

There was living in Bĕth'lĕ-hĕm at that time a very rich man amed Bō'ăz. He owned large fields that were abundant in their arvests; and he was related to the family of Ē-lĭm'e-lĕch, Nȧ-ō'mī's usband, who had died.

It was the custom in Ĭs'ra-el when they reaped the grain not to ather all the stalks, but to leave some for the poor people, who ɔllowed after the reapers with their sickles and gathered what was :ft. When Nȧ-ō'mī and Ruth came to Bĕth'lĕ-hĕm, it was the ıme of the barley harvest; and Ruth went out into the fields to lean the grain which the reapers had left. It so happened that ɪe was gleaning in the field that belonged to Bō'ăz, this rich man.

Bō'ăz came out from the town to see his men reaping, and he aid to them, "The Lord be with you"; and they answered him, The Lord bless you." And Bō'ăz said to his master of the reapers, 'Who is this young woman that I see gleaning in the field?"

The man answered, "It is the young woman from the land of ⅤΙō'ab, who came with Nȧ-ō'mī. She asked leave to glean after ɪe reapers and has been here gathering grain since yesterday."

Then Bō'ăz said to Ruth, "Listen to me, my daughter. Do n[ot]
go to any other field, but stay here with my young women. N[o]
one shall harm you; and when you are thirsty, go and drink at o[ur]
vessels of water."

Then Ruth bowed to Bō'ăz and thanked him for his kindnes[s]
all the more kind because she was a stranger in Iş'ra-el. Bō'ăz said

"I have heard how true you have been to your mother-in-law
Nȧ-ō'mī, in leaving your own land and coming with her to th[is]
land. May the Lord, under whose wings you have come, give yo[u]
a reward!" And at noon, when they sat down to rest and to ea[t]
Bō'ăz gave her some of the food. And he said to the reapers:

"When you are reaping, leave some of the sheaves for her; an[d]
drop out some sheaves from the bundles, where she may gathe[r]
them."

That evening Ruth showed Nȧ-ō'mī how much she had gleane[d]
and told her of the rich man Bō'ăz, who had been so kind to he[r]
And Nȧ-ō'mī said, "This man is a near relation of ours. Stay i[n]
his fields as long as the harvest lasts." And so Ruth gleaned in th[e]
fields of Bō'ăz until the harvest had been gathered.

At the end of the harvest Bō'ăz held a feast on the threshin[g]
floor. And after the feast, by the advice of Nȧ-ō'mī, Ruth wen[t]
to him and said to him, "You are a near relation of my husband an[d]
of his father, Ê-lĭm'e-lĕch. Now will you not do good to us fo[r]
his sake?"

And when Bō'ăz saw Ruth, he loved her; and soon after this h[e]
took her as his wife. And Nȧ-ō'mī and Ruth went to live in hi[s]

home; so that Nă-ō'mĭ's life was no more bitter, but pleasant. And Bō'ăz and Ruth had a son, whom they named Ō'bed; and later Ō'bed had a son named Jĕs'se; and Jĕs'se was the father of Dā'vid, the shepherd boy who became king. So Ruth, the young woman of Mō'ab, who chose the people and the God of Is'ra-el, became the mother of kings.

Story Fifteen

I SAMUEL I : I to 3 : 21

The Little Boy with a Linen Coat

SĂM'SON the strong man (see Story Twelve) ruled Is'ra-el as the thirteenth of the judges; and after him came Ē'lĭ as the fourteenth judge. Ē'lĭ was also the high priest of the Lord in the Tabernacle at Shī'lōh.

While Ē'lĭ was the priest and the judge, a man was living at Rā'mah in the mountains of Ē'phră-ĭm, whose name was Ĕl'kă-nah. He had two wives, as did many men in that time. One of these wives had children, but the other wife, whose name was Hăn'nah, had no child.

Every year Ĕl'kă-nah and his family went up to worship at the house of the Lord in Shī'lōh, which was about fifteen miles from his home. And at one of these visits Hăn'nah prayed to the Lord, saying:

"O Lord, if thou wilt look upon me, and give me a son, he shall be given to the Lord as long as he lives."

The Lord heard Hăn'nah's prayer and gave her a little boy; and she called his name Săm'u-el, which means, "Asked of God," because he had been given in answer to her prayer. While he was still a little child, she brought him to Ē'lĭ, the priest, and said to him:

"My Lord, I am the woman who stood here praying. I asked God for this child; and now I have promised that he shall be the Lord's as long as he lives. Let him stay here with you and grow up in God's house."

So the child Săm'u-el stayed at Shī'lōh and lived with Ē'lī the priest in one of the tents beside the Tabernacle.

And every year Săm'u-el's mother Hăn'nah made for her boy a little linen coat, just like those worn by the priests; and brought it to him at the Tabernacle. So Săm'u-el growing up in God's house looked like a young priest, and as one of the priests, he helped Ē'lī in the work of the Tabernacle. He lit the lamps, and opened the doors, and prepared the incense, and waited on Ē'lī, who was now growing old and was almost blind.

Săm'u-el was all the more a help and a comfort to Ē'lī because his own sons, who were priests, were very wicked young men. Ē'lī had not trained them to do right, nor punished them when they did wrong, when they were children; so they grew up to become evil, to disobey God's law, and to be careless in God's worship. Ē'lī's heart was very sad over the sins of his sons; but now that he was old he could do nothing to control them.

It had been a long time since God had spoken to men, as in other days God had spoken to Mō'şeş, to Jŏsh'u-à, and to Gĭd'e-on. The men of Ĭş'ra-el were longing for the time to come when God would speak again to his people as of old.

One night Săm'u-el, while yet a child, was lying down upon his bed in a tent beside the Tabernacle; he heard a voice calling him by name. It was the Lord's voice, but Săm'u-el did not know it.

He answered, "Here I am!" and then he ran to Ē'lī, saying, "Here I am. You called me; what do you wish me to do?"

And Ē'lī said, "My child, I did not call you. Go and lie down again."

Săm'u-el lay down, but soon again heard the voice calling to
m, "Săm'u-el! Săm'u-el!"

Again he rose up and went to Ē'lī, and said, "Here I am; for I am
ıre that you called me."

"No," said Ē'lī, "I did not call you. Lie down again."

A third time the voice was heard; and a third time the boy rose
p from his bed and went to Ē'lī, sure that Ē'lī had called him. Ē'lī
ow saw that this was the Lord's voice that had spoken to Săm'u-el.
Ie said:

"Go, lie down once more; and if the voice speaks to you again,
ıy 'Speak, Lord, for thy servant heareth.'"

Săm'u-el went and lay down, and waited for the voice. It spoke
ȿ if someone unseen were standing by his bed, and saying, "Săm'-
-el! Săm'u-el!"

Then Săm'u-el said to the Lord, "Speak, Lord, for thy servant
eareth."

And the Lord said to Săm'u-el:

"Listen to what I say. I have seen the wickedness of Ēlī's sons.
ınd I have seen that their father did not punish them when they
ⱱere doing evil. I am going to give to them such a punishment
hat the story shall make everyone's ears tingle who hears it."

Săm'u-el lay in his room until the morning. Then he arose and
ⱱent about his work as usual, preparing for the daily worship and
•pening the doors. He said nothing of God's voice until Ē'lī asked
ıim. Ē'lī said to him:

"Săm'u-el, my son, tell me what the Lord said to you last night.
Hide nothing from me."

And Săm'u-el told Ē'lī all that God had said, though it was a sad
nessage to Ē'lī. And Ē'lī said, "It is the Lord; let him do what
eems good to him."

And then the news went through all the land that God had
ȿpoken once more to his people. And Hăn'nah, the lonely mother
n the mountains of Ē'phră-ĭm, heard that her son was the prophet
·o whom God spoke as his messenger to all Ĭṣ'ra-el.

From that time God spoke to Săm'u-el, and Săm'u-el gave God's
ⱱord to the twelve tribes.

How the Idol Fell Down Before
the Ark

WHILE the old priest Ē′lī was still the judg though he was now very feeble, the Phĭ-lĭs′tĭn came up against Ĭs′ra-el from the plain beside th sea. A battle was fought and many of the Ĭs′ra el-ītes were slain. Then the chiefs of the peopl said: "We have been beaten in the battle, because the Lord was n with us. Let us take with us against our enemies the Ark of th Covenant from the Tabernacle; then the Lord will be among us.

So they went to Shī′lōh and they took out from the Holy o Holies in the Tabernacle the Ark of the Covenant, and the tw sons of Ē′lī the priest went with the ark to care for it. When th ark was brought into the camp of the Ĭs′ra-el-ītes, all the men of wa gave a great shout, so that the earth rang with the sound.

And when the Phĭ-lĭs′tīnes heard the shouting, they wonder what caused it, and someone told them that it was because the Go of the Ĭs′ra-el-ītes had come into their camp. The Phĭ-lĭs′tīne were afraid, and they said to each other:

"Woe unto us, for such a thing as this has never been seen! Wh shall save us from this great God who sent plague on the Ē-ġȳp′ tians? Let us be bold and act like men and fight, so that we ma not be made servants to the Ĭs′ra-el-ītes, as they have been to us!

The next day there was a great battle. The Phĭ-lĭs′tīnes over came the Ĭs′ra-el-ītes and slew thousands of them. They killed th two sons of Ē′lī, and they took the ark of the Lord away with then into their own land.

On the day of the battle Ē′lī, old and blind, was sitting besid the door of the Tabernacle, his heart trembling for the ark of th Lord. A man came from the army running, with his garments torr and with earth on his head as a sign of sorrow. As the man cam near the city and brought the news of the battle, a great cry ros up from the people. When Ē′lī heard the noise, he said:

"What does this noise mean? What has happened?"
The man came before Ē'lī, and said:
"I have just come from the army. There has been a great battle.
ra-el has fled before the Phĭ-lĭs'tīneş, and very many of the people
ve been killed. Your two sons are dead, and the ark of God has
en taken by the enemy."
When the old man heard this last word, that the ark of God was
ken, he fell backward from his seat and dropped dead upon the
ound. And all the land mourned and wept over the loss of the
k more than over the victory of the Phĭ-lĭs'tīneş.
The Phĭ-lĭs'tīneş took the ark of God down to Ăsh'dŏd, one of
eir chief cities. They set it in the temple of Dā'gon, their fish-
aded idol. The next morning, when they came into the temple,
e image of Dā'gon was lying upon its face before the ark of the
ord. They stood the image up again; but on the next morning,
ot only was Dā'gon fallen down before the ark, but the hands and
e head of Dā'gon had been cut off and were lying on the floor.
Besides all this, in the city of Ăsh'dŏd, where the ark had been
ken, all the people began to have boils and sores. They saw in
is the hand of the God of Ĭş'ra-el, and they sent the ark to Găth,
other of their cities. There, too, the people broke out with boils
d sores. They sent the ark to Ĕk'rŏn, but the people of that city
id:
"We will not have the ark of God among us. Send it back to
s own land, or we shall all die."
Then the rulers of the Phĭ-lĭs'tīneş resolved to send back the ark
f God into the land of Ĭş'ra-el. They placed it upon a wagon,
d before the wagon they yoked two cows. The cows had calves,
ut they tied the calves at home, in order to find whether the cows
ould go home to their calves or would take the ark away. But
e cows took the road which led away from their own calves,
raight up the hills toward the land of Ĭş'ra-el, and they turned
either to the right hand nor the left.
The cows drew the ark up to the village of Bĕth=shē'mesh, where
e people were reaping their wheat harvest on the hillsides. They
w the ark and were glad. The cows stopped beside a great stone

in the field. Then the men of Bĕth=shē'mesh cut up the wagon, and with it made a fire, and on the stone as an altar offered the two cows as an offering to the Lord.

But the men of Bĕth=shē'mesh opened the ark and looked into it. This was contrary to God's command, for none but the priests were allowed to touch the ark. God sent a plague upon the people of that place and many of them died, because they did not deal reverently with the ark of God.

They were filled with fear and sent to the men of Kĭr'jath=jē'a-rĭm, asking them to take the ark away. They did so, and for twenty years the ark stood in the house of a man named Ā-bĭn'a-dăb in Kĭr'jath=jē'a-rĭm.

They did not take the ark back to Shĭ'lōh, for after the death of Ē'lī, the place was deserted, the Tabernacle fell into ruins, and no man lived there again.

Story Seventeen I SAMUEL 7 : 2-1?

The Last of the Judges

WHEN the ark of God was taken and the Tabernacle fell into ruins, Săm'u-el was still a boy. He went to his father's house at Rā'mah, which was in the mountains, about four miles north of Jē-ru'sa-lĕm. Rā'mah was the home of Săm'u-el after this as long as he lived, which was many years.

For some years, while Săm'u-el was growing up, there was no judge in Ĭs'ra-el, and no head of the tribes. The Phĭ-lĭs'tĭnes ruled the people and took from them a large part of their harvests, their sheep, and their oxen. Often in their need they thought of the ark of the Lord, standing alone in the house at Kĭr'jath=jē'a-rĭm. And the eyes of all the people turned to the young Săm'u-el growing up at Rā'mah. For Săm'u-el walked with God, and God spoke to

Săm′u-el, as God had spoken to Ā′bră-hăm and to Mō′sĕs and to
Jŏsh′u-à.

As soon as Săm′u-el had grown up to be a man, he began to go
among the tribes and to give to the people everywhere God's word
to them. And this was what Săm′u-el said:

"If you will really come back with all your heart to the Lord
God of Ĭs′ra-el, put away the false gods, the images of Bā′al, and of
Ăsh-ē′rah, and seek the Lord alone and serve him, then God will
set you free from the Phĭ-lĭs′tĭnĕs."

After Săm′u-el's words the people began to throw down the
idols and to pray to the God of Ĭs′ra-el. And Săm′u-el called the
people from all the land to gather in one place, as many as could
come. They met at a place called Mĭz′pah, in the mountains of
Bĕn′ja-mĭn, not far from Jĕ-ru′sà-lĕm.

There Săm′u-el prayed for the people, and asked God to forgive
their sin in turning away from God to idols. They confessed their
wrongdoings and made a solemn promise to serve the Lord, and to
serve the Lord only.

The Phĭ-lĭs′tĭnĕs upon the plain beside the Great Sea heard of
this meeting. They feared that the Ĭs′ra-el-ītes were about to break
away from their rule, and they came up with an army to drive the
Ĭs′ra-el-ītes away to their homes and keep them under the rule of
the Phĭ-lĭs′tĭnĕs.

When the Ĭs′ra-el-ītes saw the Phĭ-lĭs′tĭnĕs coming against them,
they were greatly alarmed. The Phĭ-lĭs′tĭnĕs were men of war,
with swords and shields and spears, and they were trained in fighting; while the men of Ĭs′ra-el had not seen war. It was more than
twenty years since their fathers had fought the Phĭ-lĭs′tĭnĕs and
twice had been beaten by them. They had neither weapons nor
training and they felt themselves helpless against their enemies.
They looked to Săm′u-el, just as children would look to a father,
and they said to him, "Do not cease praying and crying to the Lord
for us, that he may save us from the Phĭ-lĭs′tĭnĕs."

Then Săm′u-el took a lamb and offered it up to the Lord as a
burnt offering for the people, and he prayed mightily that God
would help Ĭs′ra-el; and God heard his prayer.

Just as the Phĭ-lĭs′tĭnĕs were rushing upon the helpless men of

Ĭṣ'ra-el, there came a great storm with rolling thunder and flashing
lightning. Such storms do not come often in that land, and this
was so heavy that it frightened the Phĭ-lĭs'tĭneṣ. They threw down
their spears and swords in sudden terror and ran away.

The men of Ĭṣ'ra-el picked up these arms and gathered such other
weapons as they could find, and they followed the Phĭ-lĭs'tĭneṣ and
killed many of them and won a great victory over them. By this
one stroke, the power of the Phĭ-lĭs'tĭneṣ was broken and they lost

their rule over Ĭṣ'ra-el. And it so happened that the place where
Săm'u-el won this great victory was the very place where the Ĭṣ'ra-
el-ītes had been beaten twice before, the place where the ark of
God had been taken, as we read in the last story. On the battlefield
Săm'u-el set up a great stone to mark the place, and he gave it the
name Ĕb'en=ē'zĕr, which means "The Stone of Help."

"For," said Săm'u-el, "this was the place where the Lord helped
us."

After this defeat the Phĭ-lĭs'tĭneṣ came no more into the land of
Ĭṣ'ra-el in the years while Săm'u-el ruled as judge over the tribes.
He was the fifteenth of the judges, and the last. He went throughout the land, and people everywhere brought to him their questions and their differences for Săm'u-el to decide, for they knew
that he was a good man and would do justly between man and man.

From each journey he came back to Rā'mah. There was his home,
and there he built an altar to the Lord.

Săm'u-el lived many years and ruled the people wisely, so that
all trusted in him. He taught the Ĭṣ'ra-el-ītes to worship the Lord
God and to put away the idols, which so many of them had served.
While Săm'u-el ruled, there was peace in all the tribes and no
enemies came from the lands around to do harm to the Ĭṣ'ra-el-ītes.
But the Phĭ-lĭs'tĭneṣ were still very strong and held rule over some
parts of Ĭṣ'ra-el near their own land, although there was no war.
Săm'u-el was not a man of war, like Gĭd'e-on or Jĕph'thah, but a
man of peace, and his rule was quiet, though it was strong.

Story Eighteen
I SAMUEL 8 : I to 10 : 27

The Tall Man Who Was Chosen King

WHEN Săm'u-el, the good man and the wise
judge, grew old, he made his sons judges in Ĭṣ'-
ra-el, to help him in the care of the people. But
Săm'u-el's sons did not walk in his ways. They
did not try always to do justly. When men
brought matters before them to be decided, they would decide
for the one who gave them money and not always for the one who
was in the right.

The elders of all the tribes of Ĭṣ'ra-el came to Săm'u-el at his
home in Rā'mah, and they said to him, "You are growing old, and
your sons do not rule as well as you have ruled. All the lands
around us have kings. Let us have a king also, and do you choose
the king for us."

This was not pleasing to Săm'u-el, not because he wished to rule,
but because the Lord God was their king, and he felt that for

Ĭṣ'ra-el to have such a king as those who ruled the nations around them would be turning away from the Lord. Săm'u-el prayed to the Lord; the Lord said to him, "Listen to the people in what they ask, for they have not turned away from you; they have turned away from me in asking for a king. Let them have a king, but tell them of the wrong that they are doing, and show them what trouble their king will bring upon them."

Then Săm'u-el called the elders of the people together, and he said to them, "If you have a king, as do the nations around, he will take your sons away from you, and will make some of them soldiers and horsemen and men to drive his chariots. He will take others of your sons to wait on him, to work in his fields, and to make his chariots and his weapons for war. Your king will take the best of your fields and your farms, and will give them to the men of his court who are around him. He will make your daughters cook for him and make bread and serve in his palace. He will take a part of your sheep and your oxen and your asses. You will find that he will be your master and you shall be his servants. The time shall come when you will cry out to the Lord on account of the king that you have chosen, and the Lord will not hear you." But the people would not follow Săm'u-el's advice. They said, "No, we will have a king to reign over us, so that we may be like other nations, and our king shall be our judge and shall lead us out to war."

It was God's will that Ĭṣ'ra-el should be a quiet, plain people, living alone in the mountains, serving the Lord, and not trying to conquer other nations. But they wished to be a great people, to be strong in war, and to have riches and power. And the Lord said to Săm'u-el, "Do as the people ask, and choose a king for them."

Then Săm'u-el sent the people to their homes, promising to find a king for them.

There was at that time in the tribe of Běn'ja-mĭn a young man named Saul, the son of Kĭsh. He was a very large man and noble looking. From his shoulders he stood taller than any other man in Ĭṣ'ra-el. His father Kĭsh was a rich man, with wide fields and many flocks. Some asses that belonged to Kĭsh had strayed away and Saul went out with a servant to find them. While they were looking for the asses, they came near Rā'mah, where Săm'u-el lived.

he servant said to Saul, "There is in this city a man of God whom ll men honor. They say that he can tell what is about to happen, or he is a seer. Let us go to him and give him a present. Perhaps e can tell us where to find the asses."

In those times a man to whom God made known his will was alled a seer; in later times he was called a prophet.

So Saul and his servant came to Rā'mah and asked for the seer; nd while they were coming, the seer, Săm'u-el, met them. The lay before the Lord had spoken to Săm'u-el, and had said:

"Tomorrow, about this time, I will send you a man out of the ribe of Běn'ja-min, and you shall make him the prince of my people, and he shall save my people from the Phĭ-lĭs'tĭneș."

And when Săm'u-el saw this tall and noble-looking young man coming to meet him, he heard the Lord's voice saying:

"This is the man of whom I spoke to you. He is the one that hall rule over my people."

Then Saul came near to Săm'u-el, not knowing who he was, nd he said, "Can you tell me where the seer's house is?" And Săm'u-el answered Saul: "I am the seer; come with me up to the ill. We are to have an offering and a feast there. As for the asses that were lost three days ago, do not be troubled about them, for they have been found. But on whom is the desire of all Iș'ra-el? Is it not on you and on your father's house?" Saul could not think what the seer meant in those last words. He said, "Is not my tribe of Běn'ja-min the smallest of all the tribes? And is not my family the least of all the families in the tribe? Why do you say such things to me?"

But Săm'u-el led Saul and his servant into the best room at his house; at the table, where thirty had been invited, he gave Saul the best place, and he put before him the choicest of the meat, and he said, "This has been kept for you of all those invited to the feast."

That night Saul and his servant slept in the best room, which was on the roof of Săm'u-el's house. And the next morning Săm'u-el sent the servant on while he spoke with Saul alone. He brought out a horn filled with oil and poured the oil on Saul's head, and said:

"The Lord has anointed you to be prince over his land and his people."

Then he told Sạul just what he would find on the way, where
he would meet certain people, and what he must do. He said:

"When you come to the tomb where Rā'chel is buried, two men
will meet you and will say to you, 'The asses for which you were
looking have been found, and now your father is looking for you.'
Then under an oak you will meet three men carrying three kids,
three loaves of bread, and a skin bottle full of wine; and these men
will give you as a present two loaves of bread. Next you will meet
a company of prophets, men full of God's Spirit, with instruments
of music, and the Lord's Spirit shall come upon you and a new
heart shall be given to you. All these things will show you that
God is with you. Now go, and do whatever God tells you to do."

And it came just as Săm'u-el had said. These men met Sạul,
and when the prophets came near, singing and praising God, Sạul
joined them and also sang and praised the Lord. And in that hour
a new spirit came to Sạul. He was no more the farmer's son, for in
him was the soul of a king.

He came home, and told at home how he had met Săm'u-el, and
that Săm'u-el said to him that the asses had been found. But he
did not tell them that Săm'u-el had poured oil upon his head and
said that he was to be the king of Ĭs'ra-el.

Then Săm'u-el called all the people to the meeting place at Mĭz'-
pah. And he told them that they had wished for a king, and God
had chosen a king for them.

"Now," said Săm′u-el, "let the men of the tribes pass by, each tribe and each family by itself."

The people passed by Săm′u-el, and when the tribe of Běn′ja-mĭn came, out of all the tribes Běn′ja-mĭn was taken; out of Běn′ja-mĭn one family, and out of that family Sạul's name was called. But Sạul was not with his family; he had ridden away. They found him and brought him out; and when he stood among the people, his head and shoulders rose above them all. And Săm′u-el said: "Look at the man whom the Lord has chosen! There is not another like him among all the people!" And all the people shouted, "God save the king! Long live the king!"

Then Săm′u-el told the people what should be the laws for the king and for the people to obey. He wrote them down in a book, and placed the book before the Lord. Then Săm′u-el sent the people home, and Sạul went back to his own house at a place called Gĭb′e-ah, and with Sạul went a company of men to whose hearts God had given a love for the king. So after two hundred years under the fifteen judges, Ĭs′ra-el now had a king. But among the people there were some who were not pleased with the new king, because he was an unknown man from the farm. They said, "Can such a man as this save us?" They showed no respect to the king and in their hearts looked down upon him. But Sạul said nothing and showed his wisdom by appearing not to notice them.

Part Third

STORIES OF THE THREE GREAT KINGS OF ISRAEL

How Saul Saved the Eyes of the Men of Jabesh

SAUL was now the king of all the twelve tribes of Ĭs'ra-el, but he did not at once in his manner of life set up the state of a king. He lived at home and worked in the fields on his father's farm, just as he had always done.

One day, while Saul was plowing in the field with a yoke of oxen, a man came running with sad news. He said that the Ăm'mon-ītes, a fierce people living near the desert on the east, beyond the Jôr'dan, had come up against Jā'besh in Gĭl'e-ăd, led by their king, Nā'hăsh. The people in that city were too few to fight the Ăm'mon-ītes, and they said, "We will submit to your rule, if you will promise to spare our lives."

And Nā'hăsh, the king of the Ăm'mon-ītes, said to the people of Jā'besh, "You shall live, but within seven days I will come with my soldiers and I will put out the right eye of every man in your city."

When a city was taken by its enemies in those times, such cruel deeds were common. Often all the people in it, young and old, were slain without mercy. The men of Jā'besh sent a messenger to go to Saul as swiftly as possible and to tell him of the terrible fate that was hanging over them.

When Saul heard of it, the spirit of a king rose within him. He killed the oxen that he was driving, cut them into twelve pieces, and sent swift messengers through all the land, to say to every fighting man in the twelve tribes, "Whoever will not come out after Saul and after Săm'u-el, so shall it be done to his oxen."

And the Lord gave to all the people the spirit of obedience to their king. At once a great army gathered at a place called Bē'zĕk, and Saul sent word to Jā'besh, saying, "Tomorrow, by the time the sun is hot, you will be set free from all fear of the Ăm'mon-ītes."

Saul and his men marched swiftly over the mountains of Bĕn'ja-

215

mĭn and down into the Jôr'dan valley. They walked across the
river where it was shallow and climbed the mountains of Gĭl'e-ăd.
There they fell furiously upon the Ăm'mon-ītes, early in the morning, killed many of them and scattered the rest, so that not even
two of their men could be found together.

We read in the last story that when Saul was made king, some
men were not pleased and were unwilling to submit to him. Now
that a great victory had been won under Saul as leader, the people
said with one voice, "Where are those men who would not honor
our king? Bring them out and let them be put to death."

But King Saul said, "There shall not a man be put to death this
day, for today the Lord has set his people free from their enemies."
Săm'u-el was with Saul, and he said, "Let us go to Gĭl'găl, where
Jŏsh'u-à encamped long ago when our fathers crossed the Jôr'dan;
and there let us set up the kingdom again."

They came to Gĭl'găl and offered sacrifices to the Lord and worshiped. There Săm'u-el gave up to the new king the rule over the
land and spoke words of farewell. He said to the people:

"I have done as you asked me, and have given you a king. Your
king stands before you now. I am old and gray-headed, and I
have lived before you from my youth up to this day. Here I am;
now, in the presence of the Lord and of his anointed king, is there
any man whom I have wronged? Have I taken any man's ox or
ass? Have I taken a present from any man to make me favor him
as judge? If I have robbed any man, let him speak, and I will pay
him all that I have taken."

And all the people said to Săm'u-el, "You have ruled justly and have wronged no man and have robbed no man."

And Săm'u-el said, "The Lord is witness and his anointed, the king, is witness that I have taken nothing from any man."

And all the people said, "He is witness."

Then Săm'u-el called to their minds all that God had done for his people since he had led them out of Ē'ġypt; how he had saved them from their enemies and had given them judges. And he said, "Now the Lord has set a king over you. If you will fear the Lord and will serve him, then it shall be well with you. But if you disobey the Lord, then God will punish you."

Then Săm'u-el called upon God, and God sent thunder and rain on that day, showing his power. The people were filled with fear, and they cried to Săm'u-el, "Pray to the Lord for us, for we have done wrong in asking for a king."

"Yes," said Săm'u-el, "you have done wrong; but if you from this time do right and seek the Lord, God will not forsake you. He will forgive you and bless you. I will always pray for you and will teach you the right way. But if you do evil, God will destroy you and your king. So fear the Lord and serve him faithfully."

After this Săm'u-el went again to his own house at Rā'mah, and Saul ruled the people from Ġĭb'e-ah, the home of his family.

Story Two   I SAMUEL 13 : 1 to 14 : 46

The Brave Young Prince

THE PEOPLE had hoped that when they should have a king to lead them in war they might break the power of the Phĭ-lĭs'tĭnes, who were still rulers over a large part of the land. But after Saul had been king two years, the Phĭ-lĭs'tĭnes seemed to be stronger than ever. They held many walled towns on the hills, and from these their warriors went out robbing the villages and taking away the crops from the farmers, so that the men of Ĭṣ'ra-el were kept very poor and in great fear.

The Phĭ-lĭs'tĭneṣ would not allow the Ĭṣ'ra-el-ītes to do any work in iron, in order to keep them from making swords and spears for themselves. When a man wished to have his iron plowshare sharpened or to have a new one made, he must go to the Phĭ-lĭs'tĭneṣ for the work. So when Saul gathered an army, scarcely any of the men could find swords or spears, and Saul and his son Jŏn'a-than were the only ones who wore suits of armor to protect them from the darts of the enemy.

Saul gathered together a little army, of which a part was with him at Mĭch'mash and another part with his son Jŏn'a-than at Gĭb'e-ah, five miles to the south. Jŏn'a-than, who was a very brave young man, led his band against the Phĭ-lĭs'tĭneṣ at Gē'ba, halfway between Gĭb'e-ah and Mĭch'mash, and took that place from them. The news of this fight went through the land, and the Phĭ-lĭs'tĭneṣ came up the mountains with a great army, having chariots and horsemen. Saul blew a trumpet and called the Ĭṣ'ra-el-ītes to the old camp at Gĭl'găl, down in the valley of the Jôr'dan; and many came, but they came trembling with fear of the Phĭ-lĭs'-tĭneṣ.

Săm'u-el had told him not to march from Gĭl'găl until he should come to offer a sacrifice and to call upon God. But Săm'u-el delayed coming, and Saul grew impatient, for he saw his men scattering. At last Saul could wait no longer. He offered a sacrifice himself, though he was no priest. But while the offering was still burning on the altar, Săm'u-el came. He said to Saul, "What is this that you have done?"

And Saul answered, "I saw that my men were scattering, and I feared that the enemy might come down upon me, so I offered the sacrifice myself, since you were not here."

"You have done wrong," said Săm'u-el. "You have not kept God's commands. If you had obeyed and trusted the Lord, he would have kept you in safety. But now God will find some other man who will do his will, a man after his own heart, and God will in his own time take the kingdom from you and give it to him."

And Săm'u-el left the camp and went away, leaving Saul. Saul led his men, only six hundred, up the mountains to Gē'bȧ, the place which Jŏn'a-than had taken. Across the valley near Mĭch'mash was the host of the Phĭ-lĭs'tĭneṣ in plain sight. One morning Jŏn'-a-than and the young man who waited on him went down the hill toward the camp of the Phĭ-lĭs'tĭneṣ. This servant of Jŏn'a-than was called his armor-bearer, because he carried Jŏn'a-than's shield and sword and spear, to have them ready when needed.

Jŏn'a-than could see the Phĭ-lĭs'tĭneṣ just across the valley. He said, "If the Phĭ-lĭs'tĭneṣ say to us, 'Come over,' we will go and fight them, even though we two are alone, for we will take it as a sign that God will help us."

The Phĭ-lĭs'tĭneṣ saw the two Ĭṣ'ra-el-ītes standing on a rock across the valley and they called to them, "Come over here, and we will show you something."

Then Jŏn'a-than said to his armor-bearer, "Come on, for the Lord has given them into our hand."

Then they crossed the valley and came suddenly up to the Phĭ-lĭs'tĭneṣ and struck them down right and left, without giving them a moment. Some fell down, but others ran away, and as soon as their fellow soldiers saw them running, they, too, became frightened, and everybody began to run to and fro. Some fought the men who were running away; and before many minutes, the Ĭṣ'ra-el-ītes on the hill across the valley could see the Phĭ-lĭs'tĭneṣ fighting and killing each other, the men running in every direction and their army melting away.

Then Saul and his men came across the valley and joined in the
fight; and other Ĭṣ'ra-el-ītes who were in the camp of the Phĭ-lĭs'-
tĭneṣ, and under their control, rose against them; and the tribes
near at hand came forth and pursued them as they fled. So on that
day a great victory was won over the Phĭ-lĭs'tĭneṣ.

But a great mistake was made by King Saul on the day of the
victory. He feared that his men would turn aside from following
the Phĭ-lĭs'tĭneṣ to seize the spoil in their camp, and when the battle
began, King Saul said, "Let the curse of God light on any man
who takes food until the evening. Whoever takes any food before
the sun goes down shall die, so that there may be no delay in destroying our enemies."

So on that day no man ate any food until it was evening, and
they were faint and feeble from hunger. They were so worn out
that they could not chase the Phĭ-lĭs'tĭneṣ farther, and many of the
Phĭ-lĭs'tĭneṣ escaped. That afternoon, as they were driving the
Phĭ-lĭs'tĭneṣ through a forest, they found honey on the trees; but
no man tasted it, because of Saul's oath before the Lord, that whoever took a mouthful of food should be put to death.

But Jŏn'a-than had not heard of his father's command. He took
some honey and was made stronger by it. They said to Jŏn'a-than,
"Your father commanded all the people not to take any food until
the sun goes down, saying, 'May the curse of God come upon anyone who eats anything until the evening.'" When Jŏn'a-than
heard of his father's word, he said, "My father has given us all
great trouble; for if the men could have taken some food, they
would have been stronger to fight and to kill their enemies."

On that night Saul found that Jŏn'a-than had broken his command, though he knew it not at the time. He said, "I have taken
an oath before the Lord, and now, Jŏn'a-than, you must die, though
you are my own son."

But the people would not allow Jŏn'a-than to be put to death,
even to keep Saul's oath. They said, "Shall Jŏn'a-than die, after
he has done such a great deed, and won the victory and saved the
people? Not a hair of his head shall fall, for he has done God's
work this day!"

And they rescued Jŏn'a-than from the hand of the king and set him free. A great victory had been won, but Saul had already shown that he was not fit to rule, because he was too hasty in his acts and his words and because he was not careful to obey God's command.

The Phĭ-lĭs'tineş after this battle stayed for a time in their own land beside the Great Sea and did not trouble the Iş'ra-el-ītes upon the mountains.

Story Three   I SAMUEL 15 : 1-35

Saul's Great Sin and His Great Loss

AFTER the great victory over the Phĭ-lĭs'tĭneş, Saul led his men against the enemies of Iş'ra-el on every side of the land. He drove back the Mō'ab-ītes to their country east of the Dead Sea and the Ăm'mon-ītes to the desert regions across the Jôr'dan. He fought the Ē'dom-ītes on the south and the kings of Zō'bah in the far north. For a time the land of Iş'ra-el was free from its oppressors.

On the south of the land, in the desert where the Iş'ra-el-ītes had journeyed for forty years, were living the wild and wandering Ăm'a-lĕk-ītes, a people who had sought to harm the Iş'ra-el-ītes soon after they came out of Ē'ġўpt, and had killed many of their people when they were helpless on their journey. For this God had said that Iş'ra-el should have war against the Ăm'a-lĕk-ītes until they were destroyed.

The time had now come for God's word against the Ăm'a-lĕk-ītes to be fulfilled, and Săm'u-el said to Saul, "Thus says the Lord, the God of hosts, go down and make war against the Ăm'a-lĕk-ītes and destroy them utterly."

Then Saul called out the men of war in all the tribes, and they marched southward into the desert where many years before their fathers had lived for forty years. There Saul made war on the

Ăm'a-lĕk-ītes and took their city and destroyed it. But he did not do what God had commanded him. He brought Ā'găg, the king of the Ăm'a-lĕk-ītes, and many of his people as prisoners, and a great train of their sheep and oxen, intending to keep them. Then the word of the Lord came to Săm'u-el, saying, "It would have been better never to have chosen Saul as king, for he does not obey my commands."

All that night Săm'u-el prayed to the Lord, and the next day he went to meet Saul. When Saul saw him, he said, "May the blessing of the Lord be upon you. I have done what the Lord commanded me to do."

Then said Săm'u-el, "If you have obeyed God's command and destroyed all the Ăm'a-lĕk-ītes and all that they possessed, what is the meaning of this bleating of the sheep and the bellowing of the oxen which I hear?"

"They have brought them from the Ăm'a-lĕk-ītes," answered Saul, "for the people spared the best of the sheep and of the oxen, to offer in sacrifice to the Lord your God. All the rest we have utterly destroyed." This he said to excuse his wrongdoing and to put the blame for his disobedience to God's command on the people.

Then Săm'u-el said, "I will tell you what God said to me last night. When you were humble in your own sight, God chose you to be king over Ĭs'ra-el. He sent you on a long journey to the southward into the desert and said to you, 'Go and utterly destroy the Ăm'a-lĕk-ītes and leave nothing of them.' Why did you not obey God's word but did seize their oxen and sheep and save many of their people alive, disobeying God's voice?"

And Saul said, "I have done as God commanded, and have destroyed the Ăm'a-lĕk-ītes. But the people took some things that should have been destroyed, to offer in sacrifice to the Lord."

And Săm'u-el said, "Is the Lord as well pleased with offerings as he is with obeying his words? To obey is better than sacrifice, and to listen to God's word is more precious than to place offerings on his altar. To disobey God's word is as evil as to worship idols. You have refused to obey the voice of the Lord, and the Lord will take away your kingdom from you."

Saul saw now how great was the harm that he had done and he said, "I have sinned in not obeying God's word; but I was afraid of the people and yielded to them. Now forgive my sin. Come with me, and I will worship the Lord."

"No," said Săm'u-el, "I will not go with you, for God will refuse you as king."

As Săm'u-el turned away, Saul took hold of his garment, and it tore in his hand. And Săm'u-el said, "Even so has God torn the kingdom away from you; and he will give it to a man that is better than you are. And God is not like a man, to say one thing and do another. What God has said shall surely come to pass."

Saul begged Săm'u-el so hard not to leave him, but to give him honor in presence of the people, that Săm'u-el went with Saul and Saul worshiped the Lord with Săm'u-el.

After this Săm'u-el went to his house at Rā'mah, and he never again met Saul as long as he lived; but he mourned and wept for Saul, because he had disobeyed the Lord, and the Lord had rejected him as king.

The Shepherd Boy of Bethlehem

WHEN Săm′u-el told Saul that the Lord would take away the kingdom from him, he did not mean that Saul should lose the kingdom at once. He was no longer God's king; and as soon as the right man in God's sight should be found, and should be trained for his duty as king, then God would take away Saul's power and would give it to the man whom God had chosen. But it was many years before all this came to pass.

Săm′u-el, who had helped in choosing Saul as king, still loved him and he felt very sorry to find Saul disobeying God's commands. He wept much and mourned for Saul. But the Lord said to Săm′u-el:

"Do not weep and mourn any longer over Saul, for I have refused him as king. Fill the horn with oil and go to Běth′lĕ-hĕm in Jū′dah. There find a man named Jĕs′se, for I have chosen a king among his sons."

But Săm′u-el knew that Saul would be very angry if he should learn that Săm′u-el had named any other man as king in his place. He said to the Lord, "How can I go? If Saul hears of it, he will kill me."

Then the Lord said to Săm′u-el, "Take a young cow with you, and tell the people that you have come to make an offering to the Lord. And call Jĕs′se and his sons to the sacrifice. I will tell you what to do; and then you shall anoint the one whom I name to you."

Săm′u-el went over the mountains southward from Rā′mah to Běth′lĕ-hĕm, about ten miles, leading a cow. The rulers of the town were alarmed at his coming, for they feared that he had come to judge the people for some evildoing.

But Săm′u-el said, "I have come in peace to make an offering and to hold a feast to the Lord. Make yourselves ready and come to the sacrifice."

224

And he invited Jĕs'se and his sons to the service. When they had made themselves ready, they came before Săm'u-el. He looked at the sons of Jĕs'se very closely. The oldest was named Ê-lī'ab, and he was so tall and noble looking that Săm'u-el thought: "Surely this young man must be the one whom God has chosen." But the Lord said to Săm'u-el:

"Do not look on his face nor on the height of his body; for I have not chosen him. Man judges by the outward looks, but God looks at the heart."

Then Jĕs'se's second son, named Shăm'mah, passed by. And the Lord said, "I have not chosen this one." Seven young men came, and Săm'u-el said:

"None of these is the man whom God has chosen. Are these all your children?"

"There is one more," said Jĕs'se, "the youngest of all. He is a boy in the field caring for the sheep."

And Săm'u-el said:

"Send for him; for we will not sit down until he comes." So after a time the youngest son was brought in. His name was Dā'vid, a word that means "Darling," and he was a beautiful boy, perhaps fifteen years old, with fresh cheeks and bright eyes.

As soon as the young Dā'vid came, the Lord said to Săm'u-el: "Arise; anoint him, for this is the one whom I have chosen."

Then Săm'u-el poured oil on Dā'vid's head, in the presence of all his brothers. But at that time no one knew the anointing to mean that Dā'vid was to be the king. Perhaps they thought that Dā'vid was chosen to be a prophet like Săm'u-el.

From that time the Spirit of the Lord came upon Dā'vid; and he began to show signs of coming greatness. He went back to his sheep on the hillsides around Bĕth'lĕ-hĕm, but God was with him. Dā'vid grew up strong and brave; not afraid of the wild beasts which prowled around and tried to carry away his sheep. More than once he fought with lions and bears and killed them, when they seized the lambs of his flock. And Dā'vid, alone all day, practiced throwing stones in a sling, until he could strike exactly the place for which he aimed. When he swung his sling, he knew that the stone would go to the very spot at which he was throwing it.

And, young as he was, Dā'vid thought of God, and prayed to God. And God talked with Dā'vid and showed to Dā'vid his will. And Dā'vid was more than a shepherd and a fighter of wild beasts. He played upon the harp and made music, and sang songs about the goodness of God to his people.

One of these songs of Dā'vid we have all heard and perhaps know so well that we can repeat it. It is called "The Shepherd Psalm":

"The Lord is my shepherd; I shall not want.
He maketh me to lie down in green pastures:
He leadeth me beside the still waters.
He restoreth my soul:
He leadeth me in the paths of righteousness for his name's sake.
Yea, though I walk through the valley of the shadow of death,
I will fear no evil: for thou art with me;
Thy rod and thy staff they comfort me.
Thou preparest a table before me in the presence of mine enemies:
Thou anointest my head with oil; my cup runneth over.
Surely goodness and mercy shall follow me all the days of my life:
And I will dwell in the house of the Lord for ever."

Some think that Dā'vid made this Psalm, while he was himself a shepherd, tending his flock. But it seems rather like the thoughts of a man than of a boy; and it is more likely that long after those days, when Dā'vid was a king and remembered his youth and his

flock in the fields, that he saw how God had led him, just as he had led his sheep; and then he wrote this Psalm.

But while the Spirit of God came to Dā'vid among his sheep, that Spirit left King Saul, because he no longer obeyed God's words. Then Saul became very unhappy and gloomy in his feelings. There were times when he seemed to lose his mind, and a madness would come upon him; and at almost all times Saul was sad and full of trouble, because he was no more at peace with God.

The servants around Saul noticed that when someone played on the harp and sang, Saul's gloom and trouble passed away and he became cheerful. At one time Saul said:

"Find someone who can play well, and bring him to me. Let me listen to music; for it drives away my sadness."

One of the young men said:

"I have seen a young man, a son of Jĕs'se in Bĕth'lĕ-hĕm, who can play well. He is handsome in his looks and agreeable in talking. Then I have heard that he is a brave young man, who can fight as well as he can play; and the Lord is with him."

Then Saul sent a message to Jĕs'se, Dā'vid's father. He said:

"Send me your son Dā'vid, who is with the sheep. Let him come and play before me."

Then Dā'vid came to Saul, bringing with him a present for the king from Jĕs'se. When Saul saw him, he loved him, as did everybody who saw the young Dā'vid. And Dā'vid played on the harp and sang before Saul. And Dā'vid's music cheered Saul's heart and drove away his sad feelings.

Saul liked Dā'vid so well that he made him his armor-bearer; and Dā'vid carried the shield and spear and sword for Saul when the king was before his army. But Saul did not know that Dā'vid had been anointed by Săm'u-el. If he had known it, he would have been very jealous of Dā'vid.

After a time Saul seemed well, and Dā'vid left him, to be a shepherd once more at Bĕth'lĕ-hĕm.

The Shepherd Boy's Fight with the Giant

ALL THROUGH the reign of Saul there was constant war with the Phĭ-lĭs'tĭneṣ, who lived upon the lowlands southwest of Ĭṣ'ra-el. At one time, when Dā'vid was still with his sheep, a few years after he had been anointed by Săm'u-el, the camp of the Phĭ-lĭs'tĭneṣ and the Ĭṣ'ra-el-ītes were set against each other on opposite sides of the valley of Ē'lah ready to fight each other. In the army of Ĭṣ'ra-el were the three oldest brothers of Dā'vid, who were soldiers under King Saul.

Every day a giant came out of the camp of the Phĭ-lĭs'tĭneṣ, and dared someone to come from the Ĭṣ'ra-el-ītes' camp and fight with him. The giant's name was Gȯ-lī'ath. He was nine feet high; and he wore armor from head to foot, and carried a spear twice as long and as heavy as any other man could hold; and his shield-bearer walked before him. He came every day and called out across the little valley:

"I am a Phĭ-lĭs'tĭne, and you are servants of Saul. Now choose one of your men and let him come out and fight with me. If I kill him, then you shall submit to us; and if he kills me, then we shall give up to you. Come, now, send out your man!"

But no man in the army, not even King Saul, dared to go out and fight with the giant. The Ĭṣ'ra-el-ītes were mostly farmers and shepherds and were not fond of war, as were the Phĭ-lĭs'tĭneṣ. Then, too, very few of the Ĭṣ'ra-el-ītes had swords and spears, except such rude weapons as they could make out of their farming tools. Forty days the camps stood against each other, and the Phĭ-lĭs'tĭne giant continued his call.

One day old Jĕs'se, the father of Dā'vid, sent Dā'vid from Bĕth'lĕ-hĕm to visit his three brothers in the army. Dā'vid came, spoke to his brothers, and gave them a present from his father.

228

While he was talking with them, Gȯ-lī'ath, the giant, came out as before in front of the camp, calling for someone to fight with him.

The Ĭṣ'ra-el-ītes said to one another, "If any man will go out and kill this Phĭ-lĭs'tĭne, the king will give him a great reward and a high rank; and the king's daughter shall be his wife."

And Dā'vid said, "Who is this man that speaks in this proud manner against the armies of the living God? Why does not someone go out and kill him?"

Dā'vid's brother Ê-lī'ab said to him, "What are you doing here, leaving your sheep in the field? I know that you have come down just to see the battle."

But Dā'vid did not care for his brother's angry words. He was thinking out some way to kill this boasting giant. While all the men were in terror, this boy thought of a plan. He believed that he knew how to bring down the big warrior, despite all his armor.

Finally, Dā'vid said: "If no one else will go, I will go out and fight with this enemy of the Lord's people."

They brought Dā'vid before King Ṣaul. Some years had passed since Saul had met Dā'vid, and Dā'vid had grown from a boy to a man, so that Ṣaul did not know him as the shepherd who had played on the harp before him in other days.

Ṣaul said to Dā'vid, "You cannot fight with this giant. You are very young; and he is a man of war, trained from his youth."

And Dā'vid answered King Ṣaul, "I am only a shepherd, but I have fought with lions and bears, when they have tried to steal my sheep. And I am not afraid to fight with this Phĭ-lĭs'tĭne. The Lord saved me from the lion's jaw and the bear's paw, and he will save me from this enemy, for I shall fight for the Lord and his people."

Then Ṣaul put his own armor on Dā'vid, a helmet on his head and a coat of mail on his body and a sword at his waist. But Ṣaul was almost a giant, and his armor was far too large for Dā'vid.

Dā'vid said: "I am not used to fighting with such weapons as these. Let me fight in my own way."

So Dā'vid took off Ṣaul's armor; for Dā'vid's plan to fight the giant did not need an armor, but did need a quick eye, a clear head, a sure aim, and a bold heart; and all these Dā'vid had, for God had given them to him. Dā'vid's plan was very wise. It was to make Gō-lī'ath think that his enemy was too weak for him to be on his guard against him; and while so far away that the giant could not reach him with sword or spear, to strike him down with a weapon which the giant would not expect and would not be prepared for.

Dā'vid took his shepherd's staff in his hand, as though that were to be his weapon. But out of sight, in a bag under his mantle, he had five smooth stones carefully chosen and a sling— the weapon he knew how to use. Then he came out to meet the Phĭ-lĭs'tĭne. The giant looked at the youth and despised him.

"Am I a dog," he said, "that this boy comes to me with a staff! I will give his body to the birds of the air and the beasts of the field."

And the Phĭ-lĭs'tĭne cursed Dā'vid by the gods of his people. And Dā'vid answered him:

"You come against me with a sword and a spear and a dart; but I come to you in the name of the Lord of hosts, the God of the armies of Iş'ra-el. This day will the Lord give you into my hand; I will strike you down and take off your head; and the hosts of the Phĭ-lĭs'tĭneş shall be dead bodies, to be eaten by the birds and the beasts; so that all may know that there is a God in Iş'ra-el, and that he can save in other ways besides with sword and spear."

And Dā'vid ran toward the Phĭ-lĭs'tĭne, as if to fight him with his shepherd's staff. But when he was just near enough for a good aim, he took out his sling and hurled a stone aimed at the giant's forehead. Dā'vid's aim was good, the stone struck the Phĭ-lĭs'tĭne in his forehead. It stunned him and he fell to the ground.

While the two armies stood wondering and scarcely knowing what had caused the giant to fall so suddenly, Dā'vid ran forward, drew out the giant's own sword, and cut off his head.

Then the Phĭ-lĭs'tĭneş knew that their great warrior, in whom they trusted, was dead. They turned to fly back to their own land; and the Iş'ra-el-ītes followed after them and killed them by the hundred and thousand, even to the gates of their own city of Găth.

So in that day Dā'vid won a great victory; and stood before all the land as the one who had saved his people from their enemies.

The Little Boy Looking for the Arrows

FTER Dā'vid had slain the giant, he was brought before King Saul, still holding the giant's head. Saul did not remember in this bold fighting man the boy who a few years before had played in his presence. He took him into his house and made him an officer among his soldiers. Dā'vid was as wise and as brave in the army as he had been when facing the giant, and very soon he was in command of a thousand men. All the men loved him, both in Saul's court and in his camp, for Dā'vid had the spirit that drew all hearts toward him.

When Dā'vid was returning from his battle with the Phǐ-lǐs'-tǐnes, the women of Ĭṣ'ra-el came to meet him out of the cities, with instruments of music, singing and dancing, and they sang:

> "Saul has slain his thousands,
> And Dā'vid his ten thousands."

This made Saul very angry, for he was jealous and suspicious in his spirit. He thought constantly of Săm'u-el's words, that God would take the kingdom from him and would give it to one who was more worthy of it. He began to think that perhaps this young man, who had come in a single day to greatness before the people, might try to make himself king.

His former feeling of unhappiness again came over Saul. He raved in his house, talking as a man talks who is crazed. By this time they all knew that Dā'vid was a musician, and they called him again to play on his harp and to sing before the troubled king. But now, in his madness, Saul would not listen to Dā'vid's voice. Twice he threw his spear at him, but each time Dā'vid leaped aside and the spear went into the wall of the house.

232

Saul was afraid of Dā′vid, for he saw that the Lord was with Dā′vid, as the Lord was no longer with himself. He would have killed Dā′vid, but he did not dare kill him, because everybody loved Dā′vid. Saul said to himself, "Though I cannot kill him myself, I will have him killed by the Phĭ-lĭs′tĭneṣ."

And he sent Dā′vid out on dangerous errands of war; but Dā′vid came home in safety, all the greater and the more beloved after each victory. Saul said, "I will give you my daughter Mē′răb for your wife if you will fight the Phĭ-lĭs′tĭneṣ for me."

Dā′vid fought the Phĭ-lĭs′tĭneṣ; but when he came home from the war, he found that Mē′răb, who had been promised to him, had been given as wife to another man. Saul had another daughter, named Mĭ′chal. She loved Dā′vid and showed her love for him. Then Saul sent word to Dā′vid, saying, "You shall have Mĭ′chal, my daughter, for your wife when you have killed a hundred Phĭ-lĭs′tĭneṣ."

Then Dā′vid went out and fought the Phĭ-lĭs′tĭneṣ and killed two hundred of them; and they brought the word to Saul. Then Saul gave him his daughter Mĭ′chal as his wife; but he was all the more afraid of Dā′vid as he saw him growing in power and drawing nearer to the throne of the kingdom.

But if Saul hated Dā′vid, Saul's son, Jŏn′a-than, loved Dā′vid with all his heart. This was the brave young warrior of whom we read in Story Two of this Part, who with his armor-bearer went out alone to fight the Phĭ-lĭs′tĭne army. Jŏn′a-than saw Dā′vid's courage and nobility of soul, and loved him with all his heart. He took off his own royal robe and his sword and his bow and gave them all to Dā′vid. It grieved Jŏn′a-than greatly that his father, Saul, was so jealous of Dā′vid. He spoke to his father, and said: "Let not the king do harm to Dā′vid; for Dā′vid has been faithful to the king, and he has done great things for the kingdom. He took his life in his hand and killed the Phĭ-lĭs′tĭne, and thus won a great victory for the Lord and for the people. Why should you seek to kill an innocent man?"

For the time Saul listened to Jŏn′a-than and said, "As the Lord lives, Dā′vid shall not be put to death."

And again Dā′vid sat at the king's table, among the princes; and

when Saul was troubled again, Dā'vid played on his harp and sang before him. But once more Saul's jealous anger arose and he threw his spear at Dā'vid. Dā'vid was watchful and quick. He leaped aside and, as before, the spear fastened into the wall.

Saul sent men to Dā'vid's house to seize him; but Mī'chal, Saul's daughter, who was Dā'vid's wife, let Dā'vid down out of the window, so that he escaped. She placed an image on Dā'vid's bed and covered it with the bedclothes. When the men came, she said, "Dā'vid is ill in the bed and cannot go."

They brought the word to Saul, and he said, "Bring him to me in the bed, just as he is."

When the image was found in Dā'vid's bed, Dā'vid was in a safe place, far away. Dā'vid went to Săm'u-el at Rā'mah, and stayed with him among the men who were prophets worshiping God and singing and speaking God's word. Saul heard that Dā'vid was there and sent men to take him. But when these men came and saw Săm'u-el and the prophets praising God and praying, the same spirit came on them and they began to praise and to pray. Saul sent other men, but these also, when they came among the prophets, felt the same power and joined in the worship.

Finally, Saul said, "If no other man will bring Dā'vid to me, I will go myself and take him."

And Saul went to Rā'mah; but when he came near to the company of the worshipers, praising God and praying and preaching, the same spirit came on Saul. He, too, began to join in the songs and the prayers, and stayed there all that day and that night, wor-

hiping God very earnestly. When the next day he went again to
his home in Gĭb'e-ah, his feeling was changed for the time and he
was again friendly to Dā'vid.

But Dā'vid knew that Saul was at heart his bitter enemy and
would kill him if he could as soon as his madness came upon him.
He met Jŏn'a-than out in the field away from Saul's home. Jŏn'a-
han said to Dā'vid:

"Stay away from the king's table for a few days, and I will find
out how he feels toward you and will tell you. Perhaps even now
my father may become your friend. But if he is to be your enemy,
know that the Lord is with you and that Saul will not succeed
against you. Promise me that as long as you live you will be kind
to me, and not only to me while I live, but to my children after
me."

Jŏn'a-than believed, as many others believed, that Dā'vid would
yet become the king of Ĭs'ra-el, and he was willing to give up to
Dā'vid his right to be king, such was his great love for him. That
day a promise was made between Jŏn'a-than and Dā'vid that they
and their children, and those who should come after them, should
be friends forever.

Jŏn'a-than said to Dā'vid, "I will find how my father feels
toward you and will bring you word. After three days I will be
here with my bow and arrows, and I will send a little boy out near
your place of hiding, and I will shoot three arrows. If I say to the
boy, 'Run, find the arrows, they are on this side of you,' then you
can come safely, for the king will not harm you. But if I call out
to the boy, 'The arrows are away beyond you,' that will mean that
there is danger, and you must hide from the king."

So Dā'vid stayed away from Saul's table for two days. At first
Saul said nothing of his absence, but at last he said:

"Why has not the son of Jĕs'se come to meals yesterday and
today?"

And Jŏn'a-than said, "Dā'vid asked leave of me to go to his
home at Bĕth'lĕ-hĕm and visit his oldest brother."

Then Saul was very angry. He cried out, "You are a disobedient
son! Why have you chosen this enemy of mine as your best
friend? Do you not know that as long as he is alive, you can never

be king? Send after him and let him be brought to me, for he shall surely die!"

Saul was so fierce in his anger that he threw his spear at his own son Jŏn′a-than. Jŏn′a-than rose up from the table, so angry at his father and so anxious for his friend Dā′vid that he could eat nothing. The next day, at the hour agreed upon, Jŏn′a-than went out into the field with a little boy. He said to the boy, "Run out yonder and be ready to find the arrows that I shoot."

And as the boy was running, Jŏn′a-than shot arrows beyond him, and he called out, "The arrows are away beyond you; run quickly and find them."

The boy ran and found the arrows and brought them to Jŏn′a-than. He gave the bow and arrows to the boy, saying to him, "Take them back to the city. I will stay here awhile."

And as soon as the boy was out of sight, Dā′vid came from his hiding place and ran to Jŏn′a-than. They fell into each other's arms and kissed each other again and again, and wept together. For Dā′vid knew now that he must no longer hope to be safe in Saul's hands. He must leave home and wife and friends and his father's house, and hide wherever he could from the hate of King Saul.

Jŏn′a-than said to him, "Go in peace; for we have sworn together saying, 'The Lord shall be between you and me, and between your children and my children forever.' "

Then Jŏn′a-than went again to his father's palace, and Dā′vid went out to find a hiding place.

Where David Found the Giant's Sword

FROM his meeting with Jŏn'a-than, Dā'vid went forth to be a wanderer, having no home as long as Sạul lived. He went away so suddenly that he was without either bread to eat or a sword for defense. On his way he called at a little city called Nŏb, where the Tabernacle was then standing, although the holy ark was still in another place by itself. The chief priest, Ā-hĭm'e-lĕch, was surprised to see Dā'vid coming alone.

Dā'vid said to him, "The king has sent me upon an errand of which no one is to be told, and my men are to meet me in a secret place. Can you give me a few loaves of bread?"

"There is no bread here," said the priest, "except the holy bread from the table in the holy house. The priests have just taken it away to put new bread in its place."

"Let me have that bread," said Dā'vid, "for we are the Lord's and are holy."

So the priest gave Dā'vid the holy bread, which was to be eaten by the priests alone. Dā'vid said also, "Have you a spear or a sword, which I can take with me? The king's errand was so sudden that I had no time to bring my weapons."

"There is no sword here," said the priest, "except the sword of Gŏ-lī'ath of Găth, whom you slew in the valley of Ē'lah. It is wrapped in a cloth, in the closet with the priest's robe. If you wish that sword, you can have it."

"There is no sword like that," said Dā'vid; "give it to me." So Dā'vid took the giant's sword and five loaves of bread and went away. But where should he go? Nowhere in Sạul's kingdom would he be safe; and he went down to live among his old enemies, the Phĭ-lĭs'tĭneṣ, on the plain.

But the Phĭ-lĭs'tĭneṣ had not forgotten Dā'vid, who had slain

237

their great Gŏ-lī′ath and beaten them in many battles. They would
have seized him and killed him; but Dā′vid acted as though he were
crazy. Then the king of the Phĭ-lĭs′tĭneṣ said, "Let this poor crazy
man go! We do not want him here."

And Dā′vid escaped from among them, and went to live in the
wilderness of Jū′dah. He found a great cave, called the cave of
Ȧ-dŭl′lăm, and hid in it. Many people heard where he was, and
from all parts of the land, especially from his own tribe of Jū′ḍah,
men who were not satisfied with the rule of King Sạul, gathered
around Dā′vid. Soon he had a little army of four hundred men,
who followed Dā′vid as their captain.

All of these men with Dā′vid were good fighters and some of
them were very brave in battle. Three of these men at one time
wrought a great deed for Dā′vid. While Dā′vid was in the great
cave with his men, the Phĭ-lĭs′tĭneṣ were holding the town of Bĕth′-
lĕ-hĕm, which had been Dā′vid's home. Dā′vid said one day,
"How I wish that I could have a drink of the water from the well
that is beside the gate of Bĕth′lĕ-hĕm!"

This was the well from which he had drawn water and drank
when a boy; and it seemed to him that there was no water so good
to his taste.

Those three brave men went out together, walked to Bĕth′lĕ-
hĕm, fought their way through the Phĭ-lĭs′tĭneṣ, who were on

guard, drew a vessel of water from the well, and then fought their way back through the enemies. But when they brought the water to Dā'vid, he would not drink it. He said: "This water was bought by the blood of three brave men. I will not drink it; but I will pour it out as an offering to the Lord, for it is sacred." So Dā'vid poured out the water as a most precious gift to the Lord. Saul soon heard that Dā'vid, with a band of men, was hiding among the mountains of Jū'dah. One day while Saul was sitting in Gĭb'e-ah, out of doors under a tree, with his nobles around him, he said, "You are men of my own tribe of Bĕn'ja-mĭn, yet none of you will help me to find this son of Jĕs'se, who has made an agreement with my own son against me, and who has gathered an army and is waiting to rise against me. Is no one of you with me and against mine enemy?"

One man, whose name was Dō'eg, an Ē'dom-īte, said, "I was at the city of the priests some time ago, and saw the son of Jĕs'se come to the chief priest, Ā-hĭm'e-lĕch; and the priest gave him loaves of bread and a sword." "Send for Ā-hĭm'e-lĕch and all the priests," commanded King Saul; and they took all the priests as prisoners, eighty-five men in all, and brought them before King Saul. And Saul said to them, "Why have you priests joined with Dā'vid, the son of Jĕs'se, to rebel against me, the king? You have given him bread and a sword, and have shown yourselves his friends."

Then Ā-hĭm'e-lĕch, the priest, answered the king, "There is no one among all the king's servants as faithful as Dā'vid; and he is the king's son-in-law, living in the palace, and sitting in the king's council. What wrong have I done in giving him bread? I knew nothing of any evil that he had wrought against the king."

Then the king was very angry. He said, "You shall die, Ā-hĭm'-e-lĕch, and all your father's family, because you have helped this man, my enemy. You knew that he was hiding from me and did not tell me of him."

And the king ordered his guards to kill all the priests. But they would not obey him, for they felt that it was a dreadful deed to lay hands upon the priests of the Lord. This made Saul all the more furious, and he turned to Dō'eg, the Ē'dom-īte, the man who had told of Dā'vid's visit to the priest, and Saul said to Dō'eg, "You are the only one among my servants who is true to me. Do you kil these priests who have been unfaithful to their king."

And Dō'eg, the Ē'dom-īte, obeyed the king, and killed eighty-five men who wore the priestly garments. He went to the city of the priests, and killed all their wives and children, and burned the city.

One priest alone escaped, a young man named Ȧ-bī'a-thär, the son of Ȧ-hĭm'e-lĕch. He came to Dā'vid with the terrible news that Saul had slain all the priests, and he brought the high priest's breastplate and his robes.

Dā'vid said to him, "I saw this man Dō'eg, the Ē'dom-īte, there on that day and I knew that he would tell Saul. Without intending to do harm, I have caused the death of all your father's house. Stay with me and fear not. I will care for your life with my own."

Ȧ-bī'a-thär was now the high priest, and he was with Dā'vid and not with Saul. All through the land went the news of Saul's dreadful deed, and everywhere the people began to turn from Saul and to look toward Dā'vid as the only hope of the nation.

Story Eight   I SAMUEL 23 : 1 to 27 : 12

How David Spared Saul's Life

AFTER this Dā'vid and his men hid in many places in the mountains of Jū'dah, often hunted by Saul, but always escaping from him. At one time Jŏn'a-than, Saul's son, came to meet Dā'vid in a forest, and he said to him, "Fear not, for the Lord is with you; and Saul, my father, shall not take you prisoner. You will yet be the king of Is'ra-el, and I shall stand next to you."

And Jŏn'a-than and Dā'vid made again the promise to be true to each other and to each other's children always. Then they parted; and Dā'vid never again saw his dear friend, Jŏn'a-than.

At one time Dā'vid was hiding with a few men in a great cave near the Dead Sea, at a place called Ĕn=gē'dĭ. They were far back in the darkness of the cave, when they saw Saul come into the cave alone and lie down to sleep. Dā'vid's men whispered to him, "Now is the time of which the Lord said, 'I will give your enemy into your hand, and you may do to him whatever you please.'"

Then Dā'vid went toward Saul very quietly with his sword in his hand. His men looked to see him kill Saul, but instead, he only

cut off a part of Saul's long robe. His men were not pleased at this; but Dā'vid said to them, "May the Lord forbid that I should do harm to the man whom the Lord has anointed as king."

And Dā'vid would not allow his men to harm Saul. After a time Saul rose up from sleep and went out of the cave. Dā'vid followed him at a distance and called out to him. "My lord the king!"

Saul looked around, and there stood Dā'vid, bowing to him and holding up the piece of his royal robe. Dā'vid said to Saul, "My lord, O king, why do you listen to the words of men who tell you that Dā'vid is trying to do you harm? This very day the Lord gave you into my hand in the cave, and some told me to kill you, but I said, 'I will not do harm to my lord, for he is the Lord's anointed king.' See, my father, see the skirt of your robe. I cut it off to show you that I would do you no harm, though you are hunting after me to kill me. May the Lord judge between you and me, and may the Lord do justice for me upon you; but my hand shall not touch you."

When Saul heard these words, his old love for Dā'vid came back to him and he cried out, "Is that your voice, my son Dā'vid?" And Saul wept and said, "You are a better man than I am, for you have done good to me, while I have been doing harm to you. May the Lord reward you for your kindness to me this day! I know that it is God's will that you shall be king, and you will rule over this people. Now give to me your word, in the name of the Lord, that you will not destroy my family, but that you will spare their lives."

And Dā'vid gave his promise to Saul in the name of the Lord; and Saul led his men away from hunting Dā'vid to his palace at Gĭb'-e-ah; but Dā'vid kept still in his hiding place, for he could not trust Saul's promises to spare his life.

And it was not long before Saul was again seeking for Dā'vid in the wilderness of Jū'dah, with Ăb'nẽr, Saul's uncle, the commander of his army, and under him three thousand men. From his hiding place in the mountains Dā'vid looked down on the plain, and saw Saul's camp almost at his feet. That night Dā'vid and Ā-bĭsh'a-ī, one of Dā'vid's men, came down quietly and walked into the middle of Saul's camp, while all his guards were asleep. Saul himself was sleeping, with his spear standing in the ground at his head, and a bottle of water tied to it.

Ā-bĭsh'a-ī, Dā'vid's follower, knew that Dā'vid would not kill King Saul, and he said to Dā'vid, "God has given your enemy into your hand again. Let me strike him through to the ground at one stroke; only once; I will not need to strike twice."

But Dā'vid said, "You shall not destroy him. Who can strike the anointed of the Lord without being guilty of a crime? Let the Lord strike him, or let him die when God wills it, or let him fall in battle; but he shall not die by my hand. Let us take his spear and his water bottle, and let us go."

So Dā'vid took Saul's spear and his bottle of water, and then Dā'vid and Ā-bĭsh'a-ī walked out of the camp without awakening anyone. In the morning Dā'vid called out to Saul's men and to Ăb'nēr, the chief of Saul's army, "Ăb'nēr, where are you? Why do you not answer, Ăb'nēr?"

And Ăb'nēr answered, "Who are you, calling to the camp?" Then Dā'vid said, "Are you not a great man, Ăb'nēr? Who is like you in all Iṣ'ra-el? Why have you not kept your watch over the king? You deserve to be put to death for your neglect! See, here is the king's spear and his bottle of water!"

Saul knew Dā'vid's voice, and he said, "Is that your voice, my son Dā'vid?"

And Dā'vid answered, "It is my voice, my lord, O king. Why do you pursue me? What evil have I done? May God deal with the men who have stirred you up against me. I am not worth all the trouble you are taking to hunt for me. The king of Iṣ'ra-el is seeking for one who is as small as a flea or a little bird in the mountains!"

Then Saul said, "I have done wrong; come back, my son Dā'vid, and I will no longer try to do harm to you, for you have spared my life today!" Dā'vid said, "Let one of the young men come and take the king's spear. As I have spared your life today, may the Lord spare mine."

So Dā'vid went his way, for he would not trust himself in Saul's hands, and Saul led his men back to his home at Gĭb'e-ah. Dā'vid now was leading quite an army and was a powerful ruler. He made an agreement with the king of the Phĭ-lĭs'tĭneṣ who lived at Găth, King Ā'chish, and went down to the plain by the Great Sea, to live among the Phĭ-lĭs'tĭneṣ. And Ā'chish gave him a city called Zĭk'lăg, on the south of the tribe land of Jū'dah. To this place Dā'vid took his followers, and there he lived during the last years of Saul's reign.

The Last Days of King Saul

ONCE more the Phĭ-lĭs'tĭneş gathered together to make war on King Saul and the land of Iş'ra-el. The king of the Phĭ-lĭs'tĭneş, Ā'chish, sent for Dā'vid and said to him, "You and your men shall go with me in the army and shall fight with us against the men of Iş'ra-el."

For Dā'vid was now living in the Phĭ-lĭs'tĭne country, and under their rule. So Dā'vid came from Zĭk'lăg, with all his six hundred men, and they stood among the armies of the Phĭ-lĭs'tĭneş. But when the lords of the Phĭ-lĭs'tĭneş saw Dā'vid and his men, they said, "Why are these Iş'ra-el-ītes here? Is not this the man of whom they sang:

"'Saul slew his thousands,
And Dā'vid his ten thousands.'

Will not this man turn from us in the battle and make his peace with his king by fighting against us? This man shall not go with us to the war."

Then Ā'chish, the king of the Phĭ-lĭs'tĭneş, sent away Dā'vid and his men, so that Dā'vid was not compelled to fight against his own people. But when he came to his own city, Zĭk'lăg, he found it had been burned and destroyed; and all the people in it, the wives and children of Dā'vid's men, and Dā'vid's own wives also, had been carried away by the Ăm'a-lĕk-ītes into the desert on the south.

The Lord spoke to Dā'vid through the high priest, Ȧ-bī'a-thär, saying, "Pursue these men and you will overtake them and take back all that they have carried away."

So Dā'vid followed the Ăm'a-lĕk-ītes into the wilderness. His march was so swift that a part of his men could not endure it, but stopped to rest at the brook Bē'sôr, while four hundred men went on with Dā'vid. He found the Ăm'a-lĕk-ītes in their camp, without guards, feasting upon the spoil that they had taken. And

Dā'vid and his men fell upon them suddenly and killed all of them, except four hundred men who escaped on camels far into the desert, where Dā'vid could not follow them. And Dā'vid took from these robbers all the women and children that they had carried away from Zĭk'lăg, and among them Dā'vid's own two wives; also he took a great amount of treasure and of spoil, not only all that these men had found in Zĭk'lăg, but what they had taken in many other places.

Dā'vid divided all these things between himself and his men, giving as much to those who had stayed at the brook Bē'sôr as to those who had fought with the Ăm'a-lĕk-ītes. This treasure taken from the Ăm'a-lĕk-ītes made Dā'vid very rich; and from it he sent presents to many of his friends in the tribe of Jū'dah.

While Dā'vid was pursuing his enemies in the south, the Phĭ-lĭs'tĭnes were gathering a great host in the middle of the land, on the plain of Ĕs-dra-ē'lon, at the foot of Mount Gĭl-bō'à. Saul and his men were on the side of Mount Gĭl-bō'à, near the same spring where Gĭd'e-on's men drank, as we read in Story Ten in Part Second. But there was no one like Gĭd'e-on now, to lead the men of Ĭs'ra-el, for King Saul was old and weakened by disease and trouble; Săm'u-el had died many years before; Dā'vid was no longer by his side; Saul had slain the priests, through whom in those times God spoke to men; and Saul was utterly alone and knew not what to do, as he saw the mighty host of the Phĭ-lĭs'tĭnes on the plain. And the Lord had forsaken Saul and would give him no word in his sore need.

Saul heard that there was living at Ĕn'dôr, on the north side of the Hill Mō'reh, not far from his camp, a woman who could call up the spirits of the dead. Whether she could really do this or only pretended to do it, we do not know, for the Bible does not tell. But Saul was so anxious to have some message from the Lord, that at night he sought this woman. He took off his kingly robes and came dressed as a common man and said to her, "Bring me up from the dead the spirit of a man whom I greatly long to meet."

And the woman said, "What spirit shall I call up?"

And Saul answered, "Bring me up the spirit of Săm'u-el, the prophet."

Then the woman called for the spirit of Săm'u-el; and whether spirits had ever arisen from the dead before or not, at that time the Lord allowed the spirit of Săm'u-el to rise up from his place among the dead, to speak to King Saul.

When the woman saw Săm'u-el's spirit, she was filled with fear. She cried out, and Saul said to her, "Do not fear; but tell me whom you see."

For Saul himself could not see the spirit whom the woman saw. And she said, "I see one like a god rising up. He is an old man, covered with a long robe."

Then out of the darkness a voice came from the spirit whom Saul's eyes could not see. "Why have you troubled me and called me out of my rest?"

And Saul answered Săm'u-el, "I am in great distress, for the Phĭ-lĭs'tĭnes make war upon me and God has forsaken me. He will not speak to me either by a prophet or a priest or in a dream. And I have called upon you that you may tell me what to do." And the spirit of Săm'u-el said to Saul, "If the Lord has forsaken you and has become your enemy, why do you call upon me to help you? The Lord has dealt with you as I warned you that he would do. Because you would not obey the Lord, he has taken the kingdom away from you and your house and has given it to Dā'vid. And the Lord will give Ĭs'ra-el into the hands of the Phĭ-lĭs'tĭnes; and tomorrow you and your three sons shall be as I am, among the dead." And then the spirit of Săm'u-el the prophet passed from sight. When Saul heard these words, he fell down as one dead, for he was very weak, as he had taken no food all that day. The woman and Saul's servants who were with him raised him up and gave him food and tried to speak to him words of cheer. Then Saul and his men went over the mountain to their camp.

On the next day a great battle was fought on the side of Mount Gĭl-bō'a. The Phĭ-lĭs'tĭnes did not wait for Saul's warriors to attack them. They climbed up the mountain and fell upon the Ĭs'ra-el-ĭtes in their camp. Many of the men of Ĭs'ra-el were slain in the fight and many more fled away. Saul's three sons were killed, one of them, the brave and noble Jŏn'a-than.

When Saul saw that the battle had gone against him, that his sons were slain and that the enemies were pressing closely upon him, he called to his armor-bearer and said, "Draw your sword and kill me; it would be better for me to die by your hand than for the Phĭ-lĭs'tĭnes̱ to come upon me and slaughter me."

But the armor-bearer would not draw his sword upon his king, the Lord's anointed. Then Saul took his own sword and fell upon it and killed himself among the bodies of his own men.

On the next day the Phĭ-lĭs'tĭnes̱ came to strip off the armor and carry away the weapons of those who had been slain. The crown of King Saul and the bracelet on his arm already had been carried away; but the Phĭ-lĭs'tĭnes̱ took off his armor and sent it to the temple of their idol, Dā'gon; and the body of Saul and those of his three sons they fastened to the wall of Bĕth'shăn, a Cā'năan-īte city in the valley of the Jôr'dan.

You remember how Saul, in the beginning of his reign, had rescued the city of Jā'besh=g̱ĭl'e-ăd from the Ăm'mon-ītes. The men of Jā'besh had not forgotten Saul's brave deed. When they heard what had been done with the body of Saul, they rose up in the night and went down the mountains and walked across a shallow place in the Jôr'dan, and came to Bĕth'shăn. They took down

from the wall the bodies of Saul and his sons and carried them to Jā'besh; and that they might not be taken away again, they burned them and buried their ashes under a tree; and they mourned for Saul seven days. Thus came to an end the reign of Saul, which began well, but ended in failure and in ruin, because Saul forsook the Lord God of Iṣ'ra-el.

Saul had reigned forty years. At the beginning of his reign the Iṣ'ra-el-ītes were almost free from the Phĭ-lĭs'tĭneṣ, and for a time Saul seemed to have success in driving the Phĭ-lĭs'tĭneṣ out of the land. But after Saul forsook the Lord and would no longer listen to Săm'u-el, God's prophet, he became gloomy and full of fear and lost his courage, so that the land fell again under the power of its enemies. Dā'vid could have helped him, but he had driven Dā'vid away; and there was no strong man to stand by Saul and win victories for him. So at the end, when Saul fell in battle, the yoke of the Phĭ-lĭs'tĭneṣ was on Iṣ'ra-el heavier than at any time before.

Story Ten   II SAMUEL 1 : 1 to 4 : 12

The Shepherd Boy Becomes a King

O N THE third day after the battle on Mount Gĭl-bō'à, Dā'vid was at his home in Zĭk'lăg, on the south of Jū'dah, when a young man came into the town, running, with garments torn and earth on his head, as was the manner of those in deep grief. He hastened to Dā'vid and fell down before him. And Dā'vid said to him, "From what place have you come?"

And the young man said, "Out of the camp of Iṣ'ra-el I have escaped."

And Dā'vid said to him, "What has taken place? Tell me quickly."

Then the man answered, "The men of Iṣ'ra-el have been beaten in the battle; very many of them are slain and the rest have fled away. King Saul is dead and so is Jŏn′a-than, his son."

"How do you know that Saul and Jŏn′a-than are dead?" asked Dā′vid.

And the young man said, "I happened to be on Mount Gĭl-bō′à in the battle; and I saw Saul leaning upon his spear wounded and near death, with his enemies close upon him. And he said to me, 'Come to me and kill me, for I am suffering great pain.' So I stood beside and killed him, for I saw that he could not live. And I took

the crown that was on his head and the bracelet on his arm and I have brought them to you, my lord Dā′vid."

Then Dā′vid and all the men that were with him tore their clothes and mourned and wept and took no food on that day, on account of Saul and of Jŏn′a-than, and for the people of Ĭṣ′ra-el who had fallen by the sword.

And Dā′vid said to the young man who had brought to him the news, "Who are you? To what people do you belong?"

And he said, "I am no Ĭṣ′ra-el-īte; I am an Ăm′a-lĕk-īte."

"How was it," said Dā′vid to him, "that you were not afraid to slay the king of Ĭṣ′ra-el, the anointed of the Lord? You shall die for this deed."

And Dā′vid commanded one of his men to kill him, because he had said that he had slain the king. He may have told the truth, but it is more likely that he was not in the battle, and that after the fighting, he came upon the field to rob the dead bodies, and that he brought a false story of having slain Saul, hoping to have a reward. But as Dā'vid would not slay the anointed king, even though he was his enemy, he would not reward, but would rather punish the stranger who claimed to have slain him.

Dā'vid wrote this song over the death of Saul and Jŏn'a-than:

Thy glory, O Ĭs'ra-el, is slain upon thy high places!
How are the mighty fallen!
Tell it not in Găth.
Publish it not in the streets of Ăs'ke-lon;
Lest the daughters of the Phĭ-lĭs-tĭnes rejoice,
Lest the daughters of the heathen triumph.
Ye mountains of Gĭl-bō'a,
Let there be no dew nor rain upon you, neither fields of offerings:
For there the shield of the mighty was cast away as a vile thing,
The shield of Saul, not anointed with oil.
From the blood of the slain, from the fat of the mighty,
The bow of Jŏn'a-than turned not back,
And the sword of Saul returned not empty.
Saul and Jŏn'a-than were lovely and pleasant in their lives,
And in their death they were not divided;
They were swifter than eagles,
They were stronger than lions.
Ye daughters of Ĭs'ra-el, weep over Saul,
Who clothed you in scarlet delicately,
Who put ornaments of gold upon your apparel.
O Jŏn'a-than, slain upon thy high places!
I am distressed for thee, my brother Jŏn'a-than.
Very pleasant hast thou been unto me;
Thy love to me was wonderful,
Passing the love of women.
How are the mighty fallen,
And the weapons of war perished!

After this, at the command of the Lord, Dā'vid and his men went up from Zĭk'lăg to Hē'bron, in the middle of the tribe land of Jū'dah. And the men of Jū'dah met together at Hē'bron, and they made Dā'vid king over their tribe. And Dā'vid reigned in Hē'bron, over the tribe of Jū'dah, for seven years.

But Saul's uncle, Ăb'nēr, who had been the chief over his house and over his army, was not willing to have the kingdom go out of the family of Saul. He made a son of Saul king over all the tribes in the north of the land. This king was called Ĭsh=bō′sheth, a name which means "A worthless man." He was weak and helpless, except for the strong will and power of Ăb′nēr, who had made him king. For six years seemingly under Ĭsh=bō′sheth, but really under Ăb′nēr, the form of a kingdom was kept up, while Ĭsh=bō′sheth was living at Mā-hȧ-na′im, on the east of Jôr′dan.

Thus for a time there were two kingdoms in Ĭṣ′ra-el, that of the north under Ĭsh=bō′sheth, and that of the south under Dā′vid. But all the time Dā′vid's kingdom was growing stronger and Ĭsh=bō′-sheth's kingdom was growing weaker.

After a time Ăb′nēr was slain by one of Dā′vid's men, and at once Ĭsh=bō′sheth's power dropped away. Then two men of his army killed him and cut off his head and brought it to Dā′vid. They looked for a reward, since Ĭsh=bō′sheth had been king against Dā′vid. But Dā′vid said, "As the Lord lives, who has brought me out of trouble, I will give no reward to wicked men who have slain a good man in his own house and upon his own bed. Take these two murderers away and killed them!"

So the two slayers of the weak king, Ĭsh=bō′sheth, were punished with death. Dā′vid had not forgotten his promise to Saul to deal kindly with his children.

Story Eleven   II SAMUEL 5 : 1 to 7 : 29

The Sound in the Treetops

AFTER Dā′vid had reigned as king over the tribe of Jū′dah for seven years, and when Saul's son, Ĭsh=bō′sheth, was dead, all the men in Ĭṣ′ra-el saw that Dā′vid was the one man who was fit to be king over the land. So the rulers and elders of all the twelve tribes came to Dā′vid in Hē′bron and said to him, "We are all your brothers; and in time past, when Saul was king, it was you who led the people to war: and the Lord said, 'Dā'vid shall be the shepherd of my people and shall be prince over Ĭṣ'ra-el.' Now we are ready to make you king over all the land."

Then Dā'vid and the elders of Ĭṣ'ra-el made an agreement together before the Lord in Hē'bron; and they anointed Dā'vid as king over all the twelve tribes of Ĭṣ'ra-el, from Dăn in the far north to Bē'er=shē'bȧ in the south. Dā'vid was now thirty-seven years old, and he reigned over all Ĭṣ'ra-el thirty-three years.

He found the land in a helpless state, everywhere under the power of the Phĭ-lĭs'tĭneṣ, and with many of its cities still held by the Cā'năan-īte people. The city of Jĕ-rụ'sȧ-lĕm, on Mount Zī'ŏn, had been kept as a stronghold by a Cā'năan-īte tribe called the Jĕb'u-sītes, ever since the days of Jŏsh'u-ȧ. Dā'vid led his men of war against it, but the Jĕb'u-sītes, from their high walls and steep rocks, laughed at him.

To mock King Dā'vid, they placed on the top of the wall the blind and lame people, and they called aloud to Dā'vid, "Even blind men and lame men can keep you out of our city."

This made Dā'vid very angry, and he said to his men, "Whoever first climbs up the wall and strikes down the blind and the lame upon it, he shall be the chief captain and general of the whole army."

Then all the soldiers of Dā'vid rushed against the wall, each striving to be first. The man who was able first to reach the enemies and strike them down was Jō'ăb, the son of Dā'vid's sister Zĕr-u-ī'ah; and he became the commander of Dā'vid's army, a place which he held as long as Dā'vid lived. After the fortress on Mount Zī'ŏn was taken from the Jĕb'u-sītes, Dā'vid made it larger and stronger, and chose it for his royal house; and around it the city of Jĕ-rụ'sȧ-lĕm grew up as the chief city in Dā'vid's kingdom.

The Phĭ-lĭs'tĭneṣ soon found that there was a new king in Ĭṣ'ra-el and a ruler very different from King Sạul. They gathered their army and came against Dā'vid. He met them in the valley of Rĕph'a-ĭm, a little to the south of Jĕ-rụ'sȧ-lĕm, and won a great victory over them and carried away from the field the images of their gods; but that the Ĭṣ'ra-el-ītes might not be led to worship them, Dā'vid burned them all with fire.

A second time the Phĭ-lĭs'tĭneṣ came up and encamped in the valley of Rĕph'a-ĭm. And when Dā'vid asked of the Lord what he should do, the Lord said to him, "Do not go against them openly. Turn to one side, and be ready to come against them from under the mulberry trees; and wait there until you hear a sound overhead in the tops of the trees. When you hear that sound, it will be a sign that the Lord goes before you. Then march forth and fight the Phĭ-lĭs'tĭneṣ."

And Dā'vid did as the Lord commanded him; and again a great victory was won over the Phĭ-lĭs'tĭneṣ. But Dā'vid did not rest when he had driven the Phĭ-lĭs'tĭneṣ back to their own land. He marched with his men into the Phĭ-lĭs'tĭnes' country and took their chief city, Găth, which was called "The mother city of the Phĭ-lĭs'-tĭneṣ." He conquered all their land and ended the war of a hundred years by making all the Phĭ-lĭs'tĭne plain subject to Ĭṣ'ra-el.

Now that the land was free, Dā'vid thought that the time had come to bring the holy ark of the Lord out from its hiding place, where it had remained all through the rule of Săm'u-el and the reign of Saul. This was in Kĭr'jath=jē'a-rĭm, called also Bā'al-ē, a town on the northern border of Jū'dah. Dā'vid prepared for the ark a new Tabernacle on Mount Zī'ŏn; and with the chosen men of all the tribes, he went to bring up the ark to Mount Zī'ŏn.

They did not have the ark carried by the priests, as it had been taken from place to place in the earlier days; but they stood it on a wagon, to be drawn by oxen, driven by the sons of the man in whose house the ark had been standing, though these men were not priests. And before the ark walked Dā'vid and the men of Ĭṣ'ra-el, making music upon all kinds of musical instruments.

At one place the road was rough, and the oxen stumbled, and the ark almost fell from the wagon. Ŭz'zah, one of the men driving the oxen, took hold of the ark to steady it. God's law forbade anyone except a priest from touching the ark, and God was displeased with Ŭz'zah for his carelessness; and Ŭz'zah fell dead by the ark of the Lord.

This death alarmed Dā'vid and all the people. Dā'vid was afraid to have the ark of God come into his city. He stopped the procession and placed the ark in the house near by of a man named

O'bed=ē'dom. There it stayed three months. They were afraid that it might bring harm to O'bed=ē'dom and his family; but instead it brought a blessing upon them all.

When Dā'vid heard of the blessings that had come to O'bed=ē'dom with the ark, he resolved to bring it into his own city on Mount Zī'ŏn. This time the priests carried it as the law commanded, and sacrifices were offered upon the altar. They brought up the ark into its new home on Mount Zī'ŏn, where a Tabernacle was standing ready to receive it. Then the priests began to offer the daily sacrifices and the services of worship were held, after having been neglected through so many years.

Dā'vid was now living in his palace on Mount Zī'ŏn, and he thought of building a temple to take the place of the Tabernacle, for the ark and its services. He said to Nā'than, who was a prophet, through whom the Lord spoke to the people, "See, now I live in a house of cedar; but the ark of God stands within the curtains of a tent."

"Go, do all that is in your heart," answered Nā'than, the prophet, "for the Lord is with you."

And that night the voice of the Lord came to Nā'than, saying, "Go and tell my servant Dā'vid, thus saith the Lord, 'Since the time when the children of Is'ra-el came out of Ē'ġy̆pt, my ark has been in a tent; and I have never said to the people, build me a house of cedar.' Say to my servant Dā'vid, 'I took you from the sheep pasture, where you were following the sheep, and I have made you a prince over my people Is'ra-el, and I have given you a great name and great power. And now, because you have done my will, I will give you a house. Your son shall sit on the throne after you, and he shall build me a house and a Temple. And I will give you and

your children and your descendants, those who shall come from
you, a throne and a kingdom that shall last forever.' "

This promise of God, that under Dā'vid's line should rise a kingdom to last always, was fulfilled in Jē'ṣus Chrīst, who came long
afterward from the family of Dā'vid, and who reigns as King in
heaven and in earth.

Story Twelve   II SAMUEL 8 : I to 9 : 13

The Cripple at the King's Table

AS SOON as the kings of the nations around Iṣ'ra-el saw
that a strong man was ruling over the tribes, they
began to make war upon Dā'vid, for they feared to
see Iṣ'ra-el gaining in power. So it came to pass that
Dā'vid had many wars. The Mō'ab-ītes, who lived
on the east of the Dead Sea, went to war with Dā'vid, but Dā'vid
conquered them and made Mō'ab submit to Iṣ'ra-el. Far in the
north, the Sўr'ĭ-anṣ came against Dā'vid; but he won great victories over them and took Dȧ-mãs'cus, their chief city, and held it
as a part of his kingdom. In the south, he made war upon the
Ē'dom-ītes and brought them under his rule.

For a number of years Dā'vid was constantly at war, but at last
he was at peace, the ruler of all the lands from the great river Eū-
phrā'teṣ, on the north, down to the wilderness on the south, where
the Iṣ'ra-el-ītes had wandered; and from the great desert on the east
to the Great Sea on the west. All these lands were under the rule
of King Dā'vid, except the people of Tÿre and Sī'dŏn, who lived
beside the Great Sea on the north of Iṣ'ra-el. These people, the
Tÿr'ĭans, never made war on Iṣ'ra-el, and their king, Hī'ram, was
one of Dā'vid's best friends. The men of Tÿre cut down cedar
trees on Mount Lĕb'a-non for Dā'vid and brought them to Jĕ-rụ́-
sȧ-lĕm, and built for Dā'vid the palace which became his home.

When Dā'vid's wars were over and he was at rest, he thought of the promise that he had made to his friend Jŏn'a-than, the brave son of Saul (see Story Six in this Part), that he would care for his children. Dā'vid asked of his nobles and the men at his court, "Are there any of Saul's family living, to whom I can show kindness for the sake of Jŏn'a-than?"

They told Dā'vid of Saul's servant, Zī'bà, who had charge of Saul's farm in the country; and Dā'vid sent for him. Zī'bà had become a rich man from his care of the lands that had belonged to Saul.

Dā'vid said to Zī'bà, "Are there any of Saul's family living, to whom I can show some of the kindness which God has shown toward me?"

And Zī'bà said, "Saul's son, Jŏn'a-than, left a little boy, named Mĕ-phĭb'o-shĕth, who is now grown to be a man. He is living at Lŏ=dē'bär, on the east of Jôr'dan."

This child of Jŏn'a-than was in the arms of his nurse when the news came of the battle at Mount Gĭl-bō'à, where Jŏn'a-than was slain. The nurse fled with him, to hide from the Phĭ-lĭs'tĭnes, and in running, fell; and the child's feet were so injured that ever after he was lame.

Perhaps he was kept hidden in the distant place on the east of Jôr'dan, from fear lest Dā'vid, now that he was king, might try to kill all those who were of Saul's family; for such deeds were common in those times, when one king took the power away from another king's children.

Dā'vid sent for Mĕ-phĭb'o-shĕth, Jŏn'a-than's son; and he was brought into Dā'vid's presence, and fell down on his face before the king, for he was in great fear. And Dā'vid said to him, "Mĕ-phĭb'o-shĕth, you need have no fear. I will be kind to you, because I loved Jŏn'a-than, your father, and he loved me. You shall have all the lands that ever belonged to Saul and his family; and you shall always sit at my table in the royal palace."

Then the king called Zī'ba, who had been the servant of Saul, and said to him, "All the lands and houses that once belonged to Saul I have given to Mĕ-phĭb'o-shĕth. You shall care for them and bring the harvests and the fruits of the fields to him. But Mĕ-phĭb'o-shĕth shall live here with me and shall sit down at the king's table among the princes of the kingdom."

So Mĕ-phĭb'o-shĕth, the lame son of Jŏn'a-than, was taken into Dā'vid's palace and sat at the king's table, among the highest in the land. And Zī'ba, with his fifteen sons and his twenty servants, waited on him and stood at his command.

This kindness of Dā'vid to Mĕ-phĭb'o-shĕth might have brought trouble to Dā'vid; for Mĕ-phĭb'o-shĕth, the son of Jŏn'a-than, and the grandson of Saul, might have been the king if Dā'vid had not won the crown. By giving to Saul's grandson a place at his table, showing him honor, Dā'vid might have helped him to take the kingdom away from himself, if Mĕ-phĭb'o-shĕth had been a stronger man, with a purpose to win the throne of Ĭs'ra-el. But Dā'vid was generous, and Mĕ-phĭb'o-shĕth was grateful and was contented with his place in the palace.

The Prophet's Story of the Little Lamb

WHEN Dā'vid first became king, he went with his army upon the wars against the enemies of Ĭs'ra-el. But there came a time when the cares of his kingdom were many, and Dā'vid left Jō'ăb, his general, to lead his warriors, while he stayed in his palace on Mount Zī'ŏn.

One evening, about sunset, Dā'vid was walking upon the roof of his palace. He looked down into a garden near by and saw a woman, who was very beautiful. Dā'vid asked one of his servants who this woman was, and he said to him, "Her name is Băth'shĕ-bà, and she is the wife of U-rī'ah."

Now U-rī'ah was an officer in Dā'vid's army, under Jō'ăb; and at that time he was fighting in Dā'vid's war against the Ăm'mon-ītes, at Răb'bah, near the desert, on the east of Jôr'dan. Dā'vid sent for U-rī'ah's wife, Băth'shĕ-bà, and talked with her. He loved her, and greatly longed to take her as one of his own wives—for in those times it was not thought a sin for a man to have more than one wife. But Dā'vid could not marry Băth'shĕ-bà while her husband, U-rī'ah, was living. Then a wicked thought came into Dā'vid's heart and he formed a plan to have U-rī'ah killed, so that he could then take Băth'shĕ-bà into his own house.

Dā'vid wrote a letter to Jō'ăb, the commander of his army. And in the letter he said, "When there is to be a fight with the Ăm'mon-ītes, send U-rī'ah into the middle of it, where it will be the hottest; and manage to leave him there, so that he may be slain by the Ăm-mon-ītes."

And Jō'ăb did as Dā'vid had commanded him. He sent U-rī'ah with some brave men to a place near the wall of the city, where he

258

knew that the enemies would rush out of the city upon them; there was a fierce fight beside the wall; U-rī′ah was slain and other brave men with him. Then Jō′ăb sent a messenger to tell King Dā′vid how the war was being carried on, and especially that U-rī′ah, one of his brave officers, had been killed in the fighting.

When Dā′vid heard this, he said to the messenger, "Say to Jō′ăb, 'Do not feel troubled at the loss of the men slain in battle. The sword must strike down some. Keep up the siege; press forward, and you will take the city.' "

And after Băth′shĕ-bà had mourned for a time over her husband's death, Dā′vid took her into his palace and she became his wife. And a little child was born to them, whom Dā′vid loved greatly. Only Jō′ăb and Dā′vid and perhaps a few others, knew that Dā′vid had caused the death of U-rī′ah; but God knew it and God was displeased with Dā′vid for this wicked deed.

Then the Lord sent Nā′than, the prophet, to Dā′vid to tell him that, though men knew not that Dā′vid had done wickedly, God had seen it, and would surely punish Dā′vid for his sin. Nā′than came to Dā′vid, and he spoke to him thus:

"There were two men in one city; one was rich, and the other poor. The rich man had great flocks of sheep and herds of cattle; but the poor man had only one little lamb that he had bought. It

grew up in his home with his children, and drank out of his cup, and lay upon his lap, and was like a little daughter to him.

"One day a visitor came to the rich man's house to dinner. He did not take one of his own sheep to kill for his guest. He robbed the poor man of his lamb, and killed it, and cooked it for a meal with his friend."

When Dā'vid heard this, he was very angry. He said to Nā'than, "The man who did this thing deserves to die! He shall give back to his poor neighbor fourfold for the lamb taken from him. How cruel to treat a poor man thus, without pity for him!"

And Nā'than said to Dā'vid, "You are the man who has done this deed. The Lord made you king in place of Saul, and gave you a kingdom. You have a great house and many wives. Why, then, have you done this wickedness in the sight of the Lord? You have slain U-rī'ah with the sword of the men of Ăm'mon; and you have taken his wife to be your wife. For this there shall be a sword drawn against your house; you shall suffer for it and your wives shall suffer and your children shall suffer."

When Dā'vid heard all this, he saw, as he had not seen before, how great was his wickedness. He was exceedingly sorry; and said to Nā'than, "I have sinned against the Lord."

And Dā'vid showed such sorrow for his sin that Nā'than said to him, "The Lord has forgiven your sin; and you shall not die on account of it. But the child that U-rī'ah's wife has given to you shall surely die."

Soon after this the little child of Dā'vid and Băth'shĕ-ba, whom Dā'vid loved greatly, was taken very ill. Dā'vid prayed to God for the child's life; and Dā'vid took no food, but lay in sorrow, with his face upon the floor of his house. The nobles of his palace came to him and urged him to rise up and take food, but he would not. For seven days the child grew worse and worse, and Dā'vid remained in sorrow. Then the child died; and the nobles were afraid to tell Dā'vid, for they said to each other, "If he was in such grief while the child was living, what will he do when he hears that the child is dead?"

But when King Dā'vid saw the people whispering to one another with sad faces, he said, "Is the child dead?"

And they said to him, "Yes, O king, the child is dead."
Then Dā'vid rose up from the floor where he had been lying.
He washed his face and put on his kingly robes. He went first to
he house of the Lord and worshiped; then he came to his own
house and sat down to his table and took food. His servants wondered at this, but Dā'vid said to them, "While the child was still
alive, I fasted and prayed and wept; for I hoped that by prayer to
the Lord and by the mercy of the Lord, his life might be spared.
But now that he is dead, my prayers can do no more for him. I
cannot bring him back again. He will not come back to me, but
I shall go to him."

And after this God gave to Dā'vid and to Băth'shĕ-bà, his wife,
another son, whom they named Sŏl'o-mon. The Lord loved Sŏl'o-
mon and he grew up to be a wise man.

After God had forgiven Dā'vid's great sin, Dā'vid wrote the
Fifty-first Psalm; these are some of the verses:

> Have mercy upon me, O God, according to thy lovingkindness:
> According to the multitude of thy tender mercies blot out my
>   transgressions.
> Wash me thoroughly from my wickedness,
> And cleanse me from my sin.
> For I acknowledge my transgressions:
> And my sin is ever before me.
> Against thee, thee only, have I sinned,
> And done that which is evil in thy sight: . . .
> Purge me with hyssop, and I shall be clean:
> Wash me, and I shall be whiter than snow. . . .
> Hide thy face from my sins,
> And blot out all my evil deeds,
> Create in me a clean heart, O God;
> And renew a right spirit within me.
> Cast me not away from thy presence;
> And take not thy holy spirit from me.
> Restore unto me the joy of thy salvation;
> And uphold me with thy free spirit.
> Then will I teach wrongdoers thy ways;
> And sinners shall be converted unto thee. . . .
> For thou delightest not in sacrifice; else would I give it:
> Thou hast no pleasure in burnt offering.
> The sacrifices of God are a broken spirit:
> A broken and a contrite heart, O God, thou will not despise.

David's Handsome Son, and How He Stole the Kingdom

NOT LONG after Dā'vid's sin, the sorrows of which the prophet had foretold him began to fall upon Dā'vid. He had many wives, and his wives had many sons; but most of his sons had grown up wild and wicked, because Dā'vid had not watched over them and not taught them in their youth to love God and do God' will. He had been too busy as a king to do his duty as a father.

One of Dā'vid's sons was Ăb'sa-lŏm, whose mother was the daughter of Tăl'māi, the king of a little country called Gē'shŭr, or the north of Ĭs'ra-el. Ăb'sa-lŏm was said to be the most beautifu young man in all the land. He had long locks of hair, of which he was very proud, because all the people admired them. Ăb'sa-lŏm became very angry with Ăm'nŏn, another of Dā'vid's sons, because Ăm'nŏn had done wrong to Ăb'sa-lŏm's sister, named Tā'mar.

But Ăb'sa-lŏm hid his anger against Ăm'nŏn, and one day he invited Ăm'nŏn with all the king's sons to a feast at his house in the country. They all went to the feast; and while they were all at the table, Ăb'sa-lŏm's servants, by his orders, rushed in and killed Ăm'nŏn. The other princes, the king's sons, were alarmed, fearing that they also would be slain; and they ran away in haste. But no harm was done to the other princes, and they came back in safety to Dā'vid.

Dā'vid was greatly displeased with Ăb'sa-lŏm, though he loved him more than any other of his sons; and Ăb'sa-lŏm went away from his father's court to that of his grandfather, his mother's father, the king of Gē'shŭr. There Ăb'sa-lŏm stayed for three years; and all the time Dā'vid longed to see him, for he felt that he had now lost both sons, Ăb'sa-lŏm as well as Ăm'nŏn. And after three years Dā'vid allowed Ăb'sa-lŏm to come back to Jĕ-ru'să-

262

lĕm; but for a time would not meet him because he had caused his brother's death. At last Dā'vid's love was so strong that he could no longer refuse to see his son. He sent for Ăb'sa-lŏm and kissed him and took him back to his old place among the king's sons in the palace.

But Ăb'sa-lŏm's heart was wicked and ungrateful and cruel. He formed a plan to take the throne and the kingdom away from his father, Dā'vid, and to make himself king in Dā'vid's place. He began by living in great state, as if he were already a king, with a royal chariot and horses and fifty men to run before him. Then, too, he would rise early in the morning and stand at the gate of the king's palace, and meet those who came to the king for any cause. He would speak to each man and find what was the purpose of his coming; and he would say:

"Your cause is good and right, but the king will not hear you; and he will not allow any other man to hear you in his place. O that I were made a judge! Then I would see that right was done and that every man received his due!" And when any man bowed down before Ăb'sa-lŏm as the king's son, he would reach out his hand and lift him up and kiss him as his friend. Thus Ăb'sa-lŏm won the hearts of all whom he met, from every part of the land, until very many wished that he were king instead of Dā'vid, his father. For Dā'vid no longer led the army in war, nor did he sit as judge, nor did he go among the people; but lived apart in his palace, scarcely knowing what was being done in the land.

After four years Ăb'sa-lŏm thought that he was strong enough to seize the kingdom. He said to Dā'vid, "Let me go to the city of Hē'bron and there worship the Lord, and keep a promise which I made to the Lord while I was in the land of Gē'shŭr."

Dā'vid was pleased with this, for he thought that Ăb'sa-lŏm really meant to serve the Lord. So Ăb'sa-lŏm went to Hē'bron, and with him went a great company of his friends. A few of these knew of Ăb'sa-lŏm's plans, but most of them knew nothing. At Hē'bron Ăb'sa-lŏm was joined by a very wise man, named Ă-hĭth'-o-phĕl, one of Dā'vid's chief advisers whom he trusted.

Suddenly the word was sent through all the land by swift runners, "Ăb'sa-lŏm has been made king at Hē'bron!"

The news came to Dā'vid in the palace that Ăb'sa-lŏm had made himself king, that many of the rulers were with him, and that the people in their hearts really desired Ăb'sa-lŏm. Dā'vid did not know whom he could trust, and he prepared to escape before it would be too late. He took with him a few of his servants who chose to remain by his side, and his wives, and especially his wife Băth'shĕ-ba, and her son, the little Sŏl'o-mon.

As they were going out of the gates, they were joined by Ĭt'ta-ī, who was the commander of his guard, and who had with him six hundred trained men of war. Ĭt'ta-ī was not an Ĭs'ra-el-īte, but was a stranger in the land, and Dā'vid was surprised that he should offer to go with him. He said to Ĭt'ta-ī, "Why do you, a stranger, go with us? I know not to what places we may go or what trouble we may meet. It would be better for you and your men to go back to your own land; and may mercy and truth go with you!"

And Ĭt'ta-ī answered the king, "As the Lord God lives and as my lord the king lives, surely in what place the king shall be, whether in death or in life, there will we, his servants, be with him."

So Ĭt'ta-ī and his brave six hundred soldiers went with Dā'vid out of the city, over the brook Kĭd'ron, toward the wilderness. And soon after came Zā'dŏk and Ă-bī'a-thär, the priests, and the

Lē'vītes, carrying the holy ark of the Lord. And Dā'vid said, "Take back the ark of God into the city. If I shall find favor in the sight of the Lord, he will bring me again to see it; but if the Lord says, 'I have no pleasure in Dā'vid,' then let the Lord do with me as seems good to him."

And Dā'vid thought also that the priests might help him more in the city than if they should go away with him. He said to Zā'dŏk, "Do you go back to the city and watch; and send word to me by your son, Ā-hĭm'a-ăz, and Jŏn'a-than, the son of Ā-bī'a-thär. I will wait at the crossing place of the Jôr'dan for news from you."

So Zā'dŏk and Ā-bī'a-thär, the priests, carried the holy ark back to its Tabernacle on Mount Zī'ŏn, and watched closely, that they might send Dā'vid word of anything that would help his cause. Dā'vid walked up the steep side of the Mount Ŏl'ĭ-vĕt, on the east of Jĕ-ru'sȧ-lĕm, with his head covered and his feet bare, as one in mourning, weeping as he walked. And all the people who were with him, and those who saw him, were weeping in their sorrow over Dā'vid's fall from his high place.

On the top of the hill Dā'vid found another man waiting to see him. It was Hū'shāi, who was one of Dā'vid's best friends. He stood there in sorrow, with his garments torn and earth upon his head as a sign of grief, ready to go into the wilderness with Dā'vid. But Dā'vid said to Hū'shāi, "If you go with us, you cannot help me in any way; but if you stay in the city and pretend to be Ăb'sa-lŏm's friend, then perhaps you can watch against the advice that the wise man, Ā-hĭth'o-phĕl, gives to Ăb'sa-lŏm, and prevent Ăb'sa-lŏm from following it. Zā'dŏk and Ā-bī'a-thär, the priests, will help you, and through their sons, Ā-hĭm'a-ăz and Jŏn'a-than, you can send word to me of all that you hear."

A little past the top of the hill another man was waiting for Dā'vid. It was Zī'bà, the servant of Mĕ-phĭb'o-shĕth. You remember how kindly Dā'vid had treated Mĕ-phĭb'o-shĕth, because he was the son of Dā'vid's dear friend, Jŏn'a-than. Zī'bà had by his side a couple of asses saddled, and on them two hundred loaves of bread, and a hundred clusters of raisins, and a quantity of fruit, and a goat skin full of wine. Dā'vid said to Zī'bà, "For what purpose are all these things here?"

And Zī'bà said, "The asses are for the king; and here is food for the journey and wine for those who may grow faint and may need it in the wilderness."

And Dā'vid asked Zī'bà, "Where is your master?"

"He is in Jĕ-ru'sà-lĕm," said Zī'bà; "for he says that the kingdom may be given back to him, as he is the heir of Saul's house."

Dā'vid felt very sad as he heard that Mĕ-phĭb'o-shĕth had forsaken him, and he said to Zī'bà, "Whatever has belonged to Mĕ-phĭb'o-shĕth, shall be yours from this time."

But Dā'vid did not know that all Zī'bà's words were false, and that Mĕ-phĭb'o-shĕth had not forsaken him.

Soon after this another man came out to meet Dā'vid, but in a very different spirit from Ĭt'ta-ī, Hū'shāi, and Zī'bà. This man was Shĭm'e-ī, and he belonged to the family of King Saul. As Dā'vid and his party walked along the crest of the hill, Shĭm'e-ī walked over the hill on the other side of a narrow valley, and as he walked, he threw stones at Dā'vid and cursed him shouting, "Get out, get out, you man of blood, you wicked man! Now the Lord is bringing upon you all the wrong that you did to Saul, when he was your king. You robbed Saul of his kingdom, and now your own son is robbing you. You are suffering just as you deserve, for you are a bloody man!"

Then Ȧ-bĭsh'a-ī, the son of Zĕr-u-ī'ah, who was one of Dā'vid's men and Dā'vid's own nephew, said, "Why should this dog be allowed to bark against my lord the king? Let me go across the valley, and I will strike off his head at one blow!"

But Dā'vid said, "If it is the Lord's will that this man should curse Dā'vid, then let him curse on. My own son is seeking to take away my life, and is it strange that this man of another tribe should hate me? It may be that the Lord will look upon the wrong done to me and will do good to me."

So Dā'vid and his wives and his servants and the soldiers who were faithful to him, went on toward the wilderness and the valley of the Jôr'dan. Soon after Dā'vid had escaped from the city, Ăb'sa-lŏm came into it with his friends and a host of his followers. As Ăb'sa-lŏm drew near, Hū'shāi, Dā'vid's friend, stood by the road, crying, "Long live the king! Long live the king!"

And Ăb'sa-lŏm said to Hū'shāi, "Is this the way you treat your
riend? Why have you not stayed beside your friend Dā'vid?"
Hū'shāi said to Ăb'sa-lŏm, "Whom the Lord and his people
ave chosen, him will I follow, and with him I will stay. As I have
erved the father, so will I serve the son."
Then Hū'shāi went into the palace among the followers of
Ăb'sa-lŏm. And Ăb'sa-lŏm said to Ā-hĭth'o-phĕl, "Tell me what
o do next?"
Now Ā-hĭth'o-phĕl was a very wise man. He knew what was
est for Ăb'sa-lŏm's success, and he said, "Let me choose out twelve
housand men, and I will pursue Dā'vid this very night. We will
ome upon Dā'vid when he is tired, while only a few people are
vith him, and before he has time to form any plans or to gather an
rmy, I will kill Dā'vid, and will harm no one else; and then you
an reign as king in peace, and all the people will submit to you
vhen they know that Dā'vid is no longer living."

Ăb'sa-lŏm thought that this was wise advice; but he sent for
Hū'shāi. He told him what Ā-hĭth'o-phĕl had said, and asked for
is advice also. And Hū'shāi said, "The advice that Ā-hĭth'o-phĕl
ives is not good for the present time. You know that Dā'vid and
is men are very brave, and just now they are as savage as a bear
obbed of her cubs. Dā'vid is with his men in some safe place,
idden in a cave or among the mountains, and they will watch
gainst those who come out to seek for them and will rush upon
hem suddenly from their hiding place. Then, as soon as the news
goes through the land that Ăb'sa-lŏm's men have been beaten,
everybody will turn away from Ăb'sa-lŏm to Dā'vid. The better
plan would be to wait until you can gather all the men of war in
Ĭs'ra-el, from Dăn in the north to Bē'er=shē'bà in the south. And
hen if Dā'vid is in a city, there will be men enough to pull the city
in pieces, or if he is in the field, we will surround him on every
side." And Ăb'sa-lŏm and the rulers who were with him said to
each other, "The advice of Hū'shāi is better than the advice of
Ā-hĭth'o-phĕl. Let us do as Hū'shāi tells us to do."

So Ăb'sa-lŏm sat down in his father's palace and began to enjoy
himself while they were gathering his army. This was just what
Hū'shāi wished, for it would give Dā'vid time to gather his army

also, and he knew that the hearts of the people would soon turn from Ăb'sa-lŏm back to Dā'vid.

Hū'shāi told Zā'dŏk and Ả-bī'a-thär, the priests, of Ăb'sa-lŏm's plans, and they sent word by a young woman to their sons, Ả-hĭm'a-ăz and Jŏn'a-than, who were watching outside the city, and these young men hastened to tell Dā'vid, who was waiting beside the river Jôr'dan. Then Dā'vid and his men found a safe refuge in Mā-hả-nā'im, in the tribe of Găd, across Jôr'dan; and there his friends from all the land began to come to him.

When Ả-hĭth'o-phĕl saw that his advice had not been taken, and that Hū'shāi was preferred in his place, he knew at once that Ăb'sa-lŏm could not hold the kingdom, and that Ăb'sa-lŏm's cause was already as good as lost. He went to his home, put all his house and his affairs in order, and hanged himself; for he thought that it was better to die by his own hand than to be put to death as a traitor by King Dā'vid.

Ăb'sa-lŏm for a little time had his wish. He sat on the throne and wore the crown and lived in the palace at Jĕ-ru'sả-lĕm as the king of Ĭṣ'ra-el.

Story Fifteen

II SAMUEL 17 : 24 to 20 : 2

Absalom in the Wood; David On the Throne

THE LAND on the east of Jôr'dan, where Dā'vid found a refuge, was called Gĭl'e-ăd, a word which means "High," because it is higher than the land opposite on the west of Jôr'dan. There, in the city of Mā-hả-nā'im, the rulers and the people were friendly to Dā'vid. They brought food of all kinds and drink for Dā'vid and those who were with him; for they said, "The people are hungry and thirsty and very tired from their long journey through the wilderness."

And at this place Dā'vid's friends gathered from all the tribes of ṣ'ra-el, until around him was an army. It was not so large as the rmy of Ăb'sa-lŏm, but in it were more of the brave old warriors vho had fought under Dā'vid in other years. Dā'vid divided his rmy into three parts, and placed over the three parts Jō'ăb, Jō'ăb's ɪrother Ă-bĭsh'a-ī, and Ĭt'ta-ī, who had followed him so faithfully. Dā'vid said to the chiefs of his army and to his men, "I will go ɪut with you into the battle."

But the men said to Dā'vid, "No, you must not go with us; for f half of us should lose our lives, no one will care; but you are vorth ten thousand of us, and your life is too precious. You must tay here in the city and be ready to help us if we need help."

So the king stood by the gate of Mā-hă-nā'im while his men narched out by hundreds and by thousands. And as they went past he king, the men heard him say to the three chiefs, Jō'ăb and Ă-bĭsh'a-ī and Ĭt'ta-ī, "For my sake, deal gently with Ăb'sa-lŏm." Even to the last Dā'vid loved the son who had done to him such ǥreat wrong, and Dā'vid would have them spare his life.

A great battle was fought on that day at a place called "The Wood of Ē'phră-ĭm," though it was not in the tribe of Ē'phră-ĭm, ɪut of Găd, on the east of the Jôr'dan. Ăb'sa-lŏm's army was ɪnder the command of a man named Ăm'a-sà, who was a cousin ɪf Jō'ăb; for his mother, Ăb'ī-gail, and Jō'ăb's mother, Zĕr-ụ-ī'ah, ɪvere both sisters of Dā'vid. So both the armies were led by neph-ɪws of King Dā'vid. Ăb'sa-lŏm himself went into the battle riding ɪpon a mule, as was the custom of kings.

Dā'vid's soldiers won a great victory, and killed thousands of Ăb'sa-lŏm's men. The armies were scattered in the woods and ɪnany men were lost, so that it was said that the woods swallowed ɪp more men than the sword. When Ăb'sa-lŏm saw that his cause ɪvas hopeless, he rode away, hoping to escape. But as he was riding ɪnder the branches of an oak tree, his head, with its great mass of long hair, was caught in the boughs of the tree. He struggled to free himself, but could not. His mule ran away, and Ăb'sa-lŏm ɪvas left hanging in the air by his head.

One of Dā'vid's soldiers saw him and said to Jō'ăb, "I saw Ăb'sa-lŏm hanging in an oak."

"Why did you not kill him?" asked Jō′ăb. "If you had killed him, I would have given you ten pieces of silver and a girdle."

"If you should offer me a thousand pieces of silver," answered the soldier, "I would not touch the king's son; for I heard the king charge all the generals and the men, 'Let no one harm the young man Ăb′sa-lŏm.' And if I had slain him, you yourself would not have saved my life from the king's anger."

"I cannot stay to talk with you," said Jō′ăb; and with three darts in his hand he hastened to the place where Ăb′sa-lŏm was hanging. He thrust Ăb′sa-lŏm's heart through with the darts, and after that his followers, finding that Ăb′sa-lŏm was still living, pierced his body until they were sure that he was dead. Then they took down his body and threw it into a deep hole in the forest and heaped a great pile of stones upon it.

During his life Ăb′sa-lŏm had built for himself a monument in the valley of Kĭd′ron, on the east of Jĕ-ru̲′så-lĕm. There he had

xpected to be buried; but though the monument stood long after-
ard, and was called "Ăb'sa-lŏm's pillar," yet Ăb'sa-lŏm's body
y not there, but under a heap of stones in the wood of Ē'phră-ĭm.
After the battle Ȧ-hĭm'a-ăz, the son of the priest Zā'dŏk, came.
) Jō'ăb. Ȧ-hĭm'a-ăz was one of the two young men who brought
ews from Jĕ-ru̯'să-lĕm to Dā'vid at the river Jôr'dan, as we read
ı the last story. He said to Jō'ăb, "Let me run to the king, and
ıke to him the news of the battle."

But Jō'ăb knew that the message of Ăb'sa-lŏm's death would
ot be pleasing to King Dā'vid, and he said, "Some other time you
ıall bear news, but not today, because the king's son is dead."

And Jō'ăb called a Negro who was standing near, and said to
ım, "Go, and tell the king what you have seen."

The Negro bowed to Jō'ăb, and ran. But after a time Ȧ-hĭm'-
-ăz, the son of Zā'dŏk, again said to Jō'ăb, "Let me also run after
ıe Negro, and take news."

"Why do you wish to go, my son?" said Jō'ăb; "the news will
ot bring you any reward."

"Anyhow, let me go," said the young man; and Jō'ăb gave him
:ave. Then Ȧ-hĭm'a-ăz ran with all his might, and by a better
oad over the plain, though less direct than the road which the
Negro had taken over the mountains. Ȧ-hĭm'a-ăz outran the
Negro, and came first in sight to the watchman who was standing
ın the wall, while King Dā'vid was waiting below in the little
oom between the outer and inner gates, anxious for news of the
ıattle, but more anxious for his son, Ăb'sa-lŏm.

The watchman on the wall called down to the king, and said,
'I see another man running alone."

And the king said, "If he is alone, he is bringing a message." He
:new that if men are running away after a defeat in battle there
vould be a crowd together. Then the watchman called again,
'I see a man running alone."

And the king said, "He also is bringing some news."

The watchman spoke again, "The first runner is coming near,
ınd he runs like Ȧ-hĭm'a-ăz, the son of Zā'dŏk."

And Dā'vid said, "He is a good man, and he comes with good
ıews." Ȧ-hĭm'a-ăz came near, and cried out, "All is well!"

The first words which the king spoke were, "Is it well with th young man Ăb'sa-lŏm?"

Ă'hĭm'a-ăz was too wise to bring to the king the word of Ăb'sa lŏm's death. He left that to the other messenger, and said, "Whe Jō'ăb sent me, there was a great noise over something that had take place, but I did not stop to learn what it was."

A little later came the Negro, crying, "News for my lord th king! This day the Lord has given you victory over you enemies!"

And Dā'vid said again, "Is it well with the young man Ăb'sa lŏm?"

Then the Negro, who knew nothing of Dā'vid's feeling, an swered, "May all the enemies of my lord the king, and all that tr to do him harm, be as that young man is!"

Then the king was deeply moved. His sorrow over Ăb'sa-lŏr made him forget the victory that had been won. Slowly he walke up the steps to the room in the tower over the gate, and as h walked, he said, "O my son Ăb'sa-lŏm! my son, my son Ăb'sa-lŏm I wish before God that I had died for you, O Ăb'sa-lŏm, my son my son!"

The word soon went forth that the king, instead of rejoicin over the victory, was weeping over his son. The soldiers cam stealing back to the city, not as conquerors, but as if they had bee defeated. Everyone felt sorry for the king, who sat in the roon over the gate, with his face covered, and crying out, "O Ăb'sa-lŏm my son! my son, my son Ăb'sa-lŏm!"

But Jō'ăb saw that such great sorrow as the king showed wa not good for his cause. He came to Dā'vid and said to him, "Yo have put to shame this day all those who have fought for you an saved your life. You have shown that you love those who hat you, and that you hate those who love you. You have said by you actions that your princes and your servants, who have been tru to you, are nothing to you; and that if Ăb'sa-lŏm had lived an we had all died, you would have been better pleased. Now rise u and act like a man, and show regard for those who have fought fo you. I swear to you in the name of the Lord, that unless you d this, not a man will stay on your side, and that will be worse fo you than all the harm that has ever come upon you in all your life before this day!"

Then Dā'vid rose up, washed away his tears, and put on his robes, and took his seat in the gate as a king. After this he came from Mā-hȧ-nā'im to the river Jȯr'dan, and there all the people met him, to bring him back to his throne in Jė-rụ'sȧ-lĕm.

Among the first to come was Shĭm'e-ī, the man who had cursed Dā'vid and thrown stones at him as he was flying from Ăb'sa-lŏm. He fell on his face and confessed his crime and begged for mercy. Ȧ-bĭsh'a-ī, Jō'ȧb's brother, said, "Shall not Shĭm'e-ī be put to death, because he cursed the king, the Lord's anointed?"

But Dā'vid said, "Not a man shall be put to death this day in Ĭṣ'ra-el, for today I am king once more over Ĭṣ'ra-el. You shall not be slain, Shĭm'e-ī; I pledge you the word of a king."

And Zī'bȧ, the servant of Mė-phĭb'o-shĕth, was there with his sons and his followers; and Mė-phĭb'o-shĕth was there also to meet the king. And Mė-phĭb'o-shĕth had not dressed his lame feet nor trimmed his beard nor washed his clothes, from the day when Dā'vid had left Jė-rụ'sȧ-lĕm until the day when he returned in peace. And Dā'vid said to him, "Mė-phĭb'o-shĕth, why did you not offer to go with me?"

"My lord, O king," said Mė-phĭb'o-shĕth, "my servant deceived me. He said, 'You are lame and cannot go; but I will go in your name with the king and will help him.' And he has done me wrong with the king; but what matters it all, now that the king has come again?"

Dā'vid said, "You and Zī'bȧ may divide the property."

And Mė-phĭb'o-shĕth said, "Let him have it all, now that the king has come in peace to his own house!"

The army of Ăb'sa-lŏm had melted away and was scattered throughout all Ĭṣ'ra-el. Dā'vid was still displeased with Jō'ȧb, the chief of his army, because he had slain Ăb'sa-lŏm, contrary to Dā'vid's orders. He sent a message to Ăm'a-sȧ, who had been the commander of Ăb'sa-lŏm's army, and who was, like Jō'ȧb and Ȧ-bĭsh'a-ī, Dā'vid's own nephew. He said to Ăm'a-sȧ, "You are of my own family, of my bone and my flesh, and you shall be the general in place of Jō'ȧb."

Jō'ăb and his brother were strong men, not willing to submit to Dā'vid's rule; and Dā'vid thought that he would be safer on his throne if they did not hold so much power. Also, Dā'vid thought that to make Ăm'a-să general would please not only those who had been friends to Ăb'sa-lŏm, but many more of the people, for many feared and hated Jō'ăb.

At the river Jôr'dan almost the whole tribe of Jū'dah were gathered to bring the king back to Jĕ-ru'să-lĕm. But this did not please the men of the other tribes. They said to the men of Jū'dah, "You act as though you were the only friends of the king in all the land! We, too, have some right to Dā'vid."

The men of Jū'dah said, "The king is of our own tribe and is one of us. We come to meet him because we love him."

But the people of the other tribes were still offended, and many of them went to their homes in anger. The tribe of Ē-phră'ĭm, in the middle of the land, was very jealous of the tribe of Jū'dah and unwilling to come again under Dā'vid's rule. One man in Ē'phră-ĭm, Shē'bă, the son of Bĭch'rī, began a new rebellion against Dā'vid, which for a time threatened again to overthrow Dā'vid's power.

Ăm'a-să, the new commander of the army, called out his men to put down Shē'bă's rebellion. But he was slow in gathering his army, and Jō'ăb, the old general, went forth with a band of his own followers. Jō'ăb met Ăm'a-să, pretending to be his friend, and killed him, and then took the command. He shut up Shē'bă in a city far in the north, and finally caused him to be slain. So at last every enemy was put down; and Dā'vid sat again in peace upon his throne. But Jō'ăb, whom Dā'vid feared and hated because of many evil deeds that he had done, was, as before, the commander of the army and in great power. Jō'ăb was faithful to Dā'vid, and was a strong helper to Dā'vid's throne. Without Jō'ăb's courage and skill in Dā'vid's cause, Dā'vid might have failed in some of his wars, and especially in the war against Ăb'sa-lŏm's followers. But Jō'ăb was cruel and wicked and had many followers. Dā'vid felt that he was not fully the king while Jō'ăb lived.

But few people knew how Dā'vid felt toward Jō'ăb; and in appearance the throne of Dā'vid was now as strong as it had ever been; and Dā'vid's last years were years of peace and of power.

The Angel with the Drawn Sword
on Mount Moriah

AFTER the death of Ăb′sa-lŏm, Dā′vid ruled in peace over
Ĭs′ra-el for the rest of his life. His kingdom
stretched from the river Eū-phrā′tēs to the border
of Ē′ġypt, and from the Great Sea on the west to
the great desert on the east. But again Dā′vid did
that which was very displeasing to God. He gave orders to Jō′ăb,
who was the commander of his army, to send officers throughout
all the tribes of Ĭs′ra-el and to count all the men who could go forth
to battle.

It may be that Dā′vid's purpose was to gather a great army for
some new war. Even Jō′ăb, the general, knew that it was not
right to do this; and he said to Dā′vid, "May the Lord God make
his people an hundred times as great as they are; but are they not
all the servants of my lord the king? Why does the king command
this to be done? Surely it will bring sin upon the king and upon
the people."

But Dā′vid was firm in his purpose, and Jō′ăb obeyed him, but
not willingly. He sent men through all the twelve tribes to take
the number of those in every city and town who were fit for war.
They went throughout the land, until they had written down the
number of eight hundred thousand men in ten of the tribes, and of
nearly five hundred thousand men in the tribe of Jū′dah, who could
be called out for war. The tribe of Lē′vī was not counted, because all its members were priests and Lē′vītes in the service of the
Tabernacle; and Bĕn′ja-mĭn, on the border of which stood the city
of Jĕ-ru′să-lĕm, was not counted, because the numbering was
never finished.

It was left unfinished because God was angry with Dā′vid and
with the people on account of this sin. Dā′vid saw that he had
done wickedly, in ordering the count of the people. He prayed

275

to the Lord, and said, "O Lord, I have sinned greatly in doing this. Now, O Lord, forgive this sin, for I have done very foolishly."

Then the Lord sent to Dā'vid, a prophet, a man who heard God's voice and spoke as God's messenger. His name was Găd. Găd came to Dā'vid, and said to him, "Thus saith the Lord, You have sinned in this thing, and now you and your land must suffer for your sin. I will give you the choice of three troubles to come upon the land. Shall I send seven years of famine, in which there shall be no harvest? Or shall your enemies overcome you and win victories over you for three months? Or shall there be three days when pestilence shall fall upon the land, and the people shall die everywhere?"

And Dā'vid said to the prophet Găd, "This is a hard choice of evils to come upon the land; but let me fall into the hand of the Lord and not into the hands of men; for God's mercies are great and many. If we must suffer, let the three days of pestilence and death come upon the land."

Then the Lord's angel of death passed through the land, and in three days seventy thousand men died. And when the angel of the Lord stretched out his hand over the city of Jĕ-ru'să-lĕm, the Lord had pity upon the people, and said, "It is enough; now hold back your hand, and cause no more of the people to die."

Then the Lord opened Dā'vid's eyes and he saw the angel standing on Mount Mȯ-rī'ah, with a drawn sword in his hand, held out toward the city.

Then Dā'vid prayed to the Lord and he said:

"O Lord, I alone have sinned and have done this wickedness before thee. These people are like sheep; they have done nothing. Lord, let thy hand fall on me and not on these poor people."

Then the Lord sent the prophet Găd to Dā'vid, and Găd said to him, "Go, and build an altar to the Lord upon the place where the angel was standing."

Then Dā'vid and the men of his court went out from Mount Zī'ŏn, where the city was standing, and walked up the side of Mount Mŏ-rī'ah. They found the man who owned the rock on the top of the mountain threshing wheat upon it, with his sons; for the smooth rock was used as a threshing floor, upon which oxen walked over the heads of grain, beating out the kernels with their feet. This man was not an Ĭṣ'ra-el-īte, but a foreigner, of the race that had lived on those mountains before the Ĭṣ'ra-el-ītes came. His name was Ȧ-rau'nah.

When Ȧ-rau'nah saw Dā'vid and his nobles coming toward him, he bowed down with his face toward the ground and said, "For what purpose does my lord the king come to his servant?"

"I have come," said Dā'vid, "to buy your threshing floor, and to build upon it an altar to the Lord, that I may pray to God to stop the plague which is destroying the people."

And Ȧ-rau'nah said to Dā'vid, "Let my lord the king take it freely as a gift, and with it these oxen for a burnt offering and the threshing tools and the yokes of the oxen for the wood on the altar. All this, O king, Ȧ-rau'nah gives to the king."

"No," said King Dā'vid, "I cannot take it as a gift; but I will pay you the price for it. For I will not make an offering to the Lord my God of that which costs me nothing."

So Dā'vid gave Ȧ-rau'nah the full price for the land and for the oxen and for the wood. And there, on the rock, he built an altar to the Lord God, and on it he offered burnt offerings and peace offerings. The Lord heard Dā'vid's prayer and took away the plague from the land.

And on that rock afterward stood the altar of the temple of the Lord on Mount Mŏ-rī'ah. The rock is standing even to this day and over it a building called "The Dome of the Rock." Those who visit the place can see the spot where Dā'vid built his altar.

Solomon on David's Throne

URING the later years of Dā'vid's reign he laid up great treasure of gold and silver and brass and iron, for the building of a house to the Lord upon Mount Mŏ-rī'ah. This house was to be called "The Temple," and it was to be made very beautiful, the most beautiful building, and the richest, in all the land. Dā'vid had greatly desired to build this house while he was the king of Ĭṣ'ra-el, but God said to him:

"You have been a man of war and have fought many battles and shed much blood. My house shall be built by a man of peace. When you die, your son Sŏl'o-mon shall reign, and he shall have peace and shall build my house."

So Dā'vid made ready great store of precious things for the Temple, also stone and cedar to be used in the building. And Dā'vid said to Sŏl'o-mon, his son:

"God has promised that there shall be rest and peace to the land while you are king; and the Lord will be with you and you shall build a house, where God shall live among his people."

But Dā'vid had other sons who were older than Sŏl'o-mon; and one of these sons, whose name was Ăd-o-nī'jah, formed a plan to make himself king. Dā'vid was now very old and he was no longer able to go out of his palace and to be seen among the people of his kingdom.

Ăd-o-nī'jah gathered his friends; and among them were Jō'ăb, the general of the army, and Ȧ-bī'a-thär, one of the two high priests. They met at a place outside the wall and had a great feast, and they were about to crown Ăd-o-nī'jah as king, when word came to Dā'vid in the palace. Dā'vid, though old and feeble, was still wise.

He said, "Let us make Sŏl'o-mon king at once and thus put an end to the plan of these men."

So at Dā'vid's command, they brought out the mule on which no one but the king was allowed to ride and they placed Sŏl'o-mon

278

upon it, and with the king's guards and the nobles and the great
men, they brought the young Sŏl'o-mon down to the valley of
Gī'hon, south of the city.

And Zā'dŏk the priest took from the Tabernacle the horn filled
with holy oil that was used for anointing or pouring oil on the head
of the priests when they were set apart for their work. He poured
oil from this horn on the head of Sŏl'o-mon, and then the priests
blew the trumpets and all the people cried aloud, "God save King
Sŏl'o-mon."

All this time Ăd-o-nī'jah and Jō'ăb and their friends were not
far away, almost in the same valley, feasting and making merry,

intending to make Ăd-o-nī'jah king. They heard the sound of
trumpets and the shouting of the people. Jō'ăb said, "What is the
cause of all this noise and uproar?"

A moment later Jŏn'a-than, the son of Ă-bī'a-thär, came running in. We read of him as one of the two young men who brought
news from Jĕ-ru̯'sȧ-lĕm to Dā'vid at the river Jôr'dan. Jŏn'a-than
said to the men who were feasting:

"Our lord, King Dā'vid, has made Sŏl'o-mon king and he has
just been anointed in Gī'hon; and all the princes and the heads of
the army are with him, and the people are shouting, 'God save King
Sŏl'o-mon!' And Dā'vid has sent from his bed a message to Sŏl'o-
mon, saying, 'May the Lord make your name greater than my name
has been! Blessed be the Lord, who has given me a son to sit this
day on my throne!' "

When Ăd-o-nī'jah and his friends heard this, they were filled with fear. Every man went at once to his house, except Ăd-o-nī'jah. He hastened to the altar of the Lord and knelt before it and took hold of the horns that were on its corners in front. This was a holy place, and he hoped that there Sŏl'o-mon might then have mercy on him. And Sŏl'o-mon said, "If Ăd-o-nī'jah will do right and be true to me as the king of Ĭs̱'ra-el, no harm shall come to him; but if he does wrong, he shall die." Then Ăd-o-nī'jah came and bowed down before King Sŏl'o-mon, and promised to obey him, and Sŏl'o-mon said, "Go to your own house."

Not long after this Dā'vid sent for Sŏl'o-mon; and from his bed he gave his last advice to Sŏl'o-mon. And soon after that Dā'vid died, an old man, having reigned in all forty years, seven years over the tribe of Jū'dah at Hē'bron, and thirty-three years over all Ĭs̱'-ra-el in Jĕ-ru̯'sȧ-lĕm. He was buried in great honor on Mount Zī'ŏn, and his tomb remained standing for many years.

Story Eighteen   I KINGS 3 : 1 to 4 : 34; II CHRONICLES 1 : 1-13

The Wise Young King

SŎL'O-MON was a very young man, not more than twenty years old, when he became king and bore the heavy care of a great land. For his kingdom was larger than the twelve tribes of Ĭs̱'ra-el, from Dăn to Bē'er=shē'bȧ. On the north he ruled over all Sȳr'ĭ-ȧ, from Mount Hĕr'mon as far as the great river Eū-phrā'tēs̱. On the east, Ăm'mŏn and Mō'ab were under his power, and in the south all the land of Ē'dom, far down into the desert where the Ĭs̱'ra-el-ītes had wandered long before. The Phĭ-lĭs'tĭnes̱ on the southwest beside the Great Sea, had also been conquered and were a part of Ĭs̱'ra-el. He had no wars, as Dā'vid had before him, but at home and abroad his great realm was at peace as long as Sŏl'o-mon reigned.

Soon after Sŏl'o-mon became king, he went to Gĭb'e-on, a few miles north of Jĕ-rụ'să-lĕm, where the altar of the Lord stood until the Temple was built. At Gīb'e-on Sŏl'o-mon made offerings and worshiped the Lord God of Ĭṣ'ra-el.

And that night the Lord God came to Sŏl'o-mon and spoke to him. The Lord said, "Ask of me whatever you choose and I will give it to you."

And Sŏl'o-mon said to the Lord, "O Lord, thou didst show great kindness to my father, Dā'vid; and now thou hast made me king in my father's place. I am the only child, O Lord. I know not how to rule this great people, which is like the dust of the earth in number. Give me, O Lord, I pray thee, wisdom and knowledge, that I may judge this people and may know how to rule them aright."

The Lord was pleased with Sŏl'o-mon's choice and the Lord said to Sŏl'o-mon, "Since you have not asked of me long life nor great riches for yourself nor victory over your enemies nor great power, but have asked wisdom and knowledge to judge this people, I have given you wisdom greater than that of any king before you and greater than that of any king that shall come after you. And because you have asked this, I will give you not only wisdom, but also honor and riches. And if you will obey my words, as your father Dā'vid obeyed, you shall have long life and shall rule for many years."

Then Sŏl'o-mon awoke and found that it was a dream. But it was a dream that came true, for God gave to Sŏl'o-mon all that he had promised, wisdom and riches and honor and power and long life. Soon after this Sŏl'o-mon showed his wisdom. Two women came before him with two little babies, one dead and the other living. Each of the two women claimed the living child as her own, and said that the dead child belonged to the other woman. One of the women said, "O my lord, we two women were sleeping with our children in one bed. And this woman in her sleep lay upon her child, and it died. Then she placed her dead child beside me while I was asleep and took my child. In the morning I saw that it was not my child; but she says it is mine, and the living child is hers. Now, O king, command this woman to give me my own child." Then the other woman said, "That is not true. The dead

baby is her own and the living one is mine, which she is trying to take from me."

The young king listened to both women. Then he said, "Bring me a sword."

They brought a sword, and then Sŏl'o-mon said, "Take this sword and cut the living child in two and give half to each one."

Then one of the women cried out and said, "O my lord, do not kill my child! Let the other woman have it, but let the child live!"

But the other woman said, "No, cut the child in two and divide it between us!"

Then Sŏl'o-mon said, "Give the living child to the woman who would not have it slain, for she is its mother."

And all the people wondered at the wisdom of one so young; and they saw that God had given him understanding.

Sŏl'o-mon chose some of the great men who had helped his father Dā'vid, to stand beside his throne and do his will. Among those was a man named Bĕ-nā'iah, the son of Jĕ-hoi'a-dà. He was one of those who had come to Dā'vid while he was hiding from Saul, as we read in Story Seven of this Part. At that time Bĕ-nā'iah, while still a young man, did a very bold deed. He found a lion in a deep pit, leaped into the pit and killed the lion. For this act, Bĕ-nā′iah became famous, for few people would dare to venture so near to a lion with the weapons in use at that time. This brave man was old in Sŏl′o-mon's day, but he was still strong, and Sŏl′o-mon gave him a high place at the head of his guards.

<table>
<tr><td>

Story Nineteen

</td><td>

I KINGS 5 : 1 to 9 : 9;
II CHRONICLES 3 : 1 to 7 : 22

</td></tr>
</table>

The House of God on Mount Moriah

THE GREAT work of Sŏl′o-mon's reign was the building of the house of God, which was called "The Temple." This stood on Mount Mŏ-rī′ah, on the east of Mount Zī′ŏn, and it covered the whole mountain. King Dā′vid had prepared for it by gathering great stores of gold and silver and stone and cedar wood. The walls were made of stone and the roof of cedar.

For the building the cedar was brought from Mount Lĕb′a-non, where there were many large cedar trees. The trees were cut down and carried to Tȳre on the seacoast. There they were made into rafts in the Great Sea and were floated down to Jŏp′pà. At Jŏp′pà they were taken ashore and were carried up to Jĕ-ru′sà-lĕm. All this work was done by the men of Tȳre, at the command of their king, Hī′ram, who was a friend of Sŏl′o-mon, as he had been a friend of King Dā′vid.

All the stones for the building of the Temple were hewn into shape and fitted together before they were brought to Mount Mŏ-rī′ah. And all the beams for the roof and the pillars of cedar were carved and made to join each other; so that as the walls arose, no sound of hammer or chisel was heard; the great building rose up quietly. You remember the form of the Tabernacle which was built before Mount Sī′nāi, in the wilderness, with its court, its

Holy Place, and its Holy of Holies. The Temple was copied after the Tabernacle, except that it was larger and was a house of stone and cedar, instead of a tent.

The Tabernacle had one court around it, where the priests only could enter; but the Temple had two courts, both open to the sky, with walls of stone around them, and on the walls double rows of cedar pillars and a roof above the pillars, so that people could walk around the court upon the walls protected from the sun. The court in front was for the people, for all the men of Is'ra-el could enter it, but no people of foreign race. This was called the "Fore Court." Beyond the Fore Court was the Court of the Priests, where only the priests were allowed to walk. At the east gate of this court stood the great altar of burnt offerings, built of rough, unhewn stones, for no cut stones could be used in the altar. This altar stood on the rock which had been the threshing floor of Ā-rau′nah, where Dā′vid saw the angel of the Lord standing.

Near the altar, in the Court of the Priests, stood a great tank for water, so large that it was called "a sea." It was made of brass and stood on the backs of twelve oxen, also made of brass. From this the water was taken for washing the offerings.

Within the Court of the Priests stood the Holy House, or the Temple building, made of marble and of cedar. Its front was a high tower, called the Porch. In this were rooms for the high priest and his sons.

Back of the Porch was the Holy Place. This was a long room in which stood the table for the twelve loaves of the bread and golden altar of incense. In the Holy Place of the Tabernacle stood the golden lampstand. We are not sure whether it was in the Temple; for either in place of the lampstand, or perhaps in addition to it, Sŏl'o-mon placed ten lamps of gold in the Holy Place.

Between the Holy Place and the Holy of Holies was a great veil, as in the Tabernacle. And in the Holy of Holies the priests placed the Ark of the Covenant. This, you remember, was a box or chest, of gold, in which were kept the two stone tablets of the Ten Commandments. This Ark of the Covenant was all that stood in the Holy of Holies; and into this room only the high priest came, and he only on one day in the year, the great Day of Atonement, when the scapegoat was sent away.

Outside of the Temple building were rooms for the priests. They were built on the outer wall of the house, on the rear and the two sides, but not in front, three stories high; and were entered from the outside only.

Seven years were spent in building the Temple, but at last it was finished; and a great service was held when the house was set apart to the worship of the Lord. Many offerings were burned upon the great altar, the ark was brought from Mount Zī'ŏn and placed in the Holy of Holies, and King Sŏl'o-mon knelt upon a platform in front of the altar and offered a prayer to the Lord before all the people, who filled the courts of the Temple.

One night, after the Temple was finished, the Lord appeared to Sŏl'o-mon in a dream for the second time. And the Lord said to Sŏl'o-mon, "I have heard the prayer which you have offered to me and I have made this house holy. It shall be my house and I will dwell there. And if you will walk before me as Dā'vid, your father, walked, doing my will, then your throne shall stand forever. But if you turn aside from following the Lord, then I will leave this house and will turn from it, and will let the enemies of Ĭs'ra-el come and destroy this house that was built for me."

The Last Days of Solomon's Reign

UNDER King Sŏl'o-mon the land of Ĭṣ'ra-el arose to greatness as never before and never afterward. All the countries around Ĭṣ'ra-el, and some that were far away, sent their princes to visit Sŏl'o-mon. And everyone who saw him wondered at his wisdom and his skill to answer hard questions. It was said that King Sŏl'o-mon was the wisest man in all the world. He wrote many of the wise sayings in the Book of Proverbs and many more that have been lost. He wrote more than a thousand songs. From many lands people came to see Sŏl'o-mon's splendor in living and to listen to his wise words.

In a land more than a thousand miles from Jĕ-ru'sȧ-lĕm, on the south of Ā-rā'bĭ-ȧ, in the land of Shē'bȧ, the queen heard of Sŏl'-o-mon's wisdom. She left her home, with a great company of her nobles, riding on camels and bearing rich gifts; and she came to visit King Sŏl'o-mon. The queen of Shē'bȧ brought to Sŏl'o-mon many hard questions, and she told him all that was in her heart. Sŏl'o-mon answered all her questions and showed her all the glory of his palace and his throne and his servants and the richness of his table, and the steps by which he went up from his palace to the house of the Lord.

And when she had heard and seen all, she said:

"All that I have heard in my own land of your wisdom and your greatness was true. But I did not believe it until I came and saw your kingdom. And not half was told me; for your wisdom and your splendor are far beyond what I have heard. Happy are those who are always before you to hear your wisdom! Blessed be the Lord thy God, who has set thee on the throne of the kingdom of Ĭṣ'ra-el!"

And the queen of Shē'bȧ gave to Sŏl'o-mon great treasures of gold and sweet-smelling spices and perfumes; and Sŏl'o-mon also made to her rich presents. Then she went back to her own land.

Sŏl'o-mon's great palace, where he lived in state, stood on the southern slope of Mount Mŏ-rī'ah, a little lower than the Temple. Its pillars of cedar were very many, so that they stood like a forest; and on that account it was called "The House of the Forest of Lĕb'a-non." From this palace a wide staircase of stone led up to the Temple, and Sŏl'o-mon and his princes walked up these stairs when they went to worship.

But there was a dark side as well as a bright side to the reign of Sŏl'o-mon. His palaces, the walled cities that he built to protect his kingdom on all sides, and the splendor of his court, cost much money. To pay for these he laid heavy taxes upon his people, and from all the tribes he compelled many of the men to work on buildings, to become soldiers in his army, to labor in his fields, and to serve in his household. Before the close of Sŏl'o-mon's reign, the cry of the people rose up against Sŏl'o-mon and his rule, on account of the heavy burdens that he had laid upon the land.

Sŏl'o-mon was very wise in affairs of the world, but he had no feeling for the poor of the land nor did he love God with all his heart. He chose for his queen a daughter of Phā'raōh, the king of Ē'gўpt, and he built for her a splendid palace. And he married many other women who were the daughters of kings. These women had worshiped idols in their own homes, and to please them, Sŏl'o-mon built on the Mount of Ol'ives a temple of idols, in full view of the Temple of the Lord. So images of Bā'al and the Ăsh'ē'rah and of Chē'mŏsh, the idol of the Mō'ab-ītes, and of Mō'lech, the idol of the Ăm'mon-ītes, stood on the hill in front of Jĕ-ru'sȧ-lĕm; and to these images King Sŏl'o-mon himself offered sacrifices. How great was the shame of the good men in Ĭṣ'ra-el when they saw their king surrounded by idol priests, and bowing down upon his face before images of stone!

The Lord was very angry with Sŏl'o-mon for all this and the Lord said to Sŏl'o-mon, "Since you have done these wicked things, and have not kept your promise to serve me, and because you have turned aside from my commands, I will surely take away the kingdom of Ĭṣ'ra-el from your son and will give it to one of your servants. But for the sake of your father, Dā'vid, who loved me and obeyed my commands, I will not take away from your son all the kingdom, but I will leave to him and to his children after him one tribe."

The servant of King Sŏl'o-mon, of whom the Lord spoke, was a young man of the tribe of Ē'phră-ĭm, named Jĕr-o-bō'am. He was a very able man, and in the building of one of Sŏl'o-mon's castles, he had charge over all the work done by the men of his tribe. One day a prophet of the Lord, named Ȧ-hī'jah, met the young Jĕr-o-bō'am as he was going out of Jĕ-ru'sȧ-lĕm. Ȧ-hī'jah took off his own mantle and tore it into twelve pieces. Ten of these pieces he gave to Jĕr-o-bō'am, saying to him:

"Take these ten pieces, for thus saith the Lord, the God of Ĭṣ'ra-el, I will tear the kingdom out of the hand of Sŏl'o-mon's son and will give ten tribes to you. But Sŏl'o-mon's son shall have one tribe for my servant Dā'vid's sake, and for the sake of Jĕ-ru'-sȧ-lĕm. You shall reign over ten of the tribes of Ĭṣ'ra-el and shall have all that you desire. And if you will do my will, saith the Lord, then I will be with you, and will give to your children and children's children to rule long over this land."

When King Sŏl'o-mon heard what the prophet Ȧ-hī'jah had said and done, he tried to kill Jĕr-o-bō'am. But Jĕr-o-bō'am fled into Ē'ġўpt and stayed there until the end of Sŏl'o-mon's reign.

Sŏl'o-mon reigned in all forty years, as Dā'vid had reigned before him. He died and was buried on Mount Zī'ŏn, and Rē-ho-bō'am, his son, became king in his place.

Sometimes the reign of Sŏl'o-mon has been called "the Golden Age of Ĭṣ'ra-el," because it was a time of peace and of wide rule and of great riches. But it would be better to call it "the Gilded Age," because under all the show and glitter of Sŏl'o-mon's reign, there were many evil things, a king allowing and helping the worship of idols, a court filled with idle and useless nobles, and the poor of the land heavily burdened with taxes and labor. The empire of Sŏl'o-mon was ready to fall in pieces, and the fall soon came.

Part Fourth

STORIES OF THE KINGDOM OF ISRAEL

The Breaking Up of a Great Kingdom

HEN the strong rule of King Sŏl'o-mon was ended by his death, and his weak son, Rē'ho-bō'am, followed him as king, all the people of Iṣ'ra-el rose as one man against the heavy burdens which Sŏl'o-mon had laid upon the land. They would not allow Rē-ho-bō'am to be crowned king in Jĕ-ru'-ṣā-lĕm, but made him come to Shē'chem, in the tribe land of Ē'phră-ĭm, and in the center of the country. The people sent for Jĕr-o-bō'am, who was in Ē'ġy̆pt, and he became their leader. They said to Rē-ho-bō'am, "Your father, Sŏl'o-mon, laid upon us heavy burdens of taxes and of work. If you will promise to take away our load, and make the taxes and the work lighter, then we will receive you as king, and will serve you."

"Give me three days," said Rē-ho-bō'am, "and then I will tell you what I will do."

So Jĕr-o-bō'am and the people waited for three days, while Rē-ho-bō'am talked with the rulers and with his friends. Rē-ho-bō'am first called together the old men who had stood before the throne of Sŏl'o-mon and had helped him in his rule. He said to these men, "What answer shall I give to this people, who ask to have their burdens made light?"

And these old men said to King Rē-ho-bō'am, "If you will be wise today and yield to the people and speak good words to them, then they will submit to you and will serve you always. Tell them that you will take off the heavy burdens and that you will rule the land in kindness."

But Rē-ho-bō'am would not heed the advice of these wise old men. He talked with the young princes who had grown up with him in the palace and who cared nothing for the people or their troubles; and he said to these young men, "The people are asking

291

to have their heavy burdens taken away. What shall I say to them?"

And the young nobles said to Rē-ho-bō′am, "Say to the people this, 'My father made your burdens heavy, but I will make them heavier still. My father beat you with whips, but I will sting you with scorpions.' My little finger shall be thicker than my father's waist.' "

On the third day Jĕr-o-bō′am and all the people came to Rē-ho-bō′am for his answer. And the foolish young king did not follow the good advice of the old men who knew the people and their needs. He did as the haughty young princes told him to do, and spoke harshly to the people and said, "My father made your yoke heavy, but I will add to it and make it heavier. You will find my little finger thicker than my father's waist. My father struck you with whips, but I will sting you with scorpions." Then the people of Iṣ′ra-el were very angry against the king. They said, "Why should we submit any longer to the house of Dā′vid? Let us leave the family of Dā′vid and choose a king of our own. To your tents, O Iṣ′ra-el! Now, Rē-ho-bō′am, son of Dā′vid, care for your own house!"

Thus in one day ten of the twelve tribes of Iṣ′ra-el broke away forever from the rule of King Rē-ho-bō′am and the house of

Dā'vid. They made Jĕr-o-bō'am, of the tribe of Ē'phră-ĭm, their king. In his kingdom was all the land northward from Bĕth'el to Dăn, and also all the tribes on the east of the river Jôr'dan. His kingdom being the larger, was called Ĭṣ'ra-el; but it was also called 'the kingdom of the Ten Tribes," and because Ē'phră-ĭm was its leading tribe, it was often spoken of as "the land of Ē'phră-ĭm."

When Rē-ho-bō'am saw that he had lost his kingdom, he made haste to save his life by fleeing away from Shē'chem. He rode in his chariot quickly to Jĕ-ru̍'să-lĕm, where the people were his friends; and there he ruled as king, but only over the tribe of Jū'dah and as much of Bĕn'ja-mĭn as was south of Bĕth'el. The tribe of Sĭm'e-on had once lived on the south of Jū'dah, but some of its people were lost among the people of Jū'dah and others among the Arabs of the desert, so that it was no longer a separate tribe.

Rē-ho-bō'am ruled over the mountain country on the west of the Dead Sea, but he had no control over the Phĭ-lĭs'tĭne cities on the plain beside the Great Sea. So the kingdom of Jū'dah, as it was called, was less than one third the size of the kingdom of Ĭṣ'ra-el, or the Ten Tribes.

Dā'vid had conquered, and Sŏl'o-mon had ruled, not only the land of Ĭṣ'ra-el, but Sȳr'ĭ-à on the north of Ĭṣ'ra-el, reaching up to the great river Eū-phrā'tēṣ, and Ăm'mon by the desert on the east, and Mō'ab on the east of the Dead Sea, and Ē'dom on the south. When the kingdom was divided, all the empire of Sŏl'o-mon was broken up. The Sȳr'ĭ-anṣ formed a kingdom of their own, having Dă-măs'cus as its chief city. The Ăm'mon-ītes, the Mō'ab-ītes, and the Ē'dom-ītes all had their own kings, though the king of Mō'ab was for a time partly under the king of Ĭṣ'ra-el, and the king of Ē'dom partly under the king of Jū'dah. So the great and strong empire founded by Dā'vid and held by Sŏl'o-mon, fell apart and became six small, struggling states.

Yet all this was by the will of the Lord, who did not wish Ĭṣ'ra-el to become a great nation, but a good people. The Ĭṣ'ra-el-ītes were growing rich and were living for the world, while God desired them to be his people and to worship him only. So, when Rē-ho-bō'am undertook to gather an army to fight the Ten Tribes, and to bring them under his rule, God sent a prophet to Rē-ho-bō'am, who said to him, "Thus saith the Lord, Ye shall not go up and fight against your brothers, the children of Is̱'ra-el. Return every man to his house; for it is God's will that there should be two kingdoms."

And the men of Jū'dah obeyed the word of the Lord and left the Ten Tribes to have their own kingdom and their own king.

Story Two   I KINGS 12 : 25 to 14 : 20; 15 : 25-32

The King Who Led Israel to Sin, and the Prophet Who Was Slain by a Lion

THE LORD had told Jĕr-o-bō'am that he should become king over the Ten Tribes; and the Lord had promised Jĕr-o-bō'am that if he would serve the Lord and do his will, then his kingdom would become great and his descendants, those who should come after him, should sit long on the throne. But Jĕr-o-bō'am, though wise in worldly matters, was not faithful to the Lord God of Is̱'ra-el.

He saw that his people, though separated from the rule of King Rē-ho-bō'am, still went up to Jĕ-ru'sȧ-lĕm to worship in the Temple. Jĕr-o-bō'am said to himself:

"If my people go up to worship at Jĕ-ru'sȧ-lĕm, then after a time they will become the friends of Rē-ho-bō'am and his people; and then they will leave me or perhaps kill me, and let Rē-ho-bō'am rule again over all the land. I will build places for worship and altars in my own kingdom; and then my people will not need to go abroad to worship."

Jĕr-o-bō'am forgot that the Lord, who had given him the kingdom, could care for him and keep him, if he should be faithful to he Lord. But because he would not trust the Lord, he did that which was very evil. He chose two places, Bĕth'el in the south, on the road to Jĕ-ru̯'så-lĕm, and Dăn far in the north; and made these places of worship for his people. And for each place he made a calf of gold, and set it up; and he said to the people: "It is too far for you to go up to Jĕ-ru̯'så-lĕm to worship. Here are gods for you, at Bĕth'el and at Dăn. These are the gods which brought you up out of the land of Ē'ġẏpt. Come and worship these gods."

And as the priests of the tribe of Lē'vī would not serve in Jĕr-o-bō'am's idol temples, he took men out of all the tribes, some of them common and low men, and made them his priests. And all through the land, upon hills and high places, Jĕr-o-bō'am caused images to be set up, to lead the people in worshiping idols.

In the fall of the year there was held a feast to the Lord in Jĕ-ru̯'-så-lĕm, to which the people went from all the land. Jĕr-o-bō'am made a great feast at Bĕth'el, a few weeks later than the feast at Jĕ-ru̯'så-lĕm, in order to draw people to his idol temple at Bĕth'el, and to keep them away from the Temple of the Lord at Jĕ-ru̯'så-lĕm. At this feast King Jĕr-o-bō'am went up to the idol altar at Bĕth'el, and burned incense, which was a sweet-smelling smoke, made by burning certain gums. Thus Jĕr-o-bō'am led his people away from the Lord to idols; and ever after this, when his name is mentioned in the Bible, he is spoken of as "Jĕr-o-bō'am, who made Iṣ'ra-el to sin."

On a day when Jĕr-o-bō'am was offering incense at the altar, a man of God, a prophet, came from Jū'dah; and he cried out against the altar, saying:

"O altar, altar, thus saith the Lord, Behold, in the time to come there shall rise up a man of the house of Dā'vid, Jŏ-sī'ah by name. And Jŏ-sī'ah shall burn upon this altar the bones of the priests that have offered sacrifices to idols in this place. And this altar and this temple shall be destroyed."

The prophet from Jū'dah also said to Jĕr-o-bō'am, "I will prove to you that I am speaking in the power of the Lord; and this shall be the sign. This altar shall fall apart, and the ashes upon it shall be poured out."

When King Jĕr-o-bō'am heard this, he was very angry. He stretched out his arm toward the prophet and called to his guards, saying, "Take hold of that man!"

And instantly the hand which Jĕr-o-bō'am held out toward the prophet dried up and became helpless. And as if by an earthquake the altar before which the king stood was torn apart and the ashes fell out upon the ground. Then the king saw that this was the work of the Lord. He said to the prophet, "Pray to the Lord your God for me, that he may make my hand well again."

Then the prophet prayed to the Lord, and the Lord heard his prayer and made the king's hand well once more. Then King Jĕr-o-bō'am said to the prophet, "Come home with me and dine and rest; and I will give you a reward."

And the man of God said to the king:

"If you would give me half of your house, I will not go to your home nor eat bread nor drink water in this place. For the word of the Lord came to me, saying, 'Eat no bread and drink no water in this place; and go to your home in Jū'dah by another way.'"

So the man of God left Bĕth'el by a road different from that by which he came, and went toward his own home in the land of Jū'dah.

There was living in Bĕth'el at that time another prophet, an old man. His sons told him of the coming of the man of God from Jū'dah, what he had said and what the Lord had wrought. The old man learned from his sons which road the prophet had taken, and followed after him and found him resting under an oak tree. He said to him:

"Are you the man of God that came from Jū'dah?"

And he said, "I am." Then said the old prophet of Bĕth'el to him, "Come home with me, and have supper with me."

But the man of God said to him, "The Lord has commanded me not to eat bread or drink water in this place; and I must therefore go back to my own home in the land of Jū'dah."

Then the old man said:

"I am a prophet of the Lord as you are; and an angel spoke to me from the Lord, saying, 'Bring the prophet from Jū'dah back to your house, and let him eat and drink with you.'"

Now this was not true. It was a wicked lie. Then the prophet
rom Jū'dah went home with him and took a meal at his house.
This also was not right, for he should have obeyed what the Lord
ıad said to him, even though another man claimed to have heard
. different message from the Lord.

And even while they were sitting at the table, a word came
'rom the Lord to the old prophet who had told the lie; and he
:ried out to the prophet from Jū'dah, saying:

"Thus saith the Lord, 'Because you have disobeyed my com-
nand, and have come back to this place, and have eaten bread and
lrunk water here, therefore you shall die and your body shall not
ɔe buried in the tomb with your fathers.' "

After dinner the prophet started again to ride upon his ass back
.o his own home. And on the way a lion came out and killed
ıim. But the lion did not eat the man's body. He stood beside
ıt, and the ass stood by it also. And this was told to the old
prophet whose lies had led him to disobey the Lord! Then the
ɔld prophet came and took up his body and laid it in his own tomb
ınd mourned over him. And he said to his sons:

"When I am dead, bury me beside the body of the prophet from
the land of Jū'dah. For I know that what he spoke as the message
of God against the altar at Běth'el shall surely come to pass."

At one time the child of King Jěr-o-bō'am was taken very ill:
and his mother, the queen, went to the prophet Ă-hī'jah, the one
who had promised the kingdom to Jěr-o-bō'am, who was now an
old man and blind, to ask if the child would be well again. But
Ă-hī'jah said to her, "Tell King Jěr-o-bō'am that thus saith the
Lord to him:

"You have done evil worse than any before you; and have made graven images and have cast the Lord behind your back. Therefore the Lord will bring evil upon you and upon your house. Your sick child shall die, and every other child of yours shall be slain; and your family shall be swept away. The dogs shall eat the bodies of your children in the city, and the birds of the air shall eat these that die in the field. And in times to come God shall smite Ĭs'ra-el, and shall carry them into a land far away, because of the idols which they have worshiped."

And after this Jĕr-o-bō'am died and his son Nā'dăb began to reign in his place. But after two years Bā'a-shà, one of his servants, rose up against Nā'dăb and killed him and made himself king over Ĭs'ra-el. And Bā'a-shà killed every child of Jĕr-o-bō'am, and left not one son or daughter of Jĕr-o-bō'am alive, as Ă-hī'jah the prophet had said.

So, although Jĕr-o-bō'am was made king, as God had promised him, it came to pass that the kingdom was taken away from his family, because he did not obey the word of the Lord.

Story Three   I KINGS 15 : 33 to 17 : 24

The Prophet Whose Prayer Raised a Boy to Life

AFTER Jĕr-o-bō'am and Nā'dăb his son, Bā'a-shà reigned as king of Ĭs'ra-el. But he did as Jĕr-o-bō'am had done before him, disobeying the word of the Lord and worshiping idols. Therefore the Lord sent a prophet to Bā'a-shà, saying, "Thus saith the Lord to Bā'a-shà, king of Ĭs'ra-el, I lifted you up from the dust and made you the prince over my people Ĭs'ra-el. But you have walked in the way of Jĕr-o-bō'am, and have made Ĭs'ra-el sin. Therefore your family shall be destroyed, like the family of Jĕr-o-bō'am."

When Bā'a-shȧ died, his son Ē'lah became king; but while he was drinking wine and making himself drunk, his servant, Zĭm'rī, came in and killed him, and killed also all his family, and all the children of Bā'a-shȧ, so that not one was left.

Zĭm'rī tried to make himself king, but his reign was short, only seven days. Ŏm'rī, the general of the Iṣ'ra-el-īte army, made war upon him and shut him up in his palace. When Zĭm'rī found that he could not escape, he set his palace on fire and was burned up with it. After this there was war in Iṣ'ra-el between Ŏm'rī and another man named Tĭb'nī, each trying to win the kingdom. But at last Tĭb'nī was slain, and Ŏm'rī became king.

Ŏm'rī was not a good man, for he worshiped idols, like the kings before him. But he was a strong king and made his kingdom great. He made peace with the kingdom of Jū'dah, for there had been war between Jū'dah and Iṣ'ra-el ever since Jĕr-o-bō'am had founded the kingdom. Ŏm'rī bought a hill in the middle of the land, from a man named Shē'mēr; and on the hill he built a city which he named Sȧ-mā'rĭ-ȧ, after the name of the man from whom he had bought the hill. The city of Sȧ-mā'rĭ-ȧ became in Iṣ'ra-el what Jĕ-ru'sȧ-lĕm was in Jū'dah, the chief city and capital. Before the time of Ŏm'rī, the kings of Iṣ'ra-el had lived in different cities, sometimes in Shē'chem, and sometimes in Tĭr'zah; but after Ŏm'rī all the kings lived in Sȧ-mā'rĭ-ȧ; so that the kingdom itself was often called "the kingdom of Sȧ-mā'rĭ-ȧ."

After Ŏm'rī came his son, Ā'hăb, as king of Iṣ'ra-el, reigning in Sȧ-mā'rĭ-ȧ. He was worse than any of the kings before him. Ā'hăb took for his wife Jĕz'e-bĕl, the daughter of the king of Zī'dŏn, on the coast of the Great Sea; and Jĕz'e-bĕl brought into Iṣ'ra-el the worship of Bā'al and of the Ăsh-ē'rah, which was far more wicked than even the worship of the golden calves at Bĕth'el and Dăn. And Jĕz'e-bĕl was so bitter against the worship of the Lord God of Iṣ'ra-el that she sought out the prophets of the Lord everywhere, and slew them; so that to save their lives, the prophets hid in caves among the mountains.

You remember that when Jŏsh'u-ȧ destroyed and burned the city of Jĕr'ĭ-chō, he spoke a curse, in the name of the Lord, upon any man who should ever build again the walls of Jĕr'ĭ-chō. (See

Story Two in Part Second.)   In the days of Ā'hăb, king of Ĭs'ra-el,
five hundred years after Jŏsh'u-à, the walls of Jĕr'ĭ-chō were built
by a man named Hī'el, who came from Bĕth'el, the place of the
idol temple.   When he laid the foundation of the wall, his oldest
son, Ȧ-bī'ram, died; and when he set up the gates of the city, his
youngest son, Sē'gub, died.   Thus came to pass the word of the
Lord spoken by Jŏsh'u-à.

In the reign of King Ā'hăb a great prophet suddenly rose up,
named Ê-lī'jah.   He came from the land of Gĭl'e-ăd, beyond the
river Jôr'dan, and he lived alone out in the wilderness.   His clothing was a mantle of skin and his hair and beard were long and
rough.   Without any warning, Ê-lī'jah came into the presence of
King Ā'hăb, and said, "As the Lord God of Ĭs'ra-el lives, before
whom I stand, there shall not fall upon the ground any dew or rain
until I call for it."

And then he went away as suddenly as he had come.   At the
Lord's command he hid himself in a wild place by the brook
Chē'rĭth, which flows down from the mountains into the river
Jôr'dan.   There he drank of the water in the brook, and every day
the wild birds, the ravens, brought him food.

It came to pass as Ê-lī'jah had said, that no rain fell upon the
land, and there was not even any dew upon the grass.   Every day

the brook from which Ê-lī'jah drank grew smaller, until at last it was dry, and there was no water. Then the Lord spoke to Ê-lī'jah again and said, "Rise up, and go to Zăr'e-phăth, which is near to Zī'dŏn, by the Great Sea, on the north of the land of Ĭs'ra-el. I have commanded a widow woman there to care for you."

So Ê-lī'jah left the brook Chē'rĭth and walked northward through the land until he came near to the city of Zăr'e-phăth. There, beside the gate of the city, he saw a woman dressed as a widow picking up sticks. Ê-lī'jah said to her, "Will you bring to me some water, that I may drink?"

She went to bring him the water, and Ê-lī'jah said again, "Bring me also, I pray you, a little piece of bread to eat."

And the woman said to Ê-lī'jah, "As sure as the Lord your God lives, I have not in the house even a loaf of bread; but only one handful of meal in the barrel and a little oil in a bottle; and now I am gathering a few sticks to make a fire, that I may bake it for me and my son; and when we have eaten it, there is nothing left for us but to die."

Then the word of the Lord came to Ê-lī'jah, and he said to the woman, "Fear not; go and do as you have said; but first make me a little cake, and bring it to me, and afterward make for yourself and your son. For thus saith the Lord, the God of Ĭs'ra-el, 'The barrel of meal shall not waste nor the bottle of oil fail, until the day when the Lord sends rain upon the earth.'"

And the widow woman believed Ê-lī'jah's word. She took from her barrel the meal and from her bottle the oil and made a little cake for the prophet, and then found enough left for herself and for her son. And the barrel always had meal in it and the bottle held oil every day. And the prophet and the woman and her son had food as long as they needed it.

After this, one day the son of the widow was taken very ill, and his illness was so great that there was no breath left in him. The boy's mother said to Ê-lī'jah, "O man of God! have you come here to cause my son to die?"

And Ê-lī'jah said to her, "Give me your son."

And Ê-lī'jah carried the boy up to his own room, and laid him on the bed. Then he cried to the Lord, and said, "O Lord God,

hast thou brought trouble upon this woman, by taking away th
life of her son?"

Then he stretched himself upon the child's body three time
and cried to the Lord again, "O Lord God, I pray thee, let th
child's soul come into him again!"

And the Lord heard Ê-lī'jah's prayer, and the child becam
living once more. Then Ê-lī'jah carried the living boy back t
his mother; and she said, "Now I am sure that you are a man o
God, and that the word of the Lord God which you speak is th
truth."

Story Four   I KINGS 18 : 1-4

The Prayer That Was Answered in Fire

THREE years passed after Ê-lī'jah gave the message o
the Lord to King Ā'hăb, and in all that time no rai
fell upon the land of Iṣ'ra-el. Everywhere the brook
ceased to flow, the springs became dry, the groun
was parched, and the fields gave no harvest. Ther
was no grass for the cattle and the flocks, and there was scarcel
any food for the people.

King Ā'hăb was in great trouble. He knew that Ê-lī'jah ha
the power to call down rain; but Ê-lī'jah was nowhere to be foun
He sent men to search for him everywhere in the land, and h
asked the kings of the nations around to look for him in thei
countries; for he hoped to persuade the prophet to set the lan
free from the long drought by calling for rain.

When the land was at its worst, in the third year, Ā'hăb calle
the chief of his servants, the man who stood next to the king. Hi
name was Ō-ba-dī'ah, and, unlike Ā'hăb, he was a good man, wor
shiping the Lord, and trying to do right. Once, when Quee

ĕz'e-bĕl sought to kill all the prophets of the Lord, Ō-ba-dī'ah
iid a hundred of them in two caves, fifty in each cave, and gave
hem food and kept them in safety.

Ā'hăb said to Ō-ba-dī'ah, "Let us go through all the land, you
n one part, and I in another, and look for running streams and
ountains of water. Perhaps we can find some water, enough to
ave a part of the horses and mules, so that we may not lose them
.ll."

And as Ō-ba-dī'ah was going through his part of the country,
ooking for water, suddenly Ê-lī'jah met him. Ō-ba-dī'ah knew
Ê-lī'jah at once. He fell on his face before him and said, "Is this
ny lord Ê-lī'jah?"

And Ê-lī'jah answered him, "Yes, it is Ê-lī'jah. Go and tell
your master that Ê-lī'jah is here."

And Ō-ba-dī'ah said, "O my lord, what wrong have I done, that
you would cause King Ā-hăb to kill me? For there is not a land
where Ā'hăb has not sent for you; and now when I go to tell him
hat you are here, the Spirit of the Lord will send you away to
;ome other place, and then if Ā'hăb cannot find you, he will be
ingry at me and kill me. Do you not know that I fear the Lord
ind serve him?"

And Ê-lī'jah said, "As the Lord God lives, I will surely show
nyself to King Ā'hăb today."

So Ō-ba-dī'ah went to meet Ā'hăb and told him of Ê-lī'jah's
:oming; and Ā'hăb went to meet Ê-lī'jah. When Ā'hăb saw
Ê-lī'jah, he said to him, "Are you here, you that have brought all
this trouble upon Ĭṣ'ra-el?"

And Ê-lī'jah answered the king, "I am not the one that has
brought trouble upon Ĭṣ'ra-el. It is you and your house; for you
have turned away from the commands of the Lord and have worshiped the images of Bā'al. Now send and bring all the people
to Mount Cär'mel, and with them the four hundred prophets of
Bā'al and the four hundred prophets of the Ăsh-ē'rah, who eat at
Jĕz'e-bĕl's table."

So Ā'hăb did as Ê-lī'jah commanded and brought all the people
to Mount Cär'mel, which stands by the Great Sea. And Ê-lī'jah
stood before all the multitude, and he said to them, "How long

will you go halting and limping back and forth between two sides
not choosing either? If the Lord is God, follow him; but if Bā'al
is God, then follow him."

And the people had not a word to say. Then Ê-lī'jah spoke
again and said, "I am alone, the only prophet of the Lord here
today; but Bā'al's prophets are four hundred and fifty men. Now
let the people give us two young oxen, one for Bā'al's prophets
and one for me. Let the prophets of Bā'al take one ox and cut it
up and lay it on the altar on the wood. But let no fire be placed
under it. And I will do the same; then you call on your god, and
I will call on the Lord. And the God who sends down fire upon
his altar, he shall be the God of Iṣ'ra-el."

And the people said, "What you have spoken is right. We
will do as you say and will see who is the true God."

Then the two oxen were brought, and one was cut in pieces
and laid on the altar of Bā'al. The prophets of Bā'al stood around
the altar and cried aloud, "O Bā'al, hear us!" But there was no
answer, nor any voice. After a time the worshipers of Bā'al became furious. They leaped and danced around the altar, and they
cut themselves with swords and lances, until the blood gushed out
upon them. And Ê-lī'jah laughed at them, and mocked them,
calling out, "Call out louder, for surely he is a god! Perhaps he is
sitting still and thinking, or he has gone on a journey; or perhaps
he is asleep and must be awaked!"

But it was all in vain. The middle of the afternoon came, and
there was no answer. The altar stood with its offering, but no
fire came upon it. Then Ê-lī'jah said to all the people, "Come
near to me."

And they came near. He found an old altar to the Lord that
had been thrown down, and he took twelve stones, one for each
of the twelve tribes, and piled them up to form the altar anew.
Around the altar he dug a trench, to carry away water. Then he
cut wood and laid it on the altar, and on the wood he placed the
young ox, cut into pieces for a sacrifice. Then he said, "Fill four
barrels with water, and pour it on the offering."

The Great Sea was near at hand, in sight of all the people; and
from it they brought four barrels of water, and poured it on the

altar. He called upon them to do it again, and a third time, until the offering and the wood and the altar were soaked through and through, and the trench was filled with water.

Then, in the sight of all the people, Ê-lī′jah, the prophet, drew near, and stood all alone before the altar, and prayed in these words, "O Lord, the God of Ā′bră-hăm, of Ī′saac, and of Iṣ′ra-el, let it be known this day that thou art God in Iṣ′ra-el, and that I am thy servant, and that I have done all these things at thy word. Hear me, O Lord, hear me; that this people may know that thou, Lord, art God, and that thou hast turned their hearts back again to thyself."

Then the fire fell from the Lord and burned up the offering and the wood and the stones and the dust, and licked up the water that was in the trench. And when the people saw it, they fell on their faces, and they cried, "The Lord, he is God! The Lord, he is God!" And Ê-lī′jah said to the people, "Seize the prophets of Bā′al; let not one of them escape!"

They took them all, four hundred and fifty men; and by Ê-lī′-jah's command, they brought them down to the dry bed of the brook Kī′shŏn, at the foot of the mountain; and there Ê-lī′jah had them put to death, because they had led Iṣ′ra-el into sin.

Ā'hăb, the king, was present upon Mount Cär'mel and saw all that had been done. Ê-lī'jah now said to Ā'hăb, "Rise up; eat and drink; for there is a sound of a great rain."

While Ā'hăb was eating and drinking, Ê-lī'jah was praying upon Mount Cär'mel. He bowed down, with his face between his knees, and prayed to the Lord to send rain. After a time he sent his servant up to the top of the mountain, saying, "Go up and look toward the sea."

When the servant returned he said, "I can see nothing."

Ê-lī'jah sent him up seven times; and at the seventh time his servant said, "I see a cloud rising out of the sea as small as a man's hand."

Then Ê-lī'jah sent to Ā'hăb, saying, "Hasten; make ready your chariot before the rain stops you."

In a little while the sky was covered with black clouds, and there came a great rain. And Ā'hăb rode in his chariot to his palace at Jĕz're-el, on the eastern side of the great plain. And the power of the Lord was on Ê-lī'jah, and he ran before Ā'hăb's chariot to the gate of the city.

Thus in one day a great victory was wrought for the Lord God, and the power of Bā'al was thrown down.

Story Five   I KINGS 19 : 1-21

The Voice That Spoke to Elijah in the Mount

WHEN King Ā'hăb told his wife, Queen Jĕz'e-bĕl, of all that Ê-lī'jah had done; how the fire had fallen from heaven upon his altar and how he had slain all the prophets of Bā'al with the sword, Queen Jĕz'e-bĕl was very angry. She sent a messenger to Ê-lī'jah with these words:

"May the gods do to me as you have done to the prophets of

Bā'al, if I do not by tomorrow kill you, as you, Ê-lī'jah, have killed them!"

Ê-lī'jah saw that his life was in danger, and he found that not one man in all the kingdom dared to stand by him against the hate of Queen Jĕz'e-bĕl. He rose up and ran away to save his life. He went southward to the land of Jū'dah, but did not feel safe even there. He hastened across Jū'dah southward to Bē'er=shē'bȧ, which is on the edge of the desert, eighty miles away from Sȧ-mā'rĭ-ȧ. But not even here did Ê-lī'jah dare to stay, for he still feared the wrath of Queen Jĕz'e-bĕl. He left his servant at Bē'er= shē'bȧ, and went out alone into the desert, over which the children of Ĭṣ'ra-el had wandered four hundred years before. After he had walked all day under the sun and over the burning sand, he sat down to rest under a juniper tree. He was tired and hungry and discouraged. He felt that his work had all been in vain, that in heart the people were still worshipers of Bā'al; and he felt, too, that he had shown weakness in running away from his place of duty in fear of Queen Jĕz'e-bĕl. Ê-lī'jah cried out to the Lord and said, "O Lord, I have lived long enough! Take away my life, O Lord, for I am no better than my people!" Then, tired out, he lay down to sleep under the tree. But the Lord was very kind to Ê-lī'jah. While he was sleeping, an angel touched him and said, "Arise and eat."

He opened his eyes and saw beside him a little fire, with a loaf of bread baking upon it, and near it a bottle of water. He ate and drank and then lay down to sleep again. A second time he felt the angel touch him, and he heard a voice say, "Arise and eat; because the journey is too long for you."

He arose and ate once more. Then he went on his way, and in the strength given him by that food, he walked forty days through the desert. He came at last to Mount Hō'reb, the mountain where Mō'ṣeṣ saw the burning bush and where God spoke forth the words of the Ten Commandments. Ê-lī'jah found a cave in the side of the mountain and went into it to rest. While he was in the cave, he heard God's voice speaking to him and saying, "What are you doing here, Ê'lī'jah?"

And Ê-lī'jah said to the Lord, "O Lord God, I have been very

earnest for thee; for the people of Ĭṣ'ra-el have turned away from
their promise to serve thee; they have thrown down thine altars
and have slain thy prophets with the sword; and now I, even I
only, am left; and they are seeking my life, to take it away."

Then the Lord said to Ê-lī'jah, "Go out and stand upon the
mountain before the Lord."

Then, while Ê-lī'jah was standing upon the mountain, a great
and strong wind swept by and tore the mountains apart and broke
the rocks in pieces; but the Lord was not in the wind. Then came
an earthquake, shaking the mountains; but the Lord was not in the
earthquake. And after the earthquake a fire passed by; but the
Lord was not in the fire. And after the fire there was silence and
stillness, and Ê-lī'jah heard a low, quiet voice which he knew was
the voice of the Lord.

Then Ê-lī'jah wrapped his face in his mantle, for he feared to
look upon the form of God, and he stood at the opening of the
cave.

The voice said to him, "What are you doing here, Ê-lī'jah?"

And Ê-lī'jah said, as he had said before, "O Lord, I have been
very earnest for thee; for the people of Ĭṣ'ra-el have turned away
from their promise to serve thee; they have thrown down thine
altars and have slain thy prophets with the sword; and now I, even
I only, am left; and they are seeking my life, to take it away."

Then the Lord said to Ê-lī'jah, "Go back to the land from which
you have come, and then go to the wilderness of Dǎ-mǎs'cus and

anoint Hăz′a-el to be king over Sўr′ĭ-à; and Jē′hū, the son of
Nĭm′shī, you shall anoint to be king over Ĭṣ′ra-el; and Ê-lī′shà, the
son of Shā′phat, of the village of Ā′bel=mĕ-hō′lah, in the land Mȧ-
năs′seh, west of Jôr′dan, you shall anoint to take your place as
prophet. And it shall come to pass that those who escape from
the sword of Hăz′a-el, Jē′hū shall slay, and those that escape from
the sword of Jē′hū shall Ê-lī′shà slay. But there will be found
some, even seven thousand men in Ĭṣ′ra-el, who have not bowed
the knee to Bā′al or kissed his image with their lips."

Here we′re tasks that would take all the rest of Ê-lī′jah's life;
for, as we shall see, some of them were not completed until after
Ê-lī′jah had passed away, though Ê-lī′jah prepared the way for
them. But they gave to Ê-lī′jah what he needed most, work to
do; a friend to stand beside him, so that he would no longer be
alone; one also who would carry on his work after him; and the
knowledge that he had not lived in vain, since there were still in
the land seven thousand men who were faithful to the Lord God
of Ĭṣ′ra-el.

One of these commands Ê-lī′jah obeyed at once. He left Mount
Hō′reb, journeyed northward through the wilderness, across the
kingdom of Jū′dah, and into the land of Ĭṣ′ra-el. He found Ā′bel=
mĕ-hō′lah, in the tribe land of Mȧ-năs′seh on the west of Jôr′dan,
and there he saw Ê-lī′shà, the son of Shā′phat. Ê-lī′shà was plowing in the field, with twelve yoke of oxen in front of him; for
Ê-lī′shà was a rich man's son, and cared for a large farm.

Ê-lī′jah came to the field where Ê-lī′shà was at work, and without a word, took off his own mantle of skin and threw it upon
Ê-lī′shà's shoulders and walked away. Ê-lī′shà knew well who
this strange, rough, hair-covered man was; and he knew, too, what
it meant when Ê-lī′jah cast his mantle upon him. It was a call for
him to leave his home, to go out into the wilderness with Ê-lī′jah,
to take up the life of a prophet, to face the danger of the queen's
hate and perhaps to be slain, as many prophets had been slain
before. But Ê-lī′shà was a man of God and he did not hesitate to
obey God's call. He left his oxen standing in the field; he ran
after Ê-lī′jah and said to him, "Let me kiss my father and my
mother and then I will go with you."

Ê-lī'jah said to him, "Go back, if you wish; for what have I
done to you?"

Then Ê-lī'sha went back to the field, killed the oxen, made a
fire with the yokes and the wooden plow, roasted the flesh of the
oxen on the fire, and gave them to be eaten by the people on the
farm. This he did to show that he had left this farm forever.
Then he kissed his father and mother and left them and went forth
to live with Ê-lī'jah and to be Ê-lī'jah's helper.

Story Six   I KINGS 20 : 1-43

The Wounded Prophet and His Story

THE COUNTRY nearest to Ĭṣ'ra-el on the north was
Sўr'ĭ-à, of which the chief city and capital was Dà-
măs'cus; and several of its kings, one after another,
were named Bĕn=hā'dăd. This kingdom was far
greater and stronger than Ĭṣ'ra-el; and when Bĕn=hā'-
dăd went to make war upon King Ā'hăb, such was the fear of the
Ĭṣ'ra-el-ītes for the Sўr'ĭ-anṣ, that Ā'hăb could bring only seven
thousand men against the Sўr'ĭ-an army. The host of the Sўr'ĭ-
anṣ filled all the valleys and plains around Sà-mā'rĭ-à; but Bĕn=
hā'dăd and his chief rulers were drinking wine when they should
have been making ready for the battle; and the little army of Ĭṣ'-
ra-el won a great victory over the Sўr'ĭ-anṣ, and drove them back
to their own land.

Again the Sўr'ĭ-anṣ came against Ĭṣ'ra-el, with an army as large
as before; but again God gave to Ā'hăb and the Ĭṣ'ra-el-ītes a victory, and the Sўr'ĭ-an army was destroyed. King Bĕn=hā'dăd fled
away to his palace, and King Ā'hăb might easily have taken him
prisoner and conquered all Sўr'ĭ-à. If he had done this, all danger
from that land might have been forever removed. But Bĕn=hā'-

lăd dressed himself in sackcloth and put a rope around his waist
and came as a beggar to Ā'hăb and pleaded with him for his life
and his kingdom. Ā'hăb felt very proud to have so great a king
as Běn=hā'dăd come kneeling before him. He spared his life and
gave him back his kingdom. This was not wise; and God soon
showed to Ā'hăb what a mistake he had made.

By this time, through the teaching of Ė-lī'jah and Ė-lī'shà,
there were many prophets of the Lord in Ĭṣ'ra-el. The word of
the Lord came to one of these prophets and he said to a fellow
prophet, "Strike me and give me a wound."

But the man would not strike him, and the prophet said, "Because you have not obeyed the voice of the Lord, as soon as you
go away from me, a lion shall kill you."

And as the man was going away, a lion rushed out upon him
and killed him. Then the prophet said to another man, "Strike
me, I pray you!"

The man struck him and wounded him, so that the bloo(flowed. Then the prophet, all bloody, with his face covered, stoo(by the road as King Ā'hăb passed by, and he cried out to the king The king saw him and stopped and asked him what had happenec to him. Then the prophet said, "O king, I was in the battle; anc a soldier brought to me a prisoner, and said to me, 'Keep this man if you lose him, then your life shall go for his life, or you shall pay me a talent of silver for him.' And while I was busy here anc there, the prisoner escaped. Now, O king, do not let my life be taken for the man's life."

But the king said, "You have given sentence against yourself and it shall be so. Your life shall go for your prisoner's life."

Then the prophet threw off the covering from his face and the king saw that he was one of the prophets. And the prophet said to the king, "Thus saith the Lord, 'Because you have let go the king whom I willed to have destroyed, therefore your life shall go for his life, and your people for his people.' "

When Ā'hăb heard this, he was greatly troubled and displeased. He went to his palace in Să-mā'rĭ-à full of alarm, for he saw that he had not done wisely for his own kingdom in sparing his king- dom's greatest enemy.

Story Seven

I KINGS 21 : 1-29

What Ahab Paid for His Vineyard

KING Ā'HĂB'S home was at Să-mā'rĭ-à, the capital of the kingdom. But he had also a palace at Jĕz're-el, which overlooked the great plain of Ĕs-dra-ē'lon. And beside Ā'hăb's palace at Jĕz're-el was a vineyard, belonging to a man named Nā'bŏth. Ā'hăb wished to own this vineyard and he said to Nā'bŏth, "Let me have your vineyard, which is near my house. I would like to make of it a

:arden for vegetables. I will give you a better vineyard in place
)f it, or I will pay you the worth of it in money."

But Nā'bŏth answered the king, "This vineyard has belonged
o my father's family for many generations and I am not willing
o give it up or to leave it."

Ā'hăb was very angry when he heard this. He came into his
iouse and refused to eat; but he lay down on his bed and turned
iis face to the wall. His wife Jĕz'e-bĕl came to him and said,
'Why are you so sad? What is troubling you?"

And Ā'hăb answered her, "I asked Nā'bŏth to sell me his vineyard or to let me give him another vineyard for it, and he would
iot."

Then Jĕz'e-bĕl said to him, "Do you indeed rule over the kingdom of Ĭs'ra-el? Rise up and eat your dinner and enjoy yourself.
I will give you the vineyard of Nā'bŏth." Then Queen Jĕz'e-bĕl
sat down and wrote a letter in Ā'hăb's name and sealed it with the
king's seal. And in the letter she wrote, "Let the word be given
out that a meeting of the men of Jĕz're-el is to be held, and set
Nā'bŏth up before all the people. Have ready two men, no matter how worthless and wicked they may be, who will swear that
they heard Nā'bŏth speak words of cursing against God and
against the king. Then take Nā'bŏth out and stone him with
stones until he is dead."

Such was the fear of Queen Jĕz'e-bĕl among all the people that
they did as she gave command. They held a meeting and set
Nā'bŏth up in presence of the people; then they brought in two
men, who told lies, declaring that they had heard Nā'bŏth speak
words of cursing against God and against the king; and then they
dragged Nā'bŏth out of the city and stoned him and killed him.
Afterward they sent word to Queen Jĕz'e-bĕl that Nā'bŏth was
dead, and Jĕz'e-bĕl said to Ā'hăb, "Now you can go and take as
your own the vineyard of Nā'bŏth in Jĕz're-el; for Nā'bŏth is no
longer living; he is dead."

Then Ā'hăb rode in his chariot from Să-mā'rĭ-à to Jĕz're-el, and
with him were two of his captains, one named Jē'hū and another
named Bĭd'kär. Just as they were riding in the vineyard that had

been Nā′bŏth's, suddenly Ê-lī′jah, the prophet, with his mantle of skin, stood before them.

Ā′hăb was startled as he saw Ê-lī′jah and he called out, "Have you found me, O my enemy?"

"I have found you," answered Ê-lī′jah, "because you have sold yourself to do evil in the sight of the Lord. Just as the dogs licked up the blood of Nā′bŏth, shall dogs lick up your own blood. I will bring evil upon you and will sweep you away; and I will cut off every man child from Ā′hăb; and I will make your family like the family of Jĕr-o-bō′am, who made Iṣ′ra-el to sin. And because your wife, Jĕz′e-bĕl, has stirred you up to sin, she shall die, and the wild dogs of the city shall eat the body of Jĕz′e-bĕl by the wall of Jĕz′re-el."

When Ā′hăb heard these words of Ê-lī′jah, he saw how wickedly he had acted and he felt sorrow for his sin. He put on sackcloth and fasted and sought for mercy. And the word of the Lord came to Ê-lī′jah, saying, "Do you see how Ā′hăb has humbled himself before me and shows sorrow for his sin? Because of this, I will not bring the evil in his lifetime, but after he is dead, I will bring it upon his children."

The Arrow That Killed a King

FTER the two victories which King Ā'hăb gained over the Sȳr'ĭ-ans, there was peace between Sȳr'ĭ-à and Ĭs'ra-el for three years. But in the third year the Sȳr'ĭ-ans became strong once more, and they seized a city of Ĭs'ra-el on the east of Jôr'dan, called Rā'-moth=ḡĭl'e-ăd. At that time there was peace and friendship between the kingdoms of Ĭs'ra-el and Jū'dah; and Ā'hăb, the king of Ĭs'ra-el, sent to Jĕ-hŏsh'a-phăt, the king of Jū'dah, saying, "Do you know that Rā'moth=ḡĭl'e-ăd is ours and yet we have done nothing to take it out of the hands of the king of Sȳr'ĭ-à? Will you go up with me to battle at Rā'moth=ḡĭl'e-ăd?" And King Jĕ-hŏsh'a-phăt sent word to the king of Ĭs'ra-el, "I am with you, and my people are with your people and my horses with your horses."

So the king of Ĭs'ra-el and the king of Jū'dah gathered their armies for war against the Sȳr'ĭ-ans, and King Jĕ-hŏsh'a-phăt came to Sà-mā'rĭ-à to meet King Ā'hăb. Jĕ-hŏsh'a-phăt was a worshiper of the Lord.

He said to Ā'hăb, "Let us ask the prophets to give us the word of the Lord before we go to battle."

Then the king of Ĭs'ra-el called together his prophets, four hundred men, not prophets of the Lord, but false prophets of the idols, and he asked them, "Shall I go up to battle at Rā'moth=ḡĭl'e-ăd or shall I remain at home?"

And the prophets of the idols said, "Go up; for the Lord will give Rā'moth=ḡĭl'e-ăd to you."

But Jĕ-hŏsh'a-phăt was not satisfied with the words of these men. He asked, "Is there not here a prophet of the Lord, of whom we can ask the Lord's will?"

"There is one prophet," answered Ā'hăb; "his name is Mī'cā'iah, the son of Ĭm'lah; but I hate him, for he never prophesies any good about me, but always evil."

315

"Let not the king say that," said Jĕ-hŏsh'a-phăt. "Let us hear what Mī-cā'iah will speak."

Then King Ā'hăb sent one of his officers to bring the prophet Mī-cā'iah. And the officer said to Mī-cā'iah, "All the prophets have spoken good to the king; now, I pray you, let your words be like theirs, and do you speak good also."

And Mī-cā'iah said, "As the Lord lives, what the Lord says to me that I will speak, and nothing else."

The king of Iṣ'ra-el and the king of Jū'dah were seated together in their royal robes at an open place in front of the gate of Sà-mā'rĭ-à. And King Ā'hăb said to Mī-cā'iah, "Speak to me nothing but the truth, in the name of the Lord."

Then Mī-cā'iah said, "I saw all Iṣ'ra-el scattered upon the mountains, as sheep that have no shepherd; and the Lord said, 'These have no master; let every man go back to his own house.' "

Then the king of Iṣ'ra-el said to Jĕ-hŏsh'a-phăt, "Did I not tell you that Mī-cā'iah would prophesy about me no good, but only evil?"

For Ā'hăb knew that the words of Mī-cā'iah meant that he would be slain in the battle.

And Mī-cā'iah went on and said, "Hear thou the word of the Lord; I saw the Lord sitting on his throne and all the host of heaven standing around him, on his right hand and on his left. And the Lord said, 'Who will go and deceive Ā'hăb, so that he will go up and fall at Rā'moth=ḡĭl'e-ăd?' One spirit came forth and said, 'I will go and will be a lying spirit in the mouth of all Ā'hăb's prophets.' And the Lord said to the spirit, 'Go and deceive him.' Now, therefore, the Lord has let all these false prophets deceive you; and the Lord has spoken evil against you."

Then the king of Iṣ'ra-el said to his guards, "Take Mī-cā'iah and lead him to the governor of the city and say, 'Put this fellow in prison, and let him have nothing to eat but dry bread and water until I come again in peace.' "

And Mī-cā'iah said, "If you return at all in peace, then the Lord has not spoken by me. Hear my words, all ye people."

So the kings of Iṣ'ra-el and Jū'dah led their armies across the river Jôr'dan and up the mountains on the east, to battle at Rā'-

noth=ḡĭl′e-ăd. Ā′hăb felt afraid after the prophecy of Mī-cā′iah, ᴀnd he said to Jĕ-hŏsh′a-phăt, "I will dress as a common soldier ɔefore going into the battle; but do you wear your royal robes."
Now the king of Sўr′ĭ-à had given word to all his captains to ᴌook out especially for the king of Ĭṣ′ra-el, and to fight him and ᴋill him, even if they should kill no other man. When they saw Jĕ-hŏsh′a-phăt in his kingly garments standing in his chariot, they thought that he was King Ā′hăb, and they turned all the battle toward him. But Jĕ-hŏsh′a-phăt cried out, and then they found that he was not the king of Ĭṣ′ra-el, and they left him. In the battle one soldier of the Sўr′ĭ-anṣ drew his bow and shot an arrow,

not knowing that he was aiming at the king of Ĭṣ′ra-el. The arrow struck King Ā′hăb just between his breastplate and his lower armor. He was badly wounded, but they held him up in his chariot, so that the men might not see him fall; and his blood was running out of the wound upon the floor of the chariot, until the sun set, when Ā′hăb died. And the cry went through all the host of Ĭṣ′ra-el, "Every man to his city and every man to his country."
Then all knew that the king of Ĭṣ′ra-el was dead. They brought his body to Sà-mā′rĭ-à and buried him there. And at the pool of Sà-mā′rĭ-à they washed the king's chariot and his armor. And there the wild dogs of the city licked up Ā′hăb's blood, according to the word of the Lord spoken by Ė-lī′jah.
Thus died King Ā′hăb, the son of Ŏm′rī. He was not a bad man at heart, but he was weak in the hands of his wife, Jĕz′e-bĕl, who led him and his kingdom into evil in the sight of the Lord.

Elijah's Chariot of Fire

AFTER the death of Ā′hăb, his son Ā-ha-zī′ah reigned for only two years as king of Ĭṣ′ra-el. He fell out of a window in his palace and was injured so that he died; and as he had no son, his brother, Jĕ-hō′ram, became king in his place.

The work of Ê-lī′jah, the prophet, was now ended, and the Lord was about to take him up to heaven. Ê-lī′jah and Ê-lī′shà went together to a place called Gĭl′găl, not the place beside the river Jôr′dan where the army of Ĭṣ′ra-el was encamped under Jŏsh′u-à, but another place of the same name among the mountains, not far from Bĕth′el.

And Ê-lī′jah said to Ê-lī′shà, "Stay here, I pray you, for the Lord has sent me to Bĕth′el."

Ê-lī′shà knew that Ê-lī′jah would be taken from him very soon, and he said, "As surely as the Lord lives and as your soul lives, I will not leave you."

So Ê-lī′jah and Ê-lī′shà walked together to Bĕth′el. At Bĕth′el were living many worshipers of the Lord, who were called "sons of the prophets," because they followed the teaching of the prophets, and some of them became prophets themselves. These men came to Ê-lī′shà and said to him, "Do you know that the Lord will take away your master from you very soon?"

And Ê-lī′shà answered them, "Yes, I know it; but hold your peace; do not speak of it."

And at Bĕth′el Ê-lī′jah said to Ê-lī′shà again, "Ê-lī′shà, stay here; for the Lord has sent me to Jĕr′ĭ-chō." But Ê-lī′shà answered him, "As surely as the Lord lives and as your soul lives, I will not leave you."

So Ê-lī′jah and Ê-lī′shà walked together down the steep road from Bĕth′el to Jĕr′ĭ-chō. And at Jĕr′ĭ-chō the followers of the prophets came to Ê-lī′shà and said to him, "Do you know that the Lord will take your master away from you today?"

And he answered them, "Yes, I know it; but hold your peace and say nothing." And Ê-lī′jah said to him again, "Stay here at Jĕr′ĭ-chō, I pray you, for the Lord has sent me to the river Jôr′dan."

But Ê-lī′sha said to Ê-lī′jah once more, "As surely as the Lord lives and as your soul lives, I will not leave you."

So Ê-lī′jah and Ê-lī′sha walked from Jĕr′ĭ-chō to the river Jôr′dan, about five miles. About fifty men of the sons of the prophets who lived at Jĕr′ĭ-chō followed them at a distance. When they came to the bank of Jôr′dan, Ê-lī′jah took his mantle and wrapped it together and struck the waters. Then the waters were divided on each side and a path was made across the river; and the two prophets walked across on dry ground. And as they walked, Ê-lī′jah said, "Ask what I shall do for you, before I am taken away from you."

Ê-lī′sha answered him, "All that I ask is that your spirit shall come upon me in greater power than comes upon any other man."

And Ê-lī′jah said to him, "You have asked a great blessing; and if you see me when I am taken away, it shall come to you; but if you do not see me, it shall not come."

As they still went on and talked, suddenly a chariot of fire and horses of fire came between them and parted them; and Ê-lī′jah went up in a whirlwind on the fiery chariot to heaven.

And Ê-lī′sha saw him going up toward heaven, and he cried out, "O my father, my father, the chariot of Ĭṣ′ra-el, and the horsemen thereof!"

He meant that in losing Ê-lī′jah the kingdom had lost more than an army of chariots and horsemen. After this he saw Ê-lī′jah no more; but he caught up the mantle of Ê-lī′jah which had fallen from him. With the mantle he struck the waters of Jôr′dan, saying, "Where now is the Lord God of Ê-lī′jah?"

And as he struck the water with Ê-lī′jah's mantle, it parted on either side, and Ê-lī′sha walked across the Jôr′dan. The sons of the prophets who were standing near the river had not seen Ê-lī′-jah go up; but now they saw Ê-lī′sha walking through the river alone, and they felt that God had taken Ê-lī′jah away. They said,

"The spirit of Ê-lī'jah now rests upon Ê-lī'shà," and they came to meet him and bowed down before him as their chief. So Ê-lī'jah was taken away, but Ê-lī'shà stood in his place as the Lord's prophet.

Story Ten

II KINGS 2 : 19 to 3 : 27

A Spring Sweetened by Salt; and Water That Looked Like Blood

AFTER Ê-lī'jah had been taken up to heaven, Ê-lī'shà stayed for a time at Jĕr'ĭ-chō; for unlike Ê-lī'jah, Ê-lī'shà did not live in the wilderness, away from the people. He lived in the cities and helped many by the power which the Lord gave to him.

The people of Jĕr'ĭ-chō said to Ê-lī'shà, "This city stands in a pleasant place; but the water of its spring is very bitter and causes disease and death; and the land around it is barren, giving no fruit."

Ê-lī'shà said to them, "Bring me a small new bottle and fill it with salt."

They brought it to him, and he poured the salt into the fountain that gave water to the city and said:

"Thus saith the Lord, 'I have healed these waters; from them there shall no more be death or unfruitfulness to the land.'"

And the waters became pure and sweet from that time onward. Many believe that the fountain which still flows at the foot of the mountain near the ruins where once stood Jĕr'ĭ-chō is the one which was healed by the prophet; and it is called "The Fountain of Ê-lī'shà."

At this time Jĕ-hō'ram, the son of Ā'hăb, was king of Ĭṣ'ra-el. He reigned twelve years, not so wickedly as his father Ā'hăb had ruled, but still doing evil in the sight of the Lord. From the days of King Dā'vid the land of Mō'ab, on the east of the Dead Sea, had been under the control of Ĭs'ra-el. The land was governed by its own king but he paid every year a large sum to Ĭs'ra-el. The king of Mō'ab in the times of Ā'hăb and Jĕ-hō'ram was named Mē'shà. He had great flocks of sheep and he paid to the king of Ĭs'ra-el every year the wool of a hundred thousand sheep and of as many rams.

When King Ā'hăb was dead, the king of Mō'ab rose against Ĭs'ra-el and tried to set his land free. Then King Jĕ-hō'ram sent for King Jĕ-hŏsh'a-phăt of Jū'dah, and these two kings gathered their armies and made war on Mē'shà, the king of Mō'ab. They led their armies southward through Jū'dah and then through Ĕ'dom, on the south of the Dead Sea, and from Ĕ'dom into the land of Mō'ab; and with them was the king of Ĕ'dom, who was under the king of Jū'dah.

While they were on their march, they found no water, either for the army or for the horses.

And the king of Ĭs'ra-el said, "Alas! The Lord has brought together these three kings, only to let them fall into the hands of the king of Mō'ab!"

But the good King Jĕ-hŏsh'a-phăt said, "Is there not here a prophet of the Lord, so that he may show us the Lord's will?"

And one man said, "Ē-lī'shà, the son of Shā'phat, is here; the man who poured water on the hands of Ē-lī'jah."

And Jĕ-hŏsh'a-phăt said, "The word of the Lord is with him; let us see him."

And the three kings went to find Ē-lī'shà; but Ē-lī'shà said to

the king of Ĭṣ'ra-el, "Why do you come to me? Go to the idol prophets of your father Ā'hăb and your mother Jĕz'e-bĕl, and ask them!"

And the king of Ĭṣ'ra-el said to Ê-lī'shà, "You must help us; for the Lord has brought these three kings together, to let them fall into the hands of the king of Mō'ab."

Then said Ê-lī'shà, "As surely as the Lord of hosts lives, before whom I stand, if Jĕ-hŏsh'a-phăt, the king of Jū'dah, were not here, I would not look on you nor speak to you. But now bring me one who can play on the harp, a minstrel."

And while the minstrel made music on his harp, the power of the Lord came upon Ê-lī'shà and he said, "Thus saith the Lord, 'Make this valley full of ditches.' For the Lord tells me that you shall not see any rain nor hear any wind, yet the valley shall be filled with water; and you shall drink, and your cattle and your horses also shall drink. And the Lord shall give the Mō'ab-ītes into your hand; and you shall take their cities and cut down their trees and shall conquer their land."

And it came to pass as Ê-lī'shà had said. They dug ditches in the valley, and the next morning they found them full of water. And when the men of Mō'ab saw the water in the light of the sun, it was red like blood. They said one to another, "That is blood; the three kings have quarreled, and their armies have killed each other. Now, men of Mō'ab, hasten to take the camp of the three kings and all the treasure that is in it!"

So the men of Mō'ab came rushing unguarded and without their arms. But the army of Ĭṣ'ra-el and of Jū'dah and of Ĕ'dom met them and slew them, and won over them a great victory. From that place they went on laying waste the land of Mō'ab, until the cities were taken and the whole land was made desolate. And Mē'shà, the king of Mō'ab, was in such distress that, hoping to please the god of his land, who was called Chē'mŏsh, he took his oldest son, who was to have reigned in his place, and killed him and offered him up as a burnt offering. But all was in vain, for the Mō'ab-ītes were still held under the power of the Ĭṣ'ra-el-ītes. The story of this war between Ĭṣ'ra-el and Mō'ab is written not only in the second Book of Kings in the Bible, but also on a stone pillar, which was set up by the king of Mō'ab afterward. This pillar was found in the land of Mō'ab not many years ago and the writing upon it was read.

Story Eleven   II KINGS 4 : 1-7; 4 : 38-44; 6 : 1-7

The Pot of Oil and the Pot of Poison

IN MANY places in the land of Ĭs̲'ra-el there were living families of people who listened to the teaching of the prophets and worshiped the Lord. They were among the seven thousand in Ĭs̲'ra-el who never bowed their knees to the images of Bā'al. Ê-lī'shả went through the land meeting these people and teaching them and leading them in their worship. They were called the "sons of the prophets," and among them were some to whom God spoke, men who themselves became prophets of the Lord.

The wife of one of these men, the sons of the prophets, came one day to Ê-lī'shả and said, "O man of God, my husband is dead; and you know that he served the Lord while he lived. He was owing some money when he died; and now the man to whom he owed it has come, and he says that he will take my two sons to be his slaves, unless I pay the debt."

For in those lands, when a man owed a debt, he could be sold or his children, that the debt might be paid. Ê-lī'shả said to the woman, "What shall I do to help you? What have you in the house?"

"I have nothing in the house," answered the woman, "except a pot of oil."

Then Ê-lī'shả said to her, "Go to your neighbors and borrow of them empty jars and vessels and bowls; borrow a great many. Then go into the room and shut the door upon yourself and your sons; and pour out the oil into the vessels, and as each vessel is filled, set it aside."

The woman went out and borrowed of all her neighbors vessels that would hold oil, until she had a great many. Then she went into the house and shut the door and told her sons to bring the vessels to her one by one; and she poured out oil, filling vessel after vessel, until all were full. At last they said to her, "There is not another vessel that can hold oil."

And then the oil stopped running. If she had borrowed more vessels, there would have been more oil. She came and told Ė-lĭ'shȧ, the man of God. And he said, "Go and sell the oil; pay

the debt, and keep the rest of the money for yourself and your sons to live upon."

At another time Ė-lĭ'shȧ came to Gĭl'găl among the mountains, near Bĕth'el, and with him were some of these men, the sons of the prophets. It was a time when food was scarce, and they sought in the field for vegetables and green things to be eaten. One man by mistake brought a number of wild gourds, which were poisonous, and threw them into the pot to be cooked with the rest of the food.

While they were eating, they felt suddenly that they had been poisoned, and they cried out, "O man of God, there is death in the pot! The food is poisoned!"

Then Ė-lĭ'shȧ took some meal and threw it into the pot with the poisoned food. And he said, "Now take the food out of the pot and let the people eat of it."

They did so; and there was no longer any poison in the food.

At one time a man came bringing to the prophet a present of loaves of barley bread and some ears of new corn in the husks. There were with Ê-lī'shà that day a hundred men of the sons of the prophets, and Ê-lī'shà said to his servant, "Give this to the people for their dinner."

The servant said, "What, should I give this for a meal to a hundred men?"

And Ê-lī'shà said, "Yes, set it before them and let them eat. For thus saith the Lord, 'They shall eat and shall have enough, and shall leave some of it.'"

So he gave them the food; and every man took as much as he wished, and some was left over, according to the word of the Lord.

Once a company of these sons of the prophets went down from the mountains to a place near the river Jôr'dan and began to build a house; and Ê-lī'shà was with them. As one of the men was cutting down a tree, the head fell off from his ax, and dropped into the water. In those times iron and steel were very scarce and costly. The man said, "O my master, what shall I do, for this was a borrowed ax!"

Then Ê-lī'shà asked to be shown just where the ax head had fallen into the water. He cut off a stick of wood and threw it into the water at the place. At once the iron ax head rose to the surface of the water and floated, as if it were wood. The prophet said, "Reach out and take it," and the man took the iron, fitted it to the handle, and went on with his work.

By these works of power all the people came to know that Ê-lī'shà was a true prophet of the Lord and spoke as with the voice of the Lord of Iṣ'ra-el.

The Little Boy at Shunem

THE PROPHET Ê-lī'shà went through the land of Ĭs'ra-el, meeting in many places the people who worshiped the Lord and teaching them. On one of his journeys he visited the little city of Shụ'nem, which was on a hill looking over the great plain of Ĕs-dra-ē'-lon from the east. A rich woman who was living in that place asked him to come to her house and to take his meals there whenever he journeyed by. So, as often as Ê-lī'shà came to Shụ'nem on his journeys, he stopped for a meal or a night at this woman's home. After a time the lady said to her husband, "I see that this is a holy man of God who comes to our house so often. Let us build a little room for him on the side of the house; and let us place in the room for him a bed and a table and a stool and a candlestick; so that when he comes, it will be a home for him."

So they built the room, and as often as Ê-lī'shà passed by, he stayed there with his servant, the man who waited on him, as Ê-lī'shà himself in other days had waited upon Ê-lī'jah. The servant's name was Gē̇-hā'zī. At one time Ê-lī'shà said to the woman, "You have been very kind to me and to my helper, and have done much for us. Now, what can I do for you? Shall I ask the king to show you some favor? Or would you like anything that the chief of the army can do for you?" The woman said, "I live among my own people, and there is nothing else that I wish." Then Gē̇-hā'zī said to Ê-lī'shà, "This woman has no son."

And Ê-lī'shà said to her, "A year from this time, God will give to you a little boy."

The promise made the woman very happy; but she could scarcely believe it to be true, until the little child came. He grew up and became old enough to go with his father out into the field among the men who were reaping grain. Suddenly, in the field, the child cried out to his father, "O my head, my head!"

His father saw that he was very ill and he told one of his men to take him to his mother. He lay in his mother's arms until noon, and then he died. The mother did not tell her husband that the boy was dead; but she rode as quickly as she could to the prophet, who was on the other side of the plain, near Mount Cär'mel.

While she was yet far off, Ê-lī'shà saw her coming, and he said to Gĕ-hā'zī, his servant, "Run to meet this lady of Shụ'nem and ask her, 'Is it well with you? Is it well with your husband? Is it well with the child?'"

She answered, "It is well"; but she did not stop until she met the prophet, and then she fell down before him and took hold of his feet. Gĕ-hā'zī, the prophet's servant, did not think it was proper for her to seize him in this manner and was about to take her away. But Ê-lī'shà said to him, "Let her alone, for she is in deep trouble; and the Lord has hid it from me and has not told me."

And the woman said, "Did I ask for a son? Did I not say, 'Do not deceive me?'" Then Ê-lī'shà knew what had taken place. He said to Gĕ-hā'zī, "Take my staff and go at once to this woman's house. If you meet any man, do not stop to speak to him; and if anyone speaks to you, do not stop to answer him. But go, and lay my staff on the face of the child."

But the mother was not content to have only the servant go to her house. She wanted Ê-lī'shà himself to go; and she said, "As surely as the Lord lives and as your soul lives, I will not leave you."

Then Ê-lī'shà followed her back to Shụ'nem across the plain. On the way they met Gĕ-hā'zī coming back. He had laid the staff, as he had been told to lay it, on the face of the child; and he said, "The child is not awaked."

When Ê-lī'shà came, he found the child dead and laid upon the bed in the prophet's room, the staff upon his face. He shut the door and prayed beside the bed to the Lord. And after his prayer, he lay with his face upon the child's face and his hands on the child's hands; and as he lay, the child's body began to grow warm. Then he rose up and walked up and down in the house; and again he lay upon the child and put his arms around him. Suddenly the child began to sneeze and then he opened his eyes, alive once more.

Ê-lĭ'shȧ told his servant to call the mother, and when she came, he said to her, "Take up your son."

The mother saw that her son was alive from the dead; she fell at Ê-lĭ'shȧ's feet to show how great was her thankfulness to him, and then she took her son up in her arms and went out.

Story Thirteen   II KINGS 5 : 1-27

How a Little Girl Helped to Cure a Leper

A T ONE time, while Ê-lĭ'shȧ was living in Ĭş'ra-el, the general of the Sўr'ĭ-an army was named Nā'a-man. He was a great man in his rank and power and a brave man in battle, for he had won victories for Sўr'ĭ-ȧ. But one sad, terrible trouble came to Nā'-a-man. He was a leper. A leper was one with a disease called leprosy, which is still found in those lands. The leper's skin turns a deathly white and is covered with scales. One by one his fingers and toes, his hands, his feet, his arms and limbs decay, until at last

the man dies, and for the disease there is no cure. Yet, strange to
say, through it all, the leper feels no pain. Often he will not for
a long time believe that he has leprosy.

There was in Nā'a-man's house at Dă-măs'cus, in Sўr'ĭ-à, a
little girl who waited on Nā'a-man's wife. She was a slave girl
stolen from her mother's home in Iş'ra-el and carried away as a
captive to Sўr'ĭ-à. Even when there was no open war between
Sўr'ĭ-à and Iş'ra-el, parties of men were going out on both sides
and destroying villages on the border, robbing the people and
carrying them away to be killed or sold as slaves. But this little
girl, even though she had suffered wrong, had a kind heart, full of
sorrow for her master Nā'a-man; and one day she said to her
mistress:

"I wish that my lord Nā'a-man might meet the prophet who
lives in Să-mā'rĭ-à; for he could cure his leprosy."

Someone told Nā'a-man what the little girl had said, and Nā'a-
man spoke of it to the king of Sўr'ĭ-à. Now the king of Sўr'ĭ-à
loved Nā'a-man greatly; and when he went to worship in the
temple of his god, out of all his nobles he chose Nā'a-man as the
one upon whose arm he leaned. He greatly desired to have Nā'a-
man's leprosy cured; and he said, "I will send a letter to the king
of Iş'ra-el and I will ask him to let his prophet cure you."

So Nā'a-man, with a great train of followers, rode in his chariot
from Dă-măs'cus to Să-mā'rĭ-à, about a hundred miles. He took
with him as a present a large sum in gold and silver and many
beautiful robes and garments. He came to the king of Iş'ra-el and
gave him the letter from the king of Sўr'ĭ-à. And this was written
in the letter:

"With this letter I have sent to you Nā'a-man, my servant; and
I wish you to cure him of his leprosy."

The king of Sўr'ĭ-à supposed that as this prophet who could
cure leprosy was in Să-mā'rĭ-à, he was under the orders of the
king of Iş'ra-el and must do whatever his king told him to do; and
as he did not know the prophet, but knew the king, he wrote to
him. But the king was greatly alarmed when he read the letter.

"Am I God," he said, "to kill men and to make men live! Why
should the king of Sўr'ĭ-à send to me to cure a man of his leprosy?

Do you not see that he is trying to find an excuse for making war, in asking me to do what no man can do?"

And the king of Ĭṣ'ra-el tore his garments, as men did when they were in deep trouble. Ê-lī'sha the prophet heard of the letter and of the king's alarm, and he sent a message to the king. "Why are you so frightened? Let this man come to me, and he shall know that there is a prophet of the Lord in Ĭṣ'ra-el."

So Nā'a-man came with his chariots, his horses, and his followers and stood before the door of Ê-lī'sha's house. Ê-lī'sha did not come out to meet him but sent his servant out to him, saying: "Go and wash in the river Jôr'dan seven times, and your flesh and your skin shall become pure, and you shall be free from the leprosy."

But Nā'a-man was very angry because Ê-lī'sha had not treated with more respect so great a man as he was. He forgot, or he did not know, that by the laws of Ĭṣ'ra-el no man might touch or even come near a leper; and he said:

"Why, I supposed that of course he would come out to meet me and would wave his hand over the leper spot and would call on the name of the Lord his God, and in that manner would cure my leprosy! Are not Ăb'a-nà and Phär'par, the two rivers of Dă-măs'cus, better than all the waters in Ĭṣ'ra-el? May I not wash in them and be clean?"

And Nā'a-man turned and went away in a rage of anger. But his servants were wiser than he. They came to him, and one of them said:

"My father, if the prophet had told you to do some great thing, would you not have done it? Then why not do it, when he says, 'Wash and be clean?'"

After a little Nā'a-man's anger cooled, and he rode down the mountains to the river Jôr'dan. He washed in its water seven times, as the prophet had bidden him. And the scales of leprosy left his skin, and his flesh became like the flesh of a little child, pure and clean. Then Nā'a-man, a leper no more, came back to Ê-lī'sha's house with all his company, and he said, "Now I know that there is no God in all the earth, except in Ĭṣ'ra-el. Let me make you a present in return for what you have done for me."

But the true prophets of God never gave their message or did their works for pay; and Ê-lī'shà said to Nā'a-man:

"As surely as the Lord lives, before whom I stand, I will receive nothing."

And Nā'a-man urged him to take the present, but he refused. Then Nā'a-man asked a favor that he might be allowed to take away from the land of Ĭṣ'ra-el as much soil as could be carried on two mules, with which to build an altar; for he thought that an altar to the God of Ĭṣ'ra-el could be made only of earth from the land of Ĭṣ'ra-el; and he said:

"From this time I will offer no burnt offering or sacrifice to any other god except the God of Ĭṣ'ra-el. When I go with my master, the king of Sȳr'ĭ-à, to worship in the temple of Rĭm'mon his god, and my master leans on my arm, and I bow down to Rĭm'mon with him, then may the Lord forgive me for this, which will look as if I were worshiping another god."

And Ê-lī'shà said to him, "Go in peace."

Then Nā'a-man went on his way back to his own land. But Gê-hā'zī, the servant of Ê-lī'shà, said to himself:

"My master has let this Sȳr'ĭ-an go without taking anything from him; but I will run after him and ask him for a present."

So Gê-hā'zī ran after Nā'a-man, and Nā'a-man saw him following and stopped his chariot and stepped down to meet him. And Gê-hā'zī said to him:

"My master has sent me to you to say that just now two young men of the sons of the prophets have come to his house; will you give them a talent of silver and two suits of clothing?"

And Nā'a-man said, "Let me give you two talents of silver."

So he put two talents of silver in two bags, a talent in each bag, and gave them to Gĕ-hā'zī, and with them two suits of fine clothing; and he sent them back by two of his servants. But before they came to Ê-lī'shà's house, Gĕ-hā'zī took the gifts and hid them. Then Gĕ-hā'zī went into the house and stood before Ê-lī'shà. And Ê-lī'shà said to him, "Gĕ-hā'zī, where have you been?" And Gĕ-hā'zī answered, "I have not been at any place." And Ê-lī'shà said to him:

"Did not my heart go with you, and did I not see you when the man stepped down from his chariot to meet you? Is this a time to receive gifts of money and garments, or gifts of vineyards and olive yards and of sheep and oxen? Because you have done this wickedness, the leprosy of Nā'a-man shall come upon you and shall cling to you and to your children after you forever!"

And Gĕ-hā'zī walked out from Ê-lī'shà's presence, a leper, with his skin as white as snow.

Story Fourteen

II KINGS 6 : 8-23

The Chariots of Fire Around Elisha

THERE was constant war between Ĭṣ'ra-el and Sy̆r'ĭ-à through all the years of Ê-lī'shà, the prophet. And the king of Ĭṣ'ra-el found Ê-lī'shà a greater help than his horses and chariots. For whenever the king of Sy̆r'ĭ-à told his officers to make an attack upon any place in the land of Ĭṣ'ra-el, Ê-lī'shà would send word to the king of Ĭṣ'ra-el, saying, "Watch carefully that place, and send men to guard it, for the Sy̆r'ĭ-anṣ are coming to attack it."

And then, when the Sy̆r'ĭ-an army came to the place they were sure to find it strongly guarded so that their soldiers could do nothing. This happened so many times that the king of Sy̆r'ĭ-à at last said to his nobles, "Someone among you is secretly helping the king of Ĭṣ'ra-el and is sending him word of all our plans. Will no one tell me who the traitor is?"

And they said, "No one of us, my lord, O king, has made known your plans; but Ê-lī'shà, the prophet that is in Iṣ'ra-el, tells the king of Iṣ'ra-el the words that you speak in your own room."

Then the king of Sȳr'ĭ-à said, "Go and find where that man is, so that I may send an army to take him."

After a time the king of Sȳr'ĭ-à heard that Ê-lī'shà was staying in Dō'than. Then he sent to that place a great army, with horses and chariots. They came by night and stood in a great ring all around the city, ready to seize the prophet. In the morning the prophet's helper rose up early, and he found the city surrounded on every side by a host of men, with swords and spears. He called Ê-lī'shà in great alarm and said to him, "O my master, what shall we do?"

"Fear not," answered Ê-lī'shà, "there are more men on our side than on theirs."

And then Ê-lī'shà prayed to the Lord, saying, "O Lord, open the eyes of this young man and let him see who are with us."

Then the Lord opened the eyes of the young man, and he saw what other men could not see, that the mountain on which the city stood was covered with horses and chariots of fire, sent by the Lord to keep his prophet safe. But this the Sȳr'ĭ-ans could not see; and they came up to the gates of the city to take Ê-lī'shà. Then Ê-lī'shà prayed to the Lord, saying, "Lord, make these men blind for a little while." Then a mist came over the eyes of the Sȳr'ĭ-ans and they could not see clearly. And Ê-lī'shà went out to them and said, "This is not the right city, but I will show you the way. Follow me."

Ê-lī'shà led them from Dō'than to Sà-mā'rĭ-à and into the walls of the city, where the army of Iṣ'ra-el were standing all around them. Then Ê-lī'shà prayed, "O Lord, open the eyes of these men that they may see."

And the Lord opened their eyes and they saw the walls of Sà-mā'rĭ-à and the host of Iṣ'ra-el all around them. The king of Iṣ'ra-el was glad to have his enemies in his power; and he said to Ê-lī'shà, "My father, shall I kill them? Shall I kill them?"

But Ê-lī'shà said to him, "You shall not kill them. Would you kill helpless men whom you had taken as prisoners? Give them bread to eat and water to drink and send them home to their master."

So instead of killing the Sўr'ĭ-an soldiers or holding them as prisoners, the king of Ĭs'ra-el set plenty of food before them and gave them all that they needed. Then he sent them home to their master, the king of Sўr'ĭ-à. And after that it was a long time before the Sўr'ĭ-an armies came into the land of Ĭs'ra-el.

Story Fifteen

II KINGS 6 : 24 to 7 : 20

What the Lepers Found in the Camp

AFTER a time there was another great war between Sўr'ĭ-à and Ĭs'ra-el; and Bĕn=hā'dăd, the king of Sўr'ĭ-à, led a mighty army into the land of Ĭs'ra-el and laid siege against the city of Sà-mā'rĭ-à. So hard and so long was the siege that the people in Sà-mā'rĭ-à could find nothing to eat; many died from want of food and some killed their own children and ate them.

But through all the siege Ê-li'shà encouraged the king of Ĭṣ'ra-e‹
not to give up the city. When it seemed that there could be n‹
hope, Ê-li'shà said to the king, "Hear the word of the Lord, 'To‹
morrow, at this hour, in the gate of Sà-mā'rĭ-à, a peck of grain shal‹
be sold for sixty cents and two pecks of barley for sixty cents.' ›

One of the nobles, on whose arm the king was leaning, did no‹
believe Ê-li'shà's word and he said scornfully, "If the Lord woul‹
make windows in heaven and rain down wheat and barley, the‹
this might be." "You shall see it with your own eyes," answere‹
Ê-li'shà; "but you shall not eat any of the food."

On the next morning, about daybreak, four men that wer‹
lepers were standing together outside the gate of Sà-mā'rĭ-à. Being
lepers, they were not allowed by the laws of Ĭṣ'ra-el inside th‹
walls of the city. (We have read of leprosy and lepers in th‹
story of Nā'a-man.) These four men said to each other, "Wha‹
shall we do? If we go into the city, we must die there from th‹
want of food; if we stay here, we must die. Let us go to the camp
of the Sy̆r'ĭ-anṣ; perhaps they will let us live; and at the worst they
can do not more than kill us."

So the four men went toward the Sy̆r'ĭ-an camp; but as they
came near, they were surprised to find no one standing on guard.
They went into a tent and found it empty, as though it had been
left very suddenly, for there were food and drink, garments, and
gold and silver. As no one was there, they ate and drank all they
needed; and then they took away valuable things and hid them.

They looked into another tent and another, and found them like the first, but not a man was in sight. They walked through the camp but not a soldier was there, and the tents were left just as they had been when men were living in them.

In the night the Lord had caused the Sȳr'ĭ-ans̤ to hear a great noise, like the rolling of chariots and the trampling of horses and the marching of men. They said to each other in great fear, "The king of Ĭṣ'ra-el has sent for the Hĭt'tītes on the north and the Ė-ġȳp'tians̤ on the south to come against us."

And so great and so sudden was their terror, that in the night they rose up and fled away, leaving everything in their camp, even leaving their horses tied, and their asses and all their treasure and all their food in their tents.

After a time the lepers said to each other, "We do wrong not to tell this good news in the city. If they found it out, they will blame us for not letting them know, and we may lose our lives on account of it."

So they went up to the gate and called the men on guard. They told them how they had found the camp of the Sȳr'ĭ-ans̤, with tents standing and horses tied, but not a man left. The men on guard told it at the king's palace. But the king, when he heard it, thought that it was a trick of the Sȳr'ĭ-ans̤ to hide themselves and to draw the men out of the city so that they might take the city.

The king sent out two men with horses and chariots, and they found that not only had the camp been left, but that the road down the mountains to the river Jôr'dan was covered with garments and arms and treasures that the Sȳr'ĭ-ans̤ had thrown away in their wild flight.

The news soon spread through the city of Să-mā'rĭ-à, and in a few hours all the city was at the gate. When the food was brought in from the camp, there was abundance for all the people. And it came to pass as Ė-lī'shà had said, a peck of grain and two pecks of barley were sold for sixty cents in the gate of Să-mā'rĭ-à by noon of that day.

The king chose the noble upon whose arm he had leaned the day before to have charge of the gate. So he saw with his own eyes that which the prophet had foretold; but he did not eat of it, for the crowd was so great that the people pressed upon him, and he was trodden under their feet and killed in the throng.

Thus the king and all the city of Sȧ-mā'rĭ-ȧ knew that Ê-lī'shȧ had indeed spoken the word of the Lord.

We have seen how different from the ways of Ê-lī'jah were the ways of Ê-lī'shȧ. Ê-lī'jah lived alone in the wilderness and never came before kings except to tell them of their evil deeds and to warn them of punishment. But Ê-lī'shȧ who lived in the city, at times even in the city of Sȧ-mā'rĭ-ȧ, often sent helpful messages to the king and seemed to be his friend. Both these men were needed, Ê-lī'jah and Ê-lī'shȧ, one to destroy the evil in the land and the other to build up the good.

Story Sixteen   II KINGS 8 : 7-15; 9 : 1 to 10 : 36

Jehu, the Furious Driver of His Chariot

YOU REMEMBER that when the Lord came to the prophet Ê-lī'jah at Mount Hō'reb in the wilderness, the Lord gave to Ê-lī'jah a command to anoint or call Hăz'a-el to be king of Sўr'ĭ-ȧ and Jē'hū to be king of Ĭṣ'ra-el. But to prepare the way for these changes of rule, a long time was needed, and Ê-lī'jah was taken home to heaven before these men were called to be kings.

The time to call these men had now come, and Ê-lī'shȧ undertook the work that had been left to him by Ê-lī'jah. He went to Dȧ-măs'cus, the chief city of Sўr'ĭ-ȧ; and Bĕn=hā'dăd, the king of Sўr'ĭ-ȧ, heard that the great prophet of Ĭṣ'ra-el had come, for the fame of Ê-lī'shȧ's deeds had made his name known through all those lands.

At that time King Bĕn=hā'dăd was ill; and he sent one of his chief princes, whose name was Hăz'a-el, to ask Ê-lī'shȧ whether

he would be well again. Hăz'a-el came to meet Ê-lī'shà with a
rich present, which loaded forty camels, and he spoke to Ê-lī'shà
with great respect saying, "Your son, Bĕn=hā'dăd, king of Sўr'ï-à,
has sent me to you to ask, 'Shall I become well again from this
sickness?' "

And Ê-lī'shà said to Hăz'a-el, "You may tell Bĕn=hā'dăd that
he will get well; nevertheless, the Lord has shown me that he will
surely die."

Then Ê-lī'shà looked steadily upon Hăz'a-el's face, until Hăz'-
a-el felt ashamed, and Ê-lī'shà wept as he looked upon him.
Hăz'a-el said to him, "Why does my lord weep?" "I weep," said
Ê-lī'shà, "because I know the evil that you will do to the people
of Is̠'ra-el. You will take their castles and set them on fire; you
will kill their young men and you will destroy their children."

Hăz'a-el was surprised at this and said, "I am nothing but a dog;
and how can I do such great things?"

And Ê-lī'shà answered him, "The Lord has shown me that you
shall be king over Sўr'ï-à."

Then Hăz'a-el went to King Bĕn=hā'dăd and said to him, "The
man of God told me that you will surely be well from your sickness."

And on the next day Hăz'a-el took the cover from the bed and
dipped it in water and pressed it tightly over Bĕn=hā'dăd's face, so
that he died; and Hăz'a-el reigned in his place as king of Sўr'ï-à.
As soon as Hăz'a-el became king, he made war upon the Is̠'ra-el-
ītes; and a battle was fought at Rā'moth=ḡïl'e-ăd, the same place
where King Ā'hăb had been slain more than ten years before. In
this battle Jĕ-hō'ram, the king of Is̠'ra-el, was wounded; and he
was taken to Jĕz're-el, beside the great plain of Ĕs-dra-ē'lon, there
to recover from his wounds. Ā-ha-zī'ah, who was at that time
king of Jū'dah, and who was a nephew of Jĕ-hō'ram, went to
Jĕz're-el to visit him while he was ill from his wounds.

By this time Ê-lī'shà, the prophet, had returned from his visit
to Sўr'ï-à. He knew that the time had now come to finish the
work in Is̠'ra-el left to him by Ê-lī'jah; and he called one of the
sons of the prophets to him and said, "Rise up, and go to the camp
at Rā'moth=ḡïl'e-ăd; and take with you this little bottle of oil.

And when you reach Rā'moth=ḡĭl'e-ăd, find one of the captains of the army, Jē'hū, the son of Jĕ-hŏsh'a-phăt, the son of Nĭm'-shī, and lead him into a room alone and pour the oil on his head and say, 'Thus saith the Lord, I have anointed you as king over Iṣ'ra-el.' When you have done this, come back to me at once without waiting."

Then the young man, who was a prophet like Ê-lī'shà, took the bottle of oil in his hand and went to Rā'moth=ḡĭl'e-ăd. In the camp of Iṣ'ra-el he found the captains of the army sitting together. He came suddenly among them and said, "O captain, I have a despatch for you."

And Jē'hū, one of the captains, said to him, "To which one of us is your despatch directed?"

He said to Jē'hū, "It is for you alone, O captain."

Then the young prophet went with Jē'hū into the house and he poured the oil on his head and said, "Thus saith the Lord, the God of Iṣ'ra-el, 'I have anointed you as king over my people Iṣ'ra-el. And you shall destroy the family of Ā'hăb, because they destroyed the prophets of the Lord. And I will make the house of Ā'hăb like the house of Jĕr-o-bō'am, who made Iṣ'ra-el to sin. And the wild dogs shall eat Jĕz'e-bĕl in the city of Jĕz're-el and there shall be no one to bury her.' "

And after he had said this, the prophet opened the door and went away as suddenly as he had come. Jē'hū came back to the other captains and sat down again. One of the captains said to him, "Is all well? Why did this wild fellow call you out?"

Jē'hū said to them, "You know the man and you know what he said to me."

"No, no," they all said. "Tell us what he said."

Then Jē'hū told them what the prophet had said and that he had anointed him as king. This pleased all the captains. At once they took off their outer garments and spread them as a carpet on the stairs of the house, and at the head of the stairs they placed Jē'hū; and they blew the trumpets and called out to the army, "Jē'hū is the king!"

Jē'hū said to the captains, "Do not let anyone go out of the camp to bear word to Jĕ-hō'ram. I will go myself."

Then Jē'hū made ready his chariot and rode swiftly toward Jĕz're-el, his company riding after him. The watchman on the tower at Jĕz're-el saw him coming and he called out to King Jĕ-hō'ram, "I see a company coming toward the city."

Jĕ-hō'ram thought that they were bearing news of the war with the Sўr'ĭ-ans̩. He sent out a man on horseback to meet the company.

The man came and said, "Is all well?"

Jē'hū answered him, "What difference is it to you? Come after me."

Then the man turned and joined Jē'hū's company; and so did another man whom Jĕ-hō'ram sent when the first man did not return. And the watchman called out to Jĕ-hō'ram again, "Two men have gone out to meet the company that is drawing near, but they have not come back; and the man at the head drives like Jē'hū, the son of Nĭm'shī, for he drives furiously."

Then Jĕ-hō'ram became anxious; he sent for his chariot and went out to meet Jē'hū; and with him went Ā-ha-zī'ah, the king of Jū'dah, each in his own chariot. It came to pass that they met Jē'hū in the very place which had been the vineyard of Nā'bŏth; the same place where Ā'hăb had met Ê-lī'jah, when that same Jē'hu was standing behind Ā'hăb in his chariot. As Jĕ-hō'ram drew near to Jē'hū, he called to him, "Is all well, Jē'hū?"

"Can anything be well," answered Jē'hū, "as long as your mother Jĕz'e-bĕl lives, with all her wickedness?"

When Jĕ-hō'ram heard this, he saw that Jē'hū was his enemy. He cried out to King Ā-ha-zī'ah and turned his chariot and fled. But he was too late, for Jē'hū drew his bow with all his strength and sent an arrow to his heart. Jĕ-hō'ram fell down dead in his chariot. Then Jē'hū said to Bĭd'kär, whom he had made his chief captain, "Take away the body of Jĕ-hō'ram, and throw it into the field where the body of Nā'bŏth was thrown. Do you remember how when you and I were riding in the chariot behind Ā'hăb, his father, the Lord said, 'I have seen the blood of Nā'bŏth on this spot, and the punishment of Ā'hăb and his sons shall be in this place?'"

When Ā-ha-zī'ah, the king of Jū'dah, saw Jĕ-hō'ram fall, he, too, turned and fled. But Jē'hū pursued him and ordered his followers to kill him. So Ā-ha-zī'ah, the son of Jĕ-hŏsh'a-phăt and grandson of Ā'hăb (for his mother, Ăth-a-lī'ah, was a daughter of Jĕz'e-bĕl), he also died at the hand of Jē'hū. His servants took the body of Ā-ha-zī'ah to Jĕ-ru'sȧ-lĕm and buried it there.

When Jē'hū rode into the city of Jĕz're-el, Queen Jĕz'e-bĕl knew that her end had come; but she met it boldly, like a queen. She put on her royal robes and a crown upon her head, and sat by the window, waiting for Jē'hū to come. As he drew near, she called out to him, "Good day to you, Jē'hū, you who are like Zĭm'rī, the murderer of your master!"

You have read of Zĭm'rī, who slew King Ē'lah, and was himself burned in his palace seven days after. (See Story Three in this Part.) Jē'hū looked up to the window and called out, "Who is on my side? Who?"

And some men looked out to him and he said, "Throw her out of the window."

They threw her down, and her blood was spattered on the wall and on the horses. King Jē'hū came into the palace and sat down as master, and ate and drank. Then he said, "Take up the body of that wicked woman, Jĕz'e-bĕl, and bury her, for, though wicked, she was the daughter of a king."

But when they looked on the pavement, there was nothing left of her except her skull and the bones of her feet and her hands, for the wild dogs of the city had eaten her body. Thus the wicked life of Jĕz'e-bĕl came to an end, and the word of the Lord by the prophet Ê-lī'jah came to pass. And Jē'hū slew all the sons of Ā'hăb and their children with them, so that not one of Ā'hăb's family was left alive. When Jē'hū saw that he was safe and strong on the throne, he sent out a message to all the worshipers of Bā'al, the idol which Jĕz'e-bĕl and the house of Ā'hăb had brought into Ĭs'ra-el. This message was, "Ā'hăb served Bā'al a little, but Jē'hū will serve him much. Now let all the priests of Bā'al meet in the temple of Bā'al in Sā-mā'rĭ-à."

They came by hundreds, hoping that Jē'hū would be their friend as Ā'hăb and his family had been. But when they were all in the temple, he brought an army of his soldiers and placed them on guard around it. And when no one could escape, he gave the order, "Go into the temple and kill all the priests of Bā'al; let not one get away alive."

And this was done in a cruel manner. He killed all the prophets and priests of Bā'al and tore down the temple of Bā'al in Sā-mā'rĭ-à.

But though Jē'hū broke up the worship of Bā'al, he did not worship the Lord God of Ĭs'ra-el as he should. He continued to serve the golden calves which Jĕr-o-bō'am had set up long before at Bĕth'el and at Dăn. And the Lord sent a prophet to Jē'hū, who said to him, "Because you have done my will in destroying the house of Ā'hăb and in destroying those that worshiped Bā'al, your children to the fourth generation shall sit on the throne of Ĭs'ra-el."

On account of the many sins of the people of Ĭs'ra-el, the Lord began in the days of Jē'hū to take away the land of the Ten Tribes. Hăz'a-el, the new king of Sȳr'ĭ-à, made war on Jē'hū and conquered all the land on the east of the Jôr'dan, from the brook Är'nŏn to the land of Bā'shän in the north; so all that was left of Ĭs'ra-el was the country on the west of Jôr'dan, from Bĕth'el northward to Dăn.

Elisha and the Bow; Jonah
and Nineveh

AFTER Jē'hū, his son Jĕ-hō'a-hăz reigned in Ĭs'ra-el. He was not only a wicked but also a weak king; and under him Ĭs'ra-el became helpless in the hands of its enemies, Hăz'a-el, the fierce king of Sўr'ĭ-à and his son, Bĕn=hā'dăd the second. But when Jĕ-hō'-a-hăz died, his son Jō'ăsh became king, and under his rule Ĭs'ra-el began to rise again.

Ê-lī'shà, the prophet, was now an old man and very feeble and near to death. The young king, Jō'ăsh, came to see him and wept over him and said to him, as Ê-lī'shà himself had said to Ê-lī'jah, "My father, my father, you are to Ĭs'ra-el more than its chariots and its horsemen!"

But Ê-lī'shà, though weak in body, was yet strong in soul. He told King Jō'ăsh to bring to him a bow and arrows and to open the window to the east, looking toward the land of Sўr'ĭ-à. Then Ê-lī'shà caused the king to draw the bow, and he placed his hands on the king's hands. And as the king shot an arrow, Ê-lī'shà said, "This is the Lord's arrow of victory, of victory over Sўr'ĭ-à, for you shall smite the Sўr'ĭ-ans̤ in Ā'phek and shall destroy them utterly."

Then Ê-lī'shà told the king to take the arrows and to strike with them on the ground. The king struck them on the ground three times and then stopped striking. The old prophet was displeased at this and said, "Why did you stop? You should have struck the ground five or six times; then you would have won as many victories over Sўr'ĭ-à; but now you shall beat the Sўr'ĭ-ans̤ three times and no more."

Soon after this Ê-lī'shà died and they buried him in a cave. In the spring of the next year the bands of the Mō'ab-ītes came upon the place just as they were burying another man, and in their haste

344

to escape from the enemies, they placed the body in the cave where Ê-lǐ'shà was buried. When the body of this man touched the body of the dead prophet, life came to it, and the man stood up. Thus, even after Ê-lǐ'shà was dead, he still had power.

After the death of Ê-lǐ'shà, Jō'ăsh, the king of Ĭs'ra-el, made war upon Bĕn=hā'dăd the second, king of Sўr'ĭ-à. Jō'ăsh beat him three times in battle and took from him all the cities that Hăz'a-el, his father, had taken away from Ĭs'ra-el. And after Jō'ăsh, his son Jĕr-o-bō'am the Second reigned, who became the greatest of all the kings of the Ten Tribes. Under him the kingdom grew rich and strong. He conquered nearly all Sўr'ĭ-à and made Să-mā'rĭ-à the greatest city in all those lands.

But though Sўr'ĭ-à went down, another nation was now rising to power, Ăs-sўr'ĭ-à, on the eastern side of the river Tī'gris. Its capital was Nĭn'e-veh, a great city, so vast that it would take three days for a man to walk around its walls. The Ăs-sўr'ĭ-anş were beginning to conquer all the lands near them, and Ĭs'ra-el was in danger of falling under their power. At this time another prophet, named Jō'nah, was giving the word of the Lord to the Ĭs'ra-el-ītes. To Jō'nah the Lord spoke saying, "Go to Nĭn'e-veh, that great city, and preach to it, for its wickedness rises up before me."

But Jō'nah did not wish to preach to the people of Nĭn'e-veh, for they were the enemies of his land, the land of Ĭs'ra-el. He wished Nĭn'e-veh to die in its sins and not turn to God and live. So Jō'nah tried to go away from the city where God had sent him. He went down to Jŏp'pȧ, upon the shore of the Great Sea. There he found a ship about to sail to Tär'shish, far away in the west. He paid the fare and went aboard, intending to go as far as possible from Nĭn'e-veh.

But the Lord saw Jō'nah on the ship, and the Lord sent a great storm upon the sea, so that the ship seemed as though it would go in pieces. The sailors threw overboard everything on the ship, and when they could do no more, every man prayed to his god to save the ship and themselves. Jō'nah was now lying fast asleep under the deck of the ship, and the ship's captain came to him and said, "What do you mean by sleeping in such a time as this? Awake, rise up, and call upon your God. Perhaps your God will hear you and will save our lives."

But the storm continued to rage around the ship, and they said, "There is some man on this ship who has brought upon us this trouble. Let us cast lots and find who it is."

Then they cast lots, and the lot fell on Jō'nah. They said to him, all at once, "Tell us, who are you? From what country do you come? What is your business? To what people do you belong? Why have you brought all this trouble upon us?" Then Jō'nah told them the whole story; how he came from the land of Iṣ'ra-el and that he had fled away from the presence of the Lord. And they said to him, "What shall we do to you, that the storm may cease?" Then Jō'nah said, "Take me up and throw me into the sea; then the storm will cease and the waters will be calm; for I know that for my sake this great tempest is upon you."

But the men were not willing to throw Jō'nah into the sea. They rowed hard to bring the ship to the land, but they could not. Then they cried unto the Lord and said, "We pray thee, O Lord, we pray thee, let us not die for this man's life; for thou, O Lord, hast done as it pleased thee." At last, when they could do nothing else to save themselves, they threw Jō'nah into the sea. At once the storm ceased and the waves became still. Then the men on the ship feared the Lord greatly. They offered a sacrifice to the Lord and made promises to serve him.

And the Lord caused a great fish to swallow up Jō'nah; and Jō'nah was alive within the fish for three days and three nights. Long afterward, when Jē'ṣus was on the earth, he said that as Jō'nah was three days inside the fish, so he would be three days in the earth; so Jō'nah in the fish was like a prophecy of Chrīst. In the fish Jō'nah cried to the Lord, and the Lord heard his prayer and caused the great fish to throw up Jō'nah upon the dry land.

By this time Jō'nah had learned that some men who worshiped idols were kind in their hearts and were dear to the Lord. This was the lesson that God meant Jō'nah to learn; and now the call of the Lord came to Jō'nah a second time.

"Arise; go to Nĭn'e-veh, that great city, and preach to it what I command you."

So Jō'nah went to the city of Nĭn'e-veh, and as he entered into it, he called out to the people, "Within forty days shall Nĭn'e-veh be destroyed." And he walked through the city all day, crying out only this, "Within forty days shall Nĭn'e-veh be destroyed."

And the people of Nĭn'e-veh believed the word of the Lord as spoken by Jō'nah. They turned away from their sins and fasted and sought the Lord, from the greatest of them even to the least. The king of Nĭn'e-veh arose from his throne and laid aside his royal robes and covered himself with sackcloth and sat in ashes, as a sign of his sorrow. And the king sent out a command to his people, that they should fast and seek the Lord and turn from sin.

And God saw that the people of Nĭn'e-veh were sorry for their wickedness, and he forgave them and did not destroy their city. But this made Jō'nah very angry. He did not wish to have Nĭn'e-veh spared, because it was the enemy of his own land, and also he feared that men would call him a false prophet when his word did not come to pass. And Jō'nah said to the Lord:

"O Lord, I was sure that it would be thus, that thou wouldest spare the city; and for that reason I tried to flee away; for I knew that thou wast a gracious God, full of pity, slow to anger, and rich in mercy. Now, O Lord, take away my life, for it is better for me to die than to live."

And Jō'nah went out of the city and built a little hut on the east side of it and he sat under its roof, to see whether God would

keep the word that he had spoken. Then the Lord caused a plant
with thick leaves, called a gourd, to grow up and to shade Jō'nah
from the sun; and Jō'nah was glad and sat under its shadow. But
a worm destroyed the plant; and the next day a hot wind blew and
Jō'nah suffered from the heat; and again Jō'nah wished that he
might die. And the Lord said to Jō'nah, "You were sorry to see
the plant die, though you did not make it grow, and though it
came up in a night and died in a night. And should not I have
pity on Nĭn'e-veh, that great city, where are more than a hundred
thousand little children and also many cattle, all helpless and
knowing nothing?"

And Jō'nah learned that men and women and little children are
all precious in the sight of the Lord, though they know not God.

In most of the books of the Old Testament, we read of the
Iṣ'ra-el-īte people and of God's care of them; but we do not find
in the Old Testament much about God as the Father of all men of
every nation and every land. The book of Jō'nah stands almost
alone in the Old Testament, as showing that God loves people of
nations other than Iṣ'ra-el. Even the people of Nĭn'e-veh, who
worshiped images, were under God's love; God was ready to hear
their prayer and to save them. So the book of Jō'nah shows us
God as "our Heavenly Father."

Story Eighteen

II KINGS 15 : 8 to 17 : 41

How the Ten Tribes Were Lost

THE POWER and peace that Jū'dah enjoyed under
Jĕr-o-bō'am the Second did not last after his death.
His great kingdom fell apart, and his son Zăch-a-rī'ah
reigned only six months. He was slain in the sight of
his people by Shăl'lum, who made himself king. But
after only a month of rule, Shăl'lum himself was killed by Mĕn'a-
hĕm, who brought ten years of wickedness and of suffering to the

land, for the Ăs-sўr'ĭ-anṣ spoiled the land and took away the riches
of Ĭṣ'ra-el. Then came Pĕk-a-hī'ah, who was slain by Pē'kah, and
Hŏ-shē'à, who in turn slew Pē'kah. So nearly all the latter kings
of Ĭṣ'ra-el won the throne by murder and were themselves slain.
The land was helpless, and its enemies, the Ăs-sўr-ĭ-anṣ from
Nĭn'e-veh, won victories, carried away many of the people, and
robbed those who were left. All these evils came upon the Ĭṣ'ra-
el-ītes because they and their kings had forsaken the Lord God of
their fathers and worshiped idols.

Hŏ-shē'à was the last of the kings over the Ten Tribes; nineteen kings in all, from Jĕr-o-bō'am to Hŏ-shē'à. In Hŏ-shē'à's
time, the king of Ăs-sўr'ĭ-à, whose name was Shăl-man-ē'ṣēr,
came up with a great army against Sà-mā'rĭ-à. He laid siege against
the city; but it was in a strong place and hard to take, for it stood
on a high hill. The siege lasted three years, and before it was
ended, Shăl-man-ē'ṣēr, the king of Ăs-sўr'ĭ-à, died, and Sär'gon,
a great warrior and conqueror, reigned in his place. Sär'gon took
Sà-mā'rĭ-à and put to death Hŏ-shē'à the last king of Ĭṣ'ra-el. He
carried away nearly all the people from the land and led them into
distant countries in the east, to Mĕs-o-pŏ-tā'mĭ-à, to Mē'dĭ-à, and
the lands near the great Caspian Sea.

This Sär'gon did, in order to keep the Ĭṣ'ra-el-ītes from again
breaking away from his rule.

As in their own land, the children of Ĭṣ'ra-el had forsaken the
Lord and had worshiped idols, so after they were taken to these
distant lands, they sought the gods of the people among whom
they were living. They married the people of those lands and
ceased to be Ĭṣ'ra-el-ītes; and after a time they lost all knowledge

of their own God, who had given them his words and sent them his prophets. So there came an end to the Ten Tribes of Iṣ'ra-el, for they never again came back to their own land, and were lost among the peoples of the far east.

But a small part of the people of Iṣ'ra-el were left in their own land. The king of Ăs-sўr'ĭ-à brought to the land of Iṣ'ra-el people from other countries and placed them in the land. But they were too few to fill the land and to care for it; so that the wild beasts began to increase in Iṣ'ra-el, and many of these strange people were killed by lions which lived among the mountains and in the valleys. They thought that the lions came upon them because they did not worship the God who ruled in that land, and they sent to the king of Ăs-sўr'ĭ-à saying, "Send us a priest who can teach us how to worship the God to whom this land belongs; for he has sent lions among us, and they are destroying us."

They supposed that each land must have its own God, as the Phĭ-lĭs'tĭneṣ worshiped Dā'gon, and the Mō'ab-ītes Chē'mosh, and the Tўr'ĭ-anṣ and Zī-dō'nĭ-anṣ, Bā'al and the Ăsh-ē'rah. They did not know that there is only one God, who rules all the world and who is to be worshiped by all men.

Then the king of Ăs-sўr'ĭ-à sent to these people a priest from among the Iṣ'ra-el-ītes in his land; and this priest tried to teach them how to worship the Lord. But with the Lord's worship, they mingled the worship of idols and did not serve the Lord only, as God would have them serve him. In after time these people were called Să-măr'ĭ-tanṣ, from Să-mā'rĭ-à, which had been their chief city. They had their temple to the Lord on Mount Gĕr'ĭ-zĭm, near the city of Shē'chem, and in that city a few of them are found even in our time.

Part Fifth

STORIES OF THE PEOPLE
AND KINGDOM OF JUDAH

The First Four Kings of Judah

NOW WE turn from the story of the kingdom of Ĭs'ra-el in the north to the story of the kingdom of Jū'dah in the south. You read how the Ten Tribes broke away from the rule of King Rē-ho-bō'am and set up a kingdom of their own under Jĕr-o-bō'am. This division left the kingdom of Jū'dah very small and weak. It reached from the Dead Sea westward to the land of the Phĭ-lĭs'tĭnes on the shore of the Great Sea, and from Bē'er=shē'bȧ on the south not quite to Bĕth'el on the north; but it held some control over the land of Ē'dom on the south of the Dead Sea. Its chief city was Jĕ-ru'sȧ-lĕm, where stood the Temple of the Lord and the palace of the king.

After Rē-ho-bō'am found that he could no more rule over the Ten Tribes, he tried to make his own little kingdom strong by building cities and raising an army of soldiers. But he did not look to the Lord, as his grandfather Dā'vid had looked; he allowed his people to worship idols, so that soon on almost every hill and in almost every grove of trees there was an image of stone or wood. God was not pleased with Rē-ho-bō'am and his people, because they had forsaken him for idols. He brought upon the land of Jū'dah a great army from Ē'ġȳpt, led by Shī'shăk, the king of Ē'ġȳpt. They marched over all the land of Jū'dah, they took the city of Jĕ-ru'sȧ-lĕm, and they robbed the Temple of all the great treasure in gold and silver which Sŏl'o-mon had stored up. This evil came upon Jū'dah because its king and its people had turned away from the Lord their God.

After Rē-ho-bō'am had reigned seventeen years, he died, and his son Ȧ-bī'jah became king of Jū'dah. When Jĕr-o-bō'am, the king of Ĭs'ra-el, made war upon him, Ȧ-bī'jah led his army into the land of Ĭs'ra-el. But Jĕr-o-bō'am's army was twice as large as Ȧ-bī'jah's, and his men stood not only in front of the men of

353

Jū'dah but also behind them, so that the army of Jū'dah was in great danger of being destroyed. But Á-bī'jah told his men to trust in the Lord and to fight bravely in the Lord's name.

And God helped the men of Jū'dah against Ĭṣ'ra-el and they won a great victory; so that Jĕr-o-bō'am never again came against Jū'dah.

Á-bī'jah's reign was short, only three years; and after him came Ā'sà, his son, who was a great warrior, a great builder of cities, and a wise ruler, and better than all else he tried faithfully to serve the Lord. Against Ā'sà a great army of enemies came up from Ē-thǐ-ō'pǐa, which was south of Ē'ġy̆pt. Ā'sà drew out his little army against the Ē-thǐ-ō'pǐans at a place called Mȧ-rē'shah, in the south of Jū'dah near the desert. He had no hope of success in his soldiers, because they were so few and the enemies were so many. But Ā'sà called upon the Lord and said:

"O Lord, it makes no difference to thee whether there are few or many. Help us, O Lord, for we trust in thee; and in thy name we fight this vast multitude. O Lord, thou art our God; let not man succeed against thee."

The Lord heard Ā'sà's prayer and gave him a great victory over the Ē-thǐ-ō'pǐans. Ā'sà took again the cities in the south which had gone over to the side of the Ē-thǐ-ō'pǐans, and he brought to Jĕ-ru'sà-lĕm great riches, and flocks of sheep and herds of cattle and camels, which he had taken from his enemies.

Then the Lord sent to Ā'sà a prophet named Ăz-a-rī'ah. He said, "Hear me, King Ā'sà, and all Jū'dah and Bĕn'ja-mǐn. The Lord is with you while you are with him. If you seek him you shall find him; but if you forsake the Lord, he will forsake you. Now be strong and put away the wickedness out of the land, and the Lord shall reward your work."

Then Ā'sà rebuilt the altar of the Lord which had fallen into decay, and he called upon his people to worship. He went through the land and broke down the idols and burned them. He found that his own mother, the queen, had made an idol, and he cut it down and broke it in pieces; and he would not allow her to be queen any longer, because she had worshiped idols.

Until Ā'sà was old, he served the Lord; but in his old age he became sick, and in his sickness he did not seek the Lord. He turned to men who called themselves physicians or doctors, but they were men who tried to cure by the power of idols. This led many of Ā'sà's people to worship images, so that when he died, there were again idols throughout the land.

Ā'sà's son, Jĕ-hŏsh'a-phăt, was the next king, and he was the wisest and strongest of all the kings of Jū'dah, and ruled over the largest realm of any. When he became king, Ā'hăb was king of Ĭṣ'ra-el. Jĕ-hŏsh'a-phăt made peace with Ĭṣ'ra-el and united with the Ĭṣ'ra-el-ītes against the kingdom of Sўr'ĭ-à. He fought against the Sўr'ĭ-anṣ in the battle of Rā'moth=ḡil'e-ăd, where King Ā'hăb was slain, and afterward with Ā'hăb's son, Jĕ-hō'ram, he fought against the Mō'ab-ītes.

Jĕ-hŏsh'a-phăt served the Lord with all his heart. He took away the idols that had again arisen in the land; he called upon his people to worship the Lord, and he sent princes and priests throughout all Jū'dah to read to the people the law of the Lord and to teach the people how to serve the Lord.

The Lord gave to Jĕ-hŏsh'a-phăt great power. He ruled over the land of Ē'dom, over the wilderness on the south, and over the cities of the Phĭ-lĭs'tĭneṣ upon the coast. And Jĕ-hŏsh'a-phăt chose judges for the cities in all the land and he said to them:

"Remember that you are not judging for men, but for the Lord; and the Lord is with you and sees all your acts. Therefore fear the Lord and do his will. Do not allow men to make you presents, so that you will favor them; but be just toward all and be strong in doing right."

At one time news came to King Jĕ-hŏsh'a-phăt that some of the nations on the east and south and north, Mō'ab-ītes, Ăm'mon-ītes, and Sўr'ĭ-anṣ, had banded together against him and were encamped with a great army at En=ḡē'dī, near the Dead Sea. Jĕ-hŏsh'a-phăt called forth his soldiers, but before they went to battle, he led them to the Temple to worship the Lord. And Jĕ-hŏsh'a-phăt called upon the Lord for help, saying:

"O Lord, the God of our fathers, art not thou God in heaven? Dost thou not rule over the nations of earth? Is not power thine, so that none can stand against thee? Now, Lord, look upon these hosts who have come against thy people. We have no might against this great company, and we know not what to do; but our eyes look toward thee for help."

Then the Spirit of the Lord came upon one of the Lē'vītes, a man named Jȧ-hā'zĭ-el, and he said:

"Hear, ye men of Jĕ-ru̯'sȧ-lĕm and Jū'dah, and hear, O King Jĕ-hŏsh'a-phăt. Thus saith the Lord, 'Fear not this great host of your enemies, for the battle is not yours, but the Lord's. Go out against them; but you will not need to fight. You shall stand still and see how the Lord will save you. Do not fear, for the Lord is with you!' "

Then Jĕ-hŏsh'a-phăt and all his people worshiped the Lord, bowing with their faces on the ground. And the next day, when they marched against the enemies, the Lē'vītes walked in front, singing and praising the Lord, while all the people answered:

"Give thanks to the Lord, for his mercy endureth forever."

When the men of Jū'dah came to the camp of their enemies, they found that a quarrel had risen up among them. The Ăm'-mon-ītes and the Mō'ab-ītes began to fight with the rest of the bands, and soon all the host were fighting and killing each other. And when the men of Jū'dah came, part of the host were lying dead and the rest had fled away into the desert, leaving behind them great treasure. So it came to pass as the prophet Jȧ-hā'zĭ-el had said, they did not fight, but the Lord fought for them and saved them from their foes.

The place where this strange battle had taken place they named the valley of Bĕr'a-chah," which means "Blessing," because there hey blessed the Lord for the help that he had given them. And fterward they came back to Jĕ-ru̟'sȧ-lĕm with songs and praises nd the great riches which they had taken. And God gave to King Jĕ-hŏsh'a-phăt peace and rest from his enemies and great ower as long as he lived.

The Little Boy Who Was Crowned King

JĔ-HŎSH'A-PHĂT, the king of Jū'dah, was a good man and a wise king, but he made one mistake which brought great trouble upon his family and upon his land in after days. He married his son Jĕ-hō'ram to Ăth-a-lī'ah, the daughter of Ā'hăb and the wicked Jĕz'e-bĕl. When Jĕ-hŏsh'a-phăt died and Jĕ-hō'ram became king of Jū'dah, his wife, Ăth-a-lī'ah, led him into the wickedness of the house of Ā'hăb. Jĕ-hō'ram killed all his brothers, the sons of Jĕ-hŏsh'a-phăt, so that no one of them might rise up against him. His queen Ăth-a-lī'ah set up idols all around Jĕ-ru̟'sȧ-lĕm and in Jū'dah, and led the people in worshiping them.

The prophet Ē-lī'jah was still living in Ĭṣ'ra-el when Jĕ-hō'ram began to reign in Jū'dah. He sent to King Jĕ-hō'ram a letter containing a message from the Lord. He wrote:

"Thus saith the Lord, the God of Dā'vid, 'Because you have not walked in the ways of your father, Jĕ-hŏsh'a-phăt, but have walked in the ways of the kings of Ĭṣ'ra-el and have led the people of Jĕ-ru̟'sȧ-lĕm and of Jū'dah to turn from the Lord to idols, and because you have slain your brothers, who were better than you, therefore the Lord will strike you and your house and your people; and you shall have a terrible disease that none can cure.' '

And after this great troubles came upon Jĕ-hō'ram and his land The Ē'dom-ītes on the south, who had been under the rule of Jū'dah since the days of Dā'vid, broke away from King Jĕ-hō'ram and set up a kingdom of their own. The Phĭ-lĭs'tīneṣ on the west and the Ă-rā'bĭ-anṣ of the desert made war upon him. They broke into his palace and carried away his treasures, and killed all his children except one, the youngest.

And upon Jĕ-hō'ram himself fell a sickness that lasted many years and caused him great suffering. No cure could be found, and after long years of pain Jĕ-hō'ram died. So evil had been his reign of eight years that no one was sorry to have him die, and they would not allow his body to be buried among the kings of Jū'dah.

After Jĕ-hō'ram his youngest son, Ā-ha-zī'ah, became king. His mother was the wicked Ăth-a-lī'ah, the daughter of Jĕz'e-bĕl. Ā-ha-zī'ah reigned only one year; for while he was visiting King Jĕ-hō'ram of Ĭṣ'ra-el, his uncle, he was slain by Jē'hū; for this was the time when Jē'hū rose against the house of Ā'hăb, killed Jĕ-hō'-ram, Ā'hăb's son, and Jĕz'e-bĕl, Ā'hăb's widow, and made himself king of Ĭṣ'ra-el. But Jē'hū gave to the body of Ā-ha-zī'ah a king's burial, for he said, "He was the son of Jĕ-hŏsh'a-phăt, who sought the Lord with all his heart."

When Ăth-a-lī'ah, the mother of Ā-ha-zī'ah, heard that her son was dead, all the fierceness of her mother Jĕz'e-bĕl arose in her. She seized the princes who belonged to the family of Dā'vid and killed them, so that there was not a man of the royal line left. And she made herself the queen and ruler over the land of Jū'dah. She shut up the house of the Lord and built a temple for Bā'al; and for six years led the people of Jū'dah in all wickedness.

In the slaughter of the royal family by Ăth-a-lī'ah one little child of Ā-ha-zī'ah had been saved alive. His name was Jō'ăsh. He was a baby, only a year old when his grandmother, Ăth-a-lī'ah, seized the throne, and his aunt, a sister of Ā-ha-zī'ah and the wife of the priest Jĕ-hoi'a-dà, hid him in the Temple of the Lord and kept him safe from the hate of Queen Ăth-a-lī'ah. There he

tayed for six years, while Jĕ-hoi'a-dà, the priest, was preparing
o make him king.

When all things were ready and little Jō'ăsh was seven years
ld, Jĕ-hoi'a-dà, the priest, brought him out of his hiding place,
nd set him before the people and the rulers in the temple, and
·laced the crown upon his head. Then all the people shouted,
Long live the king! Long live the king!"

Queen Ăth-a-lī'ah heard the noise of the shouting and came out
·f her palace to see what had taken place. She saw the little boy-

cing standing by a pillar in the Temple, with the crown upon his
ead, and around him the soldiers and the people, crying aloud,
'Long live the king!"

Ăth-a-lī'ah was very angry as she saw all this. She called for
ıer servants and her soldiers to break up this gathering of the
·eople and to take the boy-king. But no one would follow her,
·or they were tired of her cruel rule and they wished to have for
·heir king one who came from the line of Dā'vid.

Jĕ-hoi'a-dà said to the soldiers, "Take this woman a prisoner
ınd carry her out of the Temple of the Lord. Let not her blood
·e spilled in the holy house."

So they seized Ăth-a-lī'ah and dragged her out of the Temple and killed her. Then Jĕ-hoi'a-dà and all the people made a promise to serve the Lord only. They tore down the house of the idol Bā'al and destroyed the images and broke its altar in pieces. They made the Temple holy once more, and set the house in order, and offered the sacrifices, and held the daily worship before the altar And all the people were glad to have a descendant of Dā'vid, one of the royal line, once more on the throne of Jū'dah.

As long as Jĕ-hoi'a-dà the good priest lived, Jō'ăsh ruled well and his people served the Lord. When King Jō'ăsh grew up, he wished to have the Temple of the Lord made new and beautiful for in the years that had passed since the Temple had been built by Sŏl'o-mon, it had grown old and had fallen into decay. Then too, Queen Ăth-a-lī'ah and the men who worshiped Bā'al had broken down the walls in many places, and they had carried away the gold and the silver of the Temple to use in the worship of Bā'al

At first King Jō'ăsh told the priests and Lē'vītes, who served in the Temple, to go through the land and ask the people for money to be spent in furnishing the Temple. But the priests and the Lē'vītes were slow in the work, and the king tried another plan for getting the money that was needed.

He caused a large box or chest to be made and had it placed at the door of the Temple, so that all would see it when they went to worship the Lord. In the lid of the box was a hole through which they dropped money into the box. And the king caused word to be sent through all the land that the princes and the people should bring gifts of money and drop them into the chest, whenever they came to the Temple.

The people were glad and brought their gifts willingly; for they all wished to have God's house made beautiful. In a short time the box was full of gold and silver. Then the king's officers opened the box and tied up the money in bags and placed the bags of money in a safe place. The box was filled with gold and silver many times, until there was money in abundance to pay for all the work needed in the Temple and for making new ornaments of gold and silver for the house.

When Jĕ-hoi'a-dà, the good priest, was very old, he died; and after his death there was no one to keep King Jō'ăsh in the right way. The princes of the land loved to worship idols and did not serve God, and they led King Jō'ăsh into wicked ways after he had done so well. God was not pleased with Jō'ăsh after he forsook the Lord, and God allowed the Sȳr'ĭ-ans̩ from the north to come upon the land. They robbed the cities and left Jō'ăsh sick and poor. Soon after the coming of the Sȳr'ĭ-ans̩, his own servants killed him and made Ăm-a-zī'ah, his son, king in his place.

Story Three   II CHRONICLES 25 : 1 to 28 : 27; ISAIAH, chapter 6

Three Kings and a Great Prophet

AM-A-ZĪ'AH was the ninth of the kings of Jū'dah, if the years of Ăth-a-lī'ah's rule be counted as a separate reign. Ăm-a-zī'ah worshiped the Lord, but he did not serve the Lord with a perfect heart. He gathered an army of three hundred thousand men, to make war on Ē'dom and bring its people again under the rule of Jū'dah. He hired also an army from Ĭs'ra-el to help him in this war; but a prophet said to him, "O king, do not let the army of Ĭs̩'ra-el go with you against Ē'dom, for the Lord is not with the people of Ĭs̩'ra-el. But go with your own men and be strong and brave; and the Lord will help you."

"But how will I get back the money that I have paid to the army of Ĭs̩'ra-el?" said Ăm-a-zī'ah to the prophet.

"Fear not," said the prophet; "the Lord is able to give you much more than you have lost."

Then Ăm-a-zī'ah obeyed the Lord and sent back the men of Ĭs̩'ra-el to their own land and went against the Ē'dom-ītes with the men of Jū'dah. The Lord gave him a great victory in the land of Ē'dom; Ăm-a-zī'ah was cruel to the people whom he conquered and killed very many of them in his anger. And when he came back from Ē'dom, he brought with him the idol gods of that land, and although they could not save their own people, Ăm-a-zī'ah set them up for his own gods and burned incense to them and bowed down before them. And when a prophet of the Lord came to him and warned him that God was angry with him and would surely punish him for his wickedness, Ăm-a-zī'ah said to the prophet, "Who has asked you to give advice to the king? Keep still, or you will be put to death!" And the prophet answered him, "I know that it is God's will that you shall be destroyed, because you will not listen to the word of the Lord."

Ăm-azī'ah's punishment was not long delayed, for soon after this, he made war upon Jō'ash, the king of Ĭṣ'ra-el, whose kingdom was far greater and stronger than his own. The two armies met at Bĕth=shē'mesh, northwest of Jĕ-ru'sȧ-lĕm. Ăm-a-zī'ah was beaten in a great battle, many of his men were slain, and Ăm-a-zī'ah himself was taken prisoner by Jō'ash, the king of Ĭṣ'ra-el. Jō'ash took the city of Jĕ-ru'sȧ-lĕm and broke down the wall and carried away all the treasures in the palace and in the Temple of the Lord. After this Ăm-a-zī'ah lived fifteen years but he never gained the power that he had lost. His nobles made a plan to kill him, and Ăm-a-zī'ah fled away from the city to escape them. But they caught him and slew him and brought his body back to Jĕ-ru'sȧ-lĕm to be buried in the tombs of the kings. His reign began well, but it ended ill, because he failed to obey the word of the Lord.

After Ăm-a-zī'ah came his son Ŭz-zī'ah, who was also called Ăz-a-rī'ah. He was the tenth king of Jū'dah. Ŭz-zī'ah was only sixteen years old when he began to reign, and he was king for fifty-two years. He did that which was right in the sight of the Lord during most of his reign. Ŭz-zī'ah found the kingdom weak and he made it strong, for the Lord helped him. He won back for Jū'dah the land of the Phĭ-lĭs'tĭneṣ, the land of the Ăm'mon-ītes on the east of Jôr'dan and of the Ȧ-rā'bĭ-anṣ on the south. He built cities and made strong walls around them, with towers full of weapons for defense against enemies. He loved the fields, and planted trees and vineyards and raised crops of wheat and barley.

But when Ŭz-zī′ah was strong and rich, his heart became proud, and he no longer tried to do God's will. He sought to have the power of the high priest as well as that of the king, and he went into the Holy Place in the Temple to offer incense upon the golden altar, which was allowed to the priests only. The high priest Ăz-a-rī′ah followed Ŭz-zī′ah into the Holy Place with the other priests and said to him:

"It is not for you to offer incense, O King Ŭz-zī′ah, nor to come into the Holy Place. This belongs to the priests alone. Go out of the Holy Place, for you have disobeyed the Lord's command; and it will not bring upon you honor, but trouble."

King Ŭz-zī′ah was standing before the golden altar with a censer in his hand. Instantly the white scales of leprosy rose upon his forehead. The priests saw in that moment that God had smitten Ŭz-zī′ah with leprosy; indeed, he felt it himself and turned to leave the Holy Place. But they would not wait for him to go out; they drove him out, for the leper's presence made the house unholy. And from that day until he died, Ŭz-zī′ah was a leper. He could no longer sit as king, but his son Jō′tham took his place; nor was he allowed to live in the palace, but he stayed in a house alone. And when he died, they would not give him a place among

the tombs of the kings; but they buried him in a field outside
Jō'tham, the eleventh king, ruled after his father's death sixteer
years. He served the Lord, but he did not stop his people fron
worshiping the idols. He was warned by his father's fate, and
was content to be a king, without trying at the same time to be a
priest and to offer incense in the Temple. God was with Jō'tham
and gave his kingdom some success.

The next king, the twelfth, was Ā'hăz, the most wicked of
all the kings of Jū'dah. He left the service of God and worshiped the images of Bā'al. Worse than any other king, he even
offered some of his own children as burnt offerings to the false
gods. In his reign the house of the Lord was shut up, and its
treasures were taken away, and it was left to fall into ruin. For
his sins and the sins of his people, God brought great suffering
upon the land. The king of Ĭṣ'ra-el, Pē'kah, came against Ā'hăz
and killed more than a hundred thousand of the men of Jū'dah,
among them the king's own son. The Ĭṣ'ra-el-ītes also took away
many more—men, women, and children—as captives. But a
prophet of the Lord in Ĭṣ'ra-el, whose name was Ō'ded, came out
to meet the rulers, and said to them:

"The Lord God was angry with Jū'dah and gave its people
into your hand. But do you now intend to keep your brothers
of Jū'dah as slaves? Have not you also sinned against the Lord?
Now listen to the word of the Lord, and set your brothers free
and send them home."

Then the rulers of Ĭṣ'ra-el gave clothing to such of the captives
as were in need and set food before them; and they sent them
home to their own land, even giving to those that were weak
among them asses to ride upon. They brought them to Jĕr'ĭ-chō,
in the valley of the Jôr'dan, and gave them to their own people.

When the Ē'dom-ītes came against Jū'dah, King Ā'hăz sent to
the Ăs-sўr'ĭ-anṣ, a great people far away, to come and help him.
The Ăs-sўr'ĭ-anṣ came, but they did not help him, for they made
themselves rulers of Jū'dah and robbed Ā'hăz of all that he had
and laid heavy burdens upon the land. At last Ā'hăz died, leaving his people worshipers of idols and under the power of the king
of Ăs-sўr'ĭ-à.

In the days of these three kings, Ŭz-zī'ah, Jō'tham, and Ā'hăz, God raised up a great prophet in Jū'dah, whose name was Ī-ṣā'iah. The prophecies that he spoke in the name of the Lord are given in the book of Ī-ṣā'iah. In the year that King Ŭz-zī'ah died, Ī-ṣā'-ah was a young man. One day, while he was worshiping in the Temple, a wonderful vision rose suddenly before his sight. He saw the form of the Lord God upon a throne, with the angels round him. He saw also strange creatures called seraphim, standing before the throne of the Lord. Each of these had six wings. With two wings he covered his face before the glory of the Lord, with two wings he covered his feet, and with two he flew through the air to do God's will. And these seraphim called out to one another, "Holy, holy, is the Lord of hosts; the whole earth is full of his glory!"

And the young Ī-ṣā'iah felt the walls and the floor of the Temple shaking at these voices; and he saw a cloud of smoke covering the house. Ī-ṣā'iah was filled with fear. He cried out, saying:

"Woe has come to me! for I am a man of sinful lips and I live among a people of sinful lips: and now my eyes have seen the King, the Lord of hosts!"

Then one of the seraphim took into his hand the tongs that were used in the sacrifices. He flew to the altar, and with the tongs took up a burning coal. Then he flew to the place where Ī-ṣā'iah was standing and pressed the fiery coal to Ī-ṣā'iah's lips; and he said, "This coal from God's altar has touched your lips, and now your sin is taken away, and you are made clean."

Then Ī-ṣā'iah heard the voice of the Lord saying, "Whom shall I send to this people? Who will bear the message of the Lord to them?"

And Ī-ṣā'iah said, "Here am I, Lord; send me!"

And the Lord said to Ī-ṣā'iah, "You shall be my prophet and shall go to this people and shall give to them my words. But they will not listen to you, nor understand you. Your words will do them no good, but will seem to make their hearts hard and their ears heavy and their eyes shut. For they will not hear with their ears, nor see with their eyes, nor understand with their hearts, nor will they turn to me and be saved."

And Ī-ṣā'iah said, "How long must this be, O Lord?"

And the Lord said:

"Until the cities are left waste without people and the house; without men to live in them; and the land shall become utterly desolate; and the people shall be taken far away into another land But out of all this there shall be a few people, a tenth part, to come back, and to rise like a new tree from the roots where the old tree has been cut down. This tenth part shall be the seed of a new people in the times to come."

By this Ī-ṣā'iah knew that, though his words might seem to do no good, yet he was to go on preaching, for long afterward a new Jū'dah should rise out of the ruins of the old kingdom and should serve the Lord.

Ī-ṣā'iah lived for many years and spoke the word of the Lord to his people until he was a very old man. He preached while four kings, perhaps also a fifth, were ruling. Some of these kings were friendly and listened to his words: but others were not willing to obey the prophet and do the will of God; and the kingdom of Jū'dah gradually fell away from the worship of the Lord and followed the people of the Ten Tribes in the worship of idols.

Story Four   II KINGS 18 : 1 to 21 : 21; II CHRONICLES
                       29 : 1 to 32 : 33; ISAIAH 35 : 1 to 38 : 22

The Good King Hezekiah

AFTER Ā'hăz, the wickedest of the kings of Jū'dah, came Hĕz-e-kī'ah, who was the best of the kings. He listened to the words of the prophet Ī-ṣā'iah and obeyed the commands of the Lord. In the first month of his reign, when he was a young man, he called together the priests and the Lē-vītes, who had the charge of the house of the Lord, and he said to them:

"My sons, give yourselves once more to the service of the Lord

nd be holy, as God commands you. Now open the doors of the
ouse of the Lord, which have been shut for these many years;
.nd take out of the house all the idols that have been placed in it;
.nd make the place clean and pure from all evil things. Because
he people have turned away from the Lord, he has been angry
vith us and has left us to our enemies; now let us go back to the
_ord and promise again to serve him. God has chosen you, my
ons, to lead in his worship; do not neglect the work that the Lord
ias given you to do."

Then the Temple was opened as of old; the idols were taken
away; the altar was made holy to the Lord, and the daily offering
vas laid upon it; the lamps were lighted in the Holy Place; the
priest stood before the golden altar offering incense; the Lē'vītes
n their robes sang the psalms of Dā'vid, while the silver trumpets
nade music; and the people came up to worship in the Temple as
hey had not come in many years.

You remember that the great Feast of the Passover kept in mind
iow the children of Ĭṣ'ra-el had come out of Ē'ġȳpt. (See Part
First, Story Twenty-three.) For a long time the people had
ceased to keep this feast, both in Jū'dah and in Ĭṣ'ra-el. King
Hĕz-e-kī'ah sent commands through all Jū'dah for the people to
come up to Jĕ-rụ'så-lĕm and to worship the Lord in this feast.
He also sent men through the land of Ĭṣ'ra-el, the Ten Tribes, to
ask the men of Ĭṣ'ra-el also to come up with their brothers of
Jū'dah to Jĕ-rụ'så-lĕm, and to keep the feast. At that time Hŏ-
shē'å, the last king of Ĭṣ'ra-el, was on the throne, the land was over-
run by the Ăs-sȳr'ĭ-anṣ, and the kingdom was very weak and near-
ing its end. Most of the people in Ĭṣ'ra-el were worshipers of idols
and had forgotten God's law. They laughed at Hĕz-e-kī'ah's
messengers and would not come to the feast. But in many places
in Ĭṣ'ra-el there were some who had listened to the prophets of
the Lord, and these came up to worship with the men of Jū'dah.
For each family they roasted a lamb, and with it ate the unleavened bread, that is, bread made without yeast, and they praised
the Lord who had led their fathers out from Ē'ġȳpt to their own
land.

After the feast, when the people had given themselves once

more to the service of God, King Hĕz-e-kī′ah began to destroy
the idols that were everywhere in Jū′dah. He sent men to break
down the images, to tear in pieces the altars to the false gods, and
to cut down the trees under which the altars stood. You remember that Mō′ṣeṣ made a serpent of brass in the wilderness. This
image had been brought to Jĕ-ru′sà-lĕm and was still kept there
in the days of Hĕz-e-kī′ah. The people were worshiping it as an
idol; and were burning incense before it. Hĕz-e-kī′ah said, "It is
nothing but a piece of brass," and he commanded that it should be
broken up. Everywhere he called upon his people to turn from
the idols, to destroy them, and to worship the Lord God.

When Hĕz-e-kī′ah became king, the kingdoms of Iṣ′ra-el and
Sўr′ĭ-à and Jū′dah, with all the lands near them, were under the
power of the great kingdom of the Ăs-sўr′ĭ-anṣ. Each land had
its own king, but he ruled under the king of Ăs-sўr′ĭ-à; and every
year a heavy tax was laid upon the people, to be paid to the Ăs-
sўr′ĭ-anṣ. After a few years, Hĕz-e-kī′ah thought that he was
strong enough to set his kingdom free from the Ăs-sўr′ĭ-an rule.
He refused to pay the tax any longer, and he gathered an army
and built the walls of Jĕ-ru′sà-lĕm higher, and made ready for a
war with the Ăs-sўr′ĭ-anṣ. But Sĕn-năch′e-rĭb, the king of Ăs-
sўr′ĭ-à, came into the land of Jū′dah with a great army and took
all the cities in the west of Jū′dah and threatened to take Jĕ-ru′sà-
lĕm also. Then Hĕz-e-kī′ah saw that he had made a mistake. He
was not able to fight the Ăs-sўr′ĭ-anṣ, the most powerful of all the
nations in that part of the world. He sent word to the king of
Ăs-sўr′ĭ-à, saying:

"I will no more resist your rule; forgive me for the past and
I will pay whatever you ask."

Then the king of Ăs-sўr′ĭ-à laid upon Hĕz-e-kī′ah and his
people a tax heavier than before. To obtain the money, Hĕz-e-
kī′ah took all the gold and silver in the Temple, all that was in his
own palace and all that he could find among the people, and sent
it to the Ăs-sўr′ĭ-anṣ. But even then the king of Ăs-sўr′ĭ-à was
not satisfied. He sent his princes to Jĕ-ru′sà-lĕm with this message:

"We are going to destroy this city and take you away into

The
FOUR GEMS
OF THE BIBLE

The Ten Commandments
The Twenty=third Psalm
The Beatitudes
The Lord's Prayer

THE TEN COMMANDMENTS

I

Thou shalt have no other gods before me.

II

Thou shalt not make unto thee any graven image, or any likeness of any thing that is in heaven above, or that is in the earth beneath, or that is in the water under the earth: thou shalt not bow down thyself to them, nor serve them: for I the Lord thy God am a jealous God, visiting the iniquity of the fathers upon the children unto the third and fourth generation of them that hate me; and shewing mercy unto thousands of them that love me, and keep my commandments.

THE TEN COMMANDMENTS

III

Thou shalt not take the name of the Lord thy God in vain; for the Lord will not hold him guiltless that taketh his name in vain.

IV

Remember the sabbath day, to keep it holy. Six days shalt thou labour, and do all thy work: but the seventh day is the sabbath of the Lord thy God: in it thou shalt not do any work, thou, nor thy son, nor thy daughter, thy manservant, nor thy maidservant, nor thy cattle, nor thy stranger that is within thy gates: for in six

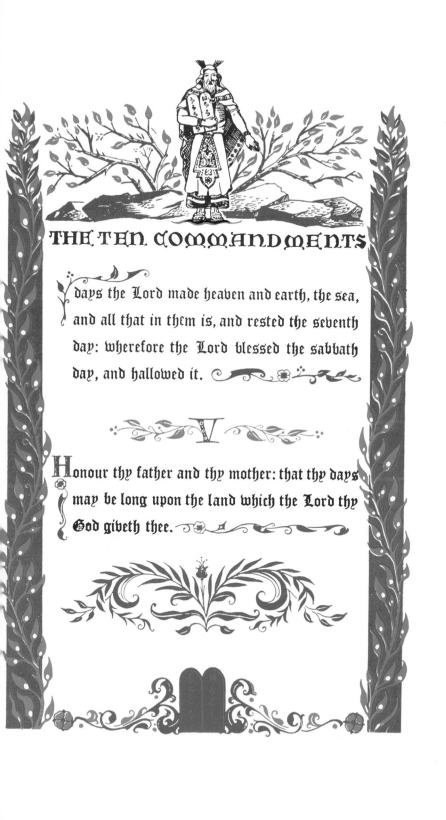

THE TEN COMMANDMENTS

days the Lord made heaven and earth, the sea, and all that in them is, and rested the seventh day: wherefore the Lord blessed the sabbath day, and hallowed it.

V

Honour thy father and thy mother: that thy days may be long upon the land which the Lord thy God giveth thee.

THE TEN COMMANDMENTS

VI

Thou shalt not kill.

VII

Thou shalt not commit adultery.

VIII

Thou shalt not steal.

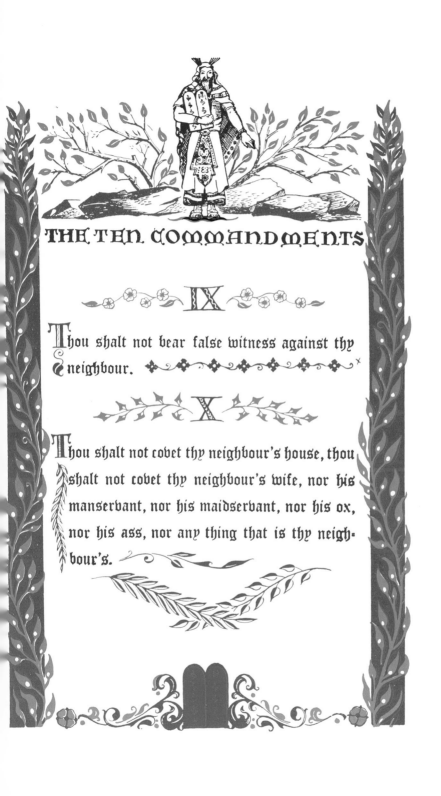

THE TEN COMMANDMENTS

IX

Thou shalt not bear false witness against thy neighbour.

X

Thou shalt not covet thy neighbour's house, thou shalt not covet thy neighbour's wife, nor his manservant, nor his maidservant, nor his ox, nor his ass, nor any thing that is thy neighbour's.

The Lord is my shepherd; I shall not want. He maketh me to lie down in green pastures: he leadeth me beside the still waters. He restoreth my soul: he leadeth me in the paths of righteousness for his name's sake. Yea, though I walk through the valley of the shadow of

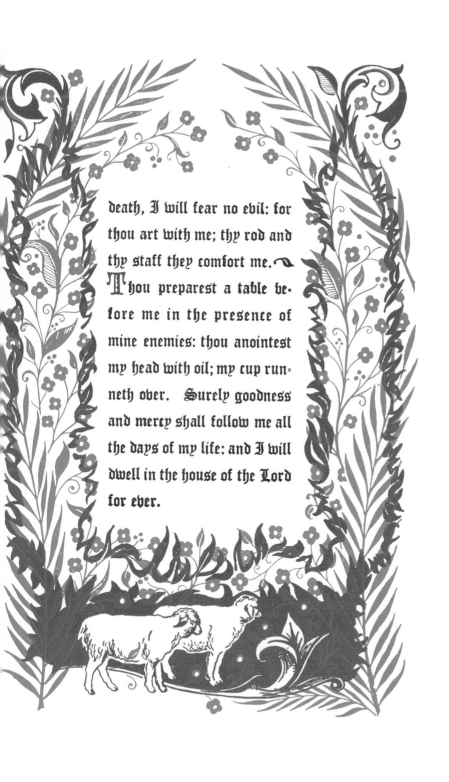

death, I will fear no evil: for thou art with me; thy rod and thy staff they comfort me. Thou preparest a table before me in the presence of mine enemies: thou anointest my head with oil; my cup runneth over. Surely goodness and mercy shall follow me all the days of my life: and I will dwell in the house of the Lord for ever.

THE BEATITUDES

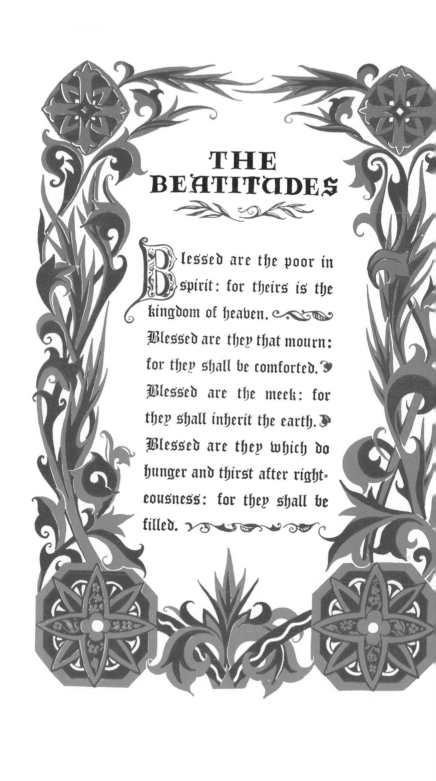

Blessed are the poor in spirit: for theirs is the kingdom of heaven. Blessed are they that mourn: for they shall be comforted. Blessed are the meek: for they shall inherit the earth. Blessed are they which do hunger and thirst after righteousness: for they shall be filled.

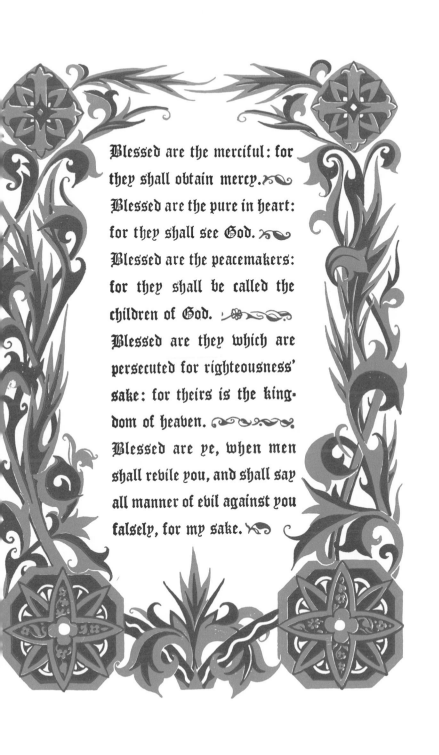

Blessed are the merciful: for they shall obtain mercy.

Blessed are the pure in heart: for they shall see God.

Blessed are the peacemakers: for they shall be called the children of God.

Blessed are they which are persecuted for righteousness' sake: for theirs is the kingdom of heaven.

Blessed are ye, when men shall revile you, and shall say all manner of evil against you falsely, for my sake.

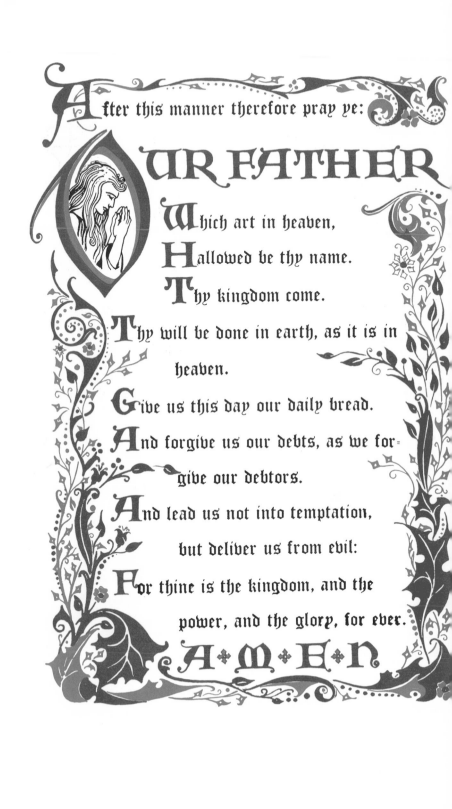

After this manner therefore pray ye:

OUR FATHER

Which art in heaven,

Hallowed be thy name.

Thy kingdom come.

Thy will be done in earth, as it is in

heaven.

Give us this day our daily bread.

And forgive us our debts, as we for-

give our debtors.

And lead us not into temptation,

but deliver us from evil:

For thine is the kingdom, and the

power, and the glory, for ever.

A · M · E · N

nother land, a land far away; as we have taken the people of ș'ra-el away and as we have carried captive other peoples. The ods of other nations have not been able to save those who trusted 1 them against us, and your God will not be able to save you. Now give yourselves up to the great king of Ăs-sўr'ĭ-à and go to he land where he will send you."

When King Hĕz-e-kī'ah heard this, he was filled with fear. He took the letter into the house of the Lord and spread it out before the altar and called upon the Lord to help him and to save his people. Then he sent his princes to the prophet Ī-șā'iah, to ask him to give them some word from the Lord. And Ī-șā'iah said: "Thus saith the Lord, 'The king of Ăs-sўr'ĭ-à shall not come to his city, nor shall he shoot an arrow against it. But he shall go back to his own land by the same way that he came. And I will cause him to fall by the sword in his own land. For I will defend his city and will save it for my own sake and for my servant Dā'vid's sake.' "

Just at that time, Sĕn-năch'e-rĭb, the king of Ăs-sўr'ĭ-à, heard that a great army was marching against him from another land. He turned away from the land of Jū'dah and went to meet these new enemies. And the Lord sent upon the army of the Ăs-sўr'-ĭ-ans a sudden and terrible plague, so that in one night nearly two hundred thousand of them died in their camp. Then King Sĕn-năch'e-rĭb hastened back to his own land, and never again came into the land of Jū'dah; nor did he again send an army there. And years after this, while he was worshiping his idol god in his temple at Nĭn'e-veh, his chief city, two of his sons came upon him and slew him with the sword. They escaped into a distant land, and Ē'sar=hăd'don, another of his sons, became king over the lands ruled by the Ăs-sўr'ĭ-ans. Thus did God save his city and his people from their enemies, because they looked to him for help.

At the time while the Ăs-sўr'ĭ-ans were in the land and the kingdom was in great danger, King Hĕz-e-kī'ah was suddenly stricken with a deadly disease. It was a tumor or a cancer, which no physician could cure; and the prophet Ī-șā'iah said to him:

"Thus saith the Lord, 'Set your house in order and prepare to leave your kingdom, for you shall die and not live.' "

But King Hĕz-e-kī'ah felt that in a time of such trouble to the land he could not be spared, especially as at that time he had no son who could take charge of the kingdom. Then Hĕz-e-kī'ah upon his bed prayed to the Lord that he might live; and he said:

"O Lord, I beseech thee, remember now how I have walked before thee in truth and with a perfect heart, and have done that which was good in thy sight. Let me live and not die, O Lord!"

The Lord heard Hĕz-e-kī'ah's prayer, and before Ī-ṣā'iah had reached the middle of the city, on his way home, the Lord said to him, "Turn again and say to Hĕz-e-kī'ah the prince of my people, 'Thus saith the Lord, I have heard your prayer, I have seen your tears; I will heal you; and in three days you shall go up to the house of the Lord. I will add to your life fifteen years and I will save this city from the king of Ăs-sȳr'ĭ-à.' "

Then Ī-ṣā'iah the prophet came again to Hĕz-e-kī'ah and spoke to him the word of the Lord; and he said, also, "Lay on the tumor a plaster made of figs, and he shall be cured."

When Hĕz-e-kī'ah heard the words of Ī-ṣā'iah, he said, "What sign will the Lord give, to show that he will cure me and that I shall again go up to the house of the Lord?"

And Ī-ṣā'iah said, "The Lord will give you a sign, and you shall choose it yourself. Shall the shadow on the dial go forward ten degrees or go back ten degrees?" Near the palace was standing a sundial, by which the time of the day was shown, for there were no clocks then. Hĕz-e-kī'ah said, "It is easy for the shadow to go forward ten degrees. Let it go back ten degrees."

Then Ī-sā'iah the prophet called upon the Lord, and the Lord heard him; and caused the shadow to go backward on the sundial ten degrees. And within three days Hĕz-e-kī'ah was well and went to worship in the house of the Lord. After this Hĕz-e-kī'ah lived fifteen years in honor. When he died, all the land mourned for him as the best of the kings.

Story Five

II KINGS 21 : 1 to 23 : 25;
II CHRONICLES 33 : 1 to 35 : 27

The Lost Book Found in the Temple

MĂ-NĂS'SEH, the fourteenth king of Jū'dah, followed the sins of his grandfather Ā'hăz, and not the good deeds of his father Hĕz-e-kī'ah. He was only twelve years old when he began to reign, too young for so great a care as the kingdom; and in his youth he turned away from the teachings of the prophet Ī-sā'iah and from the service of the Lord. He built again the altars to Bā'al and the Ăsh-ē'rah, which his father Hĕz-e-kī'ah had thrown down; he worshiped the sun and moon and stars; he set up images even in the Temple, the house of the Lord. When Mă-năs'seh grew older and had children of his own, he made them go through the fire, seeking to please the false gods. He would not listen to the prophets whom the Lord sent to warn him; and there is reason to believe—though the Bible does not say it—that he put to death the good prophet Ī-sā'iah.

And Mă-năs'seh in his wickedness reigned a long time, longer than any of the wicked kings who had gone before him; so that he led his people further away from God than even Ā'hăz, who had been as wicked as Mă-năs'seh. Because of Mă-năs'seh's sins and the sins of his people, the Lord brought upon the land the generals of the Ăs-sўr'ĭ-an army with their host. They took Mȧ-năs'seh a prisoner and bound him with chains and carried him to the city of Băb'ў-lon, where the king of Ăs-sўr'ĭ-à was then living. There Mȧ-năs'seh was kept a prisoner for a time.

While he was in prison, Mȧ-năs'seh saw how wicked he had been, and he sought the Lord. He prayed to be forgiven for his sins, and the Lord heard him. Afterward, the king of Ăs-sўr'ĭ-à allowed Mȧ-năs'seh to rule over his land again. Then Mȧ-năs'seh knew that the Lord was the only true God; and from that time he worshiped the Lord only. He took the altars and the images of the false gods out of the Temple, and built again the altar of the Lord, and caused the offerings to be laid upon it. He commanded his people to worship the Lord and to leave the idols; but they had gone too far to come back, and only a few of them followed their king's example in seeking the Lord. He could easily lead his people into sin, but he could not bring them back to God.

After a long reign of fifty-five years Mȧ-năs'seh died, and his son Ā'mon became king. He reigned only two years, but they were years of wickedness and of worshiping idols. Then his servants in his own house killed Ā'mon; but the people killed them in turn, and made his son Jŏ-sī'ah king.

Jŏ-sī'ah, the sixteenth king, was only eight years old when his father Ā'mon was slain. At first he was too young to rule over the land, and the princes of his court governed in his name. But when Jŏ-sī'ah was sixteen years old, he chose the Lord God of his father Dā'vid, the God whom Hĕz-e-kī'ah had worshiped; and he served the Lord more fully than any of the kings who had gone before him. When he was twenty years old, he began to clear away the idols and the idol temples from the land of Jū'dah. He did his work more thoroughly than it had ever been done before by Jĕ-hŏsh'a-phăt or by Hĕz-e-kī'ah; for he left in all the land not a single place where idols were worshiped. He went even beyond his own borders, into the land that had been the land of Ĭs'ra-el, from which most of the people had been carried away captive long before; and in every place he broke down the altars and burned the images, and even dug up the bones of the idol priests and burned them with their images.

He came to Běth′el, twelve miles north of Jĕ-ru̯′så-lĕm, where Jĕr-o-bō′am of Ĭṣ′ra-el had built the temple for the worship of the golden calves, two hundred years before. There, as he was burning the bones of the idol priests upon the ruins of their own altars, he found a tomb and he asked who was buried there. They said, "This is the tomb of the man of God who came from Jū′dah and warned King Jĕr-o-bō′am of one who would do these very things that you are doing."

"Let his bones rest," said King Jŏ-sī′ah. "Let no man touch the bones of the prophet."

While the men of King Jŏ-sī′ah were at work in the Temple on Mount Mŏ-rī′ah, taking away the idols and making the house pure once more, they found an old book, written upon rolls of leather. It was the book of the law of the Lord, given by Mō′ṣeṣ, but it had been hidden so long that men had forgotten it. They brought the book and read from it aloud to the king.

And when King Jŏ-sī′ah heard the words of the law and the warning of the woes that were to come upon the people for disobeying them, the king was filled with alarm. He said to the rulers, "Go and ask of the Lord for me and for all the people. Great is the anger of the Lord against us, because our fathers have disobeyed the words of the Lord written in this book." They sought for a prophet to give them the word of the Lord, and they found a woman named Hŭl′dah, living in Jĕ-ru̯′så-lĕm, to whom the word of the Lord came. She was called "a prophetess," and they brought to her the message of King Jŏ-sī′ah. And the prophetess Hŭl′dah said to them, "Thus saith the Lord, the God of Ĭṣ′ra-el, 'Go and tell the man who has sent you, Behold, I will bring evil on this place and on the people living in it, because they have forsaken the Lord and have worshiped other gods. My anger will fall upon this city and upon this land. But because King Jŏ-sī′ah has sought the Lord and has done God's will and has called upon the Lord, therefore the Lord says that he will hold back his anger against this city and this land as long as Jŏ-sī′ah lives, and he shall go down to his grave before all these evils come upon Jū′dah and Jĕ-ru̯′så-lĕm.'"

When Jŏ-sī′ah heard this, he called all the princes and the priests

and the people to meet in the Temple of the Lord.   There the
king stood by a pillar and read to all the people the words of the
book that had been found.   Then the king and all his people made
a promise to serve the Lord and to do his will, and to keep his law
with all their hearts.   And this promise they kept while Jŏ-sī'ah
lived; but that was only a few years.

All this time the kingdom of Jū'dah, like all the kingdoms
around, was a part of the greater kingdom or empire of Ăs-sўr'ĭ-à.
But the great kings of Ăs-sўr'ĭ-à had passed away, and now the
kingdom or empire of Ăs-sўr'ĭ-à was becoming weak and falling
apart.   Phā'raōh=nē'choh, the king of Ē'ġўpt, went to war with
the Ăs-sўr'ĭ-anş, and on his way passed through the land of Jū'dah
and what had once been Ĭş'ra-el before its people were carried
away captive.   Jŏ-sī'ah thought that as the king of Ăs-sўr'ĭ-à was
his overlord, he must fight against the king of Ē'ġўpt, who was
coming against him.

Phā'raōh=nē'choh, the king of Ē'ġўpt, sent a message to King
Jŏ-sī'ah, saying, "I have nothing against you, O king of Jū'dah,
and I am not coming to make war on you, but on the king of

Ăs-sўr'ĭ-à. God has sent me and commanded me to make haste.
Do not stand in my way, or you may be destroyed."

But Jŏ-sī'ah would not heed the message of the king of Ē'ġўpt.
He went out against him with his army and met him in battle on
the great plain of Ĕs-dra-ē'lon, where so many battles had been
fought before and have been fought since. There the Ē-ġўp'tianṣ
won a victory, and in the fight the archers shot King Jŏ-sī'ah. He
died in his chariot, and they brought his dead body to Jĕ-ru̱'sà-lĕm.
And all the land mourned and wept for the king whom they loved
because he had ruled wisely and well. And with the good King
Jŏ-sī'ah died the last hope of the kingdom of Jū'dah.

Story Six	II KINGS 23 : 31 to 25 : 22; II CHRONICLES 36 : 1-21; JEREMIAH 22 : 10-12; 24 : 1-10; 29 : 1-29; 36 : 1 to 43 : 13

The Last Four Kings of Judah and the Weeping Prophet

WHEN the good King Jŏ-sī'ah fell in battle, the
people of the land made his son Jĕ-hō'a-hăz
king. At that time all the kingdoms around
Jū'dah were in confusion. The great empire of
Ăs-sўr'ĭ-à had been the ruler of nearly all that
part of the world; but now it had been broken up. Nĭn'e-veh, its
chief city, had been destroyed and Ē'ġўpt, Băb-ў-lō'nĭ-a, and
other lands were at war, each striving to take the place of Ăs-sўr'-
ĭ-à as the ruler of the nations.

Phā'raōh=nē'choh, the king of Ē'ġўpt, whose warriors had slain
King Jŏ-sī'ah, became for a time the master of the lands between
Ē'ġўpt and the Eū-phrā'teṣ River. He felt that he could not trust
the young King Jĕ-hō'a-hăz, and he took his crown from him and
carried him a captive down to Ē'ġўpt, so that Jĕ-hō'a-hăz, the
seventeenth king, reigned only three months. The prophet Jĕr-e-

mī'ah, who arose during Jŏ-sī'ah's reign, spoke thus of the young king who so soon was taken away a prisoner, "Weep not for the dead King Jŏ-sī'ah nor sorrow over him, but weep for him that goeth away, the King Jĕ-hō'a-hăz, for he shall return no more nor shall he again see his own land. In the place where they have led him captive, there shall he die, and he shall look upon this land no more."

The man whom Phā'raōh=nē'choh set up as king over Jū'dah in place of Jĕ-hō'a-hăz was his brother Jĕ-hoi'a-kĭm, another son of Jŏ-sī'ah. But he was not like his father, for he lived most wickedly, and led his people back to the idols which Jŏ-sī'ah had tried to destroy. Jĕr-e-mī'ah, the prophet, spoke to him the words of the Lord and warned him that the evil way in which he was going would surely end in ruin to the king and the people. This made King Jĕ-hoi'a-kĭm very angry. He tried to kill the prophet, and to save his life, Jĕr-e-mī'ah was hidden by his friends.

Jĕr-e-mī'ah could no longer go out among the people nor stand in the Temple to speak the word of the Lord. So he wrote upon a roll God's message, and gave it to his friend Bā'rŭch to read before the people. While Bā'rŭch was reading it, some officers of the king came and took the roll away and brought it to the king. King Jĕ-hoi'a-kĭm was sitting in his palace, with the princes around him, and a fire was burning before him, for it was the winter time. The officer began to read the roll before the king and the princes, but when he had read a few pages, the king took up a knife and began cutting the leaves and throwing them into the fire. Even the princes were shocked at this, for they knew that the writing on the roll was God's word to the king and the people. They begged the king not to destroy the roll, but he would not heed them. He went on cutting up the roll and throwing it in the fire until it was all burned.

The king told his officers to take Jĕr-e-mī'ah the prophet and Bā'rŭch, who read his words; and he would have killed them if he had found them. But they were hidden, and he could not find them, for the Lord kept them in safety.

Jĕ-hoi'a-kĭm reigned a few years as the servant of the king of Ē'ġўpt. But soon the Ē-ġўp'tianș lost all the lands that they had gained outside of their own country; and the Băb-y̆-lō'ni-ans̗, under Nĕb-u-chad-nĕz'zar, rose to power over the nations and took the place of empire that had been held by the Ăs-sy̆r'ĭ-ans̗. Nĕb-u-chad-nĕz'zar was the son of the king of Băb'y̆-lon, and at first was the general of his army. He came against Jū'dah and Jĕ-ru̯'sȧ-lĕm, but Jĕ-hoi'a-kĭm did not dare to fight with him. He promised to serve Nĕb-u-chad-nĕz'zar, and, on that condition, was allowed to remain king; but no sooner had the Băb-y̆-lō'ni-an army gone away, than he broke his promise and rose against Băb-y̆'lon and tried to make himself free.

But in this King Jĕ-hoi'a-kĭm did not succeed. Instead, he lost his kingdom and his life; for either by the Băb-y̆-lō'ni-ans̗ or by his own people he was slain, and his dead body, like that of a beast, was thrown outside the gate of the city. He had reigned in wickedness eleven years, and he died in disgrace.

Jĕ-hoi'a-kĭm's young son Jĕ-hoi'a-chĭn, who was also called Cȯ-nī'ah or Jĕc-o-nī'ah, was then made king by the people. But he reigned only three months, for Nĕb-u-chad-nĕz'zar, who was now the king of Băb'y̆-lon and was conquering all the lands, came with his army and took the city of Jĕ-ru̯'sȧ-lĕm. He carried the young king a captive to Băb'y̆-lon, as Nē'choh had carried Jĕ-hō'-a-hăz a captive to Ē'ġy̆pt eleven years before. With King Jĕ-hoi'-a-chĭn were taken away many of the nobles and rulers and the best people of the land. Most of these were worshipers of the Lord, who carried with them to the land of Băb-y̆-lō'ni-ȧ a love for the Lord, and who served him there, for their trouble only drew them the closer to their God. After these captives had been taken away, the Lord showed to Jĕr-e-mī'ah in the Temple a vision of what should come to pass. Jĕr-e-mī'ah saw two baskets of figs. One basket was full of fresh, ripe figs, the best that could be found. The other basket was full of poor, decayed figs, not fit to be eaten. The Lord said, "Jĕr-e-mī'ah, what do you see?"

And Jĕr-e-mī'ah said, "Figs; the good figs very good; and the bad figs very bad; figs so bad that they cannot be eaten."

Then the Lord said to Jĕr-e-mī'ah, "Like these good figs are the captives who have been taken away to the land of Băb'y̆-lon. I will care for them and keep them and will bring them again to this land. I will give them a heart to know me; and I will be their God, and they shall be my people. And the bad figs are like those who are left in this land, the king who shall reign over them and his princes and his people. They shall suffer and shall die by the sword and by famine and by plague, until they are destroyed."

God showed Jĕr-e-mī'ah in this way that the captives in Băb'ў-lon were the hope of the nation. And afterward Jĕr-e-mī'ah sent a letter to these captives, saying, "Thus saith the Lord to those who have been carried away captive, 'Build houses and live in them; and plant gardens and eat the fruit of them; and have sons and daughters, and let your children be married in that land when they grow up. And pray the Lord to give peace to the city and the land where you are living, for you and your children shall stay there seventy years; and after seventy years they shall come again to their own land in peace. For my thoughts, saith the Lord, are thoughts of peace and kindness toward you. You shall call upon me and I will hear you. You shall seek me and find me, when you seek me with all your heart.' "

After Jĕ-hoi'a-chĭn and the captives had been taken away, Nĕb-u-chad-nĕz'zar set up as king in Jū'dah, Zĕd-e-kī'ah, the uncle of Jĕ-hoi'a-chĭn and another son of Jŏ-sī'ah. He was the twentieth and last king of the kingdom of Jū'dah. He began by promising to be true and faithful to his overlord, Nĕb-u-chad-nĕz'zar, the king of Băb'ў-lon, who had made him king. But very soon he was led by the nobles who stood around his throne to break his promise and to throw off the rule of Băb'ў-lon; also he left the worship of the Lord, as did his people, and began to pray to the idols of wood and stone that could give him no help.

Jĕr-e-mī'ah the prophet told King Zĕd-e-kī'ah that he was doing wickedly in breaking his promises and in turning from the Lord to idols. He told Zĕd-e-kī'ah that he would fail and would bring his kingdom to ruin. He said, "It is better to obey the king of Băb'ў-lon than to fight against him, for God will not bless you and your people in breaking your word. The king of Băb'ў-lon will come and will destroy this city. You shall see him face to face, and he will take you away a captive to his own land, and this city shall be destroyed."

This made the princes and nobles very angry against Jĕr-e-mī'ah. They said, "This man Jĕr-e-mī'ah is an enemy of his land and a friend to the king of Băb'ў-lon. He is a traitor, and should be put to death." Zĕd-e-kī'ah said to his nobles, "Jĕr-e-mī'ah is in your hands; you can do with him what you choose. The king cannot help him against you."

Then these men seized Jĕr-e-mī'ah and took him to the prison and threw him into a dungeon, down below the floor and filled with mud and filth, into which the prophet sank; and there they left him to die. But in the court of the king there was one kind man, a Negro named Ē'bed=mē'lech. He found Jĕr-e-mī'ah in the dungeon, and he let down to him a rope and drew him up and brought him to a safe and dry place, though still in the prison.

By this time Nĕb-u-chad-nĕz'zar, the king of Băb'ў-lon, and his army were again before the city of Jĕ-ru'så-lĕm, laying siege to it. No one could go out or come in; no food could be found for the people, and many of them starved to death. The soldiers of Nĕb-u-chad-nĕz'zar built forts and threw darts and stones, broke down the gates, and made great openings in the walls of the city.

When King Zĕd-e-kī'ah saw that the city must fall before its enemies, he tried to escape. But the men of Băb'ў-lon followed him and took him prisoner, and with him all his family, his wives

and his sons. They were all brought before King Nĕb-u-chad-nĕz′zar, so that it came to pass as the prophet had said, Zĕd-e-kī′ah saw the king of Băb′y̆-lon.

But he saw what was more terrible; he saw all his sons slain before him. Then Zĕd-e-kī′ah's eyes were put out and a blinded captive, he was dragged away to Băb′y̆-lon. The Băb-y̆-lō′ni-an soldiers killed all the leaders of the people who had led Zĕd-e-kī′ah to rebel against Nĕb-u-chad-nĕz′zar; and the rest of the people, except the very poorest in the land, they took away to the land of Băb′y̆-lon. The king of Băb′y̆-lon was friendly to Jĕr-e-mī′ah, the prophet, because of the advice that he had given to Zĕd-e-kī′ah and his people. The ruler whom Nĕb-u-chad-nĕz′zar set over the city opened the door of Jĕr-e-mī′ah's prison and allowed him to choose between going to Băb′y̆-lon with the captives or staying with the poor people in the land. Jĕr-e-mī′ah chose to stay; but not long after he was taken down to Ē′ġy̆pt by enemies to the king of Băb′y̆-lon. And there in Ē′ġy̆pt Jĕr-e-mī′ah died; some think that he was slain. His life had been sad, for he had seen nothing but evil come upon his land; and his message from the Lord had been a message of woe and wrath. Because of his sorrow, Jĕr-e-mī′ah has been called "the weeping prophet."

Nĕb-u-chad-nĕz′zar carried away all that was left of the valuable things in the Temple, and then he burned the buildings. He tore down the walls of Jĕ-ru̱′så-lĕm and set the city on fire. So all that was left of the city of Dā′vid and the Temple of Sŏl′o-mon was a heap of ashes and blackened stones. And thus the kingdom of Jū′dah ended, nearly four hundred years after Rē-ho-bō′am became its first king.

What Ezekiel Saw in the Valley

ALL THAT was now left of the people of Jū'dah was a company of captives, carried away from their own land to the land of Băb'ў-lon. Theirs was a long, sorrowful journey, with their wives and children, dragged by cruel soldiers over mountains and valleys almost a thousand miles. So hard was the journey that many of them died on the way. Babies were born, and sometimes their mothers perished from their sufferings. They could not go straight across the vast desert which lies between the land of Jū'dah and the plains of Băb-ў-lō'ni-a. They were led around this desert far to the north, through Sўr'ĭ-à, up to the Eū-phrā'tēṣ River, and then following the great river in all its windings down to the land of their captivity. There in the land of Băb-ў-lō'ni-a, or Chăl-dē'à, they found rest at last.

When they were once in their new home, the captives met with less trouble than they had feared; for the people of the land under Nĕb-u-chad-nĕz'zar, the great king, treated them kindly and gave them fields to work in as their own. The soil was rich, and they could raise large crops of wheat and barley and other grains. They planted gardens and built for themselves houses. Some of them went to live in the cities and became rich, and some were in the court of King Nĕb-u-chad-nĕz'zar and rose to high places as nobles and princes, standing next to the king in rank and honor.

And the best of all was that these captives in a strange land did not worship idols. They saw the images of the Băb-ў-lō'ni-an gods all around them, but they did not bow down to them. They worshiped the Lord God of their fathers, and the Lord only. The idol worshipers in Jū'dah had been slain, and most of the captives were good men and women, who taught their children to love and serve the Lord.

These people did not forget the land from which they had

come. They loved the land of Ĭṣ'ra-el, and they taught their children to love it by singing songs about it. Some of these songs which the captive Jewṣ sang in the land of Chăl-dē'à are in the Book of Psalms. Here is a part of one of these songs:

> "By the rivers of Bab'y-lon,
> There we sat down, yea, we wept,
> When we remembered Zĭ'ŏn.
> Upon the willow trees in the midst of that land
> We hanged up our harps.

> "For there they that led us captive asked us to sing;
> And they that wanted us asked us to be glad, saying,
> 'Sing us one of the songs of Zĭ'ŏn.'
> How shall we sing the Lord's song
> In a foreign land?

> "If I forget thee, O Jĕ-ru'sà-lĕm,
> Let my right hand forget her skill.
> Let my tongue cleave to the roof of my mouth,
> If I do not remember thee,
> If I do not prefer Jĕ-ru'sà-lĕm
> Above my chief joy."

From this time these people were called Jewṣ, a name which means "people of Jū'dah." And the Jewṣ everywhere in the world belong to this people, for they have sprung or descended from the men who once lived in the land of Jū'dah. And because they had once belonged to the twelve tribes of Ĭṣ'ra-el, and ten of the tribes had been lost, and their kingdom had forever passed away, they were also spoken of as Ĭṣ'ra-el-ītes. So from this time "people of Jū'dah," Jewṣ, and Ĭṣ'ra-el-ītes, all mean the people who had come from the land of Jū'dah, and their descendants after them.

God was good to his people in the land of Băb' y̆-lon, or Chăl-dē'à, another name by which this country was called. He sent to them prophets, who showed them the way of the Lord. One of these prophets was Dăn'iel, a young man who lived in the court of King Nĕb-u-chad-nĕz'zar. Another was a priest named Ê-zē'kĭ-el, who lived among the captive people beside a river in Chăl-dē'à, called the river Chē'bär. God gave to Ê-zē'kĭ-el wonderful isions. He saw the throne of the Lord and the strange creatures with six wings, that the prophet Ī-ṣā′iah had seen long before. (See Story Three in this Part.) And he heard the voice of the Lord telling him of what should come to his people in the years to come.

At one time the Lord lifted up Ê-zē′kĭ-el and brought him into the middle of a great valley. The prophet looked around and saw that the valley was covered with the bones of men, as though a great battle had been fought upon it, and the bodies of the slain had been left there, and they had become a vast army of dry bones.

"Son of man," spoke the voice of the Lord to Ê-zē′kĭ-el, "can these dry bones live again?"

And Ê-zē′kĭ-el answered, "O Lord God, thou knowest whether these dry bones can live."

Then the Lord said to Ê-zē′kĭ-el, "Preach to these dry bones, O son of man, and say to them, 'O ye dry bones, hear the voice of the Lord. Thus saith the Lord, I will send breath into you, and you shall live, and I will put flesh upon you and cover you with skin, and you shall be alive again and know that I am the Lord.'"

Then Ê-zē′kĭ-el spoke to the army of dry bones spread over the valley, as the Lord bade him speak. And while he was speaking, there sounded a noise of rolling thunder, and all through the field the different bones began to come together, one part to another part, until there were no more loose bones, but skeletons of bones fitted together. Then another change came. Suddenly the flesh grew over all the bones, and they lay on the ground like an army of dead men, a host of bodies without life.

Then the Lord said to Ê-zē′kĭ-el, "Speak to the wind, O son of

man; speak and say, 'Come from the four winds, O breath, and breathe upon these slain, that they may live.' "

Then Ê-zē′kĭ-el called upon the wind to come, and while he was speaking, the dead bodies began to breathe. Then they stood up on their feet, a great army of living men, filling the whole valley. Then the Lord said to Ê-zē′kĭ-el, "Son of man, these dry bones are the people of Ĭṣ′ra-el. They seem to be lost and dead and without hope. But they shall live again, for I, the Lord, will put life into them; and they shall go back to their own land and be a people once more. I, the Lord, have spoken it and I will do it."

When Ê-zē′kĭ-el told the captive people this vision, their hearts were lifted up with a new hope that they should see their own land again.

Story Eight

DANIEL 1:1 to 2:49

The Jewish Captives in the Court of the King

IN THE Book of Chronicles we read of Jĕ-hoi′a-kĭm, the wicked son of the good King Jŏ-sī′ah. While Jĕ-hoi′a-kĭm was ruling over the land of Jū′dah, Nĕb-u-chad-nĕz′zar, the great conqueror of the nations, came from Băb′ȳ-lon with his army of Chăl-dē′an soldiers. He took the city of Jĕ-ru′-så-lĕm, and made Jĕ-hoi′a-kĭm promise to submit to him as his master, a promise that Jĕ-hoi′a-kĭm soon broke. And when Nĕb-u-chad-nĕz′zar went back to his own land, he took with him all the gold and silver that he could find in the Temple; and he carried away as captives many of the princes and nobles, the best people in the land of Jū′dah.

When these Jews were brought to the land of Chăl-dē′à or

Băb′ў-lon, King Nĕb-u-chad-nĕz′zar gave orders to the prince
who had charge of his palace to choose among these Jewish captives some young men that were of noble rank and beautiful in
their looks, and also quick and bright in their minds, young men
who would be able to learn readily. These young men were to
be placed under the care of wise men, who should teach them all
that they knew and fit them to stand before the king of Băb′ў-lon,
so that they might be his helpers, to carry out his orders; and the
king wished them to be wise, so that they might give advice in
ruling the people.

Among the young men thus chosen were four Jews, men who
had been brought from Jū′dah. By order of the king the names
of these men were changed. One of them, named Dăn′iel, was
to be called Bĕl-te-shăz′zar, the other three young men were
called Shā′drach, Mē′shach, and Ȧ-bĕd′=ne-gō. These four young
men were taught in all the knowledge of the Chăl-dē′ans; and after
three years of training, they were taken into the king's palace to
stand before the king.

After they came to the palace, the chief of the princes in the
palace sent to these men as a special honor some of the dishes of
food from the king's table and some of the wine that was set apart
for the king and his princes to drink. But both the meat and the
wine of the king's table had been a part of the offerings to the idols
of wood and stone that were worshiped by the Chăl-dē′ans. These
young Jews felt that if they should take such food they, too,
would be worshiping idols. Then, too, the laws of the Jews were
very strict with regard to what kind of food might be eaten and
how it should be cooked. Food of certain kinds was called "unclean," and the Jews were forbidden to touch it.

These young Jews, far away from their own land and from
their Temple, felt that they must be very careful to do nothing
forbidden by the laws which God had given to their people. They
said to the chief of the nobles in the palace:

"We cannot eat this meat and drink this wine, for it is forbidden
by our laws."

The chief of the nobles said to Dăn′iel:

"If you do not eat the food that is given you, the king will see that you are not looking well. He will be angry with me for not giving you better care. What shall I do? I am afraid that the king may command me to be put to death."

Dăn′iel said:

"Give us vegetable food and bread. Let us eat no meat and drink no wine for ten days and see if we do not look well-fed."

The chief of the nobles, to whose care these young men had been given, loved Dăn′iel, as everyone loved him who knew him. So he did as Dăn′iel asked. He took away the meat and the wine and gave to these young Jews only vegetables and bread. At the end of ten days the four young men were brought into the room where the great King Nĕb-u-chad-nĕz′zar sat, and they bowed low before him. King Nĕb-u-chad-nĕz′zar was pleased with these four young men, more than with any others who stood before him. He found them wise and faithful in the work given to them, and able to rule over men under them. And these four men came to the highest places in the kingdom of the Chăl-dē′ans.

And Dăn′iel, one of these men, was more than a wise man. He was a prophet, like Ê-lī′jah and Ê-lī′shà and Jĕr-e-mī′ah. God gave him to know many things that were coming to pass; and when God sent to any man a dream that had a deep meaning, like Jō′seph in Story Sixteen of Part First, Dăn′iel could tell what was the meaning of the dream.

At one time King Nĕb-u-chad-nĕz′zar dreamed a dream which troubled him greatly. When he awakened, he knew that the dream had some deep meaning, but in the morning he had forgotten what the dream was. He sent for the wise men who had in times past given him the meaning of his dreams, and said:

"O ye wise men, I have dreamed a wonderful dream; but I have forgotten it. Now tell me what my dream was and then tell me what it means, for I am sure that it has a meaning."

The wise men said:

"O king, may you live forever! If you will tell us your dream, we will tell you its meaning. But we have no power to tell both the dream and also its meaning. That only the gods can know."

The king became very angry, for these men had claimed that their gods gave them all knowledge. He said:

"Tell me the dream and its meaning; and I will give you rich reward and high honor. But if you cannot tell, I shall know that you are liars, and you shall be put to death."

The wise men could not do what the king asked; and in great fury he gave command that all of them should be slain. Among these men were Dăn′iel and his three friends, Shā′drach, Mē′shach, and A-bĕd′=ne-gō; and these four Jews were to be slain with the rest of the wise men. Dăn′iel said to the chief captain, who had been sent to kill the wise men:

"Give me a little time; and I will call upon my God. I know that he will help me to tell to the king his dream and its meaning."

So time was given; and Dăn′iel and his three friends prayed to the Lord God. That night the Lord gave to Dăn′iel the secret of the king's dream and its meaning. Then Dăn′iel gave praise and thanks to the Lord; and in the morning he said to the king's captain:

"Do not kill the wise men. Take me before the king, and I will show him his dream and its meaning."

Then in haste Dăn′iel was brought before King Nĕb-u-chad-nĕz′zar. The king said to him:

"Are you able to tell me the dream that I dreamed and the meaning of it?"

Dăn′iel answered:

"The wise men of Băb′ў-lon, who look to their idol gods, cannot tell the king his dream. But there is a God in heaven who knows all things; and he has given me, his servant, to know your dream and the meaning of it. This is the dream, O king. You saw a great image, tall and noble-looking. The head of this image was of gold, his breast and his arms were of silver, his waist and his hips of brass, his legs of iron, and his feet and toes were of iron and clay mixed together. And while this great image was standing, you saw a stone cut out without hands; and the stone rolled and dashed against the feet of the image; and the whole image fell down and was broken in pieces and was crushed and ground into a powder so fine that the wind blew it away like chaff. And you saw the stone that struck the image grow until it became a mountain, and it filled the whole world. This was your dream, O king."

And Dăn'iel went on and said:

"And this, O king, is the meaning of the dream. God has shown to you what shall come to pass in the years that are to be. You are that head of gold, O king; for that head means your kingdom that now is. After your kingdom has passed away, another kingdom shall take its place; the shoulders and arms of silver. That kingdom shall be followed by another—the waist and hips of brass; and after that shall come one more kingdom, that of iron. But as you saw a stone cut out without hands, so while the last of these kingdoms shall be standing, the Lord God of heaven shall set up his kingdom. And God's kingdom, like that stone, shall be small at first, but it shall break down and destroy all those kingdoms. They shall pass away and perish before it. And as you saw the stone grow into a mountain, so God's kingdom shall become great and shall rule all the lands. And that kingdom of God shall never pass away, but shall last forever."

When King Nĕb-u-chad-nĕz'zar heard this, he was filled with wonder. He bowed down before Dăn'iel and worshiped him, as though Dăn'iel were a god. Then he gave to him great presents and made him ruler over the part of his kingdom where the city of Băb'ў-lon was standing. He gave to Shā'drach, Mē'shach, and A-bĕd'=ne-gō, Dăn'iel's friends, high offices; but Dăn-iel himself he kept in his palace, to be near him all the time.

The Golden Image and the Fiery Furnace

AT ONE time King Nĕb-u-chad-nĕz′zar caused a great image to be made and to be covered with gold. This image he set up as an idol to be worshiped, on the plain of Du′rà, near the city of Băb′ў-lon. When it was finished, it stood upon its base or foundation almost a hundred feet high, so that upon the plain it could be seen far away. Then the king sent out a command for all the princes and rulers and nobles in the land to come to a great gathering, when the image was to be set apart for worship.

The great men of the kingdom came from far and near and stood around the image. Among them, by command of the king, were Dan′iel's three friends, the young Jews, Shā′drach, Mē′shach, and A-bĕd′=ne-gō. For some reason Dăn′iel himself was not there. He may have been busy with the work of the kingdom in some other place.

At one moment in the service before the image all the trumpets sounded, the drums were beaten and music was made upon musical instruments of all kinds, as a signal for all the people to kneel down and worship the great golden image. But while the people were kneeling, there were three men who stood up and would not bow down. These were the three young Jews, Shā′drach, Mē′-shach, and A-bĕd′=ne-gō. They knelt down before the Lord God only.

Many of the nobles had been jealous of these young men because they had been lifted to high places in the rule of the kingdom, and these men, who hated Dăn′iel and his friends, were glad to find that these three men had not obeyed the command of King Nĕb-u-chad-nĕz′zar. The king had said that if anyone did not worship the golden image, he should be thrown into a furnace of fire. These men who hated the Jews came to the king and said,

389

"O king, may you live forever! You gave orders that when the music sounded everyone should bow down and worship the golden image; and that if any man did not worship, he should be thrown into a furnace of fire. There are some Jews whom you have made rulers in the land, and they have not done as you commanded. Their names are Shā'drach, Mē'shach, and A-bĕd'=ne-gō. They do not serve your gods nor worship the golden image that you have set up."

Then Nĕb-u-chad-nĕz'zar was filled with rage and fury at knowing that anyone should dare to disobey his words. He sent for these three men and said to them, "O Shā'drach, Mē'shach, and A-bĕd'=ne-gō, was it by purpose that you did not fall down and worship the image of gold? The music shall sound once more, and if you then will worship the image, it shall be well. But if you will not, then you shall be thrown into the furnace of fire to die."

These three young men were not afraid of the king. They said, "O King Nĕb-u-chad-nĕz'zar, we are ready to answer you at once. The God whom we serve is able to save us from the fiery furnace, and we know that he will save us. But if it is God's will that we should die, even then you may understand, O king, that we will not serve your gods nor worship the golden image that you have set up."

This answer made the king more furious than before. He said to his servants, "Make a fire in the furnace hotter than ever it has been before, as hot as fire can be made, and throw these three men into it."

Then the soldiers of the king's army seized the three young Jews as they stood in their loose robes, with their turbans or hats on their heads. They tied them with ropes, dragged them to the mouth of the furnace, and threw them into the fire. The flames rushed from the open door with such fury that they burned even to death the soldiers who were holding these men; and the men themselves fell down bound into the middle of the fiery furnace.

King Nĕb-u-chad-nĕz'zar stood in front of the furnace and looked into the open door. As he looked, he was filled with wonder at what he saw; and he said to the nobles around him:

"Did we not throw three men bound into the fire? How is it hen that I see four men loose, walking in the furnace, and the ourth man looks as though he were a son of the gods?"

The king came near to the door of the furnace as the fire be-:ame lower, and he called out to the three men within it:

"Shā'drach, Mē'shach, and A-bed'=ne-gō, ye who serve the Most High God, come out of the fire and come to me."

They came out and stood before the king, in the sight of all the princes and nobles and rulers; and everyone could see that they were alive. Their garments had not been scorched nor the hair singed, nor was there even the smell of fire upon them. The king, Nĕb-u-chad-nĕz'zar, said before all his rulers:

"Blessed be the God of these men, who has sent his angel and has saved their lives. I make a law that no man in all my king-doms shall say a word against their God, for there is no other god who can save in this manner. And if any man speaks a word against their God, the Most High God, that man shall be cut in pieces and his house shall be torn down." And after this the king lifted up these three young men to still higher places in the land of Băb'ў-lon.

The Tree That Was Cut Down and Grew Again

HIS is the story that King Nĕb-u-chad-nĕz'zar himself told to all the people in his great kingdom, of a strange dream that came to him, the meaning of the dream, as it was given by Dăn'iel, and how the dream came true. He said, "Nĕb-u-chad-nĕz'zar the king sends this message to all the people and nations that live in all the world. May peace be given to you! It has seemed good to me to show you the signs and wonders that the Most High God has sent to me. How great are God's works! How mighty are his wonders! His kingdom is without end, and his rule is from age to age forever and ever!

"I, King Nĕb-u-chad-nĕz'zar, was at rest in my house and was living at peace in my palace. One night a dream came to me which made me afraid, and my thoughts and my visions made me troubled in heart. I sent for all the wise men of Băb'ў-lon to come before me and to tell me the meaning of my dream. But they did not tell me what the meaning was because they could not. At last came Dăn'iel, in whom is the spirit of the holy gods; and to him I said:

"'O Dăn'iel, master of the wise men, I know that in you is the spirit of the holy gods, and that no secret is hidden from you; now tell me what is the meaning of the dream that has come to me. This was the dream:

"'I saw a tree standing upon the earth. It grew until the top of it reached up to heaven; and it was so great that it could be seen over all the earth. The leaves of it were beautiful, and its fruit was in plenty and gave food for all. The beasts in the field stood in its shadow, the birds of the heaven lived on its branches, and many people ate of its fruit.

392

" 'I saw in my dream that a Holy One came down from heaven. He cried aloud and said:

" ' "Hew down the tree and cut off its branches, shake off its leaves and scatter its fruit. Let the beasts get away from beneath it and let the birds fly from its branches. But leave the stump of the tree with its roots in the ground, with a band of iron and of brass around it and the grass of the field growing about it. Let the stump be wet with the dew from heaven and let it be among the beasts eating the grass of the field. And let seven years pass over it; that those who live may know that the Most High God rules over the kingdoms of men and gives them as is pleasing to his will." This dream I saw, and now, O Dăn'iel, whose name is Běl-te-shăz'zar, tell me what it means.' Then Dăn'iel stood wondering and was in deep trouble. And I, Něb-u-chad-něz'zar, said to him, 'Dăn'iel, let not the dream give you trouble. Fear not to tell me what is the meaning of it.'

"Then Dăn'iel said to me, 'My lord, O king, may the dream be to those who hate you and the meaning to your enemies! The tree which you saw, with green leaves and rich fruit and height reaching to heaven, and in sight of all the earth, that tree is yourself. You have become great; your power reaches up to heaven and your rule is over all the lands.

" 'And as you saw a Holy One coming down from heaven, saying, "Cut down the tree and destroy it; but leave its stump in the earth, with a band of iron and of brass until seven years pass over it," this is the meaning, O king, and it is the command of the Most High God that shall come upon my lord the king.

" 'You, O king, shall be driven away from men. You shall live with the beasts of the field; you shall be made to eat grass like oxen; and you shall be wet with the dew of heaven; seven years shall pass over you, until you know that the Most High God rules in your kingdom and gives it to the one whom he chooses. And as the Holy One gave command to leave the stump of the tree with its roots, so it shall be with you. Your kingdom shall stand and shall be sure to you and shall come back to you when you have known that he who sits in the heavens shall rule over the earth.

" 'And now, O king, take my advice and break off from your sins and do right and show mercy to the poor. It may be that God will give to you more days of peace.'

"All this Dăn'iel said to me, King Nĕb-u-chad-nĕz'zar, and it came to pass. Twelve months afterward I was walking in my kingly palace. I looked over the city and said, 'Is not this great Băb'y̆-lon that I have built for my own royal home, by my power and for my own glory?'

"While the word was in my mouth, a voice fell from heaven, saying, 'O King Nĕb-u-chad-nĕz'zar, the word has been spoken, and your kingdom is gone from you!'

"And in that hour my reason left me, and another heart was given to me, the heart of a beast instead of the heart of a man. I was driven out of my palace, and I lived among the beasts and ate grass as oxen eat it; and my body was wet with the dew of heaven, until my hair was grown like eagles' feathers and my nails like birds' claws. And at the end of seven years my mind came back to me and my reason returned. I blessed the king of heaven and praised him that lives forever. My kingdom was given to me once more, my princes and rulers came to me again, and I was again the king over all the lands.

"Now I, Nĕb-u-chad-nĕz'zar, praise and honor the king of heaven. His words are truth and his works are right; and those who walk in pride, he is able to make humble."

This was the story of the seven years' madness of King Nĕb-u-chad-nĕz'zar and of his reason and his power coming back to him again.

The Writing Upon the Wall

THE GREAT kingdom or empire of Nĕb-u-chad-nĕz'-zar was made up of smaller kingdoms which he had conquered. As long as he lived, his kingdom was strong; but as soon as he died, it began to fall in pieces. His son became king in his place, but was soon slain; nd one king followed another quickly for some years. The last ing was named Nā-bon'i-dus. He made his son Bĕl-shăz'zar ing with himself, and left Bĕl-shăz'zar to rule in the city of äb'ÿ-lon, while he was caring for the more distant parts of the ingdom.

But a new nation was rising to power. Far to the east were the ingdoms of Mē'dĭ-à and Pēr'şià. These two peoples had become ne, and were at war with Bäb'ÿ-lon, under their great leader, ÿ'rus. While Bĕl-shăz'zar was ruling in the city of Bäb'ÿ-lon, ÿ'rus and his Pēr'şian soldiers were on the outside, around the ralls, trying to take the city. These walls were so great and high hat the Pēr'şian soldiers could not break through them.

But inside the city were many who were enemies of Bĕl-shăz'zar nd were friendly with Çÿ'rus. These people opened the gates of äb'ÿ-lon to Çÿ'rus. At night he brought his army quietly into he city and surrounded the palace of King Bĕl-shăz'zar.

On that night King Bĕl-shăz'zar was holding in the palace a reat feast in honor of his god. On the tables were the golden ups and vessels that Nĕb-u-chad-nĕz'zar had taken from the Tem-le of the Lord in Jĕ-ru'så-lĕm; and around the tables were the ing, his many wives, and a thousand of his princes and nobles. hey did not know that their city was taken and that their enemies rere at the very doors of the palace.

While they were all drinking wine together, suddenly a strange hing was seen. On the wall appeared a great hand writing letters

395

and words that no one could read. Every eye was drawn to th
spot, and all saw the fingers moving on the wall and the letter
written. The king was filled with fear. His face became pal
and his knees shook. He called for the wise men of Băb'y̆-lon
who were with him in the palace, to tell what the writing meant
He said, "Whoever can read the words on the wall shall be dresse
in a purple robe and shall have a chain of gold around his neck
and he shall rank next to King Běl-shăz'zar as the third ruler in th
kingdom."

But not one of the wise men could read it, for God had no
given them the power. At last the queen of Băb'y̆-lon said t
Běl-shăz'zar, "O king, may you live forever! There is one mar
who can read this writing, a man in whom is the spirit of the holy
gods, a man whom Něb-u-chad-něz'zar, your father, made maste
of all the wise men. His name is Dăn'iel. Send for him, and h
will tell you what these words are and what they mean."

Dăn'iel was now an old man; and since the time when Něb-u
chad-něz'zar died, he had been no longer in his high place as rule
and chief adviser of the king. They sent for Dăn'iel, and he came
The king said to him, "Are you that Dăn'iel who was brough

many years ago by my father to this city? I have heard of you, that the spirit of the holy gods is upon you and that you have wisdom and knowledge. If you can read this writing upon the wall and tell me what it means, I will give you a purple robe and a gold chain and a place next to myself as the third ruler in the kingdom." And Dăn'iel answered the king, "You may keep your rewards yourself and may give your gifts to whom you please, for I do not want them; but I will read to you the writing. O king, the Most High God gave to Nĕb-u-chad-nĕz'zar this kingdom and great power and glory. But when Nĕb-u-chad-nĕz'zar became proud and boasted of his greatness, then the Lord took from him his crown and his throne and let him live among the beasts of the field until he knew that the Most High God rules over the kingdoms of men. O Bĕl-shăz'zar, you knew all this, yet you have not been humble in heart. You have risen up against the Lord, you have taken the vessels of his house, and have drunk wine in them in honor of your own gods of wood and stone; but you have not praised the Lord God who has given to you your kingdom and your power. For this reason God has sent this hand to write these words upon the wall. This is the writing, MENE, MENE, TEKEL, UPHARSIN. And this is the meaning, Numbered, Numbered, Weighed, Divided.

"MENE: God has counted the years of your kingdom and has brought it to an end.

"TEKEL: You have been weighed in the balances and have been found wanting.

"UPHARSIN: Your kingdom is divided and taken from you, and given to the Mēdes and the Pĕr'sians."

King Bĕl-shăz'zar could scarcely believe what he heard; but he commanded that the promised reward be given to Dăn'iel. And almost while he was speaking, his end came. The Pĕr'sians and the Mēdes burst into his palace; they seized Bĕl-shăz'zar and killed him in the midst of his feast.

On that night the empire or great kingdom set up by Nĕb-u-chad-nĕz'zar came to an end. A new empire arose, greater than that of Băb'ў-lon, called the Pĕr'sian Empire. And in the place of Bĕl-shăz'zar, Çy'rus, the commander of the Pĕr'sians, made an old man named Dȧ-rī'us king until the time when he was ready to take the kingdom for himself.

This empire of Pēr'ṣiȧ was the third of the world kingdoms of which we read in the Bible. The first was the Ăs-sȳr'ĭ-an kingdom, having Nĭn'e-veh for its capital. This was the kingdom that carried the Ten Tribes of Ĭṣ'ra-el into captivity. The second was the Băb-ȳ-lō'ni-an, or Chăl-dē'an kingdom, which carried the Jewṣ into captivity. The third was the Pēr'ṣian kingdom, which for two hundred years ruled all the lands named in the Bible.

Story Twelve   DANIEL, chapter 6

Daniel in the Den of Lions

THE LANDS which had been the Băb-ȳ-lō'ni-an or Chăl-dē'an empire now became the empire of Pēr'ṣiȧ; and over these Dȧ-rī'us was the king. King Dȧ-rī'us gave to Dăn'iel, who was now a very old man, a high place in honor and in power. Among all the rulers over the land Dăn'iel stood first, for the king saw that he was wise and able to rule. This made the other princes and rulers very jealous, and they tried to find something evil in Dăn'iel, so that they could speak to the king against him.

These men knew that three times every day Dăn'iel went to his room and opened the window that was toward the city of Jĕ-ru'sȧ-lĕm, and, looking toward Jĕ-ru'sȧ-lĕm, made his prayer to God. Jĕ-ru'sȧ-lĕm was at that time in ruins and the Temple was no longer standing; but Dăn'iel prayed three times each day with his face toward the place where the house of God had once stood, although it was many hundreds of miles away.

These nobles thought that in Dăn'iel's prayers they could find a chance to do him harm and perhaps cause him to be put to death. They came to King Dȧ-rī'us and said to him:

"All the rulers have agreed together to have a law made that for thirty days no one shall ask anything of any god or any man, except from you, O king; and that if anyone shall pray to any god or shall ask anything from any man during thirty days, except from you, O king, he shall be thrown into the den where the lions are kept. Now, O king, make the law and sign the writing, so that it cannot be changed, for no law among the Mēdes and Pēr'-ṣiạnṣ can be altered."

The king was not a wise man, and being foolish and vain, he was pleased with this law which would set him even above the gods. So, without asking Dăn'iel's advice, he signed the writing; the law was made and the word was sent out through the kingdom that for thirty days no one should pray to any god or ask a favor of any man.

Dăn'iel knew that the law had been made, but every day he went to his room three times and opened the window that looked toward Jĕ-ru'sȧ-lĕm and offered his prayer to the Lord, just as he had prayed in other times. These rulers were watching near by, and they saw Dăn'iel kneeling in prayer to God. Then they came to the king and said, "O King Dȧ-rī'us, have you not made a law that if anyone in thirty days offers a prayer, he shall be thrown into the den of lions?" "It is true," said the king. "The law has been made and it must stand."

They said to the king, "There is one man who does not obey the law which you have made. It is that Dăn'iel, one of the captive Jews. Every day Dăn'iel prays to his God three times, just as he did before you signed the writings of the law."

Then the king was very sorry for what he had done, for he loved Dăn'iel and knew that no one could take his place in the kingdom. All day, until the sun went down, he tried in vain to find some way to save Dăn'iel's life; but when evening came, these men again told him of the law that he had made, and said to him that it must be kept. Very unwillingly the king sent for Dăn'iel and gave an order that he should be thrown into the den of lions. He said to Dăn'iel, "Perhaps your God, whom you serve so faithfully, will save you from the lions."

They led Dăn'iel to the mouth of the pit where the lions were

kept and they threw him in; and over the mouth they placed a
stone; and the king sealed it with his own seal and with the seals
of his nobles, so that no one might take away the stone and let
Dăn'iel out of the den.

Then the king went again to his palace, but that night he was
so sad that he could not eat, nor did he listen to music as he was
used to listen. He could not sleep, for all through the night he
was thinking of Dăn'iel. Very early in the morning he rose up
from his bed and went in haste to the den of lions. He broke the
seal and took away the stone and in a voice full of sorrow he called
out, scarcely hoping to hear any answer except the roaring of the
lions, "O Dăn'iel, servant of the living God, has your God been
able to keep you safe from the lions?"

And out of the darkness in the den came the voice of Dăn'iel,
saying, "O king, may you live forever! My God has sent his
angel and has shut the mouths of the lions. They have not hurt
me, because my God saw that I had done no wrong. And I have
done no wrong toward you, O king!"

Then the king was glad. He gave to his servants orders to take
Dăn'iel out of the den. Dăn'iel was brought out safe and without
harm, because he had trusted fully in the Lord God. Then, by the
king's command, they seized those men who had spoken against
Dăn'iel, and with them their wives and their children, for the king
was exceedingly angry with them. They were all thrown into the
den, and the hungry lions leaped upon them and tore them in
pieces as soon as they fell upon the floor of the den.

It was very cruel and unjust to put to death with these men
their wives and children, who had done no wrong, either to King
Dȧ-rī'us or to Dăn'iel. But cruel and unjust as it was, such things
were very common in all the lands of that part of the world. The
lives of people were considered of little account, and children often
suffered death for their parents' crime.

After this King Dȧ-rī'us wrote to all the lands and the peoples
in the many kingdoms under his rule, "May peace be given to you
all abundantly! I make a law that everywhere among my kingdoms men fear and worship the Lord God of Dăn'iel, for he is the
living God, above all other gods, who only can save men."

And Dăn'iel stood beside King Dȧ-rī'us unto the end of his reign and afterward while Çȳ'rus the Pẽr'ṣian was king over all the lands.

Dăn'iel lived for a number of years after being saved from the lions. He had several wonderful dreams and visions, which showed him what would come to pass many years afterward, and even to the coming of Jē'ṣus Chrīst.

Story Thirteen

EZRA 1 : 1 to 3 : 7

The Story of a Joyous Journey

E HAVE seen, in the story of the kingdom of Iṣ'ra-el, or the Ten Tribes, how the great empire of Ăs-sȳr'ĭ-à arose from the city of Nĭn'e-veh, on the Tī'gris River; how it ruled all the lands and carried away the Ten Tribes of Iṣ-ra-el into captivity, from which they never came back to their own land. We saw, too, how the empire of Ăs-sȳr'ĭ-à went down and the empire of Băb'ȳ-lon, or Chăl-dē'à, arose in its place under Nĕb-u-chad-nĕz'zar. As soon as Nĕb-u-chad-nĕz'zar died, the empire of Băb'ȳ-lon began to fall, and in its place arose the empire of Pẽr'ṣià, under Çȳ'rus, who is called Çȳ'rus the Great, because of his many victories and his wide rule. His empire was much greater than either the Ăs-sȳr'ĭ-an or the Chăl-dē'an empire, for it held in its rule the land of Ê'ġȳpt, all the lands known as Ā'ṣià Mī'nor and also many lands in the far east.

Çȳ'rus, the great king, was a friend to the Jewṣ, who at this time were still living in the land of Chăl-dē'à, between the Tī'gris and Eū-phrā'tēṣ rivers. It was now seventy years since the first company of captives had been taken away from the land of Jū'dah by Nĕb-u-chad-nĕz'zar, and fifty years since the city of Jė-ru'sȧ-lem had been burned. By that time the Jewṣ were no longer

looked upon as captives in the land of Chăl-dē'à. They lived in
their own houses and tilled their own farms and were in peace.
Many of them were rich, and some of them, like Dăn'iel and
his three friends, often held high positions at the court of the
king.

You remember that in the early days of the captivity, Jĕr-e-
mī'ah the prophet wrote a letter to those who had been carried
away to Băb'ȳ-lon, telling them that after seventy years they
would come back to their own land. The seventy years were
now ended. The older men and women who had been taken
away had died in the land of Chăl-dē'à, but their children and
their children's children still loved the land of Jū'dah as their own
land, although it was so far away.

The Lord put it into the heart of Çȳ'rus, the king of Pēr'şià,
very early in his reign, to send word among the Jews that they
might now go back to their own land. This was the word, as it
was written and sent out:

"Thus saith Çȳ'rus, the king of Pēr'şià, The Lord, the God of
heaven, has given me all the kingdoms of the earth; and he has
commanded me to build him a house in Jĕ-ru'så-lĕm, in the land
of Jū'dah. Therefore, let those of the people of God who are
among you go up to Jĕ-ru'så-lĕm and help to build the house of
the Lord. And those who do not go to Jĕ-ru'så-lĕm, but stay in
the places where they are living, let them give to those who go
back to their own land gifts of gold and silver and beasts to carry
them, and goods, and also a free gift toward the building of the
house of the Lord in Jĕ-ru'så-lĕm."

At this the Jews in the land of Chăl-dē'à were very glad, for
they loved their own land and longed to see it. One of them
wrote a song at this time. It is Psalm 126:

"When the Lord turned again the captivity of Zī'ŏn,
We were like unto them that dream,
Then was our mouth filled with laughter,
And our tongue with singing:
Then said they among the nations,
'The Lord hath done great things for them,
The Lord hath done great things for us;
Whereof we are glad.

> Turn again our captivity, O Lord,
>> As the streams in the South.
> They that sow in tears
>> Shall reap in joy,
> Though he goeth on his way weeping,
>> Bearing forth the seed,
> He shall come again with joy,
>> Bringing his sheaves with him.' "

So the Jew'ĭsh people began to make ready for going back to their own land. Most of those who were rich and noble in rank stayed in the land of Chăl-dē'à and in other lands of the Pĕr'sian Empire. But though they did not go back to the land from which their fathers had come, they gave large gifts of gold and silver to help those who did go. And Çȳ'rus, the king, took from the treasure house in Băb'ȳ-lon all the vessels of the Temple that had been taken away by Nĕb-u-chad-nĕz'zar, and gave them to the Jews, to be used in the new Temple which they were soon to build. These were plates and dishes and bowls and cups of gold and silver, more than four thousand in all. So, with the gifts of the king and the gifts of their own people, and what was owned by those who went to the land of Jū'dah, the company took away a vast treasure of gold and silver.

It was a happy company of people that met together for the journey back to the land which they still called their own, though very few of them had seen it. There were forty-two thousand of them, besides their servants to help them in the journey. They traveled slowly up the Eū-phrā'tēs River, singing songs of joy, until they reached the northern end of the great desert. Then they turned toward the southwest and journeyed beside the Lĕb'a-

non Mountains, past Då-măs'cus and through Sўr'ĭ-à, until at last they came to the land of their fathers, the land of Jū'dah.

With all their joy, they must have felt sad when they saw the city of Jĕ-ru̧'så-lĕm all in ruins, its walls broken down, its houses heaps of blackened stone, its Temple burned into a heap of ashes.

As soon as they came, they found the rock where the altar of the Lord had stood, the same rock where Dā'vid had long before offered a sacrifice and the same rock upon which travelers look even in our time under the Dome of the Rock. From the smooth face of this rock they gathered up the stones and swept away the ashes and the dust. Then they built upon it the altar of the Lord, and Jŏsh'u-à, the high priest, began to offer the sacrifices which for fifty years had not been placed upon the altar. Every morning and every afternoon they laid on the altar the burnt offering, and thus gave themselves to the Lord and asked God's help.

From this time there were two branches of the Jew'ĭsh race. Those who came back to the land of Jū'dah, which was also called the land of Ĭṣ'ra-el, were called "Hē'brewş," which was an old name of the Ĭṣ'ra-el-ītes. Those who stayed in the lands abroad, in Chăl-dē'à and throughout the empire of Pēr'ṣià, were called "the Jewş of the Dispersion." There were far more of the Jewş abroad than in their own land, and they were the richer and the greater people. Many of them went up to Jĕ-ru̧'så-lĕm to visit and to worship and many others sent rich gifts; so that between the two great branches of the Jew'ĭsh people, in their own land and in other lands, there was a close friendship, and they all felt that wherever the Jewş were, they were still one people.

The Jewş who had been captives in the land of Băb'ў-lon were now free to go wherever they chose; and besides those who went back to the land of their fathers, there were many who chose to visit other lands, wherever they could find work and get gain. It was not many years before Jewş were found in many cities of the Pēr'ṣian Empire. They went also to Africa and to Europe, choosing the cities for their home rather than the country. Everywhere, in all the great cities, the "Jewş of the Dispersion" were found, besides those who were living in their own land of Ĭṣ'ra-el.

When the Jewş came back to their land, their leader was named

Zĕ-rŭb'ba-bĕl, a word which means, "One born in Băb'y̆-lon. He belonged to the family of Dā'vid and was called "the prince" but he ruled under the commands of Çy̆'rus, the great king, fc Jū'dah (which now began to be spoken of as Jū-dē'à) was a sma part, or "province" as it was called, in the great empire of Pĕr'și.

Story Fourteen
EZRA 3 : 8 to 6 : 22; HAGGAI 1 : 1 to 2:2
ZECHARIAH 4 : 6-10

The New Temple on Mount Moriah

AFTER the Jews came back to their own land, they firs built the altar upon Mount Mŏ-rī'ah, as we read ir the last story. Then they build some houses for themselves, for the winter was coming on. And early in the next year they began to build again the Temple of the Lord. Zĕ-rŭb'ba-bĕl, the prince, and Jŏsh'u-à, the priest, led in the work and the priests and Lē'vītes helped in it They gave money to masons and carpenters, and they paid men of Tȳre and Zī'dŏn, on the shore of the Great Sea, to float down cedar trees from Mount Lĕb'a-non to Jŏp'pà; and from Jŏp'pà they carried them up the mountains to Jĕ-ru'sà-lĕm for the build-ing of the house.

When they laid the first stones in the new building, the priests in their robes stood ready with trumpets and the Lē'vītes with cymbals, to praise the Lord for his goodness in bringing them once again to their own land. The singers sang:

"Praise the Lord, for he is good:
His mercy endureth forever toward Is'ra-el his people."

And all the people shouted with a great shout as the first stones were laid. But some of the priests and Lē'vītes and Jews were old men who had seen the first Temple, while it was still standing more than fifty years before. These old men wept as they thought of

he house that had been burned and of their friends who had been
lain in the destruction of the city. Some wept and some shouted,
›ut the sound was heard together, and those who heard at a dis-
ance could not tell the weeping from the shouting.

But these builders soon found enemies and were hindered in
heir work. In the middle of the land, near the cities of Shē'chem
ınd Să-mā'rĭ-à, were living the Să-măr'ĭ-tan people, some of whom
were from the old Ten Tribes, and others from the people that
ıad been brought into the land by the Ăs-sўr'ĭ-ans̩ many years
before. These worshiped the Lord, but with the Lord they worshiped other gods. These people came to the Prince Zĕ-rŭb'ba-
bĕl and said, "Let us join with you in building this house, for we
seek the Lord as you do and we offer sacrifices to him."

But Zĕ-rŭb-ba-bĕl and the rulers said to them, "You are not
with us and you do not worship as we worship. You have nothing to do with us in building the Lord's house. We will build
by ourselves to our God, the God of Ĭs̩'ra-el, as Çȳ'rus, the king
of Pĕr's̩ià, has told us to build."

This made the people of Să-mā'rĭ-à very angry. They tried to
stop the Jews̩ from building, and frightened them and wrote letters to the king, urging him to stop the work. Çȳ'rus, the king,
was a friend to the Jews̩, but he was in a land far away in the east,
carrying on war, so that he could not help them; and soon after
this he died. His son, who took his great kingdom, did not care
for the Jews̩, and he, too, died in a few years. Then a nobleman
of another family seized the throne and held it nearly a year before
he was slain. His name was Smer'dis, but he is called in the Bible
by another name, Är-tăx-ĕrx'ēs̩. While this king was reigning,
the Să-măr'ĭ-tan rulers wrote to him a letter, saying:

"Let it be known to the king that the Jews̩ have come back to
Jĕ-ru̩'să-lĕm. They are building again the city which was always
bad, and would not obey the kings when it was standing before.
If that city be built and its walls finished, then the Jews̩ will not
serve the king nor pay to him their taxes. We are true to the king
and we do not wish to see harm come to his rule. Of old time this
city was rebellious, and for that cause it was laid waste. If it is

built again, soon the king will have no power anywhere on this side of the river Eū-phrā′tēṣ.''

The King Smer′dis, or Är-tăx̱-ērx̱′ēṣ, wrote an answer to the chief men of Sȧ-mā′rĭ-ȧ, thus:

"The letter which you sent has been read to me. I have caused search to be made in the records; and I find that the city of Jĕ-rụ′-sȧ-lĕm has been in old time a strong city, with great kings ruling in it and ruling also the lands around it. I find, too, that this city did rise up and make war against the kings of empires in the past. Command the men who are building the city of Jĕ-rụ′sȧ-lĕm to stop the work; and let it not go on until an order is given from the king.''

The Sȧ-mȧr′ĭ-tanṣ and other enemies of the Jewṣ were glad to have this letter come from the great king of Pēr′ṣiȧ. They went to Jĕ-rụ′sȧ-lĕm and made the work of building the Temple and the city stop. So the foundations of the Temple lay unfinished through several years.

But after a time two prophets arose in the land of Jū-dē′ȧ. They were Hăg′ga-ī and Zĕch-a-rī′ah; and they spoke the word of the Lord to the people, telling them to go forward with the building. Hăg′ga-ī said, "Is it a time for you to dwell in richly finished houses of your own while the Lord's house lies waste? Go up to the mountain and bring wood, and build; and I will be pleased with you and will bless you, saith the Lord. The glory of this house shall be greater than the glory of the other house and in this place I will give peace, saith the Lord of hosts.''

And Zĕch-a-rī′ah, the other prophet, said, "It shall not be by might nor by power, but by my spirit, saith the Lord. The hands of Zĕ-rŭb-ba-bĕl have laid the foundation of this house, and his hands shall finish it. He shall lay the headstone with shoutings of 'Grace, grace unto it!' ''

Then Zĕ-rŭb-ba-bĕl and Jŏsh′u-ȧ and the rest of the Jewṣ began again and went on with the work. Soon after this a new king began to reign in Pēr′ṣiȧ. He was a wise man and a great ruler, whose name was Dȧ-rī′us.

King Dȧ-rī′us looked in the records of Pēr′ṣiȧ and found it

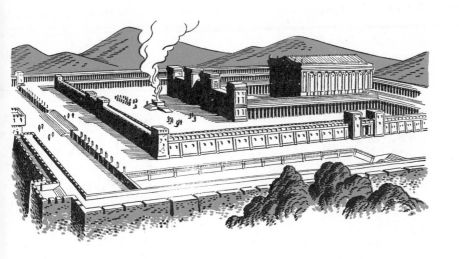

written that Çȳ'rus, the king, had commanded the Temple to be built. He wrote a letter to the rulers in all the lands around Jū-dē'à no longer to hinder the work, but to help it and to give what was needed for it. Then the Jews went on with the building in great joy; and it was finished at last, twenty-one years after it had been begun, while Zĕ-rŭb-ba-bĕl, the prince, and Jŏsh'u-à, the priest, were still ruling over the people.

The Temple, which was thus built for the second time, was like the one built by Sŏl'o-mon nearly five hundred years before; but though larger, it was not so beautiful nor costly. In front of it was an open court with a wall around it, where the people could go to worship. Next to the people's court, on higher ground, was the priests' court, where stood the altar and the laver for washing. Within this court rose the house of God, with the Holy Place and the Holy of Holies, separated by a great veil. In the Holy Place, as before, stood the table for bread, the golden lampstand, and the golden altar for incense. But in the Holy of Holies there was no Ark of the Covenant, for this had been lost and was never brought back to Jĕ-ru̇'sà-lĕm. In place of the ark stood a marble block, upon which the high priest sprinkled the blood, when he went into the Holy of Holies on the great Day of Atonement, once in each year. (See the account of the Tabernacle and its worship in Stories Twenty-seven and Twenty-eight in Part First.)

The Beautiful Queen of Persia

WHEN Dă-rī'us, the great king, died, his son Xẽr'xēṣ, who is called in the Bible Ȧ-hăṣ-ū-ē'rŭs, took his place upon the throne of Pẽr'ṣià. Ȧ-hăṣ-ū-ē'rŭs was not, like his father Dă'rī'us, a wise man. He was hasty in his temper and did many foolish acts that often brought misfortune.

At that time the palace where the king of Pẽr'ṣià lived was no longer at Băb'y̆-lon but at a city named Shu̇'shan, among the mountains of a region called Ē'lăm. King Ȧ-hăṣ-ū-ē'rŭs held at Shu̇'shan a great feast with his nobles. When the king and his company were all drunken with wine, he sent for his queen, Văsh'tī, that he might let all the nobles see how beautiful she was. Among the Pẽr'ṣianṣ it was held to be very wrong for a woman ever to allow her face to be seen by any man except her husband. Queen Văsh'tī refused to come to the feast that these drunken men might stare at her. This made the king very angry. He said that because Văsh'tī would not obey him, she should not be queen any longer, and he put her away from him and from his house.

After this King Ȧ-hăṣ-ū-ē'rŭs thought to choose another woman to be his queen instead of Văsh'tī. He sent commands throughout all the kingdom that in every land and province they should find the most beautiful young women and bring them to the royal city of Shu̇'shan. There the king would see them all, and among them he would choose the one that pleased him best and would take her as his queen. So from every land in the great empire of Pẽr'ṣià the loveliest young women were brought to Shu̇'shan, and there they were left in the care of Hĕg'a-ī, the chief of the king's palace.

At that time many Jewṣ were living in the cities of Pẽr'ṣià, for we have seen that only a small part of the Jewṣ went back to the land of Iṣ'ra-el when King Çy̆'rus allowed them to return. There

410

ʋas a Jew living in Shu̯'shan, named Môr'de-cāi. He belonged
ɔ the tribe of Bĕn'ja-mĭn, and came from the same family and line
f Sa̤ul, the first of the kings of I̤s'ra-el. At the house of Môr'-
ɛ-cāi lived his cousin, a young girl named Hả-dăs'sah, or Ĕs'thēr,
name which means "Star." Her father and mother had died, and
he had been left alone; so Môr'de-cāi took her to his house and
ɪrought her up as his own daughter. Ĕs'thēr was very beautiful
nd was as lovely in her heart as she was in her face. Among the
ɪther beautiful young women she was taken to the palace as one
ɪf those who were to be brought before the king.

When King Ȧ-hă̤s-ū-ē'rŭs saw Ĕs'thēr, the Jew'ish girl, he
ʋved her and chose her out of all the young women to be his
ɪueen, and he set upon her head the royal crown of Pēr'ṣiȧ.
Ĕs'thēr was taken into the king's palace; rooms and servants were
ɟiven to her, and she lived in the state of a queen. When the king
ʋished to see her, he sent for her, and she came to his room. No
ɪne could go to the king or could see him unless sent for. And if
ɪnyone, man or woman, came before the king without being
ɪalled, that person was seized by the guards and was led away to
ɪeath, unless the king held out toward him his golden scepter, the
ɪod which he held.

In the palace Môr'de-cāi could no longer meet his cousin
Ĕs'thēr, for no man except the king could enter the rooms set
ɑpart for the women. But Ĕs'thēr from her window could see
Môr'de-cāi as he walked by, and by her servants she could send
word to him, and in the same way could hear word from him.
Môr'de-cāi loved the lovely young queen who was to him as a
daughter and every day sat at the palace gate so that he might
hear from her.

While Môr'de-cāi was sitting by the gate, he saw two men who
were keepers of the gate often whispering together. He watched
them closely and found that they had made a plan to kill King
Ȧ-hă̤s-ū-ē'rŭs. He sent word of this to Queen Ĕs'thēr, and
Ĕs'thēr told the king of it. The men were taken, and, as Môr'de-
cāi's word was found to be true, they were both slain by being
hanged on a tree. And an account or story of all their plan, of
how they were found out by Môr'de-cāi the Jew, and how they

were punished with death, was written in the book of records of the kingdom.

After this a man named Hā'man arose to great power in the kingdom. The king gave him a seat above all the other princes and asked his advice in all matters and allowed Hā'man to do whatever he pleased. Of course everybody in the palace showed great respect to Hā'man, the man who stood next to the king. When he came near, all the men in the palace and in the city bowed down before him, and many fell on their faces, even in the very dust. But Môr'de-cāi was a worshiper of God and he would not fall upon his face before any man. Hā'man noticed that there was one man who did not bow down, as did the others around him. He said to his servants, "Who is that man sitting by the gate, who does not bow down when I pass by?"

They answered Hā'man, "That is Môr'de-cāi the Jew."

But they did not tell Hā'man, for they did not know that Môr'-de-cāi was the cousin of Queen Ĕs'thēr, and that the queen of Pēr'şià herself was a Jewess.

When Hā'man found that Môr'de-cāi was a Jew, he became very angry, not only at Môr'de-cāi, but at all his people. He hated the Jewş, and he resolved to have revenge on Môr'de-cāi, and on his account to make all Môr'de-cāi's people suffer. Hā'-man went in to the king and said to him, "O King Ā-hăş-ū-ē'rŭs, there is a certain people scattered abroad through your kingdom and apart from all other peoples. Their laws are different from those of every other nation, and they do not keep the king's laws. It is not well to allow such a people to live. If it is pleasing to the king, let a law be made that this strange people be destroyed. I will myself pay all the cost of putting them to death and will place the money in the king's treasury."

The king, living in his palace and never going out among his people, knew nothing of the Jewş, and believed Hā'man's words. He took from his hand the ring on which was the royal seal and gave it to Hā'man saying:

"Do as you please; write whatever law you wish and stamp it with the king's seal. The money is yours, and I give this strange people to you. You can do with them as you please."

Then, by Hā'man's command, a law was written and sealed with the king's seal, that on a certain day, which was the thirteenth day of the twelfth month, all the Jews in every part of Pēr'şià might be slain. Anyone who chose to kill them might do so; and those who killed them might take for their own all their money, the gold and silver and garments which they might find in the houses of the Jews.

The copies of this law were sent to every city of the empire of Pēr'şià, to be read everywhere, so that all might know that the Jews were to be destroyed. Everybody who heard of it was filled with wonder, for no one knew of any evil against the king that the Jews had done to deserve death. They could not understand why the law had been made; but everywhere the enemies of the Jews made ready to destroy them, that they might have the Jews' riches; for in those times, even as now, there was great wealth among the Jews.

The news of this terrible law came to Môr'de-cāi, as it came to all the Jews in Shu'shan. Môr'de-cāi tore his clothes, as was the manner of those in deep grief; he put on garments of sackcloth; he covered his head with ashes, and he went forth in front of the palace, crying a loud and bitter cry. Queen Ĕs'thēr saw him and heard his voice. She sent one of her servants, named Hā'tăch, to Môr'de-cāi, to find why he was in such deep trouble. Hā'tăch came to Môr'de-cāi, and Môr'de-cāi told him of the law for killing the Jews on a certain day, the thirteenth day of the twelfth month, and gave him a copy of it to show to Queen Ĕs'thēr; and he told Hā'tăch to ask the queen, in his name, to go in to King Ȧ-hăş-ū-ē'-rŭs and beg him to spare the lives of her people. Queen Ĕs'thēr heard Hā'tăch's words and sent this message to Môr'de-cāi:

"It is the rule of the palace that if any man or woman shall go in to the king in his own room, without being sent for by the king, he shall be slain unless the king holds out to him the golden scepter. But I have not been called to meet the king for thirty days."

When Môr'de-cāi heard this message, he sent word again by Hā'tăch to Queen Ĕs'thēr:

"Do not think that in the king's palace you are safe and shall escape the fate of your people. If you keep still and do nothing to save your people, God will surely save them in some other way; and you and your father's family shall be destroyed. Who can tell whether God has not raised you up and given you your royal place for such a time as this that you may save your people?"

Then Ĕs'thẽr sent this answer to Môr'de-cāi, "Go, and bring together all the Jewṣ in Shu'shan, and let them all pray for me, eating and drinking nothing, for three days. I and my maids in the palace will pray and fast also at the same time. And then I will go in to the king, even though it is against the law; and if it be God's will that I should die in trying to save my people, then I will die."

When Môr'de-cāi heard these words, he was glad, for he felt sure that God would save his people through Queen Ĕs-thẽr. For three days all the Jewṣ in Shu'shan met together, praying; and in the palace Ĕs'thẽr and her servants were praying at the same time.

The third day came, and Ĕs'thẽr dressed herself in all her robes as queen. She went out of her own rooms and across the open court, and she entered the door in front of the throne where the king was sitting. The king saw her standing before him, in all her beauty, and his heart was touched with love for her. He held out toward her the golden rod or scepter that was in his hand. Ĕs'thẽr came near and touched the top of the scepter. The king said to her:

"What do you wish, Queen Ĕs'thẽr? It shall be given to you, even to the half of my kingdom."

But Ĕs'thẽr did not at once ask for all that was in her heart. She was very wise, and she said, "If it pleases the king, I have come to ask that the king and Hā'man, the prince, shall come this day to a dinner that I have made ready for them."

The king said, "Send word to Hā'man that he haste and come to dine with the king and queen."

So that day King Ȧ-hăṣ-ū-ē'rŭs and Hā'man sat at the table with the queen. She was covered with a veil, for even Hā'man was not allowed to look upon her face. While they were sitting together, the king said, "Queen Ĕs'thẽr, is there anything that you wish? It shall be given to you, whatever it is, even to half of the kingdom."

"My wish," answered the queen, "is that the king and Hā'man shall come again to a dinner with me tomorrow."

Hā'man walked out of the palace that day happy at the honor that had come to him, but when he saw Môr'de-cāi sitting by the gate and not rising up to bow before him, all his gladness passed away, and he was angry in his heart. When he came to his own house, he told his wife Zē'resh and his friends how the king and queen had honored him, and then he said, "But all this is as nothing to me when I see that man, Môr'de-cāi the Jew, sitting at the king's gate."

But his wife said to him, "Do not let so small a matter as that trouble you. Before you go to the feast tomorrow, have a gallows made, and then ask the king to command that Môr'de-cāi be hanged upon it. The king will do whatever you wish, and then, when you have sent Môr'de-cāi to death, you can be happy at your feast with the king and the queen."

This was very pleasing to Hā'man; and on that very day he caused the gallows to be set up ready for hanging Môr'de-cāi on the next day.

It so happened that on that night the king could not sleep. He told them to read in the book of records of the kingdom, hoping that the reading might put him to sleep. They read in the book how Môr'de-cāi had told of the two men who had sought to murder the king. The king stopped the reading and said, "What reward has been given to Môr'de-cāi for saving the life of the king from these men?"

"O king," they answered, "nothing has been done for Môr'-de-cāi."

Then said the king, "Is any one of the princes standing outside in the court?"

"Yes, O king," was answered; "the noble Hā'man is in the court."

Hā'man had come in at that very moment to ask the king that Môr'de-cāi might be put to death. The king sent word to Hā'man to come in, and as soon as he entered, said to him, "What shall be done to any man whom the king wishes to honor in a special way?"

Now Hā′man thought within himself, "There is no man whom the king will wish to honor more than myself." Then he said, "The man whom the king wishes especially to honor, let him be dressed in the garments of the king, and let him sit on the horse that the king rides upon, and let the royal crown be set upon his head; let him ride through the main street of the city, and let one of the nobles call out before him, 'This is the man whom the king delights to honor.' "

Then the king said to Hā′man, "Make haste and do all this that you have said, to Môr′de-cāi the Jew, who sits in the king's gate. See that nothing it left out of what you have spoken."

Hā′man was astonished and was cut to the heart, but he did not dare to speak as he felt. He obeyed the king's command, sent for the king's horse, his robes, and his crown; dressed Môr′de-cāi like a king, mounted him on the horse, and went before him through the streets of Shụ′shan, calling aloud, "This is the man whom the king delights to honor!" And after that Hā′man hid his anger and his sorrow of heart and sat down to the feast in the queen's palace. He had not said a word to the king of having Môr′de-cāi hanged upon the gallows which he had set up the day before.

King Ȧ-hăṣ-ū-ē′rŭs knew very well that his queen had still some favor to ask; and at the feast he said to her, "What do you wish, Queen Ěs′thēr? Tell me, and I will give it to you, even though it be half of my kingdom."

Then Ěs′thēr saw that her time had come. She said to the king: "If I have found favor in your sight, O king, and if it please you, let my life be given me, and the lives of my people. For we have been sold, I and all my people, to be destroyed, to be slain, and to perish. If only we had been sold as slaves, I would have said nothing; but we are to be slain to please our enemy."

Then said the king, "Who is the man and where is he, that has dared to do this thing?"

"The enemy," said Queen Ěs′thēr, "is this wicked Hā′man!"

As the king heard this, he was so angry that he rose up from the table and walked out into the garden. In a moment he came back and saw Hā′man fallen down upon his face, begging the queen to spare his life. The king looked at him in anger, and the servants

at once covered Hā′man's face, as of one doomed to death. One
of the officers standing near said, "There stands the gallows, seventy-five feet high, which Hā′man set up yesterday for Môr′de-
cāi to be hanged upon."

"Hang Hā′man himself on it," ordered the king. So Hā′man
died upon the gallows that he had made for Môr′de-cāi.

And on that day the king gave Hā′man's place to Môr′de-cāi,
and set him over the princes. He gave to Môr′de-cāi his own ring
with its seal. And all the family of Hā′man, his sons, were put to
death for their father's evildoing, according to the cruel usage of
those times.

The law for killing the Jews on the thirteenth day of the twelfth
month had been made and sent abroad; and no law of the Pēr′ṣianṣ
could be changed. But though this law could not be taken back,
another law was made that the Jews could defend themselves
against any who might try to do them harm. When the day came,
most of their enemies feared to harm the Jews, for now they were
under the care of the king, and Môr′de-cāi, a Jew, stood next to
the king; and such of their enemies as tried to kill them on that
day were soon destroyed.

So everywhere, instead of sorrow and death, on the thirteenth
day of the twelfth month, the Jews had joy and gladness. And on
the day following, the fourteenth day of the twelfth month, the

Jews kept a feast of thanksgiving to God for his mercy in saving
them from their enemies. The same feast was kept on that day
every year afterward, and it is still kept among the Jews in all
lands, and is called the feast of Pū'rim. On that feast the story of
Ĕs'thĕr, the beautiful queen, is read by all the Jew'ish people.

Story Sixteen   EZRA 7 : 1 to 10 : 44

The Scribe Who Wrote the Old Testament

F ROM the court of the great king at Shu'shan we turn once
more to the Jews at Jĕ-ru'sà-lĕm and in Jū-dē'à. For a
long time after the first company came to the land under
Zĕ-rŭb'ba-bĕl, very few Jews from other countries
joined them. The Jews in Jū-dē'à were poor and discouraged. Many of them had borrowed money which they could
not pay, and had been sold as slaves to richer Jews. Around them
on every side were their enemies, the idol-worshiping people in
the land, and the Sà-măr'ĭ-tans on the north. These enemies
robbed them of their crops in the field and they also constantly
sent evil and false reports of them to the Pĕr'ṣian governors. Many
of the men of Ĭṣ'ra-el had married women of the land not of the
Ĭṣ'ra-el-īte race, and their children were growing up half heathen
and half Jew'ish, unable to talk in the language of their fathers,
and knowing nothing of the true God.

Ninety years after the Jews had come back to the land, Jĕ-ru'-
sà-lĕm was a small town, with many of its old houses still in ruins
and no wall around it. In those times no city could be safe from
its enemies without a wall; so that Jĕ-ru'sà-lĕm lay helpless against
bands of robbers who came up from the desert and carried away
nearly all that the people could earn.

Just at the time when the land was in the deepest need, God

raised up two men to help his people. These two men were Ĕz'rȧ and Nē-he-mī'ah. Through Ĕz'rȧ the people of Jū'dah were led back to their God, to worship him, to serve him, and especially to love God's book as they never had loved it before. And about the same time Nē-he-mī'ah gave new hope and courage and strength to the people by helping them to build a wall around Jĕ-rṳ'sȧ-lĕm. The work of these two men brought to Jū-dē'ȧ peace and plenty, and led many Jews from other lands to their own country.

Ĕz'rȧ was a priest, living in the city of Băb'ȳ-lon, though he had sprung from the family of Aả'ron, the first priest. He was also a prophet, through whom God spoke to his people. But above all, Ĕz'rȧ was a lover of God's book in a time when the book of the Lord was almost forgotten. Nearly all the books of what we call the Old Testament had been written for a long time; but in those days there were no printed books; each copy was written separately with a pen; and as the labor was great, there were very few copies of the different books of the Bible. And these copies were in different places; one book of the Bible was in one place; another book was in another place. Very few people in those times before Ĕz'rȧ had owned or had even seen the whole of the Old Testament in one book or set of books.

Ĕz'rȧ began to seek everywhere among the Jews for copies of these different books. Whenever he found one, he wrote it out and kept the copy, and also led other men to copy the books as they found them. At last Ĕz'rȧ had copies written of all the books in the Old Testament except the very latest books. They were written very nearly as we have them now, except that his copies were all in Hē'brew, the language spoken by the men who wrote most of the Old Testament.

Ĕz'rȧ put all these different books together, making one book out of many books. This great book was written on parchment, or sheepskin, in long rolls, as in old time all books were written. When the book was finished, it was called "The Book of the Law," because it contained God's law for his people, as given through Mō'șeș and Săm'u-el and Dā'vid and Ī-șā'iah, and all the other prophets.

When Ĕz'rȧ had finished writing this book of the law, he went on a long journey from Băb'ў-lon to Jū-dē'ȧ, taking with him the rolls of the book. With Ĕz'rȧ went a company of men whom he had taught to love the law, to write copies of it, to read it, and to teach it to others. These men, who gave their lives to studying and copying and teaching the law, were called "scribes," a word which means "writers."

Ĕz'rȧ was the first and the greatest of these scribes; but from his time there were many scribes among the Jews, both in Jū-dē'ȧ and in all other lands. For wherever the Jews lived, they began to read the Bible and to love it. The time came, soon after Ĕz'rȧ's day, when in every place where the Jews met to worship, at least one copy of all the books in the Old Testament was kept; so that there was no more danger that the Bible, or any part of it, would be lost.

You remember that there was only one Temple for all the Jews in the world and only one altar. Upon this one altar, and there alone, was offered the sacrifice every day. But the Jews in distant places needed to meet together for worship, and there grew up among the Jews everywhere what was called "the synagogue," a word which means "coming together." At first they met in a room, but afterward they built houses for the synagogues much like our churches. In fact, the synagogue was the church of the Jews in every city or town where Jews were found. Some of these synagogues or churches were large and beautiful, and in them the people met every week to worship God, to sing the Psalms, to hear the law and the prophets read, and to talk together about what they had heard. It was something like a prayer meeting, for any Jew who wished to speak in the meeting could do so. The men sat on mats laid on the floor; the rulers of the synagogue were on seats raised up above the rest; the women were in a gallery on one side, covered with a lattice work, so that they could see and hear, but could not be seen. And on the end of the room nearest to Jĕ-ru'sȧ-lĕm there was a large box or chest, called "the ark," within which were kept the copies of the books of the Old Testament. Thus through the synagogue-church all the Jews in the world listened to the reading of the Old Testament until very many of them knew every word of it by heart. All this came to pass from Ĕz'rȧ's work in copying and teaching the word of the Lord.

And Ĕz'rȧ wrought another work almost as great as that of giving the Bible to the world. He taught the Jew'ĭsh people, first in Ĭs'ra-el, and then in other lands, that they were the people of God, and that they must live apart from other nations. If they had gone on marrying women of other races, who worshiped other gods, after a time there would have been no Jews, and no worshipers of God. Ĕz'rȧ made some of them give up their wives of other nations, and he taught the Jews to be a people by themselves, keeping away from those who worshiped idols, even though they lived among them. Thus Ĕz'rȧ led the Jews to look upon themselves as a holy people, given up to the service of God. He taught them to live apart from other nations, with their own customs and ways of living, and very exact in obeying the law of God in the books given by Mō'ṣeṣ, even in some things that would seem small and not important. They were to be trained age after age in the service and worship of God. It was God's will that the Jews should be separate from other peoples and very strict in keeping their law, until the time should come for them to go out and preach the Gospel to all the world. But that was long after Ĕz'rȧ's day.

The Jews even now in our time continue to keep many of the rules that were given to their fathers long ago by Ĕz'rȧ; so next to Mō'ṣeṣ, Ĕz'rȧ had greater power over the Jews than any other prophet or teacher. All over the world the Jews look upon Ĕz'rȧ as the greatest man in their history except Mō'ṣeṣ. They call him "the second founder of Ĭs'ra-el."

The Nobleman Who Built the Wall of Jerusalem

HILE the good scribe Ĕz'rà was at work finding the books of the Bible, copying them, and teaching them, another great man was helping God's people in another way. This man was Nē-he-mī'ah. He was a nobleman of high rank at the court of the great King Är-tăx-ērx'ēṣ. Är-tăx-ērx'ēṣ reigned after Á-hăṣ-ū-ē'rŭs, of whom we read in the story of the beautiful Queen Ĕs'thēr.

Nē-he-mī'ah was the "cupbearer" to the king of Pēr'ṣià at Shu'-shan. It was his office to take charge of all the wine that was used at the king's table, to pour it out and hand the cup to the king. This was an important office, for he saw the king every day at his meals, and could speak with him, as very few of even the highest princes could speak. Then, too, the life of the king was in his hands, for if he were an enemy, he could have allowed poison to be put into the wine to kill the king. So the cupbearer was always a man whom the king could trust as his friend.

Nē-he-mī'ah was a Jew, and, like all the Jews, felt a great love for Jê-ru'sà-lĕm. At one time a Jew named Hà-nā-nī and certain of his friends who had come from Jê-ru'sà-lĕm, visited Nē-he-mī'ah. Nē-he-mī'ah asked them, "How are the Jews in Jê-ru'sà-lĕm doing? How does the city look?"

And they answered, "The people who are living in the land of Jū-dē'à are very poor, and are looked down upon by all around them. The wall of Jê-ru'sà-lĕm is broken down and its gates have been burned with fire."

When Nē-he-mī'ah heard this, he was filled with sorrow for his city and his people. After the Jews left him, he sat down for days and would eat nothing. He fasted and wept and prayed.

422

He said, "O Lord God of heaven, the great God, who keeps his promises to those who love him and do his will; hear, O Lord, my prayer for the people of Ĭṣ´ra-el, thy servants. We have done very wickedly, O Lord, and because of our sins, thou hast scattered us among the nations. Now, O Lord, give me grace this day in the sight of this man, the king of Pēr´ṣià, and may the king help me to do good and to help my people in the land of Ĭṣ´ra-el."

A few days after this Nē-he-mī´ah was standing beside the king's table, while the king and queen were seated at their meal. As he poured out the wine, the king saw that his face was sad, which was not usual, for Nē-he-mī´ah was of a cheerful spirit, and generally showed a happy face. The king said to him, "Nē-he-mī´ah, why do you look so sad? You do not seem to be sick. I am sure that there is something that gives you trouble. What is it? Tell me."

Then Nē-he-mī´ah was afraid that the king might be displeased with him, but he said, "Let the king live forever! Why should not my face be sad, when the city where my fathers are buried lies waste, with its walls broken down and its gates burned with fire?"

The king said, "Do you wish to ask of me any favor? Tell me what I can do to help you."

Then Nē-he-mī´ah lifted up a silent prayer to God and said, "May it please the king, I would be glad if you would send me to Jĕ-rụ´sȧ-lĕm, in the land of Jū´dah, with an order to build the walls."

The king said, "How long will the journey be? And when will you come back?"

Nē-he-mī´ah fixed upon a time, and told the king how long it would be, and he asked also that he might have letters to the men who ruled the different provinces through which he would pass for them to give him a safe journey; and also a letter to the keeper of the king's forest, to give him wood for the beams and pillars of a house which he wished to build and for repairing the Temple, and for building the wall. The king was kind to Nē-he-mī´ah and he gave him all that he asked.

Nē-he-mī´ah, with a company of horsemen and many friends,

made the long journey of almost a thousand miles to Jĕ-ru'sȧ-lĕm.
All the people were glad to have a visit from a man of such high
rank, and the whole city rejoiced at his coming. But Nē-he-mī'ah
was distressed as he saw how poor and mean and helpless the city
lay.

    One night, without telling any of the men in the city his pur-
pose, he rose up with a few of his friends, and by the light of the
moon rode on his horse around the city. There he saw in how
many places the walls were mere heaps of ruins, and gates were
broken down and burned. He found great heaps of ashes and
piles of stone, so that in some places his horse could not walk over

them. The next day he called together the rulers of the city and
the chief priests, and he said to them, "You see how poor and helpless this city lies, without walls or gates and open to all its enemies.
Come, let us build the wall of Jĕ-ru'sȧ-lĕm, so that no longer other
people may look upon us with contempt." Then he told them
how God had heard his prayer and had made the king friendly and
had sent gifts to help them. Then the people and the rulers said,
"Let us rise up and build the wall!" So at once they began the
work. Each family in Jĕ-ru'sȧ-lĕm agreed to build a part of the
wall. The high priest said that he would build one of the gates
and the wall beside it to a certain tower. Some of the rich men
built a long space, others did very little, and some would do nothing. One man built just as much of the wall as would stand in
front of his house, and no more, and another man only as much
as fronted upon his own room. One man and his daughters hired

workers to build; the goldsmiths built some, and so did the apothecaries, the men who sold medicines; and the merchants built a part. Almost all the men of the city, and some of the women, took part in the building, for the people had a mind to work.

Soon the news went abroad through Jū-dē'ȧ and the lands around that the walls of Jĕ-rṳ'sȧ-lĕm were rising from their ruins. There were many who were far from pleased as they heard this, for they hated the Jews and their God, and they did not wish to see Jĕ-rṳ'sȧ-lĕm strong, as it had been of old. The leader of these enemies was a man named Săn-băl'lat, who came from Sȧ-mā'rĭ-ȧ, where all the people were jealous of the Jews.

"What are these feeble Jews doing?" said Săn-băl'lat. "Do they intend to make their city strong? Will they pile up stones out of the rubbish of the burned city?"

And his servant Tô-bī'ah was with him, saying, "Why, if a fox should go up, he could break down their little wall."

The Ȧ-rā'bĭ-ans from the desert and the Phĭ-lĭs'tīnes from Ăsh'dŏd on the plain and the Ăm'mon-ītes from the east of Jôr'-dan, saw that if the wall should be built they could no more rob and plunder the city. They tried to form an army to come against the city and stop building. But Nē-he-mī'ah prayed to God for help, and he chose watchmen who should go around the wall and look out for the coming of the enemies. Half of Nē-he-mī'ah's men worked on the wall and the other half held the bows and spears and armor of the workers. And in some places a man would hold a spear in one hand while he spread mortar with the other. At other places men worked with their swords hanging at one side, ready for the fight any moment.

Nē-he-mī'ah rode on his horse around the wall and his servant walked beside him with a trumpet. He said, "The work is large, and you are apart from each other. Whenever you hear the sound of the trumpet, leave your work, take your arms, and go to the place where it sounds; and there the Lord will fight with us and for us."

But their enemies were not strong enough to fight the Jews; so Săn-băl'lat and Tô-bī'ah, and another of their leaders named Gē'-shem, sent a letter to Nē-he-mī'ah, saying, "Come and meet us in one of the villages on the plain near the Great Sea, and let us talk over this matter."

Now Nē-he-mī'ah knew that to go to this place and then come back again to Jĕ-ru'sȧ-lĕm would take more than a week; and he sent answer thus, "I am doing a great work and I cannot come down; why should the work stop, while I leave it, to come down and talk with you?"

Over and over again they sent for Nē-he-mī'ah, but he refused to come. Finally, Săn-băl'lat sent a letter, with this message:

"It is told among all the people, and Gē'shem says it is a fact, that you are building this city to rebel against the king of Pēr'ṣiȧ and to set up a kingdom of your own. Come now, and let us talk with you, or trouble may come to you."

Nē-he-mī'ah wrote back, "You know very well that there is no truth in all these stories. You have made them up yourselves."

Some of the Jews in the city were friendly to these enemies outside, and these men tried to frighten Nē-he-mī'ah. One of them made believe that he was a prophet and said to Nē-he-mī'ah, "Go into the Temple and hide, for in the night your enemies will come to kill you!"

"Should such a man as I am run away and hide myself?" said Nē-he-mī'ah. "No; I will not go."

So earnestly did the men of Jū'dah work that in fifty-two days after the work was begun it was finished and the gates were hung, and guards were placed within, so that no enemies might enter. Thus Jĕ-ru'sȧ-lĕm began to rise from its weakness and helplessness and once more to be a strong city.

Ezra's Great Bible Class in Jerusalem

W HEN the wall of Jĕ-ru'sȧ-lĕm was finished, Nē-he-mī'ah called together all the Jews from the villages and cities in the land to meet in Jĕ-ru'sȧ-lĕm. They met a great company with their wives and children, in an open place before the Temple. Ĕz'rȧ, the good priest and scribe, who had wrought so great a work in bringing together and writing the books of the Old Testament, was in the city at that time. They asked Ĕz'rȧ to bring the book and to read the law of the Lord to the people.

He came, carrying with him the great rolls upon which the law was written, and he stood up on a pulpit which they had built, where all the people could see him; and with Ĕz'rȧ were men whom he had taught in the law, so that they could teach it to others.

When Ĕz'rȧ stood up in the pulpit, above the heads of the people, and unrolled the scroll, all the people, who had been sitting upon the ground, rose up, while Ĕz'rȧ gave thanks to the Lord who had given to them his law. Then the people said "Amen!" with a loud voice, and they bowed until their heads touched the ground and worshiped.

Then Ĕz'rȧ began to read in the book aloud, so that as many as possible could hear. But as the people did not all understand the old Hē'brew tongue in which the book was written, men were chosen to stand by Ĕz'rȧ; and as he read each sentence, these men explained it to the people, while all the people stood listening. So, as Ĕz'rȧ read, these men told its meaning, so that the people could understand the word of the Lord.

Many of the people had never heard God's law read before, and they wept as they listened to it. But Nē-he-mī'ah, who was there as the ruler, said to them, "This day is holy to the Lord; do

427

not mourn nor weep, but rather be glad, and eat and drink and send gifts of food to those who are in need, for you are strong in the Lord and should be joyful."

And the Lē'vītes quieted the people, saying, "Hold your peace, for the day is holy. Do not weep, but be glad in the Lord."

And all the people went home to feast and to be glad, because they could hear and understand the words of God's law.

After this another meeting was held, and the people confessed their sins before God and the sins of their fathers in forsaking God's law and in not doing his will. And all the people made a solemn promise that they would keep God's law and would do his will; that they would be God's people and no more give their sons to marry women who did not worship the Lord; that they would keep holy God's day, the Sabbath; and they would give to the Lord's house for all the offerings. And they wrote the promise on a roll, and all the princes and rulers and priests signed it and placed their seals upon it.

Nē-he-mī'ah had now finished the work for which he had made the long journey to Jē-ru'så-lĕm. He went back to Shu'shan and stood once more in his place, pouring the wine at the king's table. But after some years he came again to Jē-ru'så-lĕm. He found that not all the people had fulfilled their promises to serve the Lord, and especially that the Sabbath Day was not kept as it should be. People were treading wine presses, and bringing into the city loads of grain, and selling wine and grapes and figs on the Sabbath Day. And men from the city of Tȳre, beside the Great Sea, who were not worshipers of the Lord, brought in fish and sold them on the Sabbath. When Nē-he-mī'ah saw all these evils, he was greatly displeased and said to the rulers of the city, "Why do you allow these evil things to be done, and the Sabbath Day to be broken? Were not these the very things that made God angry with our fathers, so that he let this city be destroyed? Will you bring God's anger upon us again by doing such things on God's holy day?"

Then Nē-he-mī'ah gave orders that before the sun set on the evening before the Sabbath the gates of the city should be shut and not opened until the morning after the Sabbath was over. The men came with their things to be sold and waited outside for the gates to be opened. Nē-he-mī'ah looked over the wall and saw them and said to them, "What are you doing here? If you come here again on the Sabbath, I will put you in prison!"

Then they went away and came no more upon the holy day. By such strong acts as these Nē-he-mī'ah led the people to a more faithful service of the Lord. And after this Jĕ-ru'sȧ-lĕm grew large and strong, and was full of people. Jews from other lands began to come to live in the land, until it was once more filled with cities and towns; and the hills over all the land were covered with vineyards and olive yards, and the plains were waving with fields of grain.

A little after the time of Ĕz'rȧ and Nē-he-mī'ah, Măl'a-chī arose as the last of the prophets of the Old Testament, and he said,

"Thus saith the Lord, Behold, I will send my messenger, and he shall prepare the way before me. And the Lord shall suddenly come to his Temple; behold, he cometh, saith the Lord. Behold, I will send you Ē-lī'jah, the prophet, before the great day of the Lord shall come. And he shall turn the heart of the fathers to the children, and the heart of the children to their fathers."

And with these words the Old Testament ends.

Part Sixth

THE LIFE AND
TEACHINGS
OF JESUS

The Angel by the Altar

AT THE time when the story of the New Testament began, the land of Ĭṣ'ra-el, called also the land of Jū-dē'a, was ruled by a king named Hĕr'od. He was the first of several Hĕr'ods, who at different times ruled either the whole of the land or parts of it. But Hĕr'od was not the highest ruler. Many years before this time, the Rō'mans, who came from the city of Rome in Italy, had won all the lands around the Great Sea, the sea which we call the Mĕd-ĭ-ter-rā'nē-an; and above King Hĕr'od of Jū-dē'a was the great king at Rome, who was called "Emperor," ruling over all the lands and over the land of Jū-dē'a among them. So Hĕr'od, though king of Jū-dē'a, obeyed his overlord, the emperor at Rome.

At the time when this story began, the emperor at Rome was named Au-gŭs'tus Çae'ṣar.

At this time the land where the Jews lived was full of people. Jĕ-ru'sȧ-lĕm was its largest city, and in Jĕ-ru'sȧ-lĕm was standing the Temple of the Lord, which King Hĕr'od had begun to build anew, taking the place of the old Temple built in the time of Zĕ-rŭb'ba-bĕl, which had long needed repair. There were also many other large cities besides Jĕ-ru'sȧ-lĕm. In the south was Hē'bron, among the mountains; on the shore of the Great Sea were Gā'zȧ and Jŏp'pȧ and Çaes-a-rē'a. In the middle of the land were Shē'chem and Sȧ-mā'rĭ-ȧ; and in the north were Năz'a-rĕth and Cā'nȧ; down by the shore of the Sea of Găl'ĭ-lee were Tĭ-bē'rĭ-as and Ca-pĕr'na-ŭm and Bĕth-sā'ĭ-dȧ. Far up in the north, at the foot of snowy Mount Hē'bron, was another Çaes-a-rē'a; but so that it might not be confused with Çaes-a-rē'a upon the seacoast, this city was called Çaes-a-rē'à-Phĭ-lĭp'pī, or "Phĭl'ip's Çaes-a-rē'à," from the name of one of Hĕr'od's sons.

One day, an old priest named Zăch-a-rī'as was leading the service of worship in the Temple. He was standing in front of the

golden altar of incense, in the Holy Place, and was holding in hi
hand a censer or cup full of burning coals and incense, while al
the people were worshiping in the court of the Temple, outsid
the court of the priests, where the great altar of burnt offerin
stood.

Suddenly Zăch-a-rī'as saw an angel from the Lord, standing or
the right side of the altar of incense. He felt a great fear whei
he saw this strange being with shining face; but the angel said t
him:

"Do not be afraid, Zăch-a-rī'as; for I have come from the Lor
to bring you good news. Your wife Ê-lĭṣ'a-bĕth shall have a son
and you shall name him Jŏhn. You shall be made glad, for you
son Jŏhn shall bring joy and gladness to many. He shall be grea
in the sight of the Lord; and he shall never taste wine nor strong
drink as long as he lives, but he shall be filled with God's Holy
Spirit. He shall lead many of the people of Ĭṣ'ra-el to the Lord,
for he shall go before the Lord in the power of Ê-lī'jah the prophet,
as was promised by Măl'a-chī, the last of the old prophets (see
the last story). He shall turn the hearts of the fathers to the children and those who are disobeying the Lord to do his will."

As Zăch-a-rī'as heard these words, he was filled with wonder
and could hardly believe them true. He was now an old man and
his wife Ê-lĭṣ'a-bĕth was also old; so that they could not expect to
have a child. He said to the angel:

"How shall I know that your words are true, for I am an old
man and my wife is old?"

"I am Gā'brĭ-el, that stand in the presence of God," said the
angel, "and I was sent from the Lord to speak to you and to bring
you this good news. But because you did not believe my words,
you shall become dumb and shall not be able to speak until this
which I have said comes to pass."

All this time, the people outside in the court were wondering
why the priest stayed so long in the Temple. When at last he
came out, they found that he could not speak; but he made signs
to them to tell them that he had seen a wonderful vision in the
Temple.

After the days of his service were over, Zăch-a-rī'as went to his

ɔwn home, which was near Hē′bron, a city of the priests, among
he mountains in the south of Jū-dē′à.   When his wife Ê-lĭṣ′a-bĕth
′ound that God was soon to give her a child, she was very happy
ind praised the Lord.   About six months after Zăch-a-rī′as saw
he vision in the Temple, the same angel Gā′brĭ-el was sent from
he Lord to a city in the part of the land called Găl′ĭ-lee, which'
was in the north.   The city to which the angel was sent was Năz′-
ı-rĕth.   There the angel found a young girl named Mā′rў, who
was a cousin to Ê-lĭṣ′a-bĕth.   Mā′rў was soon to be married to a
ʒood man who had sprung from the line of King Dā′vid, though
he was not himself a king, or a rich man.   He was a carpenter or
woodworker, living in Năz′a-rĕth, and his name was Jō′ṣeph.
The angel came into the room where Mā′rў was and said to her:
     "Hail, woman favored by the Lord; the Lord is with you!"
     Mā′rў was surprised at the angel's words and wondered what
they could mean.   Then the angel spoke again and said:

"Do not be afraid, Mā'rȳ. The Lord has given to you his favor and has chosen you to be the mother of a son whose name shall be Jē'ṣus, which means 'salvation,' because he shall save his people from their sins. He shall be great; and shall be called the Son of God; and the Lord shall give to him the throne of his father Dā'vid. He shall be a king and shall reign over the people of God forever; and of his rule there shall be no end."

But Mā'rȳ could not see how all this was to come to pass. And the angel said to her: "The Holy Spirit shall come upon you, and the power of the Most High God shall be over you; and the holy child which you shall have shall be called the Son of God."

Then the angel told Mā'rȳ that her cousin Ê-lĭṣ'a-bĕth was soon to have a child, through the power of the Lord. And when Mā'rȳ heard all this, she said, "I am the servant of the Lord, to do his will. Let it be to me as you have said."

When the angel had given his message and had gone away, Mā'rȳ rose up in haste and made a journey to the home of Zăch-a-rī'as and Ê-lĭṣ'a-bĕth, eighty miles away in the south country. When Ê-lĭṣ'a-bĕth saw Mā'rȳ, she was filled with the Spirit of the Lord and said, "Blessed are you among women, and blessed among men shall be your son! And why is it that the mother of my Lord comes to visit me? Blessed is the woman who believed that the promise of the Lord to her shall be made true!"

Then Mā'rȳ was filled with the Spirit of the Lord and broke out into a song of praise. She stayed with Ê-lĭṣ'a-bĕth for nearly three months, and then went again to her own home at Năz'a-rĕth.

As the angel had said, to the aged woman Ê-lĭṣ'a-bĕth was given a son. They were going to name him Zăch-a-rī'as, after his father. But his mother said, "No, his name shall be Jŏhn."

"Why?" they said. "None of your family have ever been named Jŏhn."

They asked his father Zăch-a-rī'as, by signs, what name he wished to be given to the child. He asked for something to write upon; and when they brought it, he wrote, "His name is Jŏhn."

Then all at once the power to hear and to speak came back to Zăch-a-rī'as. He spoke, praising and blessing God; and he sang a song of thanks to God, in which he said:

"You, O child, shall be called a prophet of the Most High; to go before the Lord, and to make ready his ways."

When Jŏhn was growing up, they sent him out into the desert on the south of the land, and there he stayed until the time came for him to preach to the people, for this child became the great prophet Jŏhn the Băp'tĭst.

Story Two

MATTHEW I : 18-25;
LUKE 2 : 1-39

The Manger of Bethlehem

SOON after the time when Jŏhn the Băp'tĭst was born, Jō'şeph, the carpenter of Năz'a-reth, the husband of Mā'rў, had a dream. In his dream he saw an angel from the Lord standing beside him. The angel said to him: "Jō'şeph, I have come to tell you that Mā'rў, the young woman whom you are to marry, will have a son, sent by the Lord God. You shall call his name Jē'şus, which means 'Salvation,' because he shall save his people from their sins."

Jō'şeph knew from this that this coming child was to be the King of Ĭş'ra-el, of whom the prophets of the Old Testament had spoken so many times.

Soon after Jō'şeph and Mā'rў were married in Năz'a-rĕth, a command went forth from the emperor, Au-gŭs'tus Çae'şar, through all the lands of the Rō'man empire, for all the people to go to the cities and towns from which their families had come, and there to have their names written down upon a list; for the emperor wished a list to be made of all the people under his rule. As both Jō'şeph and Mā'rў had come from the family of Dā'vid the king, they went together from Năz'a-rĕth to Bĕth'lĕ-hĕm, there to have their names written upon the list. For you remember that Bĕth'lĕ-hĕm in Jū-dē'a, six miles south of Jĕ-ru'sà-lĕm, was the place where Dā'vid was born, and where his father's family had lived for many years (see Story Four in Part Third).

It was a long journey from Năz'a-rĕth to Bĕth'lĕ-hĕm; down the mountains to the river Jôr'dan, then following the Jôr'dan almost to its end, and then climbing the mountains of Jū'dah to the town of Bĕth'lĕ-hĕm. When Jō'şeph and Mā'rў came to Bĕth'lĕ-hĕm, they found the city full of people who, like themselves, had come to have their names enrolled or written upon the list. The inn or hotel was full, and there was no room for them; for no one but themselves knew that this young woman was soon to be the mother of the Lord of all the earth. The best that they could do was to go to a stable, where the cattle were kept. There the little baby was born and was laid in a manger, where the cows and oxen were fed.

On that night some shepherds were tending their sheep in a field near Bĕth'lĕ-hĕm. Suddenly a great light shone upon them, and they saw an angel of the Lord standing before them. They were filled with fear, as they saw how glorious the angel was. But the angel said to them:

"Be not afraid; for behold, I bring you news of great joy, which shall be to all the people; for there is born to you this day in Bĕth'-lĕ-hĕm, the city of Dā'vid, a Saviour who is Chrīst the Lord, the anointed king. You may see him there, and may know him by this sign: He is a newborn baby, lying in a manger at the inn."

And then they saw that the air around and the sky above them were filled with angels, praising God and singing:

"Glory to God in the highest. And on earth peace among men in whom God is well pleased."

While they looked with wonder and listened, the angels went out of sight as suddenly as they had come. Then the shepherds said one to another:

"Let us go at once to Bĕth'lĕ-hĕm and see this wonderful thing that has come to pass, and which the Lord has made known to us."

Then as quickly as they could go to Bĕth'lĕ-hĕm, they went, and found Jō'şeph, the carpenter of Năz'a-rĕth, and his young wife Mā'rў and the little baby lying in the manger. They told Mā'rў and Jō'şeph and others, also, how they had seen the angels, and what they had heard about this baby. All who heard their story wondered at it; but Mā'rў, the mother of the child, said noth-

ing. She thought over all these things and silently kept them in her heart. After their visit, the shepherds went back to their flocks, praising God for the good news that he had sent to them.

When the little one was eight days old, they gave him a name; and the name given was "Jē′ṣus," a word which means "Salvation"; as the angel had told both Mā′rў and Jō′ṣeph that he should be named. So the very name of this child told what he should do for men; for he was to bring salvation to the world.

It was the law among the Jewṣ that after the first child was born in a family, he should be brought to the Temple; and there an offering should be made for him to the Lord, to show that this child was the Lord's. A rich man would offer a lamb, but a poor man might give a pair of young pigeons, for the sacrifice. On the day when Jē′ṣus was forty days old, Jō′ṣeph and Mā′rў brought him to the Temple; and as Jō′ṣeph the carpenter was not a rich man, they gave for the child as an offering a pair of young pigeons.

At that time there was living in Jĕ-ru̇'så-lĕm a man of God named Sĭm'ĕ-on. The Lord had spoken to Sĭm'e-on and had said to him that he should not die until the Anointed King should come, whom they called "the Chrīst," for the word Christ means "Anointed."   On a certain day the Spirit of the Lord told Sĭm'e-on to go to the Temple. He went, and was there when Jō'şeph and Mā'rÿ brought the little child Jē'şus. The spirit of the Lord said to Sĭm'e-on:

"This little one is the promised Chrīst."

Then Sĭm'e-on took the baby in his arms and praised the Lord and said:

> "Now, O Lord, thou mayest let thy servant depart,
> According to thy word, in peace
> For my eyes have seen thy salvation,
> Which thou hast given before all the peoples
> A light to give light to the nations,
> And the glory of thy people Ĭş'ra-el."

When Jō'şeph and Mā'rÿ heard this, they wondered greatly. Sĭm'e-on gave to them a blessing in the name of the Lord; and he said to Mā'rÿ, "This little one shall cause many in Ĭş'ra-el to fall and to rise again. Many shall speak against him; and sorrow like a sword shall pierce your heart also."

You know how this came to pass afterward, when Mā'rÿ saw her son dying on the cross.

While Sĭm'e-on was speaking, a very old woman came in. Her name was Ăn'nȧ, and God spoke to her as to a prophet. She stayed almost all the time in the Temple, worshiping God day and night. She, too, saw, through the Spirit of the Lord given to her, that this little child was Chrīst the Lord, and gave thanks to God for his grace.

Thus early in the life of Jē'şus God showed to a few that this little child should become the Saviour of his people and of the world.

The Star and the Wise Men

F OR SOME time after Jē'ṣus was born, Jō'ṣeph and Mā'rȳ stayed with him in Bĕth'le-hĕm. The little baby was not kept long in the stable, sleeping in the manger; for after a few days they found room in a house; and there another visit was made to Jē'ṣus by strange men who came from a land far away.

In a country east of Jū-dē'à, and many miles distant, were living some very wise men who studied the stars. One night they saw a strange star shining in the sky; and in some way they learned that the coming of the star meant that a king was soon to be born in the land of Jū-dē'à. These men felt a call of God to go to Jū-dē'à, far to the west of their own home, and there to see this newborn king. They took a long journey, with camels and horses, and at last they came to the land of Jū-dē'à, just at the time when Jē'ṣus was born at Bĕth'lĕ-hĕm. As soon as they were in Jū-dē'à, they supposed that everyone would know all about the king; and they said:

"Where is he that is born King of the Jewṣ? In the east we have seen his star; and we have come to worship him."

But no one of whom they asked had ever seen this king or had heard of him. The news of their coming was sent to Hĕr'od, the king, who was now a very old man. He ruled the land of Jū-dē'à, as you know, under the emperor at Rome, Au-gŭs'tus Çae'ṣar. (See Story One of this part.) Hĕr'od was a very wicked man; and when he heard of someone born to be a king, he feared that he might lose his own kingdom. He made up his mind to kill this new king and thus to keep his own power. He sent for the priests and scribes, the men who studied and taught the books of the Old Testament, and asked them about this Chrīst for whom all the people were looking. He said, "Can you tell me where Chrīst, the King of Iṣ'ra-el, is to be born?" They looked at the books of the prophets and then they said, "He is to be born in Bĕth'lĕ-hĕm

441

of Jū-dē'a; for thus it is written by the prophet, 'And thou, Běth'-lĕ-hěm, in the land of Jū'dah, art not the least among the princes of Jū'dah; for out of thee shall come forth one who shall rule my people Ĭs'ra-el.' "

Then Hĕr'od sent for the wise men from the east, and met them alone, and he found from them at what time the star was first seen. Then he said to them:

"Go to Běth'le-hěm, and there search carefully for the little child; and when you have found him, bring me word again, so that I also may come and worship him."

Then the wise men went on their way toward Běth'lĕ-hěm, and suddenly they saw the star again shining upon the road before them. At this they were glad and followed the star until it led them to the very house where the little child was. They came in, and there they saw the little one, with Mā'rў, its mother. They knew at once that this was the King, and they fell down on their faces and worshiped him as the Lord. Then they brought out gifts of gold and precious perfumes, frankincense and myrrh, which were used in offering sacrifices, and they gave them as presents to the royal child.

That night God sent a dream to the wise men, telling them not to go back to Hĕr'od, but to go home at once to their own land by another way. They obeyed the Lord, and found another road to their own country without passing through the city where Hĕr'od was living.

So Hĕr'od could not learn from these men who the child was that was born to be a king.

And very soon after these wise men had gone away, the Lord sent another dream to Jō'seph, the husband of Mā'rў. He saw an angel, who spoke to him, saying:

"Rise up quickly; take the little child and his mother, and go down to the land of Ē'ġўpt; for Hĕr'od will try to find the little child, to kill him."

Then at once Jō'seph rose up in the night, without waiting even for the morning. He took his wife and her baby, and quietly and quickly went with them down to Ē'ġўpt, which was on the south-

west of Jū-dē′à. There they all stayed in safety as long as the
wicked King Hĕr′od lived, which was not many months.

King Hĕr′od waited for the wise men to come back to him from
their visit to Bĕth′lĕ-hĕm; but he soon found that they had gone
to their home without bringing to him any word. Then Hĕr′od
was very angry. He sent out his soldiers to Bĕth′lĕ-hĕm. They
came, and by the cruel king's command, seized all the little children in Bĕth′lĕ-hĕm who were two years old or younger, and
killed them all. What a cry went up to God from the mothers of

Bĕth′lĕ-hĕm as their children were torn from their arms and slain!
But all this time the child Jē′ṣus, whom they were seeking, was
safe with his mother in the land of Ē′ġÿpt.

Soon after this King Hĕr′od died, a very old man, cruel to the
last. Then the angel of the Lord came again and spoke to Jō′ṣeph
in a dream, saying:

"You may now take the young child back to his own land, for
the king who sought to kill him is dead."

Then Jō′ṣeph took his wife and the little child Jē′ṣus, and started
to go again to the land of Jū-dē′à. Perhaps it was his thought to
go again to Bĕth′lĕ-hĕm, the city of Dā′vid, and there bring up the
child. But he heard that in that part of the land Är-chĕ-lā′us was
now ruling, who was a son of Hĕr′od, and as wicked and cruel as
his father. He feared to go under his rule, and instead took his

wife and the child to Năz'a-rĕth, which had been his own home
and that of Mā'rÿ his wife, before the child was born. Năz'a-rĕth
was in the part of the land called Găl'ĭ-lee, which at that time was
ruled by another son of King Hĕr'od, a king named Hĕr'od Ăn'-
tĭ-păs. He was not a good man, but was not so cruel nor bloody
as his wicked father had been.

So again Jō'şeph the carpenter, and Mā'rÿ his wife, were living
in Năz'a-rĕth. And there they stayed for many years while Jē'şus
was growing up. Jē'şus was not the only child in their house, for
other sons and daughters were given to them.

Story Four

LUKE 2 : 40-52

The Boy in His Father's House

Ē'ŞUS was brought to Năz'a-rĕth when he was a little child,
not more than three years old; there he grew up as a boy
and a young man; and there he lived until he was thirty
years of age. We should like to know many things about
his boyhood, but the Bible tells us very little. As Jō'şeph
was a workingman, it is likely that he lived in a house with only
one room, with no floor except the earth, no window except a hole
in the wall, no pictures upon the walls, and neither bedstead nor
chair nor looking-glass. They sat upon the floor or upon cushions;
they slept upon rolls of matting; and their meals were taken from
a low table, not much larger than a stool.

Jē'şus may have learned to read at the village school, which was
generally held in the house used for worship, called the "synagogue." The lessons were from rolls on which were written
parts of the Old Testament; but Jē'şus never had a Bible of his
own. From the time when he was a child, he went with Jō'şeph
to the worship in the village church, which they called "the
synagogue," twice every week. There they sat on the floor on

mats or cushions, and heard the Old Testament read and explained; while Mā'rў and the younger sisters of Jē'ṣus listened from a gallery behind a lattice screen. The Jew'ish boys of that time were taught to know almost the whole of the Old Testament by heart.

It was the custom for the Jews from all parts of the land to go up to Jĕ-ru'så-lĕm to worship at least once every year at the feast of the Passover, which was held in the spring. Some families also stayed to the feast of Pentecost, which was fifty days after Passover; and some went again in the fall to the feast of Tabernacles, when for a week all the families slept out of doors under roofs made of green twigs and bushes. When Jē'ṣus was a boy twelve years old, he was taken up to the feast of the Passover, and then for the first time he saw the holy city Jĕ-ru̇'så-lĕm and the Temple of the Lord on Mount Mȯ-rī'ah. Young as he was, his soul was stirred as he walked among the courts of the Temple and saw the altar with its smoking sacrifice, the priests in their white robes, and the Lē'vītes with their silver trumpets. Though a boy, Jē'ṣus began to feel that he was the Son of God and that this was his Father's house.

His heart was so filled with the worship of the Temple, with the words of the scribes or teachers whom he heard in the courts, and with his own thoughts, that when it was time to go home to Năz'a-rĕth, he stayed behind, held fast by his love for the house of the Lord. The company of people who were traveling together was large, and at first he was not missed. But when night came and the boy Jē'ṣus could not be found, his mother was alarmed. The next day Jō'ṣeph and Mā'rў left their company and hastened back to Jĕ-ru̇'så-lĕm. They did not at first think to go to the Temple. They sought him among their friends and kindred who were living in the city, but could not find him.

On the third day they went up to the Temple with heavy hearts, still looking for their boy. And there they found him, sitting in a company of the teachers of the law, listening to their words and asking them questions. Everybody who stood near was surprised to find how deep was the knowledge of this boy in the word of the Lord.

His mother spoke to him a little sharply, for she felt that her son
had not been thoughtful of his duty. She said:

"Child, why have you treated us in this way? Do you not
know that your father and I have been looking for you with
troubled hearts?"

"Why did you seek for me?" said Jē'ṣus. "Did you not know
that I must be in my Father's house?"

They did not understand these words, but Mā'rỹ thought often
about them afterward, for she felt that her son was no common

child and that his words had a deep meaning. Though Jē'ṣus was
wise beyond his years, he obeyed Jō'ṣeph and his mother in all
things. He went with them to Năz'a-rĕth and lived contented
with the plain life of their country home.

As the years went on, Jē'ṣus grew from a boy to a young man.
He grew, too, in knowledge and in wisdom and in the favor of
God. He won the love of all who knew him, for there was some-
thing in his nature that drew all hearts, both young and old.

Jē'ṣus learned the trade of a carpenter or worker in wood with
Jō'ṣeph; and when Jō'ṣeph died, while Jē'ṣus was still a young
man, Jē'ṣus, as the oldest son, took up the care of his mother and
his younger brothers and sisters. And so in the work of the carpenter's shop and the quiet life of a country village and the worship of the synagogue-church, the years passed until Jē'ṣus was
thirty years of age.

The Prophet in the Wilderness

E COME now to a time when Jē'ṣus, the son of Mā'rȳ, was a young man about thirty years of age. Jŏhn, the son of the old priest Zăch-a-rī'as, was six months older, but these two young men had never met, for one was in the north at Năz'a-rĕth and the other was living in the desert in the south of the land of Jū-dē'à.

Suddenly the news went through all the land of Iṣ'ra-el that a prophet had risen up and was giving to the people the word of the Lord. It was more than four hundred years since God had sent a prophet to his people; and when it was known that again a man was speaking what God had told him, and not what he had learned by studying the old writings, a thrill went through the hearts of all the people. From all parts of the land, out of cities and villages, people poured forth to the wild region beside the river Jôr'dan, where the new prophet was preaching the word of the Lord and the coming of the Messiah.

This prophet was Jŏhn, the son of Zăch-a-rī'as. He lived in the wilderness, where he was alone with God and listened to God's voice. Then he spoke to the people the words that God had given to him. In his looks and dress Jŏhn was not like other men. His garment was made of rough cloth woven from camel's hair; around his waist was a girdle of skin; and the food which he ate was dried locusts and the wild honey from the trees. And this was his message, "Turn from sin to doing right, for the kingdom of heaven is at hand, and the King is soon to come." The people came to hear his words, and when they asked him, "What shall we do?" Jŏhn said to them, "He that has two coats, let him give to him that has none; and he that has food more than he needs, let him give to him that is hungry."

The men who gathered the taxes and who were called publi-

447

cans, asked of Jŏhn, "Master, what shall we do?" And Jŏhn answered them, "Do not cheat the people nor rob them nor take more money than the law tells you to take from them."

And when the soldiers came to him, he said to them, "Do not harm anyone nor bring false charges against any; and be content with the wages that are paid to you."

There came to Jŏhn some people who were called Phăr'ĭ-seeṣ. These men made a great show of being good and of worshiping often, and of keeping the law of Mō'ṣeṣ. But in their hearts they were evil, and their goodness was not real. Jŏhn said to these men when he saw them, "O ye brood of vipers! Who has told you to escape from the wrath of God that is soon to come? Turn from your sins to God and do right. And do not say to yourselves, 'Ā'brȧ-hăm is our father,' for God is able out of these stones to raise up children to Ā'brȧ-hăm."

When men who heard the words of Jŏhn wished to give themselves up to serve God and to do his will, Jŏhn baptized them in the river Jôr′dan, as a sign that their sins were washed away. And because of this he was called "Jŏhn the Băp′tĭst." Some of the people began to ask, "Is not this man the Chrīst whom God promised long ago to send to rule over the people?"

Jŏhn heard this, and he said, "I baptize you with water, but there is one coming after me who is greater than I. He shall baptize you with the Holy Spirit and with fire. He is so high above me that I am not worthy even to stoop down and untie the strings of his shoes. This mighty one who is coming shall sift out the wheat from the chaff among the people. The wheat he will gather into his garner, but the chaff he will burn up with fire that no man can put out."

Nearly all the people in the land came to hear Jŏhn in the wilderness and were baptized by him. Among the last who came was Jē′ṣus, the young carpenter from Năz′a-rĕth. When Jŏhn saw Jē′ṣus, something within told Jŏhn that here was one greater and holier than himself. He said to Jē′ṣus, "I have need to be baptized by thee, and comest thou to me?"

Jē′ṣus answered him, "Let it be so now, for it is fitting that I should do all things that are right."

Then Jŏhn baptized Jē′ṣus, as he had baptized others. And as Jē′ṣus came up out of the water and was praying, Jŏhn saw above the head of Jē′ṣus the heavens opening and the Holy Spirit coming down like a dove and lighting upon him. And Jŏhn heard from heaven a voice saying:

"This is my beloved Son, in whom I am well pleased."

And then Jŏhn knew and told to others that this was the Son of God, the Chrīst whom God had promised to send to the people.

Jesus in the Desert and Beside the River

FROM the earliest years of Jē'ṣus the Holy Spirit of God was with him, growing as he grew. And in the hour when he was baptized and the form of a dove was seen hovering over him, Jē'ṣus was filled with the Holy Spirit as no man before him had been filled, for he was the Son of God. At that hour he knew more fully than he had ever known before the work that he should do to save men. The Spirit of God sent Jē'ṣus into the desert, there to be for a time alone with God and to plan out his work for men.

So earnest was the thought of Jē'ṣus in the desert, so full was his union with God, that for forty days he never once ate anything or felt any wish for food. But when the forty days were ended, then suddenly hunger came upon him, and he felt faint and starving, as any other man would feel who had fasted for so long a time.

At that moment Sā'tan, the evil spirit, came to Jē'ṣus, just as he comes to us, and put a thought into his mind. It was this thought:

"If you are the Son of God, you can do whatever you please and can have whatever you wish. Why do you not command that these stones be turned into loaves of bread for you to eat?"

Jē'ṣus knew that he could do this, but he knew also that this power had been given to him, not for himself, but that he might help others. He said to the evil spirit, "It is written in God's book, 'Man shall not live by bread alone, but by every word that cometh out of the mouth of God.'"

Then the evil spirit led Jē'ṣus to Jē-ru'ṣå-lĕm, the holy city, and brought him to the top of a high tower on the Temple and said to him, "Now show all the people that you are the Son of God by throwing yourself down to the ground. You know that it is written in the book of Psalms, 'He shall give his angels charge over thee; and in their hands they shall bear thee up, lest at any time thou dash thy foot against a stone.' "

But Jē'ṣus knew that this would not be right, for it would be done not to please God, but to show himself before men and as a trial of God's power when God himself had not commanded it. He answered, "It is written again, 'Thou shalt not put the Lord thy God to a trial of his power.' "

Again the evil spirit tried to lead Jē'ṣus into doing wrong, as he leads us all. He led him to the top of a high mountain and caused a vision of all the kingdoms of the world and their glory to stand before the eyes of Jē'ṣus. Then he said, "All these shall be yours; you shall be the king of all the earth if you will only fall down and worship me."

Then Jē'ṣus said to him, "Leave me, Sā'tan, thou evil spirit! For it is written, 'Thou shalt worship the Lord thy God, and him only shalt thou serve.' "

When Sā'tan found that Jē'ṣus would not listen to him, he left him; and then the angels of God came to Jē'ṣus in the desert and gave to him the food that he needed.

After this victory over the evil spirit, Jē'ṣus went again from the desert to the place at the river Jôr'dan where he had been baptized. It was near a city sometimes called Běth-ăb'a-rà, a word which means "A place of crossing," because it was one of the places where the river Jôr'dan was so shallow that the people could walk across it. The city was called also "Běth'a-nỹ beyond Jôr'dan," so that it would not be mistaken for another Běth'a-nỹ on the Mount of Ŏl'ĭveṣ, very near Jē-ru'sà-lĕm.

There Jŏhn the Băp'tĭst saw Jē'ṣus coming toward him, and he said, "Behold the Lamb of God, who takes away the sin of the world! This is the one of whom I spoke, saying, 'There is One coming after me who is greater than I.' This is the Son of God."

And again the next morning, Jŏhn the Băp'tĭst was standing with two young men, his followers. They were fishermen who had come from the Sea of Găl'ĭ-lee to hear him. One was named Ăn'drew and the other Jŏhn. Jŏhn the Băp'tĭst was walking near by, and he said again, "Behold, the Lamb of God!"

When the two young men heard this, they left Jŏhn and went

to speak with Jē'ṣus, although they had not known him before. Jē'ṣus saw that they were following him, and he said, "What is it that you wish from me?"

They said to him, "Master, we would like to know where you are staying, so that we can see you and talk with you."

Jē'ṣus said to them, "Come and see."

They went with Jē'ṣus and stayed and talked with him all the rest of that day, for it was about ten o'clock in the morning when they first saw Jē'ṣus. And these two young men went away from the meeting with Jē'ṣus, believing that Jē'ṣus was the Saviour and the King of Iṣ'ra-el. These two, Ăn'drew and Jŏhn, were the first two men, after Jŏhn the Băp'tĭst, to believe in Jē'ṣus.

Each of these two men had a brother whom he wished might know Jē'ṣus. Ăn'drew's brother was named Sī'mon, and Jŏhn's brother was named Jāmeṣ. These four men were all fishermen together upon the Sea of Găl'ĭ-lee. Ăn'drew found his brother first, and he said to him, "We have found the Anointed One, the Chrīst, who is to be the King of Iṣ'ra-el."

And Ăn'drew brought his brother to meet Jē'ṣus. Jē'ṣus saw him coming and without waiting to hear his name, he said, "Your name is Sī'mon, and you are the son of Jō'nas. But I will give you a new name. You shall be called 'The Rock.' "

The word "rock" in Hē'brew, the language of the Jewṣ, was "Çē'phas," and in Greek, the language in which the New Testament was written, it is "Petros," or Pē'tĕr. So from that time Sī'mon was called Sī'mon Pē'tĕr, that is, "Sī'mon the Rock." Sometimes his Hē'brew name is used, and he is called "Çē'phas." So now Jē'ṣus had three followers, Ăn'drew, Jŏhn, and Sī'mon Pē'tĕr. The next day as he was going back to Găl'ĭ-lee, the part of the land where his home was, he met another man named Phĭl'ĭp, also from Găl'ĭ-lee. He said to Phĭl'ĭp, "Follow me."

And Phĭl'ĭp went with Jē'ṣus as the fourth of his followers. Phĭl'ĭp found a friend, whose name was Nȧ-thăn'a-el. He came from a place in Găl'ĭ-lee, called Cā'nȧ. Phĭl'ĭp said to Nȧ-thăn'-a-el, "We have found the one of whom Mō'ṣeṣ wrote in the law, and of whom the prophets spoke, the Anointed Chrīst. It is Jē'ṣus of Năz'a-rĕth."

Nȧ-thăn'a-el lived not many miles from Năz'a-rĕth, and he did not think that such a place as Năz'a-rĕth could have in it one so great as the Chrīst, whom the Jews looked for as their king. He said to Phĭl'ĭp, "Can any good thing come out of Năz'a-rĕth?"

Phĭl'ĭp knew that if Nȧ-thăn'a-el could only meet Jē'șus and hear his words, he would believe in him, as the others believed. He said to Nȧ-thăn'a-el, "Come and see him for yourself."

And he brought Nȧ-thăn'a-el to Jē'șus. As soon as Jē'șus saw him, he said, "Here is an Iș'ra-el-īte indeed, a man without evil."

Nȧ-thăn'a-el was surprised at this, and he said to Jē'șus, "Master, how did you know me?"

"Before Phĭl'ĭp called you, when you were standing under the fig tree, I saw you," said Jē'șus.

At this Nȧ-thăn'a-el wondered all the more, for he saw that Jē'șus knew what no man could know. He said, "Master, thou art the Son of God! Thou art the King of Iș'ra-el!"

Jē'șus said to Nȧ-thăn'a-el, "Do you believe in me because I tell you that I saw you under the fig tree? You shall see greater things than these. The time shall come when you will see heaven opened and the angels of God going up and coming down through me, the Son of God."

Jē'șus now had five followers. These men and others who walked with him and listened to his words were called "disciples."

The Water Jars at the Wedding Feast

A FEW days after Jē'ṣus met his first followers or disciples at the river Jôr'dan, he came with these men to a town in Găl'ĭ-lee called Cā'nà, to be present at a wedding. In those lands a feast was always held at a wedding, and often the friends of those who were married stayed several days, eating and drinking together.

The mother of Jē'ṣus was at this wedding as a friend of the family, for Năz'a-rĕth, where she lived, was quite near to Cā'nà. Before the wedding feast was over, all the wine had been used, and there was no more for the guests to drink. The mother of Jē'ṣus believed that her son had power to do whatever he chose, and she said to him, "They have no wine."

Jē'ṣus said to her, "O woman, what have I to do with thee? My hour is not yet come."

But his mother knew that Jē'ṣus would in some way help the people in their need; and she said to the servants who were waiting at the table, "Whatever he tells you to do, be sure to do it."

In the dining hall were standing six large stone jars, each about as large as a barrel, holding twenty-five gallons. These jars held water for washing, as the Jews washed their hands before every meal and washed their feet as often as they came from walking in the street, since they wore no shoes, but only sandals. Jē'ṣus said to the servants, "Fill the water jars with water."

The servants obeyed Jē'ṣus and filled the jars up to the brim. Then Jē'ṣus spoke to them again and said, "Now pour out what you need from the jars and take it to the ruler of the feast."

They drew out from the jars some of the water which they had poured into them, and saw that it had been turned into wine. The ruler did not know from what place the wine had come, but he said to the young man who had just been married, the bridegroom,

454

'At a feast everybody gives his best wine at the beginning, and afterward, when his guests have drunk freely, he brings on wine that is not so good; but you have kept the good wine until now."

This was the first time that Jē'ṣus used the power that God had given him, to do what no other man could do. Such works as these were called "miracles," and Jē'ṣus did them as signs of his power as the Son of God. When the disciples saw this miracle, they believed in Jē'ṣus more fully than before.

After this Jē'ṣus went with his mother and his younger brothers to a place called Cȧ-pēr'na-ŭm, on the shore of the Sea of Găl'ĭ-lee.

But they stayed there only a few days, for the feast of the Passover was near, and Jē'ṣus went up to Jĕ-ru'sȧ-lĕm to attend it. You remember that the feast of the Passover was held every year to keep in mind how God had led the people of Iṣ'ra-el out of Ē'ġȳpt long before.

When Jē'ṣus came to Jĕ-ru'sȧ-lĕm, he found in the courts of the Temple men who were selling oxen and sheep and doves for the sacrifices, and other men sitting at tables changing the money of Jews who came from other lands, into the money of Jū-dē'ȧ. All this made the courts around the Temple seem like a market and not a place for the worship of God.

Jē'ṣus picked up some cord and made from it a little whip. With it he began to drive out of the Temple all the buyers and sellers. He was but one, and they were many; but such power was in his look that they ran before him. He drove out the men and the sheep and the oxen; he overturned the tables and threw on the floor the money; and to those who were selling the doves he said, "Take these things away; make not my Father's house a house for selling and buying!"

These acts of Jē'ṣus were not pleasing to the rulers of the Jews, for many of them were getting rich by this selling of offerings and changing of money. Some of the rulers came to Jē'ṣus and said to him, "What right have you to come here and do such things as these? What sign can you show that God has given to you power to rule in this place?"

Jē'ṣus said to them, "I will give you a sign. Destroy this house of God, and in three days I will raise it up."

Then said the Jews, "It has taken forty-six years to build this Temple, and it is not finished yet. Will you raise it up in three days?"

But Jē'ṣus did not mean that Temple on Mount Mȯ-rī'ah. He was speaking of himself; for in him God was dwelling as in a temple, and he meant that when they should put him to death he would rise again in three days. Afterward, when Jē'ṣus had died and risen again, his followers, the disciples, thought of what he had said and understood these words.

While Jē'ṣus was in Jė-ru'să-lĕm, one of the rulers of the Jews, a man named Nĭc-o-dē'mus, came to see him. He came in the night, perhaps because he was afraid to be seen coming in the daytime. He said to Jē'ṣus, "Master, we know that you are a teacher come from God, for no man can do these wonderful things that you do unless God is with him."

Jē'ṣus said to Nĭc-o-dē'mus, "I say to you in truth, that unless a man is born anew, he cannot see the kingdom of God."

Nĭc-o-dē'mus did not know that this meant that to be saved we must have new hearts given to us by the Lord. He said, "Why, how can a man be born twice? How can one be born again after he has grown up?"

Jē'ṣus said to him, "I tell you of a truth, that unless a man is born of water and of the Spirit, he cannot enter into the kingdom of God."

By this he meant that we must be baptized, and that God must put his Spirit in us, if we are to become God's children. Jḗ'ṣus said also, "As Mō'ṣeṣ lifted up the serpent in the wilderness, even so must the Son of Man be lifted up, that everyone who believes in him may have everlasting life. For God so loved the world that he gave his only Son, that whosoever believes in him may not perish, but may have everlasting life. For God sent not his son into the world to condemn [that is to judge] the world; but that the world through him might be saved."

We have already read how Mō'ṣeṣ lifted up the brazen serpent in the wilderness, and how that serpent pointed to Chrīst.

Story Eight
MATTHEW 14 : 3-5; MARK 6 : 17-20; LUKE 3 : 19, 20; JOHN 3 : 22 to 4 : 42

The Stranger at the Well

WHILE Jḗ'ṣus was teaching in Jḗ-ru'ṣȧ-lĕm and in the country places near it, Jŏhn the Băp'tĭst was still preaching and baptizing. But already the people were leaving Jŏhn and going to hear Jḗ'ṣus. Some of the followers of Jŏhn the Băp'tĭst were not pleased as they saw that fewer people came to their master, and that the crowds were seeking Jḗ'ṣus. But Jŏhn said to them, "I told you that I am not the Chrīst, but that I am sent before him. Jḗ'ṣus is the Chrīst, the King. He must grow greater, while I must grow less, and I am glad that it is so."

Soon after this Hĕr'od Ăn'tĭ-păs, the king of the province or land of Găl'ĭ-lee, put Jŏhn in prison. Hĕr'od had taken for his wife a woman named Hḗ-ro'dĭ-as, who had left her husband to live with Hĕr'od, which was a very wicked act. Jŏhn sent word to Hĕr'od that it was not right for him to have this woman as his wife. These words of Jŏhn made Hḗ-ro'dĭ-as very angry. She hated Jŏhn and tried to kill him. Hĕr'od himself did not hate Jŏhn so greatly, for he knew that Jŏhn had spoken the truth. But he was weak and yielded to his wife Hĕ-ro'dĭ-as. To please her, he sent Jŏhn the Băp'tĭst to a lonely prison among the mountains east of the Dead Sea, for the land in that region, as well as Găl'ĭ-lee, was under Hĕr'od's rule. There in prison Hĕr'od hoped to keep Jŏhn safe from the hate of his wife Hĕ-ro'dĭ-as.

Soon after Jŏhn the Băp'tĭst was thrown into prison, Jē'ṣus left the country near Jĕ-rṳ'sȧ-lĕm with his disciples, and went toward Găl'ĭ-lee, the province in the north. Between Jū-dē'ȧ in the south and Găl'ĭ-lee in the north lay the land of Sȧ-mā'rĭ-ȧ, where the Sȧ-măr'ĭ-tanṣ lived, who hated the Jewṣ. They worshiped the Lord as the Jewṣ worshiped him, but they had their own temple and their own priests. And they had their own Bible, which was only the five books of Mō'ṣeṣ, for they would not read the other books of the Old Testament. The Jewṣ and the Sȧ-măr'ĭ-tanṣ would scarcely ever speak to each other, so great was the hate between them.

When Jewṣ went from Găl'ĭ-lee to Jĕ-rṳ'sȧ-lĕm or from Jĕ-rṳ'-sȧ-lĕm to Găl'ĭ-lee, they would not pass through Sȧ-mā'rĭ-ȧ, but went down the mountains to the river Jôr'dan and walked beside the river, in order to go around Sȧ-mā'rĭ-ȧ. But Jē'ṣus, when he would go from Jĕ-rṳ'sȧ-lĕm to Găl'ĭ-lee, walked over the mountains, straight through Sȧ-mā'rĭ-ȧ. One morning, while he was on his journey, he stopped to rest beside an old well at the foot of Mount Gēr'ĭ-zĭm, not far from the city of Shē'chem, but nearer to a little village that was called Sȳ'chär. This well had been dug by Jā'cob, the great father or ancestor of the Ĭṣ'ra-el-ītes, many hundreds of years before. It was an old well then in the days of Jē'ṣus, and it is much older now, for the same well may be seen in that place still. Even now travelers may have a drink from Jā'cob's well.

It was early in the morning, about sunrise, when Jē'ṣus was sitting by Jā'cob's well. He was very tired, for he had walked a long journey; he was hungry, and his disciples had gone to the village near at hand to buy food. He was thirsty, too; and as he looked into the well, he could see the water, a hundred feet below, but he had no rope with which to let down a cup or a jar to draw up some water to drink.

Just at this moment a Sȧ-mȧr′ĭ-tan woman came to the well, with her water jar upon her head and her rope in her hand. Jē′ṣus looked at her, and in one glance read her soul and saw all her life. He knew that Jewṣ did not often speak to Sȧ-mȧr′ĭ-tanṣ, but he ṣaid to her, "Please give me a drink."

The woman saw from his looks and his dress that he was a Jew, and she said to him, "How is it that you, who are a Jew, ask drink of me, a Sȧ-mȧr′ĭ-tan woman?"

Jē′ṣus answered her, "If you knew what God's free gift is, and if you knew who it is that says to you, 'Give me a drink,' you would ask him to give you living water, and he would give it to you."

There was something in the words and the looks of Jē′ṣus which made the woman feel that he was not a common man. She said to him, "Sir, you have nothing to draw water with, and the well is deep. Where can you get that living water? Are you greater than our father Jā′cob, who drank from this well?"

"Whoever drinks of this water," said Jē′ṣus, "shall thirst again; but whoever drinks of the water that I shall give him, shall never thirst; but the water that I shall give him shall be in him a well of water springing up unto everlasting life."

"Sir," said the woman, "give me some of this water of yours, so that I will not thirst any more nor come all the way to this well."

Jē′ṣus looked at the woman and said to her, "Go home and bring your husband and come here."

"I have no husband," answered the woman.

"Yes," said Jē′ṣus, "you have spoken the truth. You have no husband. But you have had five husbands, and the man whom you now have is not your husband."

The woman was filled with wonder as she heard this. She saw that there was a man who knew what a stranger could not know. She felt that God had spoken to him and she said, "Sir, I see that you are a prophet of God. Tell me whether our people or the Jewṣ are right. Our fathers have worshiped on this mountain. The Jewṣ say that Jē-ru̇′sȧ-lĕm is the place where men should go to worship. Now, which of these is the right place?"

"Woman, believe me," said Jḗ'ṣus, "there is coming a time when men shall worship God in other places besides on this mountain and in Jĕ-ru̱'ṣȧ-lĕm. The time is near; it has even now come, when the true worshipers everywhere shall pray to God in spirit and in truth; for God himself is a Spirit."

The woman said, "I know that the Anointed One is coming, the Chrīst. When he comes, he will teach us all things."

Jḗ'ṣus said to her, "I that speak to you now am he, the Chrīst."

Just at this time the disciples of Jḗ'ṣus came back from the village. They wondered to see Jḗ'ṣus talking with this Sȧ-măr'ĭ-tan woman, but they said nothing.

The woman had come to draw water, but in her interest in this wonderful stranger, she forgot her errand. Leaving her water jar, she ran back to her village and said to the people, "Come, see a man who told me everything that I have done in all my life! Is not this man the Chrīst whom we are looking for?"

When the woman was gone away, the disciples urged Jḗ'ṣus to eat some of the food which they had brought. A little while before Jḗ'ṣus had been hungry, but now he had forgotten his own needs of food and drink. He said to them, "I have food to eat that you know nothing of, the food of the soul; and that food is to do the will of God and to work for him. Do you say to me that there are four months before the harvest? I tell you to look on the fields and see them white for the harvest. You shall reap and shall have a rich reward, gathering fruit to everlasting life."

Jē′ṣus meant that as this woman, bad though she may have been before, was now ready to hear his words; so they would find the hearts of men everywhere, like a field of ripe grain, ready to be won and to be saved.

Soon the woman came back to the well with many of her people. They asked Jē′ṣus to come to their town and to stay there and teach them. He went with them and stayed there two days, teaching the people, who were Sȧ-măr′ĭ-tanṣ. And many of the people in that place believed in Jē′ṣus and said, "We have heard for ourselves; now we know that this is indeed the Saviour of the world."

Story Nine   JOHN 4 : 46-54; LUKE 4 : 16-31

The Story of a Boy in Capernaum and of a Riot in Nazareth

FROM Sȳ′chär, the village near Jā′cob's well, Jē′ṣus went northward into Găl′ĭ-lee, to Cā′nȧ, the place where he had made the water into wine. The news that Jē′ṣus had come back from Jĕ-ru̇′sȧ-lĕm and was again in Găl′ĭ-lee, went through all that part of the land, and everybody wished to see the prophet who had wrought such wonders.

There was one man living in Cȧ-pẽr′na-ŭm, a town beside the Sea of Găl′ĭ-lee, who heard with great joy that Jē′ṣus was again at Cā′nȧ. He was a man of high rank, a nobleman at the court of King Hĕr′od; but he was in deep trouble over his son, who was very sick and in danger of dying. This nobleman went up the

mountains in great haste from Că-pẽr'na-ŭm to Cā'nà, to see
Jē'ṣus. He rode all night, and in the morning, when he found
Jē'ṣus, he begged him to come down to Că-pẽr'na-ŭm and cure
his son. Jē'ṣus said to the man, "You people will not believe on
me as the Saviour unless you continually see signs and wonders."

"O my lord," said the father, "do come down quickly or my
child will die."

"You may go home," said Jē'ṣus, "for your son will live."

The man believed the words of Jē'ṣus and went home, but he
did not hurry nor did he ask Jē'ṣus to go with him. The next
morning, as he was going down the mountains, his servants met
him and said, "My lord, your son is living and is better."

"At what hour did he begin to grow better?" asked the
nobleman.

"It was yesterday, at seven o'clock in the morning, when the
fever left him," they answered.

That was the very hour when Jē'ṣus had said to him, "Your son
will live." And after that the nobleman believed in Jē'ṣus, and
so did all who were living in his house.

Jē'ṣus had come to Găl'ĭ-lee to preach to the people and to tell
them of his gospel. He thought that he would begin his preaching
in the town of Năz'a-rĕth, where he had lived so many years,
where his brothers and sisters were living still, and where all the
people had known him. He loved the men who had played with
him when he and they were boys together, and he longed to give
them the first news of his gospel.

So Jē'ṣus went to Năz'a-rĕth; and, as on the Sabbath days he
had always worshiped in the synagogue-church, he went to that
place once more. He was no longer the carpenter, but the
teacher, the prophet, of whom everyone was talking, and the
church was filled with people eager to hear him and especially
hoping to see him do some wonderful works. Seated on the floor
before him were men who had known him since he was a little
boy, and perhaps some of his own sisters were looking down from
the gallery behind the lattice screen.

Jē'ṣus stood up, to show that he wished to read from the Scriptures, and the officer who had the care of the books handed him

the roll of the prophet Ī-ṣā'iah. Jē'ṣus turned to the sixty-first chapter and from it read:

"The Spirit of the Lord is upon me,
Because he hath anointed me to preach good tidings to the poor.
He hath sent me to proclaim freedom to the captives,
And recovering of sight to the blind,
To set at liberty those that are bruised,
To proclaim the year of God's grace to men."

When Jē'ṣus had read these words, he rolled up the book and gave it again to the keeper of the rolls, and sat down; for in the synagogue a man stood up to read the Bible and sat down to speak to the people. He began by saying:

"This day this word of the Lord has come to pass before you."

And then he showed how he had been sent to preach to the poor, to set the captives free, to give sight to the blind, to comfort those in trouble, and to tell to men the news of God's grace. At first the people listened with the deepest interest, and they were touched by the kind and tender words that he spoke.

But soon they began to whisper among themselves. One said, "Why should this carpenter try to teach us?" And another, "This man is no teacher! He is only the son of Jō'ṣeph! We know his brothers, and his sisters are living here." And some began to say, "Why does he not do here the wonders that they say he has done in other places? We want to see some of his miracles!"

Jē'ṣus knew their thoughts and he said, "I know that you will say to me, 'Let us see a miracle like that on the nobleman's son in Că-pēr'na-ŭm.' Of a truth, I say to you, 'No prophet has honor among his own people.'

"You remember what is told of Ê-lī'jah the prophet, when the heavens were shut up and there was no rain for three years and six months. There were many poor widows in the land of Ĭṣ'ra-el at that time, but Ê-lī'jah was not sent by the Lord to any one of them. The Lord sent him out of the land to Zăr'e-phăth, a town near Zī'dŏn, to a widow who lived there; and there he wrought his miracles.

"And in the time of Ê-lī'shȧ the prophet, there were many

lepers in Ĭṣ'ra-el that Ê-lī'shȧ might have cured; but the only lepe
that Ê-lī'shȧ made well was Nā'a-man the Sȳr'ĭ-an."

All this made the people in the church very angry; for they
cared only to see some wonderful work and not to hear the word
of Jē'ṣus. They would not listen to him; they leaped up from
their seats upon the floor; they laid hold of Jē'ṣus and dragged him

outdoors. They then took him up to the top of the hill above the
city, and they would have thrown him down to his death. But
Jē'ṣus, by the power of God, slipped quietly out of their hands
and went away, for the time for him to die had not yet come.

Very sadly Jē'ṣus went away from Năz'a-rĕth, for he had
longed to bring God's blessings to his own people. He walked
down the mountains to the city of Că-pĕr'na-ŭm, by the seashore;
there on Sabbath days he taught the people in the church.

You can read the story of Ê-lī'jah the prophet and the woman
of Zăr'e-phăth, and the story of Ê-lī'shȧ healing Nā'a-man the
Sȳr'ĭ-an. These were the stories of which Jē'ṣus spoke to the
people in the synagogue at Năz'a-rĕth.

The Baby Jesus was laid in a manger (p. 438)

Mary felt that her Son was no common child (p. 446)

Jesus began teaching the people by parables (p. 482)

Jesus said, "I am the Good Shepherd" (p. 515)

Jesus loved the little children (p. 530)

Zacchaeus tried to see Jesus (p. 533)

The Samaritan woman came back with many of her friends (p. 461)

The meal was spread upon a table (p. 547)

Jesus and Mary Magdalene (p. 567)

Peter and John looked into the Tomb (p. 566)

Jesus told the story of the Ten Young Women (p. 544)

Peter and John Before the Sanhedrin (p. 581)

The light blinded Saul's eyes (p. 594)

Barnabas went to Tarsus to find Saul (p. 607)

They came safe to shore (p. 645)

Paul loved Timothy (p. 649)

A Net Full of Fishes

WHEN Jē′ṣus was by the river Jôr′dan, a few young men came to him as followers, or disciples. We have read of these men—Ăn′drew and Jŏhn, Pē′tẽr and Phĭl′ĭp, and Nȧ-thăn′a-el. While Jē′ṣus was teaching near Jḗ-ru′sȧ-lĕm and in Sȧ-mā′rĭ-ȧ, these men stayed with Jē′ṣus; but when he came to Găl′ĭ-lee, they went again to their homes and their work, for most of them were fishermen from the Sea of Găl′ĭ-lee.

One morning, soon after Jē′ṣus came to Cȧ-pẽr′na-ŭm, he went out of the city, by the sea, followed by a great throng of people. On the shore were lying two fishing boats, one of which belonged to Sī′mon and Ăn′drew, the other to Jāmeṣ and Jŏhn and their father Zĕb′e-dee. The men themselves were not in the boats, but were washing their nets near by.

Jē′ṣus stepped into the boat that belonged to Sī′mon Pē′tẽr and his brother Ăn′drew, and asked them to push it out a little into the lake, so that he could talk to the people from it without being crowded too closely. They pushed it out; and then Jē′ṣus sat in the boat and spoke to the people as they stood upon the beach. After he had finished speaking to the people and had sent them away, he said to Sī′mon Pē′tẽr:

"Put out into the deep water and let down your nets."

"Master," said Sī′mon, "we have fished all night and have caught nothing; but if you wish, I will let down the net again."

They did as Jē′ṣus bade them; and now the net caught so many fishes that Sī′mon and Ăn′drew could not pull it up, and it was in danger of breaking. They made signs to the two brothers, Jāmeṣ and Jŏhn, who were in the other boat, for them to come and help them. They came and lifted the net, and poured out the fish. There were so many of them that both the boats were filled and began to sink.

When Sī′mon Pē′tẽr saw this, he was struck with wonder and

465

felt that it was by the power of God. He fell down at the feet of Jē'ṣus, saying, "O Lord, I am full of sin and am not worthy of all this! Leave me, O Lord."

But Jē'ṣus said to Sī'mon, and to the others, "Fear not; but follow me and I will make you from this time fishers of men."

From that time these four men, Sī'mon and Ăn'drew, Jāmeṣ and Jŏhn, gave up their nets and their work and walked with Jē'ṣus as his disciples.

On the Sabbath after this Jē'ṣus and his disciples went together to the synagogue or church and spoke to the people. They listened to him and were surprised at his teaching; for while the scribes always repeated what other scribes had said before, Jē'ṣus never spoke of what the men of old time had taught; but spoke in his own name and by his own power, saying, "I say unto you," as one who had the right to speak. Men felt that Jē'ṣus was speaking to them as the voice of God.

On one Sabbath, while Jē'ṣus was preaching, a man came into the synagogue, who had in him an evil spirit; for sometimes evil spirits came into men and lived in them, and spoke out from them The evil spirit in this man cried out, saying:

"Let us alone, thou Jē'ṣus of Năz'a-rĕth! What have we to do with thee? Hast thou come to destroy us? I know thee; and I know who thou art, the Holy One of God!" Then Jē'ṣus spoke to the evil spirit in the man, "Be still; and come out of this man!"

Then the evil spirit threw the man down and seemed as if he

would tear him apart; but he came out and left the man lying on the ground, without harm.

Then wonder fell upon all the people. They were filled with fear and said, "What mighty word is this? This man speaks even to the evil spirits, and they obey him!"

After the meeting in the synagogue Jē'ṣus went into the house where Sī'mon Pē'tēr lived. There he saw lying upon a bed the mother of Sī'mon's wife, who was very ill with a burning fever. He stood over her and touched her hand. At once the fever left her, and she rose up from her bed and waited upon them.

At sunset the Sabbath Day was over; and then they brought to Jē'ṣus from all parts of the city those who were sick and some who had evil spirits in them. Jē'ṣus laid his hands upon the sick and they became well; he drove out the evil spirits by a word and would not allow them to speak.

Story Eleven
MATTHEW 8 : 2-4; 9 : 2-8; MARK 1 : 40-45; 2 : 1-12; LUKE 5 : 12-26

A Leper, and the Man Let Down Through the Roof

AFTER the great day of teaching and healing, of which we read in the last story, Jē'ṣus lay down to rest in the house of Sī'mon Pē'tēr. But very early the next morning, before it was light, he rose up and went out of the house to a place where he could be alone, and there for a long time he prayed to God. Soon Sī'mon and the other disciples missed him and sought for him until they found him. They said, "Everybody is looking for you; come back to the city."

But Jē'ṣus said, "No, I cannot stay in Cȧ-pēr'na-ŭm. There are other places where I must preach the kingdom of God, for this is the work to which I am sent."

And Jē′ṣus went out through all the towns in that part of Găl′ĭ-lee, preaching in the churches, and curing all kinds of sickness and casting out the evil spirits. His disciples were with him, and great crowds followed him from all the land. They came to hear his wonderful words and to see his wonderful works.

While he was on this journey of preaching in Găl′ĭ-lee, a leper came to him. You remember from the story of Nā′a-man the Sўr′ĭ-an, what a terrible disease leprosy was, and still is, in those lands, and that no man could cure the leper.

This poor leper fell down before the feet of Jē′ṣus and cried out, "O Lord, if you are willing, I know that you can make me well and clean!" Jē′ṣus was full of pity for this poor man. He reached out his hand and touched him and said, "I am willing; be clean!" And in a moment all the scales of leprosy fell away, his skin became pure, and the leper stood up a well man. Jē′ṣus said to him, "Tell no one, but go to the priests, and offer the gift that the law commands, and let them see that you have been cured."

Jē′ṣus said this because he knew that if the man should tell everyone whom he met how he had been cured, such crowds would come to him for healing that he would find no time for preaching the word of God; and preaching God's word and not healing the sick was the great work of Jē′ṣus.

But this leper who had been healed did not obey the command of Jē′ṣus. He could not keep still, and told everybody whom he knew that Jē′ṣus, the great prophet, had taken away his leprosy. And it came to pass as Jē′ṣus had expected; such great crowds gathered in all the towns and villages to see Jē′ṣus and to ask him to heal their sick, that Jē′ṣus could not enter the cities to preach the gospel. He went out to the fields and the open country, and there the people followed him in great throngs.

After a time Jē′ṣus came again to Că-pēr′na-ŭm, which was now his home. As soon as the people heard that he was there, they came in great crowds to see him and to hear him. They filled the house and the court yard inside its walls and even the streets around it, while Jē′ṣus sat in the open court of the house and taught them. It was the springtime and warm, and a roof had been placed over the court as a shelter from the sun.

In the crowd listening to Jē′ṣus were not only his friends, but some that were his enemies, Phăr′ĭ-seeṣ, men making a great show of serving God, but wicked in their hearts, and scribes who taught the law, but were jealous of this new teacher, whose words were so far above theirs. These men were watching to find some evil in Jē′ṣus, so that they might lead the people away from him.

While Jē′ṣus was teaching and these men were listening, the roof was suddenly taken away above their heads. They looked up and saw that a man was being let down in a bed by four men on the walls above.

This man had a sickness called palsy, which made his limbs shake all the time and kept him helpless, so that he could neither walk nor stand. He was so eager to come to Jē′ṣus that these men, finding that they could not carry him through the crowd, had lifted him up to the top of the house and had opened the roof, and were now letting him down in his bed before Jē′ṣus.

This showed that they believed in Jē′ṣus, without any doubt whether he could cure this man of his palsy. Jē′ṣus said to the man, "My son, be of good cheer; your sins are forgiven!"

The enemies of Jē′ṣus who were sitting near heard these words, and they thought in their own minds, though they did not speak it aloud, "What wicked things this man speaks! He claims to forgive sins! Who except God himself has power to say, 'Your sins are forgiven'?"

Jē′ṣus knew their thought, for he knew all things, and he said, "Why do you think evil in your hearts? Which is the easier to say, 'Your sins are forgiven,' or to say, 'Rise up and walk?' But I will show you that while I am on earth as the Son of man, I have the power to forgive sins."

Then he spoke to the palsied man on his couch before them, "Rise up, take up your bed, and go to your house!"

At once a new life and power came to the palsied man. He stood upon his feet, rolled up the bed on which he had been lying helpless, placed it on his shoulders, and walked out through the crowd, which opened to make way for him. The man went, strong and well, to his own house, praising God as he walked.

By this Jē'ṣus had shown that, as the Son of God, he had the right to forgive the sins of men.

These enemies of Jē'ṣus could say nothing, but in their hearts they hated him more than ever, for they saw that the people believed on Jē'ṣus. They praised the Lord God and felt a holy fear toward one who could do such mighty works, and they said, "We have seen strange things today!"

Story Twelve
MATTHEW 12 : 1-14; MARK 2: 23 to 3 : 6;
LUKE 6 : 1-11; JOHN 5 : 1-18

The Cripple at the Pool, and the Withered Hand in the Synagogue

WHILE Jē'ṣus was living in Că-pẽr'na-ŭm, the time for the Passover of the Jews drew near, and Jē'ṣus went up to Jē-ru'sȧ-lĕm to keep the feast, as he had kept it a year before. You remember that at that time he drove out of the Temple the people that were buying and selling. The feast which Jē'ṣus now kept was the second Passover in the three years while Jē'ṣus was preaching.

While Jē'ṣus was at Jē-ru'sȧ-lĕm, he saw in the city, not far from the Temple, a pool called Bě-thĕṣ'da. Beside this pool were five arches or porches; and in these porches were lying a great crowd of sick and blind, helpless and crippled people. At certain times the water rose and bubbled up in the pool; and at these "troublings of the waters," the spring had power to cure diseases. We know that there are springs of water that will cure many kinds of sickness, and this may have been one of these, and its power to heal is ascribed to an angel.

On the Sabbath Day Jē'ṣus walked among these poor, helpless, and suffering people, who were waiting for the water to rise.

Jē'ṣus looked at one man, and though no one told him, he knew that this man had been a cripple, without power to walk, for almost forty years. He said to this man, "Do you wish to be made well?"

The man did not know who Jē'ṣus was. He answered, "Sir, I cannot walk; and I have no man to carry me down to the water when it rises in the pool; but while I am trying to crawl down, others crowd in before me, and the place is full, so that I cannot reach the water and be cured."

Jē'ṣus said to the man, "Rise, take up your mat and walk!"

The cripple had never heard words like these before; but as they were spoken, he felt a new power shoot through his limbs. He rose up, took the piece of matting on which he had been lying, rolled it up, and walked away toward his home!

Someone who saw him said, "Stop; this is the Sabbath Day and it is against the law for you to carry your mat!"

The man did not lay down his load. He only said, "The one who made me well said to me, 'Take up your mat and walk.'"

The Jews said, "Who was this man that told you to carry your mat on the Sabbath Day?"

The man who had been cured did not know who it was that had cured him; for there were many standing near, and Jē'ṣus, after healing the man, had walked away without being noticed. But after this Jē'ṣus met this man in the Temple and said to him, "You have been made well; do not sin against God any more, or something worse than disease will come upon you."

The man went away from the Temple and told the Jews that it was Jḗ'ṣus who had made him well. The Jews were very angry at Jḗ'ṣus because he had cured this man on the Sabbath. But Jḗ'ṣus said to them, "My Father works on all days to do good to men, and I work also."

These words made the Jews ready to kill Jḗ'ṣus, not only because, as they said, he had broken the Sabbath, but because he had spoken of God as his Father, as though he were the Son of God. He was indeed the Son of God, although they would not believe it.

After the feast of the Passover, Jḗ'ṣus went again to Cȧ-pḗr'na-ŭm in Găl'ĭ-lee, beside the lake. One Sabbath Day he was walking with his disciples through the fields of ripe grain; and the disciples, as they walked, picked the heads of grain, rubbed them in their hands, blew away the chaff, and ate the kernels of wheat. The law of the Jews allowed anyone walking through the fields to eat what he could gather with his hands, though it did not allow him to take any of the grain home. But the Phăr'ĭ-sees, whose goodness was all for show, said that it was a breaking of the Sabbath to pick the ears and to rub them in the hands on the Sabbath Day. They said to Jḗ'ṣus, "Do you see how your disciples are doing on the Sabbath what is against the law?"

Jḗ'ṣus answered them, "Have you never read what Dā'vid did when he was hungry? He went into the house of God, and took the holy bread from the table, and ate some of it, and gave some to his men, though the law said that only the priests might eat this bread. And do you not know that on the Sabbath Day the priests in the Temple do work, in killing and offering the sacrifices, yet they do no wrong? I say to you that one greater than the Temple is here; for the Son of man is lord of the Sabbath."

Jḗ'ṣus meant them to understand that he was the Son of God, that God lived in him even more fully than he lived in the Temple, and that he spoke as Lord of all.

We have read this about Dā'vid and the holy bread in the Tabernacle, of which Jḗ'ṣus spoke, in Story Seven, Part Third.

On another Sabbath Day Jḗ'ṣus went to the synagogue-church. A man was there whose hand was withered. The Phăr'ĭ-sees watched Jē'ṣus to see whether on the Sabbath Day he would make his hand well. Not that they felt for the poor man; they only wished the chance to speak evil against Jē'ṣus. Jē'ṣus knew all their thoughts, and he spoke to the man, "Rise up, and stand where all can see you!"

The man rose up from the mat where he had been sitting and stood before all the people. Then Jē'ṣus looked around upon them sternly, being sad because their hearts were so hard and cruel, and he said, "Is it against the law to do good on the Sabbath Day or to do evil? to heal a man or to try and kill a man, as you are doing? If any one of you owns a sheep, and it falls into a pit on the Sabbath Day, will he not take hold of it and lift it out? Is not a man worth more than a sheep? I say unto you that it is right to do good to men on the Sabbath Day."

And then, turning to the man, he said, "Stretch out your hand!"

The man obeyed the word of Jē'ṣus and held out his hand. At once it became strong and well, like his other hand. Many of the people were glad as they saw this; but the Phăr'ĭ-seeṣ, who hated Jē'ṣus, went out very angry; and they met together to find some plan for putting Jē'ṣus to death.

Story Thirteen   MATTHEW 9 : 9-13; chapters 5 to 8; MARK 2 : 13-17; LUKE 5 : 27-32; 6 : 12-49

The Twelve Disciples and the Sermon on the Mount

AMONG the Jewṣ there was one class of men hated and despised by the people more than any other. That was "the publicans or tax collectors." These were the men who took from the people the tax which the Rō'man rulers had laid upon the land. Many of these publicans were selfish, grasping, and cruel. They robbed the people, taking more than was right. Some of them were

honest men, dealing fairly, and taking no more for the tax than
was needful; but because so many were wicked, all the publicans
were hated alike; and they were called "sinners" by the people.

One day, when Jē'ṣus was going out of Că-pēr'na-ŭm to the
seaside, followed by a great crowd of people, he passed a publican
or taxgatherer, who was seated at his table taking money from the
people who came to pay their taxes. This man was named
Măt'thew or Lē'vī, for many Jews had two names. Jē'ṣus could
look into the hearts of men, and he saw that Măt'thew was one
who might help him as one of his disciples. He looked upon
Măt'thew and said, "Follow me!"

At once the publican rose up from his table and left it to go
with Jē'ṣus. All the people wondered as they saw one of the
hated taxgatherers among the disciples, with Pē'tēr and Jŏhn and
the rest. But Jē'ṣus knew that Măt'thew would long afterward
do a work that would bless the world forever. It was this same
Măt'thew, the publican, who many years after this wrote "The
Gospel According to Măt'thew," the book which tells us so
much about Jē'ṣus, and more than any other book gives us the
words that Jē'ṣus spoke to the people. Jē'ṣus chose Măt'thew,
knowing that he would write this book. A little while after Jē'ṣus
called him, Măt'thew made a great feast for Jē'ṣus at his house;
and to the feast he invited many tax collectors and others whom
the Jews called sinners. The Phăr'ĭ-sees saw Jē'ṣus sitting among
these people and they said with scorn to his disciples, "Why does
your Master sit at the table with tax collectors and other sinners?"

Jē'ṣus heard of what these men had said and he said, "Those
that are well do not need a doctor to cure them, but those that are
sick do need one. I go to these people because they know that
they are sinners and need to be saved. I came not to call those
who think themselves to be good, but those who wish to be made
better."

One evening Jē'ṣus went alone to a mountain not far from Că-
pēr'na-ŭm. A crowd of people and his disciples followed him;
but Jē'ṣus left them all and went up to the top of the mountain,
where he could be alone. There he stayed all night, praying to
God, his Father and our Father. In the morning, out of all his

followers, he chose twelve men who should walk with him and listen to his words, so that they might be able to teach others in turn. Some of these men he had called before; but now he called them again, and others with them. They were called "The Twelve," or "the disciples"; and after Jē'ṣus went to heaven, they were called "The Apostles," a word which means "those who were sent out," because Jē'ṣus sent them out to preach the gospel to the world.

The names of the twelve disciples, or apostles, were these: Sī'mon Pē'tēr and his brother Ăn'drew; Jāmeṣ and Jŏhn, the two sons of Zĕb'e-dee; Phĭl'ĭp of Bĕth-sā'ĭ-dà and Nȧ-thăn'a-el, who was also called Bär-thŏl'o-mew, a name which means "The Son of Thŏl-mai"; Thŏm'as, who was also called Dĭd'ȳ-mŭs, a name which means "A Twin," and Măt'thew, the publican or taxgatherer; another Jāmeṣ, the son of Al-phæ'us, who was called "Jāmeṣ the Less," to keep his name apart from the first Jāmeṣ, the brother of Jŏhn, and Lĕb-be'us, who was also called Thăd'de-us. Lĕb-be'us was also called Jū'das, but he was a different man from another Jū'das, whose name is always given last. The eleventh name was another Sī'mon, who was called "the Cā'nȧan-īte," or "Sī'mon

Zĕ-lō'tēṣ"; and the last name was Jū'das Ĭs-cắr'ĭ-ot, who was afterward the traitor. We know very little about most of these men, but some of them in later days did a great work. Sĭ'mon Pē'tēr was a leader among them; and Jŏhn, long after those times, when he was a very old man, wrote one of the most wonderful books in all the world, "The Gospel According to Jŏhn," the fourth among the Gospels.

In the sight of all the people who had come to hear Jē'ṣus, Jē'ṣus called these twelve men to stand by his side. Then, on the mountain, he preached to these disciples and to the great company of people. Jē'ṣus sat down, the disciples stood beside him, and the great crowd of people stood in front, while Jē'ṣus spoke. What he said on that day is called "The Sermon on the Mount." Mắt'thew wrote it down, and you can read it in his Gospel, in the fifth, sixth, and seventh chapters. Jē'ṣus began with these words to his disciples:

Blessed are the poor in spirit: for theirs is the kingdom of heaven.

Blessed are they that mourn: for they shall be comforted.

Blessed are the meek: for they shall inherit the earth.

Blessed are they which do hunger and thirst after righteousness: for they shall be filled.

Blessed are the merciful: for they shall obtain mercy.

Blessed are the pure in heart: for they shall see God.

Blessed are the peacemakers: for they shall be called the children of God.

Blessed are they which are persecuted for righteousness' sake: for theirs is the kingdom of heaven.

Blessed are ye, when men shall revile you, and persecute you, and shall say all manner of evil against you falsely, for my sake.

Rejoice, and be exceeding glad; for great is your reward in heaven: for so persecuted they the prophets which were before you.

Ye are the salt of the earth: but if the salt have lost his savor, wherewith shall it be salted? it is thenceforth good for nothing, but to be cast out, and to be trodden under foot of men.

Ye are the light of the world. A city that is set on an hill cannot be hid.

Neither do men light a candle, and put it under a bushel, but on a candlestick; and it giveth light unto all that are in the house.

Let your light so shine before men, that they may see your good works, and glorify your Father which is in heaven.

Here are some more of the words of Jē'ṣus in this sermon:

I say unto you, Do not be anxious for your life what ye shall eat, or what ye shall drink; nor yet for your body, what ye shall put on. Is not the life more than food, and the body than clothing?

Behold the birds of the air: for they sow not, neither do they reap, nor gather into barns; yet your heavenly Father feedeth them. Are ye not much better than they?

Which of you, by taking thought, can add one foot unto his stature?

And why take ye thought for clothing? Consider the lilies of the field, how they grow: they toil not, neither do they spin:

And yet I say unto you, That even Sŏl'o-mon in all his glory was not arrayed like one of these.

Wherefore, if God so clothe the grass of the field, which today is, and tomorrow is burned in the oven, shall he not much more clothe you, O ye of little faith?

Therefore take no thought, saying, What shall we eat? or, What shall we drink? or, Wherewithal shall we be clothed?

(For after all these things do the people of the world seek:) for your heavenly Father knoweth that ye have need of all these things.

But seek ye first the kingdom of God, and his righteousness; and all these things shall be added unto you.

Take therefore no anxious thought for the morrow: for the morrow shall take thought for the things of itself.

This is what Jē'ṣus said about prayer to our Heavenly Father:

Ask, and it shall be given you; seek, and ye shall find: knock, and it shall be opened unto you:

For every one that asketh receiveth; and he that seeketh findeth: and to him that knocketh it shall be opened.

Or what man is there of you, whom if his son ask bread, will he give him a stone?

Or if he ask a fish, will he give him a serpent?

If ye then, being evil, know how to give good gifts unto your children, how much more shall your Father which is in heaven give good things to them that ask him!

Therefore all things whatsoever ye would that men should do to you, do ye even so to them: for this is the law and the prophets.

And this was the end of the sermon:

Therefore, whosoever heareth these sayings of mine, and doeth them, I will liken him unto a wise man, which built his house upon a rock:

And the rain descended, and the floods came, and the winds blew, and beat upon that house: and it fell not: for it was founded upon a rock.

And every one that heareth these sayings of mine, and doeth them not, shall be likened unto a foolish man, which built his house upon the sand:

And the rain descended, and the floods came, and the winds blew, and beat upon that house; and it fell: and great was the fall of it.

Story Fourteen

The Captain's Servant, the Widow's Son, and the Woman Who Was a Sinner

THERE was at Că-pĕr'na-ŭm an officer of the Rō'man army, a man who had under him a company of a hundred men. They called him "a centurion," a word which means "having a hundred," but we should call him "a captain." This man was not a Jew, but was what the Jews called "a Gĕn'tile," "a foreigner," a name which the Jews gave to all people outside of their own race. All the world, except the Jews themselves, were Gĕn'tiles.

This Rō'man centurion was a good man, and he loved the Jews, because through them he had heard of God, and had learned how to worship God. Out of his love for the Jews he had built for them, with his own money, a synagogue or church, which may have been the very synagogue in which Jē'ṣus taught on the Sabbath days.

The centurion had a young servant, a boy, whom he loved greatly; and this boy was very sick with a palsy and near to death. The centurion had heard that Jē'ṣus could cure those who were sick; and he asked the chief men of the synagogue, who were called its "elders," to go to Jē'ṣus and ask him to come and cure his young servant.

The elders spoke to Jē'ṣus just as he came again to Cȧ-pēr'-na-ŭm, after the Sermon on the Mount. They asked Jē'ṣus to go with them to the centurion's house; and they said, "He is a worthy man, and it is fitting that you should help him, for though a Gĕn'-tile, he loves our people, and he has built us our church."

Then Jē'ṣus said, "I will go and heal him."

But while he was on his way, and with him were the elders and his disciples and a great crowd of people, who hoped to see the work of healing, the centurion sent some other friends to Jē'ṣus with this message:

"Lord, do not take the trouble to come to my house; for I am not worthy that one so high as thou art should come under my roof; and I did not think that I was worthy to go and speak to thee. But speak only a word where you are, and my servant shall be made well. For I also am a man under rule, and I have soldiers under me, and I say to one, 'Go,' and he goes; and to another, 'Come,' and he comes; and to my servant, 'Do this,' and he does it. You, too, have power to speak and to be obeyed. Speak the word, and my servant will be cured."

When Jē'ṣus heard this, he wondered at this man's faith. He turned to the people following him, and said, "In truth I say to you, I have not found such faith as this in all Iṣ'ra-el!"

Then he spoke to the friends of the centurion who had brought word from him: "Go and say to this man, As you have believed in me, so shall it be done to you."

Then those who had been sent went again to the centurion's house and found that in that very hour his servant had been made perfectly well.

On the day after this, Jē'ṣus, with his disciples and many people, went out from Cȧ-pēr'na-ŭm and turned southward, and came to a city called Nā'in. Just as Jē'ṣus and his disciples came near to the gate of the city, they were met by a company who were carrying out the body of a dead man to be buried. He was a young man, and the only son of his mother, and she was a widow. All the people felt sad for this woman who had lost her only son.

When the Lord Jē'ṣus saw the mother in her grief, he pitied
her, and said, "Do not weep."

He drew near and touched the frame on which they were carrying the body, wrapped round and round with long strips of linen.
The bearers looked with wonder on this stranger, and set down
the frame with its body, and stood still. Standing beside the body,
Jē'ṣus said, "Young man, I say to you, Rise up!"

And in a moment the young man sat up and began to speak.
Jē'ṣus gave him to his mother, who now saw that her son, who
had been dead, was alive again.

A great fear came upon all who had looked upon this wonderful work of Jē'ṣus. They praised God and said, "God has indeed
come to his people and has given us a great prophet!"

And the news that Jē'ṣus had raised a dead man to life again
went through all the land.

While Jē'ṣus was on this journey through southern Găl'ĭ-lee,
at one place a Phăr'ĭ-see, whose name was Sī'mon, asked Jē'ṣus to
come and dine at his house. This man did not believe in Jē'ṣus,
but he wanted to watch him, and, if possible, to find some fault
in him. He did not show Jē'ṣus the respect due to a guest, did not
welcome him, nor did he bring water to wash Jē'ṣus' feet, as was

done to people when they came in from walking. For in that land they wore no shoes or stockings, but only sandals covering the soles of their feet; and they often washed their feet when they came into the house.

At meals they did not sit up around the table, but leaned on couches, with their heads toward the table and their feet away from it. While Jē'ṣus was leaning in this manner upon his couch at the table, a woman came into the dining room, bringing a flask of ointment, such as was used to anoint people of high rank. She knelt at Jē'ṣus' feet, weeping, and began to wet his feet with her tears and then to wipe them with her long hair. She anointed his feet with the ointment and kissed them over and over again.

This woman had not been a good woman. She had led a wicked life; but by her act she showed that in her heart she was truly sorry for her sins. When Sī'mon, the Phăr'ĭ-see, saw her at the Saviour's feet, he thought within himself, though he did not say it, "If this man were really a prophet coming from God, he would have known how wicked this woman is and he would not have allowed her to touch him."

Jē'ṣus knew this man's thought and he said, "Sī'mon, I have something to say to you."

And Sī'mon said, "Master, say on."

Then Jē'ṣus said, "There was a certain lender of money to whom two men were owing. One man owed him a hundred dollars and the other owed him ten. When he found that they could not pay their debts, he freely forgave them and let them both go free. Which of these two will love that man most?"

"Why," said Sī'mon, "I suppose that the one to whom he forgave the most will love him the most."

"You are right," said Jē'ṣus. Then he turned toward the woman and added, "Do you see this woman? I came into your house; you gave me no water for my feet, but she has wet my feet with her tears and has wiped them with her hair. You gave me no kiss of welcome, but she has not ceased to kiss my feet. You did not anoint my head even with oil, but she has anointed my feet with sweet-smelling ointment. You have acted as though you owed me little, and you have loved me little; but she feels that she owes me much and she loves me greatly. I say to you, 'Her sins, which are many, are forgiven.' "

Then he spoke to the woman, "Your sins are forgiven."

Those around the table whispered to each other, "Who is this man that dares to act as God and even to forgive sins?"

But Jē′şus said to the woman, "Your faith has saved you; go in peace!"

And Jē′şus went through all that part of Găl′ĭ-lee, preaching and teaching in all the villages, telling the people everywhere the good news of the kingdom of God.

Story Fifteen

MATTHEW 13 : 1-53; MARK 4 : 1-34;
LUKE 8 : 4-18

Some Stories That Jesus Told by the Sea

AFTER Jē′şus had journeyed through the southern parts of Găl′ĭ-lee, teaching and healing the sick, he came again to Că-pēr′na-ŭm; and one day went out of the city to a place where the beach rose up gently from the water. There he sat in Sī′mon Pē′tēr's boat, as he had sat before, and spoke to a great crowd of people who stood on the beach.

At this time Jē′şus began teaching the people by parables; that is, by stories which showed the truths of the gospel. Everybody liked to hear a story; and the story would often lead people to think and to find out the truth for themselves. The first of these parables or stories that Jē′şus gave was called "The Parable of the Sower."

"Listen to me," said Jē′şus. "A sower went out to sow his seed. And as he sowed, some seeds fell by the roadside, where the ground was hard, where some of the seed was trodden down, and other seeds were picked up by the birds. Some of the seed fell where the soil was thin, because rocks were under it. These seeds grew up quickly, but when the sun became hot, they were scorched and dried up, because they did not have enough soil and moisture for their roots. Other seeds fell among briers and thorns, and the thorns kept them from growing. And some seeds fell into good ground and brought forth fruit, thirty times as many as were sown, sixty times, and even a hundred times. Whoever has ears to hear this, let him hear!" When Jē'ṣus was alone with his disciples, they said to him, "Why do you speak to the people in parables? What does this parable about the man sowing his seed mean?"

And Jē'ṣus said to them, "To you it is given to know the deep things of the kingdom of God, because you seek to find them out. But to many these things are spoken in parables, for they hear the story, but do not try to find out what it means. They have eyes, but they do not see; and they have ears, but they do not hear. For they do not wish to understand with the heart, and turn to the Lord and have their sins forgiven them. But blessed are your eyes, for they see, and your ears, for they hear. Listen now to the meaning of the Parable of the Sower.

"The sower is the one who speaks the word of God; and the seed is the word which he speaks. The seed by the roadside are those who hear; but the evil one comes and snatches away the truth, so that they forget it. The seed on the rock are those who hear the word with joy, but have no root in themselves, and their goodness lasts only for a little time. That which is sown among the thorns are they who hear, but the cares of the world, and seeking after riches and the enjoyments of this life, crowd out the gospel from their lives, so that it does them but little good. But that which is sown on the good ground are they who take the word into an honest and good heart and keep it, and bring forth fruit in their lives."

Another parable or story given by Jē′ṣus to the people was "The Parable of the Tares":

"The kingdom of God is as a man sowing good seed in his field; but while people were asleep, his enemy came and sowed tares, or weeds, among the wheat, and then went away. When the shoots of grain began to have heads of wheat, then the weeds were seen among them. The servants of the farmer came to him and said, 'Sir, did you not sow good seed in your field? How did the weeds come into it?'

"He said to them, 'An enemy has done this.'

" 'Shall we go and pick out the weeds from among the wheat?' asked the servants.

" 'No,' answered the farmer, 'for while you are pulling up the weeds, you will also root up the wheat with them. Let both grow together until the harvest; and in the time of the harvest, I will say to the reapers, "Take out the weeds first and bind them in bundles to be burned; but gather the wheat into my barn." ' "

Another parable Jē′ṣus told was that of "The Mustard Seed." He said:

"The kingdom of heaven is like a grain of mustard seed, which a man took and sowed in his field. This is the smallest of all seeds; but it grows up to be almost a tree, so that the birds light upon its branches and rest under its shadow."

Another parable was "The Leaven, or Yeast":

"The kingdom of heaven is like leaven, or yeast, that a woman mixed with dough when she was making bread. It worked through all the dough and changed it into good, light bread."

These parables Jē′ṣus told to the people as he sat in the boat and the people stood on the shore. But he did not tell them what the parables meant, for he wished them to think out the meaning for themselves. Then he sent the people away and came back to the house in the city.   There his disciples said to him, "Tell us the meaning of the parable of the weeds growing in the field."

Jē′ṣus said to them, "The one who sows the good seed is the Son of man; the field is the world; the good seed are those who belong to the kingdom of God; but the tares, the weeds, are the children of the evil one; the enemy that sowed them is Sā′tan, the devil; and the reapers are the angels.   Just as the weeds are gathered and burned in the fire, so shall it be in the end of the world. The Son of man shall send out his angels, and they shall gather out of his kingdom all that do evil and cause harm, and shall cast them into a furnace of fire; there shall be weeping and gnashing of teeth. But the people of God in that day shall shine as the sun in the kingdom of their Father."

And in the house Jē′ṣus gave to his disciples some more parables for them to think upon.   He said:

"The kingdom of heaven is like treasure which a man found hidden in a field.   He was glad when he saw it, but hid it again; and then went home and sold all that he had and bought that field with the treasure in it.

"The kingdom of heaven is like a merchant who was seeking precious pearls.   This man found one pearl of great price.   He went and sold all that he had and bought the pearl.

"Once more: the kingdom of heaven is like a net that was cast into the sea and took in fish of all kinds.   When it was full, they drew the net to the shore.   Then they sat down and picked out the good fish.   The good fish they put away for safe-keeping, but the bad fish they threw away.   So shall it be at the end of the world. The angels shall come and shall place the wicked apart from the good and shall cast them into a furnace of fire; there shall be weeping and gnashing of teeth."

"Peace, Be Still"

WHEN the evening came, after teaching all day by the sea and in the house, Jē'ṣus saw that the crowds of people were still pressing around him, and there was no time for him to rest. Jē'ṣus said, "Let us go over to the other side of the lake, where we can be alone."

So they took Jē'ṣus into the boat and began to row across the Sea of Găl'ĭ-lee. Other little boats were with them, for many wished to go with Jē'ṣus. While they were rowing, Jē'ṣus fell asleep, resting on a cushion of the boat. Suddenly a storm arose and drove great waves of water into the boat, so that it was in danger of sinking, but Jē'ṣus slept on. The disciples were very much frightened because of the storm. And they awoke him, saying, "Master, Master, we are lost! Help us or we shall perish!"

Jē'ṣus awaked and rose up and looked out upon the sea. He said to the waves, "Peace, be still!"

And at once the wind ceased, the waves were quiet, and there was a great calm. Jē'ṣus said to his disciples, "Why are you afraid? How is it that you have so little faith in me?"

They all wondered at Jē'ṣus' power and said to each other. "Who is this man whom even the winds and the sea obey?"

They came to the land on the eastern side of the lake, which was sometimes called "the country of the Găd'a-rēneṣ," from the people who lived in the large city of Găd'a-ra, which was not far away, and sometimes "Dĕ-căp'o-lĭs," the name given to that part of the country. As they were landing, a man came running down to meet them. He was one of those poor men in whose body evil spirits were living. He would not stay in any house, but slept in the graveyard among the dead. Nor did he wear any clothes. They had often chained him, but he had broken loose from his chains, and no one was able to bind him.

When this man saw Jē'ṣus afar off, he ran toward him and fell

486

down on his face before him. Jē′ṣus saw what was the trouble
with this man, and he spoke to the evil spirit in him, "Come out
of this man, vile spirit of evil!"

The spirit within the man cried with a loud voice, "What have
I to do with thee, Jē′ṣus, thou Son of the Most High God? I call
upon thee in the name of the Lord, do not make me to suffer!"

Jē′ṣus saw that this man was troubled more even than most men
who had evil spirits in them. He said to the evil one, "What is
your name?"

And the spirit said, "My name is Legion, because there are
many of us." "A legion" was a name given to an army; and in
this man was a whole army of evil spirits. There was on the
mountainside a great drove of hogs feeding. The Jews were not
allowed to keep hogs nor to eat their flesh; and the evil spirits said
to Jē′ṣus, "If we must leave this man, will you let us go into the
drove of hogs?"

Jē′ṣus gave them leave; and the evil spirits went out of the man
and went into the hogs. The whole drove, two thousand in
number, became at once wild. They rushed down a steep place
on the mountain and into the sea, and were all drowned.

The men who kept the hogs ran into the city near by, and told
all the people how the man had been made well, and what had
come to the drove of hogs, how they had been drowned. The
people came out to meet Jē′ṣus, and they were full of fear. They
saw the man who had been filled with evil spirits, now sitting at
the feet of Jē′ṣus, no longer naked, but clothed and in his right
mind. But they did not think of what Jē′ṣus had done to this man;
they thought only of the hogs that they had lost; and they begged
Jē′ṣus to go away from their land.

Jē'ṣus turned away from these people and went again to the
boat on the shore; and then the man who had been set free from
the evil spirits pleaded with Jē'ṣus that he might go with him.
But Jē'ṣus would not take him into the boat. He said:

"Go home to your friends and tell them how the Lord has had
mercy on you and has done great things for you."

The man went home and then traveled up and down all through
that land, which was called Dĕ-căp'o-lĭs, and told the people
everywhere the great things that Jē'ṣus had done for him.

And Jē'ṣus went on board the boat and crossed over the lake,
and came again to his own city of Că-pēr'na-ŭm.

Story Seventeen   MATTHEW 9 : 18-38; chapter 10; MARK 4 : 22-43;
                   LUKE 8 : 41-56; 9 : 1-5

The Little Girl Who Was Raised to Life

WHEN Jē'ṣus and his disciples landed at Că-
pēr'na-ŭm, after their sail across the lake, they
found a crowd of people on the shore waiting
for them. And a man came forward from the
throng and fell down at the feet of Jē'ṣus. He
was one of the chief men in the synagogue, and his name was
Jå-ī'rus. He said:

"O Master, come to my house at once! My little daughter is
dying; but if you will come and lay your hands upon her, she
will live."

And Jē'ṣus went with Jå-ī'rus, and his disciples followed him,
and also many people, who thronged around Jē'ṣus. In the crowd
was a poor woman who had been ill for very many years from
a sore out of which her blood ran, so that she was very weak.
Many doctors had tried to help her, but they could not; and she
had spent all her money so that she was now very poor.

This woman had heard of Jē'ṣus, and she tried to come to him, but she could not reach him in the throng of people. She said to herself, "If I can touch only his garment, I know that the touch will make me well." And as Jē'ṣus passed by, she reached out her hand and touched the hem of his robe. At that instant she felt in her body that she was cured. Jē'ṣus himself felt her touch and, turning around, said, "Who touched me?"

Pē'tēr said to him, "Master, the crowd throngs around you and presses upon you. How can you ask, 'Who touched me?'"

But Jē'ṣus said, "Someone has touched me; for I feel that power has gone out from me."

And he looked around to see who it was. Then the woman came forward, fearing and trembling over what she had done. She fell down before Jē'ṣus and told how she had touched him and had been made well. But Jē'ṣus said to her, "Daughter, be of good comfort; your faith has made you well; rise up and go in peace."

And from that hour the woman was free from her disease. All this time, while Jē'ṣus was waiting, Jå-ï'rus, the father of the dying child, stood beside Jē'ṣus in great trouble, for he feared that his child would die before Jē'ṣus could come to his house. And at that moment someone came to him and said, "It is too late; your daughter is dead; you need not trouble the Master any more."

But Jē'ṣus said to him, "Do not be afraid; only believe, and she will yet be saved to you."

Soon they came to the house where Jå-ï'rus lived; and they could hear the people weeping and crying aloud. Jē'ṣus said to them, "Why do you make such a noise? The little girl is not dead, but only asleep."

Jē'ṣus meant by this that we need not be filled with sorrow when our friends die, for death is only a sleep for a time until God shall awake them. But they did not understand this; and they would not be comforted, for they knew that the child was dead.

Jē'ṣus would not allow any of the crowd of people to go into the room where the dead child was. He took with him three of his disciples, Pē'tēr, Jāmeṣ, and Jŏhn, and the father and mother of the child, and shut out all the rest of the people. On a couch was lying the dead body of a girl, twelve years old. Taking the hand of the child into his own, he said to her, "Little girl, rise up!"

And the life of the little girl came again. She opened her eyes and sat up. Jē'ṣus told them to give her something to eat; and he said to them, "Do not tell anyone how the little girl was brought to life."

Already the crowds following him were so great that he could not teach the people in the city; and if it became known that he could raise the dead to life, the throng and the press of the multitudes would be greater. His great work was to teach and to bring life to the souls of men, rather than to heal, or even to raise the dead.

And he went out once more among the villages of Găl'ĭ-lee, teaching in the synagogues and healing the sick people who were brought to him. He pitied the people, because there was no one to give them the gospel; and they were like sheep wandering and lost without a shepherd. He said to his disciples:

"The harvest truly is great, but the workers to gather the harvest are few. Pray to the Lord of the harvest, that he may send out reapers into these harvest fields."

And after this Jē′ṣus sent out his twelve disciples to different places to preach in his name to the people. He sent them forth n pairs, two of them together, so that they could help each other. And he gave them power to heal the sick and to cast out evil pirits from men. He said to them:

"Go to the lost sheep of the house of Ĭṣ′ra-el; and as you go, preach, saying, 'The kingdom of heaven is at hand.' Heal the ick, cleanse the lepers, raise the dead, cast out the evil spirits; reely you have received, freely give. Do not take any money vith you; but at every place ask for some good man, and stay at nis house.

"And if any people will not listen to your words, when you go out of that house or out of that city, shake off the dust from your andals, as a sign; and God will judge that house or that city.

"He that hears you, hears me; and he that hears me, hears him who sent me. And if anyone will give one of these little ones a cup of cold water only, in the name of a disciple, he shall not lose nis reward."

The twelve disciples went out in pairs, as Jē′ṣus had commanded them, and preached in all the cities of Găl′ĭ-lee.

Story Eighteen

MATTHEW 11 : 2-19; 14 : 1-12; MARK 6 : 14-29; LUKE 7 : 18-35

A Dancing Girl, and What Was Given Her

YOU REMEMBER that just before Jē′ṣus went from Jĕ-ru′ṣà-lĕm to Găl′ĭ-lee, Jŏhn the Băp′tĭst was put in prison by the king, Hĕr′od Ăn′tĭ-păs. Jē′ṣus stayed in Găl′ĭ-lee for a year, and nearly all the time Jŏhn the Băp′tĭst was alone in his prison near the Dead Sea. His followers, who were now very few, came to see him and told him of the works that Jē′ṣus was doing. These were wonderful, but they were not what Jŏhn had expected Jē'ṣus to do; and in his prison, with no one to explain what Jē'ṣus was saying and doing, Jŏhn began to doubt a little whether Jē'ṣus was the Saviour whc had been promised so long. Then, too, Jŏhn's followers were inclined to feel jealous, because their master was now left alone, and all the people were seeking Jē'ṣus. Jŏhn sent two of his followers to Jē'ṣus, to ask him this question, "Are you really the Saviour who is to come, or are we to look for some other as the promised Chrīst?"

When these men came with this message from Jŏhn the Băp'-tĭst, they found Jē'ṣus in the midst of a great company of suffering people. They saw him making the sick well by his touch, giving sight to the blind, and casting out the evil spirits; and they listened to the words of Jē'ṣus as he taught the people.

When his work for the time was done, Jē'ṣus turned to the men who had come from Jŏhn and said to them, "Go and tell Jŏhn what you have seen and heard, how the blind see, the lame walk, the lepers are made clean, the deaf hear, the dead are raised to life, and the poor have good news preached to them. And blessed is that man who believes in me without doubting."

After these men had gone to bear the words of Jē'ṣus to Jŏhn, Jē'ṣus spoke to the people about Jŏhn the Băp'tĭst. He said:

"What was it that you went out into the wilderness to see? Was it a reed shaken by the wind? Was it a man dressed in rich robes? Those who are clad in splendid garments and sit at feasts are in the houses of kings. Who was the man whom you went out to see? Was he a prophet of God? I tell you that he was a prophet and more than a prophet; for he was the one who came to make men ready for the coming of the King. And I say to you, that among those who are born on the earth, there has never arisen a greater man than Jŏhn the Băp'tĭst. Yet he who is the least in the kingdom of God is greater than Jŏhn; for he can see with his own eyes what Jŏhn can only hear of from others, the works of the gospel."

All the common people who heard this were glad, for they believed that Jŏhn was a prophet, and they had been baptized by him. But the Phăr'ĭ-seeṣ and the rulers were not pleased, because they had refused to listen to Jŏhn the Băp'tĭst or to be baptized by him.

Not long after this the end came to the noble life of Jŏhn the Băp'tĭst. A great feast was held on King Hĕr'od's birthday, and all the princes and nobles of his kingdom were in the palace, eating and drinking together. While they were making merry, the young daughter of the woman Hĕ-rō'dĭ-as, who lived with Hĕr'od as his wife, came into the supper room and danced before the guests.

Hĕr'od was so greatly pleased with her dancing that he said to her, "Ask whatever you please, and I will give it to you."

He swore a solemn oath that he would give her whatever she might ask, even to the half of his kingdom. The girl went to her mother and said to her, "Tell me, what shall I ask?"

Her mother told her what to ask, and she came back with haste to the king and said, "I will ask that you give me here upon a platter the head of Jŏhn the Băp'tĭst!"

The king was very sorry that he had made the promise, but he was ashamed to break his word in the presence of his princes. He sent a man to the prison with orders that the head of Jŏhn the Băp'tĭst should be cut off and brought. It was done; and the young girl took it upon a platter and gave it to her mother, Hĕ-rō'dĭ-as.

So, as Hĕr'od's father, thirty years before, had caused all the little children of Bĕth'lĕ-hĕm to be killed, this King Hĕr'od, the son, caused Jŏhn the Băp'tĭst, one of the best of men and a great prophet, to be put to death.

The followers of Jŏhn the Băp'tĭst went to the prison and took away his body and buried it; and then they went and told Jē'sus of all that had been done. After this they were among the followers of Jē'sus.

Hĕr'od the king heard of what Jē'sus was doing, the sick healed, the blind made to see, and the dead raised to life. Everybody by this time was talking of Jē'sus and wondering who he was. Some said, "This is the prophet Ê-lī'jah come again to earth."

Others said, "If he is not Ê-lī'jah, he is surely one of the prophets of the old time who has come to life."

But Hĕr'od said, "I know who this is. It is Jŏhn the Băp'tĭst whom I killed! He has come back to life, and by him all these great works are wrought!"

And Hĕr'od was in great alarm, for he was afraid of the man whom he had slain.

Story Nineteen
MATTHEW 14 : 13-36; MARK 6 : 30-56
LUKE 9 : 10-17; JOHN, chapter 6

The Feast Beside the Sea, and What Followed It

WHEN the twelve disciples came back to Jē'sus, after preaching in his name among the villages of Găl'ĭ-lee, they told him of all that they had done and of what they had said to the people. The multitudes seeking after Jē'sus were now greater than ever before, for it was again near the time of the Passover, and very many on their way to Jĕ-ru'să-lĕm turned aside to see and to hear the great Teacher. So many people were coming and going that they could scarcely find time even to eat. Jē'sus said to the twelve:

"Come with me apart into a quiet place, away from the crowds, and let us rest for a time."

They went into the boat and rowed across the lake to an open place, where no one lived, to a place not far from the city of Bĕth-sā'ĭ-dà. But they could not be alone, for the people saw them going, and watched them from the shore and went on foot around the northern end of the lake and found them. When Jē'sus saw how eager the crowds were to hear him, he took pity on them and taught them, and healed such among them as were sick.

As it began to grow toward evening, the disciples said to Jē'sus, "This is a lonely place, and there is nothing here for such a crowd of people to eat. Send them away before it is too late and tell them to go to the towns and get food."

But Jē'ṣus said to them, "They need not go away. You can give them food to eat."

They said to him, "Shall we go into the town and buy thirty dollars' worth of bread, so that each one of them may have a little?"

Jē'ṣus turned to Phĭl'ĭp, one of his disciples, and said to him, "Phĭl'ĭp, where shall we find bread, that all these may eat?"

Jē'ṣus said this to try Phĭl'ĭp's faith, for he himself knew what he would do. Phĭl'ĭp looked at the great crowd, full five thousand men, besides women and children, and he said, "Thirty dollars' worth of bread would not be enough to give to everyone even a little piece."

Just then another of the disciples, Ăn'drew, the brother of Pē'tēr, said to Jē'ṣus, "There is a boy here who has five loaves of barley bread and two little fishes; but what use would they be among so many people?"

Jē'ṣus said to the disciples, "Go out among the people, and divide them into companies of fifty and a hundred, and tell them to sit down in order."

So the people all sat down; and upon the green grass, arranged in rows and squares in their garments of different colors, they looked like beds of flowers.

Then Jē'ṣus took into his hands the five loaves and the two fishes which the boy had brought. He looked up to heaven and blessed the food; and broke the loaves and the dried fishes and gave the pieces to the disciples. They went among the companies of people and gave to everyone bread and fish, as much as each needed. So they all ate, and had enough.

Then Jē'ṣus said, "Gather up the pieces of food that are left, so that nothing may be wasted."

Each of the disciples carried a basket among the people, and when they came to Jē'ṣus, all the twelve baskets were filled with the pieces that were left over of the five small loaves and the two fishes.

When the people saw that here was one who could give them

food, they were ready at once to make Jē′ṣus their king and to break away from the rule of the Rō′manṣ. Jē′ṣus was a King, but he would not be such a king as they wished. His kingdom was to be in the hearts of men who loved him, not a kingdom set up by the swords of soldiers. He found that his disciples were ready to help the people to make him a king even against his own will.

So Jē′ṣus first compelled his disciples to go on board the boat, though they were not willing to do so, and to row across the lake to Cȧ-pēr′na-ŭm. Then he sent away the great crowd of people who were still eager that he should be their king. And when all had gone away, and he was left alone, he went up into the mountain to pray. While he was praying in the night, a great storm arose upon the lake, and from the mountain Jē′ṣus could see his disciples working hard with their oars against the waves, although they could not see him. A little after midnight, when the storm was the highest, Jē′ṣus went to his disciples, walking upon the water, just as though the sea was dry land. The men in the boat saw a strange figure coming near them upon the sea and cried out with fear, for they thought that it must be a spirit. But Jē′ṣus called out to them, "Be of good cheer; it is I; be not afraid!" And then they knew that it was their Lord.

Pē′tēr spoke to Jē′ṣus and said, "Lord, if it be thou, let me come to thee, walking on the water." Jē′ṣus said to Pē′tēr, "Come." Then Sī′mon Pē′tēr leaped overboard from the ship and he, too, walked on the water to go to Jē′ṣus. But when he saw how great was the storm on the sea, he began to be afraid, and forgetting to trust in the word of Jē'ṣus, he began to sink. He cried out, "Lord, save me!"

And Jē'ṣus reached out his hand and caught hold of him and lifted him up, saying, "O man of little faith, why did you doubt my word?"

When Jē'ṣus came on board the boat with Pē'tẽr, at once the wind ceased and the sea was calm. The disciples wondered greatly as they saw the power of Jē'ṣus. They fell down before him and said, "In truth thou art the Son of God!" When they came to the shore and the daylight came, they saw that they were at the land of Ḡen-nĕs'a-rĕt, a plain a little to the south of Cȧ-pẽr'-na-ŭm. They went ashore; and as soon as the people saw Jē'ṣus and knew who he was, they brought their sick to him and begged that they might only touch the border of his garment; and as many as touched him, were made well.

Soon after this Jē'ṣus came again to Cȧ-pẽr'na-ŭm and went into the synagogue, which was full of people, some of whom had eaten of the five loaves a few days before. These people wished Jē'ṣus to feed them in the same way again, but Jē'ṣus said to them, "Seek not for food that passes away, but for the food that gives everlasting life, such as the Son of man can give you."

They said to him, "What sign can you show that God has sent you? Mō'ṣes gave our fathers bread from heaven, the manna in the desert. What can you do?"

You have read of the manna which fed the Ĭṣ'ra-el-ītes in the wilderness. Then Jē'ṣus said to them, "It was not Mō'ṣes, but God, who gave your fathers bread; and God gives you now the true bread from heaven, in his Son who came down from heaven, to give life to the world."

As soon as the people found that Jē'ṣus would not work wonders to please them, they turned away from him and left him, although only a few days before they would have made him a king. When Jē'ṣus saw that the great crowds of people were with him no longer, Jē'ṣus said to his twelve disciples, "Will you also go away and leave me?"

Then Sĭ'mon Pē'tẽr answered him, "Lord, to whom else can we go? for thou only hast the words that will give us everlasting life."

The Answer to a Mother's Prayer

AFTER the feeding of the five thousand and the talk which followed it in the synagogue of Că-pēr'na-ŭm, Jē'ṣus no longer sought to preach to the people in crowds, as he had preached before. He had spoken his last words to the people of Găl'ĭ-lee, and now he sought to be alone with his disciples, that he might teach them many things which they needed. Jē'ṣus knew that in a few months, less than a year, he would leave his disciples to carry on the work of preaching his gospel to the world. Before that time should come, Jē'ṣus wished to teach and train his disciples; so he tried to be apart from the people and alone with these twelve men who were close to him.

With this purpose in his mind, Jē'ṣus led his disciples away from Că-pēr'na-ŭm, across Găl'ĭ-lee westward, to the land of Tȳre and Sĭ'dŏn, near the Great Sea. On the border of this land he came to a village and entered into a house. Jē'ṣus did not wish the people to know that he was there; but he could not be hid.

A woman of that place, who was not of the Jew'ĭsh race, but belonged to the old Cā'năan-īte people, heard of Jē'ṣus' coming. She sought out Jē'ṣus, and fell down before him, and begged him to come to her house and cure her daughter, in whom was an evil spirit. At first Jē'ṣus would not answer her, for he had not come to that place to do works of healing. But she kept on crying and calling upon Jē'ṣus to help her daughter, until the disciples said, "Master, send this woman away, for she is a trouble to us, crying out after us!"

They thought that a Gĕn'tĭle woman, one who did not belong to the race of Ĭṣ'ra-el, was not worthy of the Lord's care. But Jē'ṣus wished to teach his disciples that he did care for this woman, though she was a Gĕn'tĭle and a stranger. To show them how strong was her faith, he said to her, "I am not sent to the Gĕn'tĭles, but only to the lost sheep of the house of Ĭṣ'ra-el."

498

But the woman would not be discouraged; she kept on saying, "Lord, help me!"

Jē′ṣus said to her again, "It is not fitting to take the children's bread and throw it to the dogs!"

Then the woman said, "It is true, Lord; yet the little dogs under the table eat of the children's crumbs!"

And Jē′ṣus said to her, "O woman, your faith is great! It shall be done even as you ask. Go your way; the evil spirit is sent out of your daughter."

The woman believed the words that Jē′ṣus spoke. She went to her home and there found her daughter resting upon the bed, freed from the evil spirit.

So many people sought to see Jē′ṣus in that place that he left that land with his disciples and went around Găl-ĭ-lee, and he came again to the country called Dĕ-căp′o-lĭs, on the east of the Sea of Găl′ĭ-lee. You remember that Jē′ṣus had visited this country before, when he cast the army of evil spirits out of a man into the hogs. At that time the people almost drove Jē′ṣus away from their land; but now they were glad to see him and brought their sick to him to be healed. Perhaps they had heard from the man out of whom the evil spirits had gone how kind and good and helpful Jē′sus was.

They led to Jē'ṣus a man who was deaf and could not speak
plainly. He was what we would call "tongue-tied." They asked
Jē'ṣus to cure him; but Jē'ṣus would not do his work as a sight for
men to look upon. He took the man away from the crowd and
when he was alone with him, he put his fingers into the man's ears
and touched his tongue. Then he looked up to heaven and gave a
sign and said to the man, "Be opened!"

Then the man's ears were opened and his tongue was set free,
so that he heard and spoke plainly. Jē'ṣus told the man, and those
with him, not to let others know what he had done; but they could
not keep from telling the good news to everybody. They were
full of wonder, for they had not before seen the works of Jē'ṣus;
and they said, "He has done all things well; he makes even the deaf
to hear and the dumb to speak!"

And in the land of Dĕ-căp'o-lĭs, as before in Găl'ĭ-lee, great
crowds of people came to see and hear Jē'ṣus. They followed him,
without thinking that they would need any food to eat; and Jē'ṣus
said to his disciples, "I feel a pity for this people, for they have now
been with me three days and they have nothing to eat. If I send
them home hungry, they will faint by the way, for many of them
came from far."

The disciples answered him, "How can we find bread for such
a great crowd of people, here in a desert place, so far from the
villages?"

"How many loaves of bread have you?" asked Jē'ṣus. They
said, "We have seven loaves and a few small fishes."

Then he told all the people to sit down on the ground. When
they were seated, Jē'ṣus took the seven loaves and the fishes and
gave thanks to God, and broke them and gave them to his disciples,
and they gave them to the people. Then, as before, he caused
them to gather up the food that was left, and they filled seven
large baskets with the pieces. At this time four thousand men
were fed, besides women and children. And at once after the
meal, Jē'ṣus sent the people to their homes, and with his disciples
went on board a boat and sailed across the lake to a place on the
western shore. There he stayed only a short time and then sailed
northward to Bĕth-sā'ĭ-dà, at the head of the lake.

At Bĕth-sā'ĭ-dà they brought to him a blind man, and asked him to touch his eyes. But Jē'ṣus would not heal the man while a crowd was looking on. He led the man by his hand out of the village alone. Then he spat on the man's eyes and touched them with his hands and said to him, "Can you see anything?"

The man looked up and said, "I see men; but they look like trees walking."

Then again Jē'ṣus laid his hands upon the man's eyes. He looked once more and now could see all things clearly. Jē'ṣus sent him to his home and said to him, "Do not even go into the village or tell it to anyone in the village."

For Jē'ṣus wished not to have crowds of people coming to him, but to be alone with his disciples, for he had many things to teach them.

Story Twenty-one   MATTHEW 16 : 31 to 17 : 23;
MARK 8 : 27 to 9 : 32; LUKE 9 : 18-45

The Glory of Jesus on the Mountain

FROM Bĕth-sā'ĭ-dà on the Sea of Găl'ĭ-lee, Jē'ṣus led his disciples still farther north to Çaes-a-rē'à Phĭ-lĭp'pī, at the foot of the great Mount Hēr'mon. The name of this place means "Phĭl'ĭp's Çaes-a-rē'à"; and it was so called because it was under the rule of King Hĕr'od Phĭl'ĭp, a brother of King Hĕr'od Ăn'tĭ-pǎs, who ruled in Găl'ĭ-lee; and there was another Çaes-a-rē'à on the shore of the Great Sea, south of Mount Cär'mel. At Çaes-a-rē'à Phĭ-lĭp'pī, Jē'ṣus asked his disciples this question, "Who do men say that I, the Son of man, am?" "The Son of man" was the name by which Jē'ṣus often spoke of himself.

They answered him:

"Some men say that you are Jŏhn the Băp'tĭst risen from the dead; some say that you are the prophet Ê-lī'jah or the prophet Jĕr-e-mī'ah come again to earth."

Then said Jē'ṣus, "But who do you say that I am?"

Sī'mon Pē'tēr answered for them all, saying:

"Thou art the Anointed One, the Chrīst, the Son of the livin;
God!"

Jē'ṣus said to Pē'tēr:

"Sī'mon, this has come to you not from men, but from my
Father who is in heaven. You are Pē'tēr; and upon this rock I wil
build my church, and all the powers of earth shall not overcom(
it."

For the church of Chrīst is made of those who believe wha
Pē'tēr said, that Jē'ṣus is the Chrīst, the Saviour of the World; anc
who obey Jē'ṣus as their Lord and King.

After this Jē'ṣus began to tell his disciples what things were t(
come upon him before many months. He said:

"We are going up to Jē-ru'sả-lĕm; and there the people wil
refuse to own the Son of man; and he shall suffer many wrong;
from the rulers and chief priests; and shall be killed; and on th(
third day he shall be raised to life."

But the disciples could not believe that such sad things would
come to pass with Jē'ṣus. They thought that he would reign a;
a king, and that high places in his kingdom would be given to
themselves. Pē'tēr took Jē'ṣus apart from the rest and said to him:

"Master, do not speak of such things. You will not suffer and
die. You shall be a king!"

But Jē'ṣus saw that under Pē'tēr's words was the evil one tempt-
ing him, and he said to Pē'tēr:

"Go from me, Sā'tan, evil one! You would be a stumbling-
block to me, to make me fall! You are seeking not that which
comes from God, but that which is of men!"

For Jē'ṣus knew that while all men wished him to be a king,
ruling over a kingdom on the earth, it was God's will for him to
die upon the cross to save the world from sin. Then Jē'ṣus called
the people to come near with his disciples, and he said to them all:

"If any man will come after me, let him give up his own will
and take up his cross and follow me. For whoever has a will to
save his life here, shall lose it hereafter. And whoever is willing
to give up his life for my sake, shall find it again in life everlasting.

What gain would it be to a man to have the whole world and to lose his own life? For the Son of man will come in his glory, with all the holy angels, and then he will give to every man according to his acts. And if any man is ashamed to own the Lord now, the Lord will not own him in that day!"

One night, about a week after saying those words, Jē'sus called three of his disciples, Pē'tēr, Jāmes, and Jŏhn, and with them climbed up the side of Mount Hēr'mon. At a high place on the mountain, the three disciples lay down to sleep, but Jē'sus sought his Father in prayer. While Jē'sus was praying, a great change came over him. His face began to shine as bright as the sun and his garments became whiter than snow. The three disciples awoke and saw their Lord with all this glory beaming from him.

And they saw two men talking with Jē'sus. These were Mō'ses and Ē-lī'jah, who had come down from heaven to meet Jē'sus; and they spoke with him of the death that he was to die in Jē-ru'sā-lĕm. As these men were passing from the sight of the disciples, Pē'tēr spoke, scarcely knowing what he was saying, "Master, it is good for us to be here! Let us set up here three tents for worship, one for thee and one for Mō'ses and one for Ē-lī'jah!"

While Pē'tēr was speaking, a bright and glorious cloud came over them all; and the three disciples felt a great fear as they found themselves in the cloud and no longer able to see their Master. Out of the cloud came the voice of God, saying these words:

"This is my beloved Son, in whom I am well pleased; hear ye him!"

As the disciples heard this voice, they fell upon their faces on the ground in great fear. And Jē'sus came and touched them saying, "Rise up, and do not be afraid."

Then they looked up and lo, the bright cloud had passed away, the two men were no more in sight, and Jē'sus was standing alone. They walked together down the mountain; and Jē'sus said to them very earnestly:

"Do not tell to any man what you have seen, until the Son of man is risen from the dead."

They wondered what this "rising from the dead" could mean; for even yet they could not believe that Jē'sus would die. But

they said nothing to anyone, not even to the other disciples, of what they had seen upon the mountain.

When Jē'ṣus and the three disciples came down the mountain, they found many people around the other nine disciples. As the people saw Jē'ṣus, they were filled with wonder, for some of the glory still remained upon his face, and they bowed before him. One man came to Jē'ṣus and said:

"Master, look upon my son, my only child, and have mercy upon him; for he is terribly troubled by an evil spirit. At times he cannot speak, and then he will cry out suddenly. The spirit almost tears him in pieces, and makes him fall into the fire and into the water. He foams at the mouth and grinds his teeth and pines away. And I spoke to your disciples, but they could not cast out the evil spirit."

And Jē'ṣus said:

"O ye people without faith and wandering from God, how long must I be with you? how long must I bear with you? Bring your child to me."

While they were bringing the boy to Jē'ṣus, the evil spirit in him threw him down and seemed to tear him apart; and he lay suffering and rolling on the ground. Jē'ṣus said to the boy's father:

"How long is it since this came to him?"

The father said, "Ever since he was a little child; but if you can do anything, have mercy on us and help us!"

"If I can!" said Jḗ'ṣus. "Do you not know that all things are possible to the one that believes in me?"

At once the father of the child cried out, "Lord, I do believe! Help my lack of faith!"

Then Jḗ'ṣus spoke to the evil spirit in the boy:

"Dumb and deaf spirit, come out of this child and never again enter into him!"

Then the spirit gave a cry and came out, and left the child as one dead on the ground. Indeed, many who looked at him said, "He is dead!"

But Jḗ'ṣus took him by the hand and lifted him up; and the boy stood up well, set free from the evil spirit; and Jḗ'ṣus gave him to his father. All who saw it wondered at the mighty power of the Lord.

When Jḗ'ṣus was in the house, his disciples asked him, "Why could not we cast out the evil spirit?"

And Jḗ'ṣus said to them, "Because you were wanting in faith. But this kind of evil spirit can be sent out only through prayer and fasting."

While all were wondering at the great things which Jḗ'ṣus did, he said again to his disciples:

"Let what I say to you sink down into your hearts. The time is coming when the Son of man shall be given into the hands of men; and they shall kill him; and after he is killed, on the third day he shall rise again."

But they could not understand what he meant by these words; and they were afraid to ask him.

The Little Child in the Arms
of Jesus

FROM Çaes-a-rē′à Phĭ-lĭp′pī, in the far north, Jē′ṣus went
with his disciples through Găl-ĭ-lee, but not, as at other
times, with a great multitude following him. At this
time Jē′ṣus wished no one to know of his coming, for he
had already preached to this people, and now he sought
to be alone with his disciples. They came to Că-pēr′na-ŭm; and
while they were there, the officer to whom the Jewṣ paid the tax of
half a shekel, or about thirty cents, for each man, said to Pē′tēr,
"Does not your Master pay the half shekel?"

Pē′tēr said, "Yes." But when Pē′tēr came into the house, Jē′ṣus
said to Pē′tēr, "Sī′mon, do the kings of the earth take taxes of their
own children or of strangers?"

Pē′tēr said to him, "Of strangers, but not of their own children."

And Jē′ṣus said, "Then the children of the King should be free
from the tax. But that we may not cause trouble, do you go to the
lake and cast in a hook and pull up the first fish that comes; and
when you have opened his mouth, you shall find in it a piece of
money. Take that and pay it to them for you and for me."

While Jē′ṣus was in the house, he said to his disciples, "What
was it that you were talking about among yourselves while you
were on the way?"

They looked at one another and said nothing; for on the way
they had been disputing as to who of them should have the highest
places in their Lord's kingdom. Then Jē′ṣus said to them, "If
anyone among you wishes to be first, let him be willing to be the
last of all and to be a servant of all."

And Jē′ṣus took a little child in his arms and held him up before
all his disciples, and said to them, "Unless you turn from your
ways and become like little children in spirit, you shall not enter

506

into the kingdom of heaven. Whoever shall be gentle and lowly and willing to be taught, like this little child, he shall be the greatest in the kingdom of heaven. And whoever shall receive one such little child for my sake, he receives me. Take care not to despise one of these little ones; for I say unto you, that in heaven their angels do always look upon the face of my Father who is in

heaven. For the Son of man is come to save that which was lost; and it is not the will of your Father who is in heaven that one of these little ones should perish."

And Pē'tēr said to Jē'ṣus, "Lord, how many times should I forgive a brother when he has sinned against me? Till seven times?"

Jē'ṣus said to Pē'tēr, "I do not say that you should forgive him seven times only, but seventy times seven."

Then Jē'ṣus gave to his disciples the parable or story of the Unkind Servant:

"There was once a king who had an account made with his servants of how much money they owed him. One servant was brought before the king; and he owed the king a great sum of money, ten millions of dollars. The man had nothing with which to pay his debt, and the king commanded that the man and his wife and his children should be sold as slaves for the debt. Then the servant fell down before the king and said, 'Be patient with me; give me time and I will pay all that I owe!'

"Then the king felt a pity for his servant, set him free, and let him go without any payment, giving him all that he owed.

"But that servant went out and found another servant who owed him a small sum, only ten dollars. He came to this man and took hold of him by the throat and said, 'Pay what you owe me!' The man fell down before him and said, 'Have patience with me and I will pay you!' He would not wait for the man to earn the money, but threw the man in prison, to stay there until he should pay the debt.

"When his fellow servants heard of what had been done, they were sorry for the poor debtor in prison, and came and told the king all that had been done. Then the king sent for the servant and said to him, 'You wicked servant, I forgave you all your debt when you asked me to give you time. And you should have had mercy on your fellow servant, just as I had mercy on you!' And the king was angry against the unkind servant and sent him to prison and he ordered that he should be made to suffer until he should pay all his debt. So also shall my heavenly Father do to you, if from your hearts you do not forgive your brothers who have sinned against you."

At the Feast of Tabernacles

IN THE fall of every year there was held at Jĕ-ru′sȧ-lĕm "The Feast of Tabernacles." It was kept to remind the people of the time when the Ĭṣ′ra-el-ītes came out of Ē′ġўpt and lived for forty years in the wilderness, more than a thousand years before the days when Jē′ṣus was on the earth. At this feast the people from all parts of the land came up to Jĕ-ru′sȧ-lĕm and worshiped in the Temple. And as the Ĭṣ′ra-el-ītes had lived in tents in the wilderness, the people during the feast did not sleep indoors, but made arbors and huts from green boughs on the roofs of the houses and on the hills around the city, and slept in them.

Jē′ṣus and his disciples went from Găl′ĭ-lee to Jĕ-ru′sȧ-lĕm to attend the feast.

Just as Jē′ṣus was leaving, a man who had heard him said, "Master, I will follow thee wherever thou goest."

And Jē′ṣus said to him, "The foxes have holes and the birds of the air have nests, but the Son of man has not a place where he can lay his head."

There was another man to whom Jē′ṣus had said, "Follow me." This man said, "Lord, let me go and bury my father, who is very old and must die very soon, and then I will follow thee."

Jē′ṣus said to him, "Let the dead bury their own dead; but do you go and preach the kingdom of God."

And another said, "Lord, I will follow thee; but let me first go home and say 'good-by' to those who are in my house."

Jē′ṣus said to him, "No man who has put his hand to the plow and turns back, is fit for the kingdom of God."

On his way to Jĕ-ru′sȧ-lĕm Jē′ṣus went through the country of Sȧ-mā′rĭ-ȧ, where the people hated the Jews. In one place the Sȧ-măr′ĭ-tans would not let Jē′ṣus and his disciples come into their village, because they saw that they were Jews going up to Jĕ-ru′sȧ-lĕm. The disciples were very angry at such treatment of their Master; and Jāmeṣ and Jŏhn said to him, "Lord, shall we call down

509

fire from heaven to destroy this village, as Ê-lī′jah the prophet did once?"

But Jē′ṣus would not allow them to do this to their enemies. He said to them, "Your spirit is not the spirit of my kingdom. The Son of man has not come to destroy men's lives, but to save them."

And they went to another village to find a resting place. At one town they met outside the gate ten men with the dreadful disease of leprosy, of which we read in the story of Nā′a-man. These men had heard of Jē′ṣus and his power to heal; and when they saw him, they cried out aloud, "Jē′ṣus, Master, have mercy upon us!"

Jē′ṣus said to them, "Go and show yourselves to the priests." If ever a leper became well, he went to the priest and made an offering as thanksgiving to God, and then was allowed to go to his home. These men obeyed the word of Jē′ṣus, believing that he would cure them; and as soon as they started to go to the priests, they found that they were already well. All but one of the men went on their way, but one returned and came back to Jē′ṣus and fell at his feet, giving praise to God; and this man was not a Jew, but a Sà-măr′ĭ-tan. Jē′ṣus said as he saw him, "Were there not ten cleansed? But where are the nine? Were there none who came back to give glory to God, except this stranger?"

Then he said to the man, "Rise up and go your way; your faith has saved you."

Jē′ṣus came to Jė-ru′sà-lĕm not on the first day of the feast, but in the middle, for the feast was held for a week. He stood in the Temple and taught the people, and all wondered at his words. On the last and greatest day of the feast, when they were bringing water and pouring it out in the Temple, Jē′ṣus cried aloud, "If any man thirst, let him come to me and drink! He that believes on me, out of his heart shall flow rivers of living water."

While Jē′ṣus was teaching in Jė-ru′sà-lĕm, he often went out of the city to the village of Bĕth′a-nў, on the Mount of Ŏl′ĭveṣ. There he stayed with the family of Mär′thà, her sister Mā′rў, and their brother Lăz′a-rŭs. These were friends of Jē′ṣus, and he loved to be with them. One day, while Jē′ṣus was at the house, Mā′rў sat at the feet of Jē′ṣus, listening to his words; but Mär′thà

was busy with work and full of cares. Mär′thȧ came to Jē′ṣus and said, "Master, do you not care that my sister has left me to do all the work? Tell her to come and help me!"

But Jē′ṣus said to her, "Mär′thȧ, Mär′thȧ, you are anxious and troubled about many things. Only one thing is needful; for Mā′rў has chosen the good part; and it shall not be taken away from her."

Story Twenty-four

The Man with Clay on His Face

ONE SABBATH DAY, as Jē′ṣus and his disciples were walking in Jĕ-ru′sȧ-lĕm, they met a blind man begging. This man in all his life had never seen, for he had been born blind. The disciples said to Jē′ṣus, as they were passing him, "Master, whose fault was it that this man was born blind? Was it because he has sinned, or did his parents sin?"

For the Jews thought that when any evil came, it was caused by someone's sin. But Jē'ṣus said, "This man was born blind, not because of his parents' sin or because of his own; but so that God might show his power in him. We must do God's work while it is day; for the night is coming when no man can work. As long as I am in the world, I am the light of the world."

When Jē'ṣus had said this, he spat on the ground, and mixed up the spittle with earth, making a little lump of clay. This clay Jē'ṣus spread on the eyes of the blind man, and then said to him, "Go and wash in the pool of Sī-lō'am."

The pool of Sī-lō'am was a large cistern or reservoir on the southeast of Jē-ru'ṣả-lĕm, outside the wall, where the valley of Gī'hon and the valley of the Ke'dron come together. To go to this pool the blind man, with two great blotches of mud on his face, must walk through the streets of the city, out of the gate, and into the valley. He went, and felt his way down the steps into the pool of Sī-lō'am. There he washed, and then at once his lifelong blindness passed away and he could see. When the man came back to the part of the city where he lived, his neighbors could scarcely believe that he was the same man. They said, "Is not this the man who used to sit on the street begging?"

"This must be the same man," said some; but others said, "No, it is someone who looks like him."

But the man said, "I am the very same man who was blind!"

"Why, how did this come to pass?" they asked him. "How were your eyes opened?"

"The man called Jē'ṣus," he answered, "mixed clay and put it on my eyes and said to me, 'Go to the pool of Sī-lō'am and wash,' and I went and washed, and then I could see."

"Where is this man?" they asked him.

"I do not know," said the man.

Some of the Phăr'ĭ-seeṣ, the men who made a show of always obeying the law, asked the man how he had been made to see. He said to them, as he had said before, "A man put clay on my eyes, and I washed and my sight came to me."

Some of the Phăr'ĭ-seeṣ said, "The man who hid this is not a man of God, because he does not keep the Sabbath. He makes clay and puts it on men's eyes, working on the Sabbath Day. He is a sinner."

Others said, "How can a man who is a sinner do such wonderful works?" And thus the people were divided in what they thought of Jē'ṣus. They asked the man who had been blind, "What do you think of this man who has opened your eyes?"

"He is a prophet of God!" said the man.

But the leading Jewṣ would not believe that this man had gained his sight until they had sent for his father and his mother. The Jewṣ asked them, "Is this your son, who you say was born blind? How is it that he can now see?"

His parents were afraid to tell all that they knew; for the Jewṣ had agreed that if any man should say that Jē'ṣus was the Chrīst, the Saviour, he should be turned out of the church, and not be allowed to worship any more with the people. So his parents said to the Jewṣ, "We know that this is our son and we know that he was born blind. But how he was made to see we do not know or who has opened his eyes, we do not know. He is of age; ask him, and let him speak for himself." Then again the rulers of the Jewṣ called the man who had been blind; and they said to him, "Give

God the praise for your sight. We know that this man who made clay on the Sabbath Day is a sinner."

"Whether that man is a sinner or not, I do not know," answered the man; "but one thing I do know, that once I was blind and now I see." They said to him again, "What did this man do to you? How did he open your eyes?"

"I have told you already, and you would not listen," said the man. "Why do you wish to hear it again? Do you intend to believe in him and be his followers?"

This made them very angry, and they said to the man, "You are his follower; but we are followers of Mō′ṣeṣ. We know that God spoke to Mō′ṣeṣ; but as for this fellow, we do not even know from what place he comes!"

The man said, "Why, that is a very wonderful thing! You, who are teachers of the people, do not know who this man is, or from what place he comes; and yet he has had power to open my eyes! We know that God does not hear sinners; but God hears only those who worship him and do his will. Never before has anyone opened the eyes of a man born blind. If this man were not from God, he could not do such works as these!"

The rulers of the Jews, these Phăr′ĭ-seeṣ, then said to the man, "You were born a sinner; and do you try to teach us?"

And they turned him out of the church and would not let him worship with them. Jē′ṣus heard of this; and when Jē′ṣus found him, he said to him, "Do you believe on the Son of God?"

The man said, "And who is he, Lord, that I may believe on him?"

"You have seen him," said Jē′ṣus, "and it is he who now talks with you!"

The man said, "Lord, I believe." And he fell down before Jē′ṣus and worshiped him.

The Good Shepherd and the Good Samaritan

AFTER the cure of the man born blind, Jĕ'ṣus gave to the people in Jĕ-ru'sȧ-lĕm the parable or story of "The Good Shepherd."

"Verily, verily (that is, "in truth, in truth"), I say to you, if anyone does not go into the sheepfold by the door, but climbs up some other way, it is a sign that he is a thief and a robber. But the one who comes in by the door is a shepherd of the sheep. The porter opens the door to him, and the sheep know him and listen to his call, for he calls his own sheep by name and leads them out to the pasture field. And when he has led out his sheep, he goes in front of them, and the sheep follow him, for they know his voice. The sheep will not follow a stranger, for they do not know the stranger's voice."

The people did not understand what all this meant, and Jĕ'ṣus explained it to them. He said:

"Verily, verily, I say to you, I am the door that leads to the sheepfold. If anyone comes to the sheep in any other way than through me and in my name, he is a thief and a robber; but those who are the true sheep will not hear such. I am the door; if any man goes into the fold through me, he shall be saved and shall go in and go out and shall find pasture.

"The thief comes to the fold that he may steal and rob the sheep and kill them; but I come to the fold that they may have life, and may have all that they need. I am the good shepherd; the good shepherd will give up his life to save his sheep; and I will give up my life that my sheep may be saved.

"I am the good shepherd; and just as a true shepherd knows all the sheep in his flock, so I know my own, and my own know me, even as I know the Father, and the Father knows me; and I lay

515

down my life for the sheep. Other sheep I have, which are not of this fold; them also I must lead, and they shall hear my voice, and there shall be one flock and one shepherd."

The Jews̱ could not understand these words of Jē'su̱s; but they became very angry with him, because he spoke of God as his Father. They took up stones to throw at him and tried to seize him, intending to kill him. But Jē'su̱s escaped from their hands and went away to the land beyond Jôr'dan, at the place called Bĕth-ab'a-rȧ, or "Bĕth'a-nȳ beyond Jôr'dan," the same place where he had been baptized by Jŏhn the Băp'tĭst more than two years before. From this place Jē'su̱s wished to go out through the land on the east of the Jôr'dan, a land which was called "Pē-rē'ȧ," a word that means "Beyond." But before going out himself through this land, Jē'su̱s sent out seventy chosen men from among his followers to go to all the villages and to make the people ready for his own coming afterward. He gave to these seventy the same commands that he had given to the twelve disciples, when he sent them through Găl'ĭ-lee, and sent them out in pairs, two men to travel and to preach together. He said:

"I send you forth as lambs among wolves. Carry no purse, no bag for food, no shoes except those that you are wearing. Do not stop to talk with people by the way; but go through the towns and the villages, healing the sick and preaching to the people, 'The kingdom of God is coming.' He that hears you, hears me; and he that refuses you, refuses me; and he that will not hear me, will not hear him that sent me."

And after a time the seventy men came again to Jē'ṣus, saying, 'Lord, even the evil spirits obey our words in thy name!"

And Jē'ṣus said to them, "I saw Sā'tan, the king of the evil spirits, falling down like lightning from heaven. I have given you power to tread upon serpents and scorpions; and nothing shall harm you. Still, do not rejoice because the evil spirits obey you; but rejoice that your names are written in heaven." And at that time one of the scribes—men who wrote copies of the books of the Old Testament, and studied them, and taught them—came to Jē'ṣus and asked him a question, to see what answer he would give. He said, "Master, what shall I do to have everlasting life?"

Jē'ṣus said to the scribe, "What is written in the law? You are a reader of God's law; tell me what it says."

Then the man gave this answer, "Thou shalt love the Lord thy God with all thy heart and with all thy soul and with all thy strength and with all thy mind; and thou shalt love thy neighbor as thyself."

Jē'ṣus said to the man, "You have answered right; do this and you shall have everlasting life."

But the man was not satisfied. He asked another question, "And who is my neighbor?"

To answer this question, Jē'ṣus gave the parable or story of "The Good Sȧ-mȧr'ĭ-tan." He said, "A certain man was going down the lonely road from Jē-rụ'sȧ-lĕm to Jĕr'ĭ-chō; and he fell among robbers, who stripped him of all that he had and beat him; and then went away, leaving him almost dead. It happened that a certain priest was going down that road; and when he saw the man lying there, he passed by on the other side. And a Lē'vīte also, when he came to the place and saw the man, he too went by on the other side. But a certain Sȧ-mȧr'ĭ-tan, as he was going down, came where this man was; and as soon as he saw him, he felt a pity for him. He came to the man and dressed his wounds, pouring oil and wine into them. Then he lifted him up, set him on his own beast of burden, and walked beside him to an inn. There he

took care of him all night; and the next morning he took out from
his purse two shillings and gave them to the keeper of the inn and
said, 'Take care of him; and if you need to spend more than this,
do so; and when I come again, I will pay it to you.'

"Which one of these three do you think showed himself a
neighbor to the man who fell among the robbers?"

The scribe said, "The one who showed mercy on him."

Then Jē'ṣus said to him, "Go and do thou likewise."

By this parable Jē'ṣus showed that "our neighbor" is the one
who needs the help that we can give him, whoever he may be.

Story Twenty-six   JOHN 11 : 1-55

Lazarus Raised to Life

WHILE Jē'ṣus was at Bĕth-ab'a-rà beyond Jôr'-
dan and ready to begin preaching in the land of
Pe-rē'à, he was suddenly called back to the vil-
lage of Bĕth'a-nȳ, on the Mount of Ŏl'īveṣ, near
Jē-ru'sà-lĕm. You remember that Mär'thà and
Mā'rȳ and Lăz'a-rŭs, the friends of Jē'ṣus, were living in this place.

The word came to Jē'ṣus that Lăz'a-rŭs was very ill. But
Jē'ṣus did not hurry away from Bĕth-ab'a-rà to go to Bĕth'a-nȳ.
He stayed two days, and then he said to his disciples, "Let us go
again to Jū-dē'à, near Jē-ru'sà-lĕm."

The disciples said to Jē'ṣus, "Master, when we were in Jū-dē'à
last, the people tried to stone you and to kill you; and now would
you go there again?"

Jē'ṣus said, "Our friend Lăz'a-rŭs has fallen asleep; but I go that
I may awake him out of his sleep." The disciples said, "Master,
if he has fallen asleep, he may get well."

For they thought that Jē'ṣus was speaking of taking rest in
sleep; but Jē'ṣus meant that Lăz'a-rŭs was dead. Then Jē'ṣus said
to them, "Lăz'a-rŭs is dead; and I am glad that I was not there to

:ure him of his sickness; for now you will be led to believe in me
all the more fully. But let us now go to him."

Then one of the disciples, named Thŏm′as, said to the others,
'Let us also go and die with our Master!"

So Jē′şus left Bĕth-ab′a-rà with his disciples and came to Bĕth′-
a-nÿ; and then he found that Lăz′a-rŭs had been buried four days.
Many of the Jews had come to comfort Mär′thà and Mā′rÿ in the
loss of their brother. They told Mär′thà that Jē′şus was coming,
and she went to meet him, but Mā′rÿ sat still in the house. As
soon as Mär′thà saw Jē′şus, she said to him very sadly, "Lord, if
you had been here, my brother need not have died. And even
now, I know that God will give you whatever you may ask."

Jē′şus said to her, "Your brother shall rise again."

"I know that he shall rise," said Mär′thà, "when the last day
comes, and all the dead are raised."

Jē′şus said to her, "I am the resurrection, the raising from the
dead; and I am the life. Whoever believes on me, even though
he may die, he shall live; and whoever lives and believes on me,
shall never die. Do you believe this?"

She said to him, "Yes, Lord, I believe that thou art the Chrīst,
the Son of God, the one who comes into the world."

Then Mär′thà went to her home and said to her sister Mā′rÿ,
quietly, so that no other person heard her, "The Master is here,
and he asks for you!"

At once Mā′rÿ rose up to go to Jē′şus. Her friends thought
that she was going to her brother's tomb, and they went with her.
Jē′şus was still at the place where Mär′thà had met him, near the
village. When Mā′rÿ came to him, she fell down at his feet and
said, as her sister had said, "Lord, if you had been here, my brother
need not have died!"

When Jē′şus saw Mā′rÿ weeping and the Jews weeping with
her, he also was touched, and groaned in his spirit and was filled
with great sorrow. He said, "Where have you laid him?"

They showed him the place where Lăz′a-rŭs was buried, a cave,
with a stone laid upon the door. Jē′şus wept as he stood near it,
and the Jews said, "See how he loved Lăz′a-rŭs!"

But some of them said, "If this man could open the eyes of the blind, why is it that he could not keep this man whom he loved from dying?"

Jē'ṣus, standing before the cave and still groaning within, said "Take away the stone!"

Mär'thà said, "Lord, by this time his body has begun to decay, for he has been dead four days."

Jē'ṣus said to her, "Did I not say to you that if you would believe, you should see the glory of God?"

They took away the stone as Jē'ṣus had commanded. Then Jē'ṣus lifted up his eyes toward heaven and said:

"Father, I thank thee that thou didst hear me. I know that thou dost hear me always; but because of those who are standing here I spoke, so that they may believe that thou hast sent me."

Then Jē'ṣus called out, "Lăz'a-rŭs, come forth!"

And the man who had been four days dead came out of the tomb. His body and hands and feet were wrapped round and round with grave bands, and over his face was bound a napkin.

Jē'ṣus said to those standing near, "Loose him and let him go!"

When they saw the wonderful power of Jē'ṣus in raising Lăz'a-rŭs to life, many of the people believed in Jē'ṣus. But others went away and told the Phär'ĭ-sees and rulers what Jē'ṣus had done. They called a meeting of all the rulers, the great council of the Jews, and they said, "What shall we do, for this man is doing many works of wonder? If we let him alone, everybody will believe on him and will try to make him the king; and then the Rō'mans will make war upon us and destroy our nation and our people."

But the high priest Cā'ia-phăs said, "It is better for us that one man should die for the people than that our whole nation should be destroyed. Let us put this man to death."

And to this they agreed; and from that day all the rulers made plans to have Jē'ṣus slain. But Jē'ṣus knew their purpose, for he knew all things. His time to die had not yet come, and he went away with his disciples to a city near the wilderness and not far from Bĕth-ab'a-rà, where he had been before. From there he went forth to preach in the land of Pe-rē'à, into which he had sent the seventy disciples, as we read in the last story.

Some Parables in Perea

JĒ'ŞUS went with his disciples through the land of Pe-rē'á on the east of the Jôr'dan, the only part of the Ĭs-ra-el-īte country that he had not already visited. The people had heard of Jē'ṣus from the seventy disciples whom he had sent through the land; and in every place great multitudes of people came to see him and to hear him. At one time, one man called out of the crowd and said to Jē'ṣus:

"Master, speak to my brother and tell him to give me my share of what our father left us!"

Jē'ṣus said:

"Man, who made me a judge over you, to settle your disputes? Let both of you and all of you take care to keep from being covetous, seeking what is not yours."

Then Jē'ṣus gave to the people the parable or story of "The Rich Fool."

He said:

"There was a rich farmer whose fields brought great harvests, until the rich man said to himself:

"'What shall I do? for I have no place where I can store up the fruits of my fields. This is what I will do. I will pull down my barns and will build larger ones; and there I will store all my grain and my goods. And I will say to my soul, "Soul, you have goods laid up enough to last for many years; take your ease, eat, drink, and be merry."'

"But God said to the rich man, 'Thou foolish one; this night thou shalt die, and thy soul shall be taken away from thee. And the things which thou hast laid up, whose shall they be?'"

And Jē'ṣus said, "Such is the man who lays up treasure for himself and is not rich toward God."

On one Sabbath Day, Jē'ṣus was teaching in a church. And a woman came in who for eighteen years had been bent forward

522

and could not stand up straight. When Jē'ṣus saw her, he called her, and said to her:

"Woman, you are set free from your trouble of body."

He laid his hands upon her; and she stood up straight and praised God for his mercy. But the chief man in the synagogue-church was not pleased to see Jē'ṣus healing on the Sabbath. He spoke to the people and said:

"There are six days when men ought to work; in them, you should come and be healed, and not on the Sabbath Day."

But Jē'ṣus said to him and to the others:

"Does not each one of you on the Sabbath Day loose his ox or his ass from the stall and lead him away to give him water? And should not this woman, a daughter of Ā'brȧ-hăm, who has been bound for eighteen years, be set free from her bonds on the Sabbath Day?"

And the enemies of Jē'ṣus could say nothing; while all the people were glad at the glorious works which he did.

At one place Jē'ṣus was invited to a dinner. He said to the one who had invited him:

"When you make a dinner or a supper, do not invite your friends or your rich neighbors; for they will invite you in return. But when you make a feast, invite the poor, the helpless, the lame, and the blind; for they cannot invite you again; but God will give you a reward in his own time."

And there went with Jē'ṣus great multitudes of people; and he turned and said to them:

"If any man comes after me, he must love me more than he loves his own father and his mother and wife and children, yes, and his own life also; or else he cannot be my disciple.

"For who of you, wishing to build a tower, does not first sit down and count the cost, whether he will be able to finish? For if after he has laid the foundation and then leaves it unfinished, everyone who passes by will laugh at him and say, 'This man began to build and was not able to finish.'

"Or what king going out to meet another king in war, will not sit down first and find whether he is able with ten thousand men to meet the one who comes against him with twenty thousand?

And if he finds that he cannot meet him, while he is yet a great way off, he sends his messengers and asks for peace.

"Even so, every one of you must give up all that he has, if he would be my disciple."

While Jē'ṣus was teaching, many of the publicans, those who took up the taxes from the people, came to hear him; and many others who were called "sinners" by the Phăr'ĭ-seeṣ and the scribes. The enemies of Jē'ṣus said:

"This man likes to have sinners come to see him, and he eats with them."

Then Jē'ṣus spoke a parable called "The Lost Sheep," to show why he was willing to talk with sinners. He said:

"What man of you who has a hundred sheep, if one of them is lost, does not leave his ninety and nine sheep in the field and go after the one that is lost until he finds it? And when he has found it, he lays it on his shoulders, glad to see his lost sheep again. And when he comes home, he calls together his friends and neighbors and says to them:

" 'Be glad with me; for I have found my sheep that was lost!'

"Even so," said Jē'ṣus, "there is joy in heaven over one sinner who has turned to God, more than over ninety and nine good men who do not need to turn from their sins."

Jē'ṣus gave to the people also the parable of "The Lost Piece of Money." He said:

"If any woman has ten pieces of silver and loses one piece, will she not light a lamp and sweep her house carefully until she finds

t? And when she has found it, she calls together her friends and
ier neighbors, saying:

" 'Be glad with me; for I have found the piece of silver that
had lost.'

"Even so, there is joy among the angels of God over one sinner
hat turns from his sins."

Then Jē'ṣus told another parable called "The Parable of the
'rodigal Son." A prodigal is one who spends everything that he
ias, as did the young man in this parable. Jē'ṣus said, "There was
ince a man who had two sons. The younger of his sons said to
iis father:

" 'Father, out of what you own, give to me now the share that
vill come to me.'

"Then the father divided all that he had between his two sons;
ind not many days after, the younger son took his share and went
iway into a far country; and there he wasted it all in wild and
wicked living. And when he had spent all, there arose a mighty
famine of food in that country; and he began to be in want.

"And he went to work for one of the men in that land; and this
man sent him into the fields to feed his hogs. The young man was
so hungry that he would have filled himself with the husks that
were fed to the hogs; and no one gave anything to him. At last
the young man began to think of his father's house, and he said to
himself:

" 'How many hired servants of my father's have bread enough
and to spare, while I am dying here with hunger! I will arise and
will go to my father and will say to him, "Father, I have sinned
against heaven and in your sight. I am no more worthy to be
called your son; let me be one of your hired men." '

"And he rose up, to go back to his father's house. But while
he was yet afar off, his father saw him and felt pity for him and
ran and fell on his neck and kissed him. And the son said unto
him:

" 'Father, I have sinned against heaven and in your sight. I am
no more worthy to be called your son—'

"But before he could say any more, his father called to the
servants and said:

" 'Bring out quickly the best robe and put it on him; and pu
a ring on his hand and shoes on his feet; and bring the fatted cal
and kill it; and let us eat and make merry; for this my son wa
dead and is alive again; he was lost and is found.'

"Now his elder son was in the field; and as he came and drev
nigh to the house, he heard music and dancing. And he called to
him one of the servants and asked what all this rejoicing meant
And the servant said to him:

" 'Your brother has come; and your father has killed the fatte
calf and is having a feast, because he is at home safe and sound.

"But the elder brother was angry and would not go in; and hi
father came out and urged him. But he answered his father, and
said:

" 'I have served you for these many years; and I have neve
disobeyed your commands; and yet you never gave me even a
kid, that I might make merry with my friends. But when thi
your son has come, who has wasted your living with wicked
people, you killed for him the fatted calf!'

"And the father said to him:

" 'My son, you are always with me, and all that I have is yours
But it was fitting that we should make merry and be glad; for this
your brother was dead and is alive again; he was lost and is
found.' "

By these parables Jē'ṣus showed that he came not to seek those
who thought themselves so good that they did not need him; but
those who were the sinful and the needy.

The Poor Rich Man, and the Rich Poor Man

ANOTHER story that Jē'ṣus told was that of "The Rich Man and Lăz'a-rŭs." He said:

"There was a rich man; and he was dressed in garments of purple and fine linen, living every day in splendor. And at the gate leading to his house was laid a beggar named Lăz'a-rŭs, covered with sores and seeking for his food the crusts and broken pieces that fell from the rich man's table. Even the dogs of the street came and licked his sores.

"After a time the beggar died, and his soul was carried by the angels into Ā'bră-hăm's bosom. The rich man also died, and his body was buried. And in the world of the dead he lifted up his eyes, being in misery; and far away he saw Ā'bră-hăm, and Lăz'a-rŭs resting in his bosom. And he cried out and said, 'Father Ā'bră-hăm, have mercy on me and send Lăz'a-rŭs, that he may dip the tip of his finger in water and cool my tongue."

"But Ā'bră-hăm said, 'Son, remember that you had your good things in your lifetime, and that Lăz'a-rŭs had his evil things; but now here he is comforted and you are suffering. Besides all this, between us and you there is a great gulf fixed, so that no one may cross over from us to you, and none can come from your place to us.'

"And he said, 'I pray, O father Ā'bră-hăm, if Lăz'a-rŭs cannot come to me, command that he be sent to my father's house, for I have five brothers. And let him speak to them, so that they will not come to this place of torment.'

"But Ā'bră-hăm said, 'They have Mō'ṣeṣ and the prophets; let them listen to them!'

"And he said, 'O father Ā'bră-hăm, if one should go to them from the dead, they will turn to God.'

527

"And Ā'bră-hăm said, 'If they will not hear Mō'ṣeṣ and the prophets, they will not believe, even though one should rise from the dead!'"

And this was true, for as the people would not listen to the words of Mō'ṣeṣ and the prophets about Chrīst, they would not believe, even after Jē'ṣus himself arose from the dead. There was another parable or story of Jē'ṣus, called "The Unjust Steward."

"A certain rich man had a steward, a man who took care of all his possessions. He heard that his steward was wasting his property, and he sent for him and said, 'What is this that I hear about you? You must soon give up your place and be my steward no longer.'

"Then the steward said to himself, 'In a few days I shall lose my place; and what shall I do? I cannot work in the fields, and I am ashamed to go begging from door to door. But I have thought of a plan that will give me friends, so that when I am put out of my place, some people will take me into their houses, because of what I have done for them.'

"And this was his plan. He sent for the men who were in debt to his master and said to the first one, 'How much do you owe to my master?'

"The man said, 'I owe him a thousand gallons of oil.'

"Then said the steward, 'You need only pay five hundred gallons.' Then to another he said, 'How much do you owe?'

"The man answered, 'I owe fifteen hundred bushels of wheat.' And the steward said to him, 'You need pay only twelve hundred bushels.'

"When his master heard of this which his steward had done, he said, 'That is a sharp, shrewd man, who takes care of himself.'"

And Jē'ṣus said, "Be as earnest and as thoughtful for the eternal life as men are for this present life."

Jē'ṣus did not approve the actions of this unjust steward, but he told his disciples to learn some good lessons even from his wrong deeds.

Jē'ṣus spoke another parable to show that people should pray always and not be discouraged. It was the story of "The Unjust Judge and the Widow." Jē'ṣus said:

"There was in a city a judge who did not fear God nor seek to do right; nor did he care what people thought of him. And there was a poor widow in that city who had suffered wrong. She came to him over and over again, crying out, 'Do justice for me against my enemy who has done me wrong!'

"And for a time the judge, because he did not care for the right, would do nothing. But as the widow kept on crying, at last he said to himself, 'Even though I do not fear God nor care for man, yet because this widow troubles me and will not be still, I will give her justice, or else she will wear me out by her continual crying.'"

And the Lord said, "Hear what this unjust judge says! And will not a just God do right for his own who cry to him by day and night, even though he may seem to wait long? I tell you that he will answer their prayer, and will answer it soon!"

And Jē'ṣus spoke another parable to some who thought that they were righteous and holy and set others at nought. This was the parable of "The Phăr'ĭ-see and the Tax Collector."

"Two men went up into the Temple to pray, the one a Phăr'ĭ-see, the other a publican, a tax collector. The Phăr'ĭ-see stood and prayed thus with himself, 'God, I thank thee that I am not as other men are. I do not rob. I do not deal unjustly. I am free from wickedness. I am not even like this publican. I fast twice in each week. I give to God one tenth of all that I have.' But the publican, standing afar off, would not lift up so much as his eyes unto heaven, but beat his breast, saying, 'God be merciful to me, a sinner!'

"I say unto you," said Jē'ṣus, "this man went down to his house having his sins forgiven rather than the other. For everyone that lifteth up himself shall be brought low; and he that is humble shall be lifted up."

And at this time the mothers brought to Jē'ṣus their little children, that he might lay his hands on them and bless them. The disciples were not pleased at this and told them to take their children away. But Jē'ṣus called them to him and said, "Suffer the little children to come unto me, and forbid them not, for of such is the kingdom of God. Whoever shall not receive the kingdom

of God as a little child, he shall not enter into it." And he put his hands on them and blessed them.

And a certain young man, a ruler, came running to Jḗ′sus, and said, "Good Master, what shall I do that I may have everlasting life?"

"Why do you call me good?" said Jḗ′sus. "No one is good except one, that is God. You know the commandments; keep them."

"What commandments?" asked the young man.

"Do not kill; do not commit adultery; do not steal; do not bear false witness; honor thy father and mother."

The young man said, "All these I have kept from my youth up. What do I need more than these?"

And Jḗ′sus looking on the young man, and seeing that he was so earnest in his wish to do right, loved him, and said, "If you would be perfect, one thing more you need to do. Go sell all that you have and give to the poor, and you shall have treasure in heaven. Then come and follow me."

But when he heard this, he turned and went away very sad, for he was very rich. And when Jḗ′sus saw this, he said, "How hard it is for those that are rich to enter into the kingdom of God! It is easier for a camel to go through the eye of a needle than for a rich man to enter into the kingdom of God."

At this the disciples were filled with wonder. They said, "If that be so, then who can be saved?"

And Jē'ṣus said, "The things that are impossible with men are possible with God."

And Pē'tẽr said, "Lord, we have left our homes and all that we have and have followed thee."

And Jē'ṣus answered him, "Verily, I say to you, there is no man who has left house or wife or brothers or parents or children, for the sake of the kingdom of God, who shall not have given to him many more times in this life and in the world to come life everlasting."

Then Jē'ṣus again told his twelve disciples of what was soon to come to pass, even in a few weeks. He said, "We are going up to Jē-ru'ṣà-lĕm, and there all the things written by the prophets about the Son of man shall come true. He shall be made a prisoner and shall be mocked and treated shamefully, and shall be spit upon and beaten, and shall be killed; and then the third day he shall rise again."

But they could not understand these things, and they did not believe that their Master was to die.

Story Twenty-nine

MATTHEW 20 : 20-34; MARK 10 : 35-52; LUKE 18 : 35 to 19 : 28

Jesus at Jericho

JE'SUS was passing through the land of Pe-rē'à east of the river Jôr'dan on his way to Jē-ru'ṣà-lĕm. His disciples were with him and a great multitude of people, for again the feast of the Passover was near, and the people from all parts of the land were going up to Jē-ru'ṣà-lĕm to take part in the feast; and although Jē'ṣus had said over and over again that he was to die in Jē-ru'ṣà-lĕm, still many believed that in Jē-ru'ṣà-lĕm he would make himself king and would reign over all the land.

On one day Jāmeş and Jŏhn, two of the disciples of Jē'şus, who were brothers, the son of Zĕb'e-dee, came to Jē'şus with their mother. She knelt before Jē'şus, and her two sons knelt beside her. Jē'şus said to her, "What is it that you would ask of me?"

She said to him, "Lord, grant to me that my two sons may be allowed to sit beside thy throne, one on the right hand, the other on thy left, in thy kingdom."

"You do not know what you are asking," answered Jē'şus. "Are you able to drink of the cup that I am about to drink?"

By "the cup" he meant the suffering that he was soon to endure; but this they did not understand, and they said, "We are able."

He said to them, "My cup indeed you shall drink; but to sit on my right hand and on my left is not mine to give, but it shall be given to those for whom God has made it ready."

When the other disciples heard that Jāmeş and Jŏhn had tried to get the promise of the highest places in the Lord's kingdom, they were very angry against these two brothers. But Jē'şus called them to him and he said, "You know that the rulers of nations lord it over them; and their great ones are those who bear rule. But not so shall it be among you. For whoever among you would be great, let him serve the rest. For the Son of man himself did not come to be served, but to serve others; and to give up his life that he might save many." Jē'şus with his disciples and a

great multitude drew nigh to Jĕr′ĭ-chō, which was at the foot of
the mountains, near the head of the Dead Sea.   Just outside the
city, at the gate, was sitting a blind man begging.   His name was
Bär-ti-mæ′us, which means "The Son of Tī-mæ′us."   This man
heard the noise of a crowd and he asked what it meant.   They said
to him, "Jē′ṣus of Năz′a-rĕth is passing by."   As soon as he heard
this, he began to cry out aloud, "Jē′ṣus, son of Dā′vid, have mercy
on me!"

Many people told him not to make so great a noise, but he cried
all the louder, "Jē′ṣus, son of Dā′vid, have mercy on me!"

Jē′ṣus heard his cry and stood still and said, "Call the man to
me!"

Then they came to the blind man and said, "Be of good cheer;
rise up; he calls you!"

The blind man sprang up from the ground and threw away his
outer garments and came to Jē′ṣus.   And Jē′ṣus said to him, "What
do you wish me to do to you?"

"Lord, that I might have my sight given to me," answered blind
Bär-ti-mæ′us.

Then Jē′ṣus touched his eyes and said, "Go your way; your
faith has made you well."

Then immediately sight came to his eyes and he followed Jē′ṣus,
while all the people who saw it gave thanks to God.

There was another man in Jĕr′ĭ-chō who had heard of Jē′ṣus
and greatly longed to see him.   This was a man named Zăc-chæ′us.
He was a chief man among the publicans, the men who gathered
the taxes from the people, and whom all the people hated greatly.
Zăc-chæ′us was a rich man, for many of the publicans made great
gains.   Wishing to see Jē′ṣus, and being little in size, Zăc-chæ′us
ran on before the crowd and climbed up into a sycamore tree by
the road, so that he might see Jē′ṣus as he passed by.

When Jē′ṣus came to the tree, he stopped and looked up and
called Zăc-chæ′us by name, saying, "Zăc-chæ′us, make haste and
come down, for today I must stop in your house."

At this Zăc-chæ′us was glad.   He came down at once and took
Jē′ṣus into his house.   But at this many of the people found fault.
They said, "He has gone in to lodge with a man who is a sinner!"

Because he was a publican, they counted him as a sinner. But Zăc-chæ'us stood before the Lord and said, "Lord, the half of my goods I give to the poor; and if I have wrongly taken anything from any man, I give him four times as much."

And Jē'ṣus said, "Today salvation has come to this house; for this man also is a son of Ā'bră-hăm. For the Son of man came to seek and to save that which was lost."

Jē'ṣus was now drawing nigh to Jĕ-ru'ṣȧ-lĕm, and all the people were expecting the kingdom of God to begin at once, with Jē'ṣus as its king. On this account, Jē'ṣus gave to the people "The Parable of the Pounds," saying, "A certain nobleman went to a far country, expecting there to be made a king and thence to return to his own land. Before going away, he called ten servants of his and gave to each one a pound of money, and said to them, 'Take care of this and trade with it until I come back.' [A pound was a sum in silver worth about twenty dollars.]

"But the people of his own land hated this nobleman and sent messengers to the place where he had gone, to say, 'We are not willing that this man should be king over us.'

"But in the face of this message from the people, the nobleman received the crown and the kingdom and then went back to his own land. When he had come home, he called his servants to whom he had given the pounds, so that he might know how much each had gained by trading. The first servant came before him and said, 'Lord, your pound has made ten pounds more, and is now worth two hundred dollars.'

"The king said to him, 'Well done, my good servant; because you have been found faithful in a very little, you shall bear rule over ten cities.'

"And the second came, saying, 'Your twenty dollars my lord has made a hundred dollars.' And his lord said to him, 'You shall be over five cities.'

"And another came, saying, 'Lord, here is your twenty dollars, which I have kept wrapped up in a napkin; for I feared you, because you are a harsh master; you take up what you did not lay down and you reap what you did not sow.' He said to the servant, 'Out of your own mouth I will judge you, you unfaithful servant.

If you knew that I was a harsh master, taking up what I did not lay down and reaping what I did not sow, then why did you not put my money into the bank, so that when I came I should have had my own money and its gains?' And he said to those who were standing by, 'Take away from him the pound and give it to him that has the ten pounds.'

"They said to him, 'Lord, he has two hundred dollars already!'

"But the king said, 'Unto everyone who cares for what he has, more shall be given; but the one who cares not for it, what he has shall be taken away from him.'

"And the king added, 'Those, my enemies, who would not have me to reign over them; bring them here and slay them before me.'"

And after giving this parable, Jē′ṣus went before his disciples up the mountains toward Jĕ-ru′sȧ-lĕm.

Story Thirty   MATTHEW 21 : 1-11; 26 : 6-16; MARK 11 : 1-11; 14 : 3-11;
                LUKE 19 : 29-41; 22 : 3-6; JOHN 12 : 1-19

Palm Sunday

FROM Jĕr′ĭ-chō, Jē′ṣus and his disciples went up the mountain and came to Bĕth′a-nȳ, where his friends Mär′thȧ and Mā′rȳ lived, and where he had raised Lăz′a-rŭs to life. Many people in Jĕ-ru′sȧ-lĕm heard that Jē′ṣus was there; and they went out of the city to see him, for Bĕth′a-nȳ was only two miles from Jĕ-ru′sȧ-lĕm. Some came also to see Lăz′a-rŭs, whom Jē′ṣus had raised from the dead; but the rulers of the Jews said to each other:

"We must not only kill Jē′ṣus but Lăz′a-rŭs also, because on his account so many of the people are going after Jē′ṣus and are believing on him."

The friends of Jē′ṣus in Bĕth′a-nȳ made a supper for Jē′ṣus at the home of a man named Sī′mon. He was called "Sī′mon the

Leper"; and perhaps he was one whom Jē'ṣus had cured of leprosy. Jē'ṣus and his disciples, with Lăz'a-rŭs, leaned upon the couches around the table, as the guests; and Mär'thà was one of those who waited upon them. While they were at the supper, Mā'rў, the sister of Lăz'a-rŭs, came into the room, carrying a sealed jar of very precious perfume. She opened the jar and poured some of the perfume upon the head of Jē'ṣus and some upon his feet, and she wiped his feet with her long hair. And the whole house was filled with the fragrance of the perfume.

But one of the disciples of Jē'ṣus, Jū'das Ĭs-căr'ĭ-ot, was not pleased at this. He said, "Why was such a waste of the perfume made? This might have been sold for more than forty-five dollars, and the money given to the poor!"

This he said, but not because he cared for the poor. Jū'das was the one who kept the bag of money for Jē'ṣus and the twelve, and he was a thief and took away for his own use all the money that he could steal.

But Jē'ṣus said, "Let her alone; why do you find fault with the woman? She has done a good work upon me. You have the poor always with you, and whenever you wish, you can give to them. But you will have me with you only a little while. She has done what she could; for she has come to perfume my body for its burial. And truly I say to you, that wherever the gospel shall be preached throughout all the world, what this woman has done shall be told in memory of her." Perhaps Mā'rў knew what others did not believe, that Jē'ṣus was soon to die; and she showed her love for him and her sorrow for his coming death, by this rich gift.

But Jū'das, the disciple who carried the bag, was very angry at Jē'ṣus; and from that time he was looking for a chance to betray Jē'ṣus or to give him up to his enemies. He went to the chief priests and said, "What will you give me if I will put Jē'ṣus into your hands?"

They said, "We will give you thirty pieces of silver."

And for thirty pieces of silver Jū'das promised to help them take Jē'ṣus and make him their prisoner.

On the morning after the supper at Bĕth'a-nў, Jē'ṣus called two of his disciples and said to them, "Go into the next village and at a place where two roads cross, you will find an ass tied and a colt with it. Loose them and bring them to me. And if anyone says to you, 'Why do you do this?' say 'The Lord has need of them,' and they will let them go."

They went to the place and found the ass and the colt, and they were loosing them when the owner said, "What are you doing, untying the ass?"

And they said, as Jē'ṣus had told them to say, "The Lord has need of it!"

Then the owner gave them the ass and the colt for the use of Jē'ṣus. They brought them to Jē'ṣus, on the Mount of Ŏl'ĭveṣ, and they laid some of their own clothes on the colt for a cushion, and set Jē'ṣus upon it. Then all the disciples and a very great multitude threw their garments upon the ground for Jē'ṣus to ride upon. Others cut down branches from the trees and laid them on the ground.

And as Jē'ṣus rode over the mountain toward Jĕ-ru'ṣȧ-lĕm, many walked before him waving branches of palm trees. And they all cried together:

"Blessed be the Son of Dā'vid! Blessed is he that cometh in the name of the Lord! Blessed be the kingdom of our father Dā'vid, that cometh in the name of the Lord! May the highest of God's blessings be upon the King!"

These things they said because they believed that Jē'ṣus was the Chrīst, the Anointed King, and they hoped that he would now set up his throne in Jĕ-rụ'ṣȧ-lĕm. Some of the Phăr'ĭ-seeṣ in the crowd, who did not believe in Jē'ṣus, said to him, "Master, stop your disciples!"

But Jē'ṣus said, "I tell you, that if these should be still, the very stones would cry out!"

And when he came into Jĕ-rụ'ṣȧ-lĕm with all this multitude, all the city was filled with wonder. They said, "Who is this?"

And the multitude answered, "This is Jē'ṣus, the prophet of Năz'a-rĕth in Găl'ĭ-lee!"

And Jē'ṣus went into the Temple and looked around it; but he did not stay, because the hour was late. He went again to Bĕth'-a-nў and there stayed at night with his friends.

These things took place on Sunday, the first day of the week; and that Sunday in the year is called Palm Sunday, because of the palm branches which the people carried before Jē'ṣus.

Story Thirty-one

MATTHEW 21 : 18 to 23 : 39; MARK 11 : 12 to 12 : 44; LUKE 19 : 45 to 21 : 4

The Last Visits of Jesus to the Temple

ON MONDAY morning, the second day of the week, Jē'ṣus rose very early in the morning and, without waiting to take his breakfast, went with his disciples from Bĕth'a-nў over the Mount of Ŏl'ĭveṣ toward Jĕ-rụ'ṣȧ-lĕm. On the mountain he saw at a distance a fig tree covered with leaves, and although it was early for figs to be ripe, he hoped that he might find upon it some figs fit to be eaten. Among the Jewṣ and by their law, anyone passing a tree could eat of its fruit, even though he was not the owner; but he would not be allowed to carry any away.

But when Jē'ṣus came near to this tree, he saw that there was no fruit upon it neither ripe nor green, but leaves only. Then a thought came into the mind of Jē'ṣus; and he spoke to the tree, while his disciples heard his words, "No fruit shall grow on thee from this time forever." And then he walked on his way to Jĕ-ru'ṣȧ-lĕm. We shall see later why Jē'ṣus spoke those words and what came from them.

You remember that when Jē'ṣus came to Jĕ-ru'ṣȧ-lĕm the first time after he began to preach, he found the courts of the Temple filled with people buying and selling and changing money, and he drove them all out. But that had been three years before; and now when Jē'ṣus came into the Temple on the Monday morning before the Passover, he found all the traders there once more, selling the oxen and sheep and doves for sacrifices and changing money at the tables.

And again Jē'ṣus rose up against these people who would make his Father's house a shop and a place of gain. He drove them all out; he turned over the tables of the money changers, scattering their money on the floor; he cleared away the seats of those that were selling doves; and whenever he saw anyone even carrying a jar or a basket or any load through the Temple, he stopped him and made him go back. He said to all the people, "It is written in the prophets, My house shall be called a house of prayer for all nations, but you have made it a den of robbers!"

The Jews had made it a rule that no blind man nor any lame man could go into the Temple; for they thought only those perfect in body should come before the Lord. But they forgot that God looks at hearts and not at bodies. And when Jē'ṣus found that many blind and lame people were at the doors of the Temple, he allowed them to come in, and made them all well.

And the little children, who always loved Jē'ṣus, saw him in the Temple, and they cried out, as they heard others crying, "Blessings to the Son of Dā'vid!"

The chief priests and scribes were greatly displeased as they heard the voices of these children, and they said to Jē'ṣus, "Do you hear what these are saying?"

And Jē'ṣus said, "Yes; and have you never read what is written in the Psalms, 'Out of the mouth of babes and little ones, thou hast made thy praise perfect'?"

All the common people came to hear Jē'ṣus as he taught in the Temple, and they listened to him gladly, for he gave them plain and simple teachings, with many parables or stories. But the rulers and chief priests grew more and more angry as they saw the courts of the Temple filled with people eager to hear Jē'ṣus. They tried to find some way to lay hands on Jē'ṣus and to kill him; but they dared not while all the crowds were around him.

All that day Jē'ṣus taught the people, and when night came, he went out of the city over the Mount of Ŏl'ĭveṣ to Bĕth'a-nӯ, where he was safe among his friends.

And on the next morning, which was Tuesday of the week before the Passover, Jē'ṣus again went over the Mount of Ŏl'ĭveṣ with his disciples. They passed the fig tree to which Jē'ṣus had spoken such strange words on the day before. And now the disciples saw that the tree was standing, withered and dead, with its leaves dry and rustling in the wind.

"Look, Master!" said Pē'tēr. "The fig tree to which you spoke yesterday is withered!"

And Jē'ṣus said to them all, "Have faith in God, for in truth I say to you, that if you have faith, you shall not only do this which has been done to the fig tree; but also, if you shall say to this mountain, 'Be moved away and thrown into the sea!' it shall be done. And all things, whatever they may be, that you ask in prayer, if you have faith, shall be given to you." Again Jē'ṣus went into the Temple and taught the people.

And Jē'ṣus gave another parable or story, that of "The Wedding Feast." He said:

"There was a certain king who made a great feast at the wedding of his son; and he sent out his servant to call those whom he had invited to the feast. But they would not come. Then he sent forth other servants, and said, 'Tell those who were invited that my dinner is all ready; my oxen are killed and the dishes are on the table. Say to them, "All things are ready; come to the marriage feast!" '

"But the men who had been sent for would not come. One went to his farm, another to his shop, and some of them seized the servants whom he sent, and beat them and treated them roughly; and some of them they killed. This made the king very angry. He sent his armies and killed those murderers, and burned up their city. Then he said to his servants, 'The wedding feast is ready, but those that were invited were not worthy of such honor. Go out into the streets and call in everybody that you can find, high and low, rich and poor, good and bad, and tell them that they are welcome.'

"The servants went out and invited all the people of every kind and brought them to the feast, so that all the places were filled. And to all who came they gave a wedding garment, so that everyone might be dressed as was fitting before the king.

"But when the king came in to meet his guests, he saw there a man who had not on a wedding garment. He said to him, 'Friend, why have you come to the feast without a wedding garment?'

"The man had nothing to say; he stood as one dumb. Then the king said to his officers, 'Bind him hand and foot and throw him out into the darkness, where there shall be weeping and gnashing of teeth. For in the kingdom of God many are called, but few are chosen.' "

The enemies of Jē'ṣus thought that they had found a way to bring him into trouble, either with the people, or with the Rō'-manṣ, who were the rulers over the land. So they sent to him some men, who acted as though they were honest and true, but were in their hearts seeking to destroy Jē'ṣus. These men came and they said, "Master, we know that you teach the truth and that you are not afraid of any man. Now tell what is right and what we should do. Ought our people, the Jewṣ, to pay taxes to the Rō'man emperor Çae'ṣar, or not? Shall we pay, or shall we not pay?"

And they watched for his answer. If he should say, "It is right to pay the tax," then these men could tell the people, "Jē'ṣus is the friend of the Rō'manṣ and the enemy of the Jewṣ." And then they would turn away from him. But if he should say, "It is not right to pay the tax, refuse to pay it," then they could say to the Rō'man governor that Jē'ṣus would not obey the laws, and the governor might put him in prison or kill him. So whatever answer Jē'ṣus might give, they hoped he might make trouble for himself.

But Jē'ṣus knew their hate and the thoughts of their hearts, and he said, "Let me see a piece of the money that is given for the tax."

They brought him a silver piece, and he looked at it and said, "Whose head is this on the coin? Whose name is written over it?"

They answered him, "That is Çae'ṣar, the Rō'man emperor."

"Well, then," said Jē'ṣus, "give to Çae'ṣar the things that are Çae'ṣar's, and give to God the things that are God's!"

They wondered at his answer, for it was so wise that they could speak nothing against it. They tried him with other questions, but he answered them all and left his enemies with nothing to say. Then Jē'ṣus turned upon his enemies and spoke to them his last words. He told them of their wickedness and warned them that they would bring down the wrath of God upon them.

Jē'ṣus was in the part of the Temple called "The Treasury," because around the wall were boxes in which the people dropped their gifts when they came to worship. Some that were rich gave much money; but a poor widow came by and dropped in two little coins, the very smallest, the two together worth only a quarter of a cent. Jē′ṣus said, "I tell you in truth that this poor widow has dropped into the treasury more than all the rest. For the others gave out of their plenty, but she, in her need, has given all that she had."

And with these words Jē′ṣus rose up and went out of the Temple for the last time. Never again was the voice of Jē′ṣus heard within those walls.

Story Thirty-two   MATTHEW, chapters 24; 25; MARK 8 : 1-37; LUKE 21 : 5-38

The Parables on the Mount of Olives

AFTER Jē′ṣus had spoken his last words to the people and their rulers, he walked out of the Temple with his disciples. As they were passing through the great gates on the east of the Temple, the disciples said to Jē′ṣus, "Master, what a splendid building this is! Look at these great stones in the foundation!"

Jē′ṣus answered the disciples, "Do you see these great walls? The time is coming when these buildings shall be thrown down; when not one stone that you are looking upon shall be left in its place; when the very foundations of this house and this city shall be torn up!"

These words filled the followers of Jē′ṣus with the deepest sorrow, for they loved the Temple and the city of Jĕ-ru′ṣå-lĕm, as all Jews loved it, and to them its fall seemed the ruin of the whole world. Yet they believed the words of their Master, for they knew that he was a prophet whose words were sure to come to pass, and that he was more than a prophet, even the Son of

God. They walked with Jē′ṣus down into the valley of the brook Kē′dron and up the slopes of the Mount of Ŏl′ĭveṣ. On the top of the mountain they looked down upon the Temple and the city; and then some of the disciples said to Jē′ṣus:

"Master, tell us when shall these dreadful things be? Give us some sign, that we may know when they are coming."

Then Jē′ṣus sat down with his disciples on the mountain and told them of many things that were to come upon the city and the world; how wars should arise and earthquakes and diseases should break forth; how enemies were to come and fight against Jĕ-ru′ṣà-lĕm and destroy it and scatter its people; and how trouble should come upon all the earth. And he told them that he would some time come again, as the Lord of all; and that all who believe in him should watch and be ready to meet him. Then he gave the parable of "The Ten Young Women." This was the story:

"There were ten young women who were going out one night with their lamps in their hands to meet a wedding party. Five of these young women were wise and five were foolish. Those that were foolish took with them their lighted lamps, but had no more oil than that which was in their lamps; but each of the wise young women carried also a bottle of oil. It was night, and while they were waiting for the bridal party, they all fell asleep. At midnight they were all awaked by the sudden cry, 'The bride-groom is coming! Go out to meet him!'

"Then all the young women rose up and trimmed their lamps. And the foolish ones said, 'Let us have some of your oil, for our lamps are going out.'

"But the other young women said, 'There will not be enough for us and for you too; go to those who sell, and buy oil for yourselves.'

"The young women who had no oil went away to buy; and while they were away, the bridal party came; and those that were ready, went in with them to the feast, and then the door was shut. And afterward the other young women came, knocking on the door and calling out, 'Lord, Lord, open to us!'

"But he said, 'I do not know you.'

"And he would not open the door. Watch therefore, for you do not know the day nor the hour when your Lord will come."

Jē'ṣus also gave to his disciples another parable or picture of what shall come to pass at the end of the world. He said:

"When the Son of man shall come in his glory, and all the angels of God shall come with him, then he shall sit on his glorious throne as King. And before him shall be brought together all the people of the world; and he shall divide them and make them stand apart, just as a shepherd divides the sheep from the goats. And he shall put his sheep on his right hand and the goats on his left. Then the King shall say to those on his right hand, 'Come ye whom my Father has blessed; come and take the kingdom which God has made ready for you. For I was hungry and you gave me food; I was thirsty and you gave me drink; I was a stranger and you took me into your home; I was naked and you gave me clothes; I was sick and you visited me; I was in prison and you came to me.'

"Then all those on the right of the King will say:

" 'Lord, when did we see thee hungry and feed thee? or thirsty and gave thee drink? And when did we see thee a stranger, and took thee in? or naked and gave thee clothes? And when did we see thee sick or in prison and come to thee?'

"And the King shall answer and shall say to them:

" 'Inasmuch as you did it to one of these my brothers, even the very least of them, you did it to me.'

"Then the King shall turn to those on his left hand and shall say to them:

" 'Go away from me, ye cursed ones, into the everlasting fire which has been made ready for the devil and his angels. For I was hungry and you gave me no food; I was thirsty and you gave me no drink; I was a stranger and you did not open your doors to me; I was naked and you gave me no clothes; I was sick and in prison, and you did not visit me.'

"Then shall they answer him:

" 'Lord, when did we see thee hungry or thirsty or a stranger or naked or sick or in prison, and did not help thee?'

"And the King shall say to them:

" 'Inasmuch as you did it not to one of these the least of my brothers, you did it not to me.'

"And the wicked shall go away to be punished forever; but the righteous unto everlasting life."

After these words, Jē'ṣus went with his disciples again to Bĕth'a-nў.

Story Thirty-three

MATTHEW 26 : 17-35; MARK 14 : 12-31;
LUKE 22 : 7-38; JOHN, chapters 13 to 17

The Last Supper

ON ONE of the days in the week before the Passover the disciples came to Jē'ṣus at Bĕth'a-nў and said, "Master, where shall we make ready the Passover for you to eat?"

Then Jē'ṣus called to himself the two disciples, Pē'tēr and Jŏhn, and said to them, "Go into the city, and a man carrying a pitcher of water will meet you; follow him and go into the house where he goes, and say to the head of the house, 'The Master says, "Where is my guest room, where I can eat the Passover with my disciples?" '

"And he will himself show you a large upper room, furnished; there make ready for us."

Pē'tēr and Jŏhn went into Jē-rụ'ṡå-lĕm, and soon in the street hey saw a man walking toward them carrying a pitcher of water. They followed him, went into the house where he took the pitcher, and spoke to the man who seemed to be its head:

"The Master says, 'Where is the guest room for me, where I may eat the Passover with my disciples?' "

The man led them upstairs and showed them a large upper room, with the table and the couches around it, all ready for the guests at dinner. Then the disciples went out and brought a lamb and roasted it; and made ready the vegetables and the thin wafers of bread made without yeast, for the meal.

On Thursday afternoon, Jē′șus and his disciples walked out of Bĕth′a-nȳ together, over the Mount of Ŏl′īveṣ, and into the city. Only Jē′șus, who could read the thoughts of men, knew that one of these disciples, Jū′das, had made a promise to the chief priests to lead them and their servants to Jē′șus, when the hour should come to seize him: and Jū′das was watching for the best time to do his dreadful deed. They came into the house and went upstairs to the large room, where they found the supper all ready. The meal was spread upon a table; and around the table were couches for the company, where each one lay down with his head toward the table, so near that he could help himself to the food, while his feet were at the foot of the couch, toward the wall of the room. Their feet were bare, for they had all taken off their sandals as they came in.

Jē′șus was leaning at the head of the table, and Jŏhn, the disciple whom Jē′șus loved most, was lying next to him. While they were eating, Jē′șus took bread and gave thanks. Then he broke it and passed a piece to each one of the twelve, saying:

"Take and eat; this is my body which is broken for you; do this and remember me."

Afterward, he took the cup of wine and passed it to each one, with the words:

"This cup is my blood, shed for you and for many, that their sins may be taken away; as often as you drink this, remember me."

While they were still leaning on the couches around the table, Jē′șus rose up and took off his outer robe and then tied around his waist a long towel. He poured water into a basin, and while all the disciples were wondering, he carried the water to the feet of one of the disciples and began to wash them, just as though he himself were a servant. Then he washed the feet of another disciple and then of still another. When he came to Sī'mon Pē'tẽr, Pē'tẽr said to him, "Dost thou, O Lord, wash my feet?"

Jē'ṣus said to him, "What I do, you cannot understand now, but you will understand it after a time."

"Lord, thou shalt never wash my feet," said Pē'tẽr.

"If I do not wash you," said Jē'ṣus, "then you are none of mine."

Then Pē'tẽr said, "O Lord, wash not only my feet, but my hands and my head too!"

But Jē'ṣus said to him, "No, Pē'tẽr; one who has already bathed needs only to wash his feet and then he is clean. And you are clean, but not all of you."

For he knew that among those whose feet he was washing was one, the traitor, who would soon give him up to his enemies. After he had washed their feet, he put on his garments again and leaned once more on his couch and looked around and said:

"Do you know what I have done to you? You call me 'Master' and 'Lord,' and you speak rightly, for so I am. If I, your Lord and Master, have washed your feet, you also ought to wash each other's feet; for I have given you an example that you should do to each other as I have done to you."

By this Jē′ṣus meant that all who follow him should help and
:rve each other, instead of seeking great things for themselves.
  While Jē′ṣus was talking, he became very sad and sorrowful and
iid, "Verily, verily, I say to you, that one of you that are eating
vith me shall betray me and give me up to those who will kill me."
  Then all the disciples looked round on each other, wondering
vho was the one that Jē′ṣus meant. One said and another said,
Am I the one, Lord?"
  And Jē′ṣus said, "It is one of you twelve men, who are dipping
our hands into the same dish and eating with me. The Son of
nan goes, as it is written of him; but woe to that man who betrays
im and gives him up to die. It would have been good for that
nan if he had never been born."
  While Jē′ṣus was speaking, Sī′mon Pē′tēr made signs to Jŏhn
cross the table, that he, leaning next to Jē′ṣus, should ask him who
his traitor was. So Jŏhn whispered to Jē′ṣus, as he was lying close
o him, "Lord, who is it?"
  Jē′ṣus answered, but so low that none else heard, "It is the one
o whom I will give a piece of bread after I have dipped it in the
lish."
  Then Jē′ṣus dipped into the dish a piece of bread and gave it to
ū′das Ĭs-căr′ĭ-ot, who was lying near him. And as he gave it, he
aid, "Do quickly what you are going to do."
  No one except Jŏhn knew what this meant. Not all heard what
ē′ṣus said to Jū′das; and those who heard thought that Jē′ṣus was
elling him to do something belonging to the feast, or perhaps, as
ū′das carried the money, that he should make some gift to the
oor. But Jū′das at once went out, for he saw that his plan was
cnown, and it must be carried out now or never. He knew that
fter the supper Jē′ṣus would go back to Bĕth′a-nȳ, and he went to
he rulers, told them where they might watch for Jē′ṣus on his
vay back to Bĕth′a-nȳ, and went with a band of men to a place
t the feet of the Mount of Ŏl′ĭveṣ, where he was sure Jē′ṣus would
oass.
  As soon as Jū′das had gone out, Jē′ṣus said to the eleven disciples, "Little children, I shall be with you only a little while.
 am going away; and where I go, you cannot come now. But

when I am gone away from you, remember this new command
ment that I give you, that you love one another even as I hav
loved you."

Sī'mon Pē'tẽr said to Jē'ṣus, "Lord, where are you going?"

Jē'ṣus answered, "Where I go, you cannot follow me now, bu
you shall follow me afterward."

Pē'tẽr said to him, "Lord, why cannot I follow you even now,
I will lay down my life for your sake."

Jē'ṣus said, "Will you lay down your life for me? I tell you
Pē'tẽr, that before the cock crows tomorrow morning, you wil
three times deny that you have ever known me!"

But Pē'tẽr said, "Though I die, I will never deny you, Lord!"

And so said all the other disciples; but Jē'ṣus said to them
"Before morning comes, every one of you will leave me alone
Yet I will not be alone, for my Father will be with me."

Jē'ṣus saw that Pē'tẽr and all his disciples were full of sorrow
at his words, and he said, "Let not your hearts be troubled; believ
in God, believe also in me. In my Father's house are many rooms
if it were not so, I would have told you; for I am going to mak
ready a place for you. And when it is ready, I will come again
and take you to myself, that where I am, there you may be also."

Then Jē'ṣus talked with the disciples a long time, and prayeᵈ
for them. And about midnight they left the supper room together
and came to the Mount of Ŏl'ĭveṣ.

The Olive Orchard and the High Priest's Hall

A T THE foot of the Mount of Ŏl'ĭveṣ, near the path over the hill toward Bĕth'a-nÿ, there was an orchard of olive trees, called "The Garden of Gĕth-sĕm'a-nė." The word "Gĕth-sĕm'a-nė" means "Oil Press." Jē'ṣus often went to this place with his disciples, because of its quiet shade. At this garden he stopped, and outside he left eight of his disciples, saying to them, "Sit here, while I go inside and pray."

He took with him the three chosen ones, Pē'tẽr, Jāmeṣ, and Jŏhn, and went within the orchard. Jē'ṣus knew that in a little while Jū'das would be there with a band of men to seize him; that within a few hours he would be beaten and stripped and led out to die. The thought of what he was to suffer came upon him and filled his soul with grief.

He said to Pē'tẽr and Jāmeṣ and Jŏhn:

"My soul is filled with sorrow; a sorrow that almost kills me. Stay here and watch while I am praying."

He went a little farther among the trees and flung himself down upon the ground and cried out:

"O my Father, if it be possible, let this cup pass away from me; nevertheless, not as I will, but as thou willest!"

So strong was his feeling and so great his suffering, that there came out upon his face great drops of sweat like blood, falling upon the ground. After praying for a time, he rose up from the earth and went to his three disciples; and he found them all asleep. He awaked them and said to Pē'tẽr:

"What, could you not watch with me one hour? Watch and pray, that you may not go into temptation. The spirit indeed is willing, but the flesh is weak."

551

He left them and went a second time into the woods, and he fell on his knees and prayed again, saying:

"O my Father, if this cup cannot pass away, and I must drink it, then thy will be done."

He came again to the three disciples and found them sleeping; but this time he did not wake them. He went once more into the woods and prayed, using the same words. And an angel from heaven came to him and gave him strength.

He was now ready for the fate that was soon to come, and his heart was strong. Once more he went to the three disciples and said to them:

"You may as well sleep on now and take your rest, for the hour is at hand; and already the Son of man is given by the traitor into the hands of sinners. But rise up, and let us be going. See, the traitor is here!"

The disciples awoke; they heard the noise of a crowd and saw the flashing of torches and the gleaming of swords and spears. In the throng they saw Jū′das standing, and they knew now that he was the traitor of whom Jē′ṣus had spoken the night before. Jū′das

ame rushing forward and kissed Jē′ṣus, as though he were glad
o see him. This was a signal that he had given beforehand to the
 band; for the men of the guard did not know Jē′ṣus, and Jū′das had
said to them, "The one that I shall kiss is the man that you are to
ake; seize him and hold him fast."

Jē′ṣus said to Jū′das, "Jū′das, do you betray the Son of man with
a kiss?"

Then he turned to the crowd and said, "Whom do you seek?"

They answered, "Jē′ṣus of Năz′a-rĕth."

Jē′ṣus said, "I am he."

When Jē′ṣus said this, a sudden fear came upon his enemies; they
drew back and fell upon the ground.

After a moment, Jē′ṣus said again, "Whom do you seek?"

And again they answered, "Jē′ṣus of Năz′a-rĕth."

And Jē′ṣus said, pointing to his disciples, "I told you that I am
he. If you are seeking me, let these disciples go their own way."

But as they came forward to seize Jē′ṣus, Pē′tĕr drew his sword,
and struck at one of the men in front and cut off his right ear.
The man was a servant of the high priest and his name was
Măl′chus.

Jē′ṣus said to Pē′tĕr, "Put up the sword into its sheath; the cup
which my Father has given me, shall I not drink it? Do you not
know that I could call upon my Father, and he would send to me
armies upon armies of angels?"

Then he spoke to the crowd, "Let me do this." And he
touched the place where the ear had been cut off, and it came on
again and was well. Jē′ṣus said to the rulers and leaders of the
armed men, "Do you come out against me with swords and clubs
as though I were a robber? I was with you every day in the
Temple, and you did not lift your hands against me. But the
words in the Scriptures must come to pass; and this is your hour."

When the disciples of Jē′ṣus saw that he would not allow them
to fight for him, they did not know what to do. In their sudden
alarm they all ran away and left their Master alone with his
enemies. These men laid their hands on Jē′ṣus and bound him and
led him away to the house of the high priest. There were at that
time two men called high priests by the Jewṣ. One was Ăn′nas,

who had been high priest until his office had been taken from him
by the Rō′mans and given to Cā′ia-phăs, his son-in-law. But
Ăn′nas still had great power among the people; and they brought
Jē′sus, all bound as he was, first before Ăn′nas.

Sī′mon Pē′tēr and Jŏhn, the disciple whom Jē′sus loved, had
followed after the crowd of those who carried Jē′sus away, and
they came to the door of the high priest's house. Jŏhn knew the
high priest and went in, but Pē′tēr at first stayed outside, until
Jŏhn went out and brought him in. He came in, but did not dare
to go into the room where Jē′sus stood before the high priest
Ăn′nas. In the courtyard of the house they had made a fire of
charcoal, and Pē′tēr stood among those who were warming themselves at the fire.

Ăn′nas, in the inner room, asked Jē′sus about his disciples and
teaching. Jē′sus answered him, "What I have taught has been
openly in the synagogues and in the Temple. Why do you ask
me? Ask those that heard me; they know what I said."

Then one of the officers struck Jē′sus on the mouth, saying to
him, "Is this the way that you answer the high priest?"

Jē′sus answered the officer calmly and quietly, "If I have said
anything evil, tell what the evil is; but if I have spoken the truth,
why do you strike me?"

While Ăn′nas and his men were thus showing their hate toward
Jē′sus, who stood bound and alone among his enemies, Pē′tēr was
still in the courtyard, warming himself at the fire. A woman, who
was a serving maid in the house, looked at Pē′tēr sharply and
finally said to him, "You were one of those men with this Jē′sus
of Năz′a-rĕth!"

Pē′tēr was afraid to tell the truth and he answered her,
"Woman, I do not know the man and I do not know what you
are talking about."

And to get away from her, he went out into the porch of the
house. There another woman servant saw him and said, "This
man was one of those with Jē′sus!"

And Pē′tēr swore with an oath that he did not know Jē′sus at
all. Soon a man came by, who was of kin to Măl′chus, whose ear
Pē′tēr had cut off. He looked at Pē′tēr and heard him speak and

aid, "You are surely one of this man's disciples, for your speech hows that you came from Găl'ĭ-lee."

Then Pē'tēr began again to curse and to swear, declaring that he did not know the man of whom they were speaking.

Just at that moment the loud, shrill crowing of a cock startled Pē'tēr, and at the same time he saw Jē'şus, who was being dragged hrough the hall from Ăn'nas to the council room of Cā'ia-phăs, he other high priest. And the Lord turned as he was passing and ooked at Pē'tēr.

Then there flashed into Pē'tēr's mind what Jē'şus had said on he evening before, "Before the cock crows tomorrow morning, ou will three times deny that you have ever known me."

Then Pē'tēr went out into the street and wept bitterly.

Story Thirty-five   MATTHEW 26 : 57 to 27 : 26; MARK 15 : 1 to 15; LUKE 22 : 66 to 23 : 25; JOHN 18 : 19 to 19 : 16

The Crown of Thorns

FROM the house of Ăn'nas, the enemies of Jē'şus led him away bound to the house of Cā'ia-phăs, whom the Rō'mans had lately made high priest. There all the rulers of the Jews were called together, and they tried to find men who would swear that they had heard Jē'şus say some wicked thing. This would give the rulers an excuse for putting Jē'şus to death. But they could find nothing. Some men swore one thing and some swore another; but their words did not agree.

Finally the high priest stood up and said to Jē'şus, who stood bound in the middle of the hall, "Have you nothing to say? What is it these men are speaking against you?"

But Jē'şus stood silent, answering nothing. Then the high priest spoke again, "Are you the Chrīst, the Son of God?"

And Jē'şus said, "I am; and the time shall come when you will see the Son of man sitting on the throne of power and coming in the clouds of heaven!"

These words made the high priest very angry. He said to th
rulers, "Do you hear these dreadful words? He says that he is th
Son of God. What do you think of words like these?"

They all said with one voice, "He deserves to be put to death!"

Then the servants of the high priest and the soldiers that hel
Jē'ṣus began to mock him. They spat on him, they covered hi
face, and struck him with their hands and said, "If you are
prophet, tell who it is that is striking you!"

The rulers of the Jews and the priests and the scribes passe
a vote that Jē'ṣus should be put to death. But the land of the Jew
was then ruled by the Rō'mans, and no man could be put to deatl
unless the Rō'man governor commanded it. The Rō'man gov
ernor at that time was a man named Pŏn'tĭ-us Pī'late, and he wa
then in the city. So all the rulers and a great crowd of peopl
came to Pī'late's castle, bringing with them Jē'ṣus, who was stil
bound with cords.

Up to this time Jū'das Ĭs-căr'ĭ-ot, although he had betraye
Jē'ṣus, did not believe that he would be put to death. Perhaps h
thought that Jē'ṣus would save himself from death, as he had save
others, by some wonderful work. But when he saw Jē'ṣus boun
and beaten, and doing nothing to protect himself, and when h
heard the rulers vote that Jē'ṣus should be put to death, Jū'da
knew how wicked was the deed that he had wrought. He brough
back the thirty pieces of silver that had been given to him as th
reward for betraying his Lord and he said, "I have sinned in betraying one who has done no wrong!"

But they answered him, "What is that to us?"

When Jū'das saw that they would not take back the money
and let Jē'ṣus go free, he carried the thirty pieces to the Temple and
threw them down on the floor. Then he went away and hanged
himself. And thus the traitor died.

After that the rulers scarcely knew what to do with the money
They said, "We cannot put it into the treasury of the Temple,
because it is the price paid for a man's blood."

And when they had talked together, they used it in buying a
piece of ground called "the potter's field." This they set apart as
a place for burying strangers who died in the city and had no

friends. But everyone in Jĕ-ru̅'sȧ-lĕm spoke of that place as "The Field of Blood."

It was early morning when the rulers of the Jews̱ brought Jē'ṣus to Pī'late. They would not go into Pī'late's hall, because Pī'late was not of their nation; and Pī'late came out to them and asked them, "What charge do you bring against this man?"

They answered, "If he were not an evildoer, we would not have brought him to you."

Pī'late did not wish to be troubled and he said, "Take him away and judge him by your own law!"

The Jews̱ said to Pī'late, "We are not allowed to put any man to death, and we have brought him to you. We have found this man teaching evil and telling men not to pay taxes to the Emperor Çae'ṣar, and saying that he himself is Chrīst, a king."

Then Pī'late went into his court room and sent for Jē'ṣus; and when he looked at Jē'ṣus, he said, "Are you the King of the Jews̱? Your own people have brought you to me. What have you done?"

Jē'ṣus said to him, "My kingdom is not of this world. If it were, then those who serve me would fight to save me from my enemies. But now my kingdom is not here on the earth."

Pī'late said, "Are you a king, then?"

Jē'ṣus answered him, "You have spoken it. I am a king. For this was I born and for this I came into the world, that I might speak the truth of God to men."

"Truth," said Pī'late, "what is truth?"

Then, without waiting for an answer, Pī'late went out to the rulers and the crowd and said, "I find no evil in this man."

Pī'late thought that Jē'ṣus was a harmless man, but perhaps one whose mind was weak, and he could see no reason why the rulers and the people should be so bitter against him. But they cried out all the more, saying, "He stirs up the people everywhere, from Găl'ĭ-lee even to this place."

When Pī'late heard the word "Găl'ĭ-lee," he asked if this man had come from that land. They told him that he had; and then Pī'late said, "Găl'ĭ-lee and its people are under the rule of Hĕr'od. He has come up to Jĕ-ru̅'sȧ-lĕm, and I will send this man to him."

So, from Pī'late's court room, Jē'şus was sent, still bound, t
Hĕr'od's palace. This was the Hĕr'od who had put Jŏhn th
Băp'tĭst in prison and had given his head to a dancing girl, as w
read in Story Eighteen of this part. Hĕr'od was very glad to se
Jē'şus, for he had heard many things about him; and he hoped t
see him do some wonderful thing. But Jē'şus would not worl
wonders as a show, to be looked at; and when Hĕr'od asked hin
many questions, Jē'şus would not speak a word. Hĕr'od woulc
not judge Jē'şus, for he knew that Jē'şus had done nothing wrong
so he and his soldiers mocked Jē'şus and dressed him in a gay robe
as though he were a make-believe king, and sent him back tc
Pī'late.

So Pī'late, much against his will, was compelled to decide eithe
for Jē'şus or against him. And just as Jē'şus was standing bounc
before him, a message came to Pī'late from his wife, saying, "Dc
nothing against that good man; for in this night I have suffered
many things in a dream on account of him."

Pī'late said to the Jewş, "You have brought this man to me as
one who is leading the people to evil; and I have seen that there is
no evil in him, nor has Hĕr'od; now I will order that he be beaten
with rods and then set free. For you know that it is the custom
to set a prisoner free at the time of the feast."

They set some prisoner free, as a sign of the joy at the feast.
And at that time there was in the prison a man named Bà-răb'bas,
who was a robber and a murderer.

Pī'late said to the people, "Shall I set free Jē'şus, who is called
the King of the Jewş?"

But the rulers went among the people and urged them to ask
for Bà-răb'bas to be set free.

And the crowd cried out, "Not this man, but Bà-răb'bas!"

Then Pī'late said, "What, then, shall I do with Jē'şus?"

And they all cried out, "Crucify him! Let him die on the
cross!"

Pī'late wished greatly to spare the life of Jē'şus. To show how
he felt, he sent for water and he washed his hands before all the
people, saying, "My hands are clean from the blood of this good
man!"

And they cried out, "Let his blood be on us and on our children
fter us! Crucify him! Send him to the cross!"

Then Pī′late, to please the people, gave them what they asked.
Ie set free Bȧ-răb′bas, the man of their choice, though he was a
obber and a murderer; but before giving way to the cry that he
hould send Jē′ṣus to the cross, he tried once more to save his life.
Ie caused Jē′ṣus to be beaten until the blood came upon him,
ıoping that this might satisfy the people. As Jē′ṣus was spoken
ıf as a king, the soldier who beat Jē′ṣus made a crown of thorns
ınd put it on his head and they put on him a purple robe, such as
ʋas worn by kings, and bowing down before him, they called out
o him, "Hail, King of the Jewṣ!"

Then, hoping to awaken some pity for Jē′ṣus, Pī′late brought
ıim out to the people, with the crown of thorns and the purple
∙obe upon him, and Pī′late said, "Look on this man!"

But again the cry arose, "Crucify him! Send him to the cross!"

And at last Pī′late yielded to the voice of the people. He sat
lown on the judgment seat, and gave commands that Jē′ṣus, whom
he knew to be a good man, one who had done nothing evil, should
be put to death upon the cross.

The Darkest Day of All the World

A ND SO Pŏn'tĭ-us Pī'late, the Rō'man governor, gave
order that Jē'ṣus should die on the cross. The
Rō'man soldiers then took Jē'ṣus and beat him again
most cruelly, and then led him out of the city to the
place of death. This was a place called "Gŏl'gŏ
thà" in the Jew'ĭsh language, "Căl'va-rў" in that of the Rō'mans
both words meaning "The Skull Place."

With the soldiers went out of the city a great crowd of people
some of them enemies of Jē'ṣus, glad to see him suffer; others of
them friends of Jē'ṣus, and the women who had helped him, now
weeping as they saw him, all covered with his blood and going
out to die.

But Jē'ṣus turned to them and said:

"Daughters of Jē-ru'ṣà-lĕm, do not weep for me, but weep for
yourselves and for your children. For the days are coming when
they shall count those happy who have no little ones to be slain;
when they shall wish that the mountains might fall on them,
and that the hills might cover them and hide them from their
enemies!"

They had tried to make Jē'ṣus bear his own cross, but soon
found that he was too weak from his sufferings and could not carry
it. They seized a man who was coming out of the country into
the city, a man named Sī'mon; and they made him carry the cross
to its place at Căl'va-rў.

It was a custom among the Jewṣ to give to men about to die by
the cross some medicine to deaden their feelings, so that they
would not suffer so greatly. They offered this to Jē'ṣus, but when
he had tasted it and found what it was, he would not take it. He
knew that he would die, but he wished to have his mind clear and
to understand what was done and what was said, even though his
sufferings might be greater.

At the place Căl'va-rў they laid the cross down and stretched

Jē′ṣus upon it and drove nails through his hands and feet to fasten him to the cross; and then they stood it upright with Jē′ṣus upon it. While the soldiers were doing this dreadful work, Jē′ṣus prayed for them to God, saying, "Father, forgive them; for they know not what they do."

The soldiers also took the clothes that Jē′ṣus had worn, giving to each one a garment. But when they came to his undergarment, they found that it was woven and had no seams; so they said, "Let us not tear it, but cast lots for it, to see who shall have it." So at the foot of the cross the soldiers threw lots for the garment of Chrīst. Two men who had been robbers and had been sentenced to die by the cross, were led out to die at the same time with Jē′ṣus. One was placed on a cross at his right side and the other at his left; to make Jē′ṣus appear as the worst, his cross stood in the middle. Over the head of Jē′ṣus on his cross, they placed, by Pī′late's order, a sign on which was written:

THIS IS JESUS OF NAZARETH
THE KING OF THE JEWS

This was written in three languages: in Hē′brew, which was the language of the Jewṣ; in Lăt′in, the language of the Rō′manṣ, and in Greek, a language read by many people throughout the world. Many of the people read this writing; but the chief priests were not pleased with it. They urged Pī′late to have it changed from "The King of the Jewṣ" to "He said, I am King of the Jewṣ."

But Pī′late would not change it. He said, "What I have written, I have written."

And the people who passed by on the road, as they looked at Jē′ṣus on the cross, mocked at him. Some called out to him, "You that would destroy the Temple and build it in three days, save yourself. If you are the Son of God, come down from the cross!"

And the priests and scribes said, "He saved others, but he cannot save himself. Come down from the cross and we will believe in you!"

And one of the robbers who was on his own cross beside that of Jē′ṣus joined in the cry and said, "If you are the Chrīst, save yourself and save us!"

But the other robber said to him, "Have you no fear of God, to speak thus, while you are suffering the same fate with this man? And we deserve to die, but this man has done nothing wrong."

Then this man said to Jē'ṣus, "Lord, remember me when thou comest into thy kingdom!"

And Jē'ṣus answered him, as they were both hanging on their crosses:

"Today you shall be with me in paradise."

Before the cross of Jē'ṣus his mother was standing, filled with sorrow for her son, and beside her was one of his disciples, Jŏhn, the disciple whom he loved best. Other women besides his mother were there, his mother's sister, Mā'rў the wife of Clē'o-phăs, and a woman named Mā'rў Măg-da-lē'nĕ, out of whom a year before Jē'ṣus had sent an evil spirit. Jē'ṣus wished to give his mother, now that he was leaving her, into the care of Jŏhn, and he said to her, as he looked from her to Jŏhn, "Woman, see your son."

And then to Jŏhn he said, "Son, see your mother."

And on that day Jŏhn took the mother of Jē'ṣus home to his own house and cared for her as his own mother.

At about noon a sudden darkness came over the land and lasted for three hours. And in the middle of the afternoon, when Jē'ṣus had endured six hours of terrible pain on the cross, he cried out aloud words which meant:

"My Lord, my God, why hast thou forsaken me!" words which are the beginning of the Twenty-second Psalm, a psalm which long before had spoken of many of Chrīst's sufferings.

After this he spoke again, saying, "I am thirsty."

Someone dipped a sponge in a cup of vinegar and put it upon a reed and gave him a drink of it. Then Jē'ṣus spoke his last words upon the cross:

"It is finished! Father, into thy hands I give my spirit!"

And then Jē'ṣus died. And at that moment the veil of the Temple between the Holy Place and the Holy of Holies was torn apart by unseen hands from the top to the bottom. And the Rō'man officer who had charge of the soldiers around the cross saw what had taken place and how Jē'ṣus died, and he said, "Truly this was a good man; he was the Son of God."

After Jē'ṣus was dead, one of the soldiers, to be sure that he was

no longer living, ran his spear into the side of his dead body; and out of the wound came pouring both water and blood.

Even among the rulers of the Jews there were a few who were friends of Jē'sus, though they did not dare to follow Jē'sus openly. One of these was Nĭc-o-dē'mus, the ruler who came to see Jē'sus at night. Another was a rich man who came from the town of Är-ĭ-mă-thæ'à, and was named Jō'seph. Jō'seph of Är-ĭ-mă-thæ'à went boldly in to Pī'late and asked that the body of Jē'sus might be given to him. Pī'late wondered that he had died so soon, for often men lived on the cross two or three days. But when he found that Jē'sus was really dead, he gave his body to Jō'seph.

Then Jō'seph and his friends took the body of Jē'sus down from the cross and wrapped it in fine linen. And Nĭc-o-dē'mus brought some precious spices, myrrh and aloes, which they wrapped up with the body. Then they placed the body in Jō'seph's own new tomb, which was a cave dug out of the rock, in a garden near the place of the cross. And before the opening of the cave they rolled a great stone.

And Mā'rў Măg-da-lē'nĕ and the other Mā'rў and some other women saw the tomb and watched while they laid the body of Jē'sus in it. On the next morning, some of the rulers of the Jews came to Pī'late and said:

"Sir, we remember that that man Jē'sus of Năz'a-rĕth, who deceived the people, said while he was yet alive, 'After three days I will rise again.' Give orders that the tomb shall be watched and made sure for three days; or else his disciples may steal his body and then say, 'He is risen from the dead': and thus even after his death he may do more harm than he did while he was alive."

Pīl'ate said to them, "Set a watch and make it as sure as you can."

Then they placed a seal upon the stone, so that no one might break it; and they set a watch of soldiers at the door.

And in the tomb the body of Jē'sus lay from the evening of Friday, the day when he died on the cross, to the dawn of Sunday, the first day of the week.

The Brightest Day of All the World

ON SUNDAY morning, two days after the death and burial of Jē′ṣus, some women went very early, as soon as it was light, to the tomb in the garden. One of these women was Mā′rў Măg-da-lē′nė, another was also named Mā′rў, and another was named Sȧ-lō′mė. They were bringing some more fragrant gums and spices to place in the wrappings upon the body of Jē′ṣus.

And as they went, they said to each other, "Who will roll away for us the great stone at the door of the cave?"

But when they came to the cave, they saw that the seal was broken, the stone was rolled away, and the soldiers who had been on guard were gone. There stood the tomb of Jē′ṣus all open! They did not know that before they came to the tomb there had been an earthquake; and that an angel had come down from heaven and rolled away the stone and sat upon it. When the soldiers on guard saw the angel, with his flashing face and his dazzling garments, they fell to the ground as though they were dead, and as soon as they could rise up, they fled away from the spot in terror; so when the women came there was no man in sight.

As soon as Mā′rў Măg-da-lē′nė saw that the tomb was open, without stopping to look into it, she ran quickly to tell the disciples. A moment after she had gone, the other women looked into the tomb and they saw that the body of Jē′ṣus was not there. But they saw sitting at each end of the tomb a young man, clothed in a long white garment. Their faces shone like angels and when the women saw them, they were filled with fear. One of the angels said to them:

"Do not be afraid; you are looking for Jē′ṣus of Năz′a-rĕth, who was crucified. He is not here; he is risen, as he said that he would rise from the dead. Come, see the place where the Lord

565

lay; and then go and tell his disciples and tell Pḕ'tẽr too, that Jḕ'ṣus will go before you into Găl'ĭ-lee and you shall see him there."

Then the women went away in mingled joy and fear. They ran in haste to bring this word of the angel to the disciples.

But while these women were looking into the tomb and were listening to the angel, Mā'rỹ Măg-da-lē'nê was seeking the disciples, to tell them that the tomb was open and the body of Jḕ'ṣus was not there; for she did not know that he had risen. She found Pḕ'tẽr and Jŏhn and said to them, "They have taken away the Lord out of the tomb, and we do not know where they have laid him!"

Then Pḕ'tẽr and Jŏhn at once went as quickly as they could go, to the tomb. Jŏhn outran Pḕ'tẽr and came first to the tomb, perhaps because he was the younger. But when he saw the open door and the broken seal and the stone lying at one side, he stood still for a moment. Jŏhn stooped and looked into the cave, and he could see the linen cloths that had been wrapped around the body of Jḕ'ṣus lying together. But when Pḕ'tẽr came up, he did not wait, but pressed at once into the tomb; and then Jŏhn followed him, and he too walked into the cave. Now he could see not only the long strips of linen rolled up; but in another place, carefully folded, the napkin that had been tied over the face of Jḕ'ṣus.

Then suddenly it flashed upon the mind of Jŏhn, "Jḕ'ṣus has risen from the dead!" For he had not seen the angel nor heard his words. From that moment Jŏhn believed that Jḕ'ṣus was once more living. Both Pḕ'tẽr and Jŏhn went away to think of the strange things they had seen. And very soon Mā'rỹ Măg-da-lē'nê came back to the tomb. No one was there, for both the women and the disciples had gone away. Mā'rȳ Măg-da-lē'nĕ did not know that Jē'ṣus had risen, for she had not heard the angel's message.

She wept as she thought of her Lord, slain by wicked men and not even allowed to rest in his grave. And still weeping, she stooped and looked into the tomb. There she saw two men in white garments sitting, one at the head, the other at the feet, where the body of Jē'ṣus had lain. They were the two angels whom the other women had seen, but Mā'rȳ Măg-da-lē'nĕ did not know this. One of them said to her, "Woman, why do you weep?"

She answered, "Because they have taken away my Lord; and I do not know where they have laid him."

Something caused her to turn around; and she saw a man standing beside her. It was Jē'ṣus; but her eyes were held for a moment from knowing him. He said to her, "Woman, why do you weep?"

She supposed that he was the gardener and said, hardly looking at him, "Sir, if you have carried him out of this place, tell me where you have laid him and I will take him away."

Then the stranger spoke her name, "Mā'rȳ!" and she knew that he was Jē'ṣus, no longer dead, but living. She turned around and fell down before him, and was about to seize his feet as she said, "My Master!"

But Jē'ṣus said to her, "Do not take hold of me; I am not yet going away to my Father. But go to my brothers and say to them, I go up to my Father and to your Father, to my God and your God!"

Mā'rȳ Măg-da-lē'nĕ came and told the disciples how she had seen the Lord and how he had spoken these things to her. So this was the first time that anyone saw Jē'ṣus after he rose from the dead.

You remember that the other women, another Mā'rȳ and Să-lō'mĕ, and the rest, had not seen the risen Chrīst, but they had seen an angel, who told them that he had risen and would meet his disciples in Găl'ĭ-lee. They went into the city and were looking for the disciples, when suddenly Jē'ṣus himself stood before them and said, "All hail!" That means, "A welcome to all of you!" They fell down before him and worshiped him. And Jē′sus said to them, as he had said to Mā′rў Măg-da-lē′nĕ, only a few moments before, "Do not be afraid; but find my brothers and tell them to go into Găl′ĭ-lee and they shall see me there."

And this was the second time that Jē′sus showed himself living on that day when he arose.

On that same day two of the followers of Jē′sus were walking out of Jĕ-ru′să-lĕm to a village called Ĕm-mā′us, about seven miles away. While they were talking over the strange happenings of the day, they saw that a stranger was walking beside them. It was Jē′sus, their risen Lord, but they were held back from knowing him. The stranger said to them, "What words are these that you are speaking with each other, which seem to make you feel so sad?"

One of the two men, named Clē′o-păs, answered, "Are you even a stranger in Jĕ-ru′să-lĕm and have not heard of what things have taken place there in the last few days?"

The stranger said, "What things?"

And they said, "The things with regard to Jē′sus of Năz′a-rĕth, who was a prophet mighty in his acts and his words before God and all the people; how the chief priests and our rulers caused him to be sentenced to death and how he died on the cross. But we hoped that he was the Promised One, who was to save Ĭs′ra-el. And now it is the third day since he was put to death. And today some women of our company who were early at the tomb surprised us with the news that the tomb was empty, his body was not there; and they had seen a vision of angels, who said that Jē′sus was alive. Then some of us went to the tomb and found it just as the women had said; but they did not see him."

Then the stranger said to them, "O foolish men, and slow of heart to believe what the prophets have said! Was it not needful for the Chrīst to suffer these things and then to enter in his glory?"

Then he began with the books of Mō′sĕs, and went through the prophets and showed them in all the Scriptures the meaning of all that was told about Chrīst. And as they went on, they came to the village to which they were going, and he acted as though he would go on beyond it. Then they urged and persuaded him to stay with them. They said, "Stay with us, for it is now almost evening and the day is at its close."

And he went in with them and sat down with them to a supper. As they were about to eat, he took the loaf of bread into his hands, and blessed it and broke it and gave it to them. And at that moment their eyes were opened and they knew that he was the Lord; and he passed out of their sight. They said to each other, "Was not our heart burning within us while he talked to us on the road and while he opened to us the words of the Scriptures?"

This was the third time that Jē'şus showed himself on that day. These two men hastened to Jĕ-ru'så-lĕm that night to tell what they had seen. And they found ten of the disciples met together and saying, "The Lord has risen indeed, and has been seen by Sĭ'mon Pē'tẽr."

We do not know what Jē'şus said to Pē'tẽr; but this was the fourth time that he was seen living on that day when he arose.

On that night ten disciples and other followers of Jē'şus were together in a room, and the doors were shut. Suddenly Jē'şus himself was standing among them. He said, "Peace be unto you!"

Some of them were alarmed when they saw him and thought that he must be a spirit. But he said to them, "Why are you frightened? And why do fears come to you? Look at the wounds in my hands and my feet! Handle me and see. A spirit does not have flesh and bones, as you see that I have."

And he showed them his hands and his side. They could scarcely believe for the joy of seeing him again. He said, "Have you here anything to eat?"

They gave him a piece of broiled fish and some honey, and he ate before them. And he said, "This is what I told you while I was with you, that everything written of me in the law of Mō'şeş and in the prophets and in the Psalms must come to pass. It was needful that Christ should suffer thus and should rise from the dead, and that everywhere the gospel should be preached in his name. I will send the promise of my Father upon you; but stay in Jĕ-ru'så-lĕm after I leave you, until power shall come upon you from on high."

Then, when the disciples saw that it was really the Lord and
that he was alive from the dead, they were glad. And Jē'ṣus said
to them again, "Peace be to you, as my Father has sent me, even
so I send you. May the Spirit of God come upon you!"

And this was the fifth time that Jē'ṣus showed himself alive on
that day. This Sunday was the brightest day in all the world,
because on it Jē'ṣus rose from the dead. And that Sunday in every
year is called Easter Sunday.

| Story Thirty-eight | MATTHEW 28 : 16-20; MARK 16 : 14-20; LUKE 24 : 50-53; JOHN 20 : 26 to 21 : 25; ACTS 1 : 1-11; I CORINTHIANS 15 : 3-8 |

The Stranger on the Shore

WHEN Jē'ṣus showed himself to the disciples on
the evening of the day of his rising from the
dead, only ten of the disciples saw him, for
Jū'das was no longer among them, and Thŏm'as
the Twin (which is the meaning of his other
name, Dĭd'ў̆-mŭs) was absent. The other disciples said to
Thŏm'as, "We have seen the Lord!"

But Thŏm'as said, "I will not believe that he has risen unless
I can see in his hands the marks of the nails on the cross. I must
see them with my own eyes and put my finger upon them and put
my hand into the wound in his side, before I will believe."

A week passed away, and on the next Sunday evening the disciples were together again and at this time Thŏm'as was with
them. The doors were shut, but suddenly Jē'ṣus was seen again
standing in the middle of the room. He said, as before, "Peace
be with you."

Then he turned to Thŏm'as and said to him, "Thŏm'as, come
here, and touch my hands with your finger, and put your hand
into my side; and no longer refuse to believe that I am living, but
have faith in me!"

And Thŏm'as answered him, "My Lord and my God!"

Then Jē'şus said to him, "Because you have seen me, you have believed; blessed are they that have not seen and yet have believed."

You remember that the angels had said to the women at the tomb of Jē'şus that his disciples should go into Găl'ĭ-lee and there they would see the risen Lord. They went to Găl'ĭ-lee and waited for some days without seeing Jē'şus. Finally Pē'tēr said, "I am going fishing."

"We will go with you," said the others. There were with Pē'tēr the two brothers, Jāmeş and Jŏhn, Thŏm'as and Nă-thăn'-a-el, and two other disciples. They went out upon the lake in the fishing boat, and cast their nets all night, but found no fish. Just as the day was breaking, they saw someone standing on the beach. It was Jē'şus, but they did not know him.

He called out to them, as one friend calls to another, "Boys, have you caught anything?"

They answered him, "No."

He said to them, "Cast the net on the right side of the ship and you will find some fish."

They may have thought that standing on the shore he could see the signs of a shoal of fish, which they from the boat could not see.

But the quick eyes of Jŏhn, the beloved disciple, were the first to see who this stranger was on the shore. He said to Pē'tēr, "It is the Lord!"

When Pē'tēr heard this, he flung around him his fisherman's coat and leaped into the water and swam to the shore to meet his Lord. But the other six disciples stayed in the boat and rowed to the shore, dragging after them the net full of fishes. When they came to the land, they found burning a fire of charcoal and a fish broiling upon it and a loaf of bread beside it. They all knew now that it was the Lord Jē'şus, and he said to them, "Bring some of the fish that you have now caught."

Sī'mon Pē'tēr waded out to where the net was lying, filled with fish, and drew it to the shore. Afterward they counted the fish that were in it, and found them one hundred and fifty-three large

fishes, besides small ones. Yet the net was not broken with all
these fish in it. Jē'ṣus said to them, "Come now and breakfast."

He took the bread and gave it to them and gave them fish also;
and the seven disciples ate a breakfast with their risen Lord. This
was the third time that Jē'ṣus showed himself to his disciples in a
company after rising from the tomb, the seventh of the times that
he was seen.

After the breakfast, Jē'ṣus turned to Sī'mon Pē'tĕr, the one who
three times had denied that he knew Jē'ṣus, and he said to him,
"Sī'mon, son of Jō'nas, do you love me?"

Pē'tĕr answered him, "Yes, Lord, thou knowest that I love
thee."

Jē'ṣus said to him, "Feed my lambs."

Then after a time Jē'ṣus said again, "Sī'mon, son of Jō'nas, do
you love me?"

Pē'tĕr answered him as before, "Yes, Lord; thou knowest that
I love thee."

And Jē'ṣus said to him, "Tend my sheep."

The third time Jē'ṣus said to him, "Sī'mon, son of Jō'nas, do
you love me?"

Pē'tĕr was troubled to have this question asked again and again,
and he answered, "Lord, thou knowest all things; thou knowest
that I love thee."

Then Jē'ṣus said to him, "Feed my sheep." And Jē'ṣus added, "Follow me!"

And thus Pē'tēr, after his fall, three times declared his love to Chrīst and was again called to his place among the disciples.

After this the followers of Jē'ṣus met on a mountain in Găl'ĭ-lee, perhaps the same mountain where Jē'ṣus had before given the teachings called "The Sermon on the Mount," of which we read in Story Thirteen. More than five hundred people were gathered at this time; and there Jē'ṣus showed himself to them all. He said to them:

"All power is given to me in heaven and in earth. Go ye therefore and preach my gospel to all the nations of the earth, baptizing them in the name of the Father and of the Son and of the Holy Spirit; teaching them to keep all the commands that I have given you. And I am with you always, even to the end of the world."

This was the eighth time that Jē'ṣus was seen after he rose from the dead. The ninth was when he showed himself to Jāmeṣ, not the apostle of that name, but another Jāmeṣ, who was called "The Lord's Brother," and may have been a son of Jō'ṣeph, the carpenter of Năz'a-rĕth, and of Mā'rў his wife. We do not know what was said at this meeting; but from this time Jāmeṣ was a strong believer in Jē'ṣus.

Once more, the tenth time, the risen Saviour showed himself to all his eleven disciples. It may have been in Jḗ-rụ'ṣȧ-lĕm, for he told them not to leave the city, but to wait until God should send down upon them his Spirit, as he had promised. And Jē'ṣus said to them:

"When the Holy Spirit comes upon you, you shall have a new power and you shall speak in my name in Jḗ-rụ'ṣȧ-lĕm and in Jū-dē'ȧ and in Sȧ-mā'rĭ-ȧ, and in the farthest parts of the earth."

Jē'ṣus led his disciples out of the city and over the Mount of Ŏl'īveṣ, near to the village of Bĕth'a-nў. And he lifted up his hands in blessing upon them; and while he was blessing them, he began to rise in the air, higher and higher, until a cloud covered him and the disciples saw him no more.

While they were looking up toward heaven, they found two

men, like angels, with shining garments, standing by them. These men said:

"O ye men of Găl'ĭ-lee, why do you stand looking up into heaven? This Jē'ṣus, who has been taken up from you, shall come again from heaven to earth, as you have seen him go up from earth to heaven!"

Then the disciples were glad. They worshiped their risen Lord Jē'ṣus, now gone up to heaven; and they went again to Jĕ-ru'să-lem. And they were constantly in the Temple, praising and giving thanks to God.

Part Seventh

STORIES OF THE
EARLY CHURCH

The Church of the First Days

AFTER the Lord Jē′ṣus had gone away to heaven, the eleven disciples and a small company of those who believed in Chrīst were left alone on the earth. But they were not sad, as we should have expected them to be. They were very happy, for their Lord had left with them his promise to send power from God upon them. Every day they met together and praised God and prayed in the large upper room in Jĕ-ru′ṣȧ-lĕm where Jē′ṣus had taken his last supper with them.

The eleven disciples chose a twelfth man to take the place which had belonged to Jū′das the traitor. His name was Măt-thī′as. With these were Mā′rў, the mother of Jē′ṣus, and his brothers, and the women who had been at the cross and the tomb, and a number of others, men and women, who believed in Jē′ṣus as the Chrīst. On one occasion Pē′tẽr spoke to one hundred and twenty people. And in all the world at that time there were only about five hundred people who believed in Chrīst.

Ten days after Jē′ṣus went away to heaven, there came a day which the Jewṣ called "The Day of Pentecost," or "The Fiftieth Day," for it was just fifty days after the Feast of the Passover. On that day the believers in Chrīst were all together in the upper room praying, when suddenly a sound was heard like the rushing of a mighty wind coming straight down from the sky. And what looked like tongues of fire seemed to be over the heads of all the company. Then the Spirit of God came upon them all, and they began to speak of Chrīst and of his gospel with a power that none of them had ever known before.

This strange noise as of a sounding wind was heard all over the city, and at once a great crowd of people came together at the place, to learn what the sound meant. There they saw these people, one hundred and twenty in number, singing, praising God, and telling of his wonderful works. And there was another mar-

velous thing. These people who had heard the noise and had been drawn to the place, were Jewş from many lands, who had come up to Jĕ-rụ'så-lĕm to worship, some from the lands far in the east, others from lands in the west, and others from isles of the sea. Every man heard these believers in Jē'şus speaking in the language of the land from which he had come! It was as though in every tongue of the earth men were telling of God's wonderful work.

"What does all this mean?" asked some; and others said, "These people act as though they were drunken with wine!"

Then stood up Sī'mon Pē'tĕr, with the other apostles around him; for from that time the twelve disciples were called "apostles," which means "The men sent forth," because they were now sent out to win the world to Chrīst.

Then Pē'tĕr spoke in a loud voice to all the crowd of people, and said:

"Ye men of Jū-dē'å, and all ye that live in Jĕ-rụ'så-lĕm, listen to me. This which you see is what the prophet said long ago should come to pass, that God would pour out his Spirit upon men. This is the great day of the Lord, when everyone who shall call upon the Lord shall be saved. Jē'şus of Năz'a-rĕth, one who wrought wonders and signs among you, you did put to death on the cross, by the hands of wicked men; but God has raised him up from death. We who have seen him living declare this to you, that he whom you killed on the cross is now the Lord and the Chrīst."

Then many of the people began to see how wicked had been the deed of their people in killing Jē'şus, whom God had sent to

hem as his Son; and they cried out to Pē'tēr and to the other
postles, "Men and brethren, what shall we do?"

And Pē'tēr answered them, "Turn away from your sins, believe
n Jē'ṣus, and be baptized in his name; and your sins shall be taken
way and you shall have this power of the Holy Spirit of God."

Then a great many people believed in Jē'ṣus Chrīst as their
ṣaviour and were baptized by the apostles. And on that day three
housand were added to the church of Chrīst. And they, too, met
vith the believers daily in the upper room, and worshiped in the
Temple and listened to the teaching of the apostles.

And all the followers of Jē'ṣus were like one family of brothers
nd sisters. Those who had money gave it to help those who
vere in need, and some who had lands and houses sold them and
;ave all for those who were poor. All were happy, praising God,
oving and loved by each other. And every day more and more
)f those who were being saved were united to the Church.

Story Two   ACTS 3 : 1 to 4 : 31

The Man at the Beautiful Gate

THE TWO apostles, Pē'tēr and Jŏhn, were one day
going up to the Temple at the afternoon hour of
prayer, about three o'clock. They walked across the
court of the Ġĕn'tīleṣ, which was a large, open square
paved with marble, having on its eastern side a double
row of pillars with a roof above them, called Sŏl'o-mon's Porch.
In front of this porch was the principal entrance to the Temple,
through a gate which was called "The Beautiful Gate." At this
gate, outside the Temple, they saw a lame man sitting. He was
one who in all his life had never been able to walk; and as he was
very poor, his friends carried him every day to this place; and there
he sat, hoping that some of those who went into the Temple might
take pity on him and give him a little money.

In front of this man Pē'tĕr and Jŏhn stopped; and Pē'tĕr said, "Look at us!"

The lame man looked earnestly on the two apostles, thinking they were about to give him something. But Pē'tĕr said:

"Silver and gold have I none; but what I have, that I will give you. In the name of Jē'ṣus Chrīst of Năz'a-rĕth, walk!"

And Pē'tĕr took hold of the lame man's right hand and raised him up. At once the lame man felt a new power entering into his feet and ankle bones. He leaped up and stood upon his feet, and then began to walk, as he had never done before in all his life. He

walked up the steps with the two apostles and went by their side into the Temple, walking and leaping and praising God. The people who now saw him leaping up and running knew him, for they had seen him every day sitting as a beggar at the Beautiful Gate; and everyone was filled with wonder at the change which had come over him.

After worshiping and praising God in the Temple, the man, still holding fast to Pē'tĕr and Jŏhn, went out with them through the Beautiful Gate into Sŏl'o-mon's Porch. And in a very few minutes a great crowd of people were drawn together to the place to see the man who had been made well, and to see also the two men who had healed him.

Then Pē'tĕr stood up before the throng of people and spoke to them.

"Ye men of Ĭṣ'ra-el," he said, "why do you look wondering on this man? Or why do you fix your eyes upon us, as though by our own power or goodness we had made this man to walk? The God of Ā′bră-hăm, of Ī′ṣaac, and of Jā′cob, has in this way shown the power and the glory of his Son Jē′ṣus; whom you gave up to his enemies and whom you refused before Pŏn′tĭ-us Pī′late, when Pī′late was determined to set him free. But you refused the Holy One and the Righteous One, and chose the murderer Bȧ-răb′bas to be set free in his place; and you killed the Prince of Life, whom God raised from the dead. We who have seen him risen from the dead, declare that this is true. And the power of Jē′ṣus, through faith in him, has made this man strong. Yes, it is faith in Chrīst that has given him this perfect soundness before you all. Now, my brothers, I am sure that you did not know that it was the Son of God and your own Saviour whom you sent to the cross. Therefore, turn to God in sorrow for this great sin and God will forgive you; and in his own time he will send again Jē′ṣus Chrīst. God who has raised up his Son is ready to bless you and turn away every one of you from his sins."

While Pē′tĕr was speaking, the priests and the captain of the Temple and the rulers, came upon them; for they were angry as they heard Pē′tĕr speak these words. They laid hold of Pē′tĕr and Jŏhn, and put them into the guard room for the night. But many of those who had heard Pē′tĕr speaking believed on Jē′ṣus and sought the Lord; and the number of the followers of Chrīst rose from three thousand to five thousand.

On the next day the rulers came together; and Ăn′nas and Cā′-ia-phăs, the two high priests, were there, and with them many of their friends. They brought Pē′tĕr and Jŏhn and set them before the company. The lame man who had been healed was still by the side of the two apostles. The rulers asked them:

"By what power or through whom have you done this?"

Then Pē′tĕr spoke boldly to the priests and the rulers. He said:

"Ye rulers of the people and elders, if you are asking us about the good deed done to this man who was so helpless, how it was that he was made well, I will tell you that by the name and the power of Jē′ṣus of Năz′a-rĕth, whom you put to death on the cross, whom God raised from the dead; even by him this man stands here before you all strong and well. And there is no salvation except through Jē'ṣus Chrīst, for there is no other person under heaven who can save us from our sins."

When these rulers saw how bold and strong were the words of Pē'tēr and Jŏhn, they wondered, especially as they knew that they were plain men, not learned in books and not used to speaking in public. They remembered that they had seen these men among the followers of Jē'ṣus, and they felt that in some way Jē'ṣus had given them this power. And as the man who had been healed was standing beside them, they could say nothing to deny that a wonderful work had been done.

The rulers sent Pē'tēr and Jŏhn out of the council room, while they talked together. They said to each other:

"What shall we do to these men? We cannot deny that a wonderful work has been done by them, for everyone knows it. But we must stop this from spreading any more among the people. Let us command them not to speak to any man about the name of Jē'ṣus; and let us tell them that if they do speak, we will punish them."

So they called the two apostles into the room again and said to them, "We forbid you to speak about Jē'ṣus and the power of his name, to any man. If you do not stop talking about Jē'ṣus, we will lay hands on you and put you in prison and will have you beaten."

But Pē'tēr and Jŏhn answered the rulers:

"Whether it is right to obey you or to obey God, you yourselves can judge. As for ourselves, we cannot keep silent; we must speak of what we have seen and heard."

The rulers were afraid to do any harm to Pē'tēr and Jŏhn, because they knew that the people praised God for the good work that they had done; and they would be angry to have harm come to them. For fear of the people, they let them go. And being let go, they went to their own friends, the company who met in the upper room, and there they gave thanks to God for helping them to speak his word without fear.

The Right Way to Give and the Wrong Way

IN THOSE early days the church of Chrīst in Jĕ-ru̇'så-lĕm was like a great family; for each one was full of love for all the others. No one said of anything that he owned, "This is mine," but they had all things together, as belonging to all. Some of those who owned lands or houses sold them and brought the money and laid it down at the feet of the apostles. This was not because a rule was made commanding it; but because each member loved the rest and wished to help them. The money that was given in this free way the apostles divided among those that were poor, so that no one among those who believed in Chrīst was in need.

There was one man especially who gave away all that he had to help the church. His name was Jō'ṣeph, but he was called "Bär'-na-bǎs," which means "The One Who Encourages," because he was so helpful and cheering in his words. Bär'na-bǎs sold his land and gave the money from it to the apostles, that they might help with it those who were poor; and Bär'na-bǎs spent all his time, as well as his money, in doing good.

But there was another man in the church at Jĕ-ru̇'så-lĕm whose spirit was not that of Bär'na-bǎs, to give up all and live fully for the Lord. This man, whose name was Ăn-a-nī'as, wanted to have the name of giving all, while he kept a part for himself. Ăn-a-nī'as sold some land which he had owned, and agreed with his wife Săp-phī'rȧ to give a part of the money to the apostles for the church, and to keep back a part for themselves. This they had a right to do, or even to keep it all. But they agreed together to act as though they were giving all the money, and that was agreeing together to tell a lie.

Ăn-a-nī'as brought his money and laid it down before the

apostles. But Pē'tẽr, by the power of God, saw what was in the thought of Ăn-a-nī'as and said to him, "Ăn-a-nī'as, why has the evil spirit filled your heart to tell a lie by your act in keeping back part of the money? Before it was sold, was not the land your own? And after it was sold, was not the money in your hand? You have tried to tell a lie, not to man, but to God; and God will judge you."

As Pē'tẽr spoke these words, Ăn-a-nī'as fell down before him, and in a moment was lying dead upon the floor. The young men in the meeting took up his dead body and wrapped it with long rolls of cloth and carried it out and buried it, as was the manner of the Jews.

After three hours had passed, Săp-phī'rà, the wife of Ăn-a-nī'as, came into the room where Pē'tẽr was. She did not know that her husband was dead, for no one had told her; such was the fear upon all.

Pē'tẽr said to her, "Tell me, did you sell the land for so much?" And he named the sum that Ăn-a-nī'as had placed before him.

Săp-phī'rà said, "Yes, that was the price of the land."

But Pē'tẽr said to her, "How is it that you two people agreed together to bring down God's anger upon you? Those who have buried your husband are at the door, and they shall carry you out also!"

Then Săp-phī'rà fell down, struck dead by the power of God.

The young men coming in found her dead; and they carried out her body and buried it beside her husband. A great fear came upon all the church and upon all who heard how Ăn-a-nī'as and Săp-phī'rȧ died. After that no one dared to try to deceive the apostles in their gifts to the Lord's church.

And every day the apostles went to the Temple; and standing in Sŏl'o-mon's Porch, they preached to the people about Jē'ṣus and salvation through his name. They wrought many wonders also in healing the sick. From the houses those that were sick were brought out into the street, lying on beds and couches, so that as the apostle Pē'tēr passed by, his shadow might fall on them. And from the villages around Jĕ-ru'sȧ-lĕm they brought people that had diseases or were held by evil spirits; and by the power of God in the apostles they were all made well.

All these wonderful works brought great multitudes to hear the apostles, as they spoke in Sŏl'o-mon's Porch. Very many believed in Chrīst as they heard, and men and women in great numbers were added to the church.

But all these things, the wonders wrought, the crowds brought together, and the people believing in Chrīst, gave great offense to the high priest and the rulers: for they were the ones who had led in sending Jē'ṣus Chrīst to the cross only a few months before. These rulers sent their officers, who seized all the twelve apostles and thrust them into the common prison of the city. But at night an angel of the Lord came and opened the doors of the prison and brought the apostles out and said:

"Go stand in the Temple and speak to the people all the words of this life."

Then, very early in the morning, just at the breaking of the day, they went into the Temple and preached to the people. On that day the high priest and all the rulers met together and sent to the prison house to have the apostles brought before them. But the officers who were sent did not find them in the prison. They came back to the rulers and said:

"This prison we found shut and locked and the keepers standing at the doors; but when we opened the doors and went inside, we found none of the prisoners there!"

When the captain of the Temple and the rulers heard this, they wondered greatly; for they could not understand it. Then came someone who said, "The men whom you put in prison are standing in the Temple and are teaching the people!"

Then the captain of the Temple went with his officers and again took the apostles, but without doing them any harm, for they were afraid that the people would stone them if they dealt harshly with these men, whom all held in high honor. They brought them into the hall where the rulers were met together. The high priest said to them:

"We told you not to speak in this name or about that man; and now you have filled Jĕ-ru'sȧ-lĕm with your teaching, and you are trying to bring the blood of this man upon us."

But Pē'tĕr, in the name of all the apostles, answered:

"We must obey God rather than men. You put Jē'ṣus to death, hanging him upon the cross. But the God of our fathers raised him and lifted him up to be at his right hand as a Prince and a Saviour, to give the forgiveness of sins. And we declare these things; and God's Holy Spirit tells us that they are true."

When the rulers heard these words, they were made very angry and thought of causing the apostles to be slain. But there was among them one very wise man, named Gȧ-mā'lĭ-el, a man who was held in honor by all the people. Gȧ-mā'lĭ-el asked to have the apostles sent out of the hall, while he would speak to the rulers. Gȧ-mā'lĭ-el then said:

"Ye men of Ĭṣ'ra-el, be careful in what you do to these men. If what they say comes from themselves alone, it will soon pass away; but if it be of God, you cannot destroy it, and you may even find yourselves to be fighting against God. My advice to you is: do no harm to these men and let them alone."

The rulers agreed with these words. They sent for the apostles and caused them to be beaten; then they commanded them again not to speak in the name of Jē'ṣus, and they let them go. The apostles went forth from the meeting of the rulers, happy in suffering for the name of Jē'ṣus. And in the Temple and among the homes of the people they did not cease from preaching Jē'ṣus as the Saviour and the Lord.

Stephen with the Shining Face

W E HAVE read how the members of the church in Jĕ-rụ'sȧ-lĕm gave their money freely to help the poor. This free giving led to trouble, as the church grew so fast; for some of the widows who were poor were passed by; and their friends made complaints to the apostles. The twelve apostles called the whole church together and said:

"It is not well that we should turn aside from preaching and teaching the word of God, to sit at tables and give out money. But, brethren, choose from among yourselves seven good men, men who have the Spirit of God and are wise, and we will give this work to them, so that we can spend our time in prayer and in preaching the gospel."

This plan was pleasing to all the church; and they chose seven men to take charge of the gifts of the people and to see that they were sent to those who were in need. The first man chosen was Stē'phen, a man full of faith and of the Spirit of God; and with him were Phĭl'ĭp and five other good men. These seven men they brought before the apostles; and the apostles laid their hands on their heads, setting them apart for their work of caring for the poor.

But Stē'phen did more than to look after the needy ones. He began to preach the gospel of Chrīst, and to preach with such power as made everyone who heard him feel the truth. Stē'phen saw, before any other man in the church saw, that the gospel of Chrīst was not for Jewṣ only but for all men; that all men might be saved if they would believe in Jē'ṣus; and this great truth Stē'phen began to preach with all his power.

Such preaching as this, that men who were not Jewṣ might be saved by believing in Chrīst, made many of the Jewṣ very angry. They called all the people who were not Jewṣ "Gĕn'tĭleṣ," and

587

they looked upon them with hate and scorn; but they could not answer the words that Stē'phen spoke. They roused up the people and the rulers and set them against Stē'phen, and at last they seized Stē'phen and brought him before the great council of the rulers They said to the rulers:

"This man is always speaking evil words against the Temple and against the law of Mō'ṣeṣ. We heard him say that Jē'ṣus of Năz'a-rĕth shall destroy this place and shall change the laws that Mō'ṣeṣ gave to us!"

This was partly true and partly false; but no lie is so harmful as that which has a little truth with it. Then the high priest said to Stē'phen, "Are these things so?"

And as Stē'phen stood up to answer the high priest, all fixed their eyes upon him; and they saw that his face was shining, as though it were the face of an angel. Then Stē'phen began to speak of the great things that God had done for his people of Ĭṣ'ra-el in the past; how he had called Ā'brā-hăm, their father, to go forth into a new land; how he had given them great men, as Jō'ṣeph and Mō'ṣeṣ and the prophets. He showed them how the Ĭṣ'ra-el-ītes had not been faithful to God, who had given them such blessings. Then Stē'phen said:

"You are like your fathers, a people with hard hearts and stiff necks, who will not obey the words of God and his Spirit. As your fathers did, so you do also. Your fathers killed the prophets whom God sent to them; and you have slain Jē'ṣus, the Righteous One!"

As they heard these things, they became so angry against Stē'-phen that they gnashed on him with their teeth, like wild beasts. But Stē'phen, full of the Holy Spirit, looked up toward heaven with his shining face; and he saw the glory of God and Jē'ṣus standing on God's right hand and he said:

"I see the heavens opened and the Son of man standing on the right hand of God!"

But they cried out with angry voices, and they rushed upon him and dragged him out of the council room and outside the wall of the city. And there they threw stones upon him to kill him, while Stē'phen was kneeling down among the falling stones and praying:

"Lord Jē'ṣus, receive my spirit!   Lord, lay not this sin up against them!"

And when he had said this, he fell asleep in death, the first to be slain for the gospel of Chrīst.

Among those who stoned Stē'phen was a young man named Ṣaul. He showed his fierce hate against Stē'phen and against the gospel which Stē'phen preached by holding the loose garments which the slayers of Stē'phen flung off, so that they might the more easily throw the stones upon him. Ṣaul had heard Stē'phen speak; and he saw his glorious face, but he gave his help to those who killed him.

And after Stē'phen had been slain, Ṣaul went out to seize those who believed in Chrīst. He dragged men and women out of their houses and thrust them into prison. He went into the synagogues and seized them as they were worshiping and stripped off their garments and caused them to be beaten.

By the hands of Ṣaul and those who were with him the church of Chrīst, where so many had lived in love and peace, was broken up, and its members were scattered far and wide over the lands. The apostles stayed in the city and no harm came to them, for they were kept hidden, but all the rest of the believers were driven away; and for the time the church of Chrīst seemed to have come to an end.

The Man Reading in the Chariot

E HAVE seen how the first church of those who believed in Chrīst was broken up and its members were driven away by the fury and rage of its enemy, the young man Saul. But all those who were scattered went into other places, they told the people about Chrīst and his gospel. And very soon new companies of believers in Chrīst began to rise up all over the land. In place of one church in Jĕ-ru'så-lĕm there were many churches among the cities and villages of Jū-dē'å. Thus Saul, for all his hate against Chrīst, really helped in spreading the gospel of Chrīst.

Among those driven away by Saul was a man named Phīl'ĭp not Phīl'ĭp the apostle, but another Phīl'ĭp, who had been one of those chosen with Stē'phen to care for the poor. This Phīl'ĭp went down to the city of Så-mā'rĭ-å, near the middle of the land; and there he began to tell the people about Chrīst. These people were not Jews, but were of the race called Så-măr'ĭ-tans. The woman of Så-mā'rĭ-å, with whom Jē'sus talked at Jā'cob's well, was of this people.

The Lord gave to Phīl'ĭp the power to work many wonders among these Så-măr'ĭ-tans. At Phīl'ĭp's word, evil spirits came out of men. Those who had the palsy were cured, and the lame were made to walk. The Så-măr'ĭ-tans saw these things done by Phīl'ĭp and they believed that he spoke to them the words of God. Very many of them became believers in Chrīst and were baptized; and there was great joy in that city.

At that time there was in Så-mā'rĭ-å a certain man named Sī'mon, who had made the people believe that he had great power and could do wonderful things by some magic that he used. But the works wrought by Phīl'ĭp through the power of Chrīst were

590

so much greater and more wonderful than his own, that Sī'mon himself listened to the teaching of Phĭl'ĭp, claimed to believe in Jē'ṣus and was baptized. But his heart had not been touched; he thought only that Phĭl'ĭp's magic was better than his own, and he hoped to find out what it was, so that he too could use it.

The twelve apostles, you remember, were still in Jĕ-ru'sȧ-lĕm; for they did not leave the city when Ṣaul broke up the church. After a time Ṣaul ceased to trouble the church and some of the believers went back to Jĕ-ru'sȧ-lĕm. A new church grew up in that city around the apostles, though it never became as large or as wholehearted as had been the church of the early days.

News came to the apostles of the great work wrought by Phĭl'ĭp in Sȧ-mā'rĭ-ȧ, and they sent Pē'tĕr and Jŏhn to visit the new church in that place. Pē'tĕr and Jŏhn came to Sȧ-mā'rĭ-ȧ and were glad when they saw how many and how faithful were the believers in Chrīst. They prayed for them, that the same power of the Holy Spirit that had come upon the disciples in Jĕ-ru'sȧ-lĕm might come upon those in Sȧ-mā'rĭ-ȧ; and the power of the Lord came when the apostles laid their hands on the heads of the believers.

When Sī'mon saw that this strange power of God came with the laying on of the apostles' hands, he offered Pē'tĕr and Jŏhn money, saying to them, "Sell me this power, so that I may give the Holy Spirit to those on whom I lay my hands."

But Pē'tĕr said to him, "May your silver perish with you if you think to buy the gift of God with money! You do not really belong to Chrīst and your heart is not right with God. Turn away from this your sin and pray God that he will forgive you. For I see that you are yet in your sins, sins that are as bitter as gall; and you are fast bound in evil as with a chain!"

Sī'mon could not understand this, but he said, "Pray for me to the Lord, that none of these evils that you have named come upon me!"

After this Pē'tĕr and Jŏhn preached among many villages of the Sȧ-măr'ĭ-tans and then they went back to Jĕ-ru'sȧ-lĕm. Phĭl'ĭp's work in Sȧ-mā'rĭ-ȧ was now done, and an angel of the Lord spoke to him, saying:

"Rise up and leave this city; and go toward the south, on the road that goes down from Jḗ-ru̇'sȧ-lĕm to Gā'zȧ."

This was a road through a desert region, without villages or people; but Phǐl'ǐp at once obeyed the word that came from the Lord. He left Sȧ-mā'rǐ-ȧ and walked southward, until he came to the road between Jḗ-ru̇'sȧ-lĕm and Gā'zȧ. While he was on this desert road, he saw a chariot drawing near and in it was seated a black man reading from a roll. This man had come from the land of Ē'thǐ-ō'pǐȧ, in Africa, far to the south of Ē'ġȳpt. He was a nobleman of very high rank, the treasurer of the queen of the land; and though he was not a Jew, he had taken a journey of more than a thousand miles to Jḗ-ru̇'sȧ-lĕm, riding in his chariot all the way, that he might worship God in his Temple. He was now going back to his own land, and in his hands was the roll of the prophet Ī-ṣā'iah, from which he was reading aloud while he was riding on his journey.

As the chariot of this black man came in sight, the Spirit of the Lord said to Phǐl'ǐp, "Go near and stand close by the chariot."

And Phǐl'ǐp ran toward the chariot and spoke to the man and said, "Do you understand what you are reading?"

The nobleman answered him, "How can I understand it, unless someone tells me what it means? Can you show me? If you can, come up into the chariot and sit with me."

Then Phǐl'ǐp came up and sat down in the chariot. The place where he was reading was the fifty-third chapter of Ī-ṣā'iah, with words like these:

"He was led as a sheep to the slaughter,
And as a lamb before his shearer is dumb,
So he openeth not his mouth.
His story who shall tell?
For his life is taken from the earth."

These are the words that the prophet spoke of Jē'ṣus many hundreds of years before he came to the earth. Phĭl'ĭp began with those words and told the Ē-thĭ-ō'pĭ-an nobleman all about Chrīst. And the man believed and took into his heart the word of the Lord. As they went on the way, they came to some water, and the nobleman said, "See, here is water! Why may I not be baptized?"

And Phĭl'ĭp said to him, "If you believe with all your heart, you may be baptized."

And he answered, "I believe that Jē'ṣus Chrīst is the Son of God."

Then the nobleman gave order for the chariot to stand still; and Phĭl'ĭp and the man went down into the water together, and he baptized him as a follower of Chrīst. And when they came up out of the water, the Spirit of the Lord took Phĭl'ĭp away, so that the nobleman saw him no more; but he went on his way home, happy in the Lord.

Phĭl'ĭp went next to a city near the shore and there he preached; and from that place he went northward through the cities by the Great Sea, preaching in them all, until he came to Çaes-a-rē'à, and at Çaes-a-rē'à he stayed for many years.

Story Six

ACTS 9 : 1-31; 22 : 1-21; GALATIANS 1 : 11-2

The Voice That Spoke to Saul

SAUL, the young man who had taken part in the slaying o
Stē'phen, and who had scattered abroad the believers ir
Chrīst, was still the bitter enemy of the gospel. He
heard that some of those who had fled away from Jĕ-ru'-
så-lĕm had gone to Dȧ-măs'cus, a city outside of the
Jew'ish land, far in the north, and that there they were still at worł
teaching Chrīst. Saul made up his mind to destroy this new
church in Dȧ-măs'cus, as he thought he had destroyed the churcł
in Jĕ-ru'så-lĕm.

So he went to the high priest and said:

"Let me have a letter to the chief of the Jews in Dȧ-măs'cus.
I have heard that there are some followers of Jē'sus of Năz'a-rĕth
in that city; and I will go with some men and will take these
people, and I will bind them and bring them in chains to Jĕ-ru'-
så-lĕm."

The high priest gave to Saul the letters that he asked for, and
Saul found a band of men to go with him to Dȧ-măs'cus. It was a
lengthy journey of about ten days, riding on horses. While Saul
was on his way to Dȧ-măs'cus, he had time to think about Chrīst
and his gospel. He saw again in his mind Stē'phen's shining face,
and heard his words, and he thought of the sweet and patient way
in which the followers of Jē'sus had met their sufferings and their
wrongs at his hand. Deep in Saul's heart there arose a feeling
which he could not put down, that the gospel of Chrīst was true
and that it was wicked for him to fight against it. Yet he still
went on, firm in his purpose to destroy completely the church of
Chrīst.

At last he came near to Dȧ-măs'cus. Suddenly, at full noon,
a light flashed from heaven, brighter far than the sun. For the
time the light blinded Saul's eyes, and it came so suddenly upon
him that like a bolt of lightning it struck him down, and he fell
upon the ground. In the midst of the light Saul saw One whom

he had never seen before. And a strange voice came to him, saying, "Saul, Saul, why are you fighting against me?"

And Saul answered the voice, "Who art thou, Lord?" Then
the answer came, "I am Jē'sus, whom you are trying to destroy!"

Then, trembling with surprise and alarm, Saul said, "Lord, what
wilt thou have me to do?"

And the Lord said to Saul, "Rise up and go into the city, and it
shall be told you what you must do."

Those who were with Saul wondered, for they had seen a light
and had heard a sound; but had beheld no face and heard no words;
for the vision of Chrīst had come to Saul alone. They raised him
up from the ground and found that his eyes had been made blind
by the brightness of the light. They led him by the hand into the
city and took him to the house of a man named Jū'das. There
Saul stayed for three days in the deepest suffering of mind and
body. He could see nothing; and he neither ate nor drank. But
in the darkness he was praying to God and to Chrīst with all his
heart.

In the city of Dȧ-măs'cus there was a follower of Chrīst named
Ăn-a-nī'as, a good man, held in respect by all who knew him. To
this Ăn-a-nī'as the Lord spoke, calling him by name, "Ăn-a-nī'as."

And Ăn-a-nī'as answered, "Here I am, O Lord."

And the Lord said to Ăn-a-nī'as, "Rise, and go into the street
named Straight and find the house of Jū'das; and in that house ask
for a man named Saul from Tär'sus. This man Saul is praying;
and in a vision he has seen a man named Ăn-a-nī'as coming into
his room and laying his hands on him, to give him his sight."

This command from the Lord was a surprise to Ăn-a-nī'as. He answered the Lord, "Lord, I have heard from many people about this man Saul; what great evil he has done to all thy people in Jĕ-rụ'sȧ-lĕm; and here he has an order from the high priest to bind and to carry away all who call upon thy name! Shall I go and visit such a man as he?"

But the Lord said to Ăn-a-nī'as, "Go to this man; for I have chosen him to bear my name before the people of all nations, and kings, and the children of Iṣ'ra-el. And I will show him how many things he must suffer for my sake."

Then Ăn-a-nī'as went, as the Lord had bidden him. He found the house, and he came to Saul. He laid his hands on the head of Saul and he said, "Brother Saul, the Lord Jē'ṣus, who met you in the way as you were coming, has sent me, that you may have your sight and that the Holy Spirit may come upon you. Now, wait no longer, but rise up and be baptized and call upon the name of Jē'ṣus, who will wash away your sins."

Then there fell from the eyes of Saul what seemed like scales, and at once his sight came to him. Saul was baptized as one who believed in Chrīst, and food was given him and he became strong in body and in soul. Saul had gone forth to bind the disciples of Chrīst in Dȧ-măs'cus; but now he came among them, no more as an enemy, but as a brother. And he went in the synagogue-churches in Dȧ-măs'cus, where the Jews worshiped, and began to preach Jē'ṣus to them, declaring that Jē'ṣus is the Chrīst and the Son of God. And all that heard him were amazed, and they said to each other, "Is not this the same man who in Jĕ-rụ'sȧ-lĕm wrought ruin among them who believed in his name? And did he not come to this place, intending to bind the believers in Jē'ṣus and bring them before the chief priests?"

And Saul grew stronger and stronger in his spirit and in his words. None of the Jews in Dȧ-măs'cus could answer him, as he showed that Jē'ṣus is the Anointed One, the Chrīst. But he did not stay long in Dȧ-măs'cus. After a time he left the city and went away to a quiet place in the desert of Ā-rā'bĭ-ȧ, where he stayed for a year or longer, thinking upon the gospel and learning from the Lord.

And again Saul came to Dả-mãs'cus and again he preached Chrīst and salvation through his name, not only for Jews but for Gĕn'tīles, all people besides the Jews. This made the Jews in Dả-mãs'cus very angry. They formed a plan to kill Saul, and they watched the gates day and night, hoping to seize him as he went out. But Saul's friends, the disciples of Jē'ṣus, brought him by night to a house on the wall and let him down in a basket to the ground, so that he escaped from his enemies and went away in safety.

Saul now journeyed back to Jĕ-rụ'sả-lĕm. He had left it three years before, a bitter enemy of Chrīst; he came to it again a follower of Chrīst. But when Saul sought to join the believers in Jĕ-rụ'sả-lĕm, they were all afraid of him; for they could not believe that one whom they had known as the fierce destroyer of the church was now a friend to Jē'ṣus. But Bär'na-băs, the man who had given all his land to the church, believed in Saul when he heard his story, and brought him to Pē'tēr, and told how he had seen the Lord in the way, and how boldly he had preached in Dả-mãs'cus in the name of Jē'ṣus.

Then Pē'tēr took the hand of Saul and received him as a disciple of Chrīst. For a few weeks Saul stayed in Jĕ-rụ'sả-lĕm; and he preached in the synagogues of the Jews, as Stē'phen had preached before, that Jē'ṣus is the Saviour not only to Jews but also of Gĕn'tīles ("Gĕn'tīles" was the name that Jews gave to people of every other nation except their own).

When Saul preached that Gĕn'tīles might be saved in Jē'ṣus Chrīst, it made the Jews angry, just as it had made Saul himself angry in other days to hear Stē'phen preach this same gospel. They would not listen to Saul and they sought to kill him, as they had killed Stē'phen. One day Saul was praying in the Temple and the Lord came to him once again; and Saul saw Jē'ṣus and heard his voice saying, "Make haste, and go quickly out of Jĕ-rụ'-sả-lĕm, for the people here will not believe your words about me."

Then Saul said to the Lord, "Lord, they know that I put into prison and beat in the synagogues those who believed on thee. And when thy servant Stē'phen was slain, I was standing by and was keeping the garments of those who stoned him."

And the Lord said to Saul, "Go from this place; for I will send thee far away to preach to the Gĕn'tiles."

Then Saul knew that his work was not to preach the gospel to the Jews, but to the Gĕn'tiles, the people of other nations. The disciples in Jĕ-ru'sä-lĕm helped him to get away from his enemies in the city and led him down to a place called Çaes-a-rē'ä, on the seashore. There Saul found a ship sailing to Tär'sus, a city in Ā'sia Mī'nor. Tär'sus was Saul's birthplace and his early home. He went again to this place, and in that city he stayed for a few years, safe from the Jews. He was a tentmaker and he worked at his trade while preaching the gospel in Tär'sus. And we may be sure that Saul would not be silent about the good news of the gospel. He preached in Tär'sus and in all the places near it.

Now that Saul the enemy had become Saul the friend of the gospel, all the churches in Jū-dē'ä and Sä-mä'rĭ-ä and Găl'ĭ-lee had rest and peace. The followers of Chrīst could preach without fear; and the number of those who believed grew rapidly.

All through the land, from Găl'ĭ-lee down to the desert on the south, there were meetings of those who believed in Jē'sus as the Saviour, and the apostles Pē'tĕr and Jŏhn went among them to teach them the way of life.

Story Seven
ACTS 9 : 32 to 11 : 18

What Peter Saw by the Sea

AS THE church was now planted in many cities throughout the land of the Jews, Pē'tĕr, who was a leader among the apostles, went from place to place visiting the believers in Chrīst and preaching the gospel. At one time Pē'tĕr went down to the plain beside the Great Sea and came to a city called Lўd'dä. There Pē'tĕr found a man named Æ'ne-ăs, who had the palsy and could not walk, and who had been lying on his bed eight years. Pē'tēr said to him, Æ'ne-ăs, Jē'ṣus Chrīst makes you well; rise up and roll up your bed."

Then at once Æ'ne-ăs arose and was well; and he took up the roll of matting on which he had been lying so long and laid it away. All the people in Ly̆d'dȧ and on the plain of Shâr'on heard of this great work, and many turned to the Lord.

There had been living at Jŏp'pȧ, not far from Ly̆d'dȧ, a very good woman, whom everybody loved. She was called "The Gazelle," which is the name of a beautiful animal, like a deer. For her name in Hē'brew was Tăb'ĭ-thȧ and in Greek was Dôr'cas, words which mean "Gazelle." Tăb'ĭ-thȧ, or Dôr'cas, was a believer in Chrīst, and like her Lord, she loved the poor and helped them by her work and by her gifts.

While Pē'tēr was at Ly̆d'dȧ, Dôr'cas was taken ill and died. They laid her body in an upper room, and then they sent two men to Ly̆d'dȧ for Pē'tēr, begging him to come without delay. Pē'tēr went to Jŏp'pȧ at once; and when he came to the house where the body of Dôr'cas was lying, he found the room filled with widows and poor women, who were weeping and showing the garments which Dôr'cas had made for them.

But Pē'tēr sent them all out of the room; and when he was alone with the body of Dôr'cas, he knelt down and prayed. Then he turned to the body and said, "Tăb'ĭ-thȧ, arise!"

And she opened her eyes; and when she saw Pē'tēr, she sat up. Pē'tēr took her by the hand and raised her up; then he called into the room the widows and the believers in Chrīst and showed Dôr'-cas to them, alive and well. The news of this wonderful work, of life given to the dead, amazed all the city of Jŏp'pȧ and led many to believe in Chrīst. Pē'tēr stayed many days in Jŏp'pȧ, at the house of a man named Sī'mon, who was a tanner of hides, and lived near the sea.

At that time an officer of the Rō'man army was at Çaes-a-rē'ȧ, about thirty miles north of Jŏp'pȧ, beside the Great Sea. His name was Côr-nē'li-ŭs; and he was the commander of a company of a hundred soldiers. We would call such an officer "a captain," but in the Rō'man army he was called "a centurion." The centurion Côr-nē′lĭ-ŭs was not a Jew, but a Gĕn′tĭle. Yet Côr-nē′lĭ-ŭs did not worship idols, as did most of the Gĕn′tĭleṣ. He prayed always to the God of Ĭṣ′ra-el and feared God and gave to the poor; and he taught his family to worship the Lord.

One day, in the afternoon, Côr-nē′lĭ-ŭs was praying in his house, when an angel came to him and called him by name, "Côr-nē′lĭ-ŭs!" Côr-nē′lĭ-ŭs looked at this strange and shining being and he was filled with fear, but he said, "What is it, Lord?"

And the angel said to him, "Côr-nē′lĭ-ŭs, the Lord has seen your gifts to the people and has heard all your prayers. Now send men to Jŏp′pà and let them bring to you a man named Sī′mon Pē′tĕr. He is staying in the house of Sī′mon the tanner, who lives by the sea."

Then the angel passed out of sight, and Côr-nē′lĭ-ŭs called two servants and a soldier who worshiped the Lord. He told them what the angel had said and sent them to Jŏp′pà for Pē′tĕr. These men traveled all night, following the road southward by the Great Sea, and about noon of the next day they drew near to Jŏp′pà.

On that day, just before these men came to Jŏp′pà at noon, Pē′tĕr went up to the roof of the house to pray. He became very hungry and wished for food; but while they were making ready the dinner, he fell into a strange sleep and a vision came to him. In his vision he saw what seemed to be a great sheet let down by its four corners from above. In it he saw all kinds of beasts and birds and creeping things. Some of these were animals and birds that the Jewṣ were allowed to eat; but many others were of kinds that the old law forbade the Jewṣ to eat; and such as were forbidden, the Jewṣ called "common" and "unclean." Pē′tĕr saw in this great sheet many beasts and birds and creeping things that in his sight were common and unclean. As he looked, he heard a voice saying to him, "Rise, Pē′tĕr; kill and eat."

Pē′tĕr had always been very strict in keeping the Jew′ĭsh rules about food, and he answered, "Not so, Lord; for I have never eaten anything common or unclean."

Then he heard the voice saying to him, "What God has made clean, do not thou call common or unclean."

Three times Pē′tĕr heard these words spoken, and then the great sheet with all the living creatures in it was lifted up to heaven and passed out of his sight. Pē'tẽr knew at once that the vision and the words which he had heard must have a great meaning; but as he thought upon it, he could not see what the meaning was. While he was thinking of the vision and wondering at it, the Spirit of the Lord spoke to him, saying, "Pē'tẽr, three men are looking for you. Go down to the door and meet them; and go with them without doubting, for I have sent them."

Just at that moment the three men from Çaes-a-rē'à knocked at the door and asked for Sī'mon Pē'tẽr. Pē'tẽr met them and said to them, "I am here, the man whom you are looking for. For what purpose have you come to me?"

And they said, "Côr-nē'lĭ-ŭs, a centurion at Çaes-a-rē'à, a good man, one that fears God and is well spoken of by all the Jewş, was yesterday commanded by a holy angel to send for you and to listen to words from you."

Then Pē'tẽr called the men into the house and heard all their story, and he kept them there that night. On the next morning he went with them, and some of the believers from the church of Jŏp'pà went with the party. On the next day they came to Çaes-a-rē'à and entered into the house of Côr-nē'lĭ-ŭs. There they found Côr-nē'lĭ-ŭs waiting for them, and with him a number of his family and his friends. As Pē'tẽr came into the room, Côr-nē'lĭ-ŭs fell down at his feet and was about to worship him; but Pē'tẽr raised him up, saying, "Stand up; I myself, also, am a man and not God."

And as Pē'tẽr looked around, he saw many people that had met together; and they were all Gĕn'tīleş, men who were not Jewş. And Pē'tẽr said, "You know that it is against the law of the Jewş for a man that is a Jew to come into the house with one of another nation or to meet with him. But God has showed me that I should not call any man common or unclean. For this reason I came at once when I was sent for."

Then Côr-nē'lĭ-ŭs said, "Four days ago I was praying, at three o'clock in the afternoon, when a man stood by me, clad in shining garments, and he said to me, 'Côr-nē'lĭ-ŭs, your prayer is heard and your good deeds are known to God. Send now to Jŏp'pà and

send for Sī'mon, who is called Pē'tēr.' I sent at once for you, and you have done well to come so soon. Now we are to hear whatever God has given to you to speak to us."

Then Pē'tēr opened his mouth and began to speak; for he saw now what the vision meant which he had seen on the housetop. He said, "I see now that God cares for all men alike, not for the people of one nation only; but that in every nation those that fear God and do right are pleasing to him." Then Pē'tēr began to tell the story of Jē'ṣus; how in Jē'ṣus Chrīst everyone who believes may have his sins forgiven.

While Pē'tēr was speaking, the Holy Spirit fell on all who were in the room. And the Jewṣ who were with Pē'tēr were amazed as they saw the Spirit of God given to Ġĕn'tīleṣ. Then Pē'tēr said, "Can any man forbid that these should be baptized with water, upon whom the Spirit has come, as he came upon us?"

Then by Pē'tēr's command these Ġĕn'tīle believers with Côr-nē'lĭ-ŭs were baptized as members of Chrīst's Church. And Pē'tēr stayed with them a few days, living with Côr-nē'lĭ-ŭs and eating at his table, though he was a Ġĕn'tīle, something which Pē'tēr would never before have thought it right for him to do. Soon the news went through all the churches in Jū-dē'à that Ġĕn'tīleṣ had heard the word and had been baptized. At first the Jew'ĭsh believers could not think that this should be allowed; but when Pē'tēr had told them all the story of Cȯr-nē'lĭ-ŭs and the angel, of his own vision of the great sheet full of animals and of the Spirit coming upon the Gĕn'tīleṣ, then they all praised God and said, "So to the Gĕn'tīleṣ, as well as to the Jewṣ, God has given to turn from their sins and to be saved in Jē'ṣus Chrīst and to have everlasting life."

Story Eight

ACTS 12 : 1-24

How the Iron Gate Was Opened

YOU REMEMBER that in the years while Jē'ṣus was teaching, Jē-rṵ'så-lĕm and the part of the land near it was ruled by a Rō'man governor, whose name was Pī'late; and that he was the ruler who sent Jē'ṣus Chrīst to the cross. After some years, the emperor of Rōme, who ruled all the lands around the Great Sea, gave all the country of the Jewṣ to a man named Hĕr'od Ä-grĭp'på and made him king of Jū-dē'å. He was the nephew of the Hĕr'od who killed Jŏhn the Băp'tĭst and the grandson of the other Hĕr'od who killed all the little children of Bĕth'lĕ-hĕm, in trying to destroy the little child Jē'ṣus, as we read in Story Three of Part Sixth. Hĕr'od Ä-grĭp'på was the king of Jū-dē'å when Pē'tēr saw the vision on the housetop and preached to the Gĕn'tīleṣ.

Hĕr'od wished to please the Jewṣ in Jē-rṵ'så-lĕm; and he seized one of the apostles, Jāmeṣ, the brother of Jŏhn, one of the three disciples who had been nearest to Jē'ṣus. He caused his guards to kill Jāmeṣ with the sword, just as Jŏhn the Băp'tĭst had been killed by his uncle, Hĕr'od Ăn'tĭ-păs. When he saw how greatly this act pleased the chief priests and rulers, he laid hands on Sī'mon Pē'tēr also and put him in prison, intending at the next feast of the Passover to lead him forth and to put him to death.

Pē'tẽr, therefore, was kept in prison, with sixteen soldiers around the prison to guard him, four soldiers watching him all the time; but all the church prayed very earnestly to God for him. On the night before the day when Pē'tẽr was to be brought out to die, he was sleeping in the prison, bound with two chains, while guards before the door were watching. Suddenly a bright light shone in Pē'tẽr's cell and an angel from the Lord stood by him. The angel struck him on the side and awoke him and said, "Rise up quickly."

And as Pē'tẽr awaked and stood up, his chains fell from his hands. And the angel said to him:

"Tie your girdle about your waist and bind your sandals on your feet."

And Pē'tẽr did as he was told, scarcely knowing what he was doing. Then the angel said:

"Wrap your cloak around you and follow me."

And Pē'tẽr followed the angel, thinking that he was dreaming. They passed the first guard of the soldiers and the second; but no one stirred to hinder them. Then they came to the great iron gate on the outside of the prison; and this opened to them, as if unseen hands were turning it. They went out of the prison into the city and passed through one street. Then the angel left Pē'tẽr as suddenly as he had come to him. By this time Pē'tẽr was fully awake and he said:

"Now I am sure that the Lord has sent his angel and has set me free from the power of King Hĕr'od."

Pē'tēr thought of what he should do and where he should go; and he turned toward the house of a woman named Mā'rȳ, who was near of kin to Bär'na-băs; and who had a son named Jŏhn Märk, then a young man, the same who many years afterward wrote "The Gospel According to Märk."

At Mā'rȳ's house many were met together and they were praying for Pē'tēr.

Pē'tēr came to the house and knocked on the outside door and called to those who were within. A young woman named Rhō'dà came to the door. She listened and at once knew the voice of Pē'tēr. So glad was she that she did not think to open the door, but ran into the house and told them all that Pē'tēr was standing at the door.

They said to her, "You are crazy!"

But she said that she was sure that Pē'tēr was there, for she knew his voice. And then they said:

"It must be an angel who has taken Pē'tēr's form!"

But Pē'tēr kept on knocking; and when at last they opened the door and saw him, they were filled with wonder. With his hand he beckoned to them to listen; and he told them how the Lord had brought him out of the prison.

And Pē'tēr said to them:

"Tell these things to Jāmeṣ and to the other apostles."

And then he went away to a place where Hĕr'od and his men could not find him. The morning came, and there was a great stir among the soldiers as to what had become of Pē'tēr. Hĕr'od the king sought for Pē'tēr, but could not find him; and in his anger he ordered that the guards in the prison should be put to death. And not long after this Hĕr'od himself died so suddenly that many believed his death came from the wrath of God upon him. So Hĕr'od perished; but Pē'tēr, whom he sought to kill, lived many years, working for Chrīst.

The Jāmeṣ of whom Pē'tēr spoke when said, "Tell these things to Jāmeṣ," was not Jāmeṣ the apostle, the brother of Jŏhn, for already that Jāmeṣ had been put to death by Hĕr'od. He spoke

of another Jāmeş, a son of Jō'şeph and Mā'rў, a younger brother
of Jē'şus, one who was always called "the Lord's brother." This
Jāmeş was a very holy man and a leader of the church in Jĕ-ru'să-
lĕm, where he lived many years. Some time after this Jāmeş wrote
the book of the New Testament called "The Epistle of Jāmeş."

Story Nine

ACTS 11 : 19-30; 13 : 1 to 14 : 28

The Earliest Missionaries

W E HAVE seen how, after the death of Stē'phen,
those who were driven out of Jĕ-ru'să-lĕm
went everywhere telling of Jē'şus. Some of
these men traveled as far as to Ăn'tĭ-ŏch in
Sў̄r'ĭ-à, which was a great city, far in the north,
two hundred and fifty miles from Jĕ-ru'să-lĕm. At first they
spoke only to Jewş, preaching the word of Chrīst; but soon many
Gĕn'tīleş, people who were not Jewş, heard about the gospel and
wished to have it preached also to them. So these men began
preaching to the Gĕn'tīleş, telling them about Jē'şus Chrīst and
how to be saved.

The Lord was with the gospel, and in a little time many believed in Chrīst, a great number, both of Jewş and Gĕn'tīleş. Thus
at Ăn'tĭ-ŏch in Sў̄r'ĭ-à arose a church where Jewş and Gĕn'tīleş
worshiped together and forgot that they had ever been apart.
The news came to the mother church in Jĕ-ru'să-lĕm that in
Ăn'tĭ-ŏch Gĕn'tīleş were coming to Chrīst. As all the followers
of Chrīst in Jĕ-ru'să-lĕm were Jewş, they were not sure whether
Jewş and Gĕn'tīleş should be allowed to worship together as one
people. It was decided, after a time, that some wise man should
go from Jĕ-ru'să-lĕm to Ăn'tĭ-ŏch and see this new church of
Jewş and Gĕn'tīleş.

For this errand, they chose Bär'na-băs, the good man who had given his land to be sold to help the poor and who had brought Saul to the church when the disciples were afraid of him. So Bär'na-bäs took the long journey from Jĕ-rụ'sȧ-lĕm to Ăn'tĭ-ŏch. When he saw these new disciples, so many, so strong in their love for Chrīst, so united in their spirit and so earnest in the gospel, he was glad and he spoke to them all, telling them to stand fast in the Lord. For Bär'na-bäs was a good man, full of the Holy Spirit and of faith.

The church at Ăn'tĭ-ŏch was growing so fast that it needed men for leaders and teachers. Bär'na-bäs thought of Saul, who had once been an enemy, but was now a follower of Chrīst. Saul was at that time in Tär'sus, his early home; and to this place Bär'-na-bäs went to find him. He brought Saul to Ăn'tĭ-ŏch, and there Bär'na-bäs and Saul stayed together for a year, preaching to the people and teaching those who believed in Chrīst. It was at Ăn'tĭ-ŏch that the disciples were first called by the name Chrĭs'tiạns.

At one time some men came from Jĕ-rụ'sȧ-lĕm to Ăn'tĭ-ŏch, to whom God had showed things that should come to pass. These men were prophets, speaking from God. One of them, a man named Ăg'a-bŭs, said through the Spirit of God that a great famine, a need for food, was soon to come upon all the lands. This came as Ăg'a-bŭs the prophet had said, in the days when Clạu'dĭ-ŭs was emperor at Rōme. Over all the lands food was very scarce and many suffered from hunger.

When the followers of Chrīst in Ăn'tĭ-ŏch heard that their brethren of Jĕ-rụ'sȧ-lĕm and Jū-dē'ȧ were in need, they gave money, as each one was able, to help them; and they sent Bär'na-bäs and Saul with it. Bär'na-bäs and Saul carried the gifts of the church to Jĕ-rụ'sȧ-lĕm and stayed there for a time. When they went back to Ăn'tĭ-ŏch, they took with them the young man Jŏhn Märk, the son of Mā'rў, to whose house Pē'tẽr went when he was set free from prison, as we read in the last story.

Some time after they returned to Ăn'tĭ-ŏch, the Lord called Bär'na-bäs and Saul to go forth and preach the good news of Chrīst to the people in other lands. At one time, when the members of the church were praying together, the Spirit of the Lord spoke to them, saying, "Set Bär'na-băs and Saul apart for a special work to which I have called them."

Then the leaders of the church at Ăn'tĭ-ŏch prayed and laid their hands on the head of Bär'na-băs and Saul. And Bär'na-băs and Saul went forth, taking with them Jŏhn Märk, the young man from Jĕ-ru'să-lĕm, as their helper. They went down to the shore of the Great Sea at Sĕ-leū'çĭ-à and took a ship and sailed to the island of Çÿ'prus. In that island they visited all the cities and preached Christ in all the synagogues of the Jews.

At a place called Pā'phos, in the west of the island of Çÿ'prus, they met the Rō'man ruler of the island, a man named Sĕr'gĭ-ŭs Pau'lus. He was a good man, and he sent for Bär'na-băs and Saul, that he might learn from them of Christ. But with the ruler was a Jew named Ĕl'ÿ-măs, who claimed to be a prophet, and who opposed Bär'na-băs and Saul in their teaching and tried to persuade the ruler not to hear the gospel.

Then Saul, full of the Holy Spirit, fixed his eyes on this man Ĕl'ÿ-măs, the false prophet, and said to him, "O thou man full of wickedness, thou child of the evil one, thou enemy of the right, wilt thou not stop opposing the word of the Lord? The hand of the Lord is upon thee, and thou shalt be blind for a time, not able to see the sun!"

And at once a mist and a darkness fell upon Ĕl'ÿ-măs, and he groped about, feeling for someone to lead him by the hand. When the ruler saw the power of the Lord in bringing this stroke of blindness upon his enemy, he was filled with wonder and believed the gospel of Chrīst.

From this time Saul ceased to bear his old name and was called Paul. He was no longer Saul, but "Paul the Apostle," having all the power that belonged to Pē'tēr and Jŏhn and the other apostles.

From the island of Çȳ'prus, Paul and Bär'na-bǎs and Jŏhn Märk sailed over the sea to a place called Pēr'gà. At this place Jŏhn Märk left them and went back to his home in Jė-ru'sà-lěm. But Paul and Bär'na-bǎs went into the land of Ā'sià Mī'nor and came to a city called Ăn'tĭ-ŏch. This was not Ăn'tĭ-ŏch in Sȳr'ĭ-à, from which they had come, but another Ăn'tĭ-ŏch in a region called Pĭ-sĭd'ĭ-à. There they went into the synagogue, and Paul preached to both Jews and Ġĕn'tīles. Not many of the Jews believed Paul's words, but a great number of the Ġĕn'tīles, people who were not Jews, became followers of Chrīst. This made the Jews very angry, and they roused up against Paul and Bär'na-bǎs all the chief men of the city, and they drove Paul and Bär'na-bǎs away. They went to Ī-cō'nĭ-ŭm, another city, and there they preached the gospel with such power that many of both Jews and Ġĕn'tīles believed in Chrīst. But the Jews who would not believe stirred up the city against Paul and Bär'na-bǎs. They gathered a crowd of people, intending to seize the apostles, to do them harm, and to kill them. But they knew of the coming of their enemies, and as they had now done their work in Ī-cō'nĭ-ŭm and had planted the church, they quietly went away from the city.

The apostles Paul and Bär'na-bǎs next went to the city of Lȳs'trà, in the land of Lȳc-a-ō'nĭ-à, and there they preached the gospel. There were few Jews in that city, and they preached to the people of the land who were worshipers of idols. Among those who heard Paul speak at Lȳs'trà was a lame man, who had never been able to walk. Paul fixed his eyes on this man and saw that he had faith to be made strong. He said to him with a loud voice, "Stand up on your feet!"

And at the words the man leaped up and walked. As the people saw how the lame man had been healed, they were filled with wonder and said, in the language of their land, "The gods from heaven have come down to us in the forms of men!"

They thought that Bär'na-băs was Jū'pĭ-tēr, whom they worshiped as the greatest of the gods; and because Paul was the chief
the gods. In front of their city was a temple of Jū'pĭ-tēr; and the
speaker, they thought that he was Mēr'cŭ-rў, the messenger of
priest of the temple brought oxen and garlands of flowers and was
about to offer a sacrifice to Bär'na-băs and Paul as gods. It was
some time before the two apostles understood what the people
were doing. But when they saw that they were about to offer
sacrifice to them, Paul and Bär'na-băs rushed out among the
people and cried out, "Men, why do you do such things as these?
We are not gods, but men like yourselves. And we bring you
word that you should turn from these idols, which are nothing,
to the living God, who made the heaven and the earth and the sea
and all things. It is God who has done good to you and given you
from heaven rains and fruitful seasons, filling you with food and
gladness."

And even with words like these, they could scarcely keep the
people back from offering sacrifices to them. But after a time
some Jews came from Ī-cō'nĭ-ŭm. These Jews stirred up the
people against Paul, so that instead of worshiping him, they stoned
him and dragged out of their city what they supposed was his
dead body. Then they left him, and as the believers gathered
around, weeping, Paul rose up alive, and went again into the city.
On the next day he journeyed with Bär'na-băs to Dēr'bĕ. There
they preached the gospel and led many as disciples to Chrīst.
After this they went again to the cities where they had preached,
to Lўs'trà in Lўc-a-ō'nĭ-à, to Ī-cō'nĭ-ŭm and Ăn'tĭ-ŏch in Pĭ-
sĭd'ĭ-à, and to Pēr'gà in Păm-phўl'ĭ-à, and visited the churches
which they had founded. They encouraged the believers, telling
them to continue in the faith and saying to them that those who
would enter into the kingdom of God must expect to meet with
trouble, and that God would give them a full reward.

The Song in the Prison

AFTER Paul and Bär'na-băs brought to Ăn'tĭ-ŏch the news that the Gĕn'tīleṣ had turned to the Lord, a great question arose in the church. Some of the strict Jewṣ said, "All these Gĕn'tīle believers must become Jewṣ and keep the Jew'ĭsh laws about food and feasts and washings and offerings."

Others said that the laws were made for Jewṣ only, and that Gĕn'tīleṣ who believed in Chrīst were not called upon to live as Jewṣ. After many words on both sides, Paul and Bär'na-băs, with other believers, went up to Jĕ-ru'så-lĕm to lay this matter before the apostles and the elders of the church. They listened to Paul's story of God's great work among the Gĕn'tīleṣ, and talked about it and sought God in prayer. And at last the apostles and elders and the whole church in Jĕ-ru'så-lĕm sent a message to the Gĕn'tīleṣ who believed, telling them that Jewṣ and Gĕn'tīleṣ were alike before God, that both were saved by believing in Chrīst, and that Gĕn'tīleṣ who believed were not called upon to keep the laws given to the Jewṣ only.

The apostles sent with Paul and Bär'na-băs two men, Jū'das and Sī'las, to bring this news to the church at Ăn'tĭ-ŏch. They came and read the letter, which brought great joy to the Gĕn'tīle believers. For now the Gĕn'tīleṣ who believed in Chrīst were able to serve the Lord without obeying all the rules which the Jewṣ themselves found very hard to keep.

After a time Paul said to Bär'na-băs, "Let us go out again and visit the brethren in the cities where we preached the gospel, and see how they are doing."

Bär'na-băs was willing to go, and wished to take again with them Jŏhn Märk as their helper in the work. But Paul did not think it well to take with them the young man who went home in the middle of their journey and left them to visit strange lands

611

alone. Bär'na-bäs was determined to take Mạrk, and Pạul refused
to have him go, so at last Pạul and Bär'na-bäs separated. Bär'na-
bäs took Märk and went again to the island of Çy̆'prus. Pạul
chose as his helper Sī'las, who had come from Jĕ-ru̧'să-lĕm to Ăn'-
tĭ-ŏch, and Pạul and Sī'las went together through the lands in
Ā'şià Mī'nor which Pạul had visited on his earlier journey. Everywhere they sought out the churches which before had been
planted by Pạul and Bär'na-bäs, and they encouraged the disciples
to be faithful in the Lord.

When Pạul came to Dĕr'bĕ and Ly̆s'trà, he found a young man
named Tĭm'o-thy̆, whose mother was of the Jew'ĭsh race and a
believer in Chrīst. Tĭm'o-thy̆ had known the word of God from
his childhood; he had given his heart to Chrīst, and all the believers in Chrīst at Ly̆s'trà and Ī-cō'nĭ-ŭm knew him and spoke
well of him. Pạul asked this young man Tĭm'o-thy̆ to leave his
home and to go out with him as his helper in the gospel. Tĭm'o-
thy̆ went, and from that time was with Pạul as a friend and a
fellow worker, dearly beloved by Pạul. Pạul and Sī'las and Tĭm'-
o-thy̆ went through many lands in Ā'şià Mī'nor, preaching the
gospel and planting the church. The Spirit of the Lord would
not let them go to some places which were not yet ready for the
gospel, and they came down to Trō'ăs, which was on the sea and
opposite to the land of Măç-e-dō'nĭ-à in Europe.

While they were at Trō'ăs, a vision came to Pạul in the night.
He saw a man of Măç-e-dō'nĭ-à standing before him, pleading with
him and saying, "Come over into Măç-e-dō'nĭ-à and help us."

When Pạul told this vision to his friends, they all knew that
this was a call from the Lord to carry the gospel of Chrīst to
Măç-e-dō'nĭ-à. As soon as they could find a vessel sailing across
the sea, they went on board, and with them went a doctor named
Lu̧ke, who at this time joined Pạul. Lu̧ke stayed with Pạul for
many years, and Pạul called him "the beloved physician." Afterward Lu̧ke wrote two books which are in the Bible, "The Gospel
According to Lu̧ke" and "The Acts of the Apostles."

Pạul and his three friends set sail from Trō'ăs and on the third
day they came to the city of Phĭ-lĭp'pī, in Măç-e-dō'nĭ-à, and
there they stayed for some days. There was no synagogue in

that city and scarcely any Jews; and on the Sabbath Day Paul and his company went out of the city gate to the riverside, where was a place of prayer.   There they sat down and talked with a few women who had met together to pray.   One of these was a woman named Lўd'ĭ-à, who had come from Thȳ-a-tī'rà in Ā'şià Mĭ'nor and was a seller of purple dyes.   She was one who was seeking after God, and the Lord opened her heart to hear the words of Paul and to believe in Chrīst.   She was baptized, the first one brought to the Lord in all Europe, and all her household. Lўd'ĭ-à said to Paul and to his company, "If you count me as one who is faithful to the Lord, come into my house and stay there."

She urged them so strongly that they all went to Lўd'ĭ-à's house and made it their home while they were in the city.   One day while they were going to the place of prayer, a young woman who had in her an evil spirit met them.   She was a slave girl, and through the spirit in her, her owners pretended to tell what was to happen; and by her they made great gains of money.   As soon as she saw Paul and his friends, she cried out, "These men are servants of the Most High God, who tell you how to be saved."

And this she did day after day, following Paul and his companions.   Paul was troubled to see her held in the power of the evil spirit; and he spoke to the spirit, "I command thee in the name of Jē'şus Chrīst to come out of her!"

And in that very hour the spirit left the girl.   But with the evil spirit gone from her, there were no more gains to her masters. They were very angry and took hold of Paul and Sĭ'las and dragged them before the rulers of the city, and they said, "These men, who are Jews, are making great trouble in our city and are teaching the people to do what is against the law for Rō'mans."

And they stirred up the crowd of the lowest of the people against them.   To please the throng, the rulers stripped off the garments from Paul and Sĭ'las and commanded that they should be beaten with rods.   When they had received many cruel blows, they were thrown into the prison, and the jailor was charged to keep them carefully.   He took them, all beaten and wounded, into the dungeon, which was in the very middle of the prison, and made their feet fast in the stocks.

But about midnight Paul and Sī'las were praying and singing hymns of praise to God, and the other prisoners were listening to them. Suddenly there was a great earthquake, so that the foundations of the prison house were shaken; every door was opened and all the chains on the prisoners were loosed, and all could have gone out free if fear had not held them in their places. The jailor of the prison was suddenly roused out of sleep and saw the prison doors wide open. By the law of the Rō'mans, a man in charge of a prisoner must take his place if his prisoner escaped,

and the jailor, thinking that the men in the prison had gotten away, drew out his sword and was just going to kill himself, when Paul called out, "Do yourself no harm, for we are all here."

Then the jailor called for lights and sprang into the dungeon where Paul and Sī'las were, and, trembling with fear, fell down at their feet and cried out, "O sirs, what must I do to be saved?"

And they said, "Believe on the Lord Jē'sus Chrīst and you shall be saved, and those in your house with you."

And that night, in the prison, they spoke the word of the Lord to the jailor, and to all that were with him. The jailor washed their wounds, and he and all his family were baptized in that hour. Afterward, he brought them from the prison into his own house and set food before them. And the jailor and his household were all happy in the Lord, believing in Chrīst.

The rulers of the city knew well that they had done an unjust act in beating Paul and Sī'las and thrusting them into prison; but they did not know that Paul and Sī'las, though Jews, were also free citizens of Rōme, whom it was unlawful to beat or to put in to prison without a fair trial. In the morning the rulers sent their officers to the jailor, saying, "Let those men go." And the jailor brought their words to Paul and said, "The rulers have sent to me to let you go; now come out of the prison and go in peace."

But Paul said, "We are free citizens of Rōme, and without a trial they have beaten us and have cast us into prison. And now do they turn us out secretly? No, indeed, let those rulers come themselves and bring us out!"

The officers told these words to the rulers, and when they learned that these men were Rō'man citizens, they were frightened; for their own lives were in danger for having beaten them. They came to Paul and Sī'las and begged them to go away from the prison and from the city. Then Paul and Sī'las walked out of the prison and went to the house of Lўd'ĭ-à. They met the brethren who believed in Jē'sus and spoke to them words of comfort and of help, and then they went out of the city. In Phĭ-lĭp'pī, from this time on, there was a church which Paul loved greatly, and to which he later wrote "The Epistle to the Phĭ-lĭp'pĭ-ans."

Story Eleven   ACTS, chapter 17

Paul's Speech on the Hill

FROM Phĭ-lĭp'pī, Paul and Sī'las went to Thĕs-sa-lŏ-nī'cà, which was the largest city in Măç-e-dō'nĭ-à. There they found many Jews and a synagogue or church where the Jews worshiped. For three weeks Paul spoke at the meetings in the synagogue and showed the meaning of the Old Testament writings, that the Saviour for whom all the Jews were looking must suffer and die and rise again.

And Paul said to them: "This Jē'ṣus, whom I preach to you, is the Chrīst, the Son of God and the King of Ĭṣ'ra-el."

Some of the Jews believed Paul's teachings and a far greater number of the Greeks, the people of the city who were not Jews, became followers of Chrīst. And with them were some of the leading women of the city, so that a large church of believers in Chrīst arose in Thĕs-sa-lŏ-nī'cà.

But the Jews who would not believe in Jē'ṣus were very angry as they saw so many seeking the Lord. They stirred up a crowd of the lowest people in the city and raised a riot and led a noisy throng to the house of a man named Jā'son, with whom they supposed that Paul and Sī'las were staying. The crowd broke into the house and sought for Paul and Sī'las, but could not find them. Then they seized Jā'son, the master of the house, and some other friends of the apostles, and dragged them before the rulers of the city and cried out:

"These men who have turned the whole world upside down have come to this city, and Jā'son has taken them into his house. They are acting contrary to the laws of Çae'ṣar the emperor, for they say that there is another king, a man whose name is Jē'ṣus."

The rulers of the city were greatly troubled when they saw these riotous people and heard their words. They knew that Jā'son and his friends had done nothing against the law of the land; but to content the crowd they made the believers promise to obey the laws, and then they let them go free. The brethren of the church sent away Paul and Sī'las in the nighttime, to the city of Bĕ-rē'à, which was not far from Thĕs-sa-lŏ-nī'cà. There again they found a synagogue of the Jews, and, as in other places, Paul went into its meetings and preached Jē'ṣus, not only to the Jews, but also to the Gĕn'tīles, many of whom worshiped with the Jews.

These people were of a nobler spirit than the Jews of Thĕs-sa-lŏ-nī'cà, for they did not refuse to hear Paul's teachings. They listened with open minds, and every day they studied the Old Testament writings, to see whether the words spoken by Paul were true. And many of them became believers in Jē'ṣus, not only the Jews, but the Gĕn'tīles also.

But the news went to Thĕs-sa-lŏ-nī′cà that the word of Chrīst was being taught in Bĕ-rē′à. The Jews of Thĕs-sa-lŏ-nī′cà sent some men to Bĕ-rē′à, who stirred up the people against Pạul and Sī′las. To avoid such a riot as had arisen in Thĕs-sa-lŏ-nī′cà, the brethren in Bĕ-rē′à took Pạul away from the city, but Sī′las and Tĭm′o-thў stayed for a time.

The men who went with Pạul led him down to the sea and went with him to Ăth-ĕns. There they left Pạul alone, but took back with them Pạul's message to Sī′las and Tĭm′o-thў to hasten to him as quickly as they could come.

While Pạul was waiting for his friends in Ăth′ĕns, his spirit was stirred in him, as he saw the city full of idols. It was said that in the city of Ăth′ĕns the images of the gods were more in number than the people. Pạul talked with the Jews in the synagogue and in the public square of the city with the people whom he met. For all the people of Ăth′ĕns and those who were visiting in that city spent most of their time in telling or in hearing whatever was new. And there were in Ăth′ĕns many men who were thought very wise and who were teachers of what they called wisdom. Some of these men met Pạul and as they heard him, they said scornfully, "What does this babbler say?"

And because he preached to them of Jē′sus and of his rising from the dead, some said, "This man seems to be talking about some strange gods!"

There was in Ăth′ĕns a hill, called Märs′ Hill, where a court was held upon seats of stone ranged around. They brought Pạul to this place and asked him, saying, "May we know what is this new teaching that you are giving? You bring to our ears some strange things, and we wish to know what these things mean."

Then Paul stood in the middle of Märs' Hill, with the people of the city around him, and he said:

"Ye men of Ăth'ĕns, I see that you are exceedingly given to worship. For as I passed by, I saw an altar upon which was written these words, 'To THE UNKNOWN GOD.' That God whom you know not and whom you seek to worship, is the God that I make known to you. The God who made the world and all things that are in it is Lord of heaven and earth and does not dwell in temples made by the hands of men; nor is he served by men's hands, as though he needed anything. For God gives to all men life and breath and all things. And he has made of one blood all the peoples who live on the earth: that all men should seek God, and should feel after him and should find him; for he is not far away from any of us. For in him we live and move and have our being: even as some of your own poets have said, 'For we also are the children of God.' Since we are God's children, we should not think that God is like gold or silver or stone, wrought by the hands of men. Now God calls upon men to turn from their sins; and he tells us that he has fixed a day when he will judge the world through that man Jē'sus Chrīst whom he has chosen and whom he has raised from the dead."

When they heard Paul speak of the dead being raised, some laughed in scorn; but others said, "We will hear you again about this." After a time Paul went away from Ăth'ĕns. Very few people joined with Paul and believed on Jē'sus. Among these few was a man named Dī-ŏ-nўs'ĭ-us, one of the court that met on Märs' Hill, and a woman named Dăm'a-rĭs. A few others joined with them; but in Ăth'ĕns the followers of Chrīst were not many.

Paul at Corinth

PAUL went from Ăth'ĕns̩ to Cŏr'inth, another city in the land of Greeçe. He was alone, for his fellow workers, Sī'las and Tĭm'o-thȳ, had not yet come from Thĕs-sa-lŏ-nī'cà. But in Cŏr'inth, Pa̤ul met people who soon became his dear friends. They were a man named Aq'uĭ-là and his wife Prĭs-çil'là, who had lately come from Rōme to Cŏr'inth. Every Jew in those times was taught some trade, and Pa̤ul's trade was the weaving of a rough cloth used for making tents. It happened that Ăq'uĭ-là and Prĭs-çil'là were tent-makers also, and so Pa̤ul went to live in their house and they worked together at making tents.

On the Sabbath days Pa̤ul went into the synagogue and there preached the gospel and talked about Chrīst with the Jews̩ and also with the Greeks who worshiped God in the synagogue. Some believed Pa̤ul's words and some refused to believe, but opposed Pa̤ul and spoke against him. After a time Sī'las and Tĭm'o-thȳ came from Thĕs-sa-lŏ-nī'cà to meet Pa̤ul. They brought to him word about the church at Thĕs-sa-lŏ-nī'cà and some questions that were troubling the believers there. To answer these questions, Pa̤ul wrote from Cŏr'inth two letters, which you can read in the New Testament. They are called "The First Epistle to the Thĕs-sa-lŏ'nĭ-ans̩" and "The Second Epistle to the Thĕs-sa-lŏ'nĭ-ans̩." These two letters are the earliest of Pa̤ul's writings that have been kept. We do not know that Pa̤ul wrote any letters to churches earlier than these; but if he did write any, the letters have been lost.

Now that Sī'las and Tĭm'o-thȳ, as well as Ăq'uĭ-là and Prĭs-çil'là, were with Pa̤ul, he was no more alone and he began to preach even more earnestly than before, telling the Jews̩ that Jē'ş̩us was the Chrīst of God. When he found that the Jews̩ would not listen, but spoke evil words against him and against

619

Chrīst, Paul shook out his garment, as though he were shaking
dust from it, and he said to the Jews, "Your blood shall be upon
your own heads, not on me; I am free from sin, for I have given
you the gospel and you will not hear it. From this time I will
cease speaking to you and will go to the Gĕn'tīles."

And Paul went out of the synagogue and with him went those
who believed in Jē'sus. He found a house near to the synagogue
belonging to a man named Tī'tus, a Gĕn'tile who worshiped God,
and in that house Paul set up a church, and preached the gospel to
all who came, both Jews and Gĕn'tīles. Many who heard be-

lieved in Chrīst and were baptized; and among them was a Jew
named Crĭs'pus, who had been the chief ruler of the synagogue.
But most of those who joined the Church of Chrīst in Cŏr'inth
were not Jews, but Gĕn'tīles, men and women who turned to God
from idols. One night the Lord came to Paul in a vision and said
to him, "Paul, do not be afraid; but speak and do not hold thy
peace. I am with thee, and no one shall do thee harm; for I have
many people in this city."

And Paul stayed in Cŏr'inth a year and six months, teaching
the word of God. After a time the Jews in a great crowd rushed
upon Paul and seized him and brought him into the court before
the Rō'man governor of Greeçe, a ruler whose name was Găl'lĭ-ō.
They said to the governor, "This man is persuading people to
worship God in a way forbidden by the law."

Paul was just about to speak in answer to this charge when

Găl'lǐ-ō, the governor, spoke to the Jews, "O ye Jews, if this were
a matter of wrongdoing or of wickedness, I would listen to you.
But if these are questions about words and names and your law,
look after it yourselves, for I will not be a judge of such things."
And Găl'lǐ-ō drove all the Jews out of his court. Then some of
the Greeks seized Sŏs'the-nēs, who was the chief ruler of the
synagogue, and beat him before the judge's seat in the court room.
But Găl'lǐ-ō thought it was a quarrel over small matters.

After staying many days, Paul left the church at Cŏr'inth and
sailed away in a ship across the Æ-ġē'an Sea to Ĕph'e-sŭs, which
was a great city in Ā'siȧ Mǐ'nor. With Paul were his friends,
Ăq'uǐ-lȧ and Prǐs-çǐl'lȧ. At Ĕph'e-sŭs, Paul went into the synagogue of the Jews and talked with them about the gospel and
about Chrīst. He could stay only for a little while, although they
asked him to remain longer; but he said, "I must go away now;
but if it be the will of God, I will come again to you."

And he set sail from Ĕph'e-sŭs, but left Ăq'uǐ-lȧ and Prǐs-çǐl'lȧ
there. Paul sailed over the Great Sea to Çaes-a-rē'ȧ, in the land of
Jū-dē'ȧ. At that place he landed and from thence went up to
Jĕ-ru'sȧ-lĕm and visited the mother church. Then he journeyed
back to Ăn'tǐ-ŏch, the city from which he had set forth.

Story Thirteen

ACTS 18 : 23 to 20 : 1

Paul at Ephesus

THE apostle Paul did not stay long at Ăn'tǐ-ŏch, but
soon started out for another journey among the
churches already formed and into new fields. He
went through Sўr'ǐ-ȧ, the country around Ăn'tǐ-ŏch,
and then to the region near Tär'sus, which had been
his early home, everywhere preaching Chrīst. He crossed over
the mountains and entered into the heart of Ā'siȧ Mǐ'nor, coming

to the land of Gȧ-lā'tiȧ. The people in this land were a warm-hearted race, eager to see and to hear new things. They listened to Paul with great joy and believed at once in his teachings. Paul wrote afterward that they received him as an angel of God, as though he were Jē'ṣus Chrīst himself, and that they were ready to pluck out their own eyes and give them to him, so eager were they to have the gospel.

But soon after Paul went away, some Jew'ĭsh teachers came, saying to these new believers, "You must all become Jewṣ and take upon you the whole Jew'ĭsh law, with all its rules about things to be eaten and fasts and feast days or you cannot be saved."

And the people of Gȧ-lā'tiȧ turned quickly away from Paul's words to follow these new teachers; for they were fond of change and were not firm in their minds. There was danger that all Paul's work among them would be undone. But as soon as news came to Paul of their sudden turning from the truth of the gospel, he wrote to them a letter, "The Epistle to the Gȧ-lā'tianṣ." In this letter he called them back to Chrīst and showed them that they were free and not slaves to the old law, and he urged them to stand fast in the freedom which Chrīst had given them.

Paul went through Phrўġ'ĭ-ȧ, and from that land came again to Ĕph'e-sŭs, which he had visited before, as we read in the last story. This time he stayed in Ĕph'e-sŭs more than two years, preaching the gospel of Chrīst. At first he spoke in the synagogue of the Jewṣ, telling the Jewṣ that Jē'ṣus was the Anointed Chrīst, the King of Iṣ'ra-el, and proving it from the prophets of the Old Testament. But when the Jewṣ would no longer listen to him but spoke evil against the way of Chrīst, Paul left the synagogue and spoke every day in a schoolroom which was opened to him. His work became so well known that many people in Ĕph'e-sŭs, and in the lands around the city, heard the word of the Lord.

God gave to Paul at this time great powers of healing. They carried to the sick the cloths with which Paul had wiped the sweat from his face, and the aprons that he had worn while he was at work making tents; and the diseases left the sick, and evil spirits went out of men. These wonderful works drew great crowds to hear Paul and led many more to believe in his words.

There were in that city some Jews who wandered from place to place, pretending to drive evil spirits out of men. These men saw how great was the power of the name of Jē'ṣus as spoken by Paul, and they also began to speak in Jē'ṣus' name, saying to the evil spirits in men, "I command you to come out, in the name of Jē'ṣus, whom Paul preaches."

And the evil spirit in one man answered two of these pretenders, "Jē'ṣus I know and Paul I know; but who are you?"

And the man in whom the evil spirit was, leaped upon them and threw them down. He tore off their clothing and beat them, so that they ran out of the house naked and covered with wounds. Everybody in the city, both Jews and Greeks, heard of this, and all knew that even the evil spirits feared the name of Jē'ṣus as spoken by Paul.

And many of those who had dealt with evil spirits came and confessed their deeds and turned to the Lord. And some who had books claiming to tell how to talk with spirits brought them and burned them as bad books, although the books had cost a great sum of money. Thus the word of the Lord grew in Ĕph'e-ṣŭs, a great number believed in Chrīst, and a large church arose.

Paul now began to feel that his work in Ĕph'e-ṣŭs was nearly finished. He thought that he would go across the Æ-ġē'an Sea and visit the churches at Phĭ-lĭp'pī and Thĕs-sa-lȯ-nī'cȧ and Bĕ-rē'ȧ, in the land of Măç-e-dō'nĭ-ȧ and then the church at Cŏr'inth in Greeçe, and then go once more to Jḛ-ru'sȧ-lĕm.

"And after I have been there," said Paul, "then I must also see Rōme."

So to prepare for his coming into Măç-e-dō'nĭ-ȧ, he sent Tĭm'o-thy̆ and another friend named Ḛ-răs'tus, while he himself stayed in Ĕph'e-ṣŭs for a time longer. But soon after this a great stir arose in that city over Paul and his preaching.

In the city of Ĕph'e-ṣŭs was standing at that time an idol temple, one of the greatest and richest in all the world. Around the temple stood a hundred and twenty great columns of white marble, each column the gift of a king. And in it was an image of the goddess Dī-ăn'ȧ, which the people believed had fallen down from the sky. People came from many lands to worship the idol

image of Dī-ăn′à; and many took away with them little images
like it, made of gold or silver. The making and selling of these
little images gave work to many who wrought in gold and silver,
and brought to them great riches.

One of these workers in silver, a man named Dĕ-mē′trĭ-ŭs,
called together his fellow workmen and said to them, "You know,
my friends, that by this trade we earn our living and win riches.
And you can all see and hear that this man Paul has persuaded and
turned away many people, not only in this city but also throughout all these lands, by telling all men that those are not gods which
are made by hands. There is danger that our trade will come to
an end and danger, too, that the temple of the great goddess
Dī-ăn′à may be made of no account. It may be even that the
goddess whom all Ā′ṣià and all the world worships shall fall down
from her greatness." When the workmen heard this, they became very angry, and they set up a great cry, shouting out, "Great
is Dī-ăn′à of the Ê-phē′ṣianṣ! Great is Dī-ăn′à of the Ê-phē′-
ṣianṣ!"

And soon the whole city was in an uproar; people were running
through the streets and shouting, and a great multitude was drawn
together, most of them not knowing what had caused the crowd
and the noise. In the side of the hill near the city was a great open
place hollowed out, having stone seats around it on three sides.
It was used for public meetings and was called "the theater." Into
this place all the people rushed, until it was thronged; while Dĕ-

mē′trĭ-ŭs and his fellow workers led on the shouting, "Great is Dī-ăn′a of the Ē-phē′sians!"

They seized two of Paul's friends who were with him in the city, Gā′ius and Ăr-ĭs-tär′chus, and dragged them with them into the theater. Paul wished to go in and try to speak to the people, but the disciples of Chrīst would not let him go; and some of the chief men of the land, who were Paul's friends, sent word to him, urging and beseeching him not to venture into the theater.

The noise and the shouting and the confusion were kept up for two hours. When the throng began to grow tired and were ready to listen, the clerk of the city came forward and quieted the people and said, "Ye men of Ēph′e-sŭs, what is the need of all this riot? Is there anyone who does not know that this city guards the temple of the great goddess Dī-ăn′a and of the image that fell down from the heavens? Since these things cannot be denied, you should be quiet and do nothing rash or foolish. You have brought here these men, who are not robbers of temples, nor have they spoken evil against our goddess. If Dĕ-mē′trĭ-ŭs and the men of his trade have a charge to bring against any men, the courts are open, and there are judges to hear their case. But if there is any other business, it must be done in a regular meeting of the people. For we are in danger for this day's riot and may be brought to account for it, since there is no cause for it and no reason that we can give for this gathering of a crowd."

And after the city clerk had quieted the people with these words, he sent them away. When the riot was over and all was peaceful again, Paul met the disciples of Chrīst and spoke to them once more. He had been in Ēph′e-sŭs for three years preaching; and while there he had written, besides the epistle or letter to the Gā-lā′tians, that to the Rō′mans, and two letters to the Cŏ-rĭn′-thĭ-ans, the believers in Chrīst at Cŏr′inth in Greeçe. He now sailed away from Ēph′e-sŭs, across the Æ-ġē′an Sea to Măç-e-dō′nĭ-a, where he had preached the gospel before on his second journey.

Paul's Last Journey to Jerusalem

AFTER his three years at Ĕph'e-sŭs in Ā'ṣià Mī'nor, Paul sailed across the Æ-ġē'an Sea to Măç-e-dō'nĭ-à. There he visited again the churches in Phĭ-lĭp'pī, Thĕs-sa-lŏ-nī'cà, and Bĕ-rē'à. Then he went southward into Greeçe, and saw again the church at Cŏr'inth, to which shortly before he had written two long letters. While Paul was visiting these churches, he told them of the believers in Christ among the Jews in Jē-ru'sà-lĕm and Jū-dē'à; that many of these were very poor, and since they had become disciples of Christ, the other Jews would not help them. Therefore Paul asked the Gĕn'tile churches everywhere to send gifts to these poor people. He said in his letters:

"These people have sent the word of Christ to you; now send to them your gifts to show that you love them and to show that you thank God for the gift of his Son who saves you from your sins."

From each of the churches men were chosen to go with Paul to Jē-ru'sà-lĕm and to carry these gifts. All these men went on before and waited for Paul at Trō'ăs, on the shore of the Æ-ġē'an Sea. Paul's friend Luke, the doctor, joined him again at Phĭ-lĭp'pī, and they sailed together to Trō'ăs. There the other disciples met them and they stayed for a week.

On the evening of the first day of the week, a farewell meeting was held at Trō'ăs, for Paul and his party, who on the next day were to start on their journey to Jē-ru'sà-lĕm. The meeting was in a large upper room on the third story of a house, and it was filled with people who had come to hear Paul. While Paul was speaking, one young man, named Eū'tў-chus, who was sitting in an open window, dropped asleep, and in his sleep fell out of the window upon the ground, two stories below. He was taken up dead; but Paul went down and fell on him and placed his arms

626

around him, saying, "Do not weep for him, for his life is still in him."

Then Paul went up again and broke the bread with the believers and held with them the Lord's Supper; and then he talked again for a long time, even until the break of day. And they brought the young man, who was still living, which made them all very happy.

All the rest of the party going to Jĕ-ru'så-lĕm, except Paul, went on board the ship at Trō'ăs. But as the ship was to stop on the way at a place called Ăs-sŏs, Paul chose to go to that place on foot. At Ăs'sŏs, they took Paul on board and sailed for some days among the islands of the Æ-ġē'an Sea and stopped at Mī'lē-tus, which was not far from Ĕph'e-sŭs. Paul had not time for a visit to Ĕph'e-sŭs, but he sent for the elders of the church, asking them to come to meet him at Mī'lē-tus. They came, and Paul said to them:

"You know from the first day that I set foot in this part of Ā'sià, after what manner I was with you all the time, serving the Lord with a lowly mind and with tears and with many troubles which came upon me from the plots of the Jews. You know, too, how faithfully I spoke to you, teaching you in public and from house to house, to turn from your sins and to believe in our Lord Jē'sus Chrīst.

"And now, bound in my spirit, I am going to Jĕ-ru'så-lĕm, not knowing what shall come upon me there, except that the Holy Spirit tells me in every place that chains and troubles will meet me. But I do not hold my life of any account, as dear to me; so that I may run out my race in Chrīst, and may do the work given me by the Lord Jē'sus, to preach the good news of God's grace. And now, I know that you all, among whom I went preaching the kingdom, shall see my face no more.

"Take heed to yourselves and to all the flock which the Holy Spirit has placed in your care, as shepherds to feed the church, which the Lord Jē'sus bought with his own blood. I know that after I go away, enemies, like savage wolves, shall come among you, not sparing the flock; and also among yourselves men shall rise up speaking false words and leading away disciples after them.

Therefore watch, and remember that for three years I did not cease warning you, night and day, with tears.

"And now, I leave you with God and with the word of his grace, which is able to build you up and to make you fit to dwell among his holy ones. I have not sought among you gold or silver or fine clothing. You yourselves know that these hands of mine have worked for my own living and to help those who were with me. I have tried to show you by my own example that you should in the same way help those who are weak, and remember the words of the Lord Jē'ṣus, 'It is more blessed to give than to receive.' "

When Paul had said this, he kneeled down and prayed with them all. And they all wept and fell on Paul's neck and kissed him; for they felt very sad at his words, that they should see his face no more. They went with him to the ship and saw him sail away from them.

Paul and his company sailed among the islands and toward the land of Jū-dē'á and went ashore at Tȳre. There they found disciples, and they stayed with them a week. Some of these spoke to Paul in the Spirit of God, and told him not to go into Jĕ-ru'så-lĕm. But Paul had set his face toward that city; and when he found a ship going from Tȳre to Jū-dē'á, all the disciples, with their wives and their children, went with him out of the city; and all knelt down together on the beach and prayed, before they

parted from each other. Paul's party left the ship at a place called Ptŏl-e-mā'is, from which they walked down the shore to Çaes-a-rē'à. This was the place where years before Pē'tĕr had given the gospel to the Rō'man centurion Côr-nē'lĭ-ŭs. And there Paul found Phĭl'ĭp, the man who had preached to the Sà-măr'ĭ-tanş and to the nobleman from Ē-thĭ-ō'pĭ-à. In those old days, Paul then Saul, had been Phĭl'ĭp's enemy and had driven him out of Jĕ-ru'-sà-lĕm. Now they met as friends, and Paul stayed as a guest at Phĭl'ĭp's house.

While they were at Çaes-a-rē'à, an old man, named Ăg'a-bŭs, came down from Jĕ-ru'sà-lĕm. He was a prophet, to whom God had shown some things that were to come to pass. We have read of a prophecy by this man before. This man came to Paul and took off Paul's girdle and with it bound his own feet and hands, and he said:

"Thus saith the Spirit of God, 'So shall the Jewş at Jĕ-ru'sà-lĕm bind the man that owns this girdle and shall give him into the hands of the Gĕn'tiĭleş.'"

When they heard this, all Paul's friends, and Phĭl'ĭp and the disciples of Çaes-a-rē'à, pleaded with Paul and begged him not to go up to Jĕ-ru'sà-lĕm. But Paul answered:

"What are you doing, weeping and breaking my heart? I am ready not to be bound only, but also to die at Jĕ-ru'sà-lĕm for the name of the Lord Jē'şus."

When they saw that Paul could not be moved from his purpose, they ceased trying to persuade him, saying, "The will of the Lord be done."

After some days in Çaes-a-rē'à, Paul and his friends, with some of the believers from Çaes-a-rē'à, went up the mountains to Jĕ-ru'-sà-lĕm. So Paul was once more, and now for the last time, in the city of his people.

The Speech on the Stairs

HEN Paul and his friends came to Jĕ-ru'sȧ-lĕm, they met with the church in that city and gave the money which had been gathered among the Gĕn'tīlĕs to help those of the Jew'ĭsh believers in Chrīst who were poor. The Apostle Jāmeş, the Lord's brother, who was at the head of the church in Jĕ-ru'sȧ-lĕm, gave to Paul and his friends a glad welcome and praised God for the good work wrought among the Gĕn'tīleş.

About a week after Paul had come to Jĕ-ru'sȧ-lĕm, he was worshiping in the Temple, when some Jews from the lands around Ĕph'e-sŭs saw him. They at once stirred up a crowd and took hold of Paul, crying out:

"Men of Ĭş'ra-el, help! This is the man who teaches all men everywhere against our people and against our law and against this Temple. Besides, he has brought Gĕn'tīleş into the Temple and thus has made the holy house unclean!"

They had seen with Paul, walking in the city, one of his friends from Ĕph'e-sŭs who was not a Jew, and they started the false report that Paul had taken him into the Temple. When the Jews set up this cry against Paul, all the city was stirred up and a great crowd gathered around Paul. They dragged Paul out of the Temple into the outer court, and were about to kill him in their rage.

But in the castle on the north of the Temple was a Rō'man guard of soldiers, a thousand men under the command of an officer, whom we should call a colonel, but whom they called "the chief captain." Word came to this officer that all Jĕ-ru'sȧ-lĕm was in a riot and that a wild mob had seized the Temple. He called out companies of soldiers and their centurions, or captains, and rushed quickly into the Temple and into the midst of the crowd who were beating and trampling upon Paul. The chief

630

captain took Paul from their hands, and, thinking that he must have done something very wicked to call forth such a riot, ordered him to be fastened with two chains.

Then he asked who this man was and what he had done. All began to answer at once, some shouting one thing and some another, and as the chief captain could understand nothing in the confusion, he commanded the soldiers to take him into the castle. The crowd made a rush to seize Paul and take him away from the soldiers, but they carried him through the throng and up the stone steps that led into the castle, while all around, at the foot of the stairs, was the multitude of angry Jews, crying out, "Away with him! Kill him!"

Just as they reached the platform at the door of the castle, Paul, in a quiet manner, spoke to the chief captain in his own language, which was the Greek tongue. He said, "May I say something to you?" The officer was surprised and he answered Paul, "Do you know Greek? Are you not that man from Ē'gÿpt who some time ago rose up against the rulers and let out in the wilderness four thousand men who were murderers?"

But Paul said, "I am a Jew, of Tär'sus in Çi-lǐ'çià. I belong to no mean city. I pray you, give me leave to speak to the people."

The chief captain thought that if this man should speak to the people, he might learn something about him; so he gave him leave. Then Paul, standing on the stairs, beckoned with his hand to the crowd to show that he wished to speak. Soon everybody became quiet, for all wanted to hear; and then Paul began to speak to the people. But he did not speak in Greek, as he had spoken to the chief captain. He spoke in the Hē'brew tongue, their own language, which they loved to hear. And when they heard him speak in Hē'brew, their own tongue, they were all the more ready to listen to him. And this was what Paul said:

"Brethren and fathers, hear the words that I speak to you. I am a Jew, born in Tär'sus, of Çi-lǐ'çià, but brought up in this city at the feet of the wise teacher Gȧ-mā'lǐ-el, and taught in a strict way in the law of our fathers; and I was earnest for God, as all of you are this day. And I was a bitter enemy of the way of Christ, binding and putting in prison both men and women who believed in Jē'şus. The high priest himself knows this and all the council of the elders; for they gave me letters to our people in Dȧ-mȧs'cus. And I went on a journey to that place to bring in chains from Dȧ-mȧs'cus to Jĕ-ru̧'sȧ-lĕm those who followed Jē'şus, to punish them.

"And it came to pass as I made my journey and drew nigh to Dȧ-mȧs'cus, suddenly there shone from heaven a great light round

about me. And I fell to the ground and heard a voice saying to me, 'Sa̧ul, Sa̧ul, why are you fighting against me and trying to do me harm?' And I answered, 'Who art thou, Lord?' And he said to me, 'I am Jē'şus of Năz'a-rĕth, whom you are trying to destroy!'

"Those who were with me saw the light, but they did not hear the voice that spoke to me. And I said, 'What shall I do, Lord?' And the Lord said to me, 'Rise up and go into Dȧ-mȧs'cus and it shall be told you what things are given to you to do.'

"When I stood up, I could not see from the glory of that light, and I was led by the hands of those who were with me into

Dă-măs'cus. And a man named Ăn-a-nī'as, a man who worshiped God and kept the law, of whom all the Jews in the city spoke well, came to me and standing by me, said, 'Brother Saul, receive your sight.'

"And in that very hour I looked up and saw him. And he said to me, 'The God of our fathers hath chosen you to know his will and to see the Holy One and to hear his voice. For you shall speak in his name to all men, telling them what you have seen and heard.'

"And afterward when I came back to Jĕ-ru'să-lĕm and was praying in the Temple, I saw the Lord again, and he spoke to me, 'Go forth, and I will send you far hence to the Gĕn'tīles.'"

The Jews listened to Paul quietly until he spoke that word "Gĕn'tīles," which roused up all their wrath. They began to cry out, "Away with such a fellow from the earth! It is not fit that he should live!"

And as they flung off their garments and threw dust into the air in their rage, the chief captain ordered that Paul should be taken into the castle and beaten with rods until he should tell what dreadful thing he had done to arouse such anger. For the chief captain, not knowing the Jews' language, had not understood what Paul had said.

They took Paul into the castle and were tying him up to beat him, when Paul said to the centurion who stood by, "Have you any right to beat a Rō'man citizen who has not been tried before a judge?"

When the centurion heard this, he went in haste to the chief captain and said to him, "Take care what you do to that man, for he is a Rō'man citizen!"

Then the chief captain came and said to Paul, "Tell me, are you a Rō'man citizen?"

And Paul answered, "Yes, I am."

The chief captain said, "I bought this right to be a citizen with a great sum of money."

And Paul said to him, "But I am a free-born citizen."

When those who were about to beat Paul knew that he was a Rō'man citizen, they went away from him in haste, and the chief captain was afraid, because he had bound Paul, for no one might place a chain on a Rō'man citizen until he had been tried before a Rō'man judge.

They took Paul into the castle, but were careful not to do him any harm.

Story Sixteen

Two Years in Prison

AFTER Paul had been rescued from the Jew'ish mob, he was taken into the castle on the north of the Temple for safekeeping. The chief captain wished to know for what reasons the Jews were so bitter in their hate against Paul; and to learn this he commanded the chief priests and rulers to meet together, and brought Paul down from the castle and set him before them. Paul looked earnestly upon the council and said to them, "Brethren, I have lived trying to do the will of God all my life until this day."

The high priest, whose name was Ăn-a-nī'as, was sitting in the council, clad in the white garments worn by all priests. He was so enraged at these words that he said to those who were standing near Paul, "Strike him on the mouth!"

Paul, roused to sudden anger at such unjust words, said, "God shall strike you, O whited wall! Do you sit to judge me by the law and yet against the law command me to be struck?"

Those that were standing by, said to Paul, "Do you speak such words against the high priest of God?"

"I did not know," answered Paul, "that he was high priest. It is written in the law not to speak evil of a ruler of your people."

Paul saw that there were two parties in the council and by a few wise words he made some of the rulers friendly to him, so that they stood up and said, "We find no evil in this man. Perhaps a spirit has spoken to him, or an angel."

This made the rulers on the other side all the more furious, and such a quarrel arose between them that the chief captain feared that Paul would be torn in pieces; and he again sent down soldiers to take him by force from the council and to bring him into the castle.

On the night after this, while Paul was in his cell in the castle, the Lord stood by him and said, "Be of good cheer, Paul; for as you have spoken for me at Jĕ-rụ'så-lĕm, so shall you speak for me at Rōme."

Early on the next morning more than forty of the Jews laid a plan to kill Paul and bound themselves together by an oath, swearing that they would neither eat nor drink until they had slain him. These men came to the chief priests and said, "We have bound ourselves under a great oath that we will taste nothing until we have killed Paul. Now, do you ask the chief captain to bring Paul down again to meet the council so that they may hear him and try his case once more. And while he is on his way to the council, we will rush in and kill him."

Now Paul had a sister living in Jĕ-rụ'så-lĕm, and her son heard of this plot and came to the castle and told it to Paul. Then Paul called one of the officers and said to him, "Take this young man to the chief captain, for he has something to tell him."

So the officer brought the young man to the chief captain and said to him, "Paul, the prisoner, called me to him and asked me to bring this young man to you, for he has something to say to you."

Then the chief captain took the young man aside and asked him, "What is it that you have to say to me?"

And he said, "The Jews have agreed to ask you to bring Paul before the council again; but do not let him go, for there are more than forty men watching for him, who have sworn an oath together that they will neither eat nor drink until they have killed Paul."

The chief captain listened carefully and then sent the young man away, after saying to him, "Do not tell anyone that you have spoken of these things to me."

And after the young man had gone, the chief captain called to

him two centurions, captains over a hundred men, and he said to
them, "Make ready two hundred soldiers to go as far as Çaes-a-
rē'à and seventy men on horseback and two hundred men with
spears, at nine o'clock at night."

And he told them also to have ready horses for Paul, so that
he might send him safe to Fē'lĭx, the governor of the land, at
Çaes-a-rē'à. And he wrote a letter in this manner:

"Clau'dĭ-ŭs Lў'sĭ-as sends greeting to the most noble governor
Fē'lĭx. This man was seized by the Jews and would have been
killed by them, but I came upon him with the soldiers and took
him from their hands, having learned that he was a citizen of
Rōme. And to find out the reasons why they were so strongly
against him, I brought him down to their council. But I found
that the charges against him were about questions of their law,
but nothing deserving death or prison. When I heard that there
was a plot to kill the man, I sent him at once to you and told his
enemies to go before you with their charges."

So in the night almost five hundred men were sent with a guard
for Paul. He was brought out of the castle and taken that night
as far as to An-tĭp'a-trĭs, about forty miles. On the next day the
soldiers left him, thinking him to be no longer in danger, and
returned to Jē-ru'sā-lĕm, while the horsemen rode on with him
to Çaes-a-rē'à where the governor Fē'lĭx lived. The officer in
charge gave the letter to the governor. He read the letter and
then asked Paul from what land he had come. Paul told him that
he belonged to the land of Çĭ-lĭ'çĭà in Ā'sĭà Mĭ'nor. And Fē'lĭx
said, "I will hear your case when those who bring charges against
you have come."

And he sent Paul to be kept in a castle which had once belonged to Hĕr'od. 'After five days the high priest Ăn-a-nī'as and some others came to Çaes-a-rē'à, bringing with them a lawyer named Tĕr-tŭl'lus. And when Paul was brought before them in presence of Fē'lĭx, the governor, Tĕr-tŭl'lus made a speech charging him with riot and lawbreaking, and many evil deeds. They said also that he was "a ringleader in the party of the Năz'a-rēnes," which was the name they gave to the Church of Chrīst. And the Jews all joined in the charge, saying that all these things were true. After they had spoken, the governor motioned with his hand toward Paul, showing that he might speak, and Paul began: "I know that you have been for many years a judge over this people, and for that reason I speak to you willingly. For you may know that it is only twelve days since I went up to worship at Jĕ-ru'sà-lĕm. Nor was I quarreling with anyone in the Temple nor stirring up a crowd in the Temple or the synagogues or in the city. Nor can they prove to you the things that they have said against me.

"But I do own to this, that after the way which they call 'the party of the Năz'a-rēnes,' so do I serve the God of our fathers, believing all things in the law and in the prophets, and having a hope in God that the dead shall be raised up. And I have always tried to keep my heart free from wrong toward God and toward men.

"Now, after many years, I came to bring gifts to my people and offerings for the altar. And with these they found me in the Temple, but not with a crowd, nor with a riot. But there were certain Jews from Ā'ṣià Mī'nor who ought to have been here, if they have anything against me."

Fē'lĭx knew somewhat about the Church of Chrīst, and he said, "When Lў'sĭ-as, the chief captain, shall come down, I will settle this case."

And he ordered Paul to be kept under guard, but that his friends might freely come to see him. After a few days Fē'lĭx and his wife Dru-sĭl'là, who was a Jew'ess, sent for Paul and heard from him with regard to the gospel of Chrīst. And as Paul preached to him of right living and of ruling oneself and of the judgment of God that should come upon sinners, Fē'lĭx was alarmed, and said, "Go away for this time; when a fit time comes and I am ready to listen, I will send for you."

Fē'lĭx was not a just judge, for he hoped that Paul might give him money, so that he might set Paul free; and with this in his mind, he sent for Paul and talked with him many times. Two whole years passed away and Paul was still in prison at Çaes-a-rē'à. At the end of that time Fē'lĭx was called back to Rōme and a man named Pôr'çĭ-ŭs Fĕs'tus was sent as governor in his place. Fē'lĭx wished to please the Jews, and he left Paul a prisoner.

Story Seventeen ACTS, chapters 25; 26

The Story That Paul Told
to the King

WHEN Fĕs'tus came to rule over the land of Jū-dē'à in the place of Fē'lĭx, who had kept Paul in prison so long, he went up to Jĕ-ru'sà-lĕm to visit that city. There the chief priests and the leading men spoke to him against Paul and they asked that he might be sent to Jĕ-ru'sà-lĕm to be tried. It was their plan to kill Paul on the way. But Fĕs'tus told them that Paul should be kept at Çaes-a-rē'à, and that he himself would soon go there.

"Let some of your leaders go down with me," said Fĕs'tus, "and bring your charges against him, if you have any."

When Fĕs'tus came down to Çaes-a-rē'à, he called them all together and sat upon the judge's seat and commanded Paul to be brought. Then the Jews said evil things about Paul, declaring that he had done wickedly. But they could not prove any of the things which they spoke against him. And Paul said, "I have done no wrong against the law of the Jews nor against the Temple nor against the rule of Çae'ṣar the emperor."

Fĕs'tus wished to please the Jews, for he did not know of their secret purpose to kill Paul. He said, "Are you willing to go up to Jĕ-ru'ṣà-lĕm and there be tried upon these charges before me?"

But Paul said, "I am standing before the Rō'man court where I ought to be judged. I have done no wrong to the Jews, as you know very well, and no man shall give me into their hands. I ask for a trial before Çae'ṣar, the emperor at Rōme."

It was the law throughout the Rō'man lands that any free citizen of Rōme, as Paul was, could ask to be tried at Rōme before Çae'ṣar, the emperor. When Fĕs'tus heard Paul's words, he said, "Do you ask to be tried before Çae'ṣar? Then unto Çae'ṣar you shall go."

So Paul was taken back to the prison at Çaes-a-rē'à to be sent to Rōme when his time should come. A few days after this a Jew'ĭsh ruler named À-grĭp'pà, with his sister Bĕr-nī'çĕ, came to visit Fĕs'tus. He was called "King À-grĭp'pà," and he ruled over a part of the land on the east of the river Jôr'dan. While À-grĭp'pà and Bĕr-nī'çĕ were at Çaes-a-rē'à, Fĕs'tus said to them, "There is a certain man left a prisoner by Fē'lĭx, of whom the chief priests and elders of the Jews asked, when I was at Jĕ-ru'ṣà-lĕm, that I should give orders to have him put to death, or given into their hands. I told them that the Rō'mans never give judgment against any man until he stands face to face before his enemies and can make answer to their charges. When they came down to this place and the man was brought before them, their charges were not the wicked acts that I expected to hear of; but they had some questions about their ways of worship and about somebody named Jē'ṣus, who was dead, but Paul said that he was alive. As I could not understand these questions, I asked Paul whether he would go up to Jĕ-ru'ṣà-lĕm and there be tried. But Paul asked for a trial before Çae'ṣar, and I am keeping him to be sent to the emperor at Rōme."

"I would like," said À-grĭp'pà, "to hear this man myself."

"Tomorrow," said Fĕs'tus, "you shall hear him."

So on the next day, À-grĭp'pà and his sister Bĕr-nī'çĕ and Fĕs'tus,

with the chief men of the city and the officers of the army, came in great state to the hall of judgment, and Paul was brought before them, chained to a Rō'man soldier. And after a few words by Fĕs'tus, Ȧ-grĭp'pȧ said to Paul, "You may now speak for yourself."

Then Paul spoke in words like these:

"I think myself happy, King Ȧ-grĭp'pȧ, to give answer before you of all the things charged against me by the Jews, because I am sure that you know all the Jew'ish ways and the questions about the law. I ask you, then, to hear me. My way of life from my youth all the Jews know, for I have lived among them; and if they tell the truth, they would say that I was one of those who kept the laws of our people most carefully. And now I stand here to be judged for the sake of the promise which God made to our fathers; that promise to which our twelve tribes, serving God day and night, hope to come. And on account of this hope, O king, the Jews charge me with doing evil; because I believe that Jē'sus Chrĭst rose from the dead to be the King of Ĭs'ra-el. Why should it be something you cannot believe, that God does raise the dead to life?

"In former times I really thought within myself that I ought to do many things against the name of Jē'sus of Năz'a-rĕth. And this I did in Jē-ru'sȧ-lĕm; for I shut up many good men and women in prisons, and when they were put to death, I gave my voice against them. I caused them to be beaten, and I tried to make them curse the name of Jē′ṣus; and being exceedingly mad against them, I sought for them even in cities far away.

"And as I journeyed to Dă-măs′cus with letters from the chief priests, at midday, O king, I saw on the way a light from heaven, above the brightness of the sun, shining around me and those who were with me. And as we all fell down upon the ground, I heard a voice saying to me, 'Ṣaul, Ṣaul, why are you fighting against me?'

"And I said, 'Who art thou, Lord?'

"And the Lord said, 'I am Jē′ṣus, whom you are trying to destroy. But rise up and stand upon your feet, for I have shown myself to you to make you my servant and my messenger to tell of what you have seen and of what I will show you. I will keep you safe from the Jew′ish people and from the Ġĕn′tiles, to whom I send you, to open their eyes and to turn them from darkness to light and from the power of Sā′tan, the evil one, to God, that their sins may be forgiven, and that they may receive a reward among those that are made holy by faith in me.'

"O King Ă-grĭp′pà, I did not disobey the voice from heaven, but first at Dă-măs′cus and then at Jĕ-ru′ṣà-lĕm and throughout all the land of Jū-dē′à, and also among the Ġĕn′tiles, I have spoken, telling men to turn from sin to God and to show deeds of right-doing. This is the cause why the Jews seized me in the Temple and tried to kill me. Having gained help from God, I stand unto this day, speaking to people, small and great, saying only what is given in the law of Mō′ṣes and in the prophets: that the Chrīst must suffer and die, and that he by rising from the dead should give light to our people and to the Ġĕn′tiles."

While Paul was speaking, Fĕs′tus said with a loud voice, "Paul, you are mad! Your great learning has turned you to madness!"

For Fĕs′tus, being a Rō′man, knew nothing of Jē′ṣus or of the truths which Paul spoke.

But Paul said to him, "I am not mad, most noble Fĕs′tus. I speak only sober and truthful words. The king knows of these things, and I speak freely to him. None of these things are hid-

HURLBUT'S STORY OF THE BIBLE

den from him, for these things were not done in secret. King Ȧ-grĭp′pà, do you believe the prophets? I know that you do believe."

And Ȧ-grĭp′pà said to Paul, "A little more, and you will persuade me to become a Christian!"

And Paul said, "I would before God, that whether with little or with much, that not only you, but also all that hear me this day, might become such as I am, except these chains!"

After these words, King Ȧ-grĭp′pà and Bĕr-nī′çĕ and Fĕs′tus the governor, and those who were there, went away by themselves, and they said to each other, "This man has done nothing deserving death or prison."

And Ȧ-grĭp′pà said to Fĕs′tus, "This man might have been set free if he had not asked to be tried before Çae′ṣar."

Story Eighteen

ACTS 27 : 1 to 28 : 1

Paul in the Storm

WHEN Paul chose to be tried before Çae′ṣar the emperor, which was his right as a Rō′man, it became necessary to send him from Çaes-a-rē′à in Jū-dē′à to Rōme in Ĭt′a-lў̆, where Çae′ṣar lived. In those years there were no ships sailing at regular times from city to city, but people who wished to go to places over the sea waited until they could find ships with loads sailing to those places. Paul and some other prisoners were given into the charge of a Rō′man centurion or captain named Jū′lĭ-ŭs, to be taken to Rōme. Jū′lĭ-ŭs found a ship sailing from Çaes-a-rē′à to places on the shore of Ā′ṣià Mī′nor, which would take them a part of the way to Rōme. He took Paul and the other prisoners on board this ship, and with Paul went his friends, Luke the doctor and Ăr-ĭs-tär′chus from Thĕs-sa-lŏ-nī′cà. Perhaps Tĭm'o-thў also accompanied them, but of this we are not certain.

They set sail from Çaes-a-rē'à, after Paul had been in prison more than two years; and they followed the coast northward to Sĭ'dŏn. There they stopped for a day; and Jū'lĭ-ŭs the centurion was very kind to Paul and let him go ashore to see his friends who were living there. From Sĭ'dŏn they turned to the northwest and sailed past the island of Çў'prus and then westward by the shore of Ā'ṣià Mĭ'nor. At a city called Mў'rà they left the ship and went on board another ship, which was sailing from Ăl-ĕx-ăn'-drĭ-à to Ĭt'a-lў with a load of wheat from the fields of Ē'ġўpt.

Soon a heavy wind began to blow against the ship, and it sailed very slowly for many days; but at last came to the large island of Crēte and followed its southern shore in the face of the wind until they found a harbor, and they stayed for a few days. But this harbor was not a good one, and they thought to leave it and sail to another.

Paul now said to them, "Sirs, I see that this voyage will be with great loss to the load and the ship and with great danger to the lives of us all."

And he urged them to stay where they were at anchor. But the owner of the ship and its captain thought that they might sail in safety; and Jū'lĭ-ŭs the centurion listened to them rather than to Paul. So when a gentle south wind began to blow, they set sail once more, closely following the shore of the island of Crēte. But soon the wind grew into a great storm, and the ship could not

face it and was driven out of its course. Behind the ship was a little boat and this they drew up on board; and as the ship creaked and seemed in danger of going to pieces, they tied ropes around it to hold it together.

The storm grew and drove the ship away from the island into the open sea. To make the vessel lighter, they threw overboard a part of the load; and the next day they cast into the sea all the loose ropes and everything on the ship that could be spared.

Day after day went on with no sight of the sun, and night after night with no sight of the stars. The great waves rolled over the ship and beat upon it, until those on board hardly hoped to save their lives. In their fear, for days the men and the prisoners had eaten nothing. But in the midst of the storm, Paul stood up among them and said:

"Sirs, you should have listened to me and not have set sail from Crēte, for then we might have been saved much harm and loss. But even as it is, be of good cheer; for though the ship will be lost, all of us on board shall be saved. This night there stood by me an angel of the Lord, to whom I belong and whom I serve, and the angel said to me, 'Fear not, Paul; you shall yet stand before Çae'sar; and God has given to you the lives of all those who are sailing with you.'

"Now, friends, be of good cheer; for I believe God, that it shall be even as the angel said to me. But we must cast upon some island."

When the storm had lasted fourteen days, at night the sailors thought that they were coming near to land. They dropped down the line and found that the water was one hundred and twenty feet deep; then after a little they let down the line again and found the water only ninety feet deep. They were sure now that land was near, but they were afraid that the ship might be driven upon rocks; so they threw out from the stern or rear end four anchors to hold the ship; and then they longed for the day to come.

The sailors let down the little boat, saying that they would throw out some more anchors from the bow or front of the ship, but really intending to row away in the boat and leave the ship and all on board to be destroyed. But Paul saw their purpose, and he said to the centurion, "Unless these sailors stay in the ship, none of us can be saved."

Then the soldiers cut away the ropes of the boat and let it fall off, so that the sailors could not get away. And as it drew toward daylight, Paul urged them all to take some food. He said:

"This is the fourteenth day that you have waited without any food. Now I beg of you to eat, for you need it to keep your lives safely. You will all be saved; not a hair shall fall from the head of one of you."

He took some bread and gave thanks to God before them all; then he broke it and began to eat. This encouraged all the others, so that they too took food. There were in all on board the ship, sailors and soldiers and prisoners and others, two hundred and seventy-six people. After they had eaten enough, they threw out into the sea what was left of its load of wheat, so that the ship might be lighter and might go nearer to the shore.

As soon as the day dawned, they could see land but did not know what land it was. They saw a bay with a beach, into which they thought that they might run the ship. So they cut loose the anchors, leaving them in the sea, and they hoisted up the foresail to the wind and made toward the shore. The ship ran aground and the front end was stuck fast in the sand, but the rear part began to break in pieces from the beating of the waves.

Now came another danger, just as they were beginning to hope for their lives. By the Rō'man law, a soldier who had charge of a prisoner must take his prisoner's place if he escaped from his care. These soldiers feared that their prisoners might swim ashore and get free. So they asked the centurion to let them kill all the prisoners, while they were still on board the ship. But Jū'lĭ-ŭs the centurion loved Paul, and to save Paul's life, kept them from killing the prisoners. He commanded that those who could swim should leap overboard and get first to the land. Then the rest went ashore, some on planks and some on broken pieces of the ship. And all came safe to the shore, not one life being lost.

And then they found that they were on the island of Mĕl'ĭ-tà, which is in the Great Sea, south of the larger island of Sĭç'ĭ-lў.

How Paul Came to Rome and How He Lived There

THE PEOPLE who lived on the island of Měl′ĭ-tà were very kind to the strangers who had been thrown by the sea upon their shore. It was cold and rainy, and the men from the ship were in garments drenched by the waves. But the islanders made a fire and brought them all around it and gave them good care. Very soon they found that many of the men were prisoners, who were under guard of the soldiers.

Paul gathered a bundle of sticks and placed them on the fire, when suddenly a poisonous snake came from the pile, driven out by the heat, and seized Paul's hand with its teeth. When the people saw the snake hanging from his hand, they said to each other, "This man must be a murderer. He has saved his life from the sea, but the just gods will not let him live on account of his wickedness."

But Paul shook off the snake into the fire and was not harmed. They looked to see his arm swell with poison and to see him fall down dead suddenly. But when they watched him for a long time and saw no evil come to him, they changed their minds and said that he was a god and were ready to worship him.

Near the place where the ship was wrecked were lands and buildings belonging to the ruler of the island, whose name was Pŭb′lĭ-us. He took Paul and his friends into his house and treated them very kindly. The father of Pŭb′lĭ-us was very ill with a fever and a disease called dysentery, from which people often died. But Paul went into his room and prayed by his side; then he laid his hands on him, and the sick man became well. As soon as the people of the island heard of this, many others troubled with diseases were brought to Paul and all were cured. The people of Měl′ĭ-tà after this gave great honor to Paul and those who were with him; and when they sailed away, they put on the ship as gifts for them all things that they would need for the remainder of the journey.

The centurion found at anchor by the island a ship from Ăl-ex-ăn'drĭ-à on its way to Ĭt'a-lў, which had been waiting there through the winter. The name of this ship was "The Twin Brothers." After three months on the isle, the centurion sent on board this ship his soldiers and prisoners, with Pạul's friends; and they sailed away from Mĕl'ĭ-tà. After stopping at a few places on their voyage, they left the ship at Pū-tē'o-lī, in the south of Ĭt'a-lў, and from that place they were led toward Rōme. The church at Rōme, to which Pạul had written a letter in other days, heard that he was coming, and some of the brethren went out to meet him a few miles from the city. When Pạul saw them and knew that they were glad to meet him, even though he was in chains, he thanked God and took heart once more. He had long wished to go to Rōme, and now he came into the city at last, but as a prisoner, chained to a Rō'man soldier.

When they came to Rōme, the good centurion Jū'lĭ-ŭs gave his prisoners to the captain of the guard in the city; but from the kind words spoken by Jū'lĭ-ŭs, Pạul was allowed to go to a house by himself, though with the soldier who guarded him always at his side. After three days in Rōme, Pạul sent for the chief men among the Jews of the city to meet in his house, because he could not go to the synagogue to meet with them. When they came, he said to them:

"Brethren, though I have done no harm to our people or against our law, yet I was made a prisoner in Jė-rụ'sà-lĕm and given into the hands of the Rō'mans. When the Rō'mans had given me a trial, they found no cause for putting me to death and wished to set me free. But the Jews spoke against me, and I had to ask for a trial before Çae'sar, though I have no charge to bring against my own people. I have asked to see you and to speak with you, because for the hope of Ĭs'ra-el that I am bound with this chain "

They said to Pạul, "No letters have come to us from Jū-dē'à nor have any of the brethren brought to us any evil report of you.

But we would like to hear from you about this people who follow Jḗ'ṣus of Năz'a-rĕth, for they are a people everywhere spoken against."

So Paul named a day, and on the day they came in great number to Paul's room. He talked with them, explaining the teaching of the Old Testament about Chrīst, from morning until evening. Some believed the words of Paul and others refused to believe. And when they would not agree, Paul said to them as they were leaving, "Truly indeed did the Holy Spirit say of this people, in the words of Ī-ṣa'iah the prophet, 'Hearing ye shall hear, and shall not understand, and seeing ye shall see, and yet not see. For this

people's heart is become hard, and their ears are dull, and their eyes they have shut; for they are not willing to see, nor to hear, nor to understand, nor to turn from their sins to God.' But know this, that the salvation of Chrīst is sent not alone to you Jews, but also to the Gĕn'tīleṣ; and they will listen to it, even though you do not."

And after this Paul lived two years in the house which he had hired. Every day a soldier was brought from the camp, and Paul was chained to him for all that day. And the next day another soldier came; each day a new soldier was chained to Paul. And to each one Paul spoke the gospel, until after a time many of the soldiers in the camp were believers in Chrīst; and when these soldiers were sent away, they often carried the gospel with them to other lands. So Paul, though a prisoner, was still doing good and working for Chrīst.

Then, too, some of Paul's friends were with him in Rōme. The young Tĭm'o-thy̆, whom Paul loved to call his son in the gospel, and Lṵke, the doctor, of whom he wrote as "the beloved physician," were there, perhaps in the same house. Ăr-ĭs-tär'chus of Thĕs-sa-lŏ-nī'cȧ, who had been with him in the ship and in the storm, was still with Paul. Märk, the young man who years before went with Päul and Bär'na-băs on their first journey from Ăn'tĭ-ŏch, visited Paul in Rōme.

At one time, when Paul had been a prisoner nearly two years, a friend came to see him from Phĭ'lĭp'pī in Măç-e-dō'nĭ-ȧ. His name was Ê-păph-ro-dī'tus, and he brought to Paul a loving message from that church and also gifts to help Paul in his need. In return, Paul wrote to the church at Phĭ-lĭp'pī a letter, "The Epistle to the Phĭ-lĭp'pī-anṣ," full of tender and gentle words. It was taken to the church by Ê-păph-ro-dī'tus and by Tĭm'o-thy̆, whom Paul sent with him, perhaps because in Rōme Ê-păph-ro-dī'tus was very ill, and Päul may have thought it better not to have him go home alone.

In Rōme a man named Ȯ-nĕs'ĭ-mŭs met Paul. He was a runaway slave who belonged to a friend of Paul, named Phĭ-lē'mon, living at Cȯ-lŏs'sĕ in Ā'ṣiȧ Mī'nor, not far from Ĕph'e-sŭs. Paul led Ȯ-nĕs'ĭ-mŭs to give his heart to Chrīst, and then, although he would have liked to keep him as a helper, he sent him back to Phĭ-lē'mon, his master. But he asked Phĭ-lē'mon to take him, no longer as a slave, but as a brother in Chrīst. This he wrote in a letter which he sent by Ȯ-nĕs'ĭ-mŭs, called "The Epistle to Phĭ-lē'mon." Ȯ-nĕs'ĭ-mŭs carried at the same time another letter to the church at Cȯ-lŏs'sĕ. This letter is "The Epistle to the Cȯ-lŏs'sĭ-anṣ." And about the same time Paul wrote one of the greatest and most wonderful of all his letters, "The Epistle to the Ê-phē'ṣianṣ," which he sent to the church in Ĕph'e-sŭs. So all the world has been richer ever since Paul's time by having the four letters which he wrote while he was a prisoner at Rōme.

It is thought, though it is not certain, that Paul was set free from prison after two years; that he lived a free man, preaching in many lands for a few years; that he wrote during those years the First Epistle to Tĭm'o-thў, whom he had sent to care for the church at Ĕph'e-sŭs, and the Epistle to Tī'tus, who was over the churches in the island of Crēte; that he was again made a prisoner and taken to Rōme; and from his Rō'man prison wrote his last letter, the Second Epistle to Tĭm'o-thў, and that soon after this wicked Emperor Nē'rō caused him to be put to death. Among his last words in the letter to Tĭm'o-thў were these:

"I have fought a good fight; I have run my race; I have kept the faith; and now there is waiting for me the crown which the Lord himself shall give me."

Story Twenty   REVELATION 1 : 9-20; 4 : 1 to 5 : 14

The Throne of God

YOU REMEMBER the apostle Jŏhn, "the disciple whom Jē'ṣus loved." When Jŏhn was an old man, he was made a prisoner by a cruel emperor of Rōme and was kept in a little island called "the isle of Păt'mos," which is in the Æ-ġē'an Sea, not far from Ĕph'e-sŭs. While Jŏhn was shut up on this island, the Lord Jē'ṣus Chrīst came to him and showed him some things which were to come to pass.

It was on the Lord's Day, the first day of the week, when suddenly Jŏhn heard behind him a loud voice, as loud as the sound of a trumpet. He turned to see from whom the voice came; and then he saw seven golden candlesticks standing and among them One whom Jŏhn knew at once as his Lord, Jē'ṣus Chrīst. Yet Chrīst, as he saw him, was far more glorious than he had been while living as a man on the earth. He was dressed in a long white garment, with a girdle of gold over his breast; his hair and his face were so shining that they seemed as white as snow; his eyes flashed

like fire; his feet were like polished brass, glowing as a furnace; and his voice sounded like the rushing of a mighty torrent of waters. In his right hand were held seven stars; and a glory came from him brighter than the sun.

When Jŏhn saw his Lord in all this splendor, he fell at his feet in great terror. Then he felt the right hand of Chrīst laid upon him; and he heard his voice, saying:

"Fear not; I am the first and the last and the Living One. I was dead and now I am alive for evermore. Write the things which you have seen and other things which I will show you, and send them to the seven churches in Ā'şià. The seven stars which you see in my hands are the ministers of the seven churches; and the seven candlesticks standing around me are the seven churches."

Then the Lord gave to Jŏhn the words of a letter which he commanded Jŏhn to write to the seven churches in that part of Ā'şià, of which churches that of Ĕph'e-sŭs was the first. To each church was to be sent a different letter, the word of the Lord Jē'şus to that church, praising it for some things and rebuking it for others. When these words had been given to the churches, Jŏhn saw a door opened in heaven; and he heard a voice like the sound of a trumpet, saying to him, "Come up to this place and I will show thee things that shall come to pass."

Then at once Jŏhn was taken up to heaven and he saw the throne of God and One sitting upon it whom he could scarcely see for the dazzling glory around him. And over the throne was a rainbow of many colors. Around the throne were twenty-four thrones and upon them sat twenty-four old men, the elders of the church, dressed in white, with crowns of gold on their heads. Out of the throne came lightning and thunder and the sound of voices. Before the throne was a sea of glass like crystal, and beside the throne were four strange living creatures, each having six wings. And these living ones were saying, "Holy, holy, holy, is the Lord God, the Almighty, which was and which is and which is to come."

And then the elders would fall down and worship him who sits on the throne and lay their crowns at his feet and say, "Thou art worthy, O God, our Lord, to have the honor and the glory and the power; for thou didst create and make all things."

Then Jŏhn saw in the right hand of the One sitting on the throne a book in the form of a roll, written on both sides and sealed with seven seals. And a mighty angel called out with a loud voice, "Who is worthy to open the book and to loose its seals?"

And no one in all the heaven or on the earth or under the earth was able to open the book or to loosen its seals. Then Jŏhn began to weep, because there was found no one worthy to open the book or even to look upon it. But one of the twenty-four elders spoke to Jŏhn, saying, "Weep not; see, the Lion of the tribe of Jū'dah, he who came from Dā'vid, has won the right to open the book and its seven seals."

Then before the throne and among the elders and the four living creatures, Jŏhn saw standing the Lamb of God, Jē'ṣus Chrīst, with the wounds of the cross upon him, in hands and feet and side. He came and took the book from the right hand of the One who was sitting on the throne. And as he took the book, the four living creatures and the twenty-four elders all fell down before the throne. Each held a harp and a golden bowl full of incense, such as was used in the Temple, as a sign of the prayers of God's people. And they all sang a new song, with the words:

"Worthy is the Lamb who was slain to have the power and riches, and wisdom, and might, and honor, and glory, and blessing."

The City of God

AGAIN Jŏhn saw the throne of God, and before it and before the Lamb of God stood a multitude of people so great that no man could count them. They were dressed in white robes, branches of palm were in their hands, and they cried with a loud voice saying, "Salvation unto our God upon the throne and unto the Lamb."

And all the angels were standing around the throne and around the four living creatures and around the seats of the twenty-four elders; and the angels fell down on their faces and worshiped God, saying, "Amen: Blessing, and glory, and thanksgiving, and honor, and power, and might, be unto our God for ever and ever."

Then one of the elders spoke to Jŏhn and said, "Who are these dressed in white robes? and whence did they come?"

And Jŏhn answered, "My Lord, thou knowest who they are and whence they came, but I do not know."

Then the elder said, "These are they who have come up out of great trouble and sorrow, and have washed their robes and made them white in the blood of the Lamb. For that cause they are before the throne of God, and they serve him day and night in his temple; and he that sits upon the throne shall spread his tent over them. They shall hunger no more, neither shall they thirst any more, nor shall the heat of the sun strike upon them. But the Lamb who is in the midst of the throne shall lead them as a shepherd and shall guide them unto fountains of waters of life. And God shall wipe away every tear from their eyes."

After this, Jŏhn heard a great voice out of the throne, saying, "Behold, the house of God is with men; and God shall dwell among men and they shall be his people and he shall be their God. God shall wipe away all tears from their eyes; and there shall be no more death; neither . . . weeping or crying nor pain any more."

And He that was sitting upon the throne said, "Behold, I make all things new. I will give to him who is thirsty of the fountain of the water of life freely."

Then Jŏhn seemed to be standing upon a great and high mountain; and he saw a glorious city, the new Jĕ-ru͟'så-lĕm, coming down out of heaven from God, having the glory of God. Over the city was a rich light, like that which glows in some precious stone, clear as crystal. Around the city was a lofty wall, and on

each side of the wall were three gates; for the city was foursquare, having twelve gates in all. Beside each gate stood an angel, and on the gates were written the names of the twelve tribes of Is͟'ra-el. And the wall had twelve foundations, and on them were written the names of the twelve apostles of the Lord. The wall was like jasper, and the city was built of pure gold, but a gold which seemed clear like glass. The twelve gates were twelve pearls; each one of the gates was one great pearl. And the street of the city was pure gold, as clear as glass.

Jŏhn could see no Temple in the city, and it needs none; for the Lord God and Jē's͟us Chrīst the Lamb of God are its Temple. And the city has no need of the sun nor of the moon to shine upon it, for the glory of God gives it light and the Lamb of God is as a lamp in it. And the gates of the city shall not be shut by day, for there shall be no night there.

And the nations of men shall walk in the light of this city, and the kings of the earth bring their glory into it; and all the honor and glory of the nations of earth shall be brought into it.   And into it shall never come anything that is evil or unclean or anyone who does what God hates or anyone who makes a lie.   But they only shall come into it whose names are written in the Lord's book.

And Jŏhn saw a river of water of life, clear as crystal, coming forth from the throne of God and of the Lamb, and flowing through the street of the city.   On each side of the river was growing the tree of life, bearing its fruit every month, twelve times in the year; and the leaves of the tree were to heal all people of their diseases.   And in the city the Lord God and the Lamb shall reign as kings.

When Jŏhn had seen and heard all these things, he fell down to worship the angel who had showed them to him.   But the angel said to him, "Do not worship me, for I am a fellow servant with you and with your brethren the prophets, and with those who keep the word of the book: worship God."

And the angel said to Jŏhn, "Do not seal up the words of what you have heard and seen, but tell them to all men.   And the Spirit and the bride, the Church of Chrīst, say 'Come.'   And let him that hears, say 'Come.'   And let him that is thirsty come; and whoever will let him take the water of life freely."

Hurlbut's
BIBLE LESSONS

For Young and Old

QUESTIONS AND ANSWERS
ON THE OLD TESTAMENT
AND THE NEW TESTAMENT

Comprising a Complete Course of Study
designed to carry one through the Old
Testament in one year, and through the
New Testament in one year.

BY JESSE LYMAN HURLBUT, D.D.

SUGGESTIONS FOR TEACHING

1. Let the teacher read over in advance the questions and answers of the lesson, note their relation to the story as told in *The Story of the Bible*, and to some extent fit the story to the lesson which is to be taught.

2. Tell the story (or stories) of the day's lesson to the children, following the plan given in the book. Use very simple words and avoid those which are in any sense technical or above the mind of a child.

3. After telling the story for the day, the boys and girls may be divided into classes, and assistants may teach the questions and answers. But before the close of the session, it would be well to ask all the questions, and have the answers given by the pupils.

4. In order to complete each course, both Old and New Testament, within a year, it may be necessary to omit some of the lessons where the Sunday school is closed for the summer months. To complete the course of each year in such classes, the Reviews at the end of each series of lessons may be omitted, although they will be valuable as summaries of the important facts of the lesson.

Some teachers may prefer to omit from the Old Testament lessons some of the following lessons in order to complete the course in a year: Lesson Twenty-eight, "David and Absalom"; Thirty, "The Temple"; Thirty-six, "Elisha and Jonah"; Thirty-eight and Thirty-nine, "The Early Kings of Judah"; Forty-three, "Queen Esther." These are suggested for omission, not because they are unimportant or uninteresting, but because some lessons must be omitted for lack of time. In order to complete the course in one year in the New Testament lessons, the following may be omitted: Sixteen, "The Mother's Prayer"; Twenty, "The Good Shepherd"; Twenty-three, "Jesus and the Little Children"; Twenty-six and Twenty-seven, "The Last Teachings."

PREFACE

A N early acquaintance with the great truths of the Bible is regarded as the basis of good citizenship. Perhaps one of the best ways to inscribe the lessons of the Bible on the hearts of young people is by the question and answer method. And so this lesson book was prepared in order to meet a need realized in Dr. Hurlbut's own work as a pastor; a need that is felt by many pastors and workers among the young.

In the home, in the Sunday school, and in the church are boys and girls of all ages. It is impracticable to give to all this varied company the same teaching. The lessons that are admirably adapted for young people in their teens are utterly unsuited to the younger boys and girls. Moreover, it is impossible to find satisfactory lessons which can be taught to the young children except by one especially trained for the work, and such instructors are hard to find.

After various experiments, the author adopted in his own teaching the following plan. He divided the boys and girls into two groups: the first group including all over nine years old, the second group all those under nine.

He selected twelve Bible stories following in succession, beginning with the story of Adam and Eve. On each of these stories he prepared a catechism of very simple questions and answers. He told the story to all present in simple language, explaining that while the story was told to all it was for the special benefit of the younger children; but he noticed that even the oldest boys and girls listened to it with equal interest.

After the Bible story and the singing of a hymn, the second group withdrew to another room. There the boys and girls were divided into classes and taught the questions and answers. A copy of the leaflet containing the questions and answers of the story for the day was given to each child, to be taken home and reviewed by parents or the older members of the family.

By separating the children into two grades, the older young

4

people could receive instruction suited to their age, and the youngest were also provided for.

So many pastors and others requested copies of the leaflets containing the questions and answers that it seemed desirable to publish them. They were completed upon the entire Bible story, and then brought together in this book for the use of teachers.

These lessons may be used in classes of the Sunday school, by teachers who desire a more consecutive treatment of the Bible story than is given in curriculum, and by parents.

The questions and answers do not embrace all the stories in the book, however. A selection was made of what seemed to be the most important subjects, affording weekly lessons for one year (with allowance for vacations) in the Old Testament, and another year in the New Testament.

In the hope that these lessons may aid the boys and girls of today, who are to be the men and women of tomorrow, to gain a definite knowledge of the Word of God, these lessons are sent forth.

OLD TESTAMENT
LESSONS

OLD TESTAMENT LESSONS

Part First · From Adam to Moses

Lesson One · The Beautiful Garden

(Tell Story One in Hurlbut's Story of the Bible)

To the Teacher

Under the title of each lesson instructions are given to tell certain lessons. These numbered lessons and parts correspond with the numbered parts and lessons in *The Story of the Bible*.

The teacher may begin by asking, "Who can tell us the first verse of the Bible?" When hands are raised, call on three or four pupils to repeat the verse in turn; then let the class repeat it in unison. Explain what the verse means, that God made the world and all the things in it. Tell the story of the creation of the world; of the first man and the first woman; the Garden of Ē'dĕn, and of how Ăd'ăm and Ēve lost their home and were driven out. Then teach the class the answers to the following questions. At the close of the lesson, see that every young pupil is shown just where the questions and answers on the lesson are found. The answers should be reviewed by parents or older brothers and sisters, until the child can repeat them thoroughly, and can tell in his own language the story of the lesson.

Questions and Answers

1. What is the first verse in the Bible? **"In the beginning God created the heaven and the earth."**
2. What does this mean? **That God made all things.**
3. In how many days does the Bible tell us that God made the world? **In six days.**
4. On what day did God rest from his work? **On the seventh day.**
5. Whom did God make as the first man? **Ăd'ăm.**
6. Who was the first woman? **Ēve.**
7. What place did God give to Ăd'ăm and Ēve as their home? **The Garden of Ē'dĕn.**
8. How long did Ăd'ăm and Ēve live in the beautiful garden? **As long as they did what God told them to do.**
9. What became of them when they did not obey God's word? **They were driven out of the garden.**

9

Lesson Two · The Earliest People

(*Tell Stories Two and Three.*)

To the Teacher

1. In the story of Cāin and Ā'bĕl, explain carefully what is meant by "an altar," and how in early times people came to God in prayer. With younger boys and girls, use the word "praying," rather than "worship," and "gift to God" or "offering," rather than "sacrifice."

2. In the story of "The Great Ship," explain what "an ark" was. It was properly a chest or box; in this story, a great ship, built not to sail fast, but to float on the water, and to hold a great amount. Perhaps it was made large so that it could carry many animals and their food, and also very many people, if the people had been willing to be saved by it.

1. Who was the first child of Ād'ăm and Ēve after they were sent out of the Garden of Ē'dĕn? **Cāin.**

2. What was the name of Cāin's younger brother? **Ā'bĕl.**

3. What wicked thing did Cāin do when the two boys grew up to be men? **He killed his brother Ā'bĕl.**

4. What does the Bible tell of the earliest people who were on the earth? **They lived to be hundreds of years old.**

5. Who lived the longest of any of those people? **Mê-thu'se-lah, who lived more than nine hundred years.**

6. Were those who lived at that time good people? **Nearly all of them were very wicked.**

7. What good man lived in those times? **Ē'nŏch, who walked with God.**

8. What was the end of Ē'nŏch's life? **He did not die, but God took him to himself.**

9. What came upon the earth on account of the wickedness of its people? **A great flood.**

10. What good man with his family was saved from the flood? **Nō'ah, who built the ark.**

11. On which mountain did Nō'ah and his family leave the ark after the flood? **On Mount Âr'a-răt.**

Lesson Three · Abram
(ABOUT 2000 B.C.)

(*Tell Stories Four and Five. It might be well to end the story, for the present, to the middle of page 20, and use the story of Lot for the next lesson.*)

1. What was the name of the first large city built after the great flood? **Bā'bel, afterward called Băb'ў-lon.**

2. What happened to the people who were building a great tower in this city? **They could not understand one another's speech.**
3. What did these people of different languages do? **They went away to different lands.**
4. Who was Ā'brăm? **A good man, who prayed to God.**
5. To what did all the other people of Ā'brăm's time pray? **To gods of wood and stone.**
6. What did God tell Ā'brăm to do? **To go to a land far away.**
7. What was God's promise to Ā'brăm? **"I will be with thee, and will bless thee."**
8. To what land did Ā'brăm go, obeying God's word? **To the land of Cā'nӑan.**
9. How did Ā'brăm and his family live in the land of Cā'nӑan? **In tents, moving from place to place.**
10. What did Ā'brăm build whenever he set up his tent? **An altar for prayer to God.**

Lesson Four · Abraham and Lot
(ABOUT 1900 B.C.)

(Begin at page 20 in Story Five; tell Stories Six and Eight, omitting all of Story Seven, except to tell that Abram's name was changed to Abraham.)

1. Who was Lŏt? **He was Ā'brăm's nephew, who at first lived with Ā'brăm.**
2. Where did Lŏt live, after he left his uncle Ā'brăm? **Near the wicked city of Sŏd'om.**
3. What happened to Lŏt and his family at Sŏd'om? **They were carried away by enemies in war.**
4. How was Lŏt saved from those enemies and brought back to his home? **By Ā'brăm, who drove the enemies away.**
5. What new name did God give to A'brăm? **The name of Ā'brӑ-hăm.**
6. Who came to visit Ā'brӑ-hăm in his tent? **Angels from God.**
7. What good news did they bring to Ā'brӑ-hăm? **That he should have a son.**
8. What prayer did Ā'brӑ-hăm make to God? **That God would not destroy the wicked city of Sŏd'om.**
9. What did God promise to Ā'brӑ-hăm? **To spare the city, if he should find ten good men in it.**
10. How many good men did the angels find in Sŏd'om? **Only one, Lŏt.**
11. What came upon Sŏd'om, and the cities near it after the angels had sent Lŏt away? **A rain of fire.**

Lesson Five · Isaac and His Sons
(ABOUT 1850 B.C.)

(Tell Stories Ten, Eleven, and Twelve.)

1. What was the name of Ā′bră-hăm's son? **Ī′ṣaac.**
2. What was done with Ī′ṣaac when he was a boy? **He was laid on an altar.**
3. For what purpose was Ī′ṣaac laid on the altar? **To be given to God.**
4. When Ī′ṣaac grew up, who became his wife? **Rĕ-bĕk′ah.**
5. What kind of man was Ī′ṣaac? **He was a good man, who loved peace.**
6. Who were the two sons of Ī′ṣaac and Rĕ-bĕk′ah? **Ē′ṣau and Jā′cob.**
7. To whom did Ē′ṣau sell his right as the older son? **To his brother Jā′cob.**
8. For what price did Ē′ṣau sell his birthright? **For a bowl of food.**
9. What else did Jā′cob get that was meant for Ē′ṣau? **His father's blessing.**

Lesson Six · Jacob
(ABOUT 1825 B.C.)

(Tell Stories Thirteen and Fourteen.)

1. Who was Jā′cob? **The younger son of Ī′ṣaac.**
2. What did Jā′cob see in a dream at night, when he was far from his home? **A ladder from earth to heaven with angels on it.**
3. Whom did Jā′cob see standing on the ladder? **The Lord God.**
4. What did God say to Jā′cob at that time? **"I am with thee, and will keep thee."**
5. What promise did Jā′cob make after he saw the heavenly ladder and heard the voice of God? **"Then shall the Lord be my God."**
6. What other name was given to Jā′cob many years afterward? **The name of Iṣ′ra-el.**
7. What does the name Iṣ′ra-el mean? **The prince of God.**
8. How many sons did Jā′cob or Iṣ′ra-el have? **Twelve.**
9. What people came from Jā′cob or Iṣ′ra-el? **The children of Iṣ′ra-el, or Iṣ′ra-el-ītes.**
10. What are the Iṣ′ra-el-ītes called in the Bible? **The people of God.**
11. Why were they called "the people of God"? Because they prayed **to God when other people were praying to idols.**

Lesson Seven : Joseph in Egypt
(ABOUT 1750 B.C.)

(Tell Stories Fifteen and Sixteen.)

1. Who was Jō′seph? **One of the younger sons of Jā′cob.**
2. How did Jā′cob feel toward Jō′seph? **He loved Jō′seph more than his older sons.**
3. How did Jō′seph's older brothers feel toward him? **They hated him.**
4. How did Jō′seph's brothers treat Jō′seph? **They sold him for a slave.**
5. To what land was Jō′seph taken and sold? **To the land of Ē′ġўpt.**
6. How was Jō′seph treated as a slave in Ē′ġўpt? **He was put in prison.**
7. What is told of Jō′seph in the prison? **"The Lord was with Jō′seph."**
8. Who sent for Jō′seph in the prison? **Phā′raōh, the king of Ē′ġўpt.**
9. What did Jō′seph do for Phā′raōh? **He told him the meaning of his dreams.**
10. What did Jō′seph tell Phā′raōh was coming upon the land? **Seven years of great plenty.**
11. What would come after the seven years of plenty? **Seven years of great need.**
12. What did King Phā′raōh do when he heard these things? **He made Jō′seph ruler over all the land.**

Lesson Eight · Joseph and His Brothers
(ABOUT 1750 B.C.)

(Tell Stories Seventeen, Eighteen, and Nineteen.)

1. What did Jō′seph do after he became ruler of Ē′ġўpt, during the seven years of plenty? **He saved up all the food.**
2. What was done with the food that was saved up by Jō′seph? **The people of Ē′ġўpt were fed in the years of need.**
3. Where were Jā′cob and his other sons, the brothers of Jō′seph, living at this time? **In the land of Cā′năan.**
4. What did Jō′seph's brothers do to get food in the time of need? **They went down to Ē′ġўpt.**
5. How did Jō′seph treat his brothers when they came to him? **He gave them food but he did not tell them who he was.**
6. When they came the second time what did Jō′seph do? **He told them who he was, and he forgave them.**
7. What else did Jō′seph do for his father and his brothers? **He sent for them all to come down to Ē′ġўpt.**

8. How many were the Ĭṣ'ra-el-ītes or people of Ĭṣ'ra-el, when they came down to Ē'ġy̆pt? **Seventy people.**
9. In what part of Ē'ġy̆pt did they live? **In the land of Gō'shen.**

Lesson Nine · The Youth of Moses
(ABOUT 1750 B.C.)

(Tell Story Twenty.)

1. How long did the Ĭṣ'ra-el-ītes stay in Ē'ġy̆pt? **More than four hundred years.**
2. How did the Ē-ġy̆p'tianṣ treat the Ĭṣ'ra-el-ītes while Jō'ṣeph lived, and for a time afterward? **They were kind to the Ĭṣ'ra-el-ītes.**
3. What became of the Ĭṣ'ra-el-ītes in Ē'ġy̆pt? **They grew into a great people.**
4. How did the king of Ē'ġy̆pt who ruled many years after Jō'ṣeph's time treat the Ĭṣ'ra-el-ītes? **He was very cruel to them.**
5. How did the king treat the Ĭṣ'ra-el-ītes cruelly? **He made them work very hard.**
6. What order did the king give to keep the Ĭṣ'ra-el-ītes from growing in number? **That all their boy babies should be killed.**
7. What did one Ĭṣ'ra-el-īte mother do with her little baby boy? **She left him in a little boat on the river.**
8. Who found the baby floating in the river? **The daughter of Phā'raōh the king.**
9. What did the daughter of Phā'raōh do with the baby? **She made him her own son.**
10. What was the name of this boy? **Mō'ṣeṣ.**
11. Where did Mō'ṣeṣ go after he grew up? **To the land of Mĭd'ĭ-an.**

Lesson Ten : The Israelites Leaving Egypt
(ABOUT 1500 B.C.)

(Tell Stories Twenty-one, Twenty-two, and Twenty-three.)

1. How long was Mō'ṣeṣ in the land of Mĭd'ĭ-an? **Forty years.**
2. What was Mō'ṣeṣ at that time? **A shepherd.**
3. On which mountain did Mō'ṣeṣ see a wonderful sight? **On Mount Hō'reb, called also Mount Sī'nāi.**
4. What did Mō'ṣeṣ see on this mountain? **A bush on fire, yet not burned up.**
5. Who spoke to Mō'ṣeṣ from the burning bush? **The Lord God of Ĭṣ'ra-el.**

6. What did God tell Mō'ṣeṣ to do? **To bring his people out of Ē'ġÿpt.**
7. Who helped Mō'ṣeṣ in this work? **His brother Aâr'on.**
8. Who would not allow the Iṣ'ra-el-ītes to go out of Ē'ġÿpt? **Phā'-raōh the king.**
9. What came upon Phā'raōh and the Ē-ġyp-tianṣ until they were willing to let the Iṣ'ra-el-ītes go? **Many plagues.**
10. How were the Iṣ'ra-el-ītes at last led out of Ē'ġÿpt? **By a pillar of cloud and of fire.**

Lesson Eleven · The Israelites in the Wilderness
(ABOUT 1490 B.C.)

(Tell Stories Twenty-four, Twenty-five, Twenty-six, and Twenty-seven, but tell the story of the Tabernacle very briefly.)

1. Through which sea did God lead the Iṣ'ra-el-ītes when they came out of Ē'ġÿpt? **Through the Red Sea.**
2. Into which land did they go from Ē'ġÿpt? **Into the wilderness on the south of Cā'năan.**
3. What kind of land was this wilderness? **A land without food or water.**
4. What did God give to the people for food while they were in the wilderness? **Bread from heaven.**
5. How did God give water to the people? **From a rock.**
6. Where did God speak to the people? **From Mount Sī'nāi.**
7. What did God give to the people at Mount Sī'nāi? **The Ten Commandments.**
8. How long was Mō'ṣeṣ in the mountain with God? **Forty days.**
9. What did the Iṣ'ra-el-ītes build in the wilderness for the worship of God? **The Tabernacle.**

Lesson Twelve · From the Wilderness to Canaan
(ABOUT 1450 B.C.)

(Omit Stories Twenty-eight, Twenty-nine, Thirty. Tell Stories Thirty-one, Thirty-two, Thirty-four. Omit Story Thirty-three.)

1. To which place did the Iṣ'ra-el-ītes go after leaving Mount Sī'nāi? **To Kā'desh-bär'ne-à, near the land of Cā'năan.**
2. Whom did Mō'ṣeṣ send to go through the land and bring word about it? **Twelve men, called spies.**
3. What did most of the spies say about the land? **That the Iṣ'ra-el-ītes could not take it.**

4. Who said that the Lord would help them to go in and take the land? **Cā'leb and Jŏsh'u-à.**
5. Because the people would not believe in God and go into the land, what happened to the Ĭs̠'ra-el-ītes? **They were sent back into the wilderness.**
6. How long did they live in the wilderness? **Forty years.**
7. Where did the long journey of the Ĭs̠'ra-el-ītes end? **At the river Jôr'dan.**
8. On which mountain did Mo'ṣes die? **On Mount Nē'bò.**
9. By what name is Mō'ṣes̠ spoken of in the Bible? **Mōṣes̠, the man of God.**

Lesson Thirteen · Review of Early Bible People

(Tell as many of the stories as necessary to remind the pupils of these names.)

1. Who was the first man? **Ăd'ăm.**
2. Who was the first woman? **Ēve.**
3. What son of Ăd'ăm and Ēve killed his brother? **Cāin.**
4. What was the name of Cāin's brother whom he killed? **Ā'bĕl.**
5. Who was the oldest man that ever lived? **Mè-thu̯'se-lah.**
6. What good man was taken to heaven without dying? **Ē'nŏch.**
7. Who built the ark and was saved from the flood? **Nō'ah.**
8. Who believed God and went on a long journey when God sent him? **Ā'bră-hăm.**
9. Who was saved from the wicked city of Sŏd'om? **Lŏt.**
10. Which son of Ā'bră-hăm was laid on an altar? **Ĭ'ṣaac.**
11. Which son of Ĭ'ṣaac sold his birthright for something to eat? **Ē'ṣau.**
12. Who saw the heavenly ladder? **Jā'cob.**
13. What other name was given to Jā'cob? **Ĭs̠'ra-el.**
14. Who was sold as a slave but became a prince? **Jō'ṣeph.**
15. Who led the Ĭs̠'ra-el-ītes out of E'gypt? **Mō'ṣes̠.**

Lesson Fourteen · Review of Early Bible Places

1. What place did God give to Ăd'ăm and Ēve for their home? **The Garden of Ē'dĕn.**
2. On which mountain did the ark rest after the flood? **On Mount Âr'a-răt.**
3. What great city was built after the flood? **Bā'bel or Băb'y̆-lon.**
4. What land was promised to Ā'bră-hăm as his home? **The land of Cā'năan.**
5. Which city was destroyed by rain of fire? **Sŏd'om.**

6. In which country was Jō'ṣeph first a slave and then the ruler?
   Ē'ġy̆pt.
7. In which part of Ē'ġy̆pt did the Ĭṣ'ra-el-ītes live for four hundred
   years? **The land of Gō'shen.**
8. Through which sea did God lead the Ĭṣ'ra-el-ītes? **Through the
   Red Sea.**
9. On which mountain did God give the Ten Commandments? **Mount
   Sī'nāi.**
10. In which land did the Ĭṣ'ra-el-ītes wander forty years after coming
    out of Ē'ġy̆pt? **The wilderness.**
11. From which place did Mō'ṣeṣ send the twelve spies into the land
    of Cā'năan, and then afterward lead the Ĭṣ'ra-el-ītes back into the
    wilderness? **From Kā'desh-bär'ne-à.**
12. On which mountain did Mō'ṣeṣ die? **On Mount Nē'bô.**

Part Second · From Joshua to Samuel

Lesson Fifteen · How Jericho Was Taken
(ABOUT 1450 B.C.)

(Tell Stories One and Two in Part Second.)

---

1. Who became the ruler of the Ĭṣ'ra-el-ītes after Mō'ṣeṣ died? **Jŏsh'u-à.**
2. What did God say to Jŏsh'u-à when he took charge of the Ĭṣ'ra-el-ītes? **"Be strong and of a good courage."**
3. Where was the camp of the Ĭṣ'ra-el-ītes at that time? **Beside the river Jôr'dan.**
4. What land was in front of them across the river? **The land of Cā'năan.**
5. Which city of Cā'năan was near to the river? **The city of Jĕr'ĭ-chō.**
6. Whom did Jŏsh'u-à send to look at the city of Jĕr'ĭ-chō? **Two spies.**
7. Who hid the two spies and saved their lives? **Rā'hăb.**
8. How did God help the Ĭṣ'ra-el-ītes to cross the river Jôr'dan? **The river became dry.**
9. How did God help them to take the city of Jĕr'ĭ-chō? **Its walls fell down.**
10. What became of Rā'hăb, who had helped the spies? **Her life was saved.**

Lesson Sixteen · How the Land of Canaan Was Won
(ABOUT 1445 B.C.)

(Tell Stories Three, Four, Five, and Seven in Part Second. Omit Story Six.)

1. To which place did Jŏsh'u-à lead the Ĭṣ'ra-el-ītes after Jĕr'ĭ-chō had been taken? **To Shē'chem, in the middle of the land.**
2. What did Jŏsh'u-à do near Shē'chem? **He read God's law to the people.**
3. Where was the great battle fought between Jŏsh'u-à and the Cā'năan-ītes? **At Bĕth-hō'rŏn.**
4. What is told about this battle? **The sun and moon stood still.**
5. What did Jŏsh'u-à and the Ĭṣ'ra-el-ītes do in this war? **They took the land from the Cā'năan-ītes.**
6. What was the land of Cā'năan called after this war? **The land of Ĭṣ'ra-el.**
7. Into how many parts did Jŏsh'u-à divide the land? **Into twelve parts for the twelve tribes.**
8. After whom were these tribes named? **After the sons of Jā'cob.**

18

9. Where, near the middle of the lands, did Jŏsh'u-à set up the Tabernacle for the worship of God? **At Shī'lōh.**

10. What did Jŏsh'u-à, before he died, tell the people they must do? **Fear the Lord and serve him.**

11. What promise did the people make to Jŏsh'u-à? **"We will serve the Lord, and the Lord only."**

Lesson Seventeen · The Earlier Judges
(ABOUT 1300 B.C.)

(Tell Stories Eight, Nine, and Ten in Part Second.)

1. Did the Ĭṣ'ra-el-ītes keep the promise which they had made to serve the Lord only? **No, they forgot God and served idols.**

2. What came upon them because of their sins? **They fell under the power of their enemies.**

3. Who, many times, brought the people back to God and set them free from their enemies? **Rulers who were called "judges."**

4. How many of these judges in turn ruled over the Ĭṣ'ra-el-ītes? **Fifteen.**

5. Who was the first of the judges? **Ŏth'nĭ-el.**

6. What one of the judges was a woman? **Dĕb'o-rah, the fourth judge.**

7. What did Dĕb'o-rah do for the Ĭṣ'ra-el-ītes? **She led them to a great victory over the Cā'năan-ītes.**

8. Who was the greatest of all the judges? **Gĭd'e-on, the fifth judge.**

9. What did Gĭd'e-on do for the people? **He won victories over the Mĭd'ĭ-an-ītes.**

10. Who helped Gĭd'e-on to win his first great victory? **A band of three hundred brave men.**

Lesson Eighteen : The Latest Judges
(ABOUT 1250 B.C.)

(Omit Stories Eleven and Thirteen. Tell Stories Twelve and Fourteen in Part Second.)

1. What enemies gave to the Ĭṣ'ra-el-ītes the greatest trouble in the time of the judges? **The Phĭ-lĭs'tĭneṣ.**

2. Who began to set Ĭṣ'ra-el free from the Phĭ-lĭs'tĭneṣ? **Săm'son.**

3. For what was Săm'son famed? **For his great strength.**

4. What did Săm'son once carry away from a city? **The gates of Gāzà.**

5. What did the Phĭ-lĭs'tĭneṣ do to Săm'son when they made him prisoner? **They put out his eyes.**

6. What did Săm'son do to the Phĭ-lĭs'tĭnes̱ afterward? **He pulled down a temple upon them.**
7. What good woman came to live among the Ĭs̱'ra-el-ītes in the time of the judges? **Ruth.**
8. In which city did Ruth live? **Bĕth'lĕ-hĕm.**
9. Who was the rich man who married Ruth? **Bō'ăz.**
10. Which king was the great-grandson of Bō'ăz and Ruth? **Dā'vid.**

Lesson Nineteen · The Last of the Judges
(ABOUT 1150 B.C.)

(Omit Stories Thirteen and Fourteen in Part Second. Tell Stories Fifteen, Sixteen, Seventeen.)

1. Who was the fourteenth of the fifteen judges in Ĭs̱'ra-el? **Ē'lĭ, who was also priest.**
2. Who brought her little child to Ē'lĭ in the house of God? **Hăn'nah.**
3. What was her little boy's name? **Săm'u-el.**
4. Where did Săm'u-el grow up? **In the house of the Lord.**
5. What came to Săm'u-el while he was a child? **The voice of the Lord.**
6. What did Săm'u-el answer when the Lord spoke to him? **"Speak, Lord; for thy servant heareth."**
7. What did Săm'u-el become when he grew up to manhood? **The last of the judges in Ĭs̱'ra-el.**
8. What did Săm'u-el do as judge? **He brought the people back to God.**
9. What did the prayers of Săm'u-el give to the people? **Victory over their enemies.**
10. What is said of Săm'u-el as a ruler? **He was wise and good.**
11. Where did Săm'u-el live while he was judge? **At Rā'mah.**

Lesson Twenty · The First King of Israel
(ABOUT 1100 B.C.)

(Tell Story Eighteen in Part Second.)

1. When Săm'u-el grew old, what did the people ask him to do? **To give them a king.**
2. Why did the Ĭs̱'ra-el-ītes wish for a king? **To be like the others around them.**
3. Why was Săm'u-el not pleased at this? **Because he wished God to be the king of Ĭs̱'ra-el.**
4. What did God tell Săm'u-el to do? **To let the people have a king.**

5. Whom did God choose as the first king of Ĭṣ'ra-el? **A young man named Sạul.**
6. How did Sạul look when he was made king? **He was the tallest man of all the people.**
7. What did the people say when they saw their new king? **"Long live the king."**
8. What did Săm'u-el do for the king and the people? **He wrote the laws of the land in a book.**
9. Where did Sạul live as king? **At Gĭb'e-ah.**

Lesson Twenty-one · Review of Bible People, from Joshua to Saul

(With each name, tell enough of the story to recall it to the minds of the pupils.)

1. Who was the ruler of the Ĭṣ'ra-el-ītes after Mō'ṣeṣ died? **Jŏsh'u-à.**
2. Who hid the spies and was saved by the Ĭṣ'ra-el-ītes when her city was taken? **Rā'hăb.**
3. Who ruled the Ĭṣ'ra-el-ītes in turn after Jŏsh'u-à? **Fifteen judges.**
4. Who was the first judge? **Ŏth'nĭ-el.**
5. Who was the woman judge? **Dĕb'o-rah.**
6. Who was the greatest of the judges? **Gĭd'e-on.**
7. Which judge offered up his daughter? **Jĕph'thah.**
8. Which judge was a very strong man? **Săm'son.**
9. What old man was at the same time judge and priest? **Ē'lī.**
10. Who was the last of the judges? **Săm'u-el.**
11. Who was the mother of Săm'u-el? **Hăn'nah.**
12. Who was the first king of Ĭṣ'ra-el? **Sạul.**

Lesson Twenty-two · Review of Bible Places in Part Second

(Tell as much of each story as is necessary to recall each name to the pupils.)

1. What land was won by Jŏsh'u-à and the Ĭṣ'ra-el-ītes in war? **The land of Cā'năan.**
2. What river stopped flowing while the Ĭṣ'ra-el-ītes walked across its bed? **The Jôr'dan River.**
3. Which city was taken by the Ĭṣ'ra-el-ītes when its walls fell down? **Jĕr'ĭ-chō.**
4. Near which place did Jŏsh'u-à read the law of God to the Ĭṣ'ra-el-ītes? **Near the city of Shē'chem.**
5. At what battle do we read that the sun and moon stood still? **The battle of Bĕth-hō'rŏn.**

6. What name was given to the land of Cā'năan after it was taken by the Ĭṣ'ra-el-ītes? **The land of Ĭṣ'ra-el.**

7. Where were the Tabernacle and the ark of God placed after the land was won? **At Shī'lōh.**

8. Where did Săm'u-el live while he was judge? **At Rā'mah.**

9. Where did Saul live while he was king? **At Gĭb'e-ah.**

Part Third · From Saul to Solomon

Lesson Twenty-three · Saul as King
(ABOUT 1100 B.C.)

(Tell Stories One, Two, and Three in Part Third.)

1. How did Saul begin his rule as king of Ĭṣ'ra-el? **He began by doing brave deeds.**
2. What good things did Saul do soon after he became king? **He drove away the enemies of Ĭṣ'ra-el.**
3. Who helped Saul in his wars? **His brave son Jŏn'a-than.**
4. Over what enemies did Jŏn'a-than win a great victory? **Over the Phĭ-lĭs'tĭneṣ.**
5. Who spoke to Saul the word of the Lord? **Săm'u-el, the prophet.**
6. What is a prophet? **A man who speaks God's word.**
7. What did Saul do that was wrong? **He disobeyed God's words.**
8. What did Săm'u-el say to Saul? **"Obeying God is better than offerings."**
9. What did Săm'u-el say that the Lord would do to Saul? **That he would take the kingdom from him.**
10. How did Săm'u-el feel when he saw that Saul would not obey the Lord? **He wept for Saul.**

Lesson Twenty-four · The Boy David
(ABOUT 1085 B.C.)

(Tell Stories Four and Five in Part Third.)

1. To which place did God send Săm'u-el to find a king in the place of Saul? **To Bĕth'lĕ-hĕm.**
2. Whom did God show to Săm'u-el at Bĕth'lĕ-hĕm, as the one whom he had chosen? **A boy named Dā'vid.**
3. Whose son was Dā'vid? **The son of an old man named Jĕs'se.**
4. What was Dā'vid at this time? **He was a shepherd.**
5. What did Săm'u-el do, to show that Dā'vid was to be king? **He poured oil on his head.**
6. What did Dā'vid do while caring for his sheep? **He made music on his harp.**
7. Who sent for Dā'vid to play before him? **King Saul.**
8. With what people were the Ĭṣ'ra-el-ītes at war most of the time while Saul was king? **The Phĭ-lĭs'tĭneṣ.**
9. What Phĭ-lĭs'tĭne dared the Ĭṣ'ra-el-ītes to choose a man to fight with him? **A giant named Gȯ-lī'ath.**
10. Who fought the giant and killed him? **The boy Dā'vid.**
11. With what did Dā'vid fight the giant? **With a sling and a stone.**

Lesson Twenty-five · David and Saul
(ABOUT 1065 B.C.)

(Tell Stories Six, Seven, and Eight in Part Third.)

1. What did Saul do with Dā'vid after Dā'vid had killed the Phĭ-lĭs'-tĭne giant? **He made Dā'vid an officer in his army.**
2. Whom did Dā'vid marry after this? **A daughter of King Saul.**
3. How did King Saul feel toward Dā'vid after Dā'vid slew the giant? **He was very jealous.**
4. How did Saul show that he was jealous? **He tried to kill Dā'vid.**
5. Who loved Dā'vid greatly? **Saul's son Jŏn'a-than.**
6. What promise did Dā'vid make to Jŏn'a-than? **To be true to him and kind to his children.**
7. What did Dā'vid do on account of Saul's hate? **He hid in the wilderness.**
8. How did Dā'vid treat Saul, when he found him asleep in a cave? **He spared his life.**

Lesson Twenty-six · The End of Saul's Reign
(ABOUT 1055 B.C.)

(Tell Stories Nine and Ten in Part Third.)

1. What is said of Saul toward the latter part of his reign? **The Lord had left Saul.**
2. Why did the Lord leave Saul? **Because Saul would not obey the Lord.**
3. What happened that showed the Lord had left Saul? **There was no one to help him in his need.**
4. What people were at war with the Ĭs'ra-el-ītes nearly all the time Saul was king? **The Phĭ-lĭs'tĭnes.**
5. Where was the last battle of Saul's reign fought? **On Mount Gĭl-bō'a.**
6. Which side was beaten in the battle of Mount Gĭl-bō'a? **Saul and the Ĭs'ra-el-ītes.**
7. What brave man was killed in the battle? **Saul's son Jŏn'a-than.**
8. What did Saul do after this battle? **He killed himself.**
9. How long had Saul ruled as king? **Forty years.**
10. What did Dā'vid do when he heard of Saul's death? **He mourned for Saul and Jŏn'a-than.**
11. After Saul's death which tribe chose Dā'vid as its king? **The tribe of Jū'dah.**

Lesson Twenty-seven · David, King of Israel
(ABOUT 1055 B.C.)

(Tell Stories Eleven and Twelve in Part Third.)

1. How long did Dā'vid reign as king over the tribe of Jū'dah only? **Seven years.**
2. What did the people of the land do seven years after Saul was killed? **They made Dā'vid king over all Iṣ'ra-el.**
3. How did Dā'vid find the land when he became king? **It was weak and in the power of enemies.**
4. What great city did Dā'vid take from his enemies? **The city of Jê-ru'så-lĕm.**
5. On which mountain was the city of Jê-ru'så-lĕm? **On Mount Zī'ŏn.**
6. What did Dā'vid do with Jê-ru'så-lĕm after he had taken it? **He made it strong and lived in it.**
7. What enemies did Dā'vid drive out of the land? **The Phĭ-lĭs'tĭneṣ.**
8. What did Dā'vid bring to Jê-ru'så-lĕm? **The ark of God.**
9. What did Dā'vid win by war? **Rule over all the lands around Iṣ'ra-el.**
10. Whose son did Dā'vid treat kindly after he became king? **The son of Jŏn'a-than.**

Lesson Twenty-eight · David and Absalom
(ABOUT 1023 B.C.)

(Tell Stories Thirteen, Fourteen, and Fifteen in Part Third.)

1. What wicked thing did King Dā'vid do? **He caused one of his brave soldiers to be killed.**
2. Why was this done? **So that Dā'vid might marry the soldier's wife.**
3. Who came to Dā'vid and told him that he had done wickedly? **The prophet Nā'than.**
4. In which story did Nā'than show the king how wickedly he had acted? **In the story of a little lamb.**
5. What did Dā'vid say when Nā'than spoke to him? **"I have sinned against the Lord."**
6. What did Nā'than say should come to Dā'vid because of his sin? **He should be made to suffer.**
7. Which son of Dā'vid tried to take his kingdom from him? **Ăb'sa-lŏm.**
8. How far did Ăb'sa-lŏm succeed? **He drove Dā'vid away from Jê-ru'så-lĕm.**
9. Where was the battle fought between the men of Ăb'sa-lŏm and the men of Dā'vid? **In the wood of Ē'phră-ĭm.**

10. What happened to Ăb'sa-lŏm in the battle? **He was killed.**
11. What came to Dā'vid? **He reigned again as king.**

Lesson Twenty-nine · Solomon
(ABOUT 1015 B.C.)

(Omit Story Sixteen. Tell Stories Seventeen and Eighteen in Part Third.)

1. What did Dā'vid wish to do while he was king? **To build a temple to the Lord.**
2. Why would not God allow Dā'vid to build the Temple? **Because he had been a man of war.**
3. What did God promise to Dā'vid? **That his son should build the Temple.**
4. How long did Dā'vid reign? **Forty years, seven over Jū'dah and thirty-three over Ĭṣ'ra-el.**
5. What does the Bible say of Dā'vid as king? **He was the greatest and best of all the kings of Ĭṣ'ra-el.**
6. Whom did Dā'vid make king before he died? **His son Sŏl'o-mon.**
7. What did Sŏl'o-mon have through all his reign? **Peace in all the land.**
8. What did the Lord say to Sŏl'o-mon at night? **"Ask what I shall give you."**
9. For what did Sŏl'o-mon ask the Lord? **For wisdom to rule the people.**
10. What did God promise to give to Sŏl'o-mon besides wisdom? **Riches and honor and long life.**

Lesson Thirty · The Temple
(ABOUT 1010 B.C.)

(Tell Stories Nineteen and Twenty in Part Third.)

1. What was the greatest work in the reign of Sŏl'o-mon? **The building of the Temple.**
2. For what purpose was the Temple built? **As the house of God.**
3. Where was the Temple built? **On Mount Mô-rī'ah.**
4. Of which older building was it a copy? **The Tabernacle.**
5. What stood in front of the Temple? **An open court.**
6. What were the two rooms of the building? **The Holy Place, and the Holy of Holies.**
7. What was kept in the Holy of Holies? **The Ark of the Covenant.**
8. What was in the Ark of the Covenant? **The Ten Commandments.**

9. For what was Sŏl'o-mon known? **For his wisdom.**
10. Who came from a far country to see Sŏl'o-mon? **The queen of Shē'bà.**

Lesson Thirty-one · Review of Part Third

(*Tell enough of the stories to help the pupils in answering the questions.*)

1. Who was the first king of Ĭṣ'ra-el? **Saul.**
2. Where did Saul live as king? **At Gĭb'e-ah.**
3. What was the name of Saul's brave son? **Jŏn'a-than.**
4. Who spoke to Saul the word of the Lord? **Săm'u-el.**
5. Why was the kingdom taken from Saul? **Because he disobeyed God.**
6. Whom did God choose for king in place of Saul? **Dā'vid.**
7. Where did Dā'vid live as a boy? **At Bĕth'lĕ-hĕm.**
8. What was the name of the giant whom Dā'vid killed? **Gô-lī'ath.**
9. Where did Dā'vid hide from Saul? **In the wilderness.**
10. What people were at war with Saul and the Ĭṣ'ra-el-ītes? **The Phĭ-lĭs'tĭneṣ.**
11. Where was Saul killed? **On Mount Gĭl-bō'à.**
12. Who became king after Saul? **Dā'vid.**
13. What city did Dā'vid take from enemies and make his home? **Jĕ-rṳ'sà-lĕm.**
14. Who tried to make himself king in place of Dā'vid? **Ăb'sa-lŏm.**
15. Who was king after Dā'vid? **Sŏl'o-mon.**
16. What did Sŏl'o-mon build? **The Temple.**

Part Fourth · The Kingdom of Israel

Lesson Thirty-two · The Two Kingdoms
(ABOUT 900 B.C.)

(Tell Stories One and Two of Part Fourth.)

---

1. What took place after King Sŏl'o-mon died? **The kingdom was divided.**
2. What was the larger part called? **The kingdom of Ĭṣ'ra-el.**
3. How many of the tribes were in the kingdom of Ĭṣ'ra-el? **Ten of the twelve tribes.**
4. Who was the first king of the Ten Tribes of Ĭṣ'ra-el? **Jĕr-o-bō'am.**
5. What was the smaller part called? **The kingdom of Jū'dah.**
6. What tribes were in the kingdom of Jū'dah? **Jū'dah and Bĕn'ja-mĭn.**
7. Who was the first king of Jū'dah? **Rē-ho-bō'am the son of Sŏl'o-mon.**
8. What wicked thing did Jĕr-o-bō'am the king of Ĭṣ'ra-el do? **He led his people away from God.**
9. What did Jĕr-o-bō'am lead his people to do? **To pray to idols.**
10. What is Jĕr-o-bō'am called in the Bible? **"Jĕr-o-bō'am who made Ĭṣ'ra-el to sin."**
11. What did the prophet of God tell Jĕr-o-bō'am? **That the kingdom should be taken from his family.**

Lesson Thirty-three · Elijah
(ABOUT 850 B.C.)

(Read Story Three in Part Fourth.)

1. Who was the most wicked of all the kings of Ĭṣ'ra-el? **Ā'hăb.**
2. What was the name of Ā'hăb's wife, who led him to wickedness? **Jĕz'e-bĕl.**
3. At which city did the kings of Ĭṣ'ra-el live? **At Sà-mā'rĭ-à.**
4. What great prophet came at the time while Ā'hăb was king? **Ė-lī'jah.**
5. What did Ė-lī'jah tell King Ā'hăb? **That no rain should come upon the land.**
6. Where did Ė-lī'jah hide from King Ā'hăb? **By the brook Chē'rĭth.**
7. Who brought him food? **Wild birds called ravens.**
8. Where did God send Ė-lī'jah afterward? **To the city of Zăr'e-phăth.**
9. Who cared for Ė-lī'jah in that city? **A poor widow.**
10. What did Ė-lī'jah do for this widow? **He brought her dead son to life.**

Lesson Thirty-four · Elijah on Carmel and Horeb
(ABOUT 850 B.C.)
(Tell Stories Four and Five in Part Fourth.)

1. For how long did no rain fall on the land of Ĭṣ'ra-el? **For more than three years.**
2. At which place did Ė-lī'jah call for all the people to meet him after three years? **On Mount Cär'mel.**
3. What did Ė-lī'jah tell them to build on Mount Cär'mel? **Two altars.**
4. For whom were these altars? **One for God, and the other for the idol called Bā'al.**
5. What came upon God's altar when Ė-lī'jah prayed? **Fire from heaven.**
6. What also came in answer to Ė-lī'jah's prayer? **A great rain.**
7. Who later tried to kill Ė-lī'jah? **Queen Jĕz'e-bĕl.**
8. Where did Ė-lī'jah go to escape from Jĕz'e-bĕl? **To Mount Hō'reb in the wilderness.**
9. Who spoke to Ė-lī'jah there? **The Lord God.**
10. What did the Lord give to Ė-lī'jah? **A great work to do.**
11. Whom did Ė-lī'jah call to go with him and help him? **Ė-lī'shȧ.**

Lesson Thirty-five · The Prophet Elisha
(ABOUT 840 B.C.)
(Omit Stories Six, Seven, Eight. Tell Stories Nine, Ten, Eleven, Twelve, Thirteen in Part Fourth. In Story Ten, tell only about "The Spring Sweetened by Salt.")

1. How was the prophet Ė-lī'jah taken to heaven? **In a chariot of fire.**
2. Who took Ė-lī'jah's place as prophet? **Ė-lī'shȧ.**
3. How did Ė-lī'shȧ make the bitter water of a spring sweet? **By pouring in salt.**
4. How did Ė-lī'shȧ help a poor woman to pay a debt? **By a vessel of oil.**
5. What lady built a room in her house for Ė-lī'shȧ? **The woman of Shu'nem.**
6. What did Ė-lī'shȧ do for this woman? **He raised her son to life.**
7. Which Sŷr'ĭ-an general came to Ė-lī'shȧ? **Nā'a-man.**
8. What disease did Nā'a-man have? **He was a leper.**
9. What did Ė-lī'shȧ tell him to do? **To wash seven times in the river Jôr'dan.**
10. What took place when he had washed? **He was made well.**

Lesson Thirty-six · Elisha and Jonah
(ABOUT 800 B.C.)

(Tell Stories Fourteen and Seventeen in Part Fourth. Omit Stories Fifteen and Sixteen.)

1. With what land was Ĭṣ'ra-el often at war in the time of the Kings? **With Sўr'ĭ-a.**
2. Who greatly helped the king of Ĭṣ'ra-el by his power as a prophet? **Ė-lī'shȧ.**
3. To what place did the Sўr'ĭ-ans̤ send an army to make Ė-lī'shȧ their prisoner? **At Dō'than.**
4. What did the servant of Ė-lī'shȧ see around Ė-lī'shȧ to keep him safe from the Sўr'ĭ-ans̤? **Chariots and horses of fire.**
5. Who came to visit Ė-lī'shȧ when he was dying? **Jō'ăsh the king of Ĭṣ'ra-el.**
6. What did the dying Ė-lī'shȧ promise to the king? **Victory over the Sўr'ĭ-ans̤.**
7. What prophet was sent to preach to a great city? **Jō'nah.**
8. To what city was Jō'nah sent? **To Nĭn'e-veh.**
9. What wonderful thing happened to Jō'nah? **He was inside a great fish for three days.**
10. What did Jō'nah do afterward? **He preached to the people of Nĭn'e-veh.**

Lesson Thirty-seven · The Ten Tribes Lost; with Review of Part Four

(Read Story Eighteen in Part Fourth, and recall as much of the other stories as may be needed for the Review.)

1. How many tribes were in the kingdom of Ĭṣ'ra-el? **Ten.**
2. Who was the first king of the Ten Tribes? **Jĕr-o-bō'am.**
3. How many kings ruled over Ĭṣ'ra-el or the Ten Tribes? **Nineteen.**
4. What is said of these kings? **Nearly all of them were wicked.**
5. Who was the most wicked of all the kings of Ĭṣ'ra-el? **Ā'hăb.**
6. Who was Ā'hăb's wife? **Queen Jĕz'e-bĕl.**
7. What was the chief city in the kingdom of Ĭṣ'ra-el? **Sȧ-mā'rĭ-ȧ.**
8. What prophet lived in the times of Ā'hăb and Jĕz'e-bĕl? **Ė-lī'jah.**
9. How was Ė-lī'jah fed while hiding by a brook? **By ravens.**
10. Where did he restore to life a widow's son? **At Zăr'e-phăth.**
11. Where did he call down fire from heaven upon an altar? **On Mount Cär'mel.**
12. Where did God talk with Ė-lī'jah? **At Mount Hō'reb.**

13. How was Ė-lī′jah taken to heaven? **In a chariot of fire.**
14. Who was the prophet after Ė-lī′jah? **Ė-lī′shà.**
15. How did Ė-lī′shà make a bitter spring fresh? **By pouring in salt.**
16. What woman's son did Ė-lī′shà raise to life? **The woman of Shụ′nem.**
17. Which Sўr′ĭ-an general did Ė-lī′shà cure of leprosy? **Nā′a-man.**
18. Where were chariots and horses of fire seen around Ė-lī′shà? **At Dō′than.**
19. Who lived three days inside a great fish? **Jō′nah.**
20. To which land were the Ten Tribes carried away as prisoners? **To Ās-sўr′ĭ-à.**

Part Fifth · The Kingdom and People of Judah

Lesson Thirty-eight · The Early Kings of Judah
(FROM 900-750 B.C.)

(Tell Stories One, Two, and Three in Part Fifth.)

1. Where was the kingdom of Jū'dah? **West of the Dead Sea.**
2. What was its chief city? **Jê-ru̱'så-lĕm.**
3. How many kings reigned over the kingdom of Jū'dah? **Nineteen kings and one queen.**
4. To which family did all these kings belong? **To the family of Dā'vid.**
5. Who was the first king of Jū'dah? **Rē-ho-bō'am.**
6. Who was the greatest and strongest of the kings of Jū'dah? **Jê-hŏsh'a-phăt.**
7. What wicked woman made herself queen and ruled the land? **Ăth-a-lī'ah.**
8. Which little boy was crowned king after Ăth-a-lī'ah? **Jō'ăsh.**
9. Which king became a leper? **Ŭz-zī'ah.**
10. Which great prophet lived in Jū'dah at that time and saw the Lord in the Temple? **Ī-ṣā'iah.**

Lesson Thirty-nine · The Later Kings of Judah
(FROM 750-600 B.C.)

(Tell Stories Four, Five, and Six in Part Fifth.)

1. Who was the best of all the kings of Jū'dah? **Hĕz-e-kī'ah.**
2. From what enemies did the Lord save the city of Jê-ru̱'så-lĕm in the time of Hĕz-e-kī'ah? **From the Ăs-sy̆r'ĭ-anṣ.**
3. What bad king became good after being put in prison? **Må-năs'seh.**
4. Which king, while he was young, chose the Lord and followed him? **Jô-sī'ah.**
5. What lost book was found in the Temple in the time of Jô-sī'ah? **The book of the law.**
6. Who was the last king of Jū'dah? **Zĕd-e-kī'ah.**
7. Which prophet warned the people by Jū'dah of evils that were coming? **Jĕr-e-mī'ah.**
8. Which great king over many lands came against Jê-ru̱'så-lĕm? **Nĕb-u-chad-nĕz'zar.**
9. What did Nĕb-u-chad-nĕz'zar do? **He burned the city and the Temple.**
10. To which land did he carry away all the people of Jū'dah? **To the land of Băb-y̆-lō'nĭ-a.**

Lesson Forty · The Jews in Babylon
(ABOUT 600 B.C.)

(Tell Stories Seven, Eight, and Nine in Part Fifth.)

1. By which name were the people of Jū'dah called, after they were taken to Băb'ў-lon? **By the name Jews.**
2. Which prophet among them saw a vision? **Ē-zē'kǐ-el.**
3. Which prophet lived in the palace of King Nĕb-u-chad-nĕz'zar? **Dăn'iel.**
4. What did Dăn'iel and his Jew'ish friends in the palace refuse to eat? **The meat and wine of the king.**
5. What did God help Dăn'iel to do for King Nĕb-u-chad-nĕz'zar? **To tell him the meaning of his dreams.**
6. What did three friends of Dăn'iel refuse to do? **To bow down before a golden image.**
7. What was done to these men? **They were thrown into a furnace of fire.**
8. Whom did King Nĕb-u-chad-nĕz'zar see with those men in the fire? **The Lord God.**
9. What did God do for these men in the fire? **He kept them alive.**

Lesson Forty-one · Daniel
(ABOUT 538 B.C.)

(Tell Stories Ten, Eleven, and Twelve in Part Fifth.)

1. What came upon King Nĕb-u-chad-nĕz'zar? **He lost his mind for seven years.**
2. What became of the Băb-ў-lō'nǐ-an kingdom when Nĕb-u-chad-nĕz'zar died? **It lost its power.**
3. Who was the last king in Băb'ў-lon? **Bĕl-shăz'zar.**
4. What did Bĕl-shăz'zar see one night in his palace? **A handwriting on the wall.**
5. Who read the writing to the king? **Dăn'iel.**
6. What did the writing mean? **That his kingdom was ended.**
7. How was the kingdom ended? **The city was taken and Bĕl-shăz'zar was killed.**
8. Which kingdom took the place of the Băb-ў-lō'nǐ-an kingdom? **The kingdom of Pēr'ṣià.**
9. What was done to Dăn'iel after this? **He was thrown into a den of lions.**
10. How was Dăn'iel saved from the lions? **The Lord shut the lions' mouths.**

Lesson Forty-two · The Return from Babylon
(ABOUT 530 B.C.)

(Tell Stories Thirteen and Fourteen in Part Fifth.)

1. Who broke up the Băb-y̆-lō'nĭ-an kingdom and formed the kingdom of Pĕrṣià? **Çy̆'rus.**
2. How did Çy̆'rus, the new king, treat the Jewṣ who were in Băb'y̆-lon? **He was kind to them.**
3. What did Çy̆'rus allow the Jewṣ to do? **To go back to their own land.**
4. How long had the Jewṣ been in the land of Băb'y̆-lon? **Seventy years.**
5. What happy journey did the Jewṣ take? **To the land of Jū-dē'à.**
6. Which city did they begin to build again? **The city of Jĕ-ru̧'sà-lĕm.**
7. What house did they build? **The Temple of God.**
8. Who led the Jewṣ in their journey and their building? **Zĕ-rŭb'-ba-bĕl the ruler.**
9. Which prophets encouraged the people to build? **Hăg'ga-ī and Zĕch-a-rī'ah.**

Lesson Forty-three · Queen Esther
(ABOUT 480 B.C.)

(Tell Story Fifteen in Part Fifth.)

1. In which city did the king of Pĕr'ṣià live? **In the city of Shu̧'shan.**
2. What beautiful Jew'ĭsh girl lived in Shu̧'shan? **Ĕs'thĕr.**
3. Who cared for Ĕs'thĕr and brought her up? **Her cousin Môr'-de-cāi.**
4. Who was the king of Pĕr'ṣià at that time? **Ā-hăṣ-ū-ē'rŭs.**
5. What did king Ā-hăṣ-ū-ē'rŭs do when he saw Ĕs'thĕr? **He made her queen.**
6. Who stood next to the king in power? **A man named Hā'man.**
7. What law did Hā'man cause king Ā-hăṣ-ū-ē'rŭs to make? **That all the Jewṣ should be killed.**
8. What did Queen Ĕs'thĕr do when she heard that this law had been made? **She went to the king in his palace.**
9. What did she ask the king to do? **To spare the lives of her people.**
10. What became of Hā'man, the enemy of the Jewṣ? **He was put to death.**

Lesson Forty-four · The End of the Old Testament
(ABOUT 430 B.C.)

(Tell Stories Sixteen, Seventeen, and Eighteen in Part Fifth.)

1. Which good man came to Jĕ-rṳ'så-lĕm soon after the time of Queen Ĕs'thẽr? **Ĕz'rà the scribe.**
2. What was a scribe among the Jewṣ? **One who wrote copies of God's laws.**
3. What great work did Ĕz'rà do? **He brought together the books of the Old Testament.**
4. What did Ĕz'rà do at Jĕ-rṳ'så-lĕm? **He taught the people to obey God's law.**
5. Which other good man came while Ĕz'rà was at Jĕ-rṳ'så-lĕm? **Nĕ-he-mī'ah.**
6. What did Nĕ-he-mī'ah do? **He helped the people to build a wall around the city.**
7. Why did they need a wall around the city? **To make it strong against enemies.**
8. What was done at a great meeting of the people when the wall was finished? **The law was read to the people.**
9. Who was the last prophet of the Old Testament? **Măl'a-chī.**

Lesson Forty-five . Review of Jewish People

1. How many kings reigned over Jū'dah? **Nineteen kings and one queen.**
2. Who was the first king of Jū'dah? **Rē-ho-bō'am.**
3. Who was the greatest king? **Jĕ-hŏsh'a-phăt.**
4. Who was the youngest when he became king? **Jō'ăsh.**
5. Who was the best of the kings? **Hĕz-e-kī'ah.**
6. Which prophet saw the Lord in the Temple? **Ī-ṣā'iah.**
7. Which young king chose the Lord and followed him? **Jŏ-sī'ah.**
8. Who was the last king of Jū'dah? **Zĕd-e-kī'ah.**
9. To which land were the people of Jū'dah carried as captives? **To Băb-ў̄-lō'nĭ-a.**
10. Which prophet saw the vision of the valley of dry bones? **Ē-zē'kĭ-el.**
11. Which prophet lived in the palace of the king of Băb'ў̄-lon? **Dăn'iel.**
12. Who was the great king of Băb'ў̄-lon? **Nĕb-u-chad-nĕz'zar.**
13. Which king of Băb'ў̄-lon saw the handwriting on the wall? **Bĕl-shăz'zar.**
14. Who was kept alive when thrown into a den of lions? **Dăn'iel.**

15. How long were the Jews captives in Băb′ў-lon? **Seventy years.**
16. Who allowed the Jews to go back to their own land? **Çў′rus.**
17. Which queen saved the lives of her people? **Ĕs′thĕr.**
18. Who read the law of God to the people in Jĕ-rụ′så-lĕm? **Ĕz′rå.**
19. Who helped the Jews to build a wall around the city? **Nē-he-mī′ah.**
20. Who was the last prophet of the Old Testament? **Măl′a-chī.**

NEW TESTAMENT
LESSONS

NEW TESTAMENT LESSONS

Part First · The Story of Jesus

Lesson One · The Angel by the Altar and in Nazareth
(5 B.C.)

(Tell Story One of Part Sixth, in Hurlbut's Story of the Bible.*)*

To the Teacher

In beginning the lesson the teacher should state the subject for the day and ask one or two questions about it, to get the pupils interested. Then the teacher should tell the story from *Hurlbut's Story of the Bible*, explaining how God sent his Angel Gā′brĭ-el to Zăch-a-rī′as, the old priest in the Temple to tell him that his wife Ē-lĭṣ′a-bĕth would have a son, and that the name of the son should be Jŏhn.

Explain that Jŏhn was to be sent into the world to prepare people for the coming of Chrīst. Then tell how the same Angel Gā′brĭ-el was sent to the city of Năz′a-rĕth to a young woman named Mā′rў to tell her that she was to have a son who was to be called Jē′ṣus. Then teach the class the answers to the following questions on the subject of this lesson, and explain to the younger pupils just where to find the answers to the questions of the first lesson, and have them answer the questions in class either singly or in unison. The boys and girls should understand that the questions are to be asked them by parents or older brothers and sisters until they have fixed in their minds the story of the lesson, and are able to tell it in their own language.

1. What angel was sent by God to Jĕ-rụ′sả-lĕm? **The Angel Gā′brĭ-el.**
2. To whom was the Angel Gā′brĭ-el sent? **To a priest named Zăch-a-rī′as.**
3. What did the angel tell Zăch-a-rī′as? **That his wife should have a son.**
4. What was the name of the wife of Zăch-a-rī′as? **Ē-lĭṣ′a-bĕth.**
5. What name was to be given to this son promised to Zăch-a-rī′as and Ē-lĭṣ′a-bĕth? **The name of Jŏhn.**
6. For what did the angel say that Jŏhn, when he grew up, should make the people ready? **For the coming of the Lord.**
7. To which city was the Angel Gā′brĭ-el sent after this? **To the city of Năz′a-rĕth.**
8. To whom did the angel speak in Năz′a-rĕth? **To a young woman named Mā′rў.**
9. What did the angel tell Mā′rў? **That she should have a son.**
10. What name was to be given to her son? **The name Jē′ṣus.**

39

11.   Where did Jŏhn, the son of Zăch-a-rī′as and Ê-lĭs̟′a-bĕth live while Jŏhn was a boy?   **In the desert.**

Lesson Two · The Stable and the Shepherds
(5 B.C.)
(Tell Story Two in Part Sixth.)

Let the teacher ask, "Who can tell the name of the husband of Mā′rȳ, the young woman in Năz′a-rĕth to whom God sent his angel?" After receiving an answer, ask, "Where did Jō′s̟eph and Mā′rȳ go and where was Mā′rȳ's child born?" After the answers have been given, tell the story of the lesson and teach the pupils the answers to the questions on the lesson.   The subject should be reviewed in class until each child is able to answer the questions intelligently and to be able to tell a connected story of the lesson.   Reference may also be made to the preceding story in each class, so that the pupils learn to connect each lesson correctly with the others.

1.   Who was the husband of Mā′rȳ, the young woman in Năz′a-rĕth to whom the angel came?   **A man named Jō′s̟eph.**
2.   To what place did Jō′s̟eph and Mā′rȳ go?   **To Bĕth′lĕ-hĕm, near Jê-ru̟′sȧ-lĕm.**
3.   Where was the child of Mā′rȳ born?   **In a stable in Bĕth′lĕ-hĕm.**
4.   What name was given to this child?   **The name Jē′s̟us.**
5.   What does the word "Jē′s̟us" mean?   **It means "salvation."**
6.   Why was this name given to this child?   **Because he is the Saviour of the world.**
7.   To whom was brought the first news that the Saviour had come?   **To shepherds near Bĕth′lĕ-hĕm.**
8.   What did the shepherds do as soon as they heard the news?   **They went to Bĕth′lĕ-hĕm and saw the little child and his mother.**
9.   Who saw the child when he was brought into the Temple, knew that he was the Saviour, and took him up in his arms?   **Sĭm′e-on.**
10.   What woman also saw the child and gave thanks to God?   **Ăn′nȧ.**

Lesson Three · The Wise Men and the Star
(4 B.C.)
(Tell Story Three in Part Sixth.)

1.   What men from a distant land came to see Jē′s̟us?   **Wise Men from the East.**

2. What led them on their journey to the land where Jē′ṣus was born? **A star in the sky.**

3. What question did the Wise Men ask? **"Where is he that is born King of the Jewṣ?"**

4. Of whom did they ask this question? **Of Hĕr′od the king.**

5. Where did Hĕr′od send them? **To Bĕth′lĕ-hĕm.**

6. What did the Wise Men find in Bĕth′lĕ-hĕm? **The little child and his mother.**

7. What did they do when they saw the child? **They gave him rich gifts.**

8. What did an angel tell Jō′ṣeph to do after the Wise Men had gone away? **To take the child to Ē′ġy̆pt.**

9. Why had the child to be taken to Ē′ġy̆pt? **To save his life from King Hĕr′od.**

10. How long did Jō′ṣeph and Mā′ry̆ and the child Jē′ṣus stay in Ē′ġy̆pt? **Until King Hĕr′od died.**

11. Where did Jō′ṣeph and Mā′ry̆ take the child Jē′ṣus from Ē′ġy̆pt? **To Năz′a-rĕth.**

Lesson Four · The Boy Jesus
(A.D. 7)
(Tell Story Four in Part Sixth.)

1. Where did Jē′ṣus live while he was a boy? **In Năz′a-rĕth.**

2. To which city was he taken when twelve years old? **To Jĕ-ru̱′sȧ-lĕm.**

3. What place did the boy Jē′ṣus visit when he was in Jĕ-ru̱′sȧ-lĕm? **The Temple.**

4. What did Jē′ṣus do when Jō′ṣeph and Mā′ry̆ left Jĕ-ru̱′sȧ-lĕm to go home to Năz′a-rĕth? **He stayed in Jĕ-ru̱′sȧ-lĕm.**

5. How long was it before Mā′ry̆ and Jō′ṣeph found the boy Jē′ṣus? **Three days.**

6. Where did they find him? **In the Temple.**

7. What was Jē′ṣus doing in the Temple? **Talking with the teachers of the Bible.**

8. What is said of Jē′ṣus as a boy? **He was wise and good and loved by all.**

9. How long did Jē′ṣus live in Năz′a-rĕth? **Until he was thirty years old.**

10. At what trade did Jē′ṣus work when he became a man? **As a carpenter.**

Lesson Five · John the Baptist
(A.D. 26)

(Tell Story Five in Part Sixth.)

1. When Jḗ'ṣus was a young man in Năz'a-rĕth, who began to preach? **Jŏhn the son of Zăch-a-rī'as.**
2. Where did Jŏhn preach? **In the desert near the river Jôr'dan.**
3. Who went to hear Jŏhn preach? **All the people of the land.**
4. What did Jŏhn tell the people to do? **To turn from sin and serve God.**
5. Who did Jŏhn say was soon to come? **One greater than himself.**
6. What did Jŏhn do to those who were willing to serve God? **He baptized them in the river Jôr'dan.**
7. Who saw Jḗ'ṣus again at Bĕth-ăb'a-rà? **Jŏhn the Băp'tĭst.**
8. Who came to be baptized by Jŏhn the Băp'tĭst? **Jḗ'ṣus of Năz'-a-rĕth.**
9. What took place where Jḗ'ṣus was baptized? **The Spirit of God came upon him.**
10. What voice was heard from heaven? **"This is my beloved Son."**
11. What did this mean? **That Jḗ'ṣus was the Son of God.**

Lesson Six · Jesus in the Desert and by the River
(A.D. 27)

(Tell Story Six in Part Sixth.)

1. Where did Jḗ'ṣus go after he was baptized? **To a desert place.**
2. What happened to Jḗ'ṣus there? **He was forty days without any food.**
3. Who came to Jḗ'ṣus at that time? **Sā'tan, the evil spirit.**
4. What did Sā'tan, the evil spirit, try to persuade Jḗ'ṣus to do? **To live a selfish life.**
5. What did Jḗ'ṣus say to the evil spirit? **"Leave me, Sā'tan, thou evil spirit."**
6. Where did Jḗ'ṣus go after being tempted in the desert? **To Bĕth-ăb'a-rà, the place of his baptism.**
7. Who saw Jḗ'ṣus again at Bĕth-ăb'a-rà? **Jŏhn the Băp'tĭst.**
8. What did Jŏhn the Băp'tĭst say when he saw Jḗ'ṣus? **"Behold the Lamb of God."**
9. What did some young men do, who had been following Jŏhn the Băp'tĭst? **They followed Je'ṣus.**
10. What were these men who followed Jḗ'ṣus called? **His disciples.**

Lesson Seven · The Water Turned to Wine
(A.D. 27)

(Tell Story Seven in Part Sixth.)

1. To what place did Jḗ'ṣus and his first disciples go from Bĕth-ăb'a-rȧ? **To Cā'nȧ in Găl'ĭ-lee.**
2. What took place at Cā'nȧ? **A wedding.**
3. Who came to Jḗ'ṣus at the wedding feast? **His mother Mā'rӯ.**
4. What did she say to Jḗ'ṣus? **"They have no wine."**
5. What did Jḗ'ṣus do? **He turned water into wine.**
6. What do we call a work such as this, which no one but God can do? **A miracle.**
7. Where did Jḗ'ṣus and his disciples go when they left Cā'nȧ? **To Jḗ-ru'ṣȧ-lĕm.**
8. What did Jḗ'ṣus find in the Temple at Jḗ-ru'ṣȧ-lĕm? **People buying and selling.**
9. What did Jḗ'ṣus do to these people? **He drove them out of the Temple.**
10. Who came to talk with Jḗ'ṣus at night? **Nĭc-o-dē'mus.**
11. What did Jḗ'ṣus say to Nĭc-o-dē'mus? **"Ye must be born anew."**

Lesson Eight · Jesus at Jacob's Well
(A.D. 27)

(Tell Story Eight in Part Sixth.)

1. What was done with Jŏhn the Băp'tĭst while Jḗ'ṣus was teaching at Jḗ-ru'ṣȧ-lĕm? **He was put in prison.**
2. Who put Jŏhn the Băp'tĭst in prison? **Hĕ'rod, the wicked king.**
3. To what part of the land did Jḗ'ṣus go after this? **To Găl'ĭ-lee.**
4. Where was Găl'ĭ-lee? **In the north of the land.**
5. What part of the land did Jḗ'ṣus go through on his way to Găl'ĭ-lee? **Through Sȧ-mā'rĭ-ȧ.**
6. What were the people called who lived in that country? **Sȧ-măr'ĭ-tanṣ.**
7. At which place in Sȧ-mā'rĭ-ȧ did Jḗ'ṣus rest on his journey? **At Jā'cob's well.**
8. With whom did Jḗ'ṣus talk at Jā'cob's well? **With a Sȧ-măr'ĭ-tan woman.**
9. What did Jḗ'ṣus tell this woman that he could give her? **Living water.**
10. How did Jḗ'ṣus say that all should worship God? **In spirit and in truth.**

Lesson Nine · Jesus at Cana and Nazareth
(A.D. 28)

(Tell Story Nine in Part Sixth.)

1. Where did Jē'ṣus go after his visit to Så-mä'rĭ-à? **To Cā'nà, where he had made the water wine.**
2. Who came to see Jē'ṣus at Cā'nà? **A man of high rank.**
3. What did this man wish Jē'ṣus to do? **To cure his son, who was sick.**
4. At what place was his son lying sick? **At Cå-pēr'na-ŭm.**
5. What did Jē'ṣus say to this man of high rank? **"Go home; your son will live."**
6. What did the man find when he came to his home? **His son was getting well.**
7. Where did Jē'ṣus go soon after this miracle? **To Năz'a-rĕth, where he had lived as a boy.**
8. Why did Jē'ṣus go to Năz'a-rĕth? **To preach to the people.**
9. How did the people of Jē'ṣus' town feel when they heard his words? **They were very angry.**
10. What did they try to do? **To kill Jē'ṣus.**

Lesson Ten · Many Mighty Works
(A.D. 28)

(Tell Stories Ten and Eleven in Part Sixth.)

1. Where did Jē'ṣus go when he left Năz'a-rĕth? **To Cå-pēr'na-ŭm by the sea.**
2. From what did Jē'ṣus preach beside the sea? **From a boat.**
3. After preaching, what did Jē'ṣus help his followers to do? **To catch many fish.**
4. What four fishermen became disciples of Jē'ṣus? **Pē'tēr and Andrew, Jāmeṣ and Jŏhn.**
5. Whom did Jē'ṣus cure from a great fever? **The mother of Pē'tēr's wife.**
6. Whom did Jē'ṣus heal by a touch? **A leper.**
7. How did they bring a sick man to Jē'ṣus? **Through the roof.**
8. What did Jē'ṣus say as he made the sick man well? **"Your sins are forgiven."**
9. Why had Jē'ṣus the right to forgive sins? **Because he was the Son of God.**

Lesson Eleven · The Disciples and the Sermon on the Mount
(A.D. 28)

(Tell Stories Twelve and Thirteen in Part Sixth.)

1. What place did Jḗ′ṣus visit in the city of Jĕ-ru̇′ṣȧ-lĕm? **The pool of Bḗ-thĕṣ′dȧ.**
2. Whom did Jḗ′ṣus find there beside the pool? **A man who could not walk.**
3. What did Jḗ′ṣus say to this man? **"Take up thy bed, and walk."**
4. On what day did Jḗ′ṣus make this man well? **On the Sabbath Day.**
5. How did the Jews of Jĕ-ru̇′ṣȧ-lĕm feel toward Jḗ′ṣus when he made the man well on the Sabbath Day? **They were angry at Jḗ′ṣus.**
6. What did Jḗ′ṣus say to the rulers of the Jews? **"My Father works and I work."**
7. What other good work was done by Jḗ′ṣus on the Sabbath Day? **He cured a withered hand.**
8. What did Jḗ′ṣus do on a mountain? **He prayed all night.**
9. Whom did he choose on the next day? **His twelve disciples or apostles.**
10. What did Jḗ′ṣus preach to them and to the people? **The Sermon on the Mount.**

Lesson Twelve · The Captain's Servant and the Widow's Son
(A.D. 28)

(Tell Story Fourteen in Part Sixth.)

1. Who sent a messenger to Jḗ′ṣus, asking Him to cure his servant who was sick? **A centurion.**
2. What was a centurion? **A captain in the Rō′man army.**
3. How did the centurion say that his servant could be cured without having Jḗ′ṣus come to his house? **By Jḗ′ṣus speaking a word wherever he was.**
4. What did Jḗ′ṣus praise in this man? **His faith.**
5. To which place did Jḗ′ṣus go with his disciples? **To Nā′in.**
6. What did Jḗ′ṣus meet at the gate of the city of Nā′in? **The funeral of a young man.**
7. What did Jḗ′ṣus do to the young man who was dead? **He raised him to life.**
8. What rite did a woman perform for Jḗ′ṣus at a supper? **She washed his feet.**
9. What did Jḗ′ṣus say to this woman? **"Your sins are forgiven."**

Lesson Thirteen · The Parables, the Storm and the Wild Man
(A.D. 29)

(Tell Stories Fifteen and Sixteen in Part Sixth.)

1. How did Jē'ṣus teach by the Sea of Găl'ĭ-lee? **In parables.**
2. What is a parable? **A story showing some truth.**
3. What was the first parable given by Jē'ṣus? **The Parable of the Sower.**
4. What was the next parable that Jē'ṣus gave? **The Parable of the Wheat and the Tares.**
5. After teaching some parables, where did Jē'ṣus and his disciples go? **Across the sea in a boat.**
6. What came while Jē'ṣus and his disciples were sailing across the sea? **A great storm.**
7. What did Jē'ṣus say to the winds and the waves? **"Peace, be still."**
8. What came after Jē'ṣus had spoken these words? **A great calm.**
9. Whom did Jē'ṣus meet on the shore at the other side of the sea? **A wild man.**
10. What made this man wild? **The evil spirit in him.**
11. What did Jē'ṣus do? **He set him free from the evil spirit.**

Lesson Fourteen · The Little Girl Raised to Life
(A.D. 29)

(Tell Story Seventeen in Part Sixth.)

1. After his visit to the other side of the sea, where did Jē'ṣus go with his disciples? **To Cå-pēr'na-ŭm again.**
2. Who came to meet Jē'ṣus at the shore? **Jå-ĭ'rus.**
3. What did Jå-ĭ'rus ask Jē'ṣus to do? **To cure his sick daughter.**
4. Who met Jē'ṣus as he was on his way to the house of Jå-ĭ'rus? **A sick woman.**
5. What did this woman do? **She touched his robe.**
6. What came to the woman after touching Jē'ṣus robe? **She was made well.**
7. What happened while Jē'ṣus was going to the house of Jå-ĭ'rus? **His little girl died.**
8. What did Jē'ṣus say when he stood beside the little girl who was dead? **"Little girl, rise up!"**
9. What then took place? **The girl opened her eyes and sat up.**

Lesson Fifteen : The Death of John the Baptist
(A.D. 29)
(Tell Stories Eighteen and Nineteen in Part Sixth.)

1. Where was Jŏhn the Băp'tĭst while Jē'ṣus was preaching in Găl'ĭ-lee? **In prison.**
2. Who put Jŏhn the Băp'tĭst in prison? **The wicked King Hĕr'od.**
3. What did Jē'ṣus say of Jŏhn the Băp'tĭst while he was in prison? **"No greater man than Jŏhn has lived."**
4. What other wicked deed was done by King Hĕr'od? **He put Jŏhn the Băp'tĭst to death.**
5. Where did Jē'ṣus go with his disciples when he heard that Jŏhn the Băp'tĭst was dead? **To a quiet place by the Sea of Găl'ĭ-lee.**
6. Near which city was this place? **Near Bĕth-sā'ĭ-dà.**
7. What did Jē'ṣus do? **He gave food to a great company.**
8. How many did Jē'ṣus feed at that time? **Five thousand people.**
9. With what did Jē'ṣus feed the five thousand people? **With five loaves and two fishes.**
10. After feeding the five thousand, how did Jē'ṣus go to his disciples? **By walking on the water.**

Lesson Sixteen : The Mother's Prayer and the Four Thousand Fed
(A.D. 30)
(Tell Story Twenty in Part Sixth.)

1. To which land did Jē'ṣus go with his disciples after feeding the five thousand? **To the land of Tȳre and Sī'dŏn.**
2. Why did Jē'ṣus go to that country? **To be alone with his disciples.**
3. Who came to Jē'ṣus at that place? **A woman praying for her daughter.**
4. What did this woman ask Jē'ṣus to do for her daughter? **To set her free from an evil spirit.**
5. What did Jē'ṣus say to this woman when he cured her daughter? **"O woman, your faith is great."**
6. To which country did Jē'ṣus and his disciples go from the land of Tȳre and Sī'dŏn? **To Dĕ-căp'o-lĭs.**
7. Where was the country of Dĕ-căp'o-lĭs? **East of the Sea of Găl'ĭ-lee.**
8. What did the people in that land say of Jē'ṣus as they saw his great works? **"He has done all things well."**

9. To how many people in Dĕ-căp'o-lĭs did Jē'ṣus give food at one time? **To four thousand people.**

10. With how many loaves did Jē'ṣus feed the four thousand people? **With seven loaves.**

Lesson Seventeen · The Glory of Jesus on the Mountain
(A.D. 30)

(Tell Story Twenty-one in Part Sixth.)

1. What question did Jē'ṣus ask his disciples? **"Who do you say that I am?"**

2. Who answered Jē'ṣus' question for all the disciples? **Pē'tẽr.**

3. What did Pē'tẽr say in answer to Jē'ṣus? **"You are Christ, the Son of God."**

4. What does the word "Christ" mean? **The Anointed One, the King.**

5. On which mountain did Jē'ṣus go with three of his disciples? **On Mount Hẽr'mon.**

6. What change came upon Jē'ṣus while he was praying on the mountain? **He shone as bright as the sun.**

7. What two men of the past were seen talking with Jē'ṣus? **Mō'ṣeṣ and Ē-lī'jah.**

8. What did a voice from a cloud say? **"This is my beloved Son."**

9. What did Jē'ṣus and the three disciples find when they came down the mountain? **A child with an evil spirit.**

10. What did Jē'ṣus do to the child? **He set him free from the evil spirit.**

Lesson Eighteen : The Little Child, the Ten Lepers, and the Two Sisters
(A.D. 30)

(Tell Stories Twenty-two and Twenty-three in Part Sixth.)

1. Whom did Jē'ṣus take in his arms and hold up before the disciples? **A little child.**

2. What did Jē'ṣus say to his disciples at that time? **"Be like little children."**

4. How did Jē'ṣus say we should treat those who have been unkind to us? **We should forgive them many times.**

5. Through which country did Jē'ṣus go on his way from Găl'ĭ-lee to Jĕ-rṳ'ṣȧ-lĕm? **Through Sȧ-mā'rĭ-ȧ.**

6. Who met Jē'ṣus while he was in that country? **Ten men that were lepers.**

7. What did Jē'ṣus do to these men? **He made them all well.**
8. How many came and thanked Jē'ṣus after they were made well? **Only one.**
9. At which town did Jē'ṣus stay while he was near Jē-ru'ṣȧ-lĕm? **At Bĕth'a-nȳ.**
10. With which two sisters in Bĕth'a-nȳ did Jē'ṣus stay? **With Mär'thȧ and Mā'rȳ.**

Lesson *Nineteen* · The Man with Clay on His Face
(A.D. 30)

(Tell Story Twenty-four in Part Sixth.)

1. Whom did Jē'ṣus and his disciples meet one day in Jē-ru'ṣȧ-lĕm? **A man who had been born blind.**
2. What did Jē'ṣus do to the blind man? **He put clay on his eyes.**
3. What did Jē'ṣus tell the blind man to do? **To wash in the pool of Sĭ-lō'am.**
4. What happened to the blind man after he had washed in the pool of Sĭ-lō'am? **He could see.**
5. On which day was this blind man made to see? **On the Sabbath Day.**
6. How did the Jews feel toward Jē'ṣus when they found that he had done this on the Sabbath? **They were very angry.**
7. What did they say of Jē'ṣus? **"He is a sinner."**
8. What did the man who had been blind say of Jē'ṣus? **"He is a prophet of God."**
9. What is a prophet? **One who speaks the word of God.**
10. What did Jē'ṣus say to this man when he met him afterward? **"Do you believe on the Son of God?"**
11. How did the man answer Jē'ṣus? **"Lord, I believe."**

Lesson *Twenty* · The Good Shepherd and the Good Samaritan
(A.D. 30)

(Tell Story Twenty-five in Part Sixth.)

1. What parable or story did Jē'ṣus tell while he was in Jē-ru'ṣȧ-lĕm? **The Good Shepherd.**
2. How did Jē'ṣus say the true shepherd goes into the sheepfold? **By the door.**
3. What did Jē'ṣus say of himself? **"I am the door."**
4. What else did Jē'ṣus say of himself? **"I am the good shepherd."**
5. What did Jē'ṣus say the good shepherd does for his sheep? **He gives his life for them.**

6. To which part of the country did Jē′ṣus go from Jẻ-ru̟′sȧ-lĕm? **To Pẻ-rē′a.**
7. Where was Pẻ-rē′a? **East of the river Jôr′dan.**
8. What parable or story did Jē′ṣus tell a man in Pẻ-rē′a? **The Good Sȧ-mär′ĭ-tan.**
9. What did the Good Sȧ-mär′ĭ-tan do? **He helped a man who was in need.**
10. What did Jē′ṣus say to the man to whom he told the story? **"Go, and do likewise."**

Lesson Twenty-one · Lazarus Raised to Life
(A.D. 30)
(Tell Story Twenty-six in Part Sixth.)

1. Who sent for Jē′ṣus very suddenly, asking him to come to them? **Mär′thȧ and Mā′rẏ.**
2. To which place did they ask Jē′ṣus to come? **To Bĕth′a-nẏ, near Jẻ-ru̟′sȧ-lĕm.**
3. Why did Mär′thȧ and Mā′rẏ send for Jē′ṣus to come to Bĕth′a-nẏ? **Because their brother was very sick.**
4. What was the name of their brother? **Lăz′a-rŭs.**
5. What took place before Jē′ṣus went to Bĕth′a-nẏ? **Lăz′a-rŭs died.**
6. How long had Lăz′a-rŭs been buried when Jē′ṣus came to Bĕth′-a-nẏ? **Four days.**
7. What did Jē′ṣus do as he stood before the tomb of Lăz′a-rŭs? **"Jē′ṣus wept."**
8. What did Jē′ṣus say at the tomb of Lăz′a-rŭs? **"Lăz′a-rŭs, come forth!"**
9. What took place when Jē′ṣus had spoken these words? **Lăz′a-rŭs came out of the tomb alive.**
10. What did many of the people do when they saw this mighty work of Jē′ṣus? **Many believed on Jē′ṣus.**
11. What did the rulers of the Jews resolve to do? **To kill Jē′ṣus.**

Lesson Twenty-two : Some Parables in Perea
(A.D. 30)
(Tell Story Twenty-seven in Part Sixth.)

1. To which country did Jē′ṣus go soon after he brought Lăz′a-rŭs to life? **To Pẻ-rē′a, east of the river Jôr′dan.**
2. What did Jē′ṣus do in Pẻ-rē′a? **He went through the land teaching.**
3. Which parable or story did Jē′ṣus tell in Pẻ-rē′a? **The Lost Sheep.**

4. What did the shepherd do for the sheep that was lost? **He went after it and found it.**

5. Who seeks after us when we are lost from God? **Jē'ṣus, the Good Shepherd.**

6. Of whom did Jē'ṣus tell in another parable or story? **Of a young man who went away from home.**

7. What happened to this young man? **He became very poor.**

8. What did the young man say when he was in need? **"I will arise and will go to my father."**

9. What did the father do when his son came home? **He made him a great feast.**

10. Who is the one that forgives our sins and gives us blessings? **Our Heavenly Father.**

Lesson Twenty-three · Jesus and the Little Children
(A.D. 30)

(Tell Story Twenty-eight in Part Sixth, omitting "The Rich Man and Lazarus" and "The Unjust Steward and the Unjust Judge.")

1. Which parable or story did Jē'ṣus give about prayer? **He told of two men who prayed.**

2. Where did these two men pray? **In the Temple.**

3. How did one of these two men pray to God? **He told God how good he was.**

4. What did the other man say? **"God be merciful to me a sinner."**

5. Which of these two men did God bless? **The one who asked for mercy.**

6. Who were brought to Jē'ṣus? **Little children.**

7. What did Jē'ṣus say of the children? **Of such is the kingdom of heaven.**

8. What did Jē'ṣus do to the children? **He put his hands on them and blessed them.**

9. What question did a rich young man ask of Jē'ṣus? **"What good thing shall I do?"**

10. What did Jē'ṣus tell this man to do? **To give all he had to the poor.**

11. What else did Jē'ṣus say to him? **"Come and follow me."**

Lesson Twenty-four · Jesus at Jericho
(A.D. 30)

(Tell Story Twenty-nine in Part Sixth.)

1. Which city did Jē'ṣus visit as he was leaving the land of Pĕ-rē'a? **Jĕr'ĭ-chō.**

2. Whom did Jē'sus meet at the gate of Jĕr'ĭ-chō? **A blind man.**
3. What was the name of this blind man? **Bär-ti-mae'us.**
4. What did Bär-ti-mæ'us cry out as Jē'sus came near? **"Have mercy on me."**
5. What did Jē'sus do to blind Bär-ti-mæ'us? **He gave to him sight.**
6. With what rich man did Jē'sus stay while he was in Jĕr'ĭ-chō? **With Zăc-chae'us.**
7. What did the people think Zăc-chæ'us was? **A sinner.**
8. For what purpose did Jē'sus say that he came? **To seek and to save the lost.**
9. Which parable did Jē'sus give at that time? **The Parable of the Pounds.**
10. What does the Parable of the Pounds show us that we should do? **That we should work for Christ.**

Lesson Twenty-five · Palm Sunday
(A.D. 30)

(Tell Story Thirty in Part Sixth.)

1. To which place did Jē'sus go from Jĕr'ĭ-chō? **To Bĕth'a-nў, near Jê-ru'så-lĕm.**
2. What was made for Jē'sus in Bĕth'a-nў? **A supper.**
3. Who came to Jē'sus at this supper? **Mā'rў, the sister of Lăz'a-rŭs.**
4. What did Mā'rў do to Jē'sus? **She poured costly perfume on him.**
5. What did Jē'sus say to Mā'rў? **"She has done a good work."**
6. Which of Jē'sus' disciples agreed to sell him to his enemies? **Jū'das.**
7. What did the enemies of Jē'sus promise to give Jū'das, if he would give Jē'sus to them? **Thirty pieces of silver.**
8. Over which mountain did Jē'sus ride from Bĕth'a-nў to Jê-ru'så-lĕm? **The Mount of Ŏl'ĭveṣ.**
9. Who went with Jē'sus as he rode over the Mount of Ŏl'ĭveṣ? **A great company of people.**
10. What did the people carry and wave around Jē'sus? **Branches of palm trees.**
11. What did they call out together? **Praises to Jē'sus as king.**

Lesson Twenty-six · The Last Visits to the Temple
(A.D. 30)

(Tell Story Thirty-one of Part Sixth.)

1. Where did Jē'sus go on the morning after he rode over the Mount of Ŏl'ĭveṣ? **To the Temple in Jê-ru'så-lĕm.**

2. What did he do in the Temple? **He drove out the people who were buying and selling.**
3. What did Jē'ṣus say of the Temple? **"My house shall be called a house of prayer."**
4. Who came to hear Jē'ṣus as he was teaching in the Temple? **The common people.**
5. Where did Jē'ṣus stay at night, during those days while he was teaching in the Temple? **At Bĕth'a-nў.**
6. Which parable did Jē'ṣus give on the last day of his teaching in the Temple? **The Parable of the Wedding Feast.**
7. Who were invited to the wedding feast? **Everybody, both rich and poor.**
8. Who came to the feast? **A man without a wedding garment.**
9. What was done with the man who had no wedding garment? **He was sent away from the feast.**
10. Whose gift in the Temple did Jē'ṣus praise? **The gift of a poor woman.**

Lesson Twenty-seven · On the Mount of Olives
(A.D. 30)

(Tell Story Thirty-two of Part Sixth.)

1. To which place did Jē'ṣus go with his disciples from the Temple? **To the Mount of Ŏl'ĭveṣ.**
2. Of what did Jē'ṣus tell his disciples on the Mount? **Of things to come.**
3. What parable did he give to them at that time? **The Parable of the Ten Young Women.**
4. Where were these young women going? **To a wedding at night.**
5. What did Jē'ṣus say of these women? **Five were wise and five were foolish.**
6. Wherein were the five young women foolish? **In not taking oil for their lamps.**
7. Of what time to come did Jē'ṣus tell his disciples? **Of the time when Jē'ṣus shall sit as king.**
8. Who shall stand before Jē'ṣus at the last day? **All the people of the world.**
9. What will Jē'ṣus say in that day to those on his right hand, who have done his will? **"Come, ye that are blessed of my Father."**
10. What will he say to those on his left hand? **"Go away from me, ye wicked."**

Lesson Twenty-eight · At the Supper and in the Garden
(A.D. 30)

(Tell Stories Thirty-three and Thirty-four in Part Sixth.)

1. What meal did Jē'ṣus take with his disciples one night? **The Last Supper.**
2. What did Jē'ṣus say at the supper as he gave his disciples the bread? **"This is my body."**
3. What did he say as he gave them the cup of wine? **"This is my blood."**
4. What did Jē'ṣus do after the supper? **He washed the disciples' feet.**
5. Where did he go with the disciples on the night of the Last Supper? **To a garden.**
6. What did Jē'ṣus do in the garden? **He prayed to God.**
7. Who came to the garden to find Jē'ṣus? **Jū'das and the enemies of Jē'ṣus.**
8. What did these enemies do? **They bound Jē'ṣus and took him away.**
9. Where did they take Jē'ṣus? **To the high priest's house.**
10. What did the disciples do at that time? **They left Jē'ṣus alone.**

Lesson Twenty-nine · The Trial of Jesus
(A.D. 30)

(Tell Story Thirty-five in Part Sixth.)

1. Before whom was Jē'ṣus brought for trial? **Before the high priest Cā'ia-phăs.**
2. What did the high priest ask Jē'ṣus? **"Are you the Chrīst, the Son of God?"**
3. How did Jē'ṣus answer the high priest? **"I am."**
4. What was agreed by the rulers of the Jews? **That Jē'ṣus should be put to death.**
5. Before whom did they bring Jē'ṣus for another trial? **Before Pī'late the governor.**
6. What did Pī'late say to the Jews after he had talked with Jē'ṣus? **"I find no evil in this man."**
7. To whom did Pī'late send Jē'ṣus to be tried again? **To Hĕr'od the king of Găl'ĭ-lee.**
8. What did Hĕr'od do with Jē'ṣus? **He sent him back to Pī'late.**
9. What did the crowd of people cry out about Jē'ṣus? **"Let him be crucified."**
10. What did Pī'late at last order? **That Jē'ṣus should be put to death.**

Lesson Thirty · Jesus on the Cross
(A.D. 30)

(Tell Story Thirty-six in Part Sixth.)

1. Where was Jē′ṣus led to be put to death? **To Căl′va-rў.**
2. What did they try to make Jē′ṣus carry? **His cross.**
3. What was done with Jē′ṣus at Căl′va-rў? **He was fastened to the cross.**
4. What writing was put upon the cross above the head of Jē′ṣus? **"This is Jē′ṣus, the King of the Jewṣ."**
5. How long did Jē′ṣus live on the cross? **Six hours.**
6. How many times did he speak from the cross? **Seven times.**
7. What were the last words of Jē′ṣus before he died? **"Father, into thy hands I give my spirit."**
8. Who took down the body of Jē′ṣus from the cross? **Jō′ṣeph of Ăr-ĭ-mă-thae′à.**
9. Where was the body of Jē′ṣus buried? **In Jō′ṣeph's own tomb.**
10. How long was the body of Jē′ṣus in the tomb? **From Friday evening until Sunday morning.**

Lesson Thirty-one · The First Easter Day
(A.D. 30)

(Tell Story Thirty-seven in Part Sixth.)

1. What took place two days after Jē′ṣus died on the cross? **He became alive and came out of his tomb.**
2. Who brought the news that Jē′ṣus had risen from the dead? **Angels at his tomb.**
3. Who first saw Jē′ṣus after he rose from the dead? **Mā′rў Măg-da-lē′nė.**
4. Who saw the risen Jē′ṣus soon after Mā′ry had seen him? **Some other women.**
5. Who met the risen Jē′ṣus and walked with him on that morning? **Two of his followers.**
6. To whom did Jē′ṣus show himself next on that day? **To Pē′tĕr.**
7. How many of the disciples met that afternoon in Jē-ru̧′så-lĕm? **Ten.**
8. Who came suddenly among them, talked with them, and ate before them? **The risen Jē′ṣus.**
9. What did Jē′ṣus say when he came among the disciples? **"Peace be unto you."**
10. What is the day of the year called on which Jē′ṣus rose from the dead? **Easter Sunday.**

Lesson Thirty-two · Jesus on the Shore and on the Mountain
(A.D. 30)

(Tell Story Thirty-eight in Part Sixth.)

1. After the first Easter Day, when did the risen Jē'şus show himself again to his disciples? **On Sunday, a week later.**
2. Which of the disciples saw Jē'şus then for the first time? **Thŏm'as.**
3. Where did the disciples of Jē'şus go to meet him? **To Găl'ĭ-lee.**
4. Where was the risen Chrīst first seen in Găl'ĭ-lee? **At the shore of the Sea of Găl'ĭ-lee.**
5. What did Jē'şus say to Pē'tēr at that time? **"Feed my lambs."**
6. Where was the risen Jē'şus seen again by many of his followers? **On a mountain in Găl'ĭ-lee.**
7. How many saw Jē'şus at that time? **More than five hundred.**
8. What did Jē'şus tell his disciples to do? **To preach his gospel to all the world.**
9. Where was Jē'şus seen by his disciples for the last time? **On the Mount of Ŏl'ĭveş.**
10. What did the risen Jē'şus do on the Mount of Ŏl'ĭveş? **He went up to heaven.**
11. What promise was then given the disciples? **That Jē'şus will come again.**

Lesson Thirty-three · Review of People in the Gospel Story

1. What great prophet was born a few months before Jē'şus? **Jŏhn the Băp'tĭst.**
2. Who was the father of Jŏhn the Băp'tĭst? **Zăch-a-rī'as.**
3. Who was the mother of Jŏhn the Băp'tĭst? **Ē-lĭş'a-bĕth.**
4. Who brought the news that Chrīst would soon come? **The Angel Gā'brĭ-el.**
5. Who was the mother of Jē'şus? **Mā'rў.**
6. Who heard the first news that Jē'şus Chrīst was born? **Shepherds.**
7. Who came from a far country and brought gifts to the child Jē'şus? **Wise Men.**
8. Who took up the child Jē'şus in the Temple and gave thanks to God? **Sĭm'e-on.**
9. Who baptized Jē'şus? **Jŏhn the Băp'tĭst.**
10. Who tried to tempt Jē'şus to do wrong? **Sā'tan, the evil spirit.**
11. Who talked with Jē'şus at night in Jê-ru'să-lĕm? **Nĭc-o-dē'mus.**
12. Who met Jē'şus by a well? **The Să-măr'ĭ-tan woman.**
13. With what two sisters did Jē'şus stay near Jê-ru'să-lĕm? **With Măr'thà and Mā'rў.**

4. What was the name of the brother of these two sisters whom Jĕ'ṣus raised to life? **Lăz'a-rŭs.**
5. To which blind man did Jĕ'ṣus give sight at Jĕr'ĭ-chō? **To Bär-ti-mae'us.**
6. Which rich man at Jĕr'ĭ-chō took Jĕ'ṣus to his house? **Zăc-chae'us.**
7. Who poured costly perfume on the head of Jĕ'ṣus at a supper? **Mā'rÿ, the sister of Lăz'a-rŭs.**
8. Which disciple of Chrīst sold him to his enemies for money? **Jū'das.**
9. Which ruler ordered that Jĕ'ṣus should be put to death on the cross? **Pī'late.**
10. Who first saw Jĕ'ṣus after he rose from the dead? **Mā'rÿ Măg-da-lē'nĕ.**

Lesson Thirty-four · Review of Places in the Gospel Story

1. Where was Jĕ'ṣus born? **At Bĕth'lĕ-hĕm.**
2. To what land was he taken, that his life might be saved from King Hĕr'od? **To Ē'ġÿpt.**
3. Where did Jĕ'ṣus live as a boy? **In Năz'a-rĕth.**
4. Where was he found when he was twelve years old? **In the Temple.**
5. Where was he baptized? **In the river Jôr'dan.**
6. Where was he tempted by Sā'tan? **In the wilderness.**
7. Where was his first miracle? **At Cā'nà in Găl'ĭ-lee.**
8. In which land did Jĕ'ṣus preach during the first year of his teaching? **In Jū-dē'à.**
9. Where did Jĕ'ṣus talk with a woman by a well? **In Sà-mā'rĭ-à.**
10. Where did Jĕ'ṣus preach during the second year of his teaching? **In Găl'ĭ-lee.**
11. Where did he live while he preached in Găl'ĭ-lee? **At Cà-pēr'na-ŭm.**
12. On which sea did he still the storm? **The Sea of Găl'ĭ-lee.**
13. At which pool in Jĕ-ru'sà-lĕm did he heal a man who could not walk? **The Pool of Bĕ-thĕṣ'dà.**
14. To which other pool at Jĕ-ru'sà-lĕm did he send a blind man to wash? **To the Pool of Sĭ-lō'am.**
15. Where in Găl'ĭ-lee did he raise to life a widow's son? **At Nā'in.**
16. Where did he feed five thousand people? **Bĕth-sā'ĭ-dà.**
17. On which mountain did he show his glory? **On Mount Hĕr'mon.**
18. Where did he raise Lăz'a-rŭs to life? **At Bĕth'a-nÿ.**
19. Where did Jĕ'ṣus die on the cross? **At Căl'va-rÿ.**
20. From which mountain did Jĕ'ṣus go up to heaven? **From the Mount of Ōl'ĭveṣ.**

Part Second · Stories of the Early Church

Lesson Thirty-five · The First Days
(ABOUT A.D. 30)

(Tell Story One in Part Seventh.)

1. Where did the followers of Chrīst meet after Jē'ṣus went away to heaven? **In Jē-ru̇'sȧ-lĕm.**
2. What day came ten days after Jē'ṣus left the earth? **The Day of Pĕn'te-cŏst.**
3. What seemed to fall from heaven on all the followers of Chrīst on the Day of Pĕn'te-cŏst? **Tongues of fire.**
4. What power came upon them all? **Power from God.**
5. What did they all begin to speak? **The wonderful words of God.**
6. Who preached to the people on that day? **Pē'tẽr.**
7. What new name was given to Pē'tẽr and the other eleven disciples of Chrīst? **They were called apostles.**
8. What did the apostle Pē'tẽr tell the people to do? **To believe in Chrīst as their Saviour.**
9. How many were added to the church on that day? **Three thousand.**
10. How did all these people act toward one another? **Like brothers.**

Lesson Thirty-six · The Beautiful Gate, and the Apostles in Prison
(ABOUT A.D. 30)

(Tell Stories Two and Three in Part Seventh.)

1. Whom did Pē'tẽr and Jŏhn meet at the Beautiful Gate of the Temple? **A lame man.**
2. What did Pē'tẽr say to the lame man? **"In the name of Jē'ṣus Chrīst, walk."**
3. What did the lame man do? **He walked and leaped and praised God.**
4. Who, did Pē'tẽr say, had given to this man power to walk? **Jē'ṣus Chrīst.**
5. What did the rulers of the city tell Pē'tẽr and Jŏhn? **That they must not preach Chrīst.**
6. How did Pē'tẽr and Jŏhn answer the rulers? **"We must speak of what we know."**
7. Who gave his money to the poor in the church? **Bār'na-bȧs.**
8. Who died because they told a lie? **Ăn-a-nī'as and Săp-phī'rȧ.**
9. What did the rulers of the Jews̱ do to Pē'tẽr and Jŏhn? **They put them in prison.**
10. How were they set free from the prison? **By an angel of the Lord.**

58

Lesson Thirty-seven · Stephen and Philip
(ABOUT A.D. 35)

(Tell Stories Four and Five in Part Seventh.)

1. Which good man preached in Jĕ-ru'sȧ-lĕm? **Stē'phen.**
2. What is told of Stē'phen? **His face shone like an angel's.**
3. What did the Jews do to Stē'phen? **They stoned him to death.**
4. Who helped in the stoning of Stē'phen? **A young man named Saul.**
5. What did Saul do to the followers of Chrīst? **He beat them and put them in prison.**
6. Which worker for Chrīst was driven out of Jĕ-ru'sȧ-lĕm by Saul? **Phĭl'ĭp.**
7. To which place did Phĭl'ĭp go that he might preach the gospel? **To Sȧ-mā'rĭ-ȧ.**
8. Where did an angel send Phĭl'ĭp from Sȧ-mā'rĭ-ȧ? **To the desert.**
9. Whom did Phĭl'ĭp meet in the desert? **A man riding in a chariot.**
10. What did Phĭl'ĭp do when he met this man? **He preached Chrīst to him.**

Lesson Thirty-eight · The Voice That Spoke to Saul
(ABOUT A.D. 36)

(Tell Story Six in Part Seventh.)

1. Where did Saul go, that he might break up the church there? **To Dȧ-măs'cus.**
2. What took place when Saul was near Dȧ-măs'cus? **A light shone from heaven.**
3. Who spoke to Saul from out of the light? **The Lord Jē'sus Chrīst.**
4. What did the bright light do to Saul? **It made him blind.**
5. Who brought sight to Saul in Dȧ-măs'cus? **A follower of Chrīst named Ăn-a-nī'as.**
6. What else did Ăn-a-nī'as do to Saul? **He taught him how to be saved.**
7. What did Saul do at once when he became a believer in Chrīst? **He began preaching Chrīst.**
8. What did the Jews of Dȧ-măs'cus try to do when they found that Saul was preaching Chrīst? **They tried to kill him.**
9. How did Saul get away from the city of Dȧ-măs'cus? **He was let down in a basket.**
10. Where did Saul go from Dȧ-măs'cus? **To Jĕ-ru'sȧ-lĕm.**
11. Where did he afterward go? **To his home in Tär'sus.**

Lesson Thirty-nine · About the Apostle Peter
(ABOUT A.D. 40)

(Tell Story Seven in Part Seventh.)

1. Where did the Apostle Pē'tẽr go? **To Jŏp'pà, by the Great Sea.**
2. What did Pē'tẽr do by a prayer at Jŏp'pà? **He raised a woman to life.**
3. Who was this woman whom Pē'tẽr raised to life? **A good woman named Dôr'cas.**
4. What did God teach Pē'tẽr in a dream at Jŏp'pà? **That people of every land and nation might be saved.**
5. What did the Jews call the people of every nation except themselves? **Gĕn'tīleṣ.**
6. To which Gĕn'tīle did God send Pē'tẽr to preach the gospel? **To Côr-nē'lĭ-us, a Rō'man officer.**
7. What did Pē'tẽr and the church at Jĕ-ru̟'så-lĕm learn from this? **To preach Chrīst to the Gĕn'tīleṣ.**
8. What was done to Pē'tẽr after this at Jĕ-ru̟'så-lĕm? **He was put in prison.**
9. What did the king intend to do with Pē'tẽr on the next day? **To put him to death.**
10. What happened to Pē'tẽr on that night? **He was set free by an angel.**

Lesson Forty · The First Missionaries
(ABOUT A.D. 45)

(Tell Story Eight in Part Seventh.)

1. Where did a great church of Chrīst grow up? **At Ăn'tĭ-och in Sў̆r'ĭ-à.**
2. Who preached and taught in the church of Ăn'tĭ-och? **Bär'na-băs and Saul.**
3. For what work were Bär'na-băs and Saul sent out from Ăn'tĭ-och? **To preach the gospel in other lands.**
4. What are those who go out to other lands to preach the gospel called? **Missionaries.**
5. To which island did the missionaries and Bär'na-băs first go preaching the gospel? **To the island of Çȳ'prus.**
6. By what name was Saul called after this time? **Paul, the apostle.**
7. In which land did the missionaries, Paul and Bär'na-băs, preach after they left the island of Çȳ'prus? **In Ā'sià Mī'nor.**
8. In which city of Ā'sià Mī'nor did they begin preaching the gospel? **In Ăn'tĭ-och of Pĭ-sĭd'ĭ-à.**

9. Where were they first worshiped as gods and then stoned? **At Lỹs'trà.**

10. What did Paul and Bär'na-bäs do in all the places which they visited on this journey? **They started churches of Chrīst.**

11. Where did they go again after their journey? **To Ăn'tĭ-och in Sỹr'ĭ-à.**

Lesson Forty-one · Paul's Second Journey
(ABOUT A.D. 50)

(Tell Stories Ten, Eleven, and Twelve in Part Seventh.)

1. Who went with Paul on his second missionary journey? **Sī'las and Tĭm'o-thỹ.**

2. Which great land did they visit on this journey? **Europe.**

3. Where in Europe did they begin preaching the gospel? **In Phĭ-lĭp'pī.**

4. What was done to Paul and Sī'las at Phĭ-lĭp'pī? **They were beaten and put in prison.**

5. How were they set free from the prison at Phĭ-lĭp'pī? **By an earthquake.**

6. What did the jailor of the prison at Phĭ-lĭp'pī ask Paul and Sī'las when the earthquake came? **"What must Ī do to be saved?"**

7. What did Paul and Sī'las say to the jailor? **"Believe on the Lord Jē'ṣus Chrīst."**

8. In which city after Phĭ'lĭp'pī did they preach the gospel? **In Thĕs-sa-lô-nī'ca.**

9. Where did Paul preach a sermon on a hill? **In Ăth'ĕnṣ, on Märṣ' Hill.**

10. Where did Paul stay two years, preaching? **At Cŏr'inth.**

Lesson Forty-two · Paul's Third Journey
(ABOUT A.D. 53)

(Tell Stories Thirteen and Fourteen in Part Seventh.)

1. In what great city of Ā'ṣià Mī'nor did Paul preach on his third missionary journey? **In Ĕph'e-sŭs.**

2. What did Paul do in Ĕph'e-sŭs? **Many great works of healing.**

3. How long did Paul stay in Ĕph'e-sŭs preaching? **Three years.**

4. What arose in Ĕph'e-sŭs a little while before Paul left the city? **A great uproar against Paul.**

5. To which places in Europe where Paul had preached before, did he go after leaving Ĕph'e-sŭs? **To Phĭ-lĭp'pī and Cŏr'inth.**

6. Where did P*a*ul make a young man well, after he had fallen out of a window? **At Trō'ăs.**
7. At which place did P*a*ul send for the leaders of the church at Ĕph'e-sŭs? **At Mī-lē'tus.**
8. What did P*a*ul speak to these leaders of the church? **His farewell words.**
9. What words of Jē'sus did P*a*ul tell them to remember? **"It is more blessed to give than to receive."**
10. Where did P*a*ul end his third missionary journey? **At Jĕ-rụ'så-lĕm.**

Lesson Forty-three · Paul a Prisoner
(ABOUT A.D. 56)

(Tell Stories Fifteen, Sixteen, and Seventeen, in Part Seventh.)

1. What happened to P*a*ul as he was worshiping God in the Temple at Jĕ-rụ'så-lĕm? **He was taken by his enemies.**
2. What did these enemies of P*a*ul try to do? **To kill him.**
3. Who took P*a*ul out of the hands of his enemies? **Rō'man soldiers.**
4. Where was P*a*ul taken to be kept from his enemies? **Into the castle.**
5. What did the Lord Jē'sus say to P*a*ul at night while he was in the castle? **"Be of good cheer, P*a*ul!"**
6. Where was P*a*ul sent to be safe from the Jews? **To Çaes-a-rē'å.**
7. Before which ruler was P*a*ul brought to be tried? **Before Fē'lĭx, the governor.**
8. How long was P*a*ul kept in prison at Çaes-a-rē'å? **Two years.**
9. Before what other governor was P*a*ul brought after two years? **Before Fĕs'tus.**
10. Which king listened to P*a*ul as he told how Chrīst had saved him? **King Ä-grĭp'på.**

Lesson Forty-four · Paul in the Storm
(ABOUT A.D. 60)

(Tell Story Eighteen in Part Seventh.)

1. While P*a*ul was a prisoner, where was he sent for another trial? **To Rōme.**
2. How did P*a*ul and many other prisoners leave Çaes-a-rē'å to go to Rōme? **On board a ship.**
3. What did Paul tell those on the ship that they would meet in the voyage? **Great trouble and danger.**

4. How did the trouble and danger come to those that were in the ship? **From a great storm.**
5. How long did the storm last? **Two weeks.**
6. What did an angel say to Paul in the night while the storm was raging? **That all on the ship would be saved.**
7. What did Paul say to those on the ship? **"Be of good cheer."**
8. How were the lives of the people saved from the storm? **They were thrown upon an island.**
9. What was the name of this island? **Mĕl'ĭ-tà.**

Lesson Forty-five · Paul at Rome
(ABOUT A.D. 60)

(Tell Story Nineteen in Part Seventh. Stories Twenty and Twenty-one may be omitted.)

1. What happened to Paul on the shore at the island of Mĕl'ĭ-tà? **He was bitten by a poisonous snake.**
2. What did Paul do when the snake bit him? **He shook it off and was not harmed.**
3. What did the people of the island think when they saw that no harm had come to Paul? **They thought that he was a god.**
4. Who treated Paul and his friends kindly at Mĕl'ĭ-tà? **Pŭb'lĭ-ŭs, the ruler of the island.**
5. What did Paul do for the ruler of Pŭb'lĭ-ŭs? **He made his sick father well.**
6. Where did they sail to from the island of Mĕl'ĭ-tà? **To the land of Ĭt'a-lỹ.**
7. At which great city did Paul's long journey end? **At Rōme.**
8. How long was Paul a prisoner at Rōme? **Two years.**
9. What did he do while a prisoner? **He preached the gospel.**
10. What did Paul write at the end of his life? **"I have fought a good fight."**

Lesson Forty-six · Review on the Early Church

1. In which city were the followers of Chrīst after Jē'sus went to heaven? **Jē-ru'sà-lĕm.**
2. On what day did the Holy Spirit come upon the disciples? **The Day of Pĕn'te-cŏst.**
3. Who was the leader of the church in its early days? **The apostle Pē'tēr.**
4. Who died because they told a lie? **Ăn-a-nī'as and Săp-phī'rà.**

5. Which good man was stoned to death? **Stē′phen.**
6. Which young man helped in the stoning of Stē′phen? **Saul.**
7. Who preached in Så-mā′rī-à after Stē′phen was killed? **Phĭl′ĭp.**
8. Where did Saul become a believer in Chrīst? **At Då-măs′cus.**
9. What good woman was raised to life through the prayer of Pē′tẽr? **Dôr′cas.**
10. To which Gĕn′tīle or foreigner was Pē′tẽr sent to preach the gospel? **To Côr-nē′lĭ-ŭs.**
11. How was Pē′tẽr set free from prison in Jė-ru′så-lĕm? **By an angel.**
12. Which church sent out the first missionaries to preach the gospel? **The church at Ăn′tĭ-och.**
13. Who were the two missionaries that were sent out? **Bär′na-băs and Saul.**
14. Which island did Bär′na-băs and Saul first visit in preaching the gospel? **Çȳ′prus.**
15. By what name was Saul known after this? **Paul.**
16. Where were Paul and Bär′na-băs first worshiped and then stoned? **Lȳs′trà.**
17. In which city was the gospel first preached in Europe? **In Phĭ-lĭp′pī.**
18. Where was Paul made a prisoner? **In Jė-ru′så-lĕm.**
19. On which island was Paul shipwrecked? **Mĕl′ĭ-tà.**
20. To which city was Paul taken as a prisoner after being shipwrecked? **To Rōme.**

HISTORY

of the

BOOKS OF THE BIBLE

By JOSEPH HOWARD GRAY, D.D.

INTRODUCTION

The Bible is the most marvelous of books. Most books are written by a few people in a few months or years; the Bible was probably sixteen hundred years in composition, and may have been written by forty or fifty persons, most of whom never saw or knew one another. The people who wrote it were from all groups of society. Their work began in a desert and was finished on the shore of the Ægean Sea.

As we turn the pages of the Bible, our attention is held by the writings of the greatest legislator the world has ever known—a man who commanded six hundred thousand men, women, and children after he was eighty years old, and founded a state that thirty centuries of hostility could not overthrow. We also read the story of a man in sorrow. So weird and tender and true is this story, that nothing like it has ever been written. Still the pages turn, and we find ourselves in a king's palace, and the king himself takes down his harp and plays and sings to us. More pages turn as the stately prophets pass, telling the story of Tyre and Sidon, exulting, reproving, warning, lamenting.

In the New Testament we find the story of God's love told so tenderly, so sincerely, and so convincingly that the novelists of all the ages have not been able to approach its human appeal. "For God so loved the world, that he gave his only begotten Son." John 3:16. On we go through the marvelous story of Jesus and his disciples, his crucifixion, and Resurrection to the climax of his glorious ascension to the right hand of the Father.

The books comprising the Bible are not isolated, but together form an organic unity—one whole made up of mutually related parts, progressively advancing to the one great end: the restoration of fallen man through the love and righteousness of God.

The New Testament's twenty-seven and the Old Testament's thirty-nine books, emanating from different persons separated from each other by distance, time, space, and character, form an intertwined unity, all tending to the same end. The only answer to the mutual connection and profound unity is, "The Word of God came not in old time by the will of man, but holy men of God spake as they were moved by the Holy Ghost."

The word "Bible" is derived from the Greek "ta biblia," which means the (sacred) books.

The Bible faithfully portrays man's universal corruption and the origin of sin. It also declares the sure hope of redemption, thus meeting man's profoundest desires. It gives peace to conscience. The character of

3

Christ in the Bible shows perfect manhood and the Godhead combined. The adaptation of the Bible to man's many distresses and to his circumstances in all times and places reminds one that "the words of the Lord are pure words: as silver tried in a furnace of earth, purified seven times."

THE PENTATEUCH

The Pentateuch, as the first five books of the Bible are often called, was considered by the Hebrews as a single work, and in early times was written in one roll or book. In the Greek translation it was put into the five books now found in our Bibles. This name does not occur in Scripture and may have originated with the translators.

The Pentateuch takes its name from a Greek word that means "the five-volumed" book. It is commonly called the Five Books of Moses.

In the time of Ezra and Nehemiah it was called "The Law of Moses," or "The Book of the Law of Moses," or sometimes simply "The Book of Moses."

The division of the whole work into five books is ascribed to Greek translators because the title of each of the five separate books in our English version is derived through the Latin from the Alexandrian Greek version, and these titles of the several books are not of Hebrew but of Greek origin.

The five books of the Pentateuch form a consecutive whole. The work, beginning with the record of creation and the history of the primitive world, passes on to deal more especially with the early history of the Jewish family. It gives at length the personal history of the three great fathers of the family. It then describes how the family grew into a nation in Egypt, tells us of its oppression and deliverance, of its forty years of wandering in the wilderness, of the giving of the Law, with its enactments, both civil and religious, of the construction of the Tabernacle, of the numbering of the people, of the rights and duties of the priesthood, as well as many important events that befell the Hebrews before their entrance into the Land of Canaan. It concludes with Moses' last discourses and his death.

The Pentateuch is not a mere collection of loose fragments carelessly put together at different times, but bears evident traces of purpose and design in its composition. The five books ascribed to Moses have a peculiar place in the structure of the Bible, and an order which is doubtless the order of the experience of the people of God in all ages. Genesis is the book of origins—of the beginning of life, and of ruin through sin. Exodus is the book of redemption, the first need of a ruined race. Leviticus is the book of worship. Numbers speaks of a people on a pilgrimage to a better land. Deuteronomy is a book of instruction for those traveling pilgrims. The Pentateuch is a very human document. It shows man's struggle with himself, his aspirations, his disappointments, his devotion, his backslidings, his heroism, his weakness. But through the whole story runs the evidence of man's guidance toward a better life by the hand of a just, merciful and forbearing God.

GENESIS
The Book of Beginnings

Genesis signifies "beginnings." The book so named describes a series of "beginnings" under the title of "generations." In the first three chapters five doctrines are proclaimed:

1. The Doctrine of God.
2. The Doctrine of Creation.
3. The Doctrine of Man.
4. The Doctrine of the Fall.
5. The Doctrine of Redemption.

Therefore the book of Genesis records the "beginning" of the world and of its inhabitants, especially of man. It deals with his state of innocence, his fall, the hope of pardon and restoration, and the separation of a family from which should spring the chosen people and man's Redeemer.

The book of Genesis is an introduction to the history of redemption. Here is revealed God's creative power and wisdom. His holiness is shown in the punishment; his mercy also in forgiveness of the penitent. We learn his faithfulness to his promises. The method of access to God by sacrifice is clearly revealed.

Genesis contains the biographies of five principal persons: Adam, Noah, Abraham, Isaac, and Jacob.

I. ADAM. The creation of the world and the earliest history of mankind are contained in the first three chapters.

II. NOAH. The history of Adam's descendants to the death of Noah is given in chapters 4 to 9. Here we have the history of Cain branching off, while that of Seth and his descendants continues in genealogical succession as far as Noah. The history of Noah himself is covered in chapters 6 to 9.

III. ABRAHAM. Beginning with chapter 10 an account of Noah's posterity until the death of Abraham is given. The peopling of the earth by the descendants of Noah's three sons is related. The story of two of these is then dropped, and the line of Shem pursued only as far as Terah and Abraham. Abraham is now the prominent figure; but as Terah had two other sons, Nahor and Haran, some mention of their families is added. Abraham's meeting with the angels shows us how near men the created were to the Creator.

Lot's migration with Abraham into Canaan is mentioned, as well as the fact that he was the father of Moab and Ammon.

IV. ISAAC. Isaac's retiring and uneventful life is the subject of the fourth biography. After Isaac's death, we have the genealogy of Esau, who then drops out of the story in order that the history of the patriarchs may be carried on without intermission to the death of Joseph.

V. JACOB. From chapter 38 to the end of the book we have the eventful lives of Jacob and Joseph vividly described. Jacob's remarkable dream, his colorful romance, the kidnapping of Joseph, his rise to power and his mercy to his brothers all give us a clear picture of the times and of the men who made early history.

EXODUS
The Book of Deliverance

The word "Exodus" means "Departure." As the title indicates, this book gives the account of the Israelites' deliverance from Egypt. It is the story of those who came into Egypt and of those who were brought out of it. Exodus may be divided into two principal parts: (I) Historical (chapters 1:1 to 17:27) and (II) Legislative (chapters 19 to 50). The first group may be subdivided into the preparation for the deliverance of Israel from Egyptian bondage, and the accomplishment of that deliverance.

I. HISTORICAL. The first section gives an account of Jacob's descendants in the land of Egypt and their oppression under the new king who occupied the throne after the death of Joseph. The birth, education, and flight of Moses are related. His further training in the solitude of the Midian desert by communion with God and by the hardships of desert life are told. His solemn call to be the deliverer of his people and his return to Egypt in consequence climaxes this early portion of his life. The courage and faith of Moses are shown in his confronting Pharaoh. We are told how his first attempt to prevail upon Pharaoh to let the Israelites go failed and resulted in an increase in their burdens, and how Moses and Aaron made further preparation for their work. The institution of the Feast of the Passover is the solemn closing scene of the bondage in Egypt.

II. LEGISLATIVE. The establishment of the theocracy on Mount Sinai. The latter part of Exodus is an account of how the people were set apart to God as "a kingdom of priests and a holy nation." The Ten Commandments are given, and laws to regulate the social life of the people are declared. Instructions are recorded with respect to the Tabernacle, the Ark, the mercy seat, the altar of the burnt offerings, the separation of Aaron and his sons for the priest's office, the vestments to be worn, and the observance of the Sabbath. The delivery of the two Tables of the Law into the hands of Moses is described, as is the sin of the people who prayed to the golden calf, their rejection for their sin, and their restoration to God's favor at the intercession of Moses. Lastly, instructions for the construction of the Tabernacle are given and all matters pertaining to its service are set forth. This book, in short, is an account of the early history of Israel as a nation.

LEVITICUS
God's Call to Worship

This book is so named because it treats of the priestly order for which the tribe of the Levites was especially appointed. The book may be divided into three parts:

I. Laws relating to public worship (chapters 1 to 16). These include directions as to the different kinds of sacrifices, provision for the priests, the consecration of Aaron and his sons, the punishment of Nadab and Abihu, and the great Day of Atonement.

II. Laws relating to personal and social life (chapters 17 to 25). These include the life of the family, the relation of the sexes, the treatment of workers by their employers, and provision for the poor.

III. The blessings promised for obedience, the punishment for disobedience, and the conditions connected with voluntary vows (chapters 26 and 27).

It is universally admitted that Moses was the author of this book, and it is cited as his production in several books of Scripture. By comparing Exodus 40:17 with Numbers 1:1 we learn that this book contains the history of one month, that is, from the "first day of the first month of the second year" when the Tabernacle was erected to "the first day of the second month of the second year," when the people who were fit for war were numbered. This was 1490 B.C.

The ceremonial observances taught the Jewish people the holiness of God; the moral and social regulations were the practical outcome of it. The solution of some modern social problems may be found in such passages as chapter 19:9–18 and chapter 25. More than once Christ referred to this book as an authority.

Three times a year all males were required to appear before Jehovah at the feasts of the Passover, Pentecost, and the Tabernacles. Besides these there were the Feast of Trumpets and the Day of Atonement. These feasts were designed to keep God in the thought of the people and to promote national unity. Both feasts and Sabbaths served social as well as religious ends, especially for servants and the poor.

N U M B E R S
The Book of the Wilderness

This book derives its name from the fact that it records the census of the Israelites. The first of these numberings, or musterings, of the Children of Israel, took place at Mount Sinai in the second year after their departure from Egypt. The second was made in the plains of Moab near the end of their forty years' wandering in the wilderness. The first is described in chapters 1 to 4 and the second in chapter 26.

We find in this book records of some of the most memorable events in the history of the Children of Israel. Some are referred to in the New Testament. Our Lord applies to himself the typical lifting up of the brazen serpent (compare Numbers 21:9 with John 3:14). The prophecy of Balaam, "There shall come a star out of Jacob, and a sceptre shall rise out of Israel," Numbers 24:17, is regarded as referring to the coming of the Messiah.

Numbers may be divided into the following divisions:

I. The preparations for the departure from Sinai. Chapter 10.

II. The journey from Sinai to the borders of Canaan (chapter 10:11–14). Here is described the order of march and Moses' appeal to his father-in-law, Hobab, to accompany them on their journey—a request probably made because Hobab's experience in desert life would be valuable in finding good camp sites and in dealing with wandering tribes the Israelites might encounter.

III. A brief account of laws and events during the forty years' wandering in the wilderness is contained in chapters 15 to 19.

IV. The history of the last year, from the second arrival of the Israelites in Kadesh until they reach "the plains of Moab by Jordan near Jericho" is covered by chapters 20 to 36.

The book of Numbers is rich in fragments of ancient poetry, some of them of great beauty, which throw an interesting light on the character of the times in which they were composed. The book concludes with a recapitulation of the various encampments of the Israelites in the desert, the command to destroy the Canaanites, the boundaries of the Promised Land and designation of the men appointed to divide it, the appointment of the cities of the Levites and the cities of refuge, and further directions respecting heiresses.

DEUTERONOMY
The Book of God's Law

This book consists chiefly of three discourses by Moses shortly before his death. It derives its name from the fact that it is a repetition of the Law. These discourses were delivered to all Israel, in the plains of Moab on the eastern side of the Jordan. The time was the eleventh month of the last year of the wanderings of the Israelites, the fortieth year after their Exodus from Egypt.

I. In the first discourse Moses briefly, but earnestly, warns the people against the sins because of which their fathers failed to enter the Promised Land. He tries to impress upon them the lesson of obedience, that they might be ready to enter into the land. With this in view, he recapitulates the main events of the forty years in the wilderness.

II. The second discourse enters more fully into the precepts of the Law; it may well be taken as the main address to which the first discourse is an introduction.

III. The third discourse is given almost entirely to a discussion of the solemn sanctions of the Law, with special emphasis on its blessing and its curse. Here Moses spoke in conjunction with the elders of the people, with the priests and Levites, whose business it would be to carry out the ceremony that was prescribed in anticipation of the people's settlement in the Holy Land. The place for this ceremony was the sacred spot where the first altar to God had been erected on the summit of Ebal. Then the twelve tribes were to be divided between the two hills, Gerizim and Ebal (Deuteronomy 27:12, 13).

When he had finished the discourses, Moses encouraged the people and Joshua, the new leader, to go over the Jordan and take possession of the land. He then wrote this Law, and delivered it to the Levites to be kept in the Ark of the Covenant, as a perpetual witness against the people; and he commanded them to read it to all Israel when the people assembled at the Feast of Tabernacles, every seventh year. By the command of Jehovah, who appeared in the cloud to Moses and Joshua when they presented themselves at the door of the Tabernacle, Moses added to the Book of the Law a song, which the people were requested to learn, as a witness of Jehovah against them. This "Song of Moses" recounts the blessings of God and his righteous ways.

JOSHUA

This is the first book of the second, or historical, section of the Old Testament. The historical division consists of twelve books that give the history of the Hebrew nation from the time it entered the land under the leadership of Joshua to the time of Nehemiah, the last of the Old Testament historians. During this period Israel passed through theocracy and into the monarchy, from the United Kingdom under David and Solomon through the time in which Judah and Israel were independent states to the fall and captivity of both Kingdoms and post-Exilic times. The book is named Joshua because he is the central figure, the successor of Moses who became the new leader of Israel.

The book may be divided into three parts: (I) The conquest of Canaan; (II) The partition of Canaan; (III) Joshua's farewell.

PART I deals with preparations for war and the passage of the Jordan, the capture of Jericho, the conquest of the south, the conquest of the north, and a recapitulation.

PART II tells the territory assigned to Reuben, Gad, and half the portion of Manasseh, the lot of Caleb and of the tribe of Judah, the country of Ephraim and the rest of Manasseh's territory. The portions of Simeon, Zebulun, Issachar, Asher, Naphtali, and Dan. Six cities of refuge are appointed and forty-eight cities are assigned to Levi. The departure of the trans-Jordanic tribes to their homes is described.

PART III relates Joshua's convocation of the people and his first address, his second address at Shechem, and his death. This book shows that Joshua's faith stood the test. He acts promptly upon the command of God. Not to himself, but to God, he gives the glory. In time of defeat and disappointment he turns to God in humiliation and prayer. He is loyal to God's commandments and seeks to win the people to similar loyalty. In the closing words of his life with great earnestness he urges the people to trust in God, recalling God's help in the past, and promising, with absolute confidence, the continuance of that help in the future.

Some Canaanites remained in the land because Israel failed to obey God's command to drive them out, and after the death of Joshua they made considerable trouble for Israel. During the following three hundred years, until the days of David, idolatry had the upper hand much of the time and greatly interfered with the national development of Israel. Not until David did the Israelites get all the land allotted them.

JUDGES

This book brings us to the second stage of the theocracy, the name of the system of the government in the days of the judges. God himself was supposed to be the direct ruler of the brotherhood of the twelve tribes that were under a religious constitution with a common sanctuary. Nevertheless, the people became indifferent to God, their only unifying force. They were in a state of anarchy, and therefore very slow in their development as a nation. Not until the days of David did Israel become a really great nation. The Book of Judges divides itself into two parts:

I. The oppressions that brought about the rise of the judges is described in chapters 1 and 2 and the first seven verses of chapter 3. The idolatrous races had not been driven wholly from the land. Among these the Israelites settled. They intermarried with them, imitated their idolatrous practices, and became degenerate, an easy prey, therefore, to the attacks of the other nations and tribes. It was to meet such attacks that the judges were raised up. They were at first deliverers, and then, in the quieter times, governors and judges.

II. The times from Othniel to Samson are covered in chapters 3:5 to 16:31. Israel's idolatrous defections brought upon them divine retribution in the form of oppressions by those nations whose god they worshiped. We have the account of seven of these oppressions and the manner of Israel's deliverance. (1) Oppression by the Mesopotamians from the northeast. This continued for eight years, when Israel was delivered by Othniel. (2) Oppression by Moabites from the southeast, after forty years of peace. Deliverance came through Ehud. (3) Oppression by the Philistines from the southwest after the Israelites had enjoyed the mercy of God for eighty years. They were delivered by Shamgar. (4) Oppression by the Canaanites from the north, which continued for twenty years, with final deliverance by Deborah and Barak. (5) Oppression by the Midianites from the east after a peaceful period of forty years. Israel was delivered in an unusual way by Gideon. Following him, the judgeship fell to Abimelech, Tola, and Jair. (6) Oppression by the Ammonites from the east. Israel was delivered by Jephthah and then enjoyed peace for thirty-one years. (7) Oppression by the Philistines. This lasted for forty years, then deliverance came through Samson. The four principal judges, Barak, Gideon, Jephthah, and Samson, are included among the heroes of faith in Hebrews 11:32. They believed in God and his divine power, and God honored that faith.

RUTH

The Book of Ruth originally formed the closing part of The Book of Judges. This book derives its name from the leading figure set forth in the narrative. In Judges the story is of battle and warriors, of turbulence and sin. In Ruth all is repose and peace. From the gentle and womanly pathos of its opening chapter, the story of Ruth is a charming picture in the changing panorama of history. Its fascination seems all the greater as the scenes it records have receded into the remote past. The ancient narrator tells us that a severe famine in the land of Judah, caused perhaps by the occupation of the land by the Moabites under Eglon, induced Elimelech, a native of Bethlehem Ephratah, to emigrate into the land of Moab. With him went his wife, Naomi, and his two sons, Mahlon and Chilion. Elimelech and his sons died in the land of Moab. At the end of ten years the widowed Naomi, having heard that there was plenty again in Judah, resolved to return to Bethlehem, and with her returned her daughter-in-law, Ruth. "Whither thou goest, I will go, and where thou lodgest, I will lodge; thy people shall be my people, and thy God my God; where thou diest, I will die, and there will I be buried; the Lord do so to me, and more also, if aught but death part thee and me," was the expression of the unalterable attachment of the young Moabite widow to the mother, to the land, and to the religion of her lost husband.

They arrived at Bethlehem at the beginning of barley harvest, and Ruth, going out to glean for the support of her mother-in-law and herself, chanced to go into the field of Boaz, a wealthy kinsman of her father-in-law, Elimelech. The story of Ruth's virtues and of her kindness and fidelity to her mother-in-law, and of her preference for the land of her husband's birth had gone before her. Immediately upon learning who the strange young woman was, Boaz treated her with the utmost kindness and respect and sent her home laden with the grain which she had gleaned. Encouraged by this consideration, Naomi instructed Ruth to ask that Boaz should perform the duty of her husband's near kinsman, the purchase of the inheritance of Elimelech and taking Ruth as his wife. But there was a nearer kinsman than Boaz, and it was necessary that he should have the option of redeeming the inheritance for himself. He, however, declined, fearing to mar his own inheritance, upon which, with all due solemnity, Boaz took Ruth to be his wife, amid the blessings and congratulations of their neighbors.

Neither the exact date of the composition of the book nor the name of the author is positively known. From internal evidence it appears, however, that it was written after the establishment of the monarchy in Israel, and there is much reason for reliance upon the opinion of some of the best critics that it was the work of Samuel himself.

I S A M U E L

This book marks the beginning of a new era in the history of Israel. It records the lives of the last two judges, Eli and Samuel, and the beginning of the monarchy under Saul. In the Septuagint the books of Samuel and the books of the Kings are designated Books of the Kingdom. In the Vulgate they are entitled the books of the Kings. In the Hebrew the two books of Samuel form one book. Since the death of Samuel is recorded in the first book, chapter 25:1, it is evident he could not have been the author of what followed. Ancient opinion favors the view that Samuel was the author of I Samuel, chapters 1 to 24 and that Nathan and Gad were the writers of the rest of that book. The fact that the books of Samuel contain no record of David's death has led to the opinion that they were compiled prior to his death.

This book falls into two parts, the first of which gives the events of the closing days of the judgeship, in which Samuel is the active agent; and the second of which deals with the monarchy under Saul.

I. SAMUEL, THE LAST OF THE JUDGES (chapters 1 to 8). Five things are noted regarding Samuel: his birth; his childhood promise; his dedication to God by his mother Hannah; his ministry as a child; his call and reception of the divine communication of the judgment upon the house of Eli, the high priest. This is followed by the account of the defeat of Israel by the Philistines, and of the judgeship of Samuel. His victory over the Philistines is described. The people insisted on being like other nations and demanded a king. The Lord and Samuel warned them against this step, in which they would assume the prerogative of Jehovah, but they were permitted to act in the matter, and the judgeship came to an end.

II. THE MONARCHY. The reign of Saul is chronicled in chapters 9 to 31. Saul was the people's choice. He belonged to the tribe of Benjamin and was anointed king by Samuel. Events in Saul's reign to the time of his rejection are described. He delivered Jabesh-gilead and enlisted a select band of soldiers to meet the Philistines, but in usurping the priestly office at Gilgal he brought upon himself Samuel's reproval and God's rejection. His second rejection is recorded in chapters 14 to 16. Then follows an account of Jonathan's bravery and Saul's attempt to deceive Samuel regarding Amalek. Saul is again rejected, and Agag, king of Amalek, is killed. Next comes the story of Saul and David. David is anointed. He slays the giant Goliath, after which he is taken into the court of Saul, where he marries Saul's daughter. Between David and Jonathan a lasting friendship is formed. Saul's jealousy compels David to become an outlaw. David gathers about him a loyal band, twice spares Saul's life, and defeats the Philistines and the Amalekites. In the closing chapters, Saul, troubled and fearful, seeks the witch of Endor and communes with the spirit of Samuel. Then he fights his last battle, is defeated, and falls on his own sword.

II S A M U E L

David, who had already been anointed king by Samuel upon Saul's death, came to the throne. It is with his reign that this Second Book of Samuel deals. There are two divisions: (I) David as the king of Judah, and (II) David as the king of all Israel.

I. DAVID, THE KING OF JUDAH (chapters 1 to 4). A royal line was established by David that was to hold the throne of Judah in a continuous dynasty through the time that it remained an independent state following the disruption of the kingdom. David was the king of Judah alone for seven years. The other tribes refused to unite under him and maintained the house of Saul, placing Ishbosheth upon their throne. David's capital was at Hebron. Following the conflict between Judah and Israel, Abner, of the house of Saul, proposed a union of the tribes. In reporting frankly the misconduct of persons who were highly reverenced among the people, the sacred writer demonstrates his impartial sincerity. In the fall of David we behold the strength and prevalence of human corruption, and in the repentance and recovery the extent and efficacy of divine grace.

II. DAVID, KING OF ALL ISRAEL (chapters 5 to 24). The chronology of this part of the Second Book of Samuel may be arranged as follows: (I) The most important events up to the time of bringing of the Ark to Jerusalem were the union of the tribes under David, the taking of Jerusalem from the Jebusites, the establishment of Jerusalem as the capital, defeat of the Philistines, the bringing of the Ark to Jerusalem, and David's determination to build a Temple. (2) The most important events up to the time of Absalom's rebellion (chapters 8 to 18) were David's defeat of the Philistines, the Moabites, and the Assyrians; his kindness to Mephibosheth, the lame son of Jonathan; his great sin with Bath-sheba, wife of Uriah, who became the mother of Solomon; Absalom's crime, flight, and return; Absalom's rebellion against his father; David's crushing of the rebellion; Absalom's death, and David's mourning. One of the most pathetic scenes of the Bible is that of David's grief over Absalom.

III. DAVID'S LAST YEARS (chapters 19 to 24). Following his return to Jerusalem after the death of Absalom, four things are recorded: Sheba's sedition; the famine; defeat of the Philistines and David's psalm of thanksgiving; sin of numbering the people and the penalty. Therefore we see that the two books of Samuel cover the last period of the theocracy and almost two reigns of the monarchy. The book has many noble passages, such as David's lament over Saul and Jonathan, intercession of the wise woman of Tekoah on behalf of Absalom, David's sorrow for the death of his ungrateful son, his songs of praise and faith, and story of the "three mighty men" at the well of Bethlehem. Jerusalem was David's capital. Since the days of Joshua, Jerusalem alone had defied the arms of Israel. Situated in an impregnable position, and with the tradition of Melchizedek, priest of the God Most High, David thought it was best suited to be the nation's capital. He took it, brought in the Ark of God, and made plans for building the Temple.

I KINGS

The two books of Kings formed but one in the Jewish Scriptures. The style is quite uniform, the same forms of expression are used in speaking of the same things. We have no way of knowing who the compiler was. It was ascribed to Jeremiah by Jewish tradition, but aside from this there is no reason for assuming Jeremiah to be the author. The author makes frequent reference to historical records: "The book of the Acts of Solomon," "The Chronicles of the Kings of Judah," "The History of Samuel the Seer," and so forth.

The book of Kings tells of the golden age of Israel's history. It was the era of David and Solomon. David was a warrior; Solomon was a builder. David made the kingdom; Solomon built the Temple. This was the age of Homer, the beginnings of Greek history. Egypt had declined. Babylon and Assyria were weak. Israel was the most powerful kingdom in the world. The Hebrew nation brought to a world of idol worshipers the idea of one true God.

I. Closing Days of David's Reign (chapters 1:1 to 2:10). Three things are recorded in these opening chapters: Adonijah's attempt to usurp the throne; the coronation of Solomon; David's charge to Solomon. David's death closes the account of one of the greatest men of Israel and of the world, the sweet singer of Israel whose psalms have lifted men's souls to God, grounded the faith of believers, comforted the disconsolate, and lifted up those that were bowed down.

II. Kingship of Solomon (chapters 2:11 to 11:43). At Gibeon, Solomon prayed earnestly for wisdom and was assured that and much more. This was followed by an exhibition of wisdom. The construction and dedication of the Temple was the great work of his reign. David had made his contribution to the Temple, and Hiram, king of Tyre, aided Solomon in furnishing materials. The Temple was the visible symbol of Jehovah's presence, centralizing the nation religiously. Other important features of the book are God's covenant with Solomon, Solomon's fame and prosperity, Solomon's apostasy and the judgment pronounced.

III. Division of the Kingdom (chapters 12 to 22). This occurred upon the death of Solomon, when ten of the tribes revolted and Israel and Judah became independent states. (1) The Kingdom of Judah. The closing chapters of the book are taken up with the history of the two kingdoms. That of Judah is carried through the reign of Jehoshaphat, which closes the reigns of Rehoboam, Abijam, Asa, and Jehoshaphat. Under the last occurred the first of the three great revivals during Judah's history. (2) The Kingdom of Israel. The history of this kingdom is traced to the reign of Ahaziah, the son of Ahab. But the hero of the book is Elijah. His simple faith, the faith which he inspired in others and his unflinching courage are examples for all time. God's vindication of his servant is an encouragement to all who put their trust in him and should point the way for all Christians.

II KINGS

What has been said in the introduction to I Kings applies largely to this book also. It records the reigns of fifteen kings of Judah, beginning with Ahaziah and ending with Zedekiah, and of eleven kings of Israel, beginning with Jehoram and ending with Hoshea. Of the former, Hezekiah and Josiah are the most notable. Jehu, with his strange mixture of zeal for the Lord and following the bad example of Jeroboam, is the most memorable among the kings of Israel. This book traces the two kingdoms contemporaneously, as is done in I Kings.

I. The Kingdom of Israel (chapters 1 to 17). The history of Israel is followed through the remaining periods of this kingdom. (1) During the reign of the last two kings of the second period, Ahaziah and Jehoram, Elijah and Elisha continue their labors in behalf of Israel. (2) In the third period Jehu brought to an end Jezebel and the house of Ahab and destroyed the prophets of Baal. Idolatry, which had been firmly rooted during the previous periods, was slightly checked in this third period. During the reign of Jeroboam II, the period of Jonah the prophet, Israel enjoyed considerable prosperity. Five kings reigned during the closing period of Israel. In 721 B.C. Samaria was overthrown by the Assyrians, and the people were carried into captivity.

II. The Kingdom of Judah (chapters 8:16 to 25:30). The record of I Kings closed with the reign of Jehoshaphat, and II Kings resumes the history of this kingdom with the second period. During the extended span from Jehoram to Hezekiah, Judah was committed to idolatry until the reign of Hezekiah. It was given a great impulse by Jehoram, the son-in-law of Ahab and Jezebel of Israel. It was during the reign of Uzziah that Isaiah began his ministry of prophecy. The second great revival occurred under Hezekiah. This may have been influenced by the fall of Israel, which happened during the sixth year of Hezekiah's reign. Under Manasseh, Judah fell into the worst period of her idolatry, but the godly king Josiah, assisted by Jeremiah the prophet, brought about a true religious reform. This was the third and last revival. From Jehoahaz to Zedekiah, Judah rapidly declined. Associated with these kings was Jeremiah, who saw many captives carried away in 606 B.C., and the destruction of Jerusalem by Nebuchadnezzar and the exile of its people to Babylon. Like all the prophets, Jeremiah never fails to swing from present gloom to future glory. God has not broken his covenant and will not do so.

I CHRONICLES

The books of Chronicles are genealogies and records of the reign of David, organization of worship, the reign of Solomon, the Temple, Solomon's wealth and power, and the history of Judah after the secession of the ten tribes.

Chronicles, Ezra, and Nehemiah are a unified series of works. Constant Jewish tradition was that Ezra was the author. It is thought that he wrote Ezra and Nehemiah first and then wrote Chronicles in order to connect the story of the restoration with preceding history. It is presumable that the books of Chronicles were made up of records the writer found already in existence, and that he selected his material as the Holy Spirit gave him guidance.

The genealogies that we find in the first nine chapters present to us a picture of the resettling of the land. Those who had returned from the captivity were entitled to the lands formerly held in their own families. These genealogies showed the people's title to land and office. According to the Old Testament, the land had been apportioned to families and could not be sold in perpetuity out of the family. If sold, it would be returned to the original family in jubilee year. The priesthood was hereditary in families. A priest would be succeeded by his son. Such was the law of the land. So it was with the kingly line of David. The most precious of all promises was that the Messiah would come from David's family. The most interesting of these genealogies is the tracing of David's line. These genealogies may not be exciting reading, but they form the framework of the Old Testament that binds the whole Bible together and gives it unity. Following the genealogies the book may be divided into three sections:

I. Saul's Overthrow and Death (chapter 10).

II. David Becomes King Over Israel. Chapter 11 is a record of David's mighty men. In chapter 12:23–40 are listed the men of Israel who made David king. David's prosperity is described in chapter 14. The first twenty-four verses of chapter 15 tell of the preparations of bringing the Ark to Jerusalem and the remainder of the chapter deals with its establishment there.

III. The Temple. We are told of David's desire to build the Lord's house, and of his preparation for it. Then follows David's instruction of Solomon in God's promises and his duty in building the Temple. Being now an old man, David makes Solomon king, and gives Israel and him counsel and encouragement in building the Temple. Again David exhorts the people, and both people and princes willingly offered their aid in the building of the Temple. David offers prayer and thanksgiving, and the people blessed God and offered sacrifice. So was Solomon made king, and David died, "and he died in a good old age, full of days, riches, and honor."

II CHRONICLES

The second book of Chronicles continues the history begun in First Chronicles. While the books of Samuel and the Kings trace the history of Israel and Judah, Chronicles covers the whole range of the history of Israel from Adam to the fall of the Kingdom of Judah. Chronicles gives greater emphasis to the divine side of the history than the other books. Many instances of God's care and guidance are shown in this book. Solomon is the principal person in Second Chronicles. The story in the first nine chapters corresponds with that of I Kings, chapters 3 to 11, with some interesting additions. An instance is the sacrifice at Gibeon. This was not merely an act of devotion on the part of Solomon, but a great public ceremony. It was on the night of that sacrifice that God appeared to him and said, "Ask what I shall give thee." And Solomon said unto God: "Thou has shewed [showed] great mercy unto David my father, and hast made me to reign in his stead. Now, O Lord God, let thy promise unto David my father be established: for thou hast made me king over a people like the dust of the earth in multitude. Give me now wisdom and knowledge, that I may go out and come in before this people: for who can judge this thy people, that is so great?" And God said to Solomon: "Because this was in thine heart, and thou hast not asked riches, wealth, or honour, nor the life of thine enemies, neither yet hast asked long life; but hast asked wisdom and knowledge for thyself, . . . wisdom and knowledge is granted unto thee; and I will give thee riches, and wealth, and honour." (II Chronicles 2:7–12.)

THE TEMPLE. David wanted to build the Temple, but was forbidden because he was a man of war. God helped David in his wars. However, it was not becoming for a warrior to build Jehovah's house, because the subdued nations might be bitter toward Israel's God. Solomon prepared to build the Temple, and Solomon enlisted his father's friend Hiram, the king of Tyre (see II Chronicles 2:3 and also I Kings 5:1–12). The answer of Hiram was that he would cut as much wood as should be needed out of Lebanon and send it in floats by sea to Joppa. Thence it would be carried overland to Jerusalem. The Temple was built after the general plan of the Tabernacle, every part twice the dimension. The cost has been estimated at from one to five billion dollars in our money. The Ark of the Covenant was brought into the Temple, and the glory of God filled the house. The sermon of Solomon and Solomon's prayer (in chapter 6) contain many noble expressions that are well worth anyone's faithful study.

SOLOMON AND THE QUEEN OF SHEBA. The Queen of Sheba had heard of the greatness of Solomon and came to prove him with hard questions. She came with a large company bearing many gifts. Her exclamation, "One half of the greatness of thy wisdom was not told me," indicates the impression she carried away from this meeting. The remaining chapters (10 to 36) deal with the history of the Kingdom of Judah from the time of Rehoboam to the Captivity, and records the proclamation of Cyrus permitting the return of the Jews to Jerusalem. The most important addition to the record of the kings is the account of Jehoshaphat.

E Z R A

The seventy-year Babylonian Captivity was under the Assyrian and Babylonian Kingdoms; the return of the Jews to Jerusalem was under the Persian Empire. The Book of Ezra is a continuation of the second book of Chronicles and tells of their return. It takes its name from the leader of the second of these groups of returning exiles. Ezra was both a scribe and a priest. He was a lineal descendant of Phinehas, the son of Aaron.

The Book of Ezra opens with the proclamation of Cyrus, which permitted the Jews to return to Jerusalem. It describes Cyrus as the divinely directed instrument of the repatriation. There were three returns: one led by Zerubbabel, 636 B.C., with 42,360 Jews, 7,337 servants, 200 singers, 736 horses, 245 mules, 435 camels, 6,720 asses, and 5,400 gold and silver vessels that had been taken from Jerusalem. The second was led by Ezra, 457 B.C., with 1,754 males, 100 talents of gold, and 750 talents of silver, which included offerings from the king. There was also a unit led by Nehemiah, 444 B.C., who went as governor appointed by the Persian king, with an army escort, to rebuild and fortify Jerusalem at government expense. The lot of the returning exiles was not without trouble. The Israelites who had remained in the country surrounding Jerusalem, learning of the favor of the Persians and probably wishing to share it, suggested that they be permitted to help in the rebuilding of the Temple. This Zerubbabel refused. Then the enemies of Judah and Benjamin hired what today would be called propagandists to write letters to the Persian kings saying that the returning Jews plotted against the Persians, were fortifying Jerusalem, would refuse to pay tribute, and planned revolt. Nevertheless, Darius, the king of Persia, and Artaxerxes, his successor, refused to believe these things, and the Temple and the city were rebuilt with the aid of the Persians. This was a great period in the world's history. In Greece, Athens was in her glory. Socrates and Pericles flourished. In India, Buddha was teaching. In China, Confucius was setting down his philosophy. Persian kings of this period were Cyrus, 538–529; Cambyses, 529–521; Darius I, 521–485, under whom the Temple was rebuilt; Xerxes, 485–465; and Artaxerxes I, 465–425, all great names in history.

NEHEMIAH
Rebuilding Jerusalem

Nehemiah was one of the great personalities of the Bible. His faith in God, his splendid character, his courage, his devotion to his country, his perseverance in face of opposition and ridicule, his belief in prayer, his respect for God's laws and especially for that of the Sabbath, make his life a great inspiration for those who walk in God's ways and seek to do his will.

Here is the story as told in The Book of Nehemiah: Nehemiah was the cupbearer to the king in the palace at Shushan, and there he heard of the sad condition of Judea and its people, and how, though the Temple had been rebuilt, the walls of Jerusalem were still broken down. In his distress Nehemiah turned to God with fasting, confession, and prayer, asking God to put it into the heart of the king to grant his request. Then he proceeded to action. He asked the king for permission to return to Jerusalem for the purpose of rebuilding the walls, and also for letters to the rulers of provinces through which he would have to pass. Artaxerxes not only gave Nehemiah permission and the desired letters, but also provided him with an escort of cavalry (chapter 2:5–9). Nehemiah's prayer was more than answered. Nehemiah's work was to rebuild the walls and fortify the city. When Nehemiah went to Jerusalem in 444

B.C., Ezra had already been there thirteen years. But Ezra was only a priest teaching religion to the people. Nehemiah was a civil governor, armed with authority from the king of Persia to rebuild the wall. This he did in fifty-two days. Although the exiled Jews and their children had been home nearly two hundred years, up to Nehemiah's coming they had made no progress in rebuilding Jerusalem beyond the Temple. Nehemiah and Ezra worked together to cleanse the people of their idolatrous wives, abolish usury, restore the annual festivals of the Temple worship, and enforce Sabbath observances and tithing.

ESTHER

About thirty years before the events described in The Book of Nehemiah, there ruled at Shushan the Persian king Xerxes, called in this book Ahasuerus. Now Ahasuerus gave a great feast to his nobles and the kings and princes of tributary nations. During the feast he commanded his beautiful wife Vashti to come to him that his guests might see her beauty. Vashti refused. Then Ahasuerus, being advised by his councilors that such conduct would set a bad example of disobedience for other wives, divorced her. In due time he sought a new wife from among the most beautiful women in his empire; he finally chose the Jewess Hadassah, whose name in the Persian tongue is Esther. Esther was an orphan, brought up by her cousin Mordecai. She was as wise as she was beautiful and greatly pleased the king. Her favor with her husband was increased by her warning of a plot against his life, which Mordecai had overheard. Shortly after his escape from this plot, Ahasuerus raised Haman to the office of prime minister. Mordecai promptly incurred the pompous Haman's enmity by failing to salute him; for this the new minister determined to exterminate all the Jews. He persuaded the king to give him authority to destroy a "certain people" who were spreading sedition, and letters were sent out, bearing the royal seal, to this effect all over Ahasuerus' domains.

When Mordecai informed Esther of the approaching calamity, the queen's patriotism was aroused. She resolved to save the Jews, even at the risk of her own life. After fasting and prayer for divine guidance, the resourceful woman devised a plan to save her people. Risking the king's displeasure—and the penalty of death—she presented herself before him unannounced. However, so great was his love for her, he received her kindly and asked her to make her request, promising to grant it even before he knew what it was. Her request was an invitation of himself and Haman to a banquet. While the banquet was being prepared, the king and Haman occupied themselves each with his own business. Haman boasted of favor with the royal house and prepared a gallows to hang his enemy Mordecai. The king, hearing that Mordecai had not been rewarded for saving his life, prepared to honor him. He called Haman to him and asked, "What shall be done unto the man whom the king delighteth to honour?" Haman thinking himself the man, described a spectacular reward. His hatred for Mordecai was by no means lessened when the king commanded him to do the things he had described for Mordecai. Haman dared not disobey, but wrathful and humiliated he "hasted to his house mourning" when the ceremony was over.

However, he came hopefully to the queen's banquet. How great was his dismay when Esther declared her nationality and told the king that Haman had plotted to destroy all her people! Ahasuerus in great wrath ordered Haman hanged on the same gallows he had prepared for Mordecai, recalled his orders against the Jews, and urged them to defend themselves, and made "Mordecai great in the king's house." In thankfulness for this deliverance, the Jews ordained the feast of Purim.

If there had been no Esther, it is quite probable that the restoration of Jerusalem by Ezra and Nehemiah would never have been permitted.

The ruins of the palace at Shushan have been excavated and many of the details of Esther's story verified.

The authorship of the book is unknown, but from the intimate knowledge of court life it contains, it is often ascribed to Mordecai. The Jews hold the book in veneration second only to the books of Moses.

J O B

The Book of Job is the first of the five poetical books of the Bible, the other four being The Psalms, Proverbs, Ecclesiastes, and the Song of Solomon. It is the story of a patriarchal chieftain of immense wealth and influence in the land of Uz, who was suddenly confronted by overwhelming trouble and suffering despite his piety, benevolence, and righteous life. The lesson that it teaches is the reward of constancy in the face of disaster.

The book opens with a prologue in which Satan declares to God that there is no such thing as disinterested goodness. God refutes the claim and points to Job as an example. Satan says that were Job under persecution he would turn from God. God accepts Satan's challenge and gives Job over to the torments of Satan, stipulating only that his life shall be spared. In rapid succession Job loses his wealth and his children. Then comes distressing illness to himself. Even his wife tells him to "curse God and die," but throughout his calamities Job remains constant to God. In his distress three friends, Eliphaz, Bildad, and Zophar, come to comfort him. The second division of the book consists of their counsel and of Job's replies. The speeches of the three friends follow one pattern: Job's sufferings are divine punishment for secret sins, and by inference Job is a hypocrite. Job patiently answers their arguments, noting that they too are not perfect, yet God has not brought trouble upon them.

Then up speaks Elihu, a young man, with modesty but fervor. He was angered at Job because "he justified himself rather than God," and angry at the three friends because "they had found no answer, and yet condemned Job." He emphasizes the concept that God is not a petty and capricious tyrant but that the afflictions with which men are visited are for the strengthening of their spiritual selves. Elihu's speech forms the third part of the book. The book ends with the speech of Jehovah and restoration of Job to well-earned health, happiness, and prosperity.

The authorship and date of the dramatic poem are not certainly known. In its lofty and solemn thought it is poetry of the highest order. The character of the actors is vividly brought out in their speeches. The scene is laid in the land of Uz, probably a strip of land between Arabia and Palestine extending east from Edom northerly toward the Euphrates, a fertile country once densely populated.

THE PSALMS

The book of The Psalms has been called "the prayer book of the Church." It is a collection of sacred poetry and is the most comprehensive book in the Bible, considering its marvelous scope in dealing with the great interests of the Bible, together with its historical and Messianic elements.

Five Books. The book of The Psalms, one hundred and fifty in all, comes to us in five books, each ending with a doxology in Psalms 41; 72; 89; 106; 150. BOOK ONE contains Psalms 1 to 41. Thirty-seven of the psalms in this first book are ascribed in the titles to David, distinguished by the frequent use of the name Jehovah (Lord), the covenant God. BOOK TWO comprises Psalms 42 to 72: Psalms of "the sons of Korah," 42 to 47; of David, 51 to 65, and 68 to 70. They are probably a compilation for the Tabernacle and the Temple services. Here the name Elohim (God) predominates, in one psalm (53) being altered from Jehovah (14). BOOK THREE consists of Psalms 73 to 89. 73 to 83 are ascribed to Asaph; Psalms 84, 85, and 87 to the sons of Korah. Psalm 86 is entitled "A Prayer of David." Psalm 88 is ascribed both to the sons of Korah and to Heman the Ezrahite, and Psalm 89 to Ethan the Ezrahite. BOOK FOUR contains Psalms 90 to 106. Psalm 90 is described in the title as "A Prayer of Moses the man of God." Psalms 101 and 103 are ascribed to David. All the others of Book Four are anonymous. BOOK FIVE comprises Psalms 107 to 150. Fifteen of these, according to the Hebrew titles, are Davidic. Psalms 120 to 134 are entitled "Songs of Degrees" or "Ascents." This title has also been translated, "Songs of the Upgoings," "Pilgrim Psalms," "The Traveler's Hymn Book." These psalms were probably intended to be sung by pilgrims on their way to Jerusalem.

THE VALUE OF THE PSALMS. The value of the psalms is twofold. First, they are models of devotion. Many of the portions of the Bible represent God as speaking to man, but here man is speaking to God. By the psalms we may test the innermost feelings of our hearts, and by them know whether our thoughts are healthy and true, whether they are of God or ourselves. Secondly, they give us many foreshadowings of our Lord's history, sufferings, and glory. See Psalm 22. For His glory see Psalms 2; 45; 72; 110; 132. Psalm 118:22 hints at His rejection by the Jews;

Psalm 68:18 suggests His ascension and the gift of the Spirit, and Psalm 117 is a call to the Gentiles. See also Romans 15:11.

Many of the psalms have various descriptions such as Michtam, "golden poem," or Maschil, "choice ode." The title of Psalm 4 means Neginoth, "stringed instruments," and in the title of the Sixth and the Twelfth Psalms, we have Sheminith, "the octave bass," indicating that they were for male voices.

On Alamoth, Psalm 46, is translated "after the manner of maidens," that is, a soprano song. Muth-labben in the introduction to Psalm 9 probably means that it is to be set to the tune "Death of the Son."

The word "Selah" appears seventy-one times in The Psalms, and three times in The Book of Habakkuk. It probably indicates a pause in the music, perhaps a rest in the vocal part while the instrumental music continued. "To the chief," a phrase occurring fifty-five times, probably refers to the leader of the Temple choir or of the instrumental music.

The Psalms have been classified as follows:

1. Didactic Psalms: on the character of good and bad men, their happiness and misery: 1; 5; 7; 9; 12; 14; 15; 17; 24; 25; 32; 34; 36; 37; 50; 52; 53; 58; 73; 75; 84; 91; 92; 94; 112; 121; 125; 127; 128; 133; on the excellency of the divine law, 19; 119; on the vanity of human life, 39; 49; 90; on the duty of rulers, 82; 101; on humility, 131.

2. There are psalms of praise and adoration, acknowledgments of God's goodness and mercy, and particularly of his care of good men: 23; 34; 36; 91; 100; 103; 107; 117; 121; 145; 146; acknowledgments of his power, glory, and attributes generally: 8; 19; 24; 29; 33; 47; 50; 65; 66; 76; 77; 93; 95; 97; 99; 104; 111; 113; 115; 134; 139; 147; 148; 150.

3. Psalms of thanksgiving: for mercies to individuals: 9; 18; 22; 30; 34; 40; 75; 103; 108; 116; 138; 144; for mercies to the Israelites generally, 46; 48; 65; 66; 68; 76; 81; 85; 98; 105; 124; 126; 129; 135; 136; 149.

DEVOTIONAL PSALMS: expressive of penitence, called emphatically the seven Penitential Psalms: 6; 32; 38; 51; 102; 130; 143; expressive of trust under affliction: 3; 16; 27; 31; 54; 56; 57; 61; 62; 71; 86; expressive of extreme dejection, though not without hope: 13; 22; 69; 77; 88; 143; prayers in times of severe distress: 4; 5; 11; 28; 41; 55; 59; 64; 70; 109; 120; 140; 141; 143; prayers when deprived of public worship: 42; 43; 63; 84; prayers asking help in consideration of the uprightness of his cause: 7; 17; 26; 35; prayers in time of affliction and persecution: 44; 60; 74; 79; 80; 83; 89; 94; 102; 129; 137; prayers of intercession: 20; 67; 122; 132; 144.

PSALMS EMINENTLY PROPHETICAL: 2; 16; 22; 40; 45; 68; 69; 72; 97; 110; 118, mostly Messianic.

HISTORICAL PSALMS: 78; 105; 106.

David was known as "the sweet psalmist of Israel" (II Samuel 23:1) by a people whose hearts were full of gratitude for his utterances.

Only thirty-four of the psalms are without titles. The superscriptions of the others indicate:

1. The liturgical character of the psalm, e.g., "For the precentor, or

chief musician" or the musical or religious features of the psalm, "a maschil," "a shiggaion," "a michtam," "a prayer," or "a song of praise," etc.

2. The instrument to be used in playing the accompaniment to the psalm.

3. The measure or melody to which it was to be sung.

4. The event that prompted the composition of the psalm or the occasion on which it was to be used.

5. The author. The following are named in the superscriptions in the Hebrew Bible, as authors of the psalms: Moses (one), Solomon (two), Asaph (twelve), Heman the Ezrahite (one), Ethan the Ezrahite (one), the sons of Korah (ten), and David (seventy-three). An anonymous psalm, in some cases, may, it is thought, be ascribed to the author of the preceding psalm. David, no doubt, wrote some of the anonymous psalms. We speak of certain psalms as the psalms of David because David was the principal writer or compiler. A few of them were in existence before David's time and were greatly enlarged by David and further added to from generation to generation, reaching completion in the time of Ezra.

The instruments used included stringed instruments, mainly the harp and psaltery; wind instruments as the flute, pipe, horn, and trumpet; percussion instruments, as the timbrel and cymbal. David's orchestra was composed of four thousand players (I Chronicles 23:5).

The most conspicuous and persistent thought running through the book is the psalmist's trust in God. We have in this book songs of praise, trust, lamentations, reflections on God's providence, expressions of faith, resignation, joy in God's presence, psalms of personal circumstances of the psalmist, psalms historical, and royal psalms. Others are didactic in character, having reference to matters of religion or morality. The theology of the book of The Psalms does not differ from that of the prophetical books. The use of the psalms was twofold. They were used in the public services of the Israelites and also in their private devotions.

The chief lessons of the psalms are as follows:

1. The presence and resistance of the enemy and prayer for deliverance.

2. The recital of God's dealings with the nation, his grace and goodness.

3. Appeals to the world to praise God. The response to which has become world-wide, for people of all denominations worship God in these venerable psalms.

4. The world, man, and God's rule over all.

5. The coming of Christ, his suffering and glory.

The greatest favorite among the psalms is Psalm 23; the most Messianic, 22; the shortest, 117; those most appealing to the discouraged, 34 and 37; the most penitential, 51; the psalm of the millennium, 72; the psalm for the traveler, 121. The longest psalm is 119. It is also the longest chapter in the Bible. There are 176 verses, and every verse, except three, mentions God's word, under one or another of these names: law, testimonies, judgments, statutes, commandments, precepts, word, ordinances, or ways.

PROVERBS

The book of The Psalms is primarily a book of devotion; Proverbs is a book of practical ethics, a collection of wise sayings, mostly by Solomon, about the practical affairs of life. These proverbs may be grouped into five parts by the introductions to each group of chapters: (1) The Proverbs of Solomon, 1 to 9. (2) The Proverbs of Solomon, 10 to 24. (3) The Proverbs of Solomon, probably copied by Hezekiah, 25 to 29. (4) The words of Agur, 30. (5) The words of King Lemuel, 31. Nothing is known of Agur except that to him is ascribed the authorship of the proverbs in the thirtieth chapter. Some have said that King Lemuel is possibly another name for Solomon; however, this is not at all certain. Solomon bears about the same relation to Proverbs that David does to The Psalms.

A proverb is a short, pithy, axiomatic saying, either by way of antithesis or comparison. The proverbs are unconnected and are designed to serve as instruction to the young. Such wise and practical thoughts in this form are likely to stick in the mind. The book of Proverbs is, therefore, a "collection of maxims, woven into a didactic poem around the general topic Wisdom, the eternal companion and delight of God, making a popular system of ethics." Solomon was a great king, famous for his riches and also for his wisdom. As a young king, when he felt the burdens of the kingdom upon him, he prayed for "an understanding heart" (I Kings 3:4–15). He wrote 1,005 songs and 3,000 proverbs. He lectured on natural science and zoölogy (I Kings 4:32–34). His wisdom drew people from different parts of the land to hear him, "And there came of all people to hear the wisdom of Solomon, from all kings of the earth, which had heard of his wisdom." By this passage we see that his intellectual attainments were the wonder of his time. Three books of the Bible are attributed to him, which give to all posterity his great lessons of life. He wrote about wisdom, righteousness, fear of God, knowledge, morality, chastity, diligence, self-control, trust in God, tithes, the right use of riches, consideration toward the poor, control of the tongue, kindness to enemies, choice of companions, avoidance of bad women, praise of good women, training of children, industry, honesty, avoidance of idleness, sin of laziness, justice, helpfulness, humanity, contentment, cheerfulness, reverence, and common sense.

ECCLESIASTES

The Hebrew name of the book is Koheleth, which means "Preacher." It is intended to mean Solomon as seen in the statement, "Words of Koheleth, the son of David, king in Jerusalem." The ancient interpreters regarded Solomon as the author. This is a book of man, "under the sun," reasoning about life; it is the best man can do, with the knowledge that there is a holy and just God, and that he will bring everything into judgment. The key phrases are "under the sun," "I perceived," "I said in my heart." Inspiration gives that which is accurate, but the conclusions and the reasonings are, after all, man's. Life devoted altogether to worldly things is truly "vanity." The problem presented by this book is the problem of every life. It deals with the interpretation of life. The author deals with these standpoints, hence the book falls into two parts: (I) The materialistic interpretation of life (chapters 1 to 10). What is the highest good aside from all the ruling principles of the future and of God. (II) Life interpreted from the standpoint of such ruling principles as the future and God, and the coming Judgment (chapters 11 and 12). This is quite different, and life takes on a different meaning. "It is not all of life to live, nor all of death to die." There is a future, and a righteous God to be taken into account. Eternity may be the keynote of this book. All the earthly pursuits and pleasures, separate and apart from a sure hope of immortality, are utterly insufficient to bring real happiness to mankind. Solomon, with all his great wisdom, was not sure of one thing—and that one thing was the future. There were many hints in the Old Testament of the future life, but it was not until the coming of Christ that immortality was brought to light by his Resurrection from the dead. Solomon was in position to see earthly life at its best. He could explore it from every angle of pleasure, for he enjoyed life's richest honors; but in the end his heart was overwhelmed with its emptiness. It was far from satisfying, and there was a longing for something beyond what he had ever seen or enjoyed in life. All through the book there is a longing for that which he has not yet known. The starving human heart and the mournful spirit with their craving after something not yet found to satisfy is very prominent throughout the entire book. This condition is always prevalent without the knowledge of Christ and the vision of the future. Let us compare Solomon and Jesus. Solomon used his vast powers and great riches to minister to his own pleasures, and this book in which we find his philosophy of life has a very sad note. He tells us that all is vanity and vexation of spirit. Jesus also had great powers, and these he used not to minister to his own pleasures but to help the poor and suffering whom he contacted as he "went about doing good." Jesus talked not of the vanity of life, but of his joy. Even up to and under the shadow of the cross he expressed that joy.

SONG OF SOLOMON

In the Hebrew this book is called The Song of Songs, that is, the most beautiful of songs. As a poem, it is considered by scholars who are familiar with the structure of Hebrew poetry a superb composition. It is intended to display the victory of constant and humble love over the temptations of wealth and royalty. The tempter is Solomon; the object of his seductive endeavors is a Shulammite shepherdess, who, surrounded by the glories of the court and fascinations of great splendor, pines for the shepherd from whom she has been involuntarily separated. The flatteries and promises of the king are unavailing, and the constancy of the shepherdess triumphs. She is reunited to her lover, and together they return home, visiting on their way the tree beneath whose shade they first plighted their troth. Many eminent writers, however, have maintained that the book is an allegory, intended to set forth the love of Christ for the Church. Looking at this song from the position of the Old Testament, its idea is: "Thy Maker is thy husband." Identical with this is the New Testament idea: "The bride the Lamb's wife."

I S A I A H

The first of the Major Prophets is Isaiah. It has been said of him that "in some of his rhapsodies he reaches heights unequaled by Shakespeare, Milton, or Homer." He is quoted more times in the New Testament than any other prophet. Isaiah was called to the prophetic office during the reign of Uzziah, king of Judah, and his labors extended to the time of Hezekiah, a period of twenty-two years, or longer. Some scholars advance the opinion that he lived through the reign of Hezekiah and into that of Manasseh. Rabbinic tradition says that Isaiah's father, Amoz, was a brother of King Amaziah, which would make him first cousin of King Uzziah and grandson of King Joash and thus of royal blood. Isaiah's prophecy of the coming of a Saviour is very definite: "A virgin shall conceive, and bear a son, and shall call his name Immanuel." "Immanuel," the name of the wonderful Child who would save and establish David's kingdom, means "God with us." Apparently speaking of the immediate deliverance from the Assyrian power, the prophet was in reality speaking of greater deliverance, in later times, by the Messiah. Some of Isaiah's prophecies, occasioned by a historic event, have reference both to the event and to the future that is foreshadowed. The fifty-third chapter of Isaiah and the Twenty-third Psalm are probably the best loved chapters in the entire Old Testament. The latter is a psalm of God's care for his people and the former is a picture of the Suffering Saviour. Isaiah's prophecy is written in the past tense: He "was" despised, and so forth, as if it had already come to pass. Most prophecies are uttered in the future tense, but in some of Isaiah's rhapsodies he seems to have been transported into the future and speaks as if he were an eyewitness.

Certain passages in Isaiah stand out with special interest. Chapters 1 to 5 contain Isaiah's prophecies in the reigns of Uzziah and Jotham. Chapters 6 and 7 were written in the reign of Ahaz, when he was threatened by the forces of Pekah, king of Israel, and Rezin, king of Syria. Chapter 9:8 and chapter 10:4 contain a prophecy in the same reign against the king of Israel. Chapter 25 gives a glowing account of Messianic blessings. Chapters 37 and 39 were composed when the Assyrian was near with a force that seemed irresistible. The last chapters are supposed to have been written in the time of the Babylonian Captivity. Isaiah wrote other books (II Chronicles 26:22 and 32:32), which have not been preserved to us. He was a historian as well as a prophet.

JEREMIAH

Jeremiah lived about sixty years after the death of Isaiah. Isaiah had saved Jerusalem from the Assyrians; Jeremiah tried to save it from the Babylonians. He failed. Jeremiah was the son of Hilkiah, a priest of Anathoth. He began his ministry in the thirteenth year of the reign of Josiah, king of Judah. To escape the persecution of his fellow townsmen, including his own family, and to have a wider field for his ministry, Jeremiah came to Jerusalem. The finding of the Book of the Law at this time (II Kings 22:8) must have affected him as greatly as it did Josiah. In Jeremiah, Josiah had a strong ally in carrying forward his religious reforms. Following the death of Josiah, the former corruption reappeared, and from that time on to the fall of Judah, Jeremiah had to battle with the forces arrayed against him and his prophetical labors. Jeremiah lived through these terrible forty years that mark the close of the monarchy. He was brought into contact with the last five kings of Judah—Josiah, Jehoahaz, Jehoiakim, Jehoiachin, and Zedekiah. At the fall of the kingdom he was treated with consideration by Nebuchadnezzar, king of Babylon. He was permitted to remain in the land with the remnant and was taken by them to Egypt, where, according to tradition, he spent the remainder of his days. He was contemporary with the four prophets, Zephaniah, Habakkuk, Ezekiel, and Daniel. Jeremiah has been called "the weeping prophet," and perhaps because of his tender nature it has been assumed that he was a weakly man. The truth is quite contrary. There was no man more courageous or heroic in Judah.

This book is lacking in systematic arrangement. However, the following is given: (1) The call of Jeremiah (chapter 1); (2) the sinfulness of the Jews (chapters 2 to 24); (3) review of the nations: (a) the geographical scope (chapters 46 to 49); (b) captivity predicted (chapter 25); (c) historical appendix (chapters 26 to 29); (4) the promise of better times (chapters 30 to 35): (a) exiles assured (chapters 30 and 31); (b) type of the restoration (chapters 32 and 33); (c) fall of Jerusalem predicted (chapter 34); (d) reward of the Rechabites (chapter 35); (5) conclusion: (a) burning of the roll by the king (chapter 36); (b) Baruch instructed (chapter 44).

LAMENTATIONS

This book sounds like a funeral dirge over the destruction of Jerusalem, and probably should be regarded as an appendage to Jeremiah. The last chapter of Jeremiah, which describes the burning of Jerusalem and the beginning of the Babylonian Exile, should be read as an introduction to this book. The author's name is not mentioned in this book; it has, however, been ascribed to Jeremiah. In this book are contained the utterances of Jeremiah's sorrow over the capture of Jerusalem and the destruction of the Temple. It consists of five chapters, each of which is a separate poem, complete in itself, and having a distinct subject. It is one of the most exquisitely beautiful of the Sacred Books. It enters largely into the order of the Latin Church for the services of Passion Week. An examination of the five poems will enable us to judge how far each stands by itself, how far they are connected as parts forming a whole. We should deal with them as they are, not forcing our own meanings into them, looking on them not as prophetic or didactic or historical, but simply as lamentations, exhibiting, like other elegies, the different phases of a pervading sorrow.

E Z E K I E L

Ezekiel, the son of Buzi, was a prophet of the Captivity. Like his predecessor, Jeremiah, he was a priest. One tradition makes Ezekiel the servant of Jeremiah. He was taken captive in the captivity of Jehoiachin, eleven years before the destruction of Jerusalem, and was a member of a community of Jewish exiles who settled on the banks of the Chebar, a river or stream of Babylonia. It was by this river "in the land of the Chaldeans" that God's message first reached him (chapters 1 and 3). His call took place in "the fifth year of King Jehoiachin's captivity," 595 B.C., "in the thirtieth year, in the fourth month." His labors seem to have extended over a period of twenty-two years, or to the twenty-seventh year of the Captivity. The arrangement of the book is precise, having as the central point of the predictions the destruction of Jerusalem, and the predictions are so related that every part refers to what precedes. The book naturally divides itself into two parts. The first part (chapters 1 to 24) consists of prophecies prior to the fall of Jerusalem. This group of prophecies may be cataloged as follows: (1) Fifth year of the Exile (chapters 1 to 7); (2) The sixth year of the Exile (chapters 8 to 19) wherein visions of the Temple and the city occur and scenes in Jerusalem are typically represented; (3) to the ninth year of the Exile (chapters 20 to 23) with descriptions of the sins of the nation and its approaching end, and restoration assured; (4) the ninth year of the Exile (chapter 24), with the siege of Jerusalem predicted and described. The second part contains prophecies after the fall of Jerusalem (chapters 25 to 48). Here are listed: (1) Judgment on heathen nations (chapters 25 to 32); (2) Israel's future (chapters 33 to 39), the watchman, Edom condemned, the vision of dry bones and union with Israel and Judah, and the fall of Gog and Magog; (3) Visions (chapters 40 to 48) of the Temple, people and city, and the times of the Gospel and of the Holy Spirit.

D A N I E L

The Book of Daniel was written partly in Hebrew and partly in the Chaldaic language. It is called the apocalypse of the Old Testament. To the old prophets, Daniel stands, in some sense, as a commentator; to succeeding generations as the herald of immediate deliverance. The book is divided into two nearly equal parts. The first of these contains chiefly historical incidents, while the second is entirely apocalyptic. The prophecies contained in the latter part extend from the days of Daniel to the general resurrection. Chapters 2; 7; and 9 should be studied together. Chapters may be listed as follows: The first six chapters of Daniel are mainly historical. The first four cover the reign of Nebuchadnezzar from the time Daniel and his friends, Shadrach, Meshach, and Abed-nego, came to the court. The chief incidents are Daniel's interpretation of the king's dream as a vision of the four world empires; the raising of the king's idol, the refusal of Daniel's friends to worship it and their condemnation to the fiery furnace, their deliverance and the king's amazement; Nebuchadnezzar's second dream, and Daniel's interpretation of it, the king's madness and recovery. Chapter 5 deals with the reign of Belshazzar. It describes the dissolute court, the handwriting on the wall, and the fall of Babylon, 538 B.C. In chapter 6 the beginning of the Persian dynasty under Darius and Cyrus is described, the prophet's deliverance from the lions, and his favor in the Persian court.

Chapters 7 to 12 are largely prophetic. Chapters 7 and 8 are a continuation of the prophecy in chapter 2 concerning the four world empires, chapter 9 is the prophecy of the coming of the Messiah, and chapters 10 to 12 are predictions of the troubles and tribulations ahead with a promise of the final resurrection.

HOSEA

Hosea, whose name signifies "Safety" or "Saviour," is called at the beginning of the book the son of Beeri, but we know nothing about his life. He is considered the first of the Minor Prophets. His book is set during the reign of Uzziah, Jotham, Ahaz, and Hezekiah, kings of Judah, but in the same sense its writing is limited to the reign of Jeroboam II, king of Israel, which was contemporaneous only with forty years of the reign of Uzziah. Hosea's prophetic career probably extended from 784 to 725 B.C., a period of fifty-nine years. There is general consent among commentators that the prophecies of Hosea were delivered in the Kingdom of Israel. The book of Hosea contains two parts. The first three chapters give what is generally, and probably correctly, considered a series of allegories directed against the idolatries of Israel. It is sometimes disputed whether the marriage of the prophet was a fact or an allegorical vision, but in either case it is illustrative of the relations of idolatrous Israel to her covenant God. The remaining chapters are chiefly occupied with denunciations against Israel, especially Samaria, for the worship of idols that prevailed there. Hosea's warnings are mingled with tender, pathetic expostulations. He shows a joyous faith in the coming Redeemer. The book earnestly teaches the unquenchable love of Jehovah for his erring people, the Israelites.

J O E L

Joel, of whom we know little, was the son of Pethuel. He probably lived in Judah, for his commission was for Judah, and he makes frequent mention of Judah and Jerusalem. He may have lived during the reign of Uzziah, thus being contemporary with Hosea and Amos. The book deals with (1) Judah's devastation. A call to prayer and fasting. It was a situation that was designed to cause the nation to pause in her spiritual decline. (2) Judgment and the promised blessing (chapter 2). The former is at hand, and it is time for repentance both to avert the calamity and to receive a great spiritual blessing. (3) The message to the heathen nations and to Zion (chapter 3). The enemies of Judah are specified and condemned, while Zion will be blessed.

A M O S

Amos was called to the prophetic office while a shepherd in Tekoa, a few miles south of Bethlehem. Although he lived in the Southern Kingdom, he prophesied for Israel. He was a man of the common people, without training in the schools of the prophets. The time is clearly indicated as during the reign of Uzziah in Judah and of Jeroboam II in Israel. The book falls into four parts, the first three being messages of judgments: (1) Judgments pronounced on six heathen nations, Syria, Tyre, Ammon, Philistia, Edom, and Moab. (2) Judgments pronounced on Judah and Israel. (3) Judgments variously represented. (4) The scattering and gathering of Israel. The captivity of the ten tribes is foretold, and the Messianic Kingdom and the calling of the Gentiles predicted. Compare Amos 9:11 and Acts 15:16.

O B A D I A H

The time of this book is uncertain, but it is commonly placed at 586 B.C. when the Babylonians destroyed Jerusalem, and the Edomites helped. Some place it earlier. There are some who are of the opinion that Obadiah was the same person who was governor of Ahab's house and who hid and fed one hundred prophets whom Jezebel would have destroyed. The book is a prophecy of the destruction of Edom.

J O N A H

The personal history of Jonah is brief and very well known. He is mentioned in II Kings 14:25, as prophesying in Israel, and predicting the success of Jeroboam. This is doubtless the oldest book of the Minor Prophets. This book tells how Jonah, fleeing by sea from the command of God to go to Nineveh and "cry against its wickedness," was overtaken by a great storm. The sailors threw him overboard, and he was swallowed by a great fish. While in this strait he repented of his disobedience and called upon God. He was cast ashore and preached to the people of Nineveh, who repented of their wickedness and were spared by God. This book is remarkable as being the record of a prophet sent, in that age, to the Gentiles. Jonah had no idea that the Ninevites would repent or that repentance would avert the judgment, as his proclamation contained nothing of repentance or mercy.

M I C A H

Micah lived in a town on the Philistine border named Moresheth. It was about thirty miles southwest of Jerusalem. Micah was preaching there about the same time Isaiah preached in Jerusalem and Hosea in Israel. The time was about 740–700 B.C., in the reigns of Jotham, Ahaz, and Hezekiah. Jotham and Hezekiah were good kings, but Ahaz was extremely wicked. Micah was contemporary with Isaiah, and part time with Hosea, whose ministry was closing as Micah was beginning his. Micah prophesied for and declared the fall of both kingdoms. His messages were against Jerusalem and Samaria, the two capitals that were largely responsible for the sins of the people. He lays the responsibility of the idolatrous, desperate, sinful condition of society at the feet of the rulers. He accuses them of corruption, bribery, injustice, oppression of the poor, and robbery. Calamity, doom, and captivity were near at hand. A few of the people would be saved, and for them there would be a glorious future. Micah saw some of his prophecies come true. In 734 B.C., a few years after he began his prophecy, the northern part of Israel was invaded by the Assyrians. It was only thirteen years later, 721, that Samaria fell, and afterwards Lachish, near Micah's home, was devastated by Sennacherib. But in Micah's old age came the great deliverance of Jerusalem. The outstanding feature of Micah's book is the naming of Bethlehem as the birthplace of the Messiah (chapter 5:2).

N A H U M

Nineveh, the capital of the Assyrian Empire, had ruled the world for three hundred years. The Assyrians destroyed Israel in 721 B.C. and also threatened Judah. The books of Jonah and Nahum should be read consecutively. It was one hundred and fifty years earlier that Jonah had been sent to Nineveh to warn the people to repent. The burden of Nahum's prophecy was the destruction of Nineveh, which was remarkably fulfilled. The Medes and Babylonians, 607 B.C., destroyed Nineveh; in this they were aided by a sudden rise of the Tigris, which carried away a large part of the wall. The destruction was so complete that when Alexander the Great fought the Battle of Arbela near by, 331 B.C., no one knew of the site of Nineveh. This is a graphic description of the destruction of the proud city.

HABAKKUK

Habakkuk prophesied approximately about the twelfth or thirteenth year of the reign of Josiah. He witnessed the invasion of Nebuchadnezzar when the first captives were carried away to Babylon, and it is the overthrow of that nation which is the subject of this prophecy. Thus we find three prophets divinely appointed to speak the judgment of Jehovah against three nations: Obadiah, the doom of Edom; Nahum, the doom of Assyria; Habakkuk, the doom of Babylon. The latter is the crucible in which Judah is to be refined from her idolatry. "The just shall live by his faith" (Habakkuk 2:4) is a window in this book of prophecy through which those in Habakkuk's day could look into the immediate future.

The prophet's prayer (chapter 3) is one of the greatest prayers of the Bible, and one of the finest productions of all literature.

ZEPHANIAH

Zephaniah lived in the reign of Josiah, 639–608 B.C. He was a great-great grandson of Hezekiah, a kinsman of King Josiah. His book contains furious denunciations of the sins of his own people. Without mentioning the Messiah directly, bright promises relating to him permeate the whole book. His message rang with impending judgment on the idolatrous nations Philistia, Moab, Ammon, Egypt, Assyria, and Judah; Judah shall be restored and Jehovah will yet be victorious over the idols of all other nations.

HAGGAI

The opening words of this book gives us the date. The actual year was the second year of Darius I, that is, 520 B.C., and it was on the first day of the sixth month that Haggai began to deliver his message to Zerubbabel, the governor of Jerusalem, and to Joshua, the high priest (chapter 1). Like Joel, he spoke in an unpromising time. A spirit of lethargy had fallen upon the people. Fifteen years before, the foundations of the Temple had been laid, but in all these years nothing had been done. The Samaritans, to whom Zerubbabel had refused permission to help in the building, set themselves to frustrate his purpose. They invoked the help of King Artaxerxes, and the work was stopped. The early enthusiasm of the people had faded, and in its place was a spirit of apathy and selfishness. It was against such that Haggai spoke. Haggai's message was effective. The leaders and the people "obeyed the voice of the Lord their God," and the building of the Temple was resumed. It was completed in about four years, and dedicated in the sixth year of the reign of Darius, 516 B.C.

ZECHARIAH

Zechariah was called to the prophetic office in the second year of Darius, 520 B.C., almost immediately after the call of Haggai. He and his people had been restored by Cyrus to their native land after their exile in Babylon. In this reëstablishment in Palestine the matter of first importance was the rebuilding of the Temple and the reorganization of the religion and its appointments. The work on the Temple had been interrupted and the people had fallen into a state of indifference, and their once fervent zeal had diminished. It was the mission of Haggai and Zechariah to stimulate the people to resume the building of the Temple. More than any other prophet except Isaiah, Zechariah gives a Messianic note to his prophecy. This is one of the greatest Messianic prophecies in the Old Testament.

MALACHI

Malachi gives the final message to a disobedient nation. Nothing is known of his personal history. The remnant of the Jews had been home about one hundred years, and they were prone to neglect the house of God. The priesthood was degenerate. The sacrifices were inferior. Tithes were neglected. Divorce was common. Malachi assures the people that the Messiah is coming. Four hundred years later the Messiah came. So the Old Testament closes with prophecies of the Messiah, his person, work, and his forerunner. The last words of the Old Testament form a description of the Messiah who actually did not come until four hundred years later.

THE INTERVAL BETWEEN THE OLD AND NEW TESTAMENTS

The history of the Hebrews and the things they accomplished in the period between the Old and the New Testaments have been delivered to us by the books of the Maccabees, Josephus, and other writings of a secular source.

Judea remained subject to the kings of Persia for about two hundred years. Afterwards it was annexed to the province of Syria, and the administration of affairs was in the hands of the high priest, subject to the control of the provincial rulers. In 335 B.C. Alexander, king of Macedonia, began to lay waste the Persian Empire. When he had overthrown the Persian army, Syria and neighboring countries fell under his power, and Tyre was taken after a long, stubborn resistance.

Alexander permitted the Jews to pursue the free enjoyment of their laws and religion and exempted them from tribute during their Sabbatical year. When he had built the city of Alexandria, he made room for a great many Jews there and gave them the same privileges allowed to his Greek subjects. Alexander reigned twelve years. Upon his death, his dominions were divided among his generals, and Judea became a bone of contention between the kings of Syria and Egypt. Ptolemy Soter, the king of Egypt, had thousands of Jews brought into that country, settled them there, and treated them with kindness. He gave them equality with the Greeks of Alexandria. Greek was the common language of that country, and it was quickly learned by the Jews. Thus Greek became the native language of their children born there. These Greek-speaking Jews in time came to be called Hellenists, or Grecian Jews, a name which after a while was applied to all Jews speaking Greek in foreign countries. These Grecian Jews had synagogues in Alexandria, where they used Greek translations of the writings of Moses and the prophets.

In 277 B.C. Ptolemy Philadelphus, a son of Ptolemy Soter, was king. He employed seventy-two Jews to translate the Holy Scriptures out of the original Hebrew into the Greek language. This was done in the seventieth year of his reign. This translation, called the Septuagint because it was the work of some seventy scholars, contributed largely to the spread of the knowledge of true religion through the western part of the world.

The Jewish nation had been subject to the kings of Egypt for about eighty years. Then it became, by conquest of Antiochus the Great, subject to the kings of Syria, but the Jews had been enjoying the privilege of being governed by their own laws under the high priest and council of the nation. In time God raised up one of the noble family of the Asmoneans. Mattathias, a priest, with the help of his five sons, killed those who were sent by King Antiochus to compel them to offer abominable sacrifices. They were followed by many, and a thousand perished. After that Mattathias gathered about him a number of faithful men and undertook to deliver the people and to restore the worship of the Lord God of Israel. Being old, the work was too hard, and he did not live to see its completion. His eldest son, Judas, succeeded his father to command the army, with the assistance of his brother Simon, a very prudent man. The motto which he placed on his banner was "Who is like unto thee, O Lord, among the gods?" (Exodus 15:11). The Hebrew words are Mi Camaka Baalin Jehovah. It is said that from the initial letters of these words, M. C. B. J. is to be derived the word Maccabi or Maccabee. This became the surname of the family.

In 165 B.C., after having been victorious several times over the troops of Antiochus, Judas Maccabaeus gained possession of Jerusalem. The first thing he did was to repair and to purify the Temple for the worship of God. In 161 B.C. Demetrius sent Nicanor with a great army against Judas Maccabaeus, whom he hoped to take by surprise. They engaged in battle and General Nicanor was killed. King Demetrius sent another army of twenty thousand men against Judas Maccabaeus who had only eight hundred men with him. Nevertheless, he engaged in battle, and Judas Maccabaeus was killed. His brother Jonathan, chosen general to succeed him, entered into an alliance with the Romans. This, according to Josephus, was the first league that was ever known between the Jews and the Romans.

In 153 B.C. Alexander Balos, the son of King Antiochus Epiphanes, entered Syria with an army and was careful to cultivate the friendship of Jonathan, and to oblige him conferred on him the priesthood. In 152 Jonathan wore the holy vestments on the seventh month of the one hundred and sixtieth year of the Grecian kingdom at the Feast of the Tabernacles.

In 65 B.C. there were violent contests for the throne that had a weakening effect on the Jews and made them poorly prepared to withstand the growing power of Rome, which in the same year subjugated Syria and soon afterwards conquered Egypt. In 63 Pompey marched an army into Judea, took Jerusalem, and made the country tributary to Rome, although it was still governed by Maccabean princes. It was during the reign of the later princes that Herod Antipater, an Idumean by birth, secured a position of power and influence in the land. After his death his son Herod the Great so ingratiated himself with the Romans that he was appointed to the position of king of Judea in place of Antigonus. Because the people were so attached to the Maccabean kings, Herod the Great had some difficulty in possessing the kingdom. He had to come against Jerusalem with an army of sixty thousand men, and it was half a year before he took the city by storm. He murdered many of the inhabitants. In a short time he put to death Antigonus, thus ending the Asmonean dynasty, which had existed 126 years. Herod was a man of ability and ambition, but he was a cruel tyrant. He would gain his end by any unscrupulous means. He got rid of all the Asmonean family. He put to death his wife and two of his own sons. He degraded the high priesthood. To gain popularity and fame he enlarged and beautified the Temple at Jerusalem, thus making it in some respects a more magnificent Temple than that of Solomon. In many cities he erected heathen temples. He also built many public works, such as bridges, roads, baths, aqueducts, and harbors, all of which were paid for by heavy taxation. It was in the thirty-sixth year of the reign of Herod the Great, while Augustus was emperor at Rome that the Saviour was born at Bethlehem in Judea. Herod was succeeded in the government of the greater part of Palestine by his son, Archelaus, who was so cruel and unjust that in the tenth year of his reign complaint was made against him by the Jews, and Augustus banished him to Vienne in Gaul, where he died. Cyrenius, the president of Syria, was sent to reduce the countries over which Archelaus had reigned to a Roman province, and a governor of Judea was appointed under the title of procurator, subordinate to the president of Syria. The Jews were still allowed the privilege of worship without molestation. At this time the universal power of Rome gave assurance of internal peace and facilitated communication between the different parts of the then known world. For a time, at least, it opened a wider field for broadcasting the gospel. Therefore, Providence and prophecy bring us to the "fulness of time," when the expected Saviour of the World should be born. Here we have a brief history of the Hebrews for the interval between the Old and the New Testaments.

MATTHEW

The great theme of the New Testament is Christ and his work. Throughout the centuries his coming had been predicted. Although the Jews expected the Messiah's advent, few looked forward to his coming with eagerness. Those who did await him, expected a temporal rather than a religious leader. The Jewish nation had multiplied and found prosperity since the return from Babylon. In splendid fashion the people had rebuilt the Temple, and most of the rites and ceremonies had been restored, but real, vital, spiritual religion was lacking. Our word "gospel" is the Anglo-Saxon of the Greek "good tidings." If compounded of "good" and "spell" (story), it exactly represents the original. If, however, as one commentator thinks, it means "God's spell," the word embodies the fuller New Testament phrases "the gospel of God," or "of Christ," the source and substance of the good tidings. The Gospels give the teachings of Christ and the facts of his life, death, and Resurrection. The four Gospels are four biographies of Christ. They give us four different and truthful views of Christ. The first three are very much alike and for that reason these are called Synoptic Gospels, that is, those which see alike. The Gospel of Matthew was written for the Jew. It may be called the Gospel for the Kingdom. Although the book of Matthew follows in the main a chronological order, its material is grouped rather by subjects. It gives Christ's discourses quite fully as, for example, the Sermon on the Mount, and those discourses on the Second Coming of Christ and the end of the world. The genealogy of Jesus is traced back to David, thus showing His royal descent, and His claims of the Messiahship are established by prophecy. Then follows an account of Jesus' preparation for and induction into His ministry. Then there is the laying down of the new law for the Church in the Sermon on the Mount (chapters 5 to 7), and events in historical order recounting His miracles. The appointment of apostles to preach the Kingdom marks an important step in Jesus' career. Then is set forth the doubts and opposition excited by his activity in the minds of many, among John the Baptist's disciples, and among the Pharisees, followed by a series of parables on the nature of the Kingdom. The varying effect of Christ's ministry on his countrymen, on Herod, on the people of Gennesaret, on scribes, and Pharisees, and on multitudes whom He feeds and his sympathetic and spiritual reactions contrast dramatically with the personal note in his revelation to the disciples of the sufferings that awaited him and his directions as to their conduct when this time arrived. Then followed the events of Christ's journey to Jerusalem, his triumphal entrance into the city, the opposition of the priests and denunciation of the Pharisees. Matthew then records the last discourses; Jesus as Lord and Judge of

Jerusalem; and the book ends with the solemn story of the Passion and the glad news of the Resurrection.

MARK

The Gospel According to Mark opens with John the Baptist's cry, "Prepare ye the way of the Lord," and quickly goes on to the baptism of Jesus, his temptation, and the beginning of his ministry. Before the first chapter ends we find Jesus on a preaching tour of Galilee, after having called to discipleship Peter and Andrew and John and James and performed many miracles. The story turns swiftly, with great crowds of people assembling to hear the new teachings and to see the miracles that this new preacher is performing. The skeptics go away amazed, glorifying God and saying, "We never saw it on this fashion." But the Pharisees and scribes sought to trap Jesus, for he observed not their ceremonial laws, and with such answers as "the sabbath was made for man, and not man for the sabbath" confounded their philosophy. By this time He had assembled the Twelve and was teaching the multitudes by parables that they could understand and remember: the candle under the bushel, the sower, the mustard seed. His preaching he interspersed with miracles of healing of mind, of body, and even raising of the dead, as Jairus' daughter.

Jesus was now in Herod's country, and that ruler, hearing of His miracles, was greatly troubled, for he supposed Him to be John the Baptist, whom he had murdered, risen from the dead. Jesus sent out the Twelve to preach and to heal. The apostles gathered themselves together unto Jesus, and told him all things, both what they had done and what they had taught. A multitude was continually following Jesus, and at this time he performed the miracle of the five loaves and the two fishes in order to feed the people. At this time, too, he walked upon the water to his followers' storm-tossed ship and then stilled the waves.

The Pharisees, still pursuing Jesus, were again openly critical of him because of his disregard for their ceremonial traditions. Jesus not only rebuked them, but almost immediately thereafter healed the daughter of a Greek woman—a foreigner—which must have still further vexed the bigoted Pharisees. Again Jesus fed a multitude with seven loaves. Yet the Pharisees demanded a sign of His divine office. After this Jesus set out for Caesarea Philippi, and on the way told his disciples of his coming death and Resurrection. Six days later he took Peter and James and John and went to a high mountain where He was transfigured and communed with Moses and Elias.

Again Jesus told his disciples of his impending death and Resurrection, but not for a moment did this impending suffering slaken his ardor. He vigorously refuted the Pharisees' position on divorce, he exalted the innocence of children, he preached charity to the rich man. All this time he was healing and comforting. Then Mark describes the triumphal entry into Jerusalem, Christ's purification of the Temple, his arguments with the churchmen, and his pronouncement of the great commandment: "Love one another." Then comes the Last Supper, Christ's betrayal, his trial with Pilate's weak defense, his crucifixion, burial, Resurrection, and final appearance to his disciples. As for the disciples, "they went forth, and preached every where."

L U K E

The Gospel of St. Luke is said to have been written for the Greeks. Sometimes styled the Gospel of the Son of Man, Luke's delineation of the life and works of Christ adapts itself to the Greek ideal of the perfect man. Greek philosophy concerned itself with mankind rather than race or nation, and Luke's account, as in the genealogy of Jesus to Adam, makes him the son of mankind rather than the son of the Jewish race, as does Matthew's genealogy, which goes back only to King David, the Jew. Greek philosophy sought to create the perfect man through development of intelligence. Luke's Gospel appealed to the thoughtful, cultured, philosophic Greek mind by offering a complete and orderly story, emphasizing the qualities of philosophy, wisdom, reason, and beauty which would appeal to it. In writing the book he produced what has been called "the most beautiful book ever written." It is quite natural that Luke should adopt the viewpoint and style which he did. A native of Antioch, a city strongly impregnated with Greek ideals, he was probably the best educated of the apostles. Moreover, he was not born a Jew, for he is not counted among "them of the circumcision" by Paul (Colossians 4:11 and chapter 14). He was a physician and reputed to be an artist. His own personality coincided with the Greek ideal of the well-rounded, evenly balanced man. Luke, writing with great clearness, tells in a swiftly moving story the events of Christ's life in chronological sequence. The book begins with an account of the birth of John the Baptist and the events preceding the birth of Jesus. The birth of Jesus and the touching story of Simeon's blessing of the child follow. "And Jesus increased in wisdom and stature, and in favour with God and man." Next we find Jesus arguing with the priests in the Temple and astounding them by his wisdom. His baptism and temptation are related, and then begins the story of his ministry and his miracles. The account of Christ's trial and crucifixion is told with the dramatic directness of a well-trained journalist. The events following his burial and his Resurrection differ slightly in detail, but not in tenor from the other Gospels.

J O H N

The book of John has been called the Gospel for the Church—the spiritual Gospel. It is unlike the others. Christ is the divine Word— the God-Man. The divine Christ is the basis of faith. The divinity of Christ is established by six great miracles recorded only by John.

In several respects this Gospel is unique. It contains spiritual discourses recorded only by John. It alone gives an account of Jesus' early Judean ministry. It is the Gospel without a parable.

John was the disciple who was very near to Jesus, one of the three who were very close to Him. John was a native of the town of Bethsaida in Galilee. His father, Zebedee, was a fisherman, as was his brother James. John had once been a disciple of John the Baptist, but when the great preacher directed his attention to Christ, John at once attached himself to the Lord. He was one of his first disciples and is spoken of as "the disciple whom Jesus loved." He continued to reside at Jerusalem after the Ascension of the Lord, and removed, it is believed, to Ephesus about A.D. 65, where he exercised a powerful influence in spreading Christianity through Asia Minor. About A.D. 95 he was banished by the Emperor Domitian to the isle of Patmos, where he had the vision described in the book of Revelation. He afterwards returned to Ephesus, where he died in the third year of the reign of Trajan, A.D. 100, being then, it is thought, about ninety-four years of age. Ephesus and Patmos are claimed by various writers as the place at which this Gospel was written. The weight of evidence, however, seems to be in favor of Ephesus. Probably the date was about A.D. 78.

The contents of this Gospel of John may be arranged thus:

I. Eternity and Deity of Jesus. Jesus, the Light of the World, the incarnation, John's testimony, first disciples—John, Andrew, Simon, Philip, and Nathanael, water turned into wine, brief sojourn in Capernaum.

II. A Series of Incidents. Jesus cleanses the Temple, miracles in Jerusalem, Nicodemus, Jesus' ministry in lower Jordan, the Samaritan woman, the nobleman's son, a Sabbath miracle at Jerusalem, the feeding of five thousand, Jesus again at Jerusalem, the woman taken in adultery, Jesus continues discourse on his deity, Jesus heals a man born blind, the Good Shepherd, Feast of Dedication, beyond Jordan, Lazarus raised from the dead, the supper at Bethany, triumphal entry, Greeks desire to see Jesus, unbelief, Jesus' final Temple message, the Last Supper, house of many mansions, on way to Gethsemane, intercessory prayer, Jesus' arrest, his trial, Peter's denial, the crucifixion, blood and water, burial, the tomb of Jesus, Mary Magdalene goes to the tomb, Peter and John run to the tomb, Jesus appears to Mary Magdalene, Jesus appears to the Eleven, purpose of the book, Jesus appears to the seven, "And there are also many other things which Jesus did, the which, if they should be written every one, I suppose that even the world itself could not contain the books that should be written."

THE ACTS OF THE APOSTLES

The Acts of the Apostles gives us the story of the formation and expansion of the Church. We have the story of the spread of the gospel of Christ from Jerusalem to Rome. During the generation of the apostles, the gospel was preached in all directions until it reached every nation which was then known. Colossians 1:23. In the New Testament we read of its expansion over Palestine, and to Antioch in the north, westward through Asia Minor and then to Greece, and on to Rome. The Acts deals mainly with the activities of the early apostles in spreading the gospel, particularly the missionary labors of Paul. Paul was called the apostle to the Gentiles, which included all nations other than Jews. The important subject of the book is the extension of the gospel of Christ to the Gentile world. All through the Old Testament we have the story of God's dealing with the Hebrew nation, and the passing on through them of his blessing to all other nations. The prophets of old prophesied through the ages and looked forward in great hope toward the great day when God would use the Hebrew nation to be a blessing to all other nations. In this book of The Acts this great work among the nations is started and is soon to spread to all peoples, creating an international, as well as a national, household of God.

The book of The Acts of the Apostles is described as a second treatise by Luke. Its contents are such as to be of utmost consequence to the whole Church. They are the fulfilment of the promise of the Father by the descent of the Holy Spirit. The results of that outpouring are the dispersion of the gospel among Jews and Gentiles. We know little of Luke. His name is mentioned three times in the New Testament. In Colossians 4:14 he is called the "beloved physician," and in two other places (Philemon 24, and II Timothy 4:11) he is mentioned by Paul. The only Gentile writer of the Bible, he is believed to have been a native of Antioch, a man of culture and scientific education.

The book may be divided into two sections: (I) From Pentecost to the labors of Paul (chapters 1 to 12), with the following topics treated: The ascension and the preparations for Pentecost, Day of Pentecost, from Pentecost to the death of Stephen, persecution and dispersion, Saul's persecution of the church, labors of Philip, conversion of Saul, Peter at Joppa, the church at Antioch, martyrdom of James. (II) Paul, the apostle to the Gentiles (chapters 13 to 28), in which the following subjects are discussed: The First Missionary Journey, the council at Jerusalem, the Second Missionary Journey, the Third Missionary Journey, Paul's arrest and imprisonment at Rome.

In the first division of the book Jerusalem is the center, and Peter the prominent figure. In the second section Antioch is the center and Paul is the man of importance.

Paul was born in Tarsus of noted family, honored with Roman citizenship, and educated in Jerusalem. After his conversion, he spent three years preaching in Arabia and then journeyed to Tarsus and Antioch. In his missionary work he spent fifteen years in travel over Asia Minor and in Greece. His travels were interrupted by five years of imprisonment in Cæsarea and Rome. Released, he began his travels again in the East and finally returned to Rome.

ROMANS

The Epistle of Paul to the Romans has been called, next to the four Gospels, the most important book in the world. Perhaps it is because Paul gives a clear explanation of the understanding of the nature of the gospel. The theme of Romans is the "gospel of God." It has also been called "the great systematic statement of Christianity." The Epistle to the Romans was written some four years before Paul came to Rome as a prisoner. At the time of its writing Paul was personally unknown to this church, whose founder is unknown. This epistle suggests that the Roman church was quite strong and had existed for some time. It was distinctive in that its faith was extensively known. It seems evident from certain passages that the Gentile portion of the church may have exceeded in number the Jewish, although this is uncertain. Paul's main insistence is that man's justification before God rests, not on the law of Moses, but on the mercy of Christ. Paul wrote this letter to let the Roman brethren know that he was on his way. He arrived three years after this letter was written. Chapters 1 and 2 show the universal need of the gospel. Paul states the case in the opening chapter by declaring his interest in visiting the Romans in order to confirm their faith. Since he was prevented from doing so, he is sending by Phoebe this letter which sets forth in such comprehensive manner the doctrines of grace. It is the most systematic of the didactic epistles and treats especially the great doctrines that grounded the Reformation, the doctrine of justification by faith. The book falls into two general sections: (I) The world under sin and condemnation (chapters 1 to 3). Here Paul says that the pagan world is under condemnation, that the whole Jewish world is under condemnation, that all have sinned and that the whole world is under condemnation. (II) The world under grace (chapters 4 to 16). This part includes discourses on justification by faith, the believer's life in Christ, the salvation of Israel, Christian graces.

We find that the indwelling Spirit means not only that our sins are forgiven, but that there is an impartation of new life that makes us more than conquerors.

The climax of the apostle is reached in the eighth chapter of Romans as he wrote, "For I am persuaded"; he has the assurance, he is certain that there can come no separation. In mentioning some of the things that might separate, he speaks of "death" and "life" and, stressing, as it has been said, that sometimes life is a more dangerous separating force than death. The unseen powers, "angels, principalities," to all facts of the today, "things present," to the future, "things to come," Paul declares that there is no separation "from the love of God, which is in Christ Jesus."

FIRST CORINTHIANS

The First Epistle of Paul to the Corinthians is mainly about church disorders, such as factions in the church, immorality, lawsuits, meat

offered to idols, certain abuses of the Lord's Supper, false apostles, problems about marriage, disorderly conduct of assemblies, women's part in
the church, and heresies about the Resurrection. About three years after
Paul had left Corinth, while he was at Ephesus, a delegation of the leaders
of the Corinthian church was sent to Ephesus to consult Paul about the
church difficulties that are mentioned above. The resulting epistle was
written about A.D. 57. Paul had to contend with Judaizing teachers and
tendencies in some of these churches. It will be remembered that Paul
and Barnabas were sent as commissioners by the church at Antioch to the
council at Jerusalem, which was convened for the purpose of considering
the standing of Gentiles in the church, and the Judaistic requirements
being made of them. Paul was successful in that controversy in support
of the Gentiles and in the compromise he proposed. The bigotry of the
Jews and worldliness of the Gentiles of the Corinthian church, disorders,
and dissensions called forth this letter. A party spirit had grown up in
the church, the tendency being to select religious leaders, some choosing
Paul, some Apollos, and some Cephas. This epistle was designed to
correct this error, which Paul does by declaring "all are yours," whether
Paul or Apollos be your teachers. Paul received word concerning these
disturbing matters pertaining to marriage, eating of meat offered to idols,
the Lord's Supper, the wrong attitude to spiritual gifts, and the precious
doctrine of the Resurrection. These things are handled in Paul's masterly
manner in this epistle. He puts the matter of eating of meat on the high
plane of Christian example and service. Mistaken views of the Resurrection call forth the one great treatment of that essential doctrine. To those
aspiring to certain gifts, Paul points out what is far greater in the line of
Christian graces, the preëminence of love, the greatest of all gifts. Love
remains, for "love never faileth." The most powerful force in the uni-
verse, it is the essence of God's nature. It is irresistible, undying, and
eternal. The subject matter of this epistle may be gathered under four
heads:

I. The essential unity of the church (chapters 1 to 4), under the
topics unity threatened by the party spirit, unity in the cross of Christ,
many workers but only one foundation.

II. Disorders and disturbing problems (chapters 5 to 11), discussing
matters relating to marriage, eating of meat, and the Lord's Supper.

III. Coveting the greatest spiritual gifts and graces as opposed to
shallow ambitions (chapters 12 to 14).

IV. Doctrine of the Resurrection (chapter 15). The grounding of
faith in Christ is fully explained and illustrated. "Therefore, my beloved
brethren, be ye stedfast, unmovable, always abounding in the work of
the Lord, forasmuch as ye know that your labour is not in vain in the
Lord."

Thus the final appeal of the Resurrection is to steadfastness in the work
of the Lord. The Resurrection of Jesus from the dead is one of the most
important and best established facts in history.

SECOND CORINTHIANS

The Second Epistle to the Corinthians gives us Paul's vindication of his apostleship, the glory of his ministry, and the long martyrdom of his life. Soon after Paul had written his First Epistle to the Corinthians a great riot occurred in Ephesus (Acts, chapter 19), in which Paul nearly lost his life. He left Ephesus and went into Macedonia on his way to Corinth. In Macedonia, while waiting to hear some word from Corinth, and in anxiety and much suffering, he met Titus, who was returning from Corinth. Titus told Paul that his letter had accomplished much good, but that some among the leaders of the church were questioning Paul's apostleship. Some were denying that Paul was a genuine apostle of Jesus Christ. Then Paul wrote his second epistle and sent it on ahead, by Titus, expecting that he himself would reach Corinth soon. To those in this church who were disposed to call in question Paul's apostleship, denying that there had been vested in him apostolic authority, it was imperative that Paul set forth his credentials and establish his claims as an apostle of Jesus Christ. This is one of the most important sections of this book. He declares in no uncertain terms the ground of his authority and treats ironically the criticisms of himself by the false teachers of this church. The letter deals with three climactic themes: (I) The spirit of fellowship and service. The loving relationship subsisting between the church and the apostle. Their mutual coöperation in Christian service. (II) The principle, privilege, and duty of Christian giving. Paul was raising funds for the support of the poor believers in Jerusalem and was calling upon these churches to give according as the Lord had prospered them. (III) A defense of his apostleship. The credentials of a true apostle. Paul's apostleship as related to the divine revelations that had been made to him. His thorn in the flesh to protect him against self-exaltation because of these revelations.

The epistle closes with a warning and an exhortation.

GALATIANS

Galatia, in central Asia Minor, is the region of Paul's First Missionary Journey. Its exact borders are uncertain, but it included Iconium, Lystra, Derbe, and probably Pisidian Antioch. An account of Paul's work there, in chapters 13 and 14 of The Acts, is a good introduction to this epistle. The Galatians were a group of the migrating hordes of nomadic tribes that surged out of the country north of the Black Sea in the third century B.C. and settled in Asia Minor, while their fellows pushed westward and eventually settled in what is now France. They were highly emotional, impulsive, and changeable, as may readily be seen from a reading of Acts, chapter 14. First the Galatians worshiped Paul. Then they stoned him and, supposing him to be dead, left him outside the city wall. We find that Paul's work in Galatia had been very successful. Great crowds of people, most of them Gentiles, had accepted Christ. However, after Paul had left Galatia, certain Jewish teachers came teaching a doctrine that Gentiles could not be Christians without keeping the Law of Moses. The emotional and impulsive Galatians listened to this teaching with the same enthusiasm with which they had at first received Paul's message. When Paul heard that some of the Galatians were so fickle as to accept the doctrine, he wrote the epistle to the Galatians. This was about A.D. 60. The theme of Galatians is the vindication of the gospel of the grace of God from any admixture of law—conditions that qualify its character of pure grace. The Judaizers were a sect of Jewish Christians who were not willing to accept the teachings of the apostles on the question. Acts, chapter 15, describes the council at Jerusalem and the results of its findings with regard to Gentile Christians. Many churches were troubled and unsettled by these teachers who were determined to stamp Christ with the Jewish trademark. The expansion of Christianity from a Jewish sect into a world-wide religion was the consuming passion of the Apostle Paul. For this he labored for thirty years. To save these Christians from the demoralizing influence of this Judaizing legalism, Paul announces and establishes the doctrine of justification by faith and urges them not to be misled by false teachers. He sets before them Christ and his redemption as the only way of salvation and urges them to stand fast in the liberty of the gospel. In this stirring epistle Paul discusses the following topics: Perverters of the gospel and an unsettled church, his apostleship and apostolic authority, his divine call and labors, the ground of justification, the bewitching of the church, his correction of perverted teachings bearing on justification and the works of the Law, faith and justification of Abraham prior to the Law, the Law and the Covenant distinguished, allegory of bondwoman and freewoman, the church exhorted and enjoined.

E P H E S I A N S

Paul spent his life in teaching the Gentiles that they could become Christians without becoming Jewish proselytes. This the Jews did not like generally, for to them the Mosaic Law was binding upon all. Therefore they were bitterly prejudiced against the uncircumcised Gentiles.

This is one of the prison epistles, written from Paul's Roman prison cell, A.D. 61-63. It was written to an important church in an important city. Commercially, Ephesus was one of the leading cities of Asia Minor, and under the Romans, the capital of the entire province of Asia. It was celebrated for its temple and the goddess for whom it was constructed— Diana of the Ephesians. The temple was one of the Seven Wonders of the World. Different views have been advanced as to the design of Paul's letter. Some have said that the author desired to lift the church to a sense of unity by picturing her to herself as the body of Jesus Christ, and by holding up before her at the same time a much higher conception of Jesus than the church had known hitherto. Several other views have been advanced for the reason for this epistle, but suppose we listen to the author as he gives us his reason. "I therefore, the prisoner of the Lord, beseech you that ye walk worthy of the vocation wherewith ye are called." The design is practical. It is an appeal to the sense of the great salvation to be enjoyed by all believers who exalt their Redeemer, and their appreciation of the dignity of the Church and the unity of the people of God. It is a challenge to attain to a pure and exalted form of living. Unlike some of the other epistles, it was not written to correct some doctrinal error, but for the confirmation of the Church in its spiritual unity as the body of Christ, having on the whole armor of God. This epistle bears a strong resemblance to the Epistle to the Colossians. This may be because these epistles were written about the same time. Both letters were carried to their respective churches by Tychicus. The fact that the subject of the Ephesians is broader and more general than is the more specific theme of Colossians has led to the opinion that Colossians was written first, pointing out that "progress is generally from the briefer to the more lengthy form."

The epistle has two main parts:

I. Doctrines of Christianity (chapters 1 to 3), in which the following topics are presented: The believer's selection and adoption, person and work of Christ, the equal share of the Gentiles in the blessings of the gospel, and Paul's commission to establish this truth in preaching the unsearchable riches of Christ.

II. The exemplification of these doctrines (chapters 4 to 6), which discourses on the unity of the Church, the body of Christ, unity in the diversity of gifts, many gifts but all related and reciprocal in one service, the spotless Church in Jesus Christ, full protection with the Christian armor.

This epistle holds before the Church a greater vision of the length, breadth, depth, and height of the love of Christ. The conclusion of the epistle has a personal touch that is worth our notice. The apostle speaks of the Ephesians being in prayer and supplication for all saints, and now we find that personal touch in the revealing word, "And for me or on my behalf, that utterance may be given unto me, that I may open my mouth boldly, to make known the mystery of the gospel."

PHILIPPIANS

The letter to the Philippians is a missionary letter. It is unique among the writings of the Apostle Paul because of the personal note that runs through it. A definite date for its composition cannot be given. It is one of the prison letters, as also are the letters to the Ephesians, Colossians, and to Philemon. It may be that all were written at the same time. This particular letter was addressed to the saints in Christ Jesus who were in Philippi, a city of proconsular Macedonia, taken by Philip of Macedon, who named it after himself. It was here that the celebrated battle was fought in which Brutus and Cassius were defeated, 42 B.C., and the Roman Republic was overthrown. Augustus, the new emperor, in appreciation, made it a Roman colony. The gospel was first preached in Europe in this city. There Paul and Silas had their unusual experience in jail that resulted in the jailer's conversion. Paul founded the church at Philippi, and on several occasions it contributed to his necessities. It is said that Luke, the beloved physician, was its pastor for the first six years. It could have been Luke's home, where he practiced medicine. Who knows but that he might have had much to do with the development of the character of the church. The story in the sixteenth chapter of The Acts of the Apostles is good preliminary reading for this letter. When Paul wrote this letter, about A.D. 61–63, he was in Rome. It was nearly ten years after he had founded the church at Philippi, and he had not been back there in three or four years. He had not heard from the church for some time. Paul wondered how the Philippians were getting along. Had they forgotten him? Then Epaphroditus came from Philippi with an offering of money for Paul. Paul was deeply touched. He was in great need. The messenger had almost lost his life in this ministry, and Paul looked after his welfare until he recovered. Then he sent him back with this beautiful letter full of love and song. Paul expresses his gratitude and sets before them Christ as the great exemplar. He commends the Philippians, and in no part of the epistle is there any word of censure. The first two chapters are given to a discussion of the mind and the characteristics of Christ. Then follow discourses on the believers' spiritual goal as expressed by the apostle's aspirations, the gain of losing all else for Christ, encouragement to press toward the mark for the prize, and recommendation to cultivate things that are true, honest, pure, and lovely. Paul shows how the simple things of life are linked to those of eternity. We note the familiar passage where we find human responsibility revealed in these words.

COLOSSIANS

Colossæ was a city of Phrygia. It will be recalled that some of those who were present on the Day of Pentecost were from Phrygia (Acts 2:10). Paul had gone through this country on his Second and Third Missionary Journeys. Colossians was one of the four letters written during his imprisonment at Rome, A.D. 62–63, the others being Ephesians, Philippians, and Philemon. It was Epaphras who brought to Paul an account of the religious conditions in Asia, and it is thought that he was the founder of the church at Colossæ. The spiritual life of this church was seriously endangered by the Gnostic philosophy of that time. The Gnostics held that matter was essentially evil, while God was wholly good. Hence the creation of matter was accounted for by some other creative power than that of God, who could not be conceived as creating evil. When some of these Gnostics became interested in Christianity, they brought with them their Gnostic theories. Then Christ became to them a serious problem. They could not believe him to be a man with a material body, which would make him evil. One faction believed that he had only the appearance of a material body. This would make him spirit only, and this theory denied the humanity of Christ. Another set admitted his humanity, that he was in every way human. When Epaphras brought this report to Paul the latter recognized the danger that confronted this church and then wrote this letter to them. It sets forth Christ as the supreme Head of the Church. Between Jesus and God there is no other intervening creative power. Jesus is the express image of God. It is he who is the Creator of all things. Colossians was written, not for that day only, but for a warning for the Church in all days. Paul exposes the shallowness of Gnostic philosophy, and gives warning to the Church not to be deceived by it. In this epistle Paul is attempting a logical refutation of the Gnostics, and, following the introduction or greeting, the epistle is divided rather sharply into six parts, several with subdivisions; they are as follows: (I) The apostle's prayer. "In whom we have redemption through his blood, even the forgiveness of sins." (II) The exaltation of Christ. (*a*) the seven superiorities of Christ. "For it pleased the Father that in him should all fulness dwell." (*b*) The reconciling work of Christ. "And you, that were sometime alienated and enemies in your mind by wicked works, yet now hath he reconciled." (*c*) The mystery of the indwelling Christ. "Even the mystery which hath been hid from ages and from generations, but now is made manifest to his saints: to whom God would make known what is the riches of the glory of this mystery among the Gentiles; which is Christ in you, the hope of glory." (III) The Godhead incarnate in Christ, in whom the believer is incomplete. (*a*) The danger from enticing words. (*b*) The twofold warning against philosophy and legality. (*c*) Nothing can be added to completeness. (*d*) Law observances were abolished in Christ. (*e*) Warning against false mysticism. (IV) The believer's union with Christ, now and hereafter. (V) Christian living, the fruit of union with Christ. (VI) Christian fellowship.

I T H E S S A L O N I A N S

This is the epistle of the Second Coming. The church in Thessalonica was founded about A.D. 51 on Paul's Second Missionary Journey, after he left Philippi (Acts 17:1-9). Thessalonica was named by Cassander in honor of his wife, Thessalonice, the sister of Alexander the Great. It is now called Salonika. It was on Paul's Second Missionary Journey that he and Silas visited this city. We are told, in Acts 17:1-9, how Paul preached to the Jews in their synagogue on the death and Resurrection of Jesus, how incensed the Jews became, and the departure of the missionaries to Berea. But Paul's preaching bore fruit, and a great multitude believed, both Jews and Greeks. Timothy was left here while Paul proceeded to Athens. During these labors at Thessalonica, Paul had undoubtedly instructed the people on the Second Coming of Christ. They had misunderstood these teachings, and the idea became fixed in their minds that Jesus was coming soon. The result was that many ceased to work, looking upon work as not necessary if Christ were to appear soon.

Others bemoaned the fact that many who had died in Christ would not be present to witness the glory of that great event. Paul was in Corinth working at his trade at tentmaking. He sent for Timothy and Silas to come to him. From them he learned the manner in which the Thessalonian church had confused his teaching on the Second Coming of Christ. In this letter he seeks to correct their mistaken views, telling them that the time of Christ's coming is not known. When he does come, those who are asleep in Jesus will be raised from the dead to participate in the glory of it, and those living will be changed, and both the resurrected and the living will meet Christ in the air. Therefore, this epistle gives us very important instruction on one of the greatest subjects of the Bible. It will be noticed that at the close of each chapter reference is made to our Lord's return. Paul's work in Thessalonica, though but for a short time, created a great stir. His enemies accused him of turning the world upside down. A great multitude of Greeks and chief women believed. The success of his work was heralded all over Greece. The epistle may be divided into three parts: (I) Character and engagement of the church. The true church is characterized by earnestness and loyalty. The influence of the church at Thessalonica exemplifying such qualities will be an example to believers in Macedonia and Achaia. (II) Character and ministry of the Apostle Paul. (III) The Second Coming of our Lord. The claims of the present life and service upon the believer while waiting for his Lord. He should not be indifferent to these claims. The status of the righteous dead or living in regard to that event when it occurs. The effect this great doctrine and glorious hope should have upon Christians.

II T H E S S A L O N I A N S

The second letter to the Thessalonians was written evidently soon after Paul's first letter to that church. The occasion may have been the return of the bearer of the former letter and his report, which represented the church there as being full of faith and love and unshaken in the midst of persecutions. Their only error, needing correction, was that Paul's description of Christ's Second Coming in First Thessalonians (chapters 4:13; 5:2) led them to believe that Christ's Second Coming was actually imminent. Some, professing to know by the spirit, caused Paul to write in II Thessalonians 2:2: "That ye be not soon shaken in mind, or be troubled, neither by spirit, nor by word, nor by letter as from us, as that the day of Christ is at hand." Others declared that when Paul was with them he had said so. Some ceased to mind their daily work and cast themselves on the charity of others as if their only duty was to look for Christ's immediate coming. Paul therefore tells the people that before the Lord shall come there must first be a great apostasy and the man of sin be revealed. Paul also tells them that neglect of daily business will bring only scandal on the church and is contrary to his own practice among them: "For yourselves know how ye ought to follow us: for we behaved not ourselves disorderly among you; neither did we eat any man's bread for nought; but wrought with labour and travail night and day, that we might not be chargeable to any of you: not because we have not power, but to make ourselves an ensample unto you to follow us." Believers must withdraw from such disorderly walkers. Paul admonishes: "Now we command you, brethren, in the name of our Lord Jesus Christ, that ye withdraw yourselves from every brother that walketh disorderly, and not after the tradition which he received of us."

After the salutation, Paul's letter discusses the following topics: Comfort in persecution. Paul commends the Thessalonians' faith, love, patience, amidst persecutions. Paul corrects their error as to Christ's immediate coming, and foretells that the man of sin (who is usually spoken of as the Antichrist) must first rise and perish. He exhorts to orderly conduct, prays to the God of peace in their behalf, and bestows his blessing.

Paul probably visited Thessalonica subsequently (Acts 20:4) on his way to Asia. The disorderly people of whom Paul writes seem to have been certain lazy persons who, taking advantage of the charitable disposition of some of the members of the Thessalonian church, used as an excuse for idleness their expectation of the immediate coming of Christ.

I TIMOTHY

First and Second Timothy and Titus are called the Pastoral Epistles. The prevailing thought is that I Timothy was written in Macedonia about A.D. 65, a short time prior to Paul's death, which occurred about 68. His imprisonment in Rome, 62–63, was followed, it is believed, by a fourth journey, and it is during that time that this epistle was written.

Timothy was a native of Lystra (Acts 16:1). His mother was a Jewess, and his father a Greek. His mother's name was Eunice, and his grandmother's name was Lois. He was converted under Paul and became a companion of Paul on his Second Missionary Journey, about A.D. 51 (Acts 16:3). He was set apart for the work by the elders and by Paul, whom he accompanied to Troas, Philippi, Thessalonica, and Berea. He waited at Berea until Paul sent for him to come to Athens. Then Paul sent him back to Thessalonica. When he returned, Paul had gone to Corinth. Whether Timothy reached Rome before Paul's death is not known. Paul loved him devotedly and was lonesome without him. Within the apostolic generation Ephesus became the numerical center of Christendom, the region where Christianity won its quickest laurels. There must have been hundreds of pastors. In Acts 20:17 they are called elders; in this epistle they are called bishops. In New Testament times these are different names for the same office, corresponding to "pastor."

An interesting sidelight on Timothy's early life, when his mother had carefully instructed him in the Old Testament Scriptures, is revealed by Paul in the following: "When I call to remembrance the unfeigned faith that is in thee, which dwelt first in thy grandmother Lois, and thy mother Eunice; and I am persuaded that in thee also. Wherefore I put thee in remembrance that thou stir up the gift of God, which is in thee. . . . For

God hath not given us the spirit of fear; but of power, and of love, and of a sound mind." II Timothy 1:5-7. The epistle is divided as follows: Paul's charge to Timothy. The office of the minister and steward in dealing with official matters, with regard to spiritual principles, in following after righteousness, how to preach to the rich. "But they that will be rich fall into temptation and a snare, and into many foolish and hurtful lusts, which drown men in destruction and perdition. . . . Fight the good fight of faith, lay hold on eternal life, whereunto thou art also called, and hast professed a good profession before many witnesses. . . . That thou keep this commandment without spot, unrebukeable, until the appearing of our Lord Jesus Christ."

II T I M O T H Y

The book of The Acts closes with Paul a prisoner (in his own hired house) in Rome, where "he received all that came in unto him," in about A.D. 63. It is commonly thought that he was acquitted, returned to Greece and Asia Minor, and was later rearrested and taken back to Rome. He was executed about 66 or 67. This epistle to Timothy was written while Paul was awaiting martyrdom. One object of writing this epistle was to request Timothy to come to him speedily ("Do thy diligence to come shortly unto me."), because his other friends had left him—all but his faithful comrade Luke. "For Demas hath forsaken me, having loved this present world, and is departed unto Thessalonica; Crescens to Galatia, Titus unto Dalmatia. Only Luke is with me. Take Mark, and bring him with thee: for he is profitable to me for the ministry. And Tychicus have I sent to Ephesus." He desired the presence of Timothy and Mark (the old alienation having been completely healed) that they might bring cheer to him in his trials and aid him in the work of the ministry. With strong expressions of affectionate regard, he addresses this epistle to his "son" Timothy, a series of earnest exhortations to steadfastness, diligence, and patience in his work; to courage and constancy under persecutions; and to the exercise of all personal virtues; encouraging him by calling to mind his early training in piety and in the knowledge of the Scriptures; reminding him of some who had proved unfaithful in the hour of trial; warning both Timothy and his flock against false teachers, vain controversies, and false professors, the increase of whom is predicted; foretelling the grievous times that were yet to come; and enforcing his solemn charge to Timothy to be vigilant, faithful, and zealous in the discharge of his ministry, by the consideration that his own course was nearly run and the time of his departure was at hand. This epistle contains a noble view of the consolation that Christians enjoy in the midst of suffering and in the prospect of death. The holiest spiritual affection to God and Christ is not only consistent with human friendships, but productive of them.

In the approaching corruption of Christianity, Paul directs Timothy to the true conservative principle of its purity; not new miracles nor a fresh revelation, but the doctrine in which Timothy had been instructed, and those Scriptures which make the man of God perfect, thoroughly furnished unto all good works. This epistle may be divided into three parts: (I) Fundamentals of Christian character and service. Soundness of doctrine, Christian endurance, rightly dividing the word of truth. (II) Coming perilous times. Last words of the great apostle to the Gentiles. (III) His closing injunction to Timothy. His triumphant testimony to his faith in Jesus Christ.

T I T U S

The Epistle of Titus was probably written about A.D. 65 from Macedonia. In point of time it lies between the two Epistles to Timothy. Titus is not mentioned in The Acts, and nothing more is known of him except what we find in the epistles of Paul. We learn that he was a Greek by birth (Galatians 2:3) who had been converted to Christianity by the instrumentality of Paul. He went up with Paul and Barnabas to Jerusalem, and afterwards accompanied Paul on his travels, being sent by him on various important missions. He is repeatedly mentioned by the apostle in terms of approbation and affection. Because he was the son of Gentile parents, and therefore in a different position from that of Timothy, he was not circumcised. Circumcision in his case would have involved, as Paul reasoned, a compromise of principle, especially if performed at the bidding of the Judaizing party. At the time when this epistle was written, Titus had been left by the apostle on the island of Crete, that he might establish and regulate the churches there. It is not easy to determine when this occurred; some have supposed that Paul may have landed at Crete on his voyage from Corinth to Ephesus, mentioned in Acts 18:18, 19. We know nothing of the first introduction of the gospel into Crete, but as there were Jews from that island among Peter's audience on the Day of Pentecost (Acts 2:11), it is probable that the Christian faith was carried thither by converts from among them. It appears also from this epistle that Paul had labored there, probably with considerable success. There is a striking resemblance between this epistle and the First Epistle to Timothy. This epistle is particularly remarkable, as it compresses into a very short compass a large amount of instruction, embracing doctrine, morals, and discipline. Its contents are as follows: After an apostolic salutation, declaring the object for which Paul had invested Titus with special authority, he describes the qualifications required in those who were to be ordained to the ministry and that were the more necessary on account of the dangerous principles of the false teachers whom they had to oppose, and the general character of the Cretans. Paul next describes the instructions that were to be given to various classes of persons, enjoining on the aged and the young the virtues that ought to distinguish them; exhorting Titus, himself a young man, to set a pattern in his own conduct of the virtues he was to inculcate; teaching servants to be obedient and faithful, for the salvation of the gospel was designed for all orders and classes of mankind, making them holy in this life and preparing them for the higher and better life. Titus is then instructed to enjoin obedience to rulers, and a peaceable and gentle behavior to all men; remembering their own former sinfulness, and their salvation through the free grace of God.

P H I L E M O N

The Epistle to Philemon, about A.D. 62, was a private letter concerning a runaway slave. This is an inspired model of private Christian correspondence that was addressed by the Apostle Paul to Philemon, one of his converts who resided at Colossæ, a well-to-do man in whose house church services were held. Philemon may have been a deacon or elder in the church. Apphia was supposed to have been his wife, Archippus may have been his son, and Onesimus was his slave in bonds. When Paul was at Ephesus, turning the "world upside down," Philemon might have met him and become one of Paul's converts. He was not only a convert, but seems to have become a great friend to Paul. On one visit Paul became known to Onesimus the slave. Time passed on and Paul was a prisoner in Rome, "in his own house." In the meantime an exciting event occurred in the home of Philemon. Because of some hardship, young Onesimus broke away and hastened to Rome. To appreciate this letter we must bear in mind a few things about the Roman law. (1) The Roman law gave the slave no right of asylum, but granted him the privilege of making an appeal. (2) The Roman slave had the privilege of fleeing to his master's friend, not for concealment but for intercession. (3) The owner of a slave in Roman times was absolute in his possession, yet he might be besought by a friend whom he counted as a partner. (4) It was also agreed that a Roman slave could be adopted by his master as his son; only thus could he be freed.

Onesimus had found his way to Rome and to Paul and was converted. After a time, Paul, thinking that it was right that Onesimus should be returned to his master, wrote this beautiful and persuasive letter in order to secure for him a kind reception. "A few friendly lines," someone has said, "so full of wit, of earnest trustful affection, that makes this short epistle shine among the rich treasures of the New Testament as a pearl of exquisite fineness." After an affectionate word from himself and Timothy, the apostle expresses thankfulness after hearing of the good reputation that Philemon as a Christian enjoyed. Then he gracefully introduces the main subject of his letter: requesting as "Paul the aged," now a prisoner for their common faith, what we might expect of an apostle. Acknowledging the fault of Onesimus, he mentions the happy change that had taken place in him and hints that his flight had been overruled for his master's benefit as well as his own; and entreats that he may be received back, no longer as a slave, but as a beloved Christian brother. Paul then delicately proposes to make good any loss Philemon might have sustained, saying, "If thou count me therefore a partner, receive him as myself. If he hath wronged thee, or oweth thee ought, put that on mine account." This short letter is invaluable, as it offers an example of humility, courteousness, and freedom, in the intercourse of Christian friendship. We cannot but suppose that the gentleness and address of the apostle's pleading were effectual. The Bible gives no hint as to how or in what manner Philemon received his runaway slave. Tradition tells us that Philemon did receive him, and acted on Paul's veiled hint and gave Onesimus his freedom. There is also a tradition that Onesimus afterwards became a bishop in the church at Berea. Fifty years later Ignatius speaks of an Onesimus as bishop in Ephesus. Near the close of the letter Paul says, "Having confidence in thy obedience I wrote unto thee, knowing that thou wilt also do more than I say."

H E B R E W S

The Epistle to the Hebrews stands side by side with Romans and Corinthians as one of the major messages to the Church since Pentecost. It holds a unique place not only because of the people to whom it was addressed but because in it there is a great wealth of Old Testament allusions and illustrations, throwing more light on the ancient times and unfolding a more intimate connection between the Old and the New Testaments. The authorship of this epistle is not definitely known, and for many years the Apostle Paul was considered the author. This epistle was probably written before the destruction of the Temple in A.D. 70.

We may divide the book into two principal parts. The first was intended to explain the meaning and the inferiority of the Jewish dispensation; the second aimed to confirm and comfort Jewish believers in their religious profession.

I. Having noticed that the Mosaic and the Christian dispensation both proceed from the same divine Author, the writer shows the surpassing excellency of the Christian dispensation, as being introduced by the Messiah. (1) Greater than prophets, and even than angels; notwithstanding His humiliation unto death, which, so far from diminishing His glory, was the very means of accomplishing His great work of redemption (chapter 1:2). (2) Superior to Moses, their venerated lawgiver, who nevertheless was but a servant. Here the writer solemnly warns the Hebrew Christians, lest they should lose through unbelief that present rest and final glory, of which the Canaan into which Joshua had led their forefathers was but a type, chapters 3:1 to 4:13. (3) Then, as the Jews rightly attached the highest importance to their priesthood and sacrifices, the writer expatiates at length upon the superior excellence and efficacy of the priesthood and sacrifice of Christ. He shows that the necessary qualifications of a high priest, namely, that he should be appointed by God and be able to sympathize with men, were found in the Lord Jesus: "For we have not an high priest which cannot be touched with the feeling of our infirmities; but was in all points tempted like as we are, yet without sin. Let us therefore come boldly unto the throne of grace, that we may obtain mercy, and find grace to help in time of need." Having cited from the prophecy concerning the supreme and eternal priesthood of the Messiah as typified by Melchizedek, he then reveals that the Levitical temporary services in a wordly sanctuary are inferior to the intercession of Christ in the presence of God above and contrasts the oft-repeated Jewish sacrifices with the intrinsic and perpetual efficacy of the one perfect and all-sufficient propitiation (chapters 9:1 to 10:18).

II. Upon this reasoning the practical application is grounded. The writer exhorts the Hebrews to steadfastness in hope, faith, and mutual encouragement. He points out the dangers of apostasy. Then he reminds them of their fortitude and faithful adherence under former trials; he shows the indispensable necessity of maintaining a life of faith. After describing the nature of faith, the writer proves it to have been the main principle of religion in every age; and illustrates the powerful operation and triumphant efficacy in a long line of heroes and martyrs, from Abel to the close of the Old Testament dispensation and, above all, in Jesus Christ himself. He warns the people against bartering, like Esau, their spiritual privileges for present gratifications. In conclusion, he gives specific precepts on various practical duties and closes with salutations and a beautifully comprehensive benediction embodying the chief theme of the epistle—the "everlasting covenant" and the dignity and glory of Jesus the Mediator.

J A M E S

There were three persons named James in the life of Christ—the son of Zebedee, the son of Alphæus, and the Lord's brother. The last of the three is commonly regarded as the writer of this epistle. This book was probably written near the close of his life, about A.D. 60. Those to whom the epistle was written were in trying circumstances; so the inspired writer begins with encouragements and counsels specially suited to their condition. He then describes the nature of true religion, its origin and its effects on the heart and the conduct; he enjoins sincere and impartial love, without reference to outward condition and circumstances; and exposes the hypocrisy of the man who pretends to have faith while his works do not answer to his words. James quotes Scripture examples to show that the faith which God had approved had always been evidenced by works. Then, to check some prevailing evils arising from a fondness for becoming teachers and censors, he gives cautions and rebukes on those subjects. He exhibits, in a series of striking metaphors, the evils of an unbridled tongue and contrasts the disputatious, envious, and angry spirit of the schools of earthly wisdom with the pure, peaceful, gentle, and beneficent character of that which is of heavenly origin. He exposes the effects of the spirit of the world, as exhibited in the conduct of those who are under its influence, and exhorts to submission to God and resistance to the Devil. He calls sinners and hypocrites to repent, and to humble themselves before God. He warns Christians against speaking evil, censuring, or sitting in judgment on one another. He reproves the presumption of those who formed their wordly projects without any sense of their dependence on God, and the covetousness and oppression of the rich. Then, returning to the suffering Christians, he encourages them to patience by the prospect of the Lord's coming; cautions them against swearing; recommends prayer as the best resource in sorrow, and praise as the best expression of joy; gives special directions to the sick; enjoins mutual confessions of faults and intercessions for one another, the efficacy of which he illustrates in the case of Elijah. Finally, he urges the duty of seeking to save an erring brother. The epistle well illustrates the importance of comparing Scripture with Scripture. According to James, Abraham was justified by works, James 2:21; according to Paul, by faith, Romans 4:9. Yet there is no contradiction, but a deep interior harmony. There is no conflict between this doctrine of faith and works and Paul's doctrine of justifying faith as opposed to the works of the law. The two things are wholly different and these two writers are emphasizing two entirely different things. Paul treats the means of justification; James the evidence, or spiritual expression of it. One may be right from the standpoint of Paul's theological position and wholly wrong from the practical standpoint of the position of James. Paul was in full accord with the viewpoint of James, and James was likewise in full agreement with the viewpoint of Paul.

One notices four things in this epistle: The believer's attitude toward trial, temptation, and a true religious life. The essential relation of faith to works. Things exemplified by the true believer. The substance of true riches.

FIRST EPISTLE OF PETER

The writer of this epistle was Peter, whose original name was Simeon or Simon. He wrote this epistle about A.D. 60 or 64. Peter was the son of Jonas and a native of Bethsaida, on the Sea of Galilee. At the time of his first appearance in the Gospel history he was married and living at Capernaum. Like the sons of Zebedee, he was a fisherman. He was brought to Jesus by his brother Andrew, who had been a disciple of John the Baptist, but was led by his master's testimony to attach himself to the Divine Teacher. For some time after this, the two brothers continued to follow their business until they were summoned by our Lord to be in constant attendance upon him. From that time on they were his devoted followers. The numerous facts told about Peter during his attendance upon our Saviour throw much light on his character at that period. His sincere piety, ardent attachment to his Master, and zeal for his honor, seem to have been blended with rashness and inconstancy; but, after his fall and restoration, and when "endued with power from on high," a great change is noticeable in him. He fully justifies the appellation that our Lord had bestowed on him, Cephas or Petros; the former an Aramaic, the latter a Greek word, both signifying a stone or rock.

This epistle appears to have been written from "Babylon" (chapter 5:13), which some have taken for a mystical name for Rome. Although this epistle is brief, it gives us a clear summary, both of the consolations and instructions needful for the encouragement and direction of a Christian in his journey to heaven, elevating his thoughts and desires to that happiness, and strengthening him against all opposition in the way. The heads of doctrine contained in this epistle are many; but the main ones are these three: faith, obedience, and patience. To establish in believing, to direct in doing, and to comfort in suffering are his precepts. Often the author set before his readers the matchless example of the Lord Jesus and the greatness of his suffering. Peter tells us a great deal about Christ, and he tells it very completely. Although the epistle has a practical design, it is also evangelical. It points everywhere to Christ; to his atonement as foretold by prophets, contemplated by angels appointed before the foundation of the world; to his Resurrection, Ascension, and gift of the Spirit; his example as a suffering Saviour, and the awful solemnities of the Last Judgment. Like Paul, Peter urges the doctrines of the gospel as the great motives to holiness and patience.

SECOND EPISTLE OF PETER

The Second Epistle of Peter is addressed to all believers. Like the earlier letter, it is especially intended for those who need encouragement. It is of solemn interest in that it was written not long before the apostle's death as a martyr. As in the former epistle, he exhorts his followers to be patient under persecution; so here he exhorts them to perseverance in truth in the midst of prevailing error and infidelity. The best perseverance is, as he tells them, progressive piety. Decisive evidence of the truth of the Scripture doctrine is given also by undeniable testimony of fulfilled prophecy. In terms most energetic and awful he warns false teachers and those who were beginning to yield to their seductions of their guilt and danger, and assures them that the Second Coming of Christ, though long delayed, through long suffering, is as certain as the fact of the Deluge. He then shows the bright side of the same truth and bids Christians to be diligent and holy. He appeals to the teachings of Paul to confirm his views. He points to the fact that men had taken his teaching so as to make it countenance most pernicious practices, an evil to be remedied not by neglecting those Scriptures, but by increased teachableness and a humble spirit.

We treasure the last words of great men. In the immediate prospect of martyrdom, holiness appears to Peter of first importance, and steadfastness the greatest blessing. His last precept is, "grow in grace, and in the knowledge of our Lord and Saviour Jesus Christ." His last testimony is to the divinity of his Lord, "Grow in the grace and knowledge of our Lord and Saviour Jesus Christ. To him be glory both now and for ever."

THE FIRST EPISTLE OF JOHN

This epistle was written by the Apostle John, probably A.D. 90. This sacred writing, though called an epistle, is more like a discourse on the doctrines and duties of Christianity. It seems to have been addressed to believers generally, especially to Gentiles and residents in Asia Minor, among whom John himself had labored. John did not think it was necessary to prefix his name; but its remarkable similarity in style and tone to the other writings of the same author confirm the testimony of the early Christians that John was the author. It was supposed to have been written from Ephesus. Evidently one object of this epistle was to counteract errors already prevalent. Other topics are introduced and discussed.

We are taught the true nature of fellowship with God. He is light and love; fellowship implies conformity to him. Man must be purified and redeemed, man must be holy, we must love one another. If Christ is denied, all these blessings are lost. We are taught the blessedness and duties of sonship. Not only fellowship, but adoption is our privilege in Christ. God is righteous; as his children, we too must be righteous. Christ came to take away sin; and in him is no sin; to him we must be conformed. He gave his life for us, and herein his love is our model. Having his spirit we shall share his other blessings. Again, if Christ is denied, in his human nature especially, then these blessings are lost. The author began with the truth that God is Light, and thence shows what fellowship with Him and sonship involve; now he gives another view. God is Love. Love is His essence and was manifested in the mission and character of his Son and is the necessary condition of sonship to God and one another. Faith in Christ, such confidence as casts out fear, are all among the results that revelation secures.

Here we see fellowship maintained by Christ's advocacy. "These things write I unto you, that ye sin not. And if any man sin, we have an advocate with the Father, Jesus Christ the righteous: and he is the propitiation for our sins: and not for our's only, but also for the sins of the whole world."

John was in the position to speak more positively about Jesus than a multitude of others. He was in his life for three years. He maintained the most intimate relationship with him and saw every expression of his human nature. He saw him die on the cross. These facts will outweigh all the superficial and hazy speculations of Gnosticism. John declares positively four great truths: the incarnation of Jesus; the fact of sin; the fact of propitiation and pardon; the fact of regeneration. These four truths may be reduced to two in the analysis of the epistle: (1) The incarnate Christ the ground of the believer's spiritual life. He was seen and heard by the disciples. He was the Light of the World and is the believer's light in which to walk. (2) The significance and consciousness of regeneration. Sin and the regenerated life. Christ our Advocate with the Father. Regeneration expressed in love. Love for one another and for God and God's love for us. Faith in the incarnate Christ the ground of the consciousness of regeneration.

SECOND EPISTLE OF JOHN

The Second Epistle of John was written probably at Ephesus about the end of the first century—a letter to a Christian woman. The other apostles had all passed on years before, and John alone was left. He was an old, old man, and the last surviving companion of Jesus. The best biographies in literature are largely made up of personal letters. And so we find that the New Testament consists, to a great extent, of personal correspondence. The epistles were all written to churches or individuals, and there was the local coloring with the general application. Many of them were written to individuals. The first thing that we learn from the letters of John is the lesson of humility. John could just as well have called himself apostle or made much of the fact that he was the one who sat next to the Master, and perhaps was the dearest of the Twelve. But he does none of this: He just speaks of himself in plain words, as one of the very humblest of the Church of Christ. John did not have any of that glaring fanaticism of the exalted I, such as the self-exaggeration of Simon Magus or Lucifer. He was more like the meek and lowly Jesus. The next lesson that we learn is Christian friendship. John addresses this sister in terms of tenderest regard, and yet a regard that was sacredly guarded. "Whom I love in the truth; . . . for the truth's sake, which dwelleth in us, and shall be with us for ever." Then we have the example of a Christian family, for this sister to whom John wrote this epistle had children, and John refers to them as walking in the truth. And so salvation may be claimed for the whole family as well as for oneself. "Believe on the Lord Jesus Christ, and thou shalt be saved, and thy house." We have here an example of a true Christian life, and we find that two things especially enter into it, obedience and holy aspiration. The Christian life is first of all obedience to God. For "this is love, that we walk after his commandments." Doctrine is the final test of reality. "Look to yourselves, that we lose not those things which we have wrought, but that we receive a full reward." With regard to the false teachers, these were the same set of men referred to in I John 2:18-29. They were going from place to place, preying on the churches, and teaching in the name of Christ doctrines that were utterly subversive to the Christian faith. This letter was written to warn the "elect lady" against showing hospitality to such teachers.

THIRD EPISTLE OF JOHN

The third letter of John was addressed to a well-known disciple of whom we have read in the New Testament. He was probably a man of some means, at least independent, and of great help to the brethren. This letter was addressed to the well-beloved Gaius, "whom I love in the truth."

This is in all probability the same person mentioned in Romans 16:23, and in I Corinthians 1:14. Gaius appears to have been an eminent Christian, particularly distinguished for his hospitality to Christian evangelists or missionaries. The apostle expresses his affectionate joy at this and other evidences of his piety; cautions him against one Diotrephes, noted for his ambition and turbulence; and recommends Demetrius for his friendship; deferring other matters to a personal interview. There are many beautiful points in this letter identical with the previous one.

There are other distinctive and important points. There is the fine testimony to a faithful life. "Beloved, thou doest faithfully whatsoever thou doest to the brethren, and to strangers." It is not a brilliant life, but it is a faithful one. The Christian is true to every one of his obligations; he is a faithful servant of the Master. One may never be brilliant or great, but at the last our rewards will not be for greatness, our services, or our talents; they will be for our faithfulness. "Well done, good and faithful servant; . . . enter thou into the joy of thy lord." This epistle is of special interest because of the insight it affords us of the Christian churches in the closing years of the first century. As someone has said, "It helps us to see what these churches were, not as we idealize them, but in their actual everyday condition, with their excellencies and defects, their noble, and ignoble figures, their meek and their ambitious members, the errors into which they might be betrayed; their varied, mixed, and stirring life. It shows us something, too, of their independence, of the kind of ministry that was in exercise among them, and their relation to it, of their order also and administration." This epistle speaks of three individuals and a class of individuals. It is addressed to Gaius, a man who had extended to John a Christian kindness; now John entreats him to do the same for some brethren engaged in missionary work for which they received no remuneration. "Because that for his name's sake they went forth, taking nothing of the Gentiles. We therefore ought to receive such, that we might be fellow helpers to the truth." Verses 7 and 8. The second individual referred to is Diotrephes. This man Diotrephes had treated John unkindly and had taken a high-handed position in threatening others if they acted otherwise. Verses 9, 10. John denounces him and expects to do so in person. The third individual is Demetrius, whom John commends for his goodness and loyalty, saying, "Demetrius hath good report of all men, and of the truth itself: yea, and we also bear record; and ye know that our record is true." Verse 12.

JUDE

We have here a little epistle of only twenty-five verses. This epistle is full of the most solemn warnings and loftiest spiritual lessons. The author may have been the Jude or Judas referred to in the fourteenth chapter of John as Judas, "not Iscariot," and describing himself here as Jude, the servant of Jesus Christ and the brother of James. The epistle is addressed "to them that are sanctified by God the Father, and preserved

in Jesus Christ, and called." Then follows the writer's salutation: "Mercy
unto you, and peace, and love, be multiplied." "Mercy" is the divine
fountain of all our blessings. "Peace" is the stream that flows from that
fountain. "Love" is the expression of divine fellowship toward all His
redeemed children. The epistle naturally divides itself into the following
sections:

(I) Certain references to salvation and the gospel of our Lord Jesus
Christ. Verse 3. (II) Warnings against false brethren who had crept in
among them and were exercising a destructive influence in the church.
Verses 4–13. (III) An announcement of the Second Coming of Christ,
quoted from Enoch (verses 14–16), together with warnings (verses 17–
19). (IV) An exhortation to true followers of Christ. Verses 20, 21.
(V) Counsels about Christian service and soul-winning. Verses 22, 23.
(VI) A glorious doxology. Verses 24, 25.

I. "Beloved, when I gave all diligence to write unto you of the common
salvation, it was needful for me to write unto you, and exhort you that
ye should earnestly contend for the faith which was once delivered unto
the saints." Verse 3. Here are two phrases of striking significance:
(a) "The common salvation," the salvation which belongs alike to the
Jew and the Gentile which is for every sinner, "Whosoever will, let him
take the water of life freely." And again (b) "The faith which was once
(for all) delivered unto the saints." The writer's idea is that God's word
of salvation has been proclaimed once as His final word, and as the same
one gospel, that He ever will offer to lost men. Jude reminds them
that they must "earnestly contend" for his faith. The enemy will try to
destroy it in many different ways but remember that Jesus Christ and
His word are "the same yesterday, and today, and forever."

II. Jude exposes some false brethren: (a) certain men had crept in
unawares and were spreading the gospel of denial of the Lord God, and
our Lord Jesus Christ. (b) The particular character of their teachings
was, "turning the grace of God into lasciviousness," verse 4. Jude speaks
of them in verse 8 as, "filthy dreamers." (c) They were also intolerant
of all spiritual authority, self-willed and scornful of those who were over
them. They "despise dominion, and speak evil of dignities," verse 8. They
tried to break up the peace and harmony of the church. (d) Jude gives
us three types of these wicked men in the eleventh verse: (1) Cain who
represents the unbelieving man, who presumes to approach God in his
own way. (2) Balaam is the second type, representing the world. (3) The
third type is Core (Korah) who rebelled against the authority of Moses.
Note the series of the awful and magnificent metaphors mixed with the
fiery eloquence in verses 12, and 13. And now we come to the doxology:
"Now unto him that is able to keep you from falling, and to present you
faultless before the presence of his glory with exceeding joy, To the only
wise God our Saviour, be glory and majesty, dominion and power, both
now and ever. Amen."

REVELATION

The Revelation of John. This book is styled the Apocalypse or Revelation (i.e., the revealing or unveiling of that which has been hidden), as consisting of matters revealed to John by our Lord Jesus Christ. This took place when John was on Patmos, a small rocky island in the Ægean Sea. It is impossible to determine definitely whether John's banishment to this island was in the reign of Domitian or Nero. The accepted opinion is that John saw this vision toward the end of the reign of Domitian. This book greatly resembles those of Ezekiel and of Daniel, and belongs to the class of literature known as apocalyptic. It is the design of the book of Revelation that requires special attention. The book is often read or studied without regard to the existing conditions. It is held apart from John's time and the fact has been overlooked that it was peculiarly adapted to his time. It was a time of persecution, whether it be the time of Nero or Domitian. It is designed to assure a suffering Church that Rome, with all her mighty power, will fail in her attempt to crush the Kingdom of Christ, and that, on the contrary, that Kingdom will triumph, and in the conquest of the gospel, Christ will be enthroned in his universal kingship; "that after every attempt has been made by the beast and dragon, and every vial of wrath has been emptied, the marriage Supper of the Lamb will be celebrated, and with His bride, the Church, will inaugurate the new and blessed day."

The book of Revelation could be divided as follows: Chapter 1. Introduction. Vision of the Seven Candlesticks and Christ. Chapters 2 and 3. Letters to the seven churches of Asia. Chapter 4. Vision of heaven, throne, elders, cherubim. Chapter 5. The sealed book and Christ. Chapter 6. Opening of the seals. The first seal. White horse rider. Conquering. Second seal. Red horse rider. War. Take peace from earth. Third seal. Black horse rider. Oppression. Fourth seal. Pale horse rider. Sword, famine, pestilence. Fifth seal. Martyrs and their cry. Sixth seal. Signs in sun, moon, heavens. The great day of wrath. Chapter 7. Sealing of great white robed multitude of 144,000. Chapter 8. Seventh seal. Seven trumpets. First trumpet. Hail, fire. Third part trees and grass destroyed. Second trumpet. Burning mountain in sea. Third part of life destroyed. Third trumpet. Burning star. Rivers become wormwood. Fourth trumpet. Sun, moon, stars, smitten in third part. Chapter 9. First woe. Fifth trumpet. Fallen star. Locusts from the abyss. Torment five months. Second woe. Sixth trumpet. Satanic horsemen from Euphrates. Repented not. Chapter 10. Angel with little book. Seven thunders. Chapter 11. Temple measured. Two olive trees. Witnesses. Third woe. Seventh trumpet. Chapter 12. Sun-clothed woman. Man child dragon; flight. Chapter 13. Beast from the sea beat from the earth, blasphemy, persecutions. Chapter 14. Glorified 144,000, warning, angels, harvest winepress. Chapter 15. Seven vials of wrath. Chapter 16. First vial. Sores on man and beast. Second vial. Poured on sea death. Third vial. On rivers turned to blood. Fourth vial. Poured on sun.

Men scorched. Repented not. Fifth vial. On throne of beast. Torment. Repent not. Sixth vial. On Euphrates. Kings of the East. Three unclean spirits. Seventh vial. On air. It is done. Great city divided. Cities fall. Men blaspheme. Chapter 17. The Scarlet woman and her fate. Chapter 18. Fall of Babylon world's lament. Chapter 19. Heavenly chorus over the fall of Babylon. The Word and the white horse army. Conflict with the beast. Victory. Chapter 20. Satan bound a thousand years. Millennium. Apostasy. Judgment of great white throne. Chapter 21. New heaven and earth. New Jerusalem. Chapter 22. River of Life. Closing words.